The World Trading System

The World Trading System

Law and Policy of International Economic Relations

Second Edition

John H. Jackson

The MIT Press
Cambridge, Massachusetts
London, England

This book was set in Palatino on the Monotype "Prism Plus" PostScript Imagesetter by Asco Trade Typesetting Ltd., Hong Kong.

Printed and bound in the United States of America.

Library of Congress Cataloging-in-Publication Data

Jackson, John Howard, 1932–
The world trading system : law and policy of international economic relations / John H. Jackson. — 2nd ed.
p. cm.
Includes bibliographical references and index.
ISBN 0-262-10061-4 (alk. paper). — ISBN 0-262-60027-7 (alk. paper)
1. General Agreement on Tariffs and Trade (Organization)
2. General Agreement on Tariffs and Trade (1947) 3. Tariffs—Law and legislation. 4. Foreign trade regulation. 5. International economic relations. I. Title.
K4602.2 1997
341.7′543—dc21 97-15310
CIP

10 9 8

Contents

Preface ix
Acknowledgments xi

1 The Policies and Realities of International Economic Regulation 1
1.1 Law, Politics, and the Dismal Science 1
1.2 The Policy Assumptions of the International Economic System 11
1.3 Competing Policy Goals and Noneconomic Objectives 21
1.4 International Law and International Economic Relations: An Introduction 25
1.5 The Tangled Web: Is There a Warp and a Woof? 28

2 The International Institutions of Trade: The WTO and the GATT 31
2.1 The Bretton Woods System and Its Context 31
2.2 The Flawed Constitutional Beginnings of GATT 35
2.3 The World Trade Organization and the Uruguay Round 44
2.4 The Obligations of GATT and Their Legal Setting 49
2.5 The GATT and WTO as Institutions 58
2.6 GATT, the Trade Negotiation Rounds, and the WTO 73

3 National Institutions 79
3.1 Introduction 79
3.2 The United States Constitution and Its Effects on Trade Relations 81
3.3 United States Law and International Trade 89
3.4 The Variety of National Constitutions and Their Impact on the International Trading System 99

4 Rule Implementation and Dispute Resolution 107
4.1 The Effectiveness of International Law 107
4.2 GATT as Prologue to Dispute-Settlement Procedures 112
4.3 Legal Process and Trade Disputes in GATT and the WTO 120
4.4 The WTO Dispute-Settlement Process 124
4.5 National Procedures for Citizen Initiation of International Economic Disputes 127
4.6 Looking at the Future of Dispute Settlement and Rule Application in the WTO 133

5 Tariff and Nontariff Barriers 139
5.1 Import Restrictions and GATT/WTO Obligations 139
5.2 GATT Bindings and Tariff Negotiations 142
5.3 Classification for Tariff Purposes 150
5.4 Valuation for Customs Purposes 151
5.5 Quantitative Restrictions and Other Nontariff Measures 153

6 The Most-Favored-Nation Policy 157
6.1 Most-Favored-Nation Obligation and Its Politics 157
6.2 The Meaning of MFN 160
6.3 Exceptions to MFN and Potential for Bilateralism 163
6.4 Rules of Product Origin 167
6.5 MFN, Bilateralism, and Possible Trends: Some Conclusions 169

7 Safeguards and Adjustment Policies 175
7.1 The Policies and History of the Escape Clause and the International Structure for Safeguards 175
7.2 The Escape Clause in GATT/WTO and the United States 181
7.3 The Escape Clause: Legal Prerequisites and Practice 184
7.4 The Escape Clause: Remedies and Procedures 191
7.5 The Escape-Clause MFN Question 195
7.6 Law and Practice Regarding Adjustment 199
7.7 Export Restraints, Agreements, and Arrangements 203
7.8 Reforms and the Uruguay Round Safeguards Text 209

8 National Treatment Obligations and Nontariff Barriers 213
8.1 The Policies and History of the National Treatment Obligation 213
8.2 The Contours and Application of the GATT Obligation 214
8.3 De Facto or Implicit Discrimination 216

8.4 Border Tax Adjustments 218
8.5 Technical Standards 221
8.6 Government Procurement 224

9 Competing Policies and Ingenious Devices 229
9.1 Protecting the Value of Tariff Concessions and Competing Policies 229
9.2 National Security 229
9.3 The General Exceptions and Legislation for Health and Welfare 232
9.4 Pollution and Regulation of the Manufacturing Process 235
9.5 Restrictive Business Practices 238
9.6 Balance-of-Payments Exceptions and Currency Obligations 241
9.7 Other Policies for Future Consideration: Investment and Labor Standards 244

10 Unfair Trade and the Rules of Dumping 247
10.1 The Level Playing Field and the Policies of Managing Interdependence 247
10.2 The Policies of Antidumping Rules 251
10.3 The Antidumping Rules and Their Sources 255
10.4 Dumping Margins and Less Than Fair Value 261
10.5 The Material Injury Test 266
10.6 Remedy and Reflection on Dumping Rules and Policies 272
10.7 Beyond Dumping and Subsidies 274

11 The Perplexities of Subsidies in International Trade 279
11.1 Introduction: The Policies 279
11.2 Evolution of the Rules on Subsidies and Countervailing Duties in National and International Law 285
11.3 Defining Subsidies and "Actionable Subsidies" 293
11.4 Perspectives and Reflections on the Subsidies Subject 300

12 The Uruguay Round "New Subjects": Extending the Scope and Competence of the World Trading System 305
12.1 Introduction 305
12.2 Trade in Services in the Uruguay Round 306
12.3 Intellectual Property Rights 310
12.4 Agriculture 313
12.5 Agreement on Trade-Related Investment Measures 316

13 Economies with Special Circumstances 319
13.1 Economies That Do Not Well Fit the Rules of the World Trading System 319
13.2 The Generalized System of Preferences 322
13.3 State Trading and the GATT System 325
13.4 Nonmarket Economies and Economies in Transition in China and Russia 328
13.5 The United States and Nonmarket/Transition Economies 332
13.6 Unfair Trade Practice Laws and Nonmarket/Transition Economies: Antidumping and Countervailing Duties 334

14 Conclusions and Perspectives 339
14.1 The "Trade Constitution" 339
14.2 How the System Works 341
14.3 Weaknesses of the Trade Constitution: Are They Now Corrected? 342
14.4 Some Fundamental Policy Questions 345
14.5 Regulating International Economic Behavior: The Broader Framework for Policy Analysis 347
14.6 Some Conclusions 350

Notes 353
Index 429

Preface

During the course of preparing a first edition of this book, several important national statutes were adopted on the subject of international economic relations (particularly in the United States) and a new (eighth) trade round of negotiation in the context of GATT was launched. More recently, that negotiation was completed, and most national governments involved in it have now ratified the results and are implementing them. The U.S. 1994 Uruguay Round Agreements Act is an example.

Because the subject moves so rapidly, it is my goal in this book to focus on the core fundamentals, particularly the legal rules and constraints that shape the institutions and policies of international trade. Now that the Uruguay Round has been completed and the difficult work of implementing it has begun (a decades-long process, perhaps), it seemed necessary to revise this book to take account of these developments. To make room for additional text in this revised edition, however, it seemed wise to cut back on the space allocated to endnotes. I have done this, with the understanding that scholars who wish to pursue matters that could be aided by the more extensive endnotes in the first edition will almost surely find the first edition in an accessible library; at least in the United States.

Acknowledgments

I would like to thank the Ford Foundation and the William W. Cook endowment of the University of Michigan Law School for support of many of the expenses of the research leading to this book.

I would also like to thank many other individuals who provided a remarkable amount of able assistance in the preparation of this book. A number of colleagues and other scholars, as well as practitioners, have kindly assisted me by reviewing various parts of draft manuscript material and engaging in extensive discussions of some of the points. Among these, I particularly thank Professor Alan Deardorff of the Economics Department at the University of Michigan, with whom I have jointly taught several seminars that have focused on some of the subjects of this book, including subsidies and safeguards. Needless to say, the discussions in those seminars, as well as in a number of other contexts, have been exceedingly valuable. In addition, I received very helpful comments on portions of the manuscript from Professor William Davey at the University of Illinois; Gary N. Horlick, a partner at O'Melveny & Myers, Washington, D.C.; Ake Linden and Ernst-Ulrich Petersmann of the WTO Secretariat in Geneva; Professor Meinhard Hilf, Hamburg University, Germany; Professor Mitsuo Matsushita, Seikei University, Japan; Edward J. Krauland, a partner in Steptoe & Johnson, Washington, D.C.; and Professor William J. Adams, University of Michigan, Economics Department.

During the course of many years of preparing both the first edition of this book and the second edition, I have been very fortunate to have the able assistance of Erika Hrabec, and the diligent and able research assistance of a number of very capable students. Particularly, during work on the first edition, I was very ably assisted by Ross Denton and Edwin Vermulst; during work on the second edition, by Koen Van de Casteele, Maurits Lugard, Lisa Murray, and John Zitko.

1 The Policies and Realities of International Economic Regulation

1.1 Law, Politics, and the Dismal Science

The pace of international economic activity and the developing interdependence of national economies is head spinning. Governments increasingly find it difficult to implement worthy policies concerning economic activity because such activity often crosses borders in ways that escape the reach of much of national government control. This can be true for subjects as diverse as insurance, brokerage, product health and safety standards, environmental protection, banking, securities and investment, professional services such as medical or law, and many more.

Responding to these difficulties, the contracting parties (CPs) of the General Agreement on Tariffs and Trade (GATT) and certain other nations launched the eighth major trade negotiating round at a ministerial meeting in Punta del Este, Uruguay, in September 1986. For eight years, more than one hundred twenty nations participated in the largest and most complex negotiation concerning international economics in history (some would say the largest and most complex negotiation ever). The results of the Uruguay Round (UR) of negotiations were formally signed in Marrakesh, Morocco, on 15 April 1994. By the end of 1994, 76 countries had ratified the UR agreements, and the World Trade Organization (WTO) came formally into being on January 1, 1995, with that number of members. Other members came into the WTO, so that by the end of the second year of WTO's existence (end of 1996), the total number of members was 129. In addition, 34 nations were at that time negotiating for accession. It can thus be expected that within a relatively short period of time, 160 nations or independent customs territories will be members of the WTO.[1]

The Uruguay Round results are embodied in a document of some twenty-six thousand pages, most of which are detailed schedules of tariff, services trade, and other concessions. For the first time, the GATT system includes major agreements on trade in services and on trade-related intellectual property questions. Other portions of the agreement address subjects as diverse as antidumping, agricultural trade, subsidies, technical standards, textiles, and customs valuation. Included in this agreement are two important institutional measures: the charter for a World Trade Organization, and a new set of dispute-settlement procedures, both designed to assist in the effective implementation of the substantive rules established in the agreements.

The Uruguay Round results fulfill the original agenda to a remarkable degree, although with some gaps. A list of the important achievements of the Uruguay Round includes:

1. Services: The General Agreement on Trade in Services (GATS, or the services agreement) is a major new chapter in GATT history. Although in some ways seriously flawed, this text now offers an overall "umbrella" concept for trade in services that, it is hoped, will allow an ongoing negotiating process for additional detail (probably at least a fifty-year process) to occur. In this respect the structure of the new WTO is vital.

2. Intellectual property: The Trade-Related Intellectual Property (TRIP) Agreement is a splendid achievement, bringing considerable new international rule discipline to the level of protection for patents, copyrights, trade secrets, and similar intellectual property subjects, even though some of the specialists or particular interest groups appeared disappointed by certain gaps in the text.

3. Agriculture: The result in agriculture is in many respects meager, certainly as measured against the Punta (and U.S.) aspirations. But nevertheless, for the first time, there is a realistic expectation for trade-rule discipline over agricultural trade (especially subsidies and border restrictions). Like most other subjects of the Uruguay Round, further attention to agriculture will be needed in the years ahead, but the Uruguay Round has achieved an important start.

4. Subsidies/Countervailing duties: The results include a new subsidies code, again not without flaw, but with an overall conceptual approach that much improves the Tokyo Round Code. Worries about this code focus on the ambiguity of several "exceptions" clauses which could lead to abuse.

5. Textiles: Textiles are covered in the Uruguay Round with a "phase-out" agreement for the special textile regime (always an embarrassment to GATT), to be accomplished over a decade. Again, many feel that the tex-

tile agreement is flawed—the phaseout is considered either too slow or too fast—but the direction seems right.

6. Standards: Trade rules for product standards are further addressed, after the accomplishment of the Tokyo Round Code. It has become obvious that standards questions are much more complex than many thought, with some fundamental policy differences (such as the clash of environmentalist interests with trade-policy goals). The Uruguay Round text provides the next group of improvements, although more attention will be needed.

7. Safeguards: One of the major failures of the Tokyo Round in 1979 was its inability to achieve an agreement on safeguards and escape-clause measures. In this respect, the Uruguay Round succeeded where the Tokyo Round failed, and a very impressive and ambitious Safeguards Code is one of the Uruguay Round results. It not only provides guidelines and criteria for normal escape-clause use, it also establishes a rule against the use of voluntary export restraints of various kinds. If this agreement is satisfactorily implemented, it could be an impressive addition to world trading discipline.

8. Market access: The Uruguay Round results include impressive advances in so-called market access, including a reduction in the use of quotas (and a shift of quotas to tariffs), as well as very substantial tariff cutting (some say the most of any round). Some of the most substantial tariff cutting has been accomplished by developing countries; but in addition, important advances have been made in reducing tariffs of certain sectors to zero.

9. Developing-country integration: Developing countries are more fully integrated into the GATT/WTO system than before, given the requirement that all countries have tariff and service schedules, and the narrowing of certain less developed country (LDC) exceptions. This measure could be one of the most important features of the Uruguay Round, bringing a treaty-rule discipline to the trade policies of at least the newly industrializing countries, or NICs.

10. Dispute settlement procedures: One of the many achievements of the GATT, despite its "birth defects," has been the development over four decades of a reasonably sophisticated dispute-settlement process. A number of flaws, however, have been recognized in the process. The Uruguay Round, for the first time, establishes an overall unified dispute-settlement system for all portions of its agreements, and provides a legal text (rather than just customary practice) to carry out its procedures. These new

procedures include measures to avoid "blocking" which occurred under previous consensus decision-making rules. The agreement also provides for a new "appellate procedure" which will substitute for some of the procedures that were vulnerable to blocking.

11. WTO Charter: One of the interesting achievements of the Uruguay Round is the development of a new institutional charter for an organization that will help facilitate international cooperation concerning trade and economic relations, and fundamentally change the GATT system to accommodate the vast new terrain of trade competence that this latest round of negotiation thrust on the trading system. Some people have said that this may be the most important element of the Uruguay Round.

These developments, and many others, have led at least one commentator to note the underlying shift evident in the foreign policy of industrial democracies today—namely, economic concerns have taken center stage in foreign affairs decision making. "This is the age of the finance minister," Thomas Friedman says, "The game of nations is now geo-monopoly."[2]

One of the aspects of the world trading system that in recent years has attracted more attention from economists and policymakers, but has always been in the minds of lawyers and legal scholars, is the effect of institutions and their structure on economic development and performance. A Nobel Prize was given recently to several distinguished economic scholars who have provided enormously useful insights about the relationship of institutions to economic performance.[3] Often the attention seems to be directed to models of national economies, but most certainly many of the principles also apply at the international level. One of this book's goals is to develop an explanation of the institutional framework of the world trading system, and the economic policy principles that make up that system. This is why the institutional achievements of the Uruguay Round are so important. For the first time, we now have in place and operating with a very successful launching on 1 January 1995, an organization (WTO) that can be considered the "third leg of the Bretton Woods stool," or the previously "missing link" from international economic institutions. (This link was previously filled uneasily by the GATT, as we shall see in chapter 2.)

Perhaps a good way to begin this study is to reiterate the opening paragraphs of the first edition of this book, which pointed to certain "puzzles." These puzzles were expressed primarily in the context of trade-in-goods issues, but clearly there are analogies for the new issues of trade in services and even intellectual property.

Puzzles, or Why Do Officials Choose the Fourth-Best Option?

Puzzle: Suppose you are the minister for trade of a small Asian country that is rapidly developing. Several of your small electronic components manufacturers export their products to various countries, and you are informed that one of those importing countries has just decided to stop imports from your country. What steps can you take? As a small country, are you completely at the mercy of a larger economic power? In planning investment policies for your country designed in part to export and obtain foreign exchange to pay off a staggering external debt, what world market environment can you rely on?

Puzzle: Suppose you are advising a large multinational corporation based in the United States, and this company is exploring the feasibility of a substantial investment in a plant in a small underdeveloped country in Africa. Inexpensive labor could give products of this plant a substantial advantage on the world market, but to be economically viable this plant must ship over 80 percent of its output outside the small country which has only a tiny market for the product. A smaller plant would not be able to achieve the economies of scale necessary to make the enterprise flourish. Currently there are few government barriers to imports of the projected product into either the United States or Europe. Can you advise your client that he can depend on these circumstances continuing long enough into the future to ensure a satisfactory return on the proposed investment?

Puzzle: Economists, government policymakers, and many others tend to agree that barriers to international trade reduce world welfare and often the welfare of the countries that impose the barriers. If barriers must be imposed, such experts generally agree that a tariff (or price-effect measure) is superior to quantitative restrictions. Yet quantitative measures to reduce trade have proliferated around the world. Particularly in recent years the so-called voluntary export restraint device, whereby the exporting country, at the request of the importing country, restrains the amount of exports of a product that will be shipped to the importing country. This device seems favored even by the importing country, although it is often thought to have an even less favorable effect on the economy of the importing country than the alternative, whereby the importing country itself imposes the quantitative measures. Why is it then that governments tend to opt for the fourth best measure?

These are only a few of a large number of puzzling questions embedded in the subject of international trade today. These puzzles cannot be solved by reference to only one academic discipline, be it economics, or law, or political science. Indeed, these questions may not be solvable at all. But the only potential for discovering reasonable explanations or solutions for these and many other similar puzzles requires a pragmatic and empirical analysis of the motivating factors and circumstances of real transactions and government actions. Many different disciplines, certainly all of those mentioned, are required to assist in that process.

The Meaning of Interdependence

In a world where trade across borders constitutes an ever larger percentage of the gross domestic product of some countries, even for an internal market as large as the United States,[4] it is no wonder that government leaders, businesspeople, and almost everyone else feels some anxiety about those mysterious foreign influences that can affect daily lives so dramatically.[5]

Even these percentages do not tell the whole story. It is generally recognized that the influence of international trade on national economies has been growing for decades and can be much more profound than the percentages might indicate, both because the trade itself is often a much higher percentage of the goods-producing sectors of economies, and because a multiplier or ripple effect amplifies the consequences of such sectors expanding or contracting.[6]

In sum, the world has become increasingly interdependent. With that interdependence has come great wealth: goods are produced where their costs are lowest; consumers have more choices; institutions of production are disciplined through competition; producers can realize the advantages of economies of scale. But with interdependence has come vulnerability. National economies do not stand alone: economic forces move rapidly across borders to influence other societies. Government deficits in the United States can have an impact on its interest rate, which can push heavily indebted developing countries to the verge of "bankruptcy." An embargo or price rise implemented by major oil-producing nations can cause deep and frustrating unemployment, farm bankruptcies, and dramatic rises in the cost of living in the United States. A recession in one part of the world is rapidly felt in other parts.

How did this interdependence come about? Perhaps the technological innovations of the post–World War II era alone would have created these conditions, at least in the absence of major military conflict. The time and cost of transport have fallen rapidly, so that these barriers to greater trade flows and service exchanges have also dropped. Communications have become spectacularly instantaneous: in our living rooms we watch foreign local wars broadcast on the TV news by satellite, and it is possible now to order goods or shift huge sums of money across oceans, literally in seconds. Information systems are changing the character of markets and also affecting business techniques, such as the control of inventories, the use of borrowed money, the response to changing interest rates, and the adoption of new developments of technology. But these scientific advances have little influence if they are resisted by governments, as we observed in the cases of those governments that do resist them.[7]

We must recognize that the international institutions erected or reinstated by governments after World War II have made their contribution. If some world organizations have failed to perform in the manner contemplated by their founders, they have nevertheless contributed symbiotically to the general trend of a shrinking world made possible by scientific innovation. This is particularly the case with the economic institutions.

The 1944 Bretton Woods Conference launched the World Bank and the International Monetary Fund (IMF). A few years later came a failed attempt to add a complementary organization for trade, the ill-fated International Trade Organization (ITO) of the Havana Charter, but into the vacuum came the General Agreement on Tariffs and Trade (GATT). These institutions were later joined by others, including the Organization for Economic Cooperation and Development (OECD), the United Nations Conference on Trade and Development (UNCTAD), and some important regional systems. By the late 1960s, therefore, the liberalization of trade and financial flows promoted by this postwar system—sometimes broadly called the Bretton Woods System—had progressed far enough to foster an unprecedented surge of trade and to demonstrate the economic benefits that flow from such liberalization. But at the same time, new problems were emerging. The receding waters of tariff and other overt protection inevitably uncover the rocks and shoals of nontariff barriers and other problems. As the European Community has experienced in recent decades, creating free trade requires attention to a group of interrelated activities such as the flow of capital, the movement of labor, and the flow of technology and services. These in turn have revolutionized government methods traditionally used to control fiscal and monetary policy, taxation structure, environment regulation, product standards, and liability for product defects. The propensity for government summit meetings, both within Europe and on a worldwide basis, is obviously not unrelated to these world economic trends of interdependence. Likewise, the attempts of governments to combine their efforts through international organizations have a similar result. The question is not whether a government will play on the international scene; the question is, where will it play and with whom (that is, what forum will it work in and what other governments is it willing to let into its "club")?

The problem of international economics today, then, is largely a problem of "managing" interdependence.[8] The success of the Bretton Woods System has created a host of new problems. When economic transactions so easily cross national borders, tensions occur merely because of the differences between economic institutions as well as cultures. In addition, the freedom of border "transit" sometimes allows unscrupulous entrepreneurs to evade national government regulation. Even morally sensitive entrepreneurs their effective power enhanced when they can move activity quickly from one nation to another. Governments, by contrast, are increasingly frustrated by effective evasion of their regulatory powers. Furthermore, governments find that actions of other governments can cause them great difficulties.

Governments respond to these problems in a variety of ways. Some join other governments in an attempt to create an international regulatory system to help ameliorate the "free-for-all" aspects of international trade (such as beggar-thy-neighbor policies), or to provide a unified posture to confront the less public-spirited entrepreneurs. Another common response is to develop internal policies designed to enable their nations to better cope with the challenges of the world economy. Thus, governments adopt "industrial policies," measures to enhance "competitiveness," measures (usually at the border) to offset foreign-governmental or private actions deemed potentially damaging, or reciprocal responses of various kinds.

In considering any of these responses, however, governments participating in the Bretton Woods System (as described in the next chapter) confront international as well as national sets of rules, procedures, and principles that may narrowly constrain their options. One of the purposes of this book is to describe one part of that system: the rules of international trade as developed principally in the context of GATT, but related closely to national laws that regulate trade.

Do the Rules Work?

Let us explore one example. In recent decades the so-called injury test has been a pillar of trade policy. When this test applies, an importing country will presumably only impose restraints on imports of a particular product if it can be established that such imports are "injuring" its domestic industry, which produces like or similar products. An "injurious" import is defined as one that competes with the domestic product and thus *causes* a decline in the domestic industry.

Under international treaties as well as the domestic law of major trading countries, the injury test is elaborately defined. In some cases an independent agency is charged with ascertaining whether the detailed legal criteria for "injury" have been met, and in other cases appeal to the courts may be permitted.

Thus it was surprising and revealing when some years ago during detailed conversation about trade policy with a highly ranked trade official of a European country, this official blandly stated, "Oh, we can always find 'injury' whenever we need to for political purposes."

This comment about the ease with which detailed legal criteria can be overcome for political purposes typifies a larger dilemma of implementing international trade policy in major market-oriented countries today: the tension that is created when legal rules, designed to bring to the subject a measure of predictability and stability, are juxtaposed with the intense human needs of government to make "exceptions" to solve short-term or ad hoc problems. This tension poses difficult problems for the practitioner and the scholar. (Of course, in this respect, trade policy is surely not qualitatively different from tax policy, or unfair competition law, although it may be different in degree.)

Contours of This Study

This book is about trade policy. But it is about trade policy in the context of the legal, constitutional, institutional, and political realities that constrain it. These constraints mold policy so much that its resultant form scarcely, if at all, resembles the pure logic of the economic theorist. Yet, the economic theory is clearly part of the "reality." Without the theory, the policy would often be directionless, lurching from one inconsistent approach to another.

Thus, the purpose of this book is to examine the theory and real implementation of the policies of international trade in our contemporary world in a way that attempts to explain how the theories have been effectively constrained by the processes of real human institutions, especially legal institutions. The perspective of this book is that of a legal scholar, of course. (My "comparative advantage" would not realistically support any other perspective.) Yet the goal—not too ambitious, I hope—is to explore the multidisciplinary context of trade-policy rules. Charts, graphs, and formal mathematical proofs will be eschewed here, because fortunately I can rely on the extensive literature and expertise of generous economist friends for them. Nevertheless, I will state the basic economic propositions of international trade policy, and they will lie at the center of this exposition. However, I will also examine many other policies—sometimes called "noneconomic." Indeed, in many cases we will see a direct clash of inconsistent policies. In precisely those cases lurks the greatest challenge to government action and the law. The basic purpose of this book is to provide policymakers, practitioners, students, and scholars of many different disciplines with an integrated knowledge of the way in which the "international trade system" really operates in today's complex and interdependent world economic-legal-political environment.

Clearly the larger subject of international economics includes many topics in addition to trade in goods, some of which are now embraced in the results of the Uruguay Round, such as trade in services (examples being transport, insurance, banking, other financial services, etc.), and intellectual property. In addition, monetary issues, investment flows, and competition policy come easily to mind. But the observable fact is that the "legal system" for trade in goods, including both national and international rules, is the most intricate and elaborate system of rules that exist in the context of international economic relations.[9] This book is devoted to that system of rules, with its focus primarily on the elaborate and historically well-developed rules relating to trade in goods. One of the challenges of the next few years is determining the degree to which some of these rules can be transported to the new subject areas of the Uruguay Round results, such as services or intellectual property, and even agriculture.

Throughout this work there will be references to certain basic themes. One of these has already been stated in the previous subsection: the tension between the necessity for legal rules conducive to stability and predictability, and the human need for solutions to short-term and ad hoc problems. In another sense this dilemma is largely the well-recognized political-philosophy problem of the tug-of-war between rules and official discretion.

This chapter continues in its next sections with some further introductory reflections. In section 1.2 I turn to the basic policy assumptions that underlie most of the law and policy described in this book, starting with the doctrine of "comparative advantage." Next I look at some of the policies, often termed "noneconomic," that compete with the doctrine of comparative advantage. Certain basic concepts of international law related to international economic affairs will be introduced in section 1.4. Finally I will reconsider some of the underlying themes of this book's exploration of trade policy.

Chapters 2, 3, and 4 outline the basic "constitutional structure" of the contemporary world trading system. Chapter 2 will examine its international structure, and chapter 3 will focus on domestic governmental structures, particularly those of the United States. Chapter 4 explores the much-discussed dispute-resolution and compliance problems.

Chapters 5 through 11 then take up specific "regulatory" subjects of international trade in goods. These are the "substantive issues" of trade policy which are the core of the "system" today. Not all substantive trade policy issues can be taken up in this book, of course, but these seven chapters will cover the most significant and most frequently encountered.

Chapter 12, new in this edition, explores some of the "new" topics of the Uruguay Round, including trade in services, trade-related intellectual property, investment measures, and agriculture (which is certainly not a new issue, but has been particularly perplexing and heretofore largely left out of the effective GATT trading system). Chapter 13 looks at specific types of national economic structures that pose important challenges to the "general rules" of trade policy. First this chapter explores questions related to developing countries. Next it looks at the "economies in transition," as many of the former "nonmarket economies" are now termed. Both of these types of national economic structures pose problems to the trading system, and in some cases are not very adequately handled by the more traditional trading rules.

Finally, chapter 14 surveys the scene painted with such detail in the previous chapters, and asks some very large questions. Hypotheses are offered as answers to some of these questions, but clearly some of the questions are (at least at present) unanswerable.

1.2 The Policy Assumptions of the International Economic System

"Liberal Trade"

The starting point for any discussion of policy for the international economic system of today is the notion of "liberal trade," meaning the goal to minimize the amount of interference of governments in trade flows that cross national borders. The economic arguments concerning this central policy concept will be discussed below, but regardless of their validity or intellectual persuasiveness, there is no question that they have been influential. The basic liberal trade philosophy is constantly reiterated by government and private persons, even in the context of a justification for departing from it!

The prominent economist Paul Samuelson said that "there is essentially only one argument for free trade or freer trade, but it is an exceedingly powerful one, namely: Free trade promotes a mutually profitable division of labor, greatly enhances the potential real national product of all nations, and makes possible higher standards of living all over the globe."[10]

The GATT itself began with a preamble that includes phrases expressing goals of "raising standards of living," by, among other things, "expanding ... exchange of goods." The Leutwiler "eminent persons" Report of 1985 prepared for the GATT expressed a similar view:

> Ever since ancient times, people have found that they can increase their incomes by developing specialized skills and trading the fruits of their labor in the marketplace. A farmer may know how to sew and a tailor may know how to raise chickens—but each can produce more by concentrating on doing what each can do most efficiently.
>
> The same applies to countries. Trade allows countries to concentrate on what they can do best. No two countries are exactly alike in natural resources, climate or work force. Those differences give each country a "comparative advantage" over the others in some products. Trade translates the individual advantages of many countries into maximum productivity for all. This is the classic theory of international trade. It is still valid today.[11]

A 1970 Senate document noted that "It had been the principal goal of American foreign policy since 1934 to strive for the removal of barriers to the free flow of international trade. The original trade agreements program has been extended several times; and since 1934 the Congress, after careful scrutiny and examination, repeatedly renewed the president's advance authority to negotiate reciprocal agreements to lower trade barriers."[12]

The July 1971 Report of the President's Commission on International Trade and Investment Policy (also known as the Williams Commission), in expressing the goals of U.S. policy, included this sentence: "The ultimate goal should be to achieve for all people the benefit of an open world in which goods and capital can move freely."[13]

More recently, the developments of the Uruguay Round and its implementation have reinforced these various expressions of policy. The WTO Charter carries forward some of the phraseology of the GATT Agreement, speaking of "raising standards of living ... and expanding the production of and trade in goods and services, while allowing for the optimal use of the world's resources in accordance with the objective of sustainable development ..." The United States Uruguay Round Agreements Act of 1994 carries forth these policies.

Thus there can be little doubt of the general policy underpinnings of the post–World War II international economic system as it prevails at least among the so-called industrial-market economies. There is uncertainty, however, about what this basic policy implies in specific instances, and doubt that this basic policy is still viable in the face of changed circumstances. These are issues to which this book repeatedly returns.

Of course, this basic "economic goal" is not the only goal of international trade policy. A number of other goals can be articulated also. In some cases these other goals may be partly inconsistent with the central goal, requiring some "balancing" or "compromise." At this point I will not attempt to inventory all possible goals of international economic policy, but at least two more can be mentioned here. In the next section I describe some other policy goals, which could be classified as "noneconomic."

During the years near the end and just after World War II, as leaders of the victorious nations began formulating postwar plans for international economic institutions, one could detect in speeches and documents a strong political goal that accompanied the economic thinking of the day. The political goal arose from the view that the interwar economic problems were causes in part for World War II.[14] The Great Depression, the mishandling of policy toward Germany after World War I, and other similar inter-war circumstances weighed heavily on the minds of policymakers who wanted to design post–World War II institutions that would prevent a recurrence of these problems. For example, Harry Hawkins who was, at the time, Director of the Office of Economic Affairs of the U.S. Department of State, said in a 1944 speech, "Trade conflict breeds noncooperation, suspicion, bitterness. Nations which are economic enemies are not likely to remain political friends for long."[15] A 1945 presidential message stated: "The fundamental choice is whether countries will struggle against each other for wealth and power, or work together for security and mutual advantage.... The experience of cooperation in the task of earning a living promotes both the habit and the techniques of common effort and helps make permanent the mutual confidence on which the peace depends."[16]

Another policy underlying contemporary international economic rules and institutions has become increasingly prominent in recent decades. This is the policy of promoting economic development in countries that were not industrialized at the end of World War II. Many of the corollaries of this policy goal appear to challenge the appropriateness of rules and institutions assumed to be desirable for general "liberal trade" goals, and this development goal has lead some leaders to question the fairness of the economic institutions established during the 1940s.[17]

There are many candidates for other noneconomic policies which, in the minds of some, should influence economic policy as well as other policies. Toward the end of this book I will return to some of these, which include topics such as human rights, environmental policies, labor standards, and so on.

Ricardo and the Theory of Comparative Advantage

Peter Kenen writes: "The study of international trade and finance is among the oldest specialties within economics. It was conceived in the sixteenth century, a lusty child of Europe's passion for Spanish gold, and grew to maturity in the turbulent years that witnessed the emergence of the modern nation state. It attracted the leading economists of the eighteenth and nineteenth centuries, including David Hume, Adam Smith, David Ricardo, and John Stuart Mill...."[18]

Early theorists developed a "mercantilist" viewpoint. Under this theory, the goal of nations in their economic relations was to amass gold or other treasure, so as to maximize national power (which was not well distinguished from the wealth and power of sovereigns). The goal therefore was to "sell more to strangers yearly than we consume of theirs in value." This theory was soon attacked as flawed by Hume and Smith, among others. For one thing, mere accumulation of money did not necessarily promise better living standards or even the instruments of power (warships, etc.). For another thing, accumulating monetary assets could cause inflation, undermining a nation's world-competitive position.

Eighteenth-century classicists focused on the welfare of citizens rather than sovereigns, and noted the advantages of international trade, Adam Smith saying: "What is prudence in the conduct of every private family can scarce be folly in that of a great kingdom. If a foreign country can supply us with a commodity cheaper than we ourselves can make it, better buy it of them with some part of the produce of our own industry...."[19]

It was Ricardo, in 1817, who went a step further and developed the theory of comparative advantage, which, despite refutations from skeptical politicians, has provided a powerful intellectual underpinning, still respected by all major economists, for policies that generally stress the value of "liberal trade"—that is, of minimizing governmental interference with trade flows. We must therefore examine this theory in more detail.

The theory was originally based on a simple model of international trade, involving two countries, two traded products, and one type of input for both products.[20] Often the model uses the United Kingdom and Portugal as the countries, cloth and wine as the products, and labor as the input. Assume that in the United Kingdom a yard of cloth takes 5 hours of labor to produce, and a gallon of wine 10 hours of labor to produce. Assume that in Portugal it takes 10 hours to produce the yard of cloth and 6 hours to produce the gallon of wine. It is obvious that the United Kingdom has an absolute advantage in cloth production and Portugal an absolute advantage in wine production. The total goods produced by an available 90 hours of labor in each country, absent trade (i.e. with autarky), can be summarized as follows:

United Kingdom: 18 yards of cloth or 9 gallons of wine, or some combination of these, such as 10 yards of cloth and 4 gallons of wine.

Portugal: 9 yards of cloth or 15 gallons of wine, or some combination of these, such as 6 yards of cloth and 5 gallons of wine.

Given that citizens in both countries want both products, then without trade both countries will produce some mix of the two products, such as the following:

	United Kingdom	Portugal	Total
Cloth	10 yd	3 yd	13 yd
Wine	0 gal	10 gal	14 gal

If trade between the two countries is opened and each specializes entirely, trading for the product of the other, then the products available or produced in each can be summarized as follows:

	United Kingdom	Portugal	Total
Cloth	18 yd	0 yd	18 yd
Wine	4 gal	15 gal	15 gal

The totals for both products are larger than in the autarky case, and thus more is available for consumption in both countries under trading conditions.

The model above shows a case where each of two countries has an absolute advantage in one of the two products, and trade will help both. The question that immediately occurs, then, is, if one country has an absolute advantage in *both* goods, should these countries trade? Such a case would demonstrate the power of the theory of comparative advantage. The following table summarizes this situation, both before and after trade opens.

	United Kingdom	Portugal	Total
Labor available	90 hr	90 hr	
Labor used			
Hours per yard	5 hr	10 hr	
Hours per gallon	10 hr	10 hr	
Autarky			
Cloth	10 yd	5 yd	15 yd
Wine	4 gal	4 gal	8 gal
Trade			
Cloth	18 yd	0 yd	18 yd
Wine	0 gal	9 gal	9 gal

Thus, it is not the difference of *absolute* advantages but of *comparative* advantage that gives rise to the gains from trade. Even when the United Kingdom can produce all goods in the model with no more labor than Portugal, there is an advantage for the two countries to trade if the *ratio* of production costs of the two products differs. In this second case, wine in the United Kingdom costs 2 yards of cloth, whereas in Portugal it costs only 1 yard of cloth; thus it is worthwhile for the United Kingdom to produce cloth and to trade its excess for wine. In fact (going beyond Ricardo), with specialization one may create economies of scale so that the gains from trade would be even more than those represented in this hypothetical case.

The discussion above presents the basic model of the theory of comparative advantage, but it is appropriate to ask whether the model has been confirmed by empirical evidence. The simple model above does not lend itself easily to empirical investigation, partly because it is so simple. Derivative and additive theories complementing the model, however, have been tested with some success.[21] The apparent importance of trade to national and world economic growth and well-being is sometimes seen in statistics showing that world trade over several decades has generally grown at a faster rate than the economy as a whole.[22] Strictly speaking, however, this fact does not necessarily confirm the theory of comparative advantage, given that there are many other factors (including the significant decline of transportation costs and other "natural" barriers to trade) that could explain in part the fact.

Elaborations of the simple model, however, all seem to point in the same direction. A large number of studies, based on various plausible theories or analyses of the effects of restraints on trade, exist that show a loss in welfare for the world as a whole and often also for the countries imposing the restrictions. These restraints cause costs to be borne by the economies, usually costs that are imposed on the consumers or other users of the imported product.[23]

The theory of comparative advantage does have strong intuitive appeal. As consumers, individual citizens can easily see the advantage of international trade: it gives them greater choice of products at better prices. Travelers return home raving about their purchases. Buyers in the marketplace observe better available values in some imported goods. Of course the question remains whether Adam Smith was right when he claimed that what is good for families is also good for nations. Most assuredly one does not follow from the other. The advantages that buyers discover in individual cases may result in an overall disadvantage for a nation as a whole.

One thing does seem clear, however. Import trade provides an additional source of competition to domestic producers. Considered intuitively, and on the basis of a large number of studies, competition is almost always deemed beneficial to world or national-aggregate economic welfare. This can be seen intuitively from individual experiences in recent years with electronic consumer goods: calculators costing over $100 during the mid-1970s can now be purchased in better versions for under $8 (although surely some of this discrepancy is a result of technological innovation). The remarkable and seemingly perpetual drop in the price of computers is another example.

Yet there are also groups in a national economy that experience loss from shifts to freer trade, such as the employees who lose their jobs in a domestic industry because of competition from imports. Of course, there are numerous other reasons, including other domestic competition, why firms or whole industry sectors decline, causing job loss as well as capital investment loss. Changes of taste, changes in government procurement programs, new technology, and improved efficiency of production processes can all be mentioned. The question is, why should influences from beyond a nation's borders, ones requiring "structural adjustment changes," be treated differently from such influences from within a nation's borders?

An interesting article in the *Journal of Economic Literature* discusses some of these circumstances in the context of theories relating to "industrial policy." In the article, Norton notes that the United States is a large, integrated market with conditions similar to those of free trade among a group of smaller countries (such as in Europe). He advances the suggestion that "U.S. regional diversity has enforced a painful but therapeutic adjustment of a kind missing in Victorian Britain or contemporary Europe." Unlike the relative stagnation in Europe during recent decades, he notes that "... regional diversity has enforced a rapid adjustment in the U.S. over the past 15 years. America's transition has been perhaps more painful but surely more effective than in Europe. The result has been rapid U.S. job growth over the period, during a time when new entrants flooded the American labor market."[24]

Challenging the Theory: Conditions and Assumptions of the Theory of Comparative Advantage

One way to challenge the theory of comparative advantage is to demonstrate that some of the conditions required for it to operate do not exist in the real world, or similarly, that some assumptions on which the theory is based are not valid. A few of these conditions and assumptions will be discussed in this subsection.[25]

One of the more important arguments used to challenge the theory is that it depends on a relatively perfect competitive environment which only rarely exists. Thus, if markets are manipulated by monopolistic influences or any other situations of imperfect competition (including government regulation and other policies), the functioning of comparative advantage can be seriously impaired.[26]

The theory also is said to depend on a so-called static economic analysis. Some experts have alleged that it does not adequately take into account certain "dynamic" conditions of economic systems.[27] For example, when the importing nation's economy is in a period of declining demand, it is possible that import competition could exacerbate unemployment (at least during the time required for "adjustment" unemployment and factor shifts), which could cause an over all short-term decline in world welfare because of trade. In addition, another argument forcibly put forward in recent years is that government policies can themselves change the conditions of competition or "comparative advantage," particularly for products that require inputs that are not immutable. Immutable inputs might include sunshine, arable land, iron ore deposits, water, and so forth. But for many recent products, particularly those of "high technology," important inputs include skilled labor and expertise, transportation, communication, and availability of risk capital. A nation's endowments of these inputs can be influenced by government policy (education, roads, communication infrastructure, capital-market structures, etc.).[28]

Finally, it is sometimes said that the model is too simple and thus not realistic. It deals in its original form with only two countries, two products, and one factor of production. Obviously the real world is vastly more complicated, and different products have complex interactions of factor mobility and substitutability of demand. Economists, however, respond that this criticism of the model does not hold up. Modern elaborations of the model show that it supports the value of liberal trade in surprisingly general cases.[29]

Challenging the Theory: What Is Success?

Often statements about economic theory, including theory of international trade, seem to imply a goal of maximizing "real" wealth of more and better goods and services. Theorists note that, in a market-oriented, consumer-choice system, there is room for choices to be non-"real" or nonmaterial. Thus some prefer leisure over television sets, or esoteric music over popular concerts, or religious values and meditation over worldly goods. But it is worrisome that a purely market-driven system tends to reduce the opportunity of those choices, that somehow all the talk about "efficiency" or "competitiveness" or "gross national product" tends to overlook many of these nonmaterial choices.

This subject clearly cannot be extensively explored here. Yet it is raised in connection with international economic policies. There may indeed be a preference in some societies for preserving agricultural or nonindustrial social patterns. Likewise some societies may be prepared to pay a large price (forgoing such basics as telephones or health services) to preserve historic or aesthetic sites. These societies may be willing to do this even though it requires forcing individual citizens to relinquish choices they would prefer in the market. The international policy issue of this is whether the longer-term direction of international economic policy unnecessarily tends to make national choices about social patterns or "nonmaterial" preferences more difficult. It also raises the question of whether in some circumstances such national choices are made because the cost of these choices is somehow being thrust onto other nations that do not necessarily benefit from them.

Wealth maximizing, in the material sense, may not be as high a priority in the view of some as other goals, such as equitable distribution of income. Even though a nation as a whole may prosper with trade, particular groups within it may be seriously harmed.[30] Again the circumstance raises questions, some of which are termed "adjustment," to which I will return in later chapters (see especially chapter 7, concerning safeguards).

One example of a powerful goal that often cuts against traditional theories of international trade has been brilliantly recognized by the economist Max Corden. In his book *Trade Policy and Economic Welfare* he speaks of a preference in many societies that he terms the "conservative social welfare function": "Let us now introduce the conservative social welfare function, a concept which seems particularly helpful for understanding actual trade policies of many countries. Put in its simplest form it includes the following income distribution target: any significant absolute reductions in real incomes of any significant section of the community should be avoided.... In terms of welfare weights, increases in income are given relatively low weights and decreases very high weights."[31]

This, Corden says perceptively, helps explain the income maintenance motivation of so many tariffs in the past. Corden argues that the income maintenance motivation has a number of elements. First, it is "unfair" to allow anyone's real income to be significantly reduced—especially as the result of deliberate policy decisions—unless there are very good reasons for this and it is more or less unavoidable. Second, insofar as people are risk averters, everyone's real "income" is increased when it is known that a government will generally intervene to prevent sudden or large, unexpected income losses. The conservative social welfare function is part of a social insurance system. Third, social peace requires that no significant group's income shall fall if that of other groups is rising. Social peace might be regarded as a social good in itself or as a basis for political stability and hence for economic development. And even if social peace does not depend on the maintenance of the incomes of the major classes in the community, the survival of a government may. Finally, if a policy is aimed at a certain target, such as protecting an industry or improving the balance of payments, most governments want to minimize the adverse side effects on sectional incomes so as not to become involved in political battles incidental to their main purpose.

The Level Playing Field as a Policy Goal

Often one hears about the importance of the "level playing field" in relation to proposals for trade policy.[32] The meaning and implications of this goal are anything but clear. To a certain degree the goal may imply preserving a competitive market atmosphere for world trade, just as some large societies (notably the United States) have such a goal for their internal markets. Thus, when foreign governments intervene in the world market to favor their own national objectives, or foreign manufacturers engage in various noncompetitive practices, these activities are thought to be unfair to competing producers in other countries.

But often something more is meant by the "level playing field" idea. Even "economically competitive" actions by foreign firms are considered in some cases to be "unfair," and thus to disturb the level playing field. Certain categories of actions have for many decades been considered to be "unfair" by nations and the international rules of international trade. Among these are "dumping" and "subsidy" activities, anticompetitive and monopoly practices, as well as other actions, including patent, trademark, or copyright infringements. It is not always clear whether all the practices subsumed by trade policy experts under these categories really have a damaging impact on a world trading system, or whether they provide for uneven conditions of competition for producing firms in other nations. Yet the goal of promoting a level playing field, through national and international policies designed to inhibit dumping or subsidies, seems to have powerful political appeal (which I shall discuss in later chapters).[33]

1.3 Competing Policy Goals and Noneconomic Objectives

Even Adam Smith recognized two exceptions to his views about the value of liberal trade among nations. I have already discussed some circumstances under which nations might pursue goals that would not maximize material wealth. Goals of distributive justice and Max Corden's conservative social welfare function were mentioned in section 1.2. In this section we will look at a few of the national objectives that in a sense "compete" with the traditional goals of liberal trade theories.

The objective of "national security" is frequently recognized as justifying a departure from liberal trade policies.[34] Adam Smith recognized national security as a valid reason for such departure: "Defence," he wrote, "is more than opulence."[35] Thus a nation may feel that its national security requires an airplane (or shipbuilding) industry regardless of whether such industry has a "comparative advantage" or is even viable on world markets. Tariffs or other protection may be used by such a nation to preserve and enhance this industry. There are two problems that must always be considered in this context, however.

First, preserving or building a productive capacity for the contingency of war or for preventing a challenge to national economic survival may indeed be a valid goal, but there may be more economically efficient ways to achieve that goal. Economists argue, for example, that in certain circumstances direct subsidies may be preferable to restraints on imports.[36] Of course, the structure of domestic political and legal institutions will vitally affect the choice of means to support a domestic industry. The structure of governmental and political institutions may make it impossible or very difficult to use a direct subsidy: it is too obvious, it adds to the government budget deficit, it requires a long debate and a vote of a parliament, and so on. In such cases national leaders may succumb to the temptation to fall back on the economically less desirable but politically more feasible techniques of import restraints to achieve goals they believe are important in the national interest.

A problem inherent in the national security argument is determining its limits. Which industries (if any) are needed for security in a world of potentially instantaneous wars? It is all too easy for any economic group to argue its importance to national security as an excuse for import protection. One variation on this argument proposes that a nation must always have certain industries as part of its industrial "infrastructure." Thus, it says, a certain minimum steelmaking capacity must be maintained regardless of its efficiency or competitiveness in the world economy. This argument invokes some concepts of "industrial policy," wherein the national government makes choices and influences the structure of its economy. These arguments are much debated.[37] Some would question whether in today's world of instant communications, large transport aircraft, intercontinental missiles, and computer capabilities, a steel industry is an essential institution for national security.

A second, but related argument, is that a nation needs to avoid being too dependent on other nations (or even on the world economy). Such dependence, it says, reduces real sovereignty and makes a nation vulnerable to economic and political forces beyond its control, and to decisions made by either political or business leaders outside its borders. Thus, nations that traditionally rely on one or a few types of exports (oil, copper, sugar, etc.) may legitimately feel that the ups and downs of the world markets pose too much strain and adjustment costs to their economies. In such cases a nation will often be willing to forgo some current or short-term economic welfare in order to achieve somewhat greater security and economic stability. The argument for maintaining certain basic "core" industries may be motivated by this goal. Thus a steel industry (and sometimes an airline) becomes an attribute of sovereignty. It is debatable whether the independence argument is valid even for very small economies. It is also debatable whether in today's interdependent world such argument is realistic. Like much else, it probably has some validity.

More subtle is the possibility that a national consensus could explicitly opt for a choice of policies that would not maximize wealth (in the traditionally measurable sense, at least), but would give preference to other noneconomic goals. For example, the choice might be to preserve an agricultural way of life for groups of citizens used to it. Philosophy or aesthetics might lead a public consensus to such a preference even though it means a lower standard of living for the whole population. Likewise one can imagine (and observe) choice of religious goals (and lifestyle demands of such religion), or aesthetic choices, such as a preference for classical music and opera (with extensive subsidization of music education and musicians). There is little in international trade theory that can refute the validity of such choices on the part of nations, with perhaps one exception. It can be argued that when a nation makes an "uneconomic" choice, it should be prepared to pay the whole cost, and not pursue policies that have the effect of unloading some of the burdens of that choice onto other nations. In an interdependent world, paying the whole cost is not often easy to accomplish.

Noneconomic social policy choices might also lead a nation to try to preserve or encourage certain types of economic activity for its citizens. For example, perhaps a national preference for "white-collar" work (in clean, pleasant surroundings) can be observed. A nation, for this reason, might want to take steps to favor businesses of this type. Could it be that this will become more of a problem if the major nations begin to develop more rules for trade in services such as banking or insurance?[38] A worrisome possibility that often crops up in the context of these types of consideration, is the danger that special interest groups in a particular society can manipulate the governmental processes to favor their own economic well-being, using the excuse of broader national policy goals to buttress their petitions.

A commonly stated "exception" to liberal trade theory is the "infant industry" argument. This argument proposes the use of import barriers to enable a new or young industry to become established and viable. The barriers to imports give some shelter against foreign competition, until the industry is strong enough to meet that competition. There are several problems with this argument. Economists can argue that there are better ways to achieve the goal of promoting the new industry, such as the explicit use of subsidies.[39] (The same constraints discussed in the case of national security may apply here as well, however.) And, as with the national security arguments, there may be the problem of identifying which industries should receive the benefit of "infant" treatment. For small economies, the infant industry argument for import protection may be relatively weak: such an industry may need to depend on exports to establish the economies of scale necessary for true viability. Related to these arguments are more perplexing ones that focus on the advantage of "learning by doing" to justify governments or individual firms pursuing certain strategic policies or market share-enhancing programs.

This can lead to arguments about tariff and trade preferences which later chapters discuss.[40] One problem has been determining when an "infant" industry has reached maturity, so that it no longer merits the exceptional treatment of import protection. There is often a tendency for industries to argue for perpetual infancy status.[41]

One noneconomic goal greatly affecting national trade policies is the preservation of political or economic power. At least in a democratic nation, national leaders will be observably influenced in their trade-policy decisions by the desire to get elected or reelected. But not only political leaders manifest the desire for power. Business leaders and labor leaders can also be seen to have similar tendencies. It has been queried whether liberal trade policies render labor unions more vulnerable and reduce their power. Although it may not yet be possible to answer this query definitively, it does seem that some evidence supports an affirmative answer. (This relates to goals of distributive justice also.) But the reduction of power may occur not only to labor unions. Some industrial leaders and owners of capital may also find their power reduced. No one involved in trade policy questions can afford to ignore the often intense feelings that are engendered by these effects from international trade (or other international transactions). No one can effectively explain the specially favored place that agricultural producers have preserved in trade policy measures without reference to some of these ideas.[42] An interesting study beyond the scope of this book would analyze the gains and losses of power among national groups resulting from international economic interdependence and international trade. Do the nimble, well-managed multinational corporations find their effective power enhanced by these international economic trends?

1.4 International Law and International Economic Relations: An Introduction

International Economic Law

In recent years one has increasingly heard references to "international economic law."[43] Unfortunately, this phrase is not well defined. Scholars and practitioners have differing ideas about the meaning of this term. Some would have it cast a very wide net, and embrace almost any aspect of international law that relates to any sort of economic matter. Considered broadly, almost all international law could be called international economic law, because almost every aspect of international relations touches in one way or another on economics. Indeed, it can be argued from the latter observation that there cannot be any separate subject denominated as international economic law. A more restrained definition of international economic law, however, would embrace trade, investment, and services when they are involved in transactions that cross national borders, and those subjects that involve the establishment on national territory of economic activity of persons or firms originating from outside that territory.

In any event, clearly the subject of international trade, whether in goods or in services (or both), is at the core of international economic law. This book focuses on the rules of international trade in products, but the implications of those rules for other subjects of international economic relations should be obvious. The rules of product trade, centrally served by the GATT, are the most complex and extensive international rules regarding any subject of international economic relations that exist. As such it is natural that they would have some influence on the potential development of rules for other international economic subjects,[44] particularly the subjects developed in the Uruguay Round context, including services and intellectual property. In addition, there is mention of a "GATT for investment" and the possibility of a WTO approach for certain other subjects. For this reason there is considerable justification for focusing on the rules of product trade as reflected in the WTO/GATT system. This focus can be thought of as sort of a "case study" of the advantages and disadvantages, the positives and negatives, of an elaborate rule system at the international level.

Two unfortunate bifurcations of the subject of international economic law exist, however. One is the distinction between monetary and trade affairs. Given that both are, in a sense, "two sides of the same coin," a degree of artificiality separates them as topics. Yet international organizations, national governments, and even university departments tend to indulge in the same separation; and given that the whole world cannot be studied at once, there is great practical value in taking up the trade questions separately.

An even less fortunate distinction of subject matter is often made between international and domestic rules. This book will not indulge in that separation. In fact, the domestic and international rules and legal institutions of economic affairs are inextricably intertwined. It is not possible to understand the real operation of either of these sets of rules in isolation from the other. The national rules (especially constitutional rules) have had enormous influence on the international institutions and rules. Likewise the reverse influence can often be observed. Consequently, in this work I shall try to treat them both, and introduce them in the next two chapters.

International Law and Economic Relations

By way of introduction to the international law bearing on economic affairs, and as part of an historical introduction to it, several observations may be useful to the reader.

Sources of international law can generally be divided into "customary" or "conventional." The latter term refers to treaties, which are often termed "conventions." Customary international law is defined as rules of national behavior that can be ascertained from the practice of nations when such practice reveals that nations are acting under a sense of legal obligation (*opinio juris*).[45] Unfortunately, customary international law norms are quite often ambiguous and controversial. On many propositions of customary international law, scholars and practitioners disagree not only about their meaning but even about their existence. The traditional doctrines of establishing a norm of customary international law leave a great deal of room for such controversy.

In economic affairs, however, very few norms of customary international law are recognized. There is a heavily disputed jurisprudence relating to the taking of alien property by national governments.[46] In addition, there are some fairly well-recognized norms of the law of the sea that relate to economic matters regarding the sea.[47] Beyond these, very little exists in the way of *substantive* international law customary norms (that is, norms other than ones dealing with procedures of government-to-government relations, or of relations among firms or individuals in the few cases when international law is deemed to apply to firms or indviduals).

One view argues that there is a customary norm of economic relations that prohibits "discriminatory" action among nations. This "most-favored-nation" (MFN) ideal is embodied in many treaties, including the WTO and GATT,[48] but most scholars and practitioners do not seem to accept the argument that there is any customary international norm of MFN.[49] Thus, when dealing with international economic law, one is dealng primarily with *treaties*.

Functional Approach to International Law

A critical question, almost always asked by anyone confronted with an international law norm, is "Why does it matter?" Put another way, much cynicism exists about the importance or effectiveness of international law rules. Frequently the public can read news of violations of these rules by major and minor nations. In some cases these violations, even when admitted to be such (often bitter and inconclusive argument arises on this question), are rationalized or declared "just" by national leaders.[50] Thus the cynicism about international rules cannot be surprising.

A more careful examination of the role and effectiveness of international rules is necessary, however. First, it should be observed that not all domestic rules are always obeyed either. Observe traffic at any stop sign, or recall teacher strikes in many U.S. states where they are illegal. Then observe the cases of enterprises violating economic regulations, evading taxes, or indulging in corruption of government officials. It is apparent that international law has no monopoly on breaches and violations. It is a matter of degree. At least in stable societies it can be said that domestic laws are more often obeyed and effective than are international laws, and few scholars or practitioners of international law would try to refute that statement.

Yet many international rules are remarkably well observed. Why this is so has been the subject of much speculation which will not be repeated here.[51] Notions of reciprocity and a desire to depend on other nations observance of rules lead many nations to observe rules even when they do not want to. The critical task for this book is to evaluate realistically the role of the international as well as the national rules in influencing real behavior of nations or persons or enterprises. I will have more to say on this in later chapters.[52]

At least in the context of economic behavior, however, and particularly when that behavior is set in circumstances of decentralized decision making, as in a market economy, rules can have important operational functions. They may provide nearly the only predictability or stability to a potential investment or trade-development situation. Without such predictability or stability, trade or investment flows might be even more risky and therefore more inhibited than otherwise. If such "liberal trade" goals (for reasons already discussed in section 1.2) contribute to world welfare, then it follows that rules that assist such goals should also contribute to world welfare. To put it another way, the policies that tend to reduce some risks lower the "risk premium" required by entrepreneurs to enter into international transactions.

1.5 The Tangled Web: Is There a Warp and a Woof?

Legal scholars sometimes refer to the "seamless web" of the law.[53] The phrase connotes the notion that each legal concept is in some way related to virtually every other legal concept. It also connotes a certain skepticism of theory and of simplifying concepts—a skepticism that in many ways is characteristic of the legal profession, that often views itself as uniquely, among the learned professions, coming face to face with the complexity and coarseness of reality with the aim of solving real problems. It is sometimes said that the economist tells us what should be done, while the lawyer is left to figure out how to do it.

The converse problem can also be dangerous: there is always the risk of losing sight of the forest because one's gaze focuses on particular trees. Watch a lawyer and a social scientist argue. The lawyer often cites specific cases—the "anecdotal evidence"—to make his point. The social scientist, on the other hand, will often use statistics to make his point. There are dangers with each approach. To formulate statistics it is often necessary to develop categories for counting that are oversimplified. The specific case history can be a useful way to avoid this kind of oversimplification. On the other hand, the use of anecdotes can often seriously mislead policymakers. "Once does not make always"; the anecdotes may be atypical.

Thus the dilemma of a book like this becomes obvious. How can meaningful generalizations be stated in the short space allotted for exposition of an extraordinarily complex subject? There is always the danger of an apparently "unifying hypothesis" seriously oversimplifying the subject and thereby misleading the policymaker and problem solver. Yet without some generalization it is difficult, if not impossible, to understand the subject. Perhaps one way out of this difficulty is to state issues or questions raised by the material, without in all cases trying to formulate answers. In this book I try to do a little of both.

Several important themes or problems of the "world trade policy system" have already been introduced. The dilemma of rule versus discretion is one such theme, to which I return particularly in chapter 4. Closely associated with this theme is the question of the "effectiveness" of the trade rules: How effective are they? How effective should they be? How can they be made more effective (if that is desirable)?

The puzzle of an apparent tendency to choose second-, third-, or even fourth-best policy options has also been noted. In these cases noneconomic policy goals are often operating, sometimes without being obvious. Some of the conflicting policy goals have to do with the legal and constitutional structure of the "system." A certain constitutional political structure can impose severe constraints on decision makers, as I will show particularly in the next two chapters. For example, a constitutional requirement of parliamentary approval can often lead officials to seek nonlegislative ways to resolve problems, even if these ways appear to be less desirable (in economic theory) than the option selected. Yet there are important policy reasons for the existence of constitutional structure, for example, preventing a monopoly of power or preserving a representative form of government. Sometimes the "obstructiveness" of lawyers ("you can't do that, it's unconstitutional!") is merely the exercise of a constitutional cautionary function ("Think about the really long-term consequences of what you want to do").

One persistent theme that becomes apparent in the study of trade policy and law is the close interaction of national and international institutions. Each has a strong influence on the other, and it is impossible to understand this subject fully (and many others in today's interdependent world) without noticing and analyzing how these influences operate. The U.S. Constitution had a direct influence on the shaping of the GATT (as the next chapter will show). Vice versa, much of current U.S. trade legislation can only be understood in the context of the GATT rules.[54] The tendency for academic subject matters to separate international from national or domestic issues becomes an important source of misunderstanding.

A frequently discussed and debated topic of current trade policy is the question of what is "unfair" government or private activity. Politicians and others commonly declare, "Of course I am for liberal trade, but it must be *fair* trade. We must take action against all those unfair trade activities of *other* nations, even if that means restraining imports from them." But how do we tell what is "fair?" In chapters 10 and 11 we struggle with this theme. Closely related to it is another theme, which I call the "interface" problem. This refers to the difficulty, in the current interdependent world, of trade among different types of economies. Some of the "unfairness" problems are in reality "difference" problems. We come across this type of issue in later chapters, but again, especially in chapters 10 and 11.

Thus I have expressed a sort of "consumer warning." Do not expect too much of this book. Problems that appeared intractable before you read it will in many cases still appear intractable afterward. But I hope that this monograph will contribute at least modestly to an understanding of *why* these problems appear to be intractable, albeit primarily from the perspective of a legal scholar, but also whenever possible from the direct vantage point of a participant.

2 The International Institutions of Trade: The WTO and the GATT

2.1 The Bretton Woods System and Its Context

Introduction

The previous chapter made allusion to the importance of institutions; and indeed, a response to the "puzzles" set forth early in that chapter can only point to the impact of institutions, both international and national, on the empirically observable effects of the international trade rules and policies.[1]

We now have the WTO as the principal institution for international trade, but to understand this institution, it is necessary also to know something about its "predecessor," the GATT. Indeed, the WTO Charter makes it clear that the GATT history is significant, prescribing (in Article 16) that "the WTO shall be guided by the decisions, procedures and customary practices followed by the CONTRACTING PARTIES (expressed in all caps to signify the Contracting Parties acting jointly under the GATT agreement) to GATT 1947 and the bodies established in the framework of GATT 1947." Given that the rules of international law are framed and interpreted by "customary practice," including practice of its treaty institutions,[2] in many cases the history and practice of institutions and international law are significantly more important than might be the case in some national legal jurisdictions. Thus, in this chapter we will begin with a review of the historical background of the GATT, leading up to the WTO charter and its implementation.[3]

Although for many years the GATT has been featured in headlines and major daily newspapers as the most important treaty governing international trade relations, the fact is that the GATT treaty, as such, never came into force. How could this be? What were the institutional and historical events that occurred during the formation years of the GATT (1947–1950) that led to this state of affairs? How has this history affected the operation and the vigor of the GATT? And how will this history affect the new WTO? These are some of the issues with which we struggle in this chapter. Although the GATT treaty as such never came into force, it is necessary to clarify that the obligations of GATT were (and are) clearly binding under international law, because of the historical circumstances that this chapter describes.

The Context of Treaty Obligations for International Economic Affairs

Before embarking on a history of the GATT and the WTO, however, it may be useful to review the context of international norms relating to economic affairs. International economic relations under international law are primarily governed by treaties, rather than by customary law. In many cases, the treaties establish organizations. In these cases, a number of interesting legal questions may arise concerning the constitution and operation of the institution, as well as its authority to establish "secondary" law in the form of decisions, regulations, or possibly subsidiary treaty-type instruments.[4]

The principal governmental organizations concerning economic relations include the International Monetary Fund (IMF),[5] the International Bank for Reconstruction and Development (IBRD) or the World Bank,[6] and the GATT. These institutions comprise the Bretton Woods System. Although the GATT was not formed at the Bretton Woods Conference, the participants at the conference nevertheless contemplated the necessity of an international trade organization, or ITO. Indeed, in some ways the WTO, after many years, has become the "missing leg" of the Bretton Woods "stool," as noted earlier.

There is no dearth of organizations relating to international economic relations. Of the three thousand nine hundred governmental international organizations listed in the *Yearbook of International Organizations*, at least three hundred can be said to relate to economic matters.[7]

What does this "landscape" of international economic institutions look like? These institutions can be grouped into the following categories. The first category would include general economic institutions that are designed to address problems that appear in a variety of economic sectors and that affect many nations (but not necessarily all). The Bretton Woods System, consisting of the IMF, the World Bank, and the two World Bank affiliates,[8] as well as GATT/WTO, is the core of this category. Furthermore, two important international organizations can be included, namely, the Organization for Economic Cooperation and Development

(OECD),[9] although its membership is focused primarily on the industrial western countries, and the United Nations Conference on Trade and Development (UNCTAD),[10] which is a United Nations subsidiary and therefore has as "members" all United Nations members. The UNCTAD has been identified most prominently with developing countries issues, but is not technically limited to those. In addition, the UN's Economic and Social Council (ECOSOC) can be grouped with these.[11]

The second category of organizations includes the other United Nations specialized agencies, which tend to focus on particular problems or sectors of endeavor. For example, the Food and Agriculture Organization (FAO) addresses agricultural problems; the International Civil Aviation Organization (ICAO) deals with airline transportation; the International Labor Organization (ILO) tries to improve working and livng standards; and the International Maritime Organization is concerned with shipping.[12]

The third category is composed of the "regional" organizations. In many cases these organizations are in the form of "customs unions," "free trade areas," or interim agreements leading to one or the other. The most prominent of these organizations of course is the European Community (EC), or as it is often termed today the "EU"—European Union,[13] which currently has fifteen member states in Europe, and is perhaps the most cohesive customs union in existence.[14] In addition to the EC, however, there are a number of other regional economic organizations, with varying degrees of cohesiveness and stability. For example, in the past the European Free Trade Area (EFTA) was prominent,[15] although its role decreased after most of its members left to join the EC.[16] More recently we have seen the establishment of the North American Free Trade Agreement (NAFTA)—a very significant regional organization.[17]

A fourth category of institutions or international agreements relating to economic matters consists of a variety of international commodity agreements.[18] As of mid-1996, there were basically eighteen agreements, each devoted to a specific commodity, such as sugar, tin, and so on. Some of these agreements themselves have had checkered histories, have terminated, or are dormant.[19]

A fifth category of agreements and institutions relating to economic affairs includes a significant number of even more specialized ones. One example is the World Customs Organization (WCO), previously called the Customs Cooperation Council (CCC). The WCO is headquartered in Brussels, deals with problems of customs classification and works closely with the WTO and GATT.[20] When this organization was called the CCC, it sponsored the negotiations that led to the "International Convention on the Harmonized Commodity Description and Coding System."[21] Another is the World Intellectual Property Organization (WIPO), headquartered in Geneva, which deals with such things as patent and copyright law.[22] Even more specialized agreements govern the relations of a very small group of states to a common watershed or river (such as the U.S.-Canada Boundary Waters Agreement of 1907[23] or the Rhine River agreement[24]).

A final category includes the myriad bilateral agreements that govern economic relations. Prior to the 1950s, the friendship, commerce, and navigation (FCN) treaties were of central importance to bilateral relations;[25] but in recent decades, with the advent of multilateral treaties such as the GATT/WTO, the FCN treaties have become less important, and fewer new ones seem to be negotiated. On the other hand, in recent decades—a major program has been developed to build a web of bilateral investment treaties—at least for several industrialized countries, such as Germany, France and the U.S. These treaties are more narrowly focused than FCN treaties, but they cover many similar subjects, often providing for certain standards of compensation in the event of expropriation, as well as for other matters relating to the investment of capital from a capital-exporting country in a capital-importing country. The United States has recently embarked on such a program, and as of mid-1996 it has completed and brought into effect treaties under that program.[26] During the 1930s, there was a fairly elaborate network of reciprocal bilateral trade treaties, most of which were superseded by the GATT.[27] Numerous bilateral tax treaties also are part of this picture.

A key question is whether all these international organizations and treaties are adequate—either in number and subject-matter coverage, or in their structure and institutional makeup—to cope with the new and complex problems that have been developing in the context of greater world international economic interdependence. Furthermore, the institutional arrangements embodied in these treaties differ greatly. For instance, some of the institutions have a weighted voting system;[28] but much more common is a one-nation/one-vote system,[29] sometimes tempered by an ancillary or elite body of selected member states (for example, a council) that has additional powers. In addition, the degree to which there are measures to ensure the "effectiveness" of these treaties' norms (for example, sanctions) varies enormously from treaty to treaty, as does the effectiveness of the treaties themselves.[30]

This then is a partial road map of the landscape on which we must place the international trade system. It is complex and constantly changing, and furnishes both pitfalls and opportunities for constructive diplomacy.

2.2 The Flawed Constitutional Beginnings of GATT[31]

Early Development of International Trade Rules

The history of international cooperation to discipline national actions affecting international trade can be traced back to the beginnings of recorded history.[32] During the Middle Ages the development of the city-states and the Hanseatic League were manifestations of this long history, and the "law merchant," later to be incorporated into the Common Law of England by Lord Mansfield in the late 1700s, was another example of the search for predictability and stability in international trading relations.[33] The Treaty of Utrecht of 1713 has been described as a forerunner of GATT![34]

The development of the bilateral friendship, Commerce, navigation (FCN) treaties during the seventeenth and eighteenth centuries was an important step in regulating economic relations among the emerging nation-states.[35] These treaties also covered matters other than trade in goods, but involved clauses dealing with "most-favored-nation" status and "national treatment" that later became pillars of the GATT structure.[36]

Modern multilateral developments to regulate trade began mainly during the late nineteenth century. In 1890 a treaty was signed Concerning the Creation of an International Union for the Publication of Customs Tariffs.[37] International meetings or congresses were held in 1900, 1908, and 1913 to address problems of customs cooperation. Conferences on this matter were also organized in 1920, 1922, 1923, 1927, 1930, and 1933.[38] The 1923 International Conference on Customs Formalities, sponsored by the League of Nations, completed an International Convention Relating to the Simplification of Customs Formalities that covered many of the matters now treated in GATT. The League of Nations produced a series of studies on trade problems from 1926 to 1936 that later influenced international initiatives concerning trade.

World War II and Bretton Woods

The major initiatives leading to the establishment of the GATT were taken by the United States during World War II, in cooperation with its allies—particularly the United Kingdom. Two distinct strands of thought influenced these countries during the war. One strand concerned the program of trade agreements begun by the United States after the enactment of the 1934 Reciprocal Trade Agreements Act. Between 1934 and 1945 the United States entered into thirty-two bilateral reciprocal trade agreements,[39] many of which had clauses that foreshadowed those currently in GATT.

The second strand of thinking during the war period stemmed from the view that the mistakes made concerning economic policy during the interwar period (1920 to 1940) were a major cause of the disasters that led to World War II. The Great Depression has been partly blamed for this war, as has the harsh reparations policy toward Germany.[40] In the interwar period, particularly after the damaging 1930 U.S. tariff act was signed, many other nations began enacting protectionist measures, including quota-type restrictions, which choked off international trade. Political leaders in the United States and elsewhere made statements about the importance of establishing postwar economic institutions that would prevent these mistakes from happening again.

Thus it was that the Bretton Woods conference was held in 1944.[41] This conference was devoted to addressing monetary and banking issues. It established the charters of the International Monetary Fund and the World Bank (International Bank for Reconstruction and Development), but it did not take up the problems of trade as such. This was undoubtedly because the conference was sponsored by and under the jurisdiction of ministries of finance, whereas trade was under the jurisdiction of different ministries. (It is interesting to speculate, in light of the history of the trade conferences, how history might have been different if the Bretton Woods conference had indeed taken up the entire subject matter of economic relations, including trade.) Nevertheless, the 1944 conference is on record as having recognized the need for a comparable institution for trade, to complement the IMF monetary institutions.[42]

The United Nations and Preparations for an International Trade Organization: 1945–1948

The two strands of thinking about creating an organization for international trade began to merge in 1945. In the United States, the Congress enacted the 1945 renewal of the reciprocal trade agreements legislation for a three-year period.[43] In December of that year, the U.S. government invited a number of nations to enter into negotiations to conclude a multilateral agreement for the mutual reduction of tariffs. Also in 1945, the United Nations was formed; and in February 1946, its subordinate body, ECOSOC, at its first meeting adopted a resolution calling for a conference to draft a charter for an international trade organization.[44] The

United States at this time published a draft of a suggested ITO charter, and a preparatory committee was formed and met in October 1946, in London.

Altogether, including the London 1946 preparatory committee meeting, four preparatory meetings were held to complete a draft charter for an ITO. The various official records of these meetings total more than twenty-seven thousand pages in over one hundred volumes.[45] The second meeting was a brief limited meeting of a drafting committee at Lake Success, New York, in early 1947. The third and principal meeting was held in Geneva from April to November 1947, and was followed by the fourth meeting to complete the ITO charter, in Havana, Cuba, in 1948.

The history of the preparation of GATT is intertwined with that of the preparation of the ITO charter. The 1947 Geneva meeting was actually an elaborate conference divided into three major parts (sometimes referred to as a "three-ring circus"). One part dealt with continuing the preparation of a charter for a major international trade institution, the ITO. A second part focused on negotiating a multilateral agreement to reciprocally reduce tariffs. A third part concentrated on drafting the "general clauses" of obligations relating to the tariff obligations. The second and third parts, together, constitute the GATT—the General Agreement on Tariffs and Trade.

The general clauses of the draft GATT imposed obligations on nations to refrain from a variety of trade-impeding measures. These clauses had evolved in the United States bilateral trade agreements, and were seen as necessary to protect the value of any tariff-reducing obligations.[46] The GATT, however, was not intended to be an organization. Indeed, U.S. negotiators were called to task by committees of the U.S. Congress during 1947 for appearing to tentatively agree to draft GATT clauses that seemed to imply an organization. The U.S. president and his negotiators recognized that an ITO charter would have to be submitted to Congress for approval. But from the U.S. point of view, the GATT was being negotiated under authority of the 1945 extension of the trade agreements authority. The congressional committees pointed out that this 1945 act did not authorize the president to enter into an agreement for an organization: it only authorized agreements to reduce tariffs and other restrictions on trade. The general clauses of GATT were recognized as a necessary complement to any tariff-reduction agreement, but organizational clauses were a different matter. So the U.S. negotiators returned to Geneva and redrafted the general GATT clauses to eliminate the suggestion of an organization. Thus multilateral decisions under GATT are to be taken by the "CONTRACTING PARTIES acting jointly" and not by any "organization" body.[47]

The Geneva negotiators thus conceived of their task as preparing a draft ITO charter (to be completed in Havana in 1948), and also as negotiating the GATT (which would consist of elaborate schedules of tariff reductions appended to the general clauses of GATT). These schedules included thousands of individual tariff commitments that resulted from numerous bilateral meetings of negotiators.[48] These commitments in turn ultimately led to generalized tariff-reduction commitments that applied to all GATT members through the MFN obligation.

The GATT was to be merely a multilateral treaty, not an organization; and it was to be similar to the bilateral treaties that preceded it, but now designed to operate under the umbrella of the ITO when the ITO came into being. The general clauses of GATT were largely drawn from the chapter of the draft ITO charter that was devoted to trading rules that in turn had been heavily influenced by clauses in bilateral trade treaties. The GATT contained a clause recognizing that, after the ITO charter was completed, parallel GATT clauses would be revised to bring them into conformity with those of the ITO charter.[49] One important implication of this preparatory history linking the GATT to the ITO draft charter is that the ITO preparatory history, including in some instances the history of the Havana Conference (which occurred after some of the GATT obligations came into force), is relevant to the interpretation of GATT clauses.[50]

The draft ITO charter was completed at the 1948 Havana Conference, but the ITO never came into being. The principal reason for this was the failure of the U.S. Congress to approve it. The president submitted it to Congress in 1949, but by 1948 wartime urgency for new institutions had given way to a desire for a return to "normalcy." In addition, the 1948 U.S. elections returned a Congress that was Republican dominated, while the presidency remained in Democratic hands. Other factors undoubtedly contributed to this history,[51] and by the end of 1950 President Truman announced that he would no longer seek congressional approval of the ITO, and that ended any chance of an ITO coming into being. Although other countries could have gone ahead, at this time the United States was the preeminent economic power in the world—having emerged from the war largely unscathed—and no country desired to enter an ITO that did not include the United States. The irony was that it had been the United States that had taken the principal initiative to develop the ITO charter in the first place.[52]

The GATT and the Protocol of Provisional Application

At the beginning of this chapter I asked: How is it that the GATT as such has never come into force, and yet that it is known as the principal institution of international trade today? The answer technically lies in the Protocol of Provisional Application (PPA), through which the GATT was applied as a treaty obligation under international law. This situation was a direct result of the history I have outlined, but it takes a bit of explaining.

The GATT, including the various tariff obligations, was completed by October 1947 as the Geneva Conference drew to a close. Even though the GATT was to be subordinated to the ITO, the ITO charter was to be finished only later, in 1948. Yet many negotiators believed that the GATT should be brought into force much sooner for the following reasons. First, the GATT consisted in part of thousands of individual tariff concessions. The United Stated, for example, had committed to reduce the tariff on wooden chairs from 40 percent to 20 percent, and on leather shoes from 30 percent to 20 percent. The United Kingdom likewise agreed to reduce tariffs on soya beans, coniferous wood and timber, and many other products.[53] Although these concessions were still secret, the negotiators knew that it was inevitable that their contents would begin to creep into public knowledge, and as they did, so traders would be influenced by them. Sellers might anticipate a forthcoming tariff reduction by holding back their product until the new tariff came into force. World trade patterns could thus be seriously disrupted if a prolonged delay occurred before the tariff concessions came into force.[54]

Another reason for early implementation of the GATT influenced U.S. negotiators in particular. They were negotiating under the authority of the U.S. trade legislation that had been renewed in 1945. Under this authority they would not need to submit the GATT to Congress (in the next chapter I discuss how some members of Congress disagreed with this). But the 1945 act expired in mid-1948.[55] Thus the U.S. had strong motivation (shared by knowledgeable allies) to bring the GATT into force before this act expired. It was unlikely that this could be done if the participants waited until after the 1948 Havana Conference and the ITO charter were completed.

On the other hand, there were several difficult problems in bringing the GATT into force. Of course, some of the language of the general clauses of GATT had to be identical to the final ITO language, but this could be handled by amending the GATT at a later date to bring it into conformity with the results of the Havana conference.

More troublesome was that some nations had constitutional procedures under which they could not accept parts of the GATT (particularly some of the general clauses) without submitting this agreement to their parliaments. Given that they anticipated the necessity to submit the final draft of the ITO charter to their parliaments in late 1948 or later, they did not want to give their legislatures "two bites at the apple." They feared that to spend the political capital and effort required to get the GATT through their legislatures might jeopardize their later efforts to get the ITO passed. Hence, they preferred to take both agreements to their legislatures as a package.[56]

The solution agreed upon was the adoption of the Protocol of Provisional Application.[57] By this protocol, eight of the twenty-three original GATT signatories agreed to apply the treaty "provisionally on and after 1 January 1948," while the remaining members would do so soon after. The protocol contained two important clauses that altered the impact of the GATT itself. The protocol required only sixty-day's notice for withdrawal from the GATT, compared to the six months's required by the GATT agreement itself. This, however, was not particularly meaningful, given that withdrawal from GATT was not a very viable option in practical terms, at least for any major participant.

The more important impact of the PPA, however, was its statement of the manner of implementing GATT. Parts I and III of GATT are fully implemented without a PPA exception, but the PPA called for implementation of Part II "to the fullest extent not inconsistent with existing legislation." Part I of GATT contained the MFN and the tariff concession obligations, while Part III was mainly procedural. Part II (Articles III to XXIII) contained most of the principal substantive obligations including those relating to customs procedures, quotas, subsidies, antidumping duties, and national treatment. As to these important obligations, each GATT contracting party was entitled to "grandfather rights" for any provision of its legislation that existed when it became a party, and that was inconsistent with a GATT Part II obligation.

These "grandfather rights," or the "existing legislation" exception of the PPA, solved for most countries the problem of executive authority to agree to GATT. This exception allowed most governments, which would otherwise need to submit the GATT for legislative approval, to approve the PPA by executive or administrative authority without going to the legislature. Obviously it was understood that after the ITO charter was ready to be submitted to legislatures, the GATT would also be submitted for "definitive" application (pursuant to GATT Article XXVI). In the meantime, the GATT contracting parties could deviate from those GATT Part II obligations to which they could not adhere without legislative authority. They must accept fully the MFN obligation of Article I of GATT and the tariff cuts of Article II incorporating the tariff schedules, but in most cases the executives had authority to do this. (The United States had such authority, of course, from its 1945 trade act extension. Whether the United States had authority to fully accept and implement the GATT during 1947 to 1948 on a definitive basis without submitting it to Congress can be argued. I return to this question in the next chapter.) Governments that later joined the GATT did so on treaty terms that incorporated the same "existing legislation" exception.

Although attempts during subsequent GATT history have been made to obtain "definitive application" of the GATT, none has succeeded.[58] Thus, even until nearly the end of GATT's existence, one could witness the reliance on grandfather rights to justify certain national actions regarding international trade.[59] This legal context was an important part of the U.S. bargaining position in the Tokyo Round (1973–1979) negotiation of the Countervailing Duty Code[60] and was also a central issue of a GATT panel proceeding concerning the so-called manufacturing clause, which limited copyright protection in the United States on certain imported English-language books.[61] Gradually many of the grandfather rights, however, became extinct. New legislation did not qualify for this PPA exception, and some of the old provisions passed out of existence, or for other reasons became nonoperative or were superseded. One of the features of the WTO is the elimination of any generalized idea of grandfather rights, although one or two are probably represented by some specific new treaty clause obligations and exceptions.

The GATT Begins to Fill the Vacuum

A major hole was left in the fabric intended for post–World War II international economic institutions because the ITO did not come into being. It was only natural that the institution that did exist—the GATT—would find its role changing dramatically as nations turned to it as the forum in which an increasing number of problems of their trading relationships would be handled. More countries became contracting parties, sometimes in groups (nine in 1949, four in 1951), sometimes individually.[62] The CPs met almost every six months, usually for several weeks, and discussed a wide range of problems, including disputes about the implementation of GATT rules. Because of the fiction that GATT was not an "organization," there was considerable reluctance at first to delegate any activity even to a "committee." Gradually that reluctance faded, and soon there was even an "intercessional committee" that met between sessions of the contracting parties.[63]

No secretariat existed for the GATT. After Havana, however, an Interim Commission for the International Trade Organization (ICITO) was set up, in the typical pattern of preparing the way for a new international organization. A small staff was assembled to prepare the ground for the ITO, and this staff serviced the needs of the GATT.[64] As years passed and it became clear that the ITO was never to come into being, this staff found that all of its time was devoted to the GATT, and as such it became de facto the GATT Secretariat (technically as a kind of a "leased" group, whereby the GATT "reimbursed" the ICITO for the costs of the secretariat).

During the early 1950s the GATT CPs decided it would be necessary to review and amend the GATT, so as to prepare it for its developing role as the central international institution for trade. The CPs' ninth regular session, scheduled for 1954–1955, was designated as a "review session"; and at this exceptionally long session extensive protocols were prepared to amend the GATT—one for those parts of GATT requiring unanimity to amend, another for the other parts requiring only two-thirds acceptance. (Ultimately the latter protocol came into effect amending portions of Part II of GATT, but the protocol requiring unanimity never came into force and was withdrawn in 1967.[65])

The 1955 review session also drafted a new organizational protocol. Under this protocol an organization for trade cooperation (OTC) was to be established to provide the institutional framework for the developing organizational role of GATT. This short treaty agreement was much less elaborate than the ITO's, but even it failed to get the approval of the U.S. Congress, so the OTC was also stillborn. (However, the OTC in some ways was a model for the initial thinking about a new WTO.)[66] Thus, the GATT has limped along for nearly fifty years with almost no basic constitution designed to regulate its organizational activities and procedures. Even so, the GATT by any fair definition must be deemed to have been a de facto international organization. Through trial and error it has evolved some fairly elaborate procedures for conducting its business. That it could do so, despite the flawed basic documents on which it had to build, is a tribute to the pragmatism and ingenuity of many of its leaders over the years.

One person in particular must be singled out for his influence on the evolution of GATT: Sir Eric Wyndham White, a British citizen (knighted in 1968) who was the chief administrative officer of the UN group that provided service for the drafting conferences of the ITO and GATT. He became the first GATT executive secretary, a post he held (later embellished by the title of director-general) until he retired in 1968.[67] Although he was careful to give the appearance of playing the role of a typical international civil servant—that is, to be neutral among all parties and to avoid the appearance of taking initiatives that should be left to member states—Sir Eric nevertheless had a profound sense of the "possible" while continuously working toward achieving the basic goals of the GATT agreement. Some attribute important evolutionary steps of the GATT dispute settlement procedure to Sir Eric's actions behind the scenes. In the Kennedy Round of world trade negotiations from 1963 to 1967, Sir Eric's role was reportedly crucial, particularly in the last few weeks of the negotiation, in helping nations break a stalemate and achieve a final agreement.[68]

During the Kennedy Round period, the GATT contracting parties adopted an amendment to the GATT general clauses, which is the last such amendment to date. A protocol to add Part IV to GATT, dealing with problems of developing countries, was approved in 1965 and came into force in 1966.[69] Articles XXXVI, XXXVII, and XXXVIII of this part are primarily expressions of goals, and impose few if any concrete obligations. Nevertheless, this language has been relied on in legal and policy argumentation in GATT, and has had considerable influence.

Later sections will describe the eight major trade and tariff-negotiating rounds held through 1994 under the aegis of GATT. The next to the last of these, the Tokyo Round (1973–1979), resulted in a major expansion of the activity and competence of GATT, not through amendments to the treaty text, but through the negotiation of a series of separate instruments, sometimes called "codes," each of which was technically a standalone treaty. These codes addressed a number of nontariff measures that distort international trade flows, such as government procurement regulations and the use of product standards to restrain imports.

The codes, like the GATT agreement and its various amendments and understandings, have become part of the overall WTO agreement. Thus, in a different form, they continue to have international law application. Some of these codes will be considered in detail, given that they have important effects on the GATT rules regarding their subject.[70]

2.3 The World Trade Organization and the Uruguay Round

Fairly soon after the completion of the Tokyo Round in 1979, some diplomatic leaders had begun to think about the need for another round.[71] Already there was attention to the need of some kind of a GATT-type discipline for trade in services (a growing proportion of many national economies and of world trade), and also for a place to provide an institutional structure for intellectual property rules, given that a number of firms and policymakers felt that the World Intellectual Property Organization was inadequate for the tasks contemplated for new intellectual property agreements. Discussions were held in GATT and, at the 1982 ministerial meeting in particular, members focused considerable attention on the question of developing and encouraging a new trade round. Opposition came from various quarters. At first, the European Community was hesitant about paying attention to trade in services, but later it began to realize the importance of this for many European Community member states (such as the United Kingdom with its London financial center). Some developing countries were extremely concerned about norms that would protect intellectual property at the expense of developing country needs. Others were worried that a GATT-type discipline for services would put their own service industries at a disadvantage vis-à-vis some of the more powerful entities located in industrial countries.

In September 1986, however, in Punta del Este, Uruguay, a large ministerial meeting was held to launch a new trade round—appropriately called the "Uruguay Round." Most of the dissent was somehow overcome at this meeting, and the result was a declaration (the Punta Declaration), which included an extraordinarily ambitious agenda and launched the negotiations. Both services and intellectual property were included on this agenda, although it was not resolved at the time whether they would become a part of the GATT system or some other newly created institution. Included high on the list of priorities for the new negotiation were: bringing agricultural goods trade under GATT discipline (a problem that had persisted throughout the history of GATT but that had resisted reforms in the two previous negotiating rounds); elaborating further on the rules regarding subsidies beyond that of the Tokyo Round Code; bringing attention to the troublesome textile protectionist-type arrangements that existed uneasily in the GATT context; and a number of other issues.

Two issues that required negotiation relating to the institutions of the world trading system were developed in two negotiating groups. One group would focus on the dispute-settlement rules, particularly given that it was commonly agreed that the GATT rules had some grievous defects. The other group was called the "Future of the GATT System" or "FOGS"—which some thought quite appropriate. Early indications at the beginning of this group's work were that its intentions were quite modest. It would focus on some of the interstitial problems of the institutional questions of GATT, particularly GATT's relationship with monetary issues and the International Monetary Fund. The Punta del Este agenda did not include any indication that an entirely new trade organization was being contemplated. Negotiators had not thought through the implications of the troublesome amending clauses of the GATT, and indeed compromises in Punta del Este led negotiators to delay resolving a number of issues about the institutional structure of the final negotiating result until the end of the negotiation.

After several years of negotiation, a midterm review was held in Montreal in December 1988. This ministerial meeting was generally deemed a failure, because negotiating positions on many priority issues had not been amenable to compromise. A few problems were resolved, however, and attention was paid to the dispute-settlement process, resulting in some interim measures being implemented. One of the reasons for the problems at the Montreal meeting was that both the United States and the European Community were in positions of governmental transition. In the United States, the election of George Bush as president meant that many of the personnel and policies could change shortly. The European Community was also going through a transition, with new commissioners being installed under various portfolios. Thus, the Montreal meeting was pretty much a "hold-the-line" meeting.

Negotiations proceeded in the next few years with a target of a final conclusion at a ministerial meeting to be held in Brussels, in December 1990. By mid- to late 1989, a small amount of attention was directed toward how the Uruguay Round could be implemented;[72] and in early 1990, Canada put forth the first official government-tabled proposal for a new institution, which it called the "World Trade Organization." Later, the European Community began to support the proposal, but wanted the title of the organization to be called the "Multilateral Trade Organization" (MTO).

The Brussels meeting in 1990 also proved to be a failure, with a negotiating impasse largely centered on the agricultural sector. Once again, lower-level negotiators went back to the daily work of honing positions and proposals; and in December 1991, with great prodding by GATT's director-general, Arthur Dunkel, the various texts of negotiating proposals—such as they were in the twenty or so different negotiation groups—were pasted together into one overall draft called the "Dunkel Draft." Included in this was a proposal for a charter of an MTO. Gradually over the next year or two, countries were able to examine and reflect on the Dunkel Draft, which led to a general acceptance of most of the text, with some very hard negotiating remaining on certain key provisions (particularly in the area of agriculture).

The U.S. Congress had extended the fast-track procedures that were vital to the ultimate implementation of the Uruguay Round results, and these procedures required a general end to the negotiations in mid-December 1993. During the preceding four to five months, the negotiations became very intense and negotiators once again turned their attention to the institutional proposal. The United States was not prepared at the time to say that it would accept the new institution. A settlement was eventually reached, but only after a number of modifications in the text, many of which were designed to limit the decision-making authority of the new organization and protect the position of some of the more powerful negotiating countries that would not subject themselves to a simple majority vote on crucial matters such as those that would "change the rights and obligations" of the parties. The settlement, which was reached in 1993, included the draft charter (as well as various other texts) for a world trade organization that was finally brought into existence. This draft was signed at a ministerial meeting in Marrakesh, Morocco, on 15 April 1995, and subsequently the various nations and independent customs territories pursued their national constitutional and parliamentary processes to enable them to accept this massive agreement.

The original agenda from the Punta Declaration was, as stated above, very ambitious. Many observers, myself included, were surprised by how much of that ambition had in fact been fulfilled in December 1993. Even at half-fulfillment, the negotiation would have been the largest ever.

Legal Characteristics and Structure of the New Institution

The Uruguay Round Agreement, as contained in the Final Act, begins with the agreement on the WTO, which I will refer to throughout this book as the "charter," although technically it is not titled that. In fact, it is actually the first "chapter" of the much larger Uruguay Round Agreement. Many parts of the Uruguay Round Agreement are themselves entitled "agreements," but they are not stand-alone, and I sometimes refer to them as particular "texts," such as the "antidumping text," although many are labeled officially as "agreements."

Several extremely significant characteristics of the negotiation results should be noted. Perhaps foremost is the "single-package" idea, which the negotiators had embraced some years earlier and had resolved to make an important aspect of the negotiation. The idea was that there should be one complete elaborate text to which all those who wanted to become members of the new structure must adhere and accept. This would be in contrast to the Tokyo Round result which included specific individual agreements that were optional ("GATT à la carte"). Another characteristic that was exceedingly important was the decision to set up the Uruguay Round Final Act as a new agreement and not as an amendment to previous agreements, such as the GATT itself. Under this basic legal structure the Uruguay Round Agreement would be a new agreement that would create a new organization—the WTO—and would embrace the text of GATT and its related agreements as annexes. Thus it was not necessary to follow the amending procedure contained in the GATT Agreement, and this virtually assured that the new agreement would come into force, given that technically no minimum threshold number of countries was required, although it was understood that a substantial number, including all of the major trading countries, was necessary.

Legal Structure of the Uruguay Round Agreement

The legal structure of the Uruguay Round Agreement is perhaps best understood by presenting the agreement's table of contents. It will be noted that the agreement establishing the WTO is the umbrella that embraces all parts of the detailed texts (and technically also all of the twenty-five thousand pages of schedules). The WTO Charter is a mere ten pages long, but it has four very important annexes, which contain all of the other negotiated texts of the Uruguay Round. It will be noted that Annex 1 contains the "multilateral agreements," which are considered mandatory (i.e., all members must accept them). Annex 1 is divided into three parts that correspond to the three major basic agreements, namely, goods (GATT 1994 and its related agreements and other texts); services (GATS and its annexes); and trade-related aspects of intellectual property rights. All members are also required to accept Annex 2 (the Dispute Settlement Understanding) and Annex 3 (the Trade Policy Review Mechanism).

Annex 4 represents a small departure from the single-package idea. It contains the "plurilateral agreements," which are optional. Four are listed: two regarding agricultural subjects, which do not have much "bite," and two—civil aircraft and government procurement—that might be considered of more interest to industrial countries than to developing countries (although it is questionable).

The texts, particularly those in Annex 1A, include a number of ministerial decisions and declarations, so that interpretation of the agreement must keep them under consideration (as well as the other ingredients of interpretations, such as Annex I of GATT, termed "interpretive notes").

To a great extent, contemporary international economic interdependence can be attributed to the success of the institutions put in place just after World War II as part of the Bretton Woods System, which includes the IMF, the IBRD and the GATT. The GATT in particular has been a major force for more than four decades in greatly reducing tariff barriers to trade in industrial goods, at least among the democratic market-oriented industrial countries. And, with the successful conclusion of the Uruguay Round, the signing of GATT 1994, and the creation of the World Trade Organization, the influence of the GATT system has been extended to trade in services, intellectual property, and other important areas previously outside its purview.

The result is a full-fledged legally constituted international organization, the WTO. Its charter begins by establishing the international organization and then proceeds through the priority elements for creating it, including statements on functions and structure; provision for the highest authority in a ministerial conference to meet at least biannually; and provision for a secretariat, a director-general, and a series of subbodies, including four councils that will be described later in this chapter.

This treaty is definitively applied. No longer do we have the uneasiness and ambiguity of provisional application, under which the GATT suffered throughout its existence. The GATT continued through one year of overlap with the WTO (ending at the end of 1995, while the WTO began at the beginning of 1995). Now GATT 1947 is out of existence, although there can be "de facto application" that will continue under various legal arrangements, some of them bilateral. The institution of GATT is thus over. The substantive obligations (and some of the procedural obligations) of GATT continue, however, with the text of GATT 1994 as part of Annex 1A of the WTO. Because there is no protocol of provisional application, there are also no "grandfather rights" or "existing legislation" exceptions. In at least one situation, however, the terms of a previous grandfather right have been embodied in a special text (paragraph 3 of the preliminary notes to GATT 1994). This text carries forward a grandfather right (which the United States exercised) now stated in more general terms, but clearly aimed to benefit the United States' rules, relating to vessels in commercial applications between points in national waters. This may be the only grandfather right that was explicitly carried forward in the new Uruguay Round agreement. Thus, for general purposes, grandfather rights are fortunately now extinct.

Nevertheless, no one should expect a very "tidy" text in the Uruguay Round. A number of subtexts have been pasted together, and the relationships among them is often very unclear. Negotiating compromises required the introduction, or at least toleration, of ambiguous phrases in a number of places. The sheer complexity of the agreement assures that a variety of interpretive problems will arise. Trade policy experts generally agree, however, that the Uruguay Round is a remarkable and substantial step forward for the world trade system.

2.4 The Obligations of GATT and Their Legal Setting

What Are the Rules?

Decreasing the costs of transportation and communication has played a profound role in increasing levels of trade and interdependence during the postwar years. With the decline of tariffs to near de minimis levels in developing countries, other much more complex barriers or distortions of trade have become relatively more important. Nontariff barriers are myriad, and the ingenuity of man to invent new ones assures us that the problem of trade barriers will never go away. This is why one of the most important problems facing the world today is institutional—the question of whether national and international governmental institutions (such as the WTO/GATT) have the capacity to meet the challenges of private and governmental behavior that could undermine the world trading system and the prosperity that it brings.

Of particular interest to us in this book, and to practicing trade lawyers, is the increasing importance of laws against unfair trade practices. In some cases trade may indeed be "unfair" by some intelligible standard, but in others the suspicion arises that practices are unfair only in the eyes of the import-competing industries that would like freedom from the challenges that competition can bring. Further, a growing number of situations involve conflicts among contradictory economic, cultural, and political goals across nations. Disputes about what is "unfair," therefore, often lie in deep, fundamental differences of opinion about the appropriate economic role of governments.

There are innumerable other important and perplexing issues in international economic relations. Monetary issues take a central place among them. With fundamental shifts in the Bretton Woods System, the world has experienced considerable volatility in its exchange rates. When an exchange rate changes 20 percent or 30 percent within even one year, the effects on trade can swamp the effects of conventional instruments of commercial policy such as tariffs and quotas. Additional topics including trade in services, competition policy, the environment, and intellectual property have become increasingly important to economic relations among nations.

We are also concerned in this book with the way that national legal systems interact with international legal rules and institutions. For example, the process by which nations bind themselves to international agreements and the institutional structure of domestic institutions that implement rights and responsibilities under international law are of deep practical and intellectual significance.

Although the GATT no longer exists as an institution or even a de facto institution, the substantive obligations of the GATT and its many ancillary documents and codes remain a central part of the rule structure for the world trading system. Indeed, new issues such as trade in services or intellectual property borrow heavily from some of the concepts of the GATT (particularly MFN and national treatment). This section focuses on these GATT rules for trade in goods and serves a dual purpose.

First, it introduces the GATT treaty obligations. This constitutes an overview, because many of the particular obligations are taken up more extensively elsewhere in the book. (It will be noted that the obligations, in light of the history previously explained, were binding under international law as applied by the Protocol of Provisional Application, but now are part of the WTO Annex 1.)

Second, this section discusses several important legal and policy issues that tend to "cut across" many GATT articles and principles. For example, it examines some of the problems of ascertaining which GATT obligations apply to which nations. It also explores the question, "To whom, within a nation, do obligations apply, particularly in the context of subordinate units of government in a federal system?"

One important question that affects many other GATT/WTO issues concerns the procedures and techniques for interpreting the GATT. This subject, touched on in this section, is taken up more extensively in chapter 4 when I discuss dispute-resolution and rule application problems of GATT. Certain key legal issues, such as the issue of "self-executing" or "direct" effects of GATT law, are more closely related to problems of national domestic law. I will examine these in chapter 3, which explores national law issues.

The GATT Obligations and Code of Conduct

The central obligations of GATT are the tariff "concessions," by which contracting parties commit themselves (in Article II and the schedules) to limit the amount of tariffs they will impose on imports from other GATT contracting parties. These obligations were the original reason for negotiating the GATT agreement, and it is probably fair to say that these obligations have been the most effective obligations of the GATT. Through a series of tariff-reduction negotiations in GATT, the general average of tariffs of industrial countries on industrial goods has declined significantly during the history of GATT, to about 3.9 percent or less today.[73] Many observers believe that such a low tariff level is not a significant barrier to imports: it acts more as a low sales tax, one that most efficient producers abroad can effectively "hurdle" by increasing their productivity and decreasing their costs.[74]

A second and equally central obligation is that of most favored nation. Both of these obligations are extensively considered in other chapters (chapters 5 and 6, respectively), so I will not elaborate further here. It will be remembered that these obligations form Part I of GATT in amendments that require unanimity,[75] and are not subject to the existing legislation clause of the Protocol of Provisional Application.[76]

In Part II of GATT, Articles III through XVII comprise most of the other substantive obligations of GATT and can be thought of as the code of conduct for government behavior in regulating international trade. It will be noted that these obligations (as well as MFN) apply to all products regardless of whether such products appear in a tariff-concession schedule. This code applies to all goods, both imported and exported, although most of the rules are relevant only to imports. Most of these obligations are also treated more extensively in later chapters. They include the following:

National treatment (Article III, treated in chapter 8)

Antidumping and countervailing duties (Article VI, treated in chapters 10 and 11)

Valuation of goods for customs purposes (Article VII, treated in chapter 5)

Procedures of customs administration (Article VIII and X, treated in chapter 5)

Marks of origin (Article IX, treated in chapter 5)

Quantitative restrictions (Article XI, treated in chapter 5)

Subsidies (Article XVI, treated in chapter 11)

State trading monopolies (Article XVII, treated in chapter 13)

One policy question is whether it is beneficial to have a general code of conduct on trade. An alternative would be to apply rules only to agreed-upon lists of goods (like the tariff schedules). A variation on this idea would incorporate notions of reciprocity so that a rule would apply to a product from another contracting party only if that party also applied the rule to its imports of the same product. These variations would obviously add greatly to the complexity and therefore probably to the confusion and difficulty of predicting compliance.[77] In some of the new subject areas (particularly services, and also with regard to government procurement, and other measures), the Uruguay Round texts provide some of these variations and greater complexity.

In fact, because of the legal and sometimes not-so-legal measures taken to affect various products, the application of the GATT rules varies substantially. Under the amending rule of GATT, a contracting party was not obligated to an amendment that it did not accept (even if more than two-thirds of the CPs had accepted the amendment).[78]

Under the WTO amending procedure, this rule has been continued with some additional variations and an attempt to distinguish between amendments that would "alter rights and obligations" of member states and other more "procedural" amendments. The grandfather rights that created various exceptions in the GATT 1947 have been done away with, but possibilities for exceptions remain under the waiver authority other provisions of the GATT. Article XVI relating to subsidy obligations has had a particularly unusual history, given that under the original GATT only a few of the contracting parties were bound by one part of that article. The Tokyo Round Subsidies Code changed the effective rules for subsidies for countries that accepted it, but now of course under the single-package doctrine all members of the WTO are bound by the newly developed Uruguay Round text on subsidies, and these appear to largely supersede GATT Article XVI. It should also be noted that the GATT has a series of "interpretive notes" contained in Annex I ("i" or eye). These have status that is equivalent to the treaty text, and that must be read in conjunction with the particular articles to which they relate. Beyond that, the Uruguay Round texts include a series of understandings, ministerial decisions, and declarations that may affect one or another of the GATT (or other text) obligations, and so must always be consulted in that connection. As noted above, the Tokyo Round separate codes were not integrated into the GATT texts, so only those countries which accepted them were bound by them. After the Uruguay Round, all of these texts (as modified by the Uruguay Round negotiation) have become part of the Annex 1, which is binding on all members of the WTO. Thus, overall, one can say that the Uruguay Round has brought a much higher degree of harmonization and homogeneity in the varied obligations of the GATT.

De facto nonlegal differentiation, however, occurs when compliance with GATT legal norms varies. This subject will be addressed elsewhere, but it is well known in GATT that many countries have used "balance-of-payments tariff surcharges," which technically were inconsistent with GATT rules.[79] Likewise the proliferation of various types of "voluntary export restraints" during the last two decades often involved breaches of GATT obligations, as well as contraventions of the basic policies of GATT. These restraints raise interesting jurisprudential questions about international law, but it should be noted that the Uruguay Round "safeguards text" is designed to prohibit most voluntary export restraint arrangements.[80]

To Whom Do GATT Obligations Apply? Private Enterprises and Subordinate Government Units

The wording of GATT makes it reasonably clear that this agreement applies only to treatment of *products* (and not to services, for example, which are the subject of a separate new Uruguay Round text included in WTO Annex 1B).[81] It is also reasonably clear that the agreement applies only to *government* action and not to actions of private firms or individuals. Newer trends of international law entertain the possibility that treaties or customary international law may apply to individuals as well as to nations and international organizations. There is no longer much jurisprudential problem with these developments.[82] Nevertheless, the GATT wording is almost all phrased in such a way as to apply only to governments.[83] One important result of this circumstance is that the GATT (in contrast to the ITO charter) has very little to say about monopolistic practices of private firms, even though such practices can substantially undermine the basic policies on which GATT is based.[84] These practices have become the focus of considerable attention by those who argue that a GATT-type code or discipline is needed for them.

Whether or not treaty language is worded to apply to governments, in some legal systems it may additionally have so-called direct effect.[85] In the United States this would be called the "self-executing" effect, whereby private parties would be allowed to rely on the treaty language in private litigation in the domestic courts, in some circumstances.[86] I return to this subject in chapter 3.

Another question is: To what extent do the GATT norms apply to units of government subordinate to the nation that is the contracting party? Such units might include states in a federal system (e.g., California) or municipal or county units of various kinds. The GATT is not entirely clear on this question, but language in Article XXIV, paragraph 12 requires the contracting party to take "such reasonable measures ... available to it to ensure observance." For the United States this probably meant that the proclamation of GATT made it applicable to subordinate government units directly, and courts have so held.[87] A new Uruguay Round text (part of the mandatory Annex 1) addresses Article XXIV, paragraph 12 to make it clear that "each member is fully responsible under GATT 1994 for the observance of all provisions of GATT 1994, and shall take such reasonable measures as may be available to it to ensure such observance by regional and local governments and authorities within its territory." This does not eliminate completely the ambiguity for this issue, and it still remains to be determined what the consequences of such "responsibility" will be. Some GATT panel reports provide that even if a federal government cannot impose a mandate on a subordinate governmental unit to follow the GATT or correct its legal inconsistencies, the federal government may nevertheless be responsible to complaining WTO members, and the latter may be authorized to take "compensatory measures."[88]

GATT/WTO Legal Exceptions to the Obligations

The GATT agreement provides a large number of potential exceptions to its other norms, some of which have been altered or embellished by language in the WTO Charter itself. A simple enumeration will introduce them (many are taken up elsewhere in this book):

Waivers voted under GATT Article XXV (see below)

Balance-of-payments exceptions allowing use of quotas (Articles XII to XV)

Exceptions for developing countries in Article XVIII, and also Part IV (Articles XXXVI-XXXVIII)

The important exception for customs unions and free trade areas Article XXIV; (see chapter 6)

The Escape Clause of Article XIX (see chapter 7)

The general exceptions of Article XX, which cut across all GATT obligations, but are themselves subject to sort of "soft" MFN and national treatment requirements (see chapter 9)

National security exceptions of Article XXI (see chapter 9)

The renegotiation procedures for tariff concessions of Article XXVIII (see chapter 5)

The "opt-out" provisions of Article XXXV (see following section)

Under the new WTO Agreement, which is now the umbrella for the GATT text, it is not always clear when GATT exceptions will apply and what procedures will be necessary for them. Also, the relationships of the GATT text and exceptions to some of the other agreements and texts in Annex 1A (e.g., the antidumping, subsidies, and licensing texts) are not entirely clear. The diplomats and lawyers working in the negotiation were not able to come to sufficient agreements on how to handle these relationships in order to clarify this. Thus, considerable ambiguity exists regarding some of these questions. For example, does the national security exception of Article XXI or the general exceptions of Article XX apply to some of the ancillary texts of Annex 1A, such as safeguards texts, or the technical barriers text, or other texts mentioned above?

Two of the exceptions on the list above are sufficiently general to merit additional discussion here. These are the waiver provisions (Article XXV) and the "opt-out" provision of GATT Article XXXV. In both of these cases, the structures of the Uruguay Round agreement and the WTO umbrella text add complexity and ambiguity. I will briefly take up the waiver provision here, but the opt-out provision will be left to a later section of this chapter.

The waiver authority of the original GATT Article XXV authorizes the CONTRACTING PARTIES acting jointly to grant a waiver to any party "in exceptional circumstances not elsewhere provided." The vote required was two-thirds of those nations voting, to include a majority of all contracting parties. In practice, the "exceptional circumstance" language had not been a constraint.

It was once argued that it would be inappropriate to grant a waiver of obligations in Part I of GATT (MFN and tariff concessions) because amendment of that part required unanimous action while the waiver required a lesser vote.[89] Sufficient practice to amount to an "interpretation" of GATT has occurred to the contrary, however. In effect, some waivers have been almost the equivalent of amendments, as they have no time limits. In some cases waivers have fundamentally altered the rights and obligations of contracting parties,[90] and in other cases the right to deviate from a GATT norm has been granted on conditions that almost amount to impositions of new obligations on contracting parties.

In the WTO Charter waivers are explicitly addressed as part of Article IX on decision making. Paragraph 3 and paragraph 4 of Article IX relate to waivers and provide a new special procedure, at least for waivers for the WTO agreement itself. This calls for the ministerial conference (or general council) to allow for a time period "which shall not exceed 90 days" so that members can develop a consensus on a waiver. If a consensus is not reached, then a decision to grant a waiver shall be taken by three-fourths of the members (not just those voting). This is a fairly stringent requirement, not easily obtained. Yet the waiver could be accomplished by consensus in the absence of more than a quarter of the members.

WTO Article IX:3(b) addresses a waiver concerning the multilateral trade agreements in Annexes 1A, 1B, or 1C (GATT 1994, the Services Agreement, or Intellectual Property). In these cases, a request for a waiver will be submitted initially to the council for the particular subject (e.g., Council for Trade in Goods, regarding GATT). The submittal will be "for consideration during a time-period which will not exceed 90 days." And then at the end of this period, the relevant council "shall submit a report to the Ministerial Conference." It is then not entirely clear how the ministerial conference proceeds, but there is at least some opinion that it will proceed according to its own procedures, so that if a consensus cannot be reached, the waiver will require a vote of three-fourths of the members. The treaty text of Annex 1A contains some explanatory notes at the outset that attempt to reconcile some of the interpretive problems relating to placing GATT under the umbrella of the WTO. Explanatory note 2(b) states that references to decisions by the CONTRACTING PARTIES acting jointly in various articles shall be references to the WTO. In a list, Article XXV is not included, but the next sentence states "the other functions of the provisions of GATT 1994 signed to the CONTRACTING PARTIES acting jointly shall be allocated by the Ministerial Conference."

The WTO Charter Article XVI:3 provides that in the event of a conflict between the provisions of the WTO Agreement and the provisions of many of the multilateral trade agreements (Annex 1) "the provision of this [WTO] Agreement shall prevail to the extent of the conflict." Thus it can be argued that the WTO provision on waivers replaces the provisions on GATT Article XXV, so that the three-fourths of members vote requirement is now the rule. On the other hand, this opens up the door to a "consensus adoption" of a waiver by a much lower majority. Thus we see the evolution of institutional treaty texts! And we can also see that there will be a number of such interpretive problems that will need to be addressed by the new WTO as an institution during its formative years.

Omissions and Sectorial Exceptions

Certain subjects have been purposely omitted from GATT cognizance. We have already noted that the language of GATT applies to products but not to services (although services are now included in a new separate text on the subject).[91]

In addition, although the ITO draft charter contained a whole chapter on anticompetitive practices, the GATT included none of that language, and subsequent GATT interpretations have established the view of the CPs that it would be inappropriate to try to use GATT too fully to control such practices.[92] Likewise the WTO omits any general language concerning anticompetitive practices, although specific phrases in both the services and the intellectual property texts address particular aspects of this subject.[93]

Also, a number of "loopholes" in GATT—particular practices unanticipated when GATT was drafted—have been utilized by various governments to evade GATT obligations or to subvert the general policy thrust of GATT in order to promote liberal trade. It has been argued that the variable levy used by the European Community is one such practice—one that is argued to be technically legal under GATT as a tariff on products that are not "bound," yet one that amounts to an evasion of the idea to limit the protective effect of border measures to stable and predictable levels of tariffs.[94]

Although the GATT on its face applies to all product sectors of economic activity (with some differentiation between industrial and primary goods),[95] noncompliance with GATT rules has resulted in some sectors being effectively beyond the discipline of these rules. The most striking example of this is agriculture. So ineffective have GATT rules been with respect to trade in agricultural goods that some writers or practitioners have made the error of stating that the GATT does not legally apply to agricultural goods. One of the reasons for this state of affairs was the

Congress of the United States, which early in GATT history adopted legslation mandating certain import restrictions on some agriculture goods—such that the United States would be in violation of its GATT obligations.[96] In 1955 the U.S. government sought and obtained a GATT waiver for the requirements of this legislation.[97] This waiver was much criticized, and even though other governments may not have had legal cover of a waiver, they engage in practices similar to those covered by the waiver, arguing that what is fair for the United States must also be fair for others. One of the major objectives of the Uruguay Round was to bring GATT discipline to agricultural goods trade, and this was one of the most difficult negotiating problems of the negotiation. The resulting texts do seem to provide an important beginning for establishing that discipline, although some have suggested that the beginning is a very small one. We return to this in chapter 12.

Another sector that has been troublesome for GATT is textiles and clothing. Since 1961 world trade in textiles has basically evaded the discipline of GATT because of a series of negotiated "side agreements" that establish a special regime of quotas for trade in these products.[98] Reform of the troublesome textile regime was another important objective of the Uruguay Round, and again some progress appears to have been made by the text on textiles, albeit with a fairly long phase-in (or phaseout of the old textile regime), so that textile goods will finally be under the general discipline of GATT.[99]

2.5 The GATT and WTO as Institutions

The Nonorganization and the New Organization (GATT and the WTO)

I have already expressed my view on the importance of the legal framework of institutions for a complete understanding of the nature and application of the rules of the world trading system. As Nobel Prize winner Douglas North has written, institutions play a significant role in setting the conditions and constraints that have a profound influence on economic development.[100] Part of that framework is the subject of this section. In this section I will deal with both the GATT and the WTO. Some of the material about the GATT is perhaps only history now, but because of the WTO charter "guidance" clause (Article XVI:1, saying the WTO "shall be guided by" the decisions, procedures and practices of the GATT), the history of GATT is an important element for the interpretation and understanding of the WTO institution and other provisions.

In addition, the GATT as a treaty still exists (as GATT 1994 in Annex 1A), although its institutional role is taken over by the WTO.

Despite the original theory of the drafters of the GATT, who viewed the GATT not to be an international organization, the evolution and practice of GATT by which it was forced to assume an institutional role for which it was never intended, it effectively became a de facto organization, at least for consultation, negotiation, and application of rules regarding international trade.

In contrast, the WTO is clearly an international organization, established by treaty (as outlined in section 2.3 supra), with at least the minimal necessary clauses for institutional and organizational effectiveness. Thus many of the "birth defects" of the GATT have now been corrected. Here I take up several particular aspects of the institutional framework of the current world trading system, particularly membership, voting, and amendment.

Membership

Given that in theory GATT was not an "organization," it did not have "members." The terminology used to emphasize this theory in the agreement was "contracting party." Yet we can speak fairly of "membership" in light of the evolution of the GATT into a de facto organization.

Apart from the twenty-three nations that were original GATT CPs, nations became GATT contracting parties by one of two methods. The normal method is governed by Article XXXIII of GATT and required a two-thirds vote of approval by the existing contracting parties for a nation to be accepted into GATT. The key element in obtaining sufficient votes for accession is the candidate nation's willingness to negotiate tariff concessions that existing GATT CPs deem to be adequate to fulfill their views of "reciprocity" to the various existing GATT concessions now binding the current GATT members. It would be unfair to let a nation enter GATT and receive the advantage of over forty years of various trade concessions and obligations, which the existing membership had accepted, without requiring the new nation also to commit itself to equivalent obligations. This is sometimes referred to as "negotiating the ticket of admission."

In this respect, WTO Article XII on accession follows the GATT (and presumably will largely follow the GATT practice for the accession procedures). Of course, accession to the WTO requires acceptance of all of the multilateral agreements, so in that respect there is added complexity.

Membership in the GATT/WTO not limited to "sovereign nations"

An interesting aspect of GATT membership, which continues under the WTO Charter, is that a condition of membership need not be full national sovereignty. Instead, the language of GATT and of the WTO (Article XII) allows a "separate customs territory possessing full autonomy in the conduct of its external commercial relations and of the other matters provided for in this Agreement and the Multilateral Trade Agreements" to accede to the WTO "on terms to be agreed." Such accession, of course, involves full acceptance of Annexes 1, 2, and 3, under the single-package idea thus including the GATT, the GATS, and the Intellectual Property Agreement.

A second path to membership in GATT also existed, however. GATT Article XXVI 5(c) provides that if a parent country has accepted the GATT in respect of a dependent customs territory (such as a colony), and that customs territory later becomes independent, such territory could become a GATT contracting party merely through sponsorship by the parent country. Since GATT's creation, over fifty newly independent nations have attained membership by this route. The advantage to these nations was that they did not need to negotiate a ticket of admission.

One result of this provision was that many developing countries—that is, those that were newly independent and sponsored for contracting party status—had either no tariff schedule or very brief tariff schedules. Under the WTO, this is no longer the case. A condition of membership of the WTO is the acceptance of a schedule of concessions and commitments for both the GATT and the GATS (services). Later accession requires the negotiation of an agreement between the WTO and the applicant, as noted above, and presumably this will apply the same conditions as are applied to original membership.

The Opt-Out Clause

Article XXXV of GATT has an important measure that affects to whom a contracting party's GATT obligations apply. This article, introduced in the original 1947 GATT draft when the voting requirement for new members was reduced from unanimity to two-thirds, allowed either a prior member or a new member to "opt out" of a GATT relationship with the other at one time only—the time when the new member entered GATT.[101] This opt-out clause was used extensively against Japan when it became a member, and it has been used by other countries for a variety of reasons. Often the reason to object to a GATT relationship is political in nature, as in the case of India's original 1948 invocation of Article XXXV against South Africa.[102] This opt-out clause was carried into several of the 1979 Tokyo Round Codes and, in some cases, has been used in connection with those codes.[103]

Article XIII of the WTO charter carries forward this concept of a one-time "opt-out" between WTO members at the time one or the other first enters the agreement. There is provision for carryover of the opt-outs for the GATT which are still in effect, and it is applied now to all of the mulilateral trade agreements in Annex 1 and also Annex 2 (dispute settlement). The WTO clarifies an ambiguity present in the GATT regarding the time when notice of the opt-out must be made. This can have substantial significance. It means that an applicant may be approved for membership in the WTO, and assume that membership, but find that it will not have a treaty obligation relationship on the most important rules vis-à-vis another WTO member because that other member has opted out. Indeed, the treaty language of the WTO charter on this point suggests that an existing member might be willing to vote in favor of a new applicant's membership but, at the same time, give notice and apply the opt-out. Under existing U.S. law in mid-1996, the United States executive branch may be required to use the opt-out clause in the event of accession by certain "communist" countries. (This would leave the United States and the other country to continue a WTO/GATT relationship through bilateral agreement, but that agreement would be subject to annual or other reviews.) The WTO language is similar, but it expands the concept beyond the GATT agreement to other matters provided for in this WTO Agreement and the multilateral trade agreements annexed thereto.

Several interesting membership questions existed in connection with GATT practice, one of which was the status of the European Community in GATT. It is possible to argue that the EC is a "separate customs territory possessing full autonomy" over GATT matters, so that it could have itself become a contracting party. Yet it did not take steps to do so. The EC represented its member states (all of whom are GATT CPs) in the GATT. The Treaty of Rome, however, allocates competence over member states external trade relations with the EC institutions. The EC Commission provides a mission at GATT (now WTO) and asserts the sole right to speak on trade matters for the member states at GATT. On occasion, however, tension has developed between the EC Commission representatives and the member states because of this. In addition, in several instances it was decided that the commission did not have competence to discuss a matter at GATT, and in such cases the member states spoke and acted for themselves. When actual voting occurred in GATT (somewhat rarely), each member state cast its vote as a contracting party (supposedly coordinated by the EC), and thus the EC effectively had twelve or more votes.[104]

China was one of the original contracting parties of GATT, but arguably withdrew from GATT in 1950 (the matter is disputed).[105] In the Uruguay Round the People's Republic of China negotiated for "resumption" of its seat. China joined the GATT Multifiber Agreement in 1984, and became an observer to GATT in that same year.[106] China eagerly sought to become an original member to the new WTO which required it to become a contracting party to the GATT under the appropriate procedures (somewhat ambiguous). China did not succeed in this quest, however, and as of this writing, it is still going through the process of negotiating the appropriate agreement for its membership in the WTO.

The case of Hong Kong is also very interesting in connection with GATT membership. For many years Hong Kong has participated in GATT as a colonial entity of the United Kingdom, which is a GATT contracting party.[107] In April 1986, after declaration of the United Kingdom under Article XXVI, Hong Kong was accepted by the GATT contracting parties as a full contracting party. To become such a member, however, a determination was necessary that Hong Kong was an independent customs territory with full autonomy over its external trade relations. The United Kingdom's possession of Hong Kong and adjacent territories ends in 1997, and an agreement has already been reached between the United Kingdom and the People's Republic of China about the reversion of Hong Kong to China and Hong Kong's status thereafter. Before Hong Kong was accepted as a contracting party to GATT, assurances were received from the People's Republic of China that its status would remain sufficiently independent to fulfill the GATT Article XXVI requirement.[108] Hong Kong, as a contracting party of GATT, completed the appropriate steps to accede as an original member to the WTO and as of 1 January 1995, the effective date of the WTO, Hong Kong has been a member.

Power under GATT and the WTO

For a treaty that was not supposed to form an organization, the GATT contained clauses that appeared to authorize a very broad exercise of authority.[109] The principal body of GATT was the CONTRACTING PARTIES. A number of GATT clauses called for joint action, but Article XXV of the agreement gave general authority to the CPs to meet "from time to time for the purpose of giving effect to those provisions of this Agreement which involve joint action and, generally, with a view to facilitating the operation and furthering the objectives of this Agreement."[110] Each CP had one vote, and unless otherwise specified, a majority of votes cast controlled an issue.

From the language of GATT Article XXV it can be seen that there was the potential for very broad CP authority. In practice this authority was not exercised. Many governments (including the U.S.) could have had serious constitutional problems if the CPs purported to exercise this language of Article XXV to its limit. Nevertheless, the use of waivers has been extensive and in some cases nearly like an amendment.[111] (The degree to which the CONTRACTING PARTIES had the authority to definitively interpret the GATT in a manner binding on all contracting parties will be taken up in chapter 4.)

As we shall see below, the WTO has a more complex series of rules regarding decisions than the GATT, and there are many more checks and balances on the authority of the organization. The very broad language of Article XXV does not exist in the WTO, and presumably the provisions of GATT Article XXV (now in WTO annex 1) are now trumped by the WTO.

The CONTRACTING PARTIES of GATT carried out their business within a large number of committees, working parties, panels, and other bodies.[112] The most significant subbody of the CPs was the council, which was set up by resolution of the CONTRACTING PARTIES in 1960. The council consisted of representatives of all GATT contracting parties who wished to assume the responsibility of such membership, and met almost monthly. In part because of the formation of this group, but also because diplomacy has increasingly become a process of referring to national capitals for instructions and even voting by telex, the sessions of the CONTRACTING PARTIES as such were reduced to annual meetings that lasted only a few days. The ordinary "grist" of GATT business was carried on by the Council, supervising the many other bodies of GATT.

The WTO will clearly continue GATT's practice of having an extensive number of subordinate bodies. Indeed, instead of one council, the WTO has four—one of which is a "general council," which appears to be the most powerful and has exclusive authority to take certain actions (such as "interpretations"). Overall, the highest level of authority in the

WTO is the ministerial conference, which is mandated to meet not less than every other year. Clearly designed on the model of the GATT council, the general council will likely meet regularly and can carry out the functions of the ministerial conference in the intervals between ministerial meetings. In addition, the WTO agreement assigns other functions to the general council. Then there is a council for each of the three major agreements of Annex 1, namely, a Council for Trade in goods (GATT), a Council for Trade in Services (GATS), and a Council for Trade-Related Aspects of Intellectual Property Rights (TRIPS). These councils will each oversee the functioning of their particular agreement, but they "shall operate under the general guidance of the General Council." This appears to be an extraordinarily complex structure, and it was apparently instigated by various divergent interests in the negotiating delegations about control over the different kinds of subject matter in the three agreements of Annex 1. It remains to be seen exactly how this will work, and whether over time the four different councils will in some way tend to converge in meeting time and genda documents.

On 30 August, 1995, the date of its termination, the GATT had one hundred twenty-eight contracting parties. This obviously was no longer the "cozy group" that formed the GATT in 1947; the very size of this number made effective operation more and more difficult as the years wore on. Likewise, in the WTO (when as of January 1, 1997 the membership reached 129) similar difficulties will arise. Given the various checks and balances on the power of the WTO and its subordinate institutions, as well as the tendency to avoid centralizing power and operations in any particular part of the organization (see figure 2.1), it can be expected that the difficulties for WTO effectiveness could increase. There is already a trend among major GATT/WTO trading countries to take their business elsewhere, for example, to annual "summit" meetings, small groups of trade ministers such as the "quad group" (i.e., the United States, the EC, Japan, and Canada), certain regional arrangements, or other types of private meetings of trade ministers or major participants. Consensus remains an important element of decision making in the WTO, and it is now reinforced with particular definitions and reference to this practice which developed over the history of GATT without being described in any treaty language. This could operate to hamstring the development of the organization, or on the other hand, it could in some instances play against the interests of the most powerful members of the WTO (although there appear to be many checks against that). For these reasons it has sometimes been suggested that the GATT, and now the WTO, needs some sort of high-level "supercommittee" that can act more like an executive, and that would reflect more accurately the real power relations in the organization.

The weighted voting techniques used in the IMF and World Bank are not deemed realistic options, but a small group of nations, including the most powerful trading entities as well as representatives of major categories of other CPs, has been suggested to provide guidance for the organization. In 1975, during the Tokyo Round negotiation, a "consultative group of 18" was set up, partly with the considerations just mentioned in mind. It did not play a powerful role, however.[113]

Voting and Decision Making in the GATT and the WTO

Acting jointly, the GATT CONTRACTING PARTIES governed by majority vote on many matters; however, in much of GATT business a decided preference for "consensus" approaches developed. There was in fact some fear of voting, possibly for good reason. The voting structure, as in so many international organizations today, bears little resemblance to the real power relations of the participants. The practice in GATT generally was to avoid formal voting, although this practice was conditioned by the amending, membership, and waiver language of the agreement, so that at least for waivers, or for membership or treaty amendments, formal votes (or treaty acceptances) were considered necessary.

The WTO continues these preferences and procedures, and actually redefines and embellishes them. In Article IX on decision making, the WTO Agreement explicitly states that "the WTO shall continue the practice of decision-making by consensus followed under GATT." The footnote states that "the body concerned shall be deemed to have decided by consensus on a matter submitted for its consideration, if no Member, present at the meeting when the decision is taken, formally objects to the proposed decision." This is one of the few definitions of consensus, and will probably be influential in interpreting the word "consensus" throughout the Uruguay Round agreements, although this is not entirely certain. To some extent, this consensus idea appears to give veto power to almost any country. It should be noted, however, that it is not unanimity. Absent parties, and those present but abstaining, do not prevent consensus. Thus, countries that find it financially or politically difficult to have adequate representation at the WTO may find decisions being made that they do not want. To some extent, this procedure actually operates

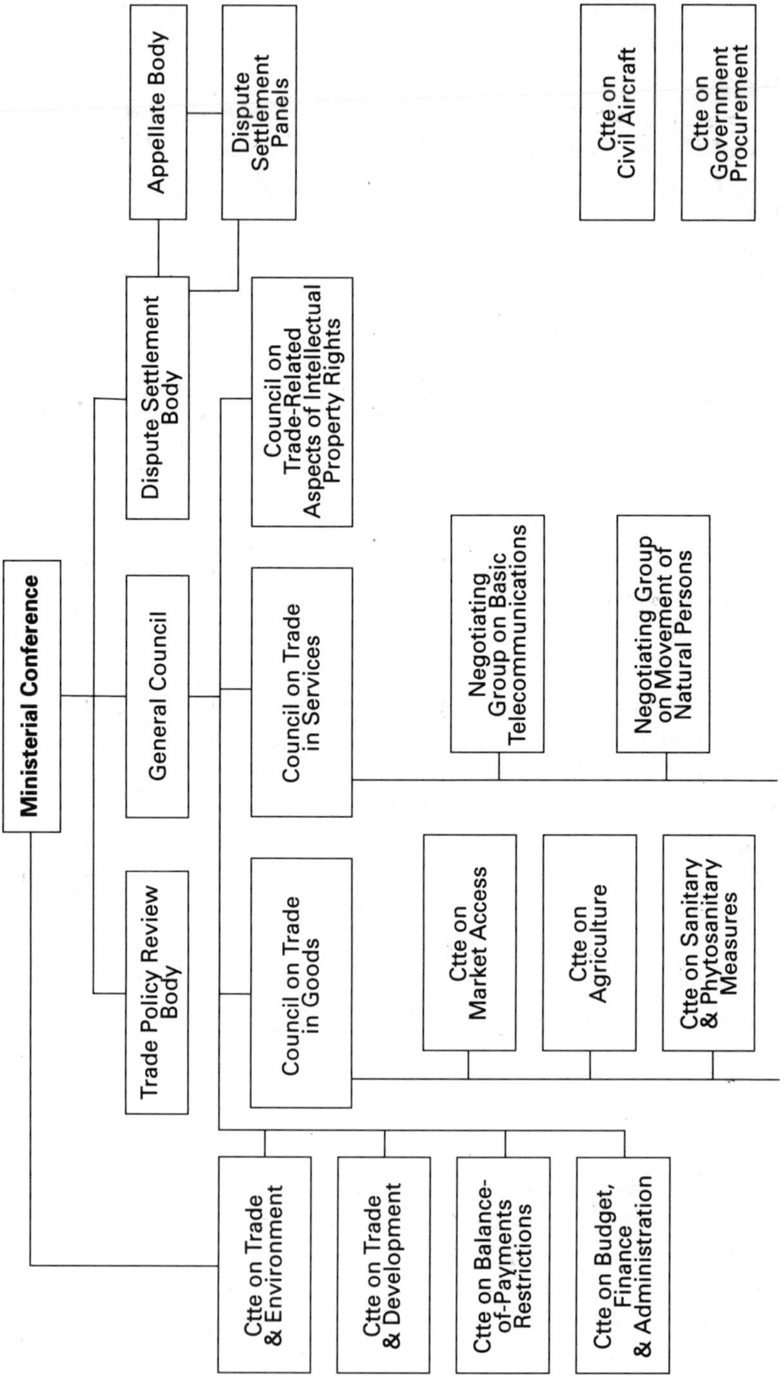
Ministerial Conference
Trade Policy Review Body
General Council
Dispute Settlement Body
Appellate Body
Dispute Settlement Panels
Council on Trade in Goods
Council on Trade in Services
Council on Trade-Related Aspects of Intellectual Property Rights
Ctte on Market Access
Ctte on Agriculture
Ctte on Sanitary & Phytosanitary Measures
Negotiating Group on Basic Telecommunications
Negotiating Group on Movement of Natural Persons
Ctte on Civil Aircraft
Ctte on Government Procurement
Ctte on Trade & Environment
Ctte on Trade & Development
Ctte on Balance-of-Payments Restrictions
Ctte on Budget, Finance & Administration

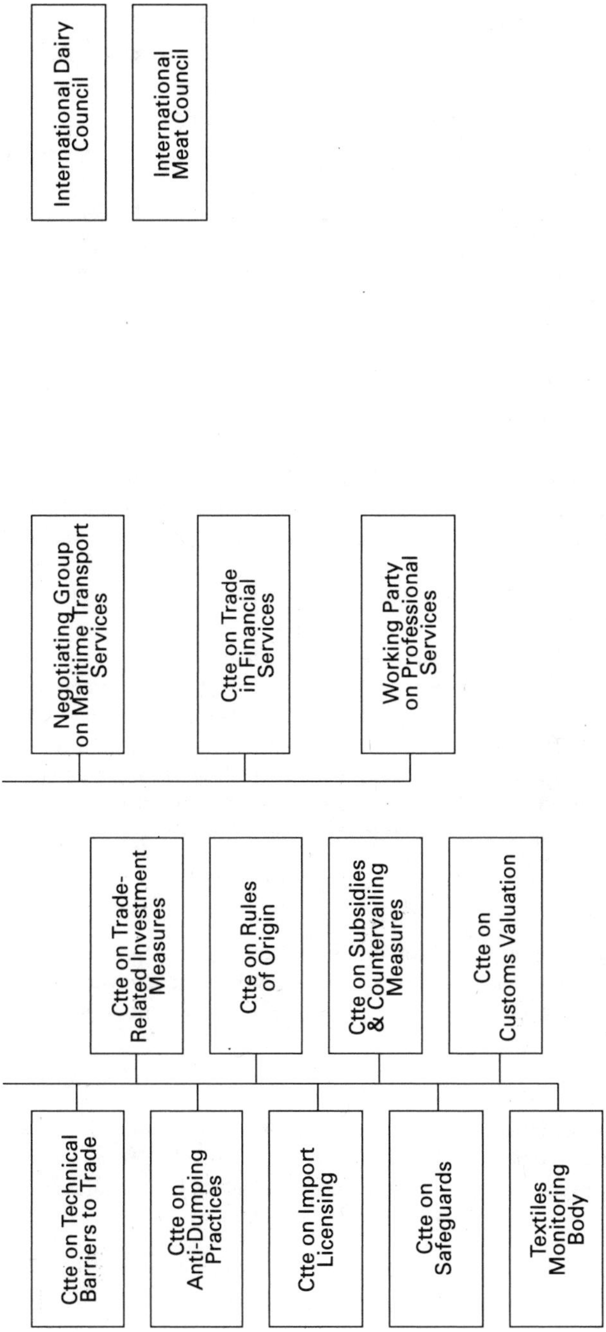

Source: WTO Focus, No. 1, Jan.–Feb, 1995, at p. 5.

Figure 2.1
WTO Structure

as sort of a weighted-voting provision, given that the larger powers will undoubtedly always have a presence at any important decision-making opportunity. The following is a brief synopsis of some of the important decision-making procedures of the new WTO Agreement.

Ordinary Decisions: Article IX:1

The WTO Charter specifies that the GATT practice of decision making by consensus is to be continued for the WTO Ministerial Conference (MC) and General Council (GC), but when consensus cannot be achieved, decisions will be made on the basis of the majority of votes cast, with each member having one vote, unless otherwise provided.

Interpretations: Article IX:2

The MC and GC have exclusive authority to adopt interpretations of the WTO Charter and the Annex 1 Multilateral Trade Agreements. Interpretations of the Annex 1 agreements are to be based on a recommendation of the Council for that agreement and require an affirmative vote from three-quarters of the overall WTO membership. Interpretations are not to be used to undermine Article X's amendment procedures.

Waivers: Article IX:3

The MC may waive an obligation under the WTO Charter and the Annex 1 Multilateral Trade Agreements. If consensus cannot be reached, the grant of a waiver requires an affirmative vote of three-quarters of the overall WTO membership. In the case of Annex 1 agreements, the waiver request is to be submitted to the relevant Council (e.g., Goods, Services, or TRIPS), which will submit a report to the MC. Article IX:4 provides that any waiver granted shall specify the exceptional circumstances justifying it and a termination date. Waivers are subject to annual MC review.

Negotiating Other Agreements: Article III:2

The WTO is to provide a forum for negotiations on agreements contained in its annexes. It may also provide a forum for other negotiations on trade relations and a framework for the implementation of the results of such negotiations, by decision of the MC.

Annex 4: Plurilateral Agreements

Decision making and amendments under these agreements is governed by the rules contained in each agreement (Articles IX:5, X:10). The MC may add trade agreements to Annex 4 by consensus; it may delete agreements from Annex 4 on the request of the members party to the agreement (Article X:9).

In addition, it is important to understand both the potential of the dispute-settlement procedures and the panel reports that result from the change or evolution of the trade rules.

In GATT some members worried about waivers being used as a sort of "easy-track" substitute for amendments. Some GATT documents discussed this problem, but the practice of GATT was rather relaxed on this point. The WTO Charter stiffens considerably the rules regarding waivers and makes explicit the power of the organization to terminate waivers (an issue of some contention in GATT. See Article IX:3).

Likewise concern was expressed in GATT about the amending rules (contained in Article XXX). The unanimity required for certain amendments had never been achieved, and the requirement otherwise of two-thirds (but not binding on holdouts) was increasingly difficult to fulfill as the number of GATT contracting parties increased. This difficulty was a major factor in the Tokyo Round negotiations, leading the participants to utilize "side" codes or agreements on a number of GATT subjects as a way to avoid the need for amendments. But these codes only bound governments that accepted them; and in the Uruguay Round it was decided that a single-package approach should be followed, so that all governments that became members of the WTO would be obligated to accept almost all of the agreements and rules. The whole package itself was accepted as a totally new treaty, thus avoiding the GATT amending procedure (and probably resulting in technical withdrawals from the old GATT). The amending rules of this new package are somewhat similar to the GATT rules, so it is possible that the inconveniences of the GATT rules will continue to be a problem. The WTO rules, however, do have some areas of greater flexibility for changing trade rules.

The legal structure of potential voting still has a great influence on any organization, no matter how hard the organization tries to avoid voting. Consensus approaches often involve negotiating to resolve differences, but such negotiation is in the context of the participants knowledge of the likely outcome if the negotiation breaks down. This can be complex and subtle. The outcome may be a vote, in which case the voting structure will in fact influence the negotiations toward a consensus. On the other hand, voting an unrealistic proposition will likely lead one or more powerful participants to ignore the vote result. This too becomes one of the constraints in a negotiation, at least when the negotiators are responsible and reasonably realistic.

A consensus approach has other problems. Strictly applied, it gives every country a veto, and thus reduces any potential initiative to the least common denominator. If not strictly applied, there will often be deference to the real "power structure" of the participants, and this in fact may give the most powerful of the group an even larger share of the power than policy or equity might dictate. During the Tokyo Round the actual negotiation often began with major decisions being made by only the United States, the European Community, and Japan. Canada or a few others might elbow their way into these discussions, but even then the vast majority of the contracting parties and other negotiating nations might be excluded from real influence on the drafting of a proposed agreement until near the end of the process—at which time it was difficult to get changes made.[114] In the Uruguay Round, the groups of "inner-participants" were considerably enlarged, but the key "quad group" continued to have considerable influence.

Likewise, the voting-consensus question has posed great problems for the GATT dispute-settlement procedure, rendering it difficult if not impossible to obtain council approval of a panel report in a dispute when a nation dissatisfied with the outcome expressed in such a report refuses to go along with a consensus for council approval.[115] This "blocking" opportunity provided the motivation for developing a new dispute-settlement procedure with an appellate body (described in chapter 4). It is in light of this particular difficulty, and the desire to prevent the continuation of the Tokyo Round "GATT à la carte" approach, that the legal steps used to bring about the implementation of the Uruguay Round results and the new WTO organization can be better understood. As noted in section 2.3, the legal approach that was taken was to essentially abandon the GATT, not try to amend it under its amending clauses. Instead, a whole new treaty was created with the WTO as the umbrella, and the remaining parts as annexes. Technically, no minimum number was required for bringing the WTO into effect and implementing the Uruguay Round, although it was clear that in practical terms they had to be accepted by all the major trading participants—and the more the better. In fact, the number that acceded, even before the WTO came into effect and in the several years following, is very large indeed as noted earlier.

A number of legal issues nevertheless remain about the interrelationship of the various parts of the Uruguay Round text (even though technically part of one massive treaty). We have already encountered some of these problems, such as the relationship of GATT 1994 and some of the particular text "agreements" related to GATT.

The membership of the WTO as of January 1, 1997, was 129, with as many as 34 other nations negotiating to join. The make-up of this membership can be roughly illustrated by the following approximate figures:[116]

Total WTO Members	129
Industrial countries	26
EU member states	15
Developing countries	73
Least developed countries	29
EU Lome ACP countries	52

(The Lome convention is one of a series (now the fourth) of trade preference treaties between the EU and the ACP (Asian-Caribbean-Pacific) states. Some numbers above are approximate and can differ with different definitions.)

Although there is not yet particular evidence of bloc voting or bloc solidarity, one can see certain risks in the overall membership structure especially if consensus decision making breaks down. Developing and least developed countries amount to more than 80 percent of the membership. The European Union casts fifteen votes itself, and if joined by Associated States and the Lome ACP countries, could conceivably muster 84 or more votes, more than 65 percent. These figures can have important influences on the WTO, even in the consensus decision-making process. For example, waivers now generally require a three-fourths vote, which could be achieved by developing countries. The overall experience and practice of GATT and now WTO voting suggest, however, more potential for paralysis than for voting abuses.

Amending the Agreements

During the Tokyo Round (1973–1979), it was generally considered impractical to amend the GATT general clauses. Thus it was deemed impossible to embody the nontariff measure results of the Tokyo Round negotiation into amendments to the GATT. Getting more than ninety (or even more than sixty) parliaments to accept the results would likely have been too time consuming. Furthermore, such an approach would effectively have given much more negotiating power to the large developing country majority.

On the other hand, the development of side codes, or stand-alone ancillary treaties, to enlarge and elaborate the GATT rules, posed technical, legal and administrative difficulties. I have written about some of these difficulties in the following terms:

> The inter-relationships between the various Codes and the GATT will become increasingly complex. Such complexity, in turn, will make it harder for the general

public to understand the GATT-MTN system, perhaps resulting in less public support for that system over time. The complexity will hurt those countries that cannot devote additional governmental expertise to GATT representation problems. In addition, such complexity inevitably will give rise to a variety of legal disputes among GATT parties. Finally, it will contribute to the belief that the richer nations can control and can manipulate the GATT system for their own advantage.[117]

The most striking characteristic [of the Tokyo Round results] is the Balkanization or fragmentation of dispute settlement under the various Agreements....[118]

One of the questions raised by the side codes, that purported to obligate only those nations that separately accept them, was the relationship of these codes to the obligations of GATT itself. The Uruguay Round, of course, took a very different approach with its "single package" concept.

The WTO Charter now provides a somewhat more complex amending process. Article X provides that amendments to the WTO Charter and the Annex 1 multilateral trade agreements may be proposed to the MC by members or councils. If consensus cannot be reached, the approval of an amendment for submission to the members requires a two-thirds vote of the overall WTO membership. Generally, amendments come into force on acceptance by two-thirds of the members. If it has been determined that the amendment will not affect member rights and obligations, it comes into force for all members at that time. Otherwise, amendments come into force only for those members accepting them, unless by a three-quarters vote of the overall WTO membership, it is decided that if a member does not accept the amendment it shall be free to withdraw or remain a member with permission of the MC. (In the case of GATS, amendments to certain provisions come into force on a two-thirds vote. For the other provisions, they come into effect for those approving them, but are subject to the same three-quarters vote procedure.)

Amendments to certain rules take effect only upon acceptance by all members: WTO decision-making and amendment rules (Articles IX, X); GATT Articles I (MFN) and II (tariff schedules); GATS Article II:1 (MFN); TRIPS Article 4 (MFN). Amendments to Annexes 2 (dispute settlement) and 3 (TPRM) can be made by MC action alone (without member acceptance), but for Annex 2, MC approval must be by consensus. Article X:8. Amendments to the plurilateral agreements in Annex 4 are governed by the rules contained in each of those agreements.

Thus, we can see that the amending procedure under the WTO Charter is quite intricate and ingenious. It obviously has been carefully tailored to the needs of the participating nations, and it is differently formulated for different parts of the major multilateral agreements and other annexes of the WTO. A particularly important characteristic is designed to protect the "sovereignty of members." When an amendment would "alter the rights and obligations" of a member that refuses to accept the amendment, that member is not bound by it. One particular procedure noted above, however, allows the ministerial conference by three-fourths vote of the members to require all to accept the amendment, withdraw from the agreement, or remain a member with the explicit consent of the ministerial conference. It is therefore very difficult to conceive of the amending provisions being used in any way to force a major trading country, such as the United States, or the EC to accept altered rights or obligations. To force the issue upon a major country could raise the possibility that such country would withdraw from the WTO, and clearly the WTO would be severely handicapped and would perhaps collapse if any of the major trading partners did so withdraw. It is very unlikely that other members of the WTO will push matters to this stage, and thus the major trading partners seem to possess a sort of de facto veto. The spirit and practice of GATT, however, has always been to try to accommodate through consensus-negotiation procedures the views of as many countries as possible, but certainly to give weight to views of countries that have great weight in the trading system. This will undoubtedly not change.

2.6 GATT, the Trade Negotiation Rounds, and the WTO

Trade Negotiation Rounds and the Evolution of GATT

An important but intermittent feature of GATT has been the series of trade negotiating rounds that it has sponsored. Through 1985, seven of these rounds (counting the 1947 original negotiating and drafting of GATT as the first) had taken place, and in September 1986 a decision was made to launch the eighth.[119] The first five of these rounds were devoted almost exclusively to tariff negotiations, although during the time of the fourth round, at the "review session" of 1954–1955, the GATT contracting parties separately drafted the protocols revising nontariff measure clauses of the agreement. The sixth round, the Kennedy Round, had as one of its goals the negotiation of nontariff measure obligations, but succeeded only in a limited way to achieve this goal. The seventh round, the 1973–1979 Tokyo Round, was more devoted to nontariff measures than to tariffs.

Over its forty-eight-year of history, GATT's most resounding success has undoubtedly been the reduction of tariff levels among the contracting parties.[120] As a result of these seven rounds, and of other activity, many tariffs on nonprimary goods imported into the industrialized contracting-party nations have been so reduced that many economists and businessmen feel that they are no longer a meaningful barrier to imports. Indeed, this very success (as mentioned in section 1.1) has been one of the causes of today's "interdependence" problems. The story regarding primary goods, particularly agricultural products, is not nearly so encouraging. Likewise many developing countries have extensive tariff or other barriers to imports (as we shall explore in a later chapter), although the WTO requirements for membership now puts some important constraints on these developing country practices, and requires a more substantial contribution to trade liberalization by the developing countries than they faced under the prior institution.

The tariff schedules are incorporated into GATT by language in Article II, and thus changes might technically be considered amendments to that article. By GATT practice, however, they generally are not considered to require unanimity. Instead, the acceptance of each contracting party whose schedule is affected is considered a prerequisite for the coming into force of those schedules.[121]

The table below gives some indication of the scope and success of the tariff-reducing activity of GATT. (The tariff averages refer to tariffs on non-primary products of industrial countries.)[122]

Round	Dates	Number of countries	Value of trade covered	Average tariff cut	Average tariffs afterward
Geneva	1947	23	$10 billion	35%	"not available"
Annecy	1949	33	Unavailable	35%	"not available"
Torquay	1950	34	Unavailable	35%	"not available"
Geneva	1956	22	$2.5 billion	35%	"not available"
Dillon	1960–61	45	$4.9 billion	35%	"not available"
Kennedy	1962–67	48	$40 billion	35%	8.7%
Tokyo	1973–79	99	$155 billion	34%	6.3%
Uruguay	1986–94	120+	$3.7 trillion	38%	3.9%

The Kennedy Round and Nontariff Measures

Although the contracting parties intended the Kennedy Round to deal with the increasingly troublesome problems of nontariff measures (NTMs), the results of that round for NTMs were very modest. Only one basic side code resulted, namely, the 1967 Antidumping (AD) Code.[123] This code had a troubled history because of U.S. constitutional and legal problems,[124] and was replaced in 1979 by a second AD code developed during the Tokyo Round.[125]

The Kennedy Round also produced a separate protocol agreement complementing the tariff protocol and embodying some NTM matters. The United States had a system of valuation of imports for customs that, for certain products, used the American selling price (ASP) technique. Under this method, imported goods were valued by reference to the price of competing domestically produced goods in the United States. This procedure was a clear violation of GATT, but the United States claimed grandfather rights for it. It applied to a few selected categories of goods, primarily shoe products and petrochemicals.[126] Other contracting parties, eager to obtain a commitment from the United States to change this system, were willing to negotiate reciprocal concessions on a variety of tariffs and a few other matters. Given that under U.S. law, changes in ASP could not be agreed to or implemented without reference to Congress, this matter and the reciprocal commitments to it were embodied in a separate protocol at the end of the Kennedy Round in 1967, so as not to hold up implementation of the main tariff protocol. This ASP side agreement was then submitted to the U.S. Congress for approval, but the Congress never concurred and the protocol died. In fact, the side agreement never reached the floor of either the House or the Senate because of various procedural devices engineered by domestic interests desiring to protect the products involved from foreign competition. This sad experience, reminiscent of congressional treatment of the ITO and the OTC,[127] was one factor leading to some foreign nation reluctance to enter into a new (Tokyo) round of negotiations during the 1970s.

The Tokyo Round: Side Agreements and the GATT (Legal Status of Agreements Resulting from the Tokyo Round)

The seventh round of negotiation, which occurred from 1973 to 1979, is called the "Tokyo Round," or sometimes the "MTN" (for multilateral trade negotiations). In this round nontariff and tariff measures were addressed extensively for the first time. Except for the original drafting of the GATT itself, the MTN results were the most far-reaching and substantively important product of the first seven major trade rounds. In addition to tariff-reduction protocols, the MTN results included nine special agreements and four "understandings."[128] The agreements were on:

1. Technical barriers to trade
2. Government procurement
3. Interpretation and application of Articles VI, XVI, and XXIII (subsidies)
4. Arrangements regarding bovine meat
5. Arrangements regarding dairy products
6. Implementation of Article VII (custom valuation)
7. Import licensing procedures
8. Trade in civil aircraft
9. Implementation of Article VI (antidumping duties)

And the understandings were on:

1. Differential and more favorable treatment, reciprocity, and fuller participation of developing countries
2. Declaration on trade measures taken for balance-of-payments purposes
3. Safeguard action for development purposes
4. Understanding regarding notification, consultation, dispute settlement, and surveillance

The overall impact of these results was to substantially broaden the scope of coverage of the GATT system.[129] The legal status of these various agreements and understandings, however, was not always clear. The nine agreements are drafted as stand-alone treaties, each with signatory clauses, and in most cases with institutional measures that include a committee of signatories with certain powers, and with a dispute settlement mechanism (part of the "Balkanization" mentioned previously). Of these agreements, seven have sufficiently precise obligations to be called "codes." The others tend to confine their terms to the development of consultation mechanisms, statements of objectives, and only a few weak provisions that actually provide binding obligations. In one case, an agreement has apparently been sufficiently troubled that the United States and some other signatories formally withdrew from it.[130]

The "understandings" have a much more ambiguous status. Not signed as independent agreements, these instruments for the most part express goals or very general obligations, or (in the case of dispute settlement) describe procedures that arguably were already followed. The CONTRACTING PARTIES adopted these understandings in November 1979.[131] The implication of some of the provisions in these understandings is such as to suggest a "waiver" from other GATT obligations, while other provisions elaborate procedures in the manner in which a "decision" under GATT Article XXV might do.[132]

As stand-alone treaties, the codes obligated only those nations that signed and ratified them. A number of questions were raised about the legal relationship of these codes to the GATT itself. First, in theory, GATT parties that did not sign the agreements were not bound by them, and no provision of a code could alter their GATT rights. Because the GATT obligations included the most-favored-nation clause, however, and if a code provided treatment for the trade of any other code signatory which was more favorable than that provided in GATT, such treatment was arguably required for the GATT member that had not signed the code. The GATT CONTRACTING PARTIES in November 1979 adopted a decision that took this position.[133] Some codes, however, did not fall within the terms of the GATT MFN clause.[134]

Some of the codes had titles that relate them to the GATT, such as the Agreement on Implementation of Article VI, and another on interpretation and application of several GATT articles. Again, nonsignatories argue that they were in no way bound by such codes. If these codes can be deemed to be "practice" of the GATT contracting parties, however, they may be evidence of an evolving interpretation of the GATT language itself.

Many of the codes had independent dispute-settlement mechanisms. This raised questions about whether a particular dispute should be brought in the general GATT procedure or in the separate code procedure. This also gave rise to questions about what happens when an interpretation of a code by a code-dispute panel differs from an interpretation on asimilar GATT issue by a GATT panel.

The WTO Agreement and its single-package result will hopefully eliminate most of the questions that are raised in the paragraphs above. All of the so-called codes are actually parts of the text of the Uruguay Round Agreement, found mostly in the annexes to the WTO. Likewise a single-dispute settlement process has been designed and set up under the dispute-settlement understanding (Annex 2). Nevertheless, Annex 4 contains some so-called plurilateral agreements, which are a slight departure from the single-package idea, allowing countries the option of whether or not to join. With respect to the four agreements in Annex 4, or other plurilateral agreements that may be added later, some of the issues described above may surface again. In addition, practice under the Tokyo Round codes, and the Understandings adopted at the end of the Tokyo Round, are part of the "guidance" referred to in WTO Article XVI, par. 1. Some of the Understandings may also continue to be "in force" as decisions or waivers carried over into the WTO by reference in Annex 1A.

3 National Institutions

3.1 Introduction

Interrelationship of National and International Institutions

The erosion of the concept of "sovereignty" in international affairs has been much commented on.[1] Perhaps in no context more than international economic affairs has this erosion actually occurred. One occasionally still hears national officials (including those from the United States) argue against international rules or foreign government demands for consultation or representation either on the basis that it "interferes with our sovereignty" or that it encroaches on the "internal affairs" of our government. But this is usually a misplaced argument in today's world. The effects of national government actions on other societies, and on general world economic conditions, are so often significant that it would seem that the time has come for all governments to be prepared at least to listen to the arguments and representations of other governments, or of citizens of other societies, before taking action that has such effects. The old, tired argument that "it is premature" for a foreign party to weigh in with its ideas, or for it to ask for consultation, before a government acts, is often only an excuse to enable the acting government to create a fait accompli situation before foreign objections can have any meaningful influence.

Apart from the above considerations, it is also clear today that any coordinated activity of governments, especially in connection with economic affairs, requires a complex set of individual governmental actions by both international and national institutions. This is particularly important, of course, for the large and powerful economies that participate in world economic affairs. For example, to achieve any meaningful initiative by the WTO requires not only action by some body of that organization, but also action by at least the United States and the European Community—and probably also by Japan, Canada, and certain other key countries. In every such case, each government responds to a complex set of internal institutional constraints. As we see in this chapter, the United States Constitution mandates certain procedures (often requiring action by both the executive and legislative bodies), and this immediately imposes a set of legal/constitutional/political constraints on any proposed course of international action.

United States Law and the International System—Synergy or Conflict?

It is not difficult to find cases in which national and international legal systems interact to influence each other. A prime example is the effect of the U.S. Constitution and laws on the GATT-ITO history.[2] The 1967 GATT Antidumping Code was also heavily influenced by U.S. legal constraints imposed on U.S. negotiators; and the difficulty of implementing that code in U.S. law because of congressional criticism illustrates the interaction point.[3]

Other countries, especially the more powerful ones, have similar problems. The EC is a particularly interesting example, because it is so influential in GATT and the WTO. Under the Treaty of Rome, the troubled and evolving nature of the EC institutions has had a constant influence on many GATT matters.[4] Controversy about appropriate competence or authority between EC institutions and member states, or between the EC Commission and the EC Council, can slow down action, or impose constraints on that action, just as it does to United States law. The Treaty of Rome cedes competence over "commercial policy" to the EC, and such policy arguably includes all matters within the scope of GATT. Commercial policy is not defined in the Treaty of Rome, nor is the competence said to be exclusive. Member states often therefore argue that certain matters are not within the exclusive competence of the EC. In such circumstances, the EC may allow member states to participate in the process alongside it.

When the European Community undertook the process of ratifying and implementing the Uruguay Round results, a controversy regarding the relative competence of the various EC institutions was taken to the Court of Justice in Luxembourg, which ruled that member states must be allowed to participate in some of the procedures. This was partly a result of the inclusion of services and intellectual property in the Uruguay Round.[5]

At the end of the Tokyo Round in 1979, a number of these issues suddenly came to prominence. In the United States, the Congress began considering legislation to approve and implement the Tokyo Round agreements. The EC, rightfully concerned that this national procedure would influence potential future interpretations of these agreements, retained legal and economic consultants located in Washington, D.C., to monitor and report to Brussels about these congressional proceedings—once again illustrating the departure from theories of strict sovereignty and traditional diplomacy. On at least one important issue, EC officials thought it was necessary to communicate with the U.S. government to influence the direction of congressional measures to be included in the Trade Agreements Act of 1979.[6]

3.2 The United States Constitution and Its Effects on Trade Relations

The Constitution and Its Constraints: Congressional Power to Regulate Commerce

The Founding Fathers who wrote the U.S. Constitution in the 1780s distrusted government and the concentration of power. Consequently, they built into the Constitution the concept of distributing power among three principal branches of the federal government (the executive, legislative, and judicial branches), and between the federal government and state governments. One consequence of this structure is a constant tension between the legislative and executive branches. This tension sometimes results in actions taken by one branch or another that may seem mysterious unless they are viewed in the context of this constitutional structure. This power struggle between the branches of the U.S. government, however is precisely what the Founding Fathers contemplated. They viewed it as a system of "checks and balances" that would prevent any one branch from becoming too powerful.

During recent decades, beginning with the economic and political crises of the 1930s, the U.S. presidency has grown considerably stronger. A Supreme Court case in 1936, the *United States v. Curtiss Wright Export Company*, even propounded the theory that the president of the United States has certain inherent powers over foreign affairs that do not depend on the Constitution![7] Although many scholars reject this theory,[8] for practical reasons the presidency has developed a preeminent role in the conduct of U.S. foreign affairs, stemming in part from clauses found in the Constitution.

With regard to international economic affairs, the Congress can point to several clauses in the Constitution to indicate that power has been delegated to it. Among these is Article I, section 8, which grants to the Congress the power to "regulate commerce with foreign Nations," and to "lay and collect Taxes, Duties, Imposts and excises."[9] Consequently, the Congress believes that it has a special power over matters of international trade, and it likes to remind the executive branch of this special power.[10]

Although the power of the presidency was enhanced by the necessities of World War II, in the postwar period this power continued to be great, particularly in foreign affairs. In 1952, however, the U.S. Supreme Court, in the case of *Youngstown Sheet and Tube Co. v. Sawyer*, held that President Truman had exceeded his power by seizing the steel mills to keep them operating in the face of a strike.[11] Constitutional language in that case was relied on to support arguments limiting presidential power in matters relating to both domestic and foreign affairs. Although there have been few cases subsequently in which the Supreme Court has limited presidential powers in foreign affairs, some lower court cases have suggested the possibility of further limitations.[12]

The Vietnam War and the Watergate crisis caused Congress to reassert its powers, especially with regard to international affairs. Consequently, during the last decade Congress has taken a number of actions that have imposed restraints on the president's authority.[13]

Treaties and Executive Agreements

As we have seen in a previous chapter,[14] treaties are the main international law method for implementing norms concerning economic relations. The way by which a nation enters into and implements treaties from a domestic law point of view thus becomes extremely significant.

The U.S. Constitution requires that treaties be submitted to the U.S. Senate for "advise and consent" (requiring a two-thirds affirmative vote) before the president can enter into them on behalf of the United States. Nevertheless, during two centuries of constitutional history, alternative forms of approval of international agreements have been developed. United States practice divides international treaty agreements into "treaties" (in the U.S. constitutional sense, agreements that must be submitted to the Senate) and "executive agreements" (all others.) From an international law standpoint, all of these instruments are treaties, but from a U.S.

constitutional perspective of its domestic law, the different terminology is significant.[15]

Executive agreements may be approved under U.S. constitutional practice in several ways: (1) they may be submitted to the Congress for approval by the passage of a statute that grants the authority to the president to accept the international agreement (many trade agreements are approved in this manner—a primary example being approval of most Tokyo Round GATT agreements by the 1979 Trade Agreements Act); (2) the Congress can pass a statute that authorizes the president in advance to negotiate, enter into, and accept for the United States an international agreement (this is the approach to tariff agreements of the Reciprocal Trade Agreements Acts); (3) a *treaty* may give the president advance delegated authority within limits to enter an executive agreement designed to implement the treaty; and finally (4) under the Constitution the president may enter into some executive agreements on his own "inherent" authority, without any participation either before or after the negotiation by the Congress as a whole or the Senate alone. These would be agreements authorized by explicit constitutional grants of authority to the president (such as his authority as commander in chief of the armed forces) or implied by the Constitution as falling under presidential authority (executive power).[16]

The first procedure mentioned above turned out to be somewhat controversial in the process of U.S. ratification of the Uruguay Round results in 1994. One important legal scholar challenged the statutory procedure contemplated as violating the "treaty clause" of the constitution. But after considerable debate—some of which is contained in published works—the Congress, including the Senate, chose to follow the statutory procedure; and indeed, the Senate vote on the implementing bill was more than two-thirds (for what comfort that may give to those challenging the procedure).[17]

Some countries, including the United States, make a distinction between international law and domestic law. This distinction concerns whether an international treaty will be treated by courts and government agencies as part of the domestic law of a country, similar to statute law. Some countries, notably the United Kingdom, are considered "dualist," meaning that their treaties do not become part of domestic law. For domestic law implementation of a treaty to occur, the Parliament must enact a statute, or some other legal instrument (such as executive decree or regulation) must be promulgated. Other countries have legal systems that tend to incorporate international agreements into domestic law without the intervention of further governmental acts.[18] These are often called "monist" systems. The United States falls in between. International agreements (including the five types just described, that is: senate treaty procedure and four types of executive agreements) can sometimes be deemed to apply automatically as "statute-like" law in domestic U.S. courts. In U.S. jurisprudence such agreements are (unfortunately) called "self-executing."[19] Some agreements, however, cannot be deemed to be domestic law, and may require further governmental acts to be implemented.

It must be recognized that a treaty norm may well be valid and binding under international law but not be part of a domestic law system. This gives rise to the possibility that the domestic law that prevails in specific cases is inconsistent with the international law treaty norm. In such a case the country concerned may be in violation of its international law obligations, although its domestic law will be "valid" in its own government institutions, including its courts. These issues can be extremely significant in connection with, for example, the WTO and the Uruguay Round results, or the 1979 Tokyo Round results and various side codes resulting from that Round.

In the 1979 act implementing the Tokyo Round, the U.S. Congress specified that the agreements resulting from that Round would not be "self-executing," and it has included similar statutory clauses and legislative history in connection with trade agreements subsequent to that including the Uruguay Round. Thus it can be seen that the legal treatment of these trade agreements may differ from country to country, giving rise to perceptions of unfairness or lack of reciprocity.[20]

A great deal of confusion exists about U.S. law relating to domestic application of international agreements, and this confusion is reflected in the court opinions and in the secondary literature.[21] In U.S. law, if an international agreement has direct statutelike ("self-executing") legal effect, then, in relation to statutes or other such agreements, the latest in time will prevail.

Presidential Powers

Even though the Congress has been reasserting its powers in connection with foreign affairs, the presidential powers are formidable, and still dominant. The president has authority to negotiate international agreements and to carry on international diplomacy. Consequently, as I have indicated, he can enter into some executive agreements on his own constitutional authority, although the number that falls into this category is rather small. More significantly, however, over the years the Congress has delegated to the president a wide variety of powers relating to international affairs. Because the president is the chief "actor" in international affairs, he may sometimes interpret these delegations "expansively," and effectively exercise great power indeed.

The extent of presidential power in international economic matters is not clear.[22] Several significant court cases have addressed the issue of the president's power to enter into international agreements, formal or informal. In the 1953 case of the *United States v. Guy Capps Inc.*, the Fourth Circuit U.S. Court of Appeals held that the president's officials exceeded presidential authority in entering an agreement with Canada concerning the importation of potatoes to the United States.[23] No explicit statutory authority for such an agreement existed, and indeed a relevant statute was deemed to require different procedures for the circumstances involved. The U.S. Supreme Court affirmed the case but did so on other grounds, and historical evidence exists that the Court intended to avoid taking a position on the presidential power issue.[24]

During the late 1960s and early 1970s, U.S. government officials "promoted" an informal understanding by which steel producers in Japan and Europe sent "unilateral" letters to the United States government containing assurances that steel shipments to the U.S. market would not exceed certain quantities. In *Consumers Union v. Kissinger*, 1974, this voluntary restraint arrangement was challenged as a violation of U.S. antitrust laws and as exceeding the president's power.[25] The antitrust portion of the lawsuit was dismissed because of lack of investigative resources by the complainant. On the *ultra vires* issue, however, the Court of Appeals for the District of Columbia circuit ruled two-to-one in favor of the president, largely on ground that the arrangement did not involve any *formal* agreement on behalf of the United States. The dissenter vehemently argued that the informality of the arrangement should not prevent the court intervention, given that the *effects* on trade were just as real as if the agreement had been formal. The Supreme Court refused to take the case; and in the 1974 trade act, the Congress enacted a provision immunizing the participants in these *past* steel arrangements from antitrust liability, in part on grounds that key congressional leaders had been consulted before the arrangement had been encouraged—and had condoned it.[26] We shall return to some of these issues in chapter 7, where I discuss voluntary restraint arrangements in general.

The Congress and International Economic Relations

It is interesting to speculate whether the Congress or the president has been more protectionist or trade restrictive. This question is not easily answered, although many would quickly answer that the Congress is the more protectionist. It is true that congressmen, senators, and a plethora of committees often seem bent on adopting a certain proposal to please specific constituent groups by restricting imports. Yet since 1945 the Congress has never adopted a *general* trade statute designed as primarily protectionist trade legislation. It is true that the Congress has sometimes adopted "riders" or other "tack-on" measures in bills principally designed for other purposes, which have restricted imports of specific product groups (such as English-language books or steel for mass transit systems). But despite threats and occasional near misses, the Congress since 1945 has usually pulled back from the brink of any overtly protectionist statute.[27] The lessons of the 1930 Smoot-Hawley Tariff still seem to have some force.[28] The 1988 Tariff Trade and Trade Act is considered by some to be rather protectionist, but close examination leads others to ambivalence on that issue.[29]

The president, on the other hand, has implemented several programs with broad and extensive import-restricting results, including programs on textiles,[30] steel,[31] and autos.[32] In terms of trade coverage or impact, the president "wins" this contest hands down. The president's action, however, is often motivated by the threat of imminent congressional action—which would be worse—if he does not act first.

The fact is that the role of the Congress in trade policy is extremely important, and to some, very troublesome. The authority of the U.S. executive branch in this subject derives principally from enactments of the Congress. A number of these are enactments that the executive branch has sought from Congress. When the Congress grants authority in this area, however, it usually extracts some "price," requiring certain procedural or judicial restraints on executive action, or mandating certain trade-policy activity that may have import-restricting consequences. (We will explore these enactments in the next section.)

Several general topics relating to the exercise of congressional authority need examination. One of these is the question of constitutional constraints on congressional delegation of authority to the president. In past decades this has been a seriously debated question, but no jurists or scholars seem to deny that *some* constitutional limitation exists on the extent to which the Congress could delegate authority to the president.

The Congress, for example, could not delegate "all legislative authority" to the president, because the Constitution sets forth a division of powers inconsistent with such sweeping delegation. No Supreme Court case since 1935, however, has held an explicit congressional delegation to be unconstitutional,[33] and the rule articulated by the Supreme Court is that as long as a delegation contains an "intelligible principle" on which the executive branch or other official shall act, the delegation will be upheld.[34] Even a 1971 delegation to the president authorizing him "to issue such orders and regulations as he may deem appropriate to stabilize prices, rents, wages, and salaries at levels not less than those prevailing on May 25, 1970..." was upheld,[35] and trade statutes commonly contain some very broadly stated principles.[36]

The Congress, however, does not often wish to delegate much authority to the president, and this is particularly noticeable in connection with authority regarding international economic matters. Although the Congress has delegated the president authority to act in certain emergencies, in matters relating to trade (particularly export controls and the negotiation of agreements on tariffs), the Congress has kept the executive on a relatively "short leash," with statutory delegations that expire and require renewal every few years. Even then, executive authority is usually hedged with many conditions and requirements, as we shall see.[37]

The Courts and International Economic Relations

Federal courts in the United States, in exercising their constitutional role of mediating the division of powers within the U.S. government, have played a relatively cautious role. With respect to foreign affairs, they seem to have given a great deal of deference to the president.[38] This deference has carried over into international economic affairs, with the Supreme Court making statements like the following in 1948.[39]

> The President, both as Commander-in-Chief and as the Nation's organ for foreign affairs, has available intelligence services whose reports neither are nor ought to be published.... The very nature of executive decisions as to foreign policy is political, not judicial. They are delicate, complex and involve large elements of prophecy.... They are decisions of a kind for which the Judiciary has neither aptitude, facilities nor responsibility and have long been held to belong in the domain of political power not subject to judicial intrusion or inquiry....[40]

The Court has also noted that the Congress, "in giving the Executive authority over matters of foreign affairs—must of necessity paint with a brush broader than it customarily wields in domestic areas."[41]

Whether it is wise for the courts to be so deferential might well be questioned in a world of growing international interdependence.[42] Such interdependence causes greater portions of government activity to be "international," and thus potentially removed from close court scrutiny. In any event, in some international economic matters, courts are not so deferential. The Congress, perhaps in part because it feels incapable of restraining the executive itself, has in a few areas delegated considerable powers of judicial review over executive branch administrative decisions. This has been particularly the case with respect to antidumping[43] and countervailing duty[44] cases, where the Court of International Trade has intruded deeply into the decisions of the U.S. Department of Commerce and the International Trade Commission (ITC).

Federal-State Relations in the United States

The United States is a federal system, and the Constitution reserves certain powers to the states. With regard to international economic matters, however, no significant constitutional limitation seems to exist on the powers of the federal government because of state powers. Thus, any valid international agreement that has direct application, or any valid federal statute or regulation regarding foreign economic affairs, will likely prevail over inconsistent state law. One well-known Supreme Court case held that a valid international agreement may even extend federal powers of regulation beyond that which would be permissible in the absence of such an agreement.[45] Several cases have addressed the matter of conflict between state law and GATT, and all such cases have recognized that the federal law—or directly applicable international agreements—regulating international commerce will prevail over state law.[46] Of course, political and comity concerns may prevent the federal government from exercising the full measure of its legal authority.[47]

Perhaps the most interesting issue in this context concerns the international Government Procurement Code negotiated in the context of GATT.[48] This code imposes international obligations on procedures by which signatory governments handle certain parts of their government purchases, requiring them to treat imports equally to domestic goods. During the negotiation the question arose whether such obligations should be applied to government subdivisions, including states in a federal system. The U.S. negotiators apparently took the position that the United States could validly enter into a commitment on the subject that would obligate state government purchases to follow the code. Negotiators from other nations, however, found more difficulty in such a provision and, in the end, the code excluded political subdivisions from its ambit.[49] The Uruguay Round updated the government procurement code, so that now there is some application to subordinate government bodies, depending on each member's schedule.

Such authority in the central government in a federal state is not common to certain other countries, however. In Canada the provinces have considerably more power over international trade,[50] and in the European Community the relationship between the EC's powers and those of the member states is an evolving question and a controversial subject.[51]

3.3 United States Law and International Trade

Introduction

Even though the president has broad and ill-defined powers in foreign affairs, in economic affairs (for reasons already discussed[52]) his inherent or direct constitutional powers are considerably constrained. The Congress normally must delegate to the president for him to be able to act. In fact, the Congress has delegated many powers to him, and "creative interpretation" on the part of the president and his lawyers has undoubtedly extended the limits of those delegations beyond what the Congress intended.

The frustration of the Congress in this respect is contained in a statement made in 1985.

> Before I get into the national security section of the new law, I want to talk about the foreign policy section for just a moment. I have with me a copy of the committee report for the supplemental appropriations bill that we took up recently. The first page of the report says that the American agricultural community is near bankruptcy because of past foreign policy controls. It went through and listed at least four different executive branch actions that called for either trade embargoes or termination of contracts on agricultural exports. It then listed recent statements by the Administration that it will never again consider embargoes on agricultural products, in full recognition that they do not work and that they harm American farmers. At the same time that this page in the committee report was being printed, the President was imposing a new trade embargo on Nicaragua. Where was the authority? The EAA has expired.
>
> The President found the authority in the International Emergency Economic Powers Act (IEEPA). So when the State Department appeared before the committee I asked, "If the EAA [Export Administration Act] had been alive and well, and if we had no contract sanctity provision, which would you have chosen, IEEPA or the EAA to impose that embargo? The official response was IEEPA. All

of the work that we have put into contract sanctity to protect American businessmen with long-term commitments in the work community goes out the window because the President at any time, through a mere whim, can invoke IEEPA.[53]

The U.S. statute books are full of a variety of delegations of authority to the president to deal with various aspects of international economic relations.[54] Furthermore, the approval of treaties has extended additional powers to the executive. The focus here will be on the trade agreements acts that concern the WTO, its various annexes including GATT, and related matters of international trade regulation.

Smoot-Hawley and Progeny

The infamous Smoot-Hawley Tariff Act of 1930 led the Roosevelt administration (elected in 1932) to consider ways to reduce the damage done to the world economy by high tariffs. Under the leadership of the Secretary of State Cordell Hull, the executive proposed and the Congress adopted a statute, the Reciprocal Trade Agreements Act of 1934, that was designed to allow the president's officials to negotiate with foreign nations for the mutual reduction of tariffs. During the debate on this act in Congress, one senator noted: "[O]ur experience in writing tariff legislation ... has been discouraging. Trading between groups and sections is inevitable. Logrolling is inevitable, and in its most pernicious form. We do not write a national tariff law. We jam together, through various unholy alliances and combinations, a potpourri or hodgepodge of section and local tariff rates, which often add to our troubles and increase world misery."[55]

The 1934 act was limited in duration, but until the mid-1960s, renewals came regularly—in 1937, 1940, 1943, 1945, 1948, 1951, 1953, 1954, 1955, 1958, and 1962.[56] In recent years these acts have concerned much besides tariff matters, and large portions of these acts have been permanently added to the statute books. The tariff negotiating authority, however, has always been limited in duration. The authority granted for the Tokyo Round expired in January 1980 (although section 1102 of the 1988 Omnibus Trade and Competitiveness Act renewed that authority, for a new round, until 1 June 1993).[57]

The basic negotiating authority of the series of trade acts has provided a two-part power to the president. First, it authorizes him to negotiate and accept an international agreement on the reduction of tariffs, specifying certain goals and certain defined limits on his authority to enter into agreement. The agreement itself is the "executive agreement pursuant to congressional authority granted in advance" that I described in the preceding section. Second, these statutes authorize the president to "proclaim" such agreements on tariffs, so that they become part of the domestic law that customs officials and others would apply to actual transactions and other events. A senate report stated in 1943: "Under the Trade Agreements Act changes in our tariff rates are made, so far as our domestic law is concerned, by the President's proclamation under the authority of the Trade Agreement Act. Changes in the Tariff rates are not made by the agreements, per se...."[58]

The 1962 renewal of trade agreements authority saw a shift in emphasis from fairly simple renewal, or date-extension legislation, to more elaborate legislation intended to deal with a number of different issues of international economics. The 1962 Trade Expansion Act set up the framework for U.S. participation in the sixth GATT trade negotiating round, the Kennedy Round, and explicitly mentioned the goal of reducing nontariff measures on the flow of trade.

From 1967 to 1975 there was a hiatus (the longest since 1934) in the trade agreements authority. This was finally corrected in the 1974 Trade act (effective in 1975), which was the framework for U.S. participation in the seventh trade round, the Tokyo Round. The 1974 act renewed the advance authority for the president to enter into tariff agreements until 5 January 1980. It also made some permanent changes to the escape clause and certain other legislative provisions. Most significantly, however, it added to the books some major titles of law concerning nontariff measures, provision for industry group liaison to the negotiators, treatment of communist or nonmarket economies, and provisions for preferential treatment for developing countries.[59]

The next major U.S. trade act was the Trade Agreements Act of 1979, which approved the agreements that resulted from the Tokyo Round Agreement under the so-called fast track procedure. In 1984 the Congress passed the Trade and Tariffs Act,[60] which made some significant changes in U.S. trade law, but did not purport either to generally overhaul that law or to establish new negotiating authority. In fact, since World War II, this statute was the first major trade act concerning imports that was not the result of a comprehensive proposal from the executive branch. Although the executive branch in 1984 wanted basically two things—renewal of the preference title concerning developing countries, and authority to negotiate a bilateral free trade area with Israel—the Congress had a number of other matters on its mind, and various pieces of draft legislation from various committees were rather suddenly pasted together near the end of the 1984 congressional session, to form the 1984 act.

Since 1984 there have been hundreds of proposals in Congress for further trade legislation, and several comprehensive or broad scope bills. When a new eighth round of negotiations was launched in September 1986, it was acknowledged that some U.S. legislation would be needed to assist U.S. participation in that round. The Congress, however, threatened to require an expensive quid pro quo for such legislation, making various proposals concerning a variety of trade policy issues, many of which proposals would have a trade limiting effect.

In mid-1988, the Omnibus Trade and Competitiveness Act[61] became law (after much maneuvering between the president and the Congress, an earlier version of the act being vetoed). This act, similar to that of 1984, was primarily a result of congressional initiative, again reflecting a considerable shift from the traditional pattern of major trade acts since 1934.

The final step in this brief overview of history was the enactment in late 1994 of the Uruguay Round Agreement Act, which authorized the president to ratify the Uruguay Round Agreement. The statute also modified a number of provisions of U.S. law, in some cases to implement the Uruguay Round Agreement, in other cases to establish certain kinds of procedures which the Congress demanded with respect to how the agreements would be administered. The processes of getting this act through the Congress, were extraordinarily complicated and politically varied. As is quite often the case, a number of special "deals" were made between the president and individual or small groups of congressmen. But in the end the statute passed with handsome majorities of two hundred eighty-eight to one hundred forty-six in the House, and seventy-six to twenty-four in the Senate.[62]

Congressional Attempts to Keep the Executive in Check: Legislative Veto Procedures and the "Fast Track"

Imagine you are a congressman, and the president comes to you and says he needs authority to negotiate with foreign nations for the reduction of nontariff measures (NTMs) which are restricting trade. The tariff problem, although not extinguished, has been largely resolved by multiple rounds of GATT negotiation, but now NTMs are proving damaging to the principles of comparative advantage and to world welfare. The president would like advance authority for NTM negotiations along the pattern of the traditional tariff authority. The problem is that nontariff measures reach deeply into the interstices of domestic policy and regulation. The Congress has fought lengthy battles on many of such issues, including environmental standards, product liability, and purity requirements for medicines. The Congress does not relish the prospect of a president changing all its work through the implementation of international agreements. So you advise the president to negotiate all he wants, but to bring back for congressional approval any agreements he completes.

The president's answer is that such a procedure is not acceptable to foreign governments, who see it as a way for U.S. negotiators to get "two bites of the apple." The negotiators and their political superiors spend "political chips" by the compromises necessary to obtain an international agreement. These will cost governments some loss of votes in the next elections, but will be worth it if they can demonstrate some advantage will ensue from the agreement. But when the delicately balanced draft agreement is submitted to Congress (or to other parliaments), then it can all come unraveled, as those bodies find clauses objectionable or feel their negotiators should have obtained more. Major portions of the results of the Kennedy Round were never approved by the U.S. Congress, and foreign officials remember this. They also remember the history of congressional refusal to approve the ITO and the OTC.[63]

What should one do? Some sort of middle way must be sought. This was the thinking of the drafters in the early 1970s as they prepared the bill that finally became the 1974 Trade Act. One idea was to turn to a procedure that had a long but controversial history in the United States—the legislative veto. This procedure basically called for the president to establish an order, regulation, or international draft agreement; submit that to the Congress; and if the Congress did not—within a specified time by a specified majority—disapprove the measures, it came into effect and became valid law. But, although many foreign governments, and a number of state governments in the United States, have used the legislative veto, the constitutional doctrine of "separation of powers" has been used to argue against it.

Early drafts of the 1974 legislation provided a fairly elaborate legislative veto provision as a way to resolve the apparent dilemma of the need for U.S. NTM negotiating credibility—that is, a procedure that improved the chance that U.S. officials could "deliver" on a commitment to accept an international agreement, while not giving the president a "blank check." Under this draft procedure, the president, before final completion of a draft international agreement,[64] would consult with the Congress, and be partly guided by their views of the draft agreement in progress. Then, when the draft agreement was completed, he would prepare proposed legislation to approve and implement it which, if the legislation was not disapproved by the Congress, would become law.

The House of Representatives accepted this procedure, but when it went to the Senate, the political atmosphere was different. The Watergate scandal had recently been uncovered, and the Senate Finance Committee was reluctant to approve delegations of authority to a President under such a cloud. (In fact, the bill did not make much progress until after President Nixon resigned and President Ford took office.) Even though there were other legislative veto procedures which were not challenged, the one relating to nontariff measures was too significant. Consequently the Senate committee drafted an alternative that became law, and this has been termed the "fast-track" procedure.

The fast-track procedure for approval of the results of international negotiations on nontariff measures was an attempt to retain the essential features of the legislative veto. In addition to the consultation requirement, the fast-track provided three essential rules: (1) a bill, when introduced, would not be amendable; (2) committees to which the bill was referred would be required to report out the bill within a short period of time;[65] and (3) debate over the bill in both Houses was limited. These rules were not statutory, however. They were included in the rules of each House of Congress, and were subject to change through parliamentary procedure that excluded the president. Thus, the procedures were not quite so stable as a statutory "legislative veto" would have been.

It should be noted that this procedure is constitutionally the same as that of adopting a statute. Further, if a statute is adopted, the statute itself cures most conceivable departures from the fast-track procedure. For example, if the proposed bill were to go beyond the scope of subject matter contemplated in the fast-track procedure, but the Congress were to adopt it anyway (and the president were to sign it), then the statute would be valid because the Constitution would be fulfilled, and the deviance would be "cured."

The fast-track procedure worked very well during the 1979 enactment of approval and implementation of the Tokyo Round results. Surprisingly, the relevant congressional committees developed a procedure for the consultation period, under which those committees played a role very similar to their role in normal legislation, with "non-mark up", and a "nonconference" to reconcile differences between the House and the Senate. These committees and the lawyers for the Congress actually developed the draft legislation, which they wanted the president to introduce for the fast-track procedure. The president's bill was almost identical to the bill developed by the Congress[66]; and, partly for this reason the bill was adopted by an astounding three hundred ninety-five to seven in the House, and ninety to four in the Senate. During the consultation period several concerns of congressional interests had resulted in negotiated changes in the draft agreements, proving the efficacy of the procedure.[67]

Subsequently, in 1983 the U.S. Supreme Court, in the case *INS v. Chadha*,[68] held that a legislative veto procedure was not permissible under the U.S. Constitution.[69] Fortunately, the trade act fast-track procedure was not threatened. Certain other trade act "vetoes," however, were subsequently changed because of this case.[70] The fast-track procedure has in fact been suggested as a plausible alternative to legislative vetoes in other types of statutes.

The trade act fast-track procedure, like the tariff authority, however, has a duration limit. Satisfaction with the procedure led the Congress in the 1979 act to extend the original time of expiry from 5 January 1980 to 5 January 1988. This procedure was considered so important that in 1986, at the beginning of negotiations between Canada and the U.S. for a free trade area, Canada insisted on the fast-track application for the negotiation results.[71] Subsequently, other nations have expressed similar views.

The 1988 Omnibus Trade and Competitiveness Act renewed the fast-track procedure for possible use in the Uruguay Round, and also in the NAFTA negotiations. It was clear that this procedure was deemed essential by foreign negotiating partners in both of those negotiations. Indeed, the deadline for the Uruguay Round fast-track motivated the negotiation deadline throughout the Uruguay Round. When the 1990 ministerial meeting scheduled to finish the Uruguay Round failed, a special procedure for extending the deadline of the fast-track was necessary (and accomplished during 1991). This fast-track then was scheduled to expire in 1993, but the newly elected Clinton administration was not prepared to move so quickly, and thus the fast-track was extended again, its final deadline requiring an agreement be signed by 15 April 1994, and indeed that was the date of signature (at Marrakesh). There is much debate about whether the fast-track should or will be used again, but it appears quite clear that it will be an essential ingredient of future trade negotiations.

GATT and the WTO in Domestic United States Law

A critical and intriguing question concerning the GATT, and, more recently, some of the codes related to GATT and the Uruguay Round Agreement, is whether these agreements have a "direct application" in the domestic law of signatory countries. As I previously noted, the answer to this question varies from country to country. The issue, for example, has been addressed in Luxembourg by the Court of Justice of the EC.[72] Here I will examine the issue insofar as it pertains to the United States.

First, about GATT. The GATT language itself was intended by negotiators to be precise enough for direct application by courts, and its phraseology is such that a U.S. court would likely find most of the GATT clauses to be "self-executing."[73] It must be remembered, however, that the GATT as such was not in effect under international law. It is the Protocol of Provisional Application that brought GATT into effect, and this protocol had language suggesting a requirement of an added governmental action to implement the GATT. Thus, this language could have been treated by a U.S. court as *not* self-executing. But (another "but"!) the President negotiated the GATT under the authority of the Trade Agreements Act renewal of 1945, which contained the typical two-part authority:—to accept an agreement and to proclaim it. In fact, the president proclaimed all of the general language of GATT except Part IV (added in the 1960s to address problems of developing countries).[74] Thus the key parts of GATT were all domestic U.S. law because they had been proclaimed, and not because they were self-executing. Courts in the United States that have had to decide the issue of GATT direct applicability have all held that GATT was part of U.S. domestic law, but usually without realizing or discussing the intermediate steps in the logic required for such finding.

For the Tokyo Round Codes, the Congress and the executive anticipated this question of direct application, and provided explicitly in the approval of the Trade Agreements Act of 1979 that the agreements approved would *not* be self-executing. This provision is not crystal clear from the language of the statute,[75] but the legislative history shows the clear intent of both the Executive (which proposed the bill), and the Congress (which adopted it), that the agreements the statutes approves are not to be self-executing. It is virtually certain that the U.S. court would therefore follow this intent.[76] Thus, the source of domestic U.S. law was the implementing statute (Trade Agreement Act of 1979) and not the agreements themselves. The agreements, however, are most certainly part of the legislative history of the statute, given that the congressional committee reports state, "This bill is drafted with the intent to permit U.S. practice to be consistent with the obligations of the agreements, as the United States understands those obligations."[77] In addition the well accepted rule in U.S. jurisprudence that courts, when confronted with several possible choices for interpreting a statute, should prefer that choice which is consistent with U.S. international obligations, must be remembered.[78] Unfortunately, some U.S. courts in the 1980s and 1990s seem to have forgotten this. Also this rule of jurisprudence is probably not required by the constitution and therefore the Congress could alter it and may have done so implicitly with certain phraseology in later statutes.

While addressing these questions of statutory interpretation, another wrinkle caused by the fast-track procedure should be noted. The legislative history for the 1979 implementing statute is different from most bills, because a bill is theoretically drafted by the president and amendments in Congress are prohibited. Thus, it can be argued that the statement of the executive branch is of primary importance.[79] However, the actual history of the process, as described, suggests a somewhat different argument. Although the congressional committee reports were issued at a time in the procedure when no amendments or changes were possible, the reports explain:

> The Committee emphasized that virtually all of the provisions of H.R. 4357 [which became the TAA of 1979] reflect the decisions of the House and Senate committees, as coordinated in the joint meetings noted above. The implementing bill was drafted in the offices of the House and Senate Legislative Counsel with the participation of staff members of the committees of jurisdiction in both Houses and representatives from the Administration. The bill reflects the understandings achieved on all issues, as explained in this report.[80]

These considerations also apply to later trade treaties negotiated and implemented during the 1980s and 1990s, including several free trade agreements and the NAFTA, and of course the Uruguay Round. In each of these cases, the U.S. implementing statute has language that would prevent a direct or "self-executing" effect of the agreements themselves in U.S. domestic jurisprudence. The statutes implementing the agreements alter domestic law, and that of course, is binding. The language of "non-direct application," particularly in the Uruguay Round implementing statute, however, is not (to say the least) crystal clear. On balance it appears to negate "self-executing", but there are certain complicated wrinkles involved for certain types of cases, for example, the relationship of the international agreements to state (subfederal) legislation.

Part of the fast-track procedure requires a statement of the president to accompany his proposed legislation when it is finally introduced in the Congress. This statement of administrative action (SAA) has a very important position for the interpretation of the statute (and indeed for the agreements). The 1994 statute explicitly states (following similar language in some of the previous trade agreement approval statutes), that "the Congress approves ... the statement of administrative action proposed to implement the agreements ..." Thus the SAA has a status perhaps even higher than that of the normal legislative history found in committee reports and debates of Congress. It is clear that this SAA was carefully negotiated between the Executive Branch, and the relevant committees of Congress.[81]

Structure of the U.S. Government for Trade Policy

Dozens of U.S. government agencies have at least some jurisdiction over various aspects of trade policy. For example, the Agriculture Department has considerable authority on matters relating to agricultural commodity trade. The Defense Department has great power in the procedures relating to export controls. The Labor Department is concerned with workers who have become unemployed because of imports. The Commerce Department has the line authority on antidumping and countervailing duty measures, while the Departments of State and the Treasury also have important roles not only in international economic affairs generally, but with respect to trade particularly.[82]

A key agency is a small one attached to the Executive Office of the President, namely the Office of the U.S. Trade Representative. The position of trade representative (originally created in the 1962 Trade Expansion Act, partly as a compromise between competing jurisdictional claims of the Departments of State and Commerce) was first called "special trade representative," or "STR." During several decades the office serving this official has become increasingly important to U.S. trade policy; and in the 1974 act the Congress upgraded the USTR position to cabinet status, one of few such positions not heading a department. The position also carries the rank of ambassador. The office of the USTR normally chairs many of the interagency committees which formulate trade policy and negotiating positions for the U.S. government, including the Trade Staff Committee (TSC) and the cabinet-level Trade Policy Committee (TPC).[83]

In addition to the many Executive Branch agencies which participate in trade policy and trade regulation, and to the interagency trade-policy committees, there is an important quasi-independent agency: the International Trade Commission (ITC). This agency of six commissioners appointed for nine-year terms, with a staff of approximately 400, is often considered closely allied to Congress. It has the task of making various factual determinations, usually on the question of whether imports are "injuring" domestic U.S. industry (as in cases of the escape clause, antidumping duties, and countervailing duties). It plays the central role in Section 337, unfair trade complaints against imports.[84]

3.4 The Variety of National Constitutions and Their Impact on the International Trading System

National Constitutions and International Economic Relations

We have already remarked how the international trading system is a complex interaction of international and national legal norms, political institutions, and economic systems. The legal and constitutional requirements on treaty-making of national governments can profoundly influence the international negotiating processes, and can sometimes impose crippling constraints on the nature of possible agreements. When international agreements are completed by the negotiators, the difficult processes of completing the ratification by national governments begins. These processes vary enormously from nation to nation. When they are completed, different legal and constitutional systems may cause the implementation of the agreements to be uneven.[85] In some systems the executive branch may be operating under laws which are "mandatory" and allow it little discretion. In others, open-ended legal authority may allow government officials considerable leeway, which can sometimes be valuable in fashioning an international settlement on some controverted point. In certain systems, private firms and citizens may have the power to invoke procedures that raise international trade issues requiring the attention by foreign nation against their will.[86] On top of all this lurk the major problems that occur when the economic systems of the various nations also differ.[87]

I have examined the U.S. national legal system at some length. A scientific approach to understanding the trading system would require a similar examination for many other countries. With over 120 members now in the WTO, however, there is no practical way to analyze the national constitutional, legal, and governmental structures of even a significant fraction of that number of countries in relation to international trade. Fortunately, for some of the key countries, other works on this subject exist.[88] However, some brief descriptions of two other major players, the EC and Japan, are useful, partly because these along with the U.S. so dominate world trade.

Of course the focus below will be on information that is relevant to international trade negotiations and implementation of those negotiations, as well as the rules applying process of the world trading system.[89]

The European Community

In recent years, the largest number of disputes under GATT rules, and generally the most acrimonious, have been those between the United States and the European Community (EC) and its Member States. The EC is a very complex institution, viewed by some as a budding "federal state," but by others as still an international organization. This institution, it is safe to say, is in a process of a difficult constitutional evolution which clearly has had an impact on what its representatives at GATT and other international fora have been able or willing to say or do. The internal difficulties of the EC have probably led to the cautious approach of the EC diplomats when dealing with other countries or international organizations and norms. There undoubtedly has been an internal political need to keep the pressures of the outside world from constraining the potential options for compromise needed internally in order to keep the whole institution from falling apart. Thus, prior to the Uruguay Round the EC has stiffly resisted an international negotiating agenda which would include attention to agricultural policies, since the EC has viewed the Common Agricultural Policy (CAP) as so centrally important to the continued viability of the EC itself.[90]

Here I can only sketch the outlines of the EC constitution as it relates to the world trading system. The starting point is to realize that essentially six entities or groups of entities play the key constitutional roles in the EC: the "commission," the "council," the "European council," the "court" (European Court of Justice and Court of First Instance), the "European parliament," and finally, the "member states" whose heads of state exercise overall political control. Each of these entities plays a distinct role, which is constantly evolving in a sort of dance of power contests and struggles, not unlike that which the United States experiences with its separation-of-powers problems between the executive and Congress.

One of the very interesting features of the EC, at least to members of the legal profession, is the degree to which the EC as a whole is heavily influenced by legal structures and concepts. Even though many of the largest member states of the EC have constitutional structures that do not permit judicial review of parliamentary action, the EC effectively has a judicial review system in which its court plays a central role. Likewise, although an unwritten constitution is a feature of one of the largest member states, the EC to which it belongs has an elaborate written constitution (the 1957 Treaty of Rome and later related treaties[91]) which is subject to definitive interpretation by the court. It appears that for a number of issues the types and styles of government that member states have become used to are not deemed appropriate in the larger continental arena. Nations which have what has been termed "one city governments", in which one city has a virtual monopoly on governmental and business decision making, as well as intellectual and cultural activity, find that their own national methods of operating (involving quiet genteel meetings at pubs and cocktail parties) no longer are feasible to the same extent when the affairs of a whole continent, involving many different languages, are at stake.

The institutional structure of the EC described below was subject to alteration as a result of two major amendments of the EC Treaty: the Single European Act (1986) and the Maastricht Treaty (1992).

The Single European Act[92] introduced the concept of an "Internal Market" by the end of 1992 based on more effective Community decision making procedures (encouraging the use of simple or qualified majority voting in the council. It also enhanced the role of the European Parliament in the decision making process,[93] it formalized the "European council" (discussed below) and it added a Court of First Instance to the European Court of Justice in Luxembourg. Finally, it introduced an embryonic community foreign policy.[94]

The Maastricht Treaty,[95] which came into effect in November 1993, introduced the "European Union" structure, based on three pillars: (1) the European Community; (2) the Common Foreign and Security Policy; and (3) Cooperation in the Field of Justice and home Affairs. While the first and most important pillar was based on the Community acquis, the second and third pillar were mostly based on inter-governmental cooperation, with no role for the European Court of Justice. The Maastricht Treaty contained detailed provisions for the establishment of an EMU (European Monetary Union) and again enhanced the role of the European Parliament.[96]

The commission is the EC's counterpart to the executives of member states. In the current EC, the commission consists of 20 commissioners, each given a certain "portfolio" of activities and generally heading a "Directorate General." The commissioners are appointed for terms of five years by the joint action of the member states with the approval of the European Parliament. The directorate generals each have a "director-general" who is more likely to be a career civil servant of the EC. This person presides over the staff. The commission totals about 16,000 employees, and has the task and competence to implement the laws and policies of the EC, and to propose law changes.[97]

The council is composed of Ministers of each of the member state, who sit as representatives, and not as civil servants or executives. The composition of the council changes with the subject discussed. For example, issues relating to agriculture would be taken up by agricultural Ministers in the so-called "Agricultural Council". Matters relating to foreign affairs by foreign affairs Ministers in the "General Counsil", and so on. The council reviews and controls the actions of the commission, except to the extent that the foundation treaties delegate direct responsibility to the commission, or to the extent that the council itself has so delegated. The "legislative" process most often consists of an interaction between the commission and the council, whereby the commission proposes, and the council must approve of a proposal before it becomes law. The European parliament is generally only consulted, although its powers were increased by the Single European Act and the Maastricht Treaty. The treaties allow the approval in some cases to be by a "qualified majority" which is less than unanimous.

Through this "legislative" process, inter alia, "regulations" and "directives" are adopted. The former are "directly applicable" in the domestic law of the members, while the latter tend to be addressed to member states, requiring some further government action at the national level in order for them to be utilized directly in cases before national courts, and so on.[98].

The "European Council" brings together the Heads of State or of Government of the member states and the President of the commission. They are assisted by the Ministers of Foreign Affairs and by a member of the commission. The European council meets at least twice a year, normally in June and December.

With direct elections, and some other modest tinkering with its authority, the Parliament has begun to play a more substantial role in EC government decision making. The Single European Act and the Maastricht Treaty gave the parliament an enhanced role with respect to EC decisions, including a modest new role in approving certain types of external relations treaties. The Maastricht Treaty further increased the role of the European parliament. It now has the right to bring actions before the European Court of Justice for the purpose of protecting its prerogatives, it may set up a temporary committee of inquiry to investigate alleged contraventions or maladministration in the implementation of Community Law, it can receive certain petitions from European citizens and it has been given the right to appoint an Ombudsamn.

The European Court of Justice (ECJ) is a central and significant part of the EC institutional structure, and has evolved into a rather strong constitutional court for the EC. Its influence is felt daily in the other EC institutions, and officials often find their discourse centered on questions about how the Court might react to this or that proposal. The ECJ has fifteen judges, and following a continental European pattern, eight advocates general who prepare cases for the court and give their opinion as to how the court should decide each case.[99] As we see below, the court decided a very important opinion in 1994 relating to the constitutional procedures for the European Union to approve the Uruguay Round results.

In 1987, the Court of First Instance was created, which initially had only jurisdiction over antitrust cases and labor disputes involving employees of the EC. As of 1994, it was also given initial jurisdiction of claims by individuals challenging EC acts.

Finally, of course, there are the member state governments, jealously trying to preserve their national sovereign power, and with some success. Currently they discuss in the IGC (Inter Governmental Conference) which further changes should be made to the European Treaty, following the amendments introduced at Maastricht. it remains to be seen how much sovereignty the governments are willing to transfer to the Community this time.

A key question for the international trading system is the treaty-making authority of the EC, and the method by which the EC can participate in such organizations as GATT. The Treaty of Rome provides that in matters relating to the conduct of "commercial policy," the EC is to have exclusive competence.[100] The negotiation of commercial agreements with third countries was to be undertaken by the commission alone, and was to be concluded by the council on behalf of the Community by a qualified majority. This exclusive power of negotiation has been jealously guarded by the commission and has often been challenged by the council acting on behalf of the member states interests.[101] Relationships with international organizations such as GATT are dealt with in specific articles.[102] Another significant question is the domestic law effect of international agreements accepted by the EC institutions. Can these become a direct part of the jurisprudence of the EC, both at the EC level (e.g., before the court in an EC matter), and at the Member State level (e.g., as directly applicable before member-state domestic courts)? The answer appears to depend on a combination of factors, but it is anything but clear how far this principle will be extended to give EC international agreements domestic law effect.[103]

Throughout most of the Uruguay Round negotiation, the EC commission took the general position that EC constitutional law allowed the European institutions to negotiate, approve, ratify and implement all subjects that were being taken up in the Uruguay Round. The issue had also come up in the Tokyo Round, but there the scope of the subject matter was considerably less, whereas in the Uruguay Round, the scope included the important new issues of services and intellectual property. It was argued by some that these new issues in particular, or certain sub parts of them, were beyond the scope of a "common commercial policy" which was delegated to the European Community institutions. The matter was taken to the European Court of Justice in Luxembourg, and its opinion stated that some parts of the Uruguay Round would necessitate the participation and approval of member states, not just the European institutions. This was a very important "constitutional decision" for the European Community. The court suggested the desirability of the EC institutions coming to some sort of an agreement or accommodation on how procedures should be designed to enable the EC to have a consistent and unified foreign policy, including such policy regarding trade.

Japan

The government of Japan differs considerably from that of either the United States or the EC. Japan has essentially a parliamentary form of government, and thus its executive is supervised by a cabinet of a number of ministers, including the prime minister, who are almost always members of the Diet (parliament) belonging to the party that has the parliamentary majority. However, most legislation in the Japanese system is drafted by the relevant ministry, and this is particularly so with respect to international trade matters dominated by MITI.[104] Thus, as compared to other governments I have discussed, there would seem to be less tension between the executive and the parliament in this system, and it would appear that the government would more likely be able to implement international agreements as well as other initiatives, since it would have considerable control over the parliamentary majority. Even in such a country however, there are institutional power rivalries and tensions. The ruling "party" has a certain apparatus for its own decision making, and this must be persuaded of the desirability of measures which require parliamentary approval. A supreme court in Japan presides over the legal conflicts, including constitutional rules. Although Japanese society has been described as less litigious than U.S. society, and operates in a social climate that tends to discourage resort to formal court processes to resolve differences. A few cases relating to international economic measures have gone to the courts in Japan, and there has been speculation that the number might increase.[105]

In the summer of 1993, when the control of the Diet shifted, the processes in the Diet and the Japanese government began to change, which this may affect some of the procedures outlined above. For example, no single party may have control and a coalition may rule, affecting the degree of cooperation with ministries.

4 Rule Implementation and Dispute Resolution

4.1 The Effectiveness of International Law

Introduction

In chapter 1 I discussed briefly some of the general concepts of international law.[1] I noted the tendency of many observers, particularly those not well acquainted with international relations or transactions, to dismiss international law rules as ineffective. I mentioned, however, that many domestic law rules are equally ineffective. Although it may be the case that international law rules are somewhat less effective than domestic law rules for those nations with stable legal systems and a generally effective central government, it is not always the case that domestic laws are implemented efficiently.[2] It is important for the policy advisor, statesman, or practitioner to accurately evaluate the real impact of the international rules, recognizing that some of those rules (often the ones that do not reach the headlines) do have considerable effect and influence on real government and business decisions.[3] For example, despite cynical statements by members of the U.S. Congress that GATT rules were "irrelevant," there are a number of proven instances when congressional committees and their staff members took considerable trouble to tailor legislative proposals to minimize the risk of a complaint to GATT. Not all of these efforts have been successful; but in other cases, Congress has been persuaded to drop a proposal because of its inconsistency with GATT provisions.[4] The U.S. executive branch also has been influenced in its action by GATT legality arguments, although it too has not always deferred to these.

In later chapters I will evaluate rules regarding trade and their effectiveness, and in the final chapter I will come back to this issue to see if any generalizations about the rules are warranted. For example, the ability of nations to unilaterally apply antidumping or countervailing duties often has a powerful influence on potential transactions or even government policy. The constraints on the nation applying these duties stem from the GATT and WTO texts on these subjects, and thus these rules have considerable utility for determining what would be the likely response of an importing country to certain dumping or subsidy-like practices in an exporting country.[5]

In addition to the difficulty of evaluating the effectiveness of existing international rules, there are several important policy issues about rule implementation, which often do not get explicitly addressed. First, should the legal system be improved to make rules more effective? Second, should new rules be added and made effective? It might seem at first that these questions are trivial and that most persons would answer them in the affirmative. Indeed, most governmental and private practitioners would probably privately answer this way. But in actual practice, they would act differently. To put this another way: realistic observations of the operation of the legal system, even as it pertains to international economic affairs, will lead one to perceive that many government and private practitioners are not all in favor of an effective international rules system![6]

Why does real (albeit concealed or implicit) opposition to the effectiveness of international rules exist? Part of the reason can be traced to the older concepts of national sovereignty. As an astute European observer put it, one reason for the difficulty of welding a more effective European Union is that national leaders would then lose a number of "photo opportunities"—that is, news coverage of summit meetings, decisions, and conflict on various issues among national leaders, playing to their constituencies with a "tough stance" against other foreign leaders. In short, power is fun, and international rules reduce the power of national leaders and government officials. The chance to go "tooting off in private jets to negotiate with other national leaders at comfortable locations or three-star restaurants" is a key plum of otherwise dull government jobs, a high former government official once indicated.

It would be unfair to implicate this type of motivation as being too much the cause of antagonism to international rules. But the international rules do cause real difficulties for national leaders. In chapter 1 I noted the problems posed for national leaders by growing international economic interdependence. It is harder to deliver on promises to constituents. Several situations lead even the wise national leader to cause his government to breach or consider breaching the international rules. One such situation is when the international "rule" is patently unfair or bad policy. This may be because it is outdated and not in tune with current actual practice and conditions. (I noted in chapter 2 the difficulty of amending GATT rules—one example of activity which created this "out-of-date" problem for some rules.[7]) It may also be because the current international rule-making process is faulty—as when voting procedures allow rules to be created that are unrealistic and that do not recognize real power relationships.[8]

Another situation in which it can be argued that rules *should* be breached is when reform of the rule is badly needed, but the international and national institutional system for some reason makes the reform impossible. It could be argued that the U.S. departure from the IMF's currency par-value system in 1971 was such a case, leading quickly to a major revision in the IMF Charter to allow "floating exchange rates," which had been advocated for decades by many eminent economists.[9]

Nevertheless, every departure from the rules carries some risks. It causes respect for the rule system itself to be weakened. It makes it easier in the next hard case to depart from the rules. If rules are viewed as one tool for ordering or improving human affairs, then weakening a rule system tends to reduce the utility of that tool in all its contexts.

Power-Oriented Diplomacy Contrasted with Rule-Oriented Diplomacy

One way to explore the questions raised above is to compare two techniques of modern diplomacy: a "rule-oriented" technique and a "power-oriented" technique. This perhaps puts the issue in too simple a dichotomy (because in practice the observable international institutions and legal systems involve some mixture of both), but it is nevertheless a useful way to examine the policy issues involved. This dichotomy can be explained as follows:

> In broad perspective one can roughly divide the various techniques for the peaceful settlement of international disputes into two types: settlement by negotiation and agreement with reference (explicitly or implicitly) to relative power status of the parties; or settlement by negotiation or decision with reference to norms or rules to which both parties have previously agreed.
>
> For example, countries A and B have a trade dispute regarding B's treatment of imports from A to B of widgets. The first technique mentioned would involve a negotiation between A and B by which the most powerful of the two would have the advantage. Foreign aid, military maneuvers, or import restrictions on other key goods by way of retaliation would figure in the negotiation. A small country would hesitate to challenge a large one on whom its trade depends. Implicit or explicit threats (e.g., to impose quantitative restrictions on some other product) would be a major part of the technique employed. Domestic political influences

would probably play a greater part in the approach of the respective negotiators in this system, particularly on the negotiator for the more powerful party.

On the other hand, the second technique suggested—reference to agreed rules—would see the negotiators arguing about the application of the rule (e.g., was B obligated under a treaty to allow free entry of A's goods in question?). During the process of negotiating a settlement it would be necessary for the parties to understand that an unsettled dispute would ultimately be resolved by impartial third-party judgments based on the rules so that the negotiators would be negotiating with reference to their respective predictions as to the outcome of those judgments and not with reference to potential retaliation or actions exercising power of one or more of the parties to the dispute.

In both techniques negotiation and settlement of disputes is the dominant mechanism for resolving differences; but the key is the perception of the participants as to what are the "bargaining chips." Insofar as agreed rules for governing the economic relations between the parties exist, a system which predicates negotiation on the implementation of those rules would seem for a number of reasons to be preferred. The mere existence of the rules, however, is not enough. When the issue is the application or interpretation of those rules (rather than the formulation of new rules), it is necessary for the parties to believe that if their negotiations reach an impasse the settlement mechanisms which take over for the parties will be designed to fairly apply or interpret the rules. If no such system exists, then the parties are left basically to rely upon their respective "power positions," tempered (it is hoped) by the good will and good faith of the more powerful party (cognizant of its long-range interests)....

All diplomacy, and indeed all government, involves a mixture of these techniques. To a large degree, the history of civilization may be described as a gradual evolution from a power-oriented approach, in the state of nature, towards a rule-oriented approach. However, never is the extreme in either case reached. In modern Western democracies, as we know them, power continues to play a major role, particularly political power of voter acceptance, but also to a lesser degree economic power such as that of labor unions or large corporations. However, these governments have passed far along the scale toward a rule-oriented approach, and generally have an elaborate legal system involving court procedures and a monopoly of force, through a police and a military, to ensure the rules will be followed. The U.S. government has indeed proceeded far in this direction, as the resignation of a recent president demonstrates. When one looks at the history of England over the last thousand years, I think that the evolutionary hypothesis from power to rule can be supported. And more recently, when one looks at the evolution of the EC, one is struck by the evolution toward a system that is remarkably elaborate in its rule structure, effectuated through a court of justice, albeit without a monopoly of force.

In international affairs, a strong argument can be made that to a certain extent this same evolution must occur, even though currently it has not progressed very far. The initiatives of the World War II and immediate postwar periods toward developing international institutions is part of this evolution, but as is true in most evolutions there have been setbacks, and mistakes have been made. Likewise, when one focuses on international economic policy, we find that the dichotomy between power-oriented diplomacy and rule-oriented diplomacy can be seen. We have tried to develop rules, in the context of the International Monetary Fund and the GATT. The success has been varied.

Nevertheless, a particularly strong argument exists for pursuing gradually and consistently the progress of international economic affairs towards a rule-oriented approach. Apart from the advantages which accrue generally to international affairs through a rule-oriented approach—less reliance on raw power, and the temptation to exercise it or flex one's muscles, which can get out of hand; a fairer break for the smaller countries, or at least a perception of greater fairness; the development of agreed procedures to achieve the necessary compromises—in economic affairs there are additional reasons.

Economic affairs tend (at least in peace time) to affect more citizens directly than may political and military affairs. Particularly as the world becomes more economically interdependent, more and more private citizens find their jobs, their businesses, and their quality of life affected if not controlled by forces from outside their country's boundaries. Thus they are more affected by the economic policy pursued by their own country on their behalf. In addition, the relationships become increasingly complex—to the point of being incomprehensible to even the brilliant human mind. As a result, citizens assert themselves, at least within a democracy, and require their representatives and government officials to respond to their needs and their perceived complaints. The result of this is increasing citizen participation, and more parliamentary or congressional participation in the processes of international economic policy, thus restricting the degree of power and discretion which the executive possesses.

This makes international negotiations and bargaining increasingly difficult. However, if citizens are going to make their demands heard and influential, a "power-oriented" negotiating process (often requiring secrecy, and executive discretion so as to be able to formulate and implement the necessary compromises) becomes more difficult, if not impossible. Consequently, the only appropriate way to turn seems to be toward a rule-oriented system, whereby the various citizens, parliaments, executives and international organizations will all have their inputs, arriving tortuously to a rule—which, however, when established will enable business and other decentralized decision makers to rely upon the stability and predictability of governmental activity in relation to the rule.[10]

Exploring These Concepts

In this chapter I will examine the rule effectiveness and implementation of the international trade system, centering on GATT and the WTO. Any effective system probably needs at least two workable procedures: a procedure of "norm formulation" or new rulemaking, and a procedure for applying and implementing those rules. An implementing/applying procedure requires a dispute-settlement mechanism as part of its tool. Somehow the existing rule must be applied to specific facts in particular cases.

Inevitably disagreement will arise about such application, that is, disagreement on the interpretation of the rule, its scope, appropriate exceptions, and so on. The dispute-settlement mechanism could be based on brute force, of course, but as I have noted above, significant reasons exist to avoid recourse to this type of behavior.

The norm application system is not totally an international procedure. National governments play extremely important roles in the process. In this chapter I will examine several very interesting procedures that have been devised in the United States and the EC to complement the international procedures of the WTO.

As mentioned earlier, the new WTO Charter includes a clause (Article XVI:1) stipulating that the WTO "shall be guided by the decisions, procedures and customary practices followed by" GATT 1947. Thus the history and jurisprudence of the GATT becomes vitally relevant to the new WTO. In this chapter I will explore part of that history with respect to a few fundamental jurisprudential concepts.

4.2 GATT as Prologue to Dispute-Settlement Procedures

One of the interesting and certainly more controversial aspects of the GATT as an institution was its dispute-settlement mechanism. It is probably fair to say that this mechanism was unique. It was also flawed, in part because of the troubled beginnings of GATT.[11] Yet these procedures worked better than might be expected, and some could argue that in fact they worked better than those of the World Court.[12] A number of interesting policy questions are raised by the experience of the procedure, not the least of that is the question of what should be the fundamental objective of the system: to solve the instant dispute (by conciliation, obfuscation, power threats, or otherwise), or to promote certain longer-term goals.

The difference of opinion about the basic purpose or goals of the dispute-settlement process in the GATT system has not often been explicit, and the same individuals sometimes express a preference for opposite poles of this difference without realizing it. Of course, the matter is more one of appropriate balance along a spectrum than it is of choosing one extreme or the other; but nevertheless it is important to understand the difference, and to describe the dichotomy helps to do so. Perhaps the following two statements help illustrate the differences I have mentioned.

> As a part of the increasingly pragmatic policies of the secretariat and the recognition by all contracting parties that legalism does not contribute to trade liberalization, emphasis has shifted from the formal role of the GATT as third-party

arbiter to its informal role as catalyst for the resolution of disputes by the disputing parties themselves.[13]

International economic policy commitments, in the form of agreed rules, have far-reaching domestic effects.... They are the element which secures the ultimate co-ordination and mutual compatibility of the purely domestic economic policies. They form the basis from which the government can arbitrate and secure an equitable and efficient balance between the diverse domestic interest: producers v. consumers, export industries v. import-competing industries.... Only a firm commitment to international rules makes possible the all-important reconciliation, which I have already alluded to, of the necessary balance on the production side and on the financial side of the national economy....[14]

There are at least two important questions here: one historical, one of future policy. The historical question is whether the GATT preparatory work and practice through the decades established a goal of dispute settlement more oriented toward "conciliation and negotiation" or toward "rule integrity." The future policy question is, Which of these *ought* be the goal? These questions relate to the "power- or rule-oriented diplomacy" discussion in section 1 of this chapter.

With regard to the first question, the record is somewhat mixed. Despite the many statements of some writers[15] and diplomats that the GATT is merely a "negotiating forum" primarily designed to "preserve a balance of concessions and obligations,"[16] considerable historical evidence exists to the contrary. At least one draftsman of GATT said at the preparatory meetings that the agreement ... should deal with these subjects in precise detail so that the obligations of member governments would be clear and unambiguous. Most of these subjects readily lend themselves to such treatment. Provisions on such subjects, once agreed upon, would be self-executing and could be applied by the governments concerned without further elaboration or international action."[17]

The original intention was for GATT to be placed in the institutional setting of the ITO, and the draft ITO charter called for a rigorous dispute-settlement procedure that contemplated effective use of arbitration (not always mandatory, however), and even appeal to the World Court in some circumstances.[18] Clair Wilcox, vice-chairman of the U.S. delegation to the Havana Conference, notes that the possibility of suspending trade concessions under this procedure was "... regarded as a method of restoring a balance of benefits and obligations that, for any reason, may have been disturbed. It is nowhere described as a penalty to be imposed on members who may violate their obligations or as a sanction to ensure that these obligations will be observed. But even though it is not so regarded, it will operate in fact as a sanction and a penalty...."[19] He further notes the procedure for obtaining a World Court opinion on the law involved in a dispute and says, "A basis is thus provided for the development of a body of international law to govern trade relationships."[20]

The shift in GATT from a committee or "working party" procedure to a "panel" procedure (see below), with its connotation of impartial third-party findings, can also be used as evidence that the practice evolved in a direction of "rule integrity"[21]; and a number of panel reports during the first several decades of GATT contained reasoning that closely resembled that of an opinion of a court of law, with reference to precedent, and so on. Then, during the 1960s, the GATT dispute-settlement procedure fell into disuse. Some contracting parties feared that invocation of the procedure would be deemed an "unfriendly act," or for other prudent policy reasons abstained from formal procedures to resolve disputes. Countries with less bargaining power, however, seemed to feel differently. Indeed, the developing countries pushed through a proposal in GATT designed to strengthen the dispute-settlement procedures as they applied in disputes with developing countries.[22] In a celebrated exercise, Uruguay brought a series of complaints against industrial countries treatment of Uruguayan exports (with mixed results).[23] It was during this 1962 case that the doctrine of "*prima facie* nullification or impairment," which has had a continuing effect in GATT, developed.

The ITO Charter would have established a rather elaborate dispute-settlement procedure,[24] but the GATT, not intended to be an "organization," had only a few paragraphs devoted to this subject.[25] Although one can argue that a number of "dispute-settlement" procedures are distributed throughout the GATT (raising the issue of what we mean by that phrase),[26] the central and formal procedures were found in Articles XXII and XXIII. The first of these simply established the right to consult with any other contracting party on matters related to the GATT—a right that does not impose a major obligation, but that is nevertheless useful.[27] I would argue such language should be interpreted to rule out the all-too-frequently heard argument against allowing a request to consult on some potential legislative or executive action, namely, that the matter was "premature."

Article XXIII was the centerpiece for dispute settlement in GATT, (and is still relevant to the WTO procedures.) It also provided for consultation as a prerequisite to invoke the multilateral GATT processes. Three features of these processes can be stressed: (1) they were usually invocable on grounds of "nullification or impairment" of benefits expected under the agreement, and did *not* depend on actual breach of legal obligation;

(2) they established the power for the CONTRACTING PARTIES to not only investigate and recommend action but to "give a ruling on the matter"; and (3) they gave the CONTRACTING PARTIES the power in appropriately serious cases to authorize "a contracting party or parties" to suspend GATT obligations to other contracting parties. Each of these features had important interpretations and implications, and although Article XXIII did not say much about them, the procedures followed to implement these principles evolved over four decades of practice into a rather elaborate process.

The key to invoking the GATT dispute-settlement mechanism was almost always "nullification or impairment,"[28] an unfortunately ambiguous phrase. It was neither sufficient nor necessary to find a "breach of obligation" under this language, although later practice has made doing so important. An early case in GATT[29] defined the nullification or impairment (N or I) phrase as including actions by a contracting party that harmed the trade of another, and that "could not reasonably have been anticipated ..." by the other at the time it negotiated for a concession.[29] Thus the concept of "reasonable expectations" was introduced, and it is almost a "contract"-type concept.[30] But even this elaboration is quite ambiguous. Consequently, a practice in GATT later developed to enumerate three situations in which the CPs and their panels might find "*prima facie* nullification or impairment." One of these situations was the breach of an obligation. The other two were the use of domestic subsidies to inhibit imports in certain cases[31] and the use of quantitative restrictions (even when they would have been otherwise legal in GATT).[32] In such cases, the burden of proof of showing that no N or I occurred as the result of the breach, subsidy, or quantitative restriction shifted to the country that breached or used those actions. Lacking a clear showing that no N or I occurred, the GATT practice assumed that the panel was obligated to make a prima facie N or I ruling, usually calling for the offending nation to make its actions conform to the GATT obligation.

At the beginning of GATT's history, disputes were generally taken up by the plenary semiannual meeting of the contracting parties. Later they would be brought to an "intercessional committee" of the CPs, and even later were delegated to a working party set up to examine either all disputes or only particular disputes brought to GATT.[33] Around 1955 a major shift in the procedure occurred, in large part because of the influence of the then director-general, Eric Wyndham-White.[34] It was decided that rather than use a working party composed of nations (so that each nation could designate the person who would represent it, subject to that government's instructions), a dispute would be referred to a panel of experts. The three or five experts would be specifically named and were to act in their own capacities and not as representatives of any government. This development, it can be argued, represented a shift from primarily a "negotiating" atmosphere of multilateral diplomacy to a more "arbitrational" or "judicial" procedure designed to arrive impartially at the truth of the facts and the best interpretation of the law. All subsequent dispute procedures in GATT (and the new WTO) have contemplated the use of a panel in this fashion.[35]

Although the CONTRACTING PARTIES were authorized (by majority vote) to suspend concessions (by way of retorsion, retaliation, or "rebalancing" of benefits—a term which is not and never has been clear), they actually did so in only one case. That instance was the result of a complaint brought by The Netherlands against the United States for the latter's use, contrary to GATT, of import restraints on imported dairy products from The Netherlands.[36] For seven years in a row, The Netherlands was authorized to utilize restraints against importation of U.S. grain,[37] although it never acted on that authorization. This had no effect on U.S. action, however. There have been other moves to seek authorization to suspend obligations.[38] Also, the United States has taken measures without authorization.[39]

During the Tokyo Round negotiation, some initiative was taken to improve the dispute-settlement processes of the GATT. The so-called Group Framework Committee of the negotiation was given this task, among others. However, in part because of the strong objection of the EC to any changes in the existing procedures, this effort did not get very far. The result was a document entitled, "Understanding Regarding Notification, Consultation, Dispute Settlement and Surveillance," which was adopted by the CONTRACTING PARTIES at their thirty-fifth session in Geneva, November 1979.[40] Like the other understandings resulting from the Tokyo Round, the precise legal status of this understanding is not clear. Unlike the Tokyo Round codes and other agreements, it is not a stand-alone treaty. It is also not a waiver under Article XXV of GATT, but is presumably adopted under the general powers of Article XXV to "facilitate the operation and further the objectives" of GATT. This document is nevertheless very interesting and also was very influential, given that along with its annex, it consisted of a detailed description of the dispute-settlement processes of GATT. It thus formed a sort of constitutional framework for these processes in the GATT prior to the WTO.

The most salient features of this restatement of procedures are the explicit provisions for a conciliatory role for the GATT director-general and for panels (with some ambiguity about whether a complainant had the right to a panel), reinforcement of the prima facie nullification or impairment concepts, outline of the work of a panel including oral and written advocacy, language permitting the use of nongovernment persons for panels while stating a preference for government persons, recognition of the practice of a panel report with statement of facts and rationale, and understanding that the report was then submitted to the CONTRACTING PARTIES for final approval.[41]

Subsequent to the 1979 understanding, much dissatisfaction was expressed in GATT about the dispute-settlement procedures. At the 1982 ministerial meeting, a new attempt to improve them was made, again with modest success. The resulting resolution suggests the possibility of departing from the tradition of requiring a consensus to approve a panel report, so that the "losing" party could not block or delay that approval,[42] but subsequent practice did not seem much improved. Later, many GATT members continued to talk of the need for improving procedures, and this subject was included in the Punta del Este declaration establishing the framework for the eighth round of trade negotiations.[43]

Many of the treaty agreements resulting from the Tokyo Round negotiations included special procedures devoted to the settlement of disputes relating to a particular agreement. Some of these followed very closely the traditional GATT procedure, and unfortunately they utilized the language "nullification or impairment." In a few cases, special "expert" groups have been called into the process to handle highly technical problems involving such things as scientific judgments.[44]

Several Cases Examined

Although the compliance record of GATT panel recommendations is very respectable (perhaps higher in percentage terms than that of the World Court),[45] much concern has been voiced in recent years about noncompliance. It is very difficult to assemble data on this question, but our explorations suggest that only about eight to ten cases in the GATT system resulted in adopted panel reports that were not followed.[46] In some cases, the concerns about the GATT processes are partly to blame: a disputing nation could block adoption of a report and then argue that no binding requirement exists for it to follow the report. Furthermore, merely counting cases does not adequately reveal the relative importance of some cases compared to others. If compliance occurs only in the relatively unimportant cases, the percentage record may look good but not be too meaningful.

In an important study by Robert Hudec (1993), the author and his colleagues provide a fairly upbeat appraisal of the GATT dispute settlement system, noting as follows:

A Statistical Profile of GATT Dispute Settlement Cases: 1948–1989[47]

1. The GATT dispute settlement procedure has been a quite successful international legal institution. The overall success rate of 88 percent, or even the 1980s success of 81 percent, means that at least four out of five valid complaints are being dealt with successfully. There is legal substance to the enterprise. Its accomplishments to this point, if not unique, are at least rare in the history of international legal institutions. Those accomplishments have laid down a strong base upon which to build.
2. The quantitative analysis of individual country performance makes it pretty clear that he GATT dispute settlement system is, at the margin, more responsive to the interests of the strong than to the interest of the weak. The evidence for this hypothesis occurs in all phases of performance—in the rates of success as complainants, in the rates of noncompliance as defendants, in the quality of outcomes achieved, and in the extent to which complainants are able to carry complaints forward to a decision.

Two cases in GATT posed some substantial problems in this regard, and in addition pointed to some of the considerations that lead nation-states to be cautious about international dispute-settlement procedures. Both of these cases involved processes brought under the 1979 so-called subsidies code of the GATT; and in both, the United States brought a complaint against the EC.[48] The cases were the Wheat Flour case—in which a panel found itself unable to rule on the critical legal issue—and the Pasta case—in which a different panel ruled in favor of the U.S. position. Neither report was adopted by the committee of signatories of the code, although the United States and the EC settled the pasta dispute.[49] A brief look at these two cases is revealing for our purposes.

The Wheat Flour case involved a 1983 complaint by the United States that EC subsidies (as much as 75 percent) to aid exports of wheat flour to third markets (including Egypt) were a violation of the code and of the GATT rules regarding export subsidies. Export subsidy rules for agricultural products differ from those for manufactured or "nonprimary" products.[50] There seemed to be little doubt that the EC subsidies would have been violating the rules if manufactured products had been involved. But the rules were less absolute regarding agricultural products, requiring only that a subsidy not result in a nation "having more than an equitable share" of world export trade. The United States argued that the EC share of the world export market had increased from 29 percent to 75 percent over a relevant period and that the EC market share in a number of important and growing markets had increased, while U.S. export share of those markets had decreased. Yet the panel, partly influenced by special characteristics of the marketing of U.S. wheat flour, including aid under the U.S. food aid program to assist developing countries, did not find that the EC had achieved "more than an equitable share." The panel refused to be guided in this case by an earlier export subsidy case in GATT history, also dealing with wheat flour, that might have been seen as a sort of precedent for a meaningful definition of "equitable share."

The 1983 Pasta case also involved a U.S. complaint against EC subsidies for exports (pasta), which in this case went to the U.S. market (particularly harming a U.S. regional pasta industry).[51] The EC claimed that its subsidies to EC pastamakers for exporting were only such as were necessary to equalize the effective cost of the more expensive European durum wheat (which EC pastamakers presumably used) with the world-market price for wheat. The EC price was higher because of its Common Agriculture Policy (CAP) program of maintaining grain prices. For the pastamakers to be able to export, they needed to have inputs at prices equivalent to those of foreign competitors, so the EC provided a "cereals refund" to make up the difference. The EC claimed, therefore, that the subsidy was really one for wheat (and thus was governed by the rules for agriculture products). The panel, however, found that the payments were made to the pasta makers for pasta exports and, more significantly, that pasta was not a primary or agricultural product, but was a processed good and therefore came under the rules for nonprimary products. In this case, the subsidies were forbidden by the code.

Both of these cases sorely tested the GATT-type processes. The Wheat Flour case is viewed by some observers as one in which the panel members, for diplomatic reasons, essentially "ducked" their responsibility. Yet it has to be recognized that the treaty language is exceedingly vague. A restrained view of judicial behavior might legitimately lead to a refusal to rule on such an issue. If no prior precedent existed, such a refusal seems fair.

The Pasta case was approached differently by its panel. Clearly the EC was surprised to find that processed agricultural goods fell afoul of the subsidy rules for nonprimary goods, and arguably would not have agreed to some of the language of the agreement if it had realized what would be the eventual result. The panel nevertheless was willing to come to that conclusion, in what was perhaps the only opinion of the GATT dispute system in which a dissenting opinion was offered. Again, a more restrained view of judicial behavior in these circumstances might lead to the conclusion that the issue is one that the interested nations should negotiate toward a solution by refining the rule. Persons with this view would argue that the nation-states did not intend to delegate so important a question (which, the EC argues, goes to central issues of its all-important Common Agricultural Policy) to a trio of disinterested panel members.

Each side had its point. But considerable ambiguity about the appropriate role of third-party decision making was evident in these cases. Therefore an institutional process is required that will effectively resolve disputes (which otherwise can fester for lengthy periods of time), and will do so in a way that reinforces rule integrity. The jurisprudence and philosophy of these processes needed considerable attention in the Uruguay Round and afterward.

It is interesting to note some of the statistics about cases brought under the GATT system. There are various inventories. The GATT Analytical Index through January 1995 contains 196 cases, but seems not to include most cases for which no panel report was issued (usually because parties settled). It also does not include cases under the separate Tokyo Round codes. A GATT document in March 1994 notes 306 disputes contained in the GATT secretariat's official inventory. Hudec's 1993 book analyses 207 complaints.[52] Another rough inventory that I compiled for many years includes many cases noted from some informal sources, including some that were never brought as a formal complaint. The disputes in this list number 418 to about mid-1994. Thus it seems plausible that in some sense the GATT system has handled over 500 disputes since its inception. These various approaches all imply a very impressive role for the GATT dispute settlement system.

Hudec's figures as well as mine suggest that a very large percentage of the formal cases under GATT and the Tokyo Round codes involved the United States (as complainant about 30 percent of case; as respondent about 25 percent, thus party in over half the cases brought). The European Community was also a major party after its formation in 1957, accounting for over 35 percent of the overall cases. Many cases were between the United States and the European Community.

4.3 Legal Process and Trade Disputes in GATT and the WTO

Legal interpretation of the GATT and WTO agreements must be considered in the context of the general principles of international law regarding interpretation of treaties. These general principles are probably best summarized today by Article XXXI of the Vienna Convention on the Law of Treaties, although this convention does not technically apply in some situations, and would not technically apply in a controversy involving a nation—such as the United States—that has not yet ratified the Vienna convention. Nevertheless, this portion of the Vienna convention is considered by many nations, including the United States, to codify generally accepted rules of customary international law, and thus is a definitive text describing those rules.[53]

The principles of treaty interpretation include "ordinary meaning" of the words, other agreements or instruments influencing the treaty which were accepted by the parties to the treaty at the time it was concluded, subsequent agreement among the parties to the treaty, "subsequent practice in the application of the treaty which establishes the agreement of the parties regarding its interpretation," and other relevant rules of international law. In some circumstances the preparatory work can also be relevant,[54] but many argue that it is strictly a subsidiary influence.

Each of these principles of interpretation plays a role for the GATT, the WTO and associated agreements. The GATT history, it must be remembered, is "guidance" for the WTO. GATT contains an annex with a series of originally agreed interpretations that are considered definitive.[55] Subsequently there have been formal agreements which purport to interpret the GATT. Among these were the Tokyo Round subsidies code and antidumping codes, although these clearly go beyond mere "interpretation." Whether these codes could influence the interpretation for GATT contracting parties that did not accept the codes is not yet clear.[56] Likewise, the Uruguay Round Final Act includes as part of the treaty text, a number of understandings, ministerial decisions and ministerial declarations, as well as assorted other documents, all of which become part of the text of the agreement, and thus influence the interpretation of the whole. The interrelationship of these various texts is also not very clear, as indicated in chapter 1.

The preparatory work of the GATT itself, as well as drafting of the amendments that came into force, have often been relied on in GATT proceedings. Indeed, a document prepared by the secretariat, entitled the "Analytical Index," lists many aspects of the preparatory work as interpretative material.[57] A major question is whether the text and preparatory work for the Havana (ITO) Charter could also be considered interpretative material for the GATT.[58] I have taken the position that it can, because it is contemporaneous with the preparation of the GATT (the Geneva conference preparations were simultaneous with the GATT drafting, with the same national negotiators involved). Even the 1948 Havana

Conference is, in my view, relevant to GATT, given that the GATT drafters clearly anticipated later changing the GATT to accord with the changes made at Havana to the corresponding provisions of the ITO charter, and that some of those changes were later incorporated into the GATT while others were not (on the grounds that the GATT language was already sufficiently similar to the Havana revisions).[59] As indicated above, however, under the Vienna Convention, preparatory work is arguably a *subsidiary* source of interpretive materials, and should not be used unless the primary sources cannot solve the interpretive questions. Nevertheless, there is a well-supported practice in the GATT to turn rather quickly to preparatory work.

The actual practice in GATT and now the WTO also played a major role in the interpretation of the agreement. Technically, to be "binding," practice must be sufficient to "establish the agreement of the parties." Exactly how far the evidence must go in this regard is not clear. In addition, it should be noted that under accepted doctrines of international law, *stare decisis* or the common-law concept of "precedent" does not apply.[60] Thus a World Court decision (formally the International Court of Justice, ICJ) in a dispute between countries A and B provides no binding precedent as such in a dispute between C and D, nor for A and C, nor even for another dispute at another time between A and B.[61] Yet, in practice, the diplomats and officials who participated in the GATT system were very influenced by precedent, and often mentioned precedents in some detail in GATT deliberations, as well as in the formal dispute-settlement panel findings. A common-law lawyer would find himself very much at home in GATT legal discussions!

From time to time GATT interpretations were made in short statements by the chairman of the contracting parties.[62] Sometimes these were offered in the context of a "consensus view" of the CPs, without any objection from any CP. At other times, interpretations were made as statements of the chair without any explicit connection to an agreement or a vote (without objection) of the CPs. In all such cases, however, it is safe to assume that the text had been carefully negotiated in advance and deemed acceptable to the interested CPs. Similarly, often dispute-settlement panel findings contained rulings interpreting the GATT application in the particular dispute, and the CPs adopted most of these findings. These findings may have been binding on the disputing parties,[63] but it can still be asked, what is the status of such "interpretative statements" as to future disputes? Although their status is quite indefinite, the procedure suggests, in Vienna

Convention phraseology, that it is one of "practice ... establishing agreement."[64] Again, this can be guidance for the WTO.

Another interesting question is whether the CONTRACTING PARTIES of GATT, under their Article XXV powers, had the authority to make a legal and definitively binding interpretation of GATT (binding on all CONTRACTING PARTIES). Some international organizations are explicitly given such power in their charters, so that an interpretation adopted by the procedure specified would carry with it a binding treaty obligation to accept the interpretation—even for nations disagreeing with the interpretation and even in the absence of sufficient practice to establish "agreement of the parties."[65] The language of GATT itself did not explicitly grant this power, although it gave authority for "joint action" with a view to "facilitating the operation and furthering the objectives of this Agreement...." This language seems broad enough to include the power to interpret, but caution is necessary for several reasons. First, because binding interpretative power for other organizations has been explicit in their charters, the absence of explicit power in the GATT could argue against the existence of that power. Second, the ill-fated ITO Charter contained explicit provisions for interpretation, whereas these provisions were not included in the GATT (because the GATT was not considered to be an "organization").[66] In the light of the Vienna Convention codification of customary international law, as well as the general language of GATT Article XXV, it seems likely that at least where there was no formal dissent by any GATT CP, various "practice" actions of the GATT would be deemed very definitive interpretations. In the case of only the majority of CPs agreeing, however, there was some ambiguity. It is quite possible that the practice of GATT during its four decades of existence has itself established an interpretation of the Article XXV powers to include the power to interpret.

This legal question, which was relatively open in the GATT, is now dramatically affected by the WTO charter. In Article IX of that text, at paragraph 2, the treaty language makes explicit a procedure for adopting "interpretations of this agreement and of the multilateral trade agreements." (We will recall that the multilateral trade agreements are those in Annex 1, which are required of all members.) The procedure specifies that upon a recommendation by a particular council overseeing the functioning of a multilateral trade agreement, a decision to adopt an interpretation shall be taken by a three-fourths majority of the members (not just of those voting). Presumably this procedure for a formal interpretation "preempts" less formal means that might be argued. Of course, interpretations do not necessarily have to be "formal" or "definitive." If they are definitive under this special procedure, then presumably they bind all parties irrevocably, as a matter of treaty text law, and not just developing through practice, or a relatively loose concept of precedent through panel reports. The procedure of GATT to have a chairman's statement of interpretation in the context of no objection by any contracting party may therefore not suffice unless at least three-fourths of the membership of the WTO is manifestly present at the meeting when this occurs. This provision of the WTO charter does not call for the use of consensus in the final step of the procedure, although the recommendations by the various councils might be by consensus in some circumstances.

No dispute involving GATT or its associated agreements has ever been taken to the World Court.[67] One may ask whether that court would have jurisdiction over such a dispute, or whether the internal GATT interpretative processes would be held to be exclusive. The ITO charter would have provided both a requirement to exclusively use dispute procedures contained within it and a reference to the World Court in certain circumstances.[68] No provisions were included in the GATT, but in any event, no GATT contracting party has been motivated so far to bring a GATT case to the World Court.[69]

The Uruguay Round text for the dispute-settlement understanding (DSU) probably reinforces this practice, because in Article 23 of the text the treaty states that "when members seek the redress of a violation of obligations or other nullification or impairment of benefits under the covered agreements, or impediment to the attainment of any objective of the covered agreements, they shall have recourse to, and abide by, the rules and procedures of this Understanding." Thus it can be argued that the parties have agreed in the WTO treaty that the WTO dispute-settlement procedure is the exclusive recourse for disputes concerning any of the WTO texts.

4.4 The WTO Dispute-Settlement Process

One of the great achievements of the Uruguay Round text—an achievement that may be the core "linchpin" of the whole trading system and the effective implementation of the Uruguay Round text—is the development of the new dispute-settlement understanding. In contrast to the meager number of paragraphs on dispute settlement found in the GATT 1947, the new DSU has thirty-five pages (including appendices) of reasonably elaborate procedures. This new text solves many of the issues that have plagued the previous GATT dispute-settlement system, although not necessarily all of them. It accomplished the following:

1. It established a unified dispute-settlement system for all parts of the GATT/WTO system, including the new subjects of services and intellectual property. No longer do different subjects have different dispute-settlement procedures, and the dispute-settlement procedures under the separate Tokyo Round Codes are no longer valid. Nevertheless, even though this was the goal, complete achievement was not entirely possible, as one of the appendices of the DSU indicates. There are certain variations and embellishments on the dispute-settlement procedures contained in some of the various texts of the Uruguay Round. The central core process, however, is unified.

2. The text reaffirms the right of a complaining government to have a panel process initiated, thus preventing blocking at that stage. The practice under GATT had reached this point, but earlier practice was vulnerable to such blocking.

3. The new text establishes an appellate procedure that will substitute for some of the council approval process of a panel report, and overcome blocking of a dispute-settlement panel report. This is extraordinarily important, and indeed one can already detect a certain nervousness on the part of sovereign members about the potential of this process. It has been described as "automaticity," meaning that under the procedure (which requires a consensus to block a dispute rather than to approve one) it is assumed that it will be virtually impossible to block a panel report. The quid pro quo is an appellate process, with the possibility of an appeal to a panel of three experts drawn from a permanent roster of seven such experts. The seven are selected for terms of four years, once renewable (and staggered). No longer will the panel process be totally ad hoc; the appellate body will presumably bring some greater degree of coherence and consistency, as well as preventing blocking. The appellate report is likewise adopted "automatically."

4. The DSU contains explicit text concerning the implementation or "compensation" phase of a dispute, when a losing party declines to adequately implement its obligations pursuant to the dispute determinations or recommendations. How significant this is, or whether it will actually work in the context of powerful trading partners, remains to be seen.

5. An extremely interesting development in the DSU that tracks some of the practice of the late years of the GATT is to separate the procedures

for "violation complaints" from those of "nonviolation complaints." The procedure for implementing the latter is significantly different from the former, in that in the latter case a country is not obligated to perform a recommendation or bring its law and practice into consistency (given that it has not violated anything). Instead, it is obligated to negotiate for and provide compensation to redress the nullified benefits.

One interesting question arising in the context of the DSU is whether a party that has been the subject of a complaint for a violation case has an international legal obligation to follow the recommendations or determinations of the panel report or appellate report that results from the process. Unlike other international tribunal proceedings, such as the World Court, the DSU does not make this entirely explicit. No one clause establishes this requirement in so many words. When one analyzes the DSU, however, it is possible to find a number of separate clauses that in context seem to strongly imply or "add up to" the obligation to conform to a panel/appellate report in violation cases. For example, DSU Article 3.1 states that "members affirm their adherence to the principles for the management of disputes heretofore applied ... and the rules and procedures as further elaborated and modified herein." Article 3.2 notes that the dispute settlement "is a central element in providing security and predictability to the multilateral trading system." Article 19 provides that a panel or appellate body "shall recommend that the member concerned bring the measure into conformity with that agreement." Article 21:1 states "prompt compliance with recommendations or rulings of the DSB is essential in order to ensure effective resolution of disputes to the benefit of all members." Likewise other clauses, in context, seem to imply an obligation to perform. Article 22 relating to compensation and suspension of concessions states "neither compensation or the suspension of concessions or other obligations is preferred to full implementation of a recommendation ..."[70]

The new DSU does not contain anything that would lead to a view that the legal effect more generally of a panel report is different from that of the practice under GATT. This suggests that again neither a *stare decisis* effect, nor any "definitive interpretation" effect (particularly given that there is an alternative procedure for a definitive interpretation) of a panel report exists. Nevertheless, the panel report remains persuasive, and presumably is part of the "practice" of the parties under the agreement.

After the first two years of operation under the DSU, there seems to be widespread opinion that the WTO Dispute Settlement procedures are quite successful. They certainly have been heavily utilized, and seem to be an increasing part of international economic diplomacy as well as a source of pride for the WTO officials and diplomats.[71] As of the end of 1996, a total of 64 complaints (termed "consultation requests") had been made, concerning 44 distinct substantive matters (some matters were subject to multiple complaints). Of these, 14 cases have been apparently settled, while two were completed (through the appellate stage) and 11 others were still "active," generally meaning that panels had been set up and were operating.[72]

Perhaps most interesting were the two Appellate Body reports that had been completed, namely: United States—Standards for Reformulated and Conventional Gasoline, complaints by Venezuela and Brazil (appellate and lower panel findings concluded that the United States should change its law to conform with its obligations); and Japan—Taxes on Alcoholic Beverages, complaints by the European Communities, Canada, and the United States (again the appellate body report and the lower panel report recommended that Japan revise its tax system on alcoholic beverages to be consistent with the GATT Article III).[73] A relatively light load for the first year of the appellate body gave the seven members a chance to study the processes and develop rules of procedure. Some of the members were not particularly expert in the GATT/WTO law and jurisprudence, so this opportunity to study has worked out reasonably well. Their future may be considerably busier!

The appellate panel reports seem to strongly reinforce the "rule orientation of the system." They also reinforce the concept that general international law principles apply to the WTO and its agreements (sometimes questions under GATT). Likewise the reports discuss in certain broad terms, the "standard of review," in one case stating that "WTO members have a large measure of autonomy to determine their own policies on the environment, including its relationship with trade."[74]

4.5 National Procedures for Citizen Initiation of International Economic Disputes

The United States and Section 301

Under traditional international law doctrines, nations were almost the only "subjects" of international law, and international procedures were open only to nation-states, or in some cases, also to international organizations. This is still generally true today, although a developing body of practice and thought permits individuals as well as business firms to be "subjects." Nevertheless, the primary international law institutions for dispute settlement, such as the World Court, are available only to nation-states and international organizations. When individuals have a complaint against a foreign nation, the traditional approach requires these individuals to have their own governments to bring up the matter in international diplomatic processes or tribunals. This is called "diplomatic protection."[75]

Under traditional practice of diplomatic protection, the nation whose citizen has urged it to take up his or her cause is the "owner" or controller of the case. If that nation refuses to proceed, the individual usually has no recourse under international law.[76] That nation's domestic law may give the individual some recourse, such as under laws regarding taking of property; but under international law national government officials have the final say as to whether to bring a citizen's complaint to the attention of an offending nation or to an international proceeding. The theory supposedly is that national policy may in some cases make it more important for a nation to refrain from pursuing its citizens' problems. A desire to preserve its good relations with a more powerful state may lead a small nation to refrain from aggravating the powerful state by supporting the complaints of a few of its citizens.

In the United States the traditional approach for an American citizen who has a complaint against actions taken by a foreign nation is to bring that complaint to the attention of the U.S. government (usually the Department of State), and try to get the U.S. government to intervene on behalf of the citizen with the foreign authorities. This was true in foreign economic matters, for example, when a foreign nation expropriated property of an American citizen. And it is true when a foreign nation violates an international treaty obligation that would otherwise protect the economic or trade interests of an American citizen or firm. Thus, if a foreign country imposes a tarrif on imports from an American firm that exceeds the limit set in its GATT obligations, the American firm will probably not find help in the courts of that foreign nation, and certainly cannot go itself directly to the GATT or WTO about the matter. It has to prod the U.S. government to take the matter up at GATT and now the WTO. Dissatisfaction with the U.S. government's handling of such complaints led the Congress to insert into the 1962 Trade Expansion Act a provision[77] that explicitly granted to the U.S. president some authority to take retaliatory actions when foreign governments harmed the trade interests of American firms.[78]

In the 1974 Trade Act the Congress overhauled this authority and set up a more regular procedure for handling these types of cases. The procedure gave American firms and citizens the right to formally petition an agency of the U.S. government to allege that American commercial interests had been harmed by illegal or unfair actions of foreign governments. This agency, the Office of the U.S. Trade Representative, was charged with the responsibility of investigating the allegations, trying to obtain redress for the U.S. citizen, and ultimately recommending various retaliatory actions to the president that were authorized by the statute. The 1979 Trade Agreements Act amended this law, as did the 1984 Tariff and Trade Act. The 1988 Omnibus Trade and Competitiveness Act also contains amendments to Section 301. (The Uruguay Round Implementing Act of 1994 made virtually no substantive changes to Section 301.) These amendments have several objectives. First, they move the responsibility for the disposition of the action from the president to the U.S. trade representative (USTR). The USTR, however, is subject to the "direction" of the president. Second, under certain circumstances, the use of Section 301 is to be nearly "mandatory," with presidential discretion reduced in certain cases of "unjustifiable" actions (for example, breach of legal obligations) by foreign governments. Certain exceptions are specified that restore some president's discretion, but on the whole, Congress "tightened" the 301 process and made it at least politically more difficult for the president *not* to retaliate. This seems a source of rather bitter criticism from foreign government officials toward the 1988 act.[79]

Thus today, the United States has a procedure that until 1984 was virtually unique in the world, under that U.S. firms and citizens could petition the U.S. government in any case involving trade or commerce, for U.S. government aid to redress foreign-nation action that is deemed to be a violation of the "rights of the United States under any trade agreement ...," or which action denies "benefits to the United States under any trade agreement ..." or which is "unjustifiable, unreasonable, or discriminatory and burdens or restricts United States commerce."

Section 301 Procedures

Section 301 of the U.S. law contains procedures that allow the government to "self-initiate" a case, or a citizen to file a petition. A citizen petition must be addressed to the United States trade representative, who must then determine within forty-five days whether to initiate an investigation. If an investigation is opened, the USTR must publish a summary of the petition, provide opportunity for a public hearing, and request consultation with the foreign country or instrumentality concerned. If the case involves a trade agreement and no mutually acceptable resolution is obtained, the Unite States must involve the dispute-settlement procedures of the agreement. Finally, the trade representative must (with certain time limits) make a published determination of what action the United States should take. The statute delegates broad powers of response to the trade representative, including suspending or withdrawing trade agreement concessions, and imposing duties, fees, or other restrictions on the offending country's trade. It makes clear that the procedure applies to trade in services as well as products, and allows responses through either MFN measures or discriminatory measures targeting the offending country.[80]

As I have noted, the 1988 Omnibus Trade and Competitiveness Act strengthened the political pressure on the U.S. executive to take concrete action in the case of "unjustifiable" foreign actions.

Several other features of the U.S. procedure should be noted. Although it is required in some cases to follow an international procedure, the U.S. government is not required to abide by the outcome of that procedure and, in some cases, does not even need to refrain from action until the international procedures are formally completed. This feature reflects considerable congressional dissatisfaction with the GATT dispute procedures.[81] Furthermore, a Section 301 case need not depend on foreign actions that violate international rules (actions that the statute usually terms "unjustifiable"): it can also be based on the statutory criteria of "unreasonableness," which gives the United States much latitude to unilaterally define practices it deems to be unfair and deserving of counter measures.[82] Finally, Section 301 does not have an "injury requirement" specifically; but, for practices not in violation of a trade agreement, it does require something that "burdens or restricts United States commerce," which might be interpreted as a kind of injury requirement.[83]

On the whole, it is apparent that the language of Section 301 is extraordinarily vague and imprecise, and partly for this reason it offers considerable discretionary power to the president to impose retaliatory measures against foreign trade. In several cases this broad power has been relied on in connection with self-initiation to justify presidential measures restricting trade in cases that do not quite fit the traditional trade actions or congressional delegations. For example, Section 301 was used as part of a package to settle a countervailing duty case concerning Canadian lumber,[84] and to impose the so-called computer-chips agreements on Japan.[85]

The Practice and Cases under Section 301

From the 1974 enactment of Section 301 until August 1996, one hundred six petitions have been directed to the Office of the USTR. Of these, twenty-five concerned the practices of the EC, with an additional eight or so concerning actions of European countries that are currently EC member states. Nineteen cases involve trade and services rather than goods, and ten concerned the protection of intellectual property. A large number, probably half, of these cases were settled by bilateral agreement or some change in practice by the foreign state. Only slightly more than a dozen have resulted in U.S. government retaliatory sanctions of some type.

The utility of the procedure does not result from the counteraction itself, but from the negotiation process assisted by the potential of counteraction—as the drafters anticipated.[86] One of the lawyers who has most often used Section 301 explains:

> In practice, a petition filed under Section 301 by a private party carries an effective threat of potential retaliation, combined with the threat of adverse publicity and a general souring of trade relations. These potential ramifications alone may bring the offending government to the bargaining table. Indeed, astutely using the threat of filing a Section 301 complaint as leverage to achieve a desired end may lead to better results than casually filing a complaint and pursuing the case through administrative channels. Conversely, a sound legal case coupled with inept commercial diplomacy by either the petitioners or the U.S. government may lead to wasted effort and negligible results. More than any other U.S. trade law, Section 301 works through feints and threats, rather than through formal legal processes.[87]

Although most of the Section 301 cases regarding products were concerned with damage to U.S. exports from a foreign government action, some of these cases involved imports to the United States. When Section 301 is used in connection with foreign practices regarding exports to the U.S., the question of overlap or conflict between Section 301 and other U.S. laws regarding unfair trade practices is raised. For example, the complaint about pasta imports from the EC argued that the EC export subsidies were unfair. Presumably the countervailing duty laws were designed for such a case. Section 301, however, does not contain all the same criteria for U.S. government response that one finds in the countervailing duty law. Section 301 does not explicitly require an injury test, although it appears to be normally interpreted to require some "injury" because of the statutory language of "burdening commerce."[88] The definition of "industry" for purposes of an injury test could also vary. Section

301 criteria may also differ in other ways from those of an unfair trade statute. Nevertheless, there is no a priori exclusion of a complaint from a Section 301 procedure merely because the facts are similar to or sufficient for a different proceeding. Since Section 301 gives the government considerably more discretion than the principal unfair trade laws (countervailing duties and antidumping duties), it is usually not preferred by complainants. Furthermore, in one set of Section 301 cases regarding steel products, the government decision was to invoke the escape-clause procedures for the complainants, in essence transferring each case to a different statutory provision and a different U.S. government agency.[89]

The "Trade Barriers Regulation" of the EC

A new 1994 EC Regulation[90] replaces the 1984 "New Commercial Policy Instrument"[91], and lays down new and improved Community procedures to ensure that the rights of the Community under international trade rules, including those established under the WTO, are effectively exercised. In particular, the Regulation aims to provide procedural means to request that the Community institutions react to obstacles to trade adopted or maintained by third countries that cause injury or otherwise adverse trade effects. The mechanism can be initiated in three ways: by a Community industry, by an individual firm, or at the request of a Member State.[92]

The EC Regulations seem to have been partly inspired by the U.S. Section 301 procedure, but as adopted, the current version has some significant differences. It would be a mistake to assume that all the same motivations were behind the EC Regulation as were behind the U.S. law. The EC Regulation is set in a very different governmental context and arguably has an important effect of altering the balance or allocation of power among EC institutions.

For example, the Commission is now authorized, before any retaliatory measures are taken, to initiate, conduct, and terminate a WTO dispute settlement procedure (subject to a "guillotine" vote of the Council),[93] whereas previously this required an affirmative decision by the Council. However, retaliatory measures such as the suspension or withdrawal of concessions, the raising of customs duties, or the introduction of quantitative restrictions can still only be taken in accordance with Article 113 EC, by qualified majority in the Council.[94]

Several interesting differences between the EC Regulation and the U.S. Section 301 law exist. First, under the Regulation, an international proceeding, if applicable, must always be invoked and followed through to its conclusion before the Regulation-contemplated counteractions may be utilized. Also, any commercial policy measure must be in accordance with the Community's international obligations. In particular, any retaliatory measure shall be in accordance with the recommendation of the DSB.[95]

Second, the Regulation provides that it "shall not apply in cases covered by other existing rules in the commercial policy field." This seems to suggest, for example, that antidumping and subsidization cases are more appropriately brought under other Regulations relating to those actions. In addition, the Regulation leaves open any other measure that may be taken in accordance with Article 113 EU.[96]

Finally, "the shift in emphasis from inward-looking protective measures to export promotion" that has come to be identified with Section 301 is not reflected in the EC instrument. Regulation 3286/94 primarily seeks to protect European firms against foreign unfair trade practices.

The "New Commercial Policy Instrument" has not been used extensively: only ten cases in ten years. However, it can be said that almost all procedures initiated under this mechanism have led to an improved situation for Community exporters.[97] Therefore, although not intensively used, the Regulation has been considered successful in promoting the Community's interests in international trade. It remains to be seen how often its successor, the "Trade Barrier Regulation," will be used and how successful it will be.

Obviously, the U.S. and the EC developments raise the question of whether they represent a trend toward more formalistic procedures available to private individuals or firms in connection with the application and enforcement of international trade rules, at least under the WTO. I will have more comment on this in the next section.

4.6 Looking at the Future of Dispute Settlement and Rule Application in the WTO

The new Uruguay Round dispute-settlement understanding is clearly a substantial improvement in the world trading system, and if it works even reasonably efficiently it should considerably enhance the predictability and rule-based nature of the trading system. Undoubtedly, certain problems will be discovered, and practice will reveal that more evolution in the procedures will be needed. Unfortunately, the WTO charter requires a full consensus for changes in the DSU, so it may be somewhat more difficult for the system to evolve and adapt to practice and experience than was the case under GATT, when everything was relatively fluid and open without much reference to treaty text.

As the system evolves, it may be useful to briefly suggest a few ideas that have been noted with respect to potential and proposed changes. First, it should be noted that the system ought to encourage settlement by disputants, giving them assistance in the process of settlement, but it should encourage that settlement primarily with reference to the existing agreed rules rather than simply with reference to the relative economic or other power that the disputants possess. The mechanism should be designed so that as time goes on, greater and greater confidence will be placed in the system and it will more often be utilized, and gradually greater responsibilities may be given to it.

In order to establish that the dispute-settlement mechanism relies primarily on reference to rules and their application, the fulcrum of a mechanism will be the opportunity to obtain an impartial and trusted decision as to the interpretation or application of a previously agreed-upon rule. To avoid tainting the process of that judgment—that is, to avoid reducing the trust placed in that decision because the process of obtaining it might be mixed with other goals—the impartial third-party decision of rule interpretations or application should be (as it most often is in the various legal systems of the world) relatively isolated from other processes, such as the process of assisting in negotiation for settlement, or the process of rule formulation (left to legislatures in typical legal systems).

It can be seen that the WTO system allows a rather impressive framework for implementing some of these principles. It can be roughly described as a five part approach outlined as follows:[98]

1. Bilateral consultations between the disputing parties, without outside presence (as now provided).

2. Conciliation process, with the assistance of trained persons probably from the secretariat, to assist the parties in resolving their dispute.

3. Panels and appellate body rulings with emphasis on impartiality of the panel members, and a separation of the panel process from the conciliation process and other political or diplomatic negotiating influences.

4. Policy body examination of the panel or appellate body reports, with the change that the approval will be virtually "automatic." However, the WTO Charter has provision for the members to act in definitive ways, such as making a decision or adopting an interpretation (even though it might differ from a panel ruling), or adopting a waiver, and so on.

5. "Sanction," with more explicit procedures for "compensatory measures." In my view, however, history suggests that sanctions, and even compensation, have limited utility and thus I doubt that this is will be a very essential part of the procedure. More important is the credibility and advisability of the panel reports in the eyes of the international community.

To make further progress in an organization with more than one hundred twenty nations will be difficult. Recognizing the divergence of opinion regarding dispute-settlement procedures even among relatively similar cultures and national legal systems, it may be necessary to turn to some alternative methods for certain types of dispute resolution. Some regional organizations have experimented with more dramatic and enforceable dispute resolution. The European Community has a constitutional court at its disposal (in Luxembourg). The 1988 Free Trade Agreement between Canada and the United States, and now NAFTA, have several far-reaching bilateral or trilateral dispute-settlement provisions that cover many GATT subjects. One of these provisions created an international panel procedure that not only substitutes for appeal to domestic courts in antidumping and countervailing duty cases in the two countries, but is empowered to issue a decision that becomes directly applicable in the domestic law of the country concerned, so as to bind the administration officials there.[99]

At some point in the future (certainly not soon), the participants in the international multilateral trade system might consider an approach to disputes and rule application that allows some modified means of direct access to procedures by individuals and private firms, perhaps after an appropriate international "filter" to prevent spurious complaints. I explained, with several coauthors, in our 1984 book:

> There are some interesting potentials in these precedents for the GATT and the international economic system, although they will probably not be readily accepted by the governments that participate in the GATT. But governments and business firms do desire greater predictability of national government economic actions in an increasingly interdependent world, and do desire greater balance and equality in actual implementation of negotiated international rules on economic matters. Those factors could lead governments to be willing to accept some sort of a mechanism by which individual citizens or firms could appeal directly to an international body like the GATT to determine whether a government obligated under the GATT or one of its codes has taken an action that is inconsistent with its international obligations....
>
> Clearly, the typical governmental reluctance to relinquish any power or to constrain its field of discretion would discourage a move in the direction of the procedures described. On the other hand, it should be recognized that there are some

advantages for governments in such a procedure. For one thing, if it were carefully designed and became reliable, governments might well find that the procedure would tend to deemphasize and depoliticize many relatively minor trade or economic complaints that now exist between nations. For example, let us assume that Mr. A, a citizen in country A, finds that his exports to country B are being restrained improperly by country B, inconsistent with country B's international obligations. Under the current procedure, Mr. A must go to his own national government and get it to take up his matter with the foreign government. Thus, his case has immediately been raised to a diplomatic level. That quite often means, by the nature of things, that it has been raised to a fairly high level of official attention and consequently of public perception. On the other hand, if an appropriate international procedure existed, when Mr. A came to his government to complain about country B, country A officials could refer Mr. A to that procedure and encourage him to use it, without taking any stand on the matter. It is quite possible that the issue could then be handled more expeditiously and routinely. The case would continue to be Mr. A's case, and [would] not become country A's case. The issue would be Mr. A versus country B, instead of Mr. A and country A versus country B.

It is the view of at least one of the authors of this book that in all probability, early versions of such a procedure would have to allow the individual governments to exercise some kind of right of veto over their own citizens' attempts to invoke the process. However, this right could be accorded to national governments as a way to make them more comfortable with experimenting with the procedure, and could be designed to gradually die out (at least for all but the most exceptional cases).[100]

Once again, we need to return to the dichotomy of policy pointed out in the first section of this chapter. A European author, in a book quoted approvingly by a major European diplomat, suggests that international resolution of disputes, at least regarding economic matters, has as its prime objective neither ascertainment of right or wrong, nor establishment of responsibility of a particular nation, but instead the most rapid cessation of the violations.[101] That author, and others,[102] stress the importance of diplomatic means and negotiating approaches to resolving disputes.

In my estimation, these viewpoints miss important policy considerations and are often misleading. In the first place, considerable utility exists in publicly designating (or threatening to do so) the "wrongdoer" in an international dispute, especially if the validity of the process that determines the wrongdoing is widely accepted. But, more significantly, it must be recognized that in most cases it is *not* the resolution of the specific dispute under consideration that is most important. Rather, it is the efficient and just future functioning of the overall system that is the primary goal of a dispute-settlement procedure. Thus, it may be more important to clarify and provide predictive guidance about the application of a rule than it is to determine that a "judgment" is acceptable to either or both parties of the immediate dispute. Indeed, in some GATT proceedings, contracting parties other than the disputants have expressed a strong interest in a dispute process because the resultant "precedent" effect of a panel ruling could affect them.[103] If the policies of a "rule-oriented diplomacy," as mentioned in section 1, make sense, they also tend to suggest a broader goal than just the settlement of a particular dispute to the satisfaction of the disputants.

These are not absolute "either/or" questions, however. There is a spectrum of utilities involved in the considerations discussed here. If a rule is too rigidly applied, so that the application is consistently ignored, that too will damage the broader international trading system. On the other hand, too much concern for the "feelings" of the parties, with too much concern for "diplomatic approaches" designed to sweep differences under the rug, or the use of studied ambiguity to "paper over" differences, will have their costs also.

Finally, other mechanisms and techniques for improving the "rule integrity" of the GATT trade system are available. One approach is called "surveillance." One technique is to have committees or working groups systematically examine the trade measures of particular countries (perhaps on a rotating basis) and comment on the GATT consistency or policy appropriateness of such measures.[104] Another is for a GATT body to report semiannually (as is now done) on the "status" of the trading system, to flag discrepancies between measures actually taken (such as "gray area" or export-restraint arrangements)[105] and GATT rules, or to raise questions about the policy appropriateness of such measures.

5 Tariff and Nontariff Barriers

5.1 Import Restrictions and GATT/WTO Obligations

The first four chapters of this book have dealt with the institutional and legal structure of the world trade system related to GATT and the WTO. Now we turn to the substantive regulatory policies of that system. In the next seven chapters I describe in turn the most important of these policies and their legal implementation both nationally and internationally. These chapters deal both with the affirmative obligations (such as tariff bindings, MFN, and national treatment) and with a series of exceptions to these obligations. In some cases, when the exceptions are most closely identified with a particular affirmative policy, they are discussed in the chapter relating to that policy.

The diplomats who wrote the GATT and the ITO charter had broadly in mind a regulatory system that would essentially inhibit the use of restrictions on imports other than tariffs, and then provide for negotiation of reduced tariff levels.[1] It was recognized that the mere agreement to reduce tariff levels could be easily evaded unless other obligations were established to prevent that evasion. A simple example would be a negotiated limit of a 10 percent tariff on bicycles but evaded by a national government that imposes a quota on bicycle imports, thus frustrating the purpose of the tariff limit to liberalize trade.

It has been said that the drafters of GATT addressed primarily five types of border barriers to imports: tariffs, quotas, subsidies, state trading, and customs procedures.[2] For tariffs, the approach was to allow them to continue but to provide for reduction negotiations. For quotas, the approach (with the experience of the 1930s well in mind) was to establish a prohibition on their use. For customs procedures, the GATT (in Articles VII–X) established norms of reasonableness, with limits on taking or delaying costly measures. With respect to subsidies and state trading, however, the drafters were not so rigorous.

State trading agencies, such as a government agency given exclusive rights to import, could be used to restrict trade in a number of ways. The agency could simply refuse to buy more than a certain quantity of the goods each year. Alternatively, it could buy goods but set a resale price for domestic buyers at a level high enough to inhibit sales and, therefore, imports. The agency could argue that in each case it did this as a matter of internal proprietary decision making, and not by government regulation, so that most GATT rules did not apply. Yet the government in most cases, certainly when it owned the agency or company, could have great "influence" on these "proprietary" decisions. The GATT rules on state trading (Article XVII) do not establish very much discipline.[3]

Likewise, domestic subsidies can be used to allow domestic producers to undersell and inhibit imports. Once again, the GATT rules on such subsidies are not very strong.[4]

This pattern of regulation—negotiating tariffs, eliminating quotas, and not enforcing too much discipline on subsidies and state trading—has been the basis of one early argument used by developing countries to suggest that the GATT was biased in favor of industrial-country trading patterns.[5]

There are some important economic and other policy reasons to favor tariffs over quotas, however. The price effect and competitive distortion caused by quotas tend to be much less transparent than those of tariffs. Quotas as well as tariffs yield "monopoly rents"—that is, the domestic producers will be able to price their goods higher, and thus will receive more profits. Although under tariffs the government captures some of these monopoly rents (from tariff payments), this often is not the case with quotas (unless the government charges for the quota licenses). Depending on how they are constructed, quotas may also allow foreign producers to pocket these added rents. In addition, the administration of quotas often is by "license," and licensing procedures lend themselves to corruption of government officials.[6] Some of these policies can also apply to use of other nontariff measures. For all these reasons, the policy preference given to tariffs has considerable rationale behind it.

The history of tariffs in the United States has been ably chronicled by well-known economists.[7] A broad characterization of that history is that U.S. tariffs were high in the early 1800s (averaging up to 60 percent), then dropped to a low of about 20 percent during the 1850s, only to climb back to high levels between 1860 and 1914. Tariffs were cut sharply in the Wilson administration (1914–1920) but then climbed again, to peak with the 1930 Smoot-Hawley Tariff.[8]

One of the true success stories of the GATT is the effect it has had on tariffs during its more than forty years of existence. The first seven GATT trade negotiating rounds[9] (through the Tokyo Round, which was completed in 1979) have resulted in an overall reduction in the weighted-average tariff on industrial products to a level of about 6.3 percent. Some estimates of the result of the Uruguay Round (where the emphasis was not on tariffs but on introducing the new subject of services) suggest that average tariffs will decline further to about 3.9 percent. In chapter 2 I presented a table which overviews the results of these prior negotiations.

The first five of these rounds negotiated tariffs on an "item-by-item" basis, under a procedure explained in section 5.2, below. The latest two rounds turned to a "linear cut" approach (as I explain in that section), and also tried to emphasize negotiations on nontariff measures. As I noted earlier,[10] the Kennedy Round was not very successful in this regard, but the Tokyo Round resulted in more than a dozen treaty agreements and "understandings" regarding nontariff measures.

Tariffs of under 5 percent ad valorem, arguably, constitute more of a "sales tax" or nuisance than an import barrier. Producers who can become sufficiently more efficient can "hurdle the tariff" by selling at a lower cost to offset the tariff. There may be special circumstances, however, in which even a low tariff could be important. For example, Canadians sometimes note that even a low tariff can have a substantial impact on an investment decision about where to locate a plant. If a substantial portion of the output from a Canadian plant must be sold in the U.S. market, a 5 percent U.S. tariff could be instrumental in leading investors to locate in the United States. so as to enhance the long-term rate of return on the capital allocated to build the plant.[11]

In addition, the low tariff is an average that could conceal a few relatively high tariffs. Some U.S. tariffs (even MFN rates), for example, are above 20 percent ad valorem (even as high as 40 percent). Such extremely high tariffs may reduce the volume of trade such that trade weighted-tariff averages do not give adequate significance to their effect. Furthermore, the depressing experience of the GATT period is that as tariffs have declined, there is reason to think that various (often ingenious) nontariff measures have been introduced or enhanced to limit imports. And for reasons discussed above, these may be less desirable from a policy standpoint than tariffs.

An interesting study by Stern and Deardorff uses a large computer model at the University of Michigan to measure the effects of the Tokyo Round tariff-cutting and Non-Tariff Barrier (NTB) agreements. Their results show four broad effects. First, employment dislocations in most countries will aggregate only a fraction of 1 percent. Second, exchange rates will change to a small extent. Third, import and, therefore, consumer prices will fall to a limited extent. Finally, economic welfare will be increased in most countries, including the major economies of the United States, the EC, and Japan. In general, however, the effects of tariff and certain NTB changes seem quite minor.[12]

Treaties relating to trade restrictions have for almost a century been concerned with the use of customs procedures as disguised import barriers in themselves. Like almost every other governmental activity, delay, excessive documentation, or arbitrary application of seemingly neutral rules can operate to prevent or inhibit business activity—and customs enforcement is no exception. The GATT treats these activities in Articles VII–X, which call for opportunity to appeal arbitrary decisions, notice of regulations, minimization of fees and formalities, and reduction of the impact of requirements for marks of origin.[13]

5.2 GATT Bindings and Tariff Negotiations

The Bindings and Their Meaning

The GATT bindings, of course, are part of the WTO Annex 1A, and consist of many thousands of pages of individual national schedules.[14]

Given that the GATT derived partly from the line of history begun with the 1934 Reciprocal Trade Agreements Act,[15] it is not surprising that commitments to limit the level of tariffs are the central feature of this agreement. The tariff commitments are called "bindings" or "concessions." They are contained for each country in that country's "schedule of tariff concessions," which in turn is incorporated into GATT by language in Article II of GATT. These schedules are voluminous: they consist of lists of product descriptions, followed by a tariff level—either specific or ad valorem[16]—that is the treaty obligation for *that product* or *that country*. A typical item might look like this:

Tariff item number	Description of products	Rate of duty
734.45	Archery equipment, and parts thereof	3.8% ad valorem
	Dolls and parts of dolls including doll clothing	
737.21	Doll clothing imported separately	8% ad valorem
737.22	Other	12% ad valorem

Because of the large number of products, and because for the major trading countries almost all products are "bound" in GATT, a schedule for a typical country will take up many pages—seven hundred fifty for the United States, for example. Also, because of a series of trade negotiations resulting in new schedules, and because the older schedules are still technically in force (and can sometimes have some effect),[17] the complete text of all the schedules for GATT comprises many volumes.

A binding is a maximum tariff: contracting parties are obligated by treaty not to allow their tariff level on a particular product to exceed the GATT binding. They may set a tariff lower than the binding, however—and sometimes they do[18]. When no binding exists, a country may charge any tariff amount it pleases, even a prohibitive tariff of 1,000 percent or more.[19] Some GATT contracting parties (especially developing countries) have had very short schedules, so that they have had wide discretion to change very high tariffs on most imports, although the Uruguay Round and WTO obligations are now more stringent in this regard.

A number of possible exceptions to the tariff-concession obligation exist. The escape clause, for example, allows temporary departure from tariff bindings (see chapter 7). Waivers by the contracting parties are another exception. In addition, the GATT agreement includes a provision that essentially allows a contracting party to withdraw a concession at any time. On doing this, however, the CP becomes obligated to grant "compensation" or "renegotiation rights" to other CPs that are affected. These renegotiation rights require that the CP withdrawing a concession either grant a different equivalent concession, or be prepared to endure equivalent withdrawals of concessions from other CPs regarding the exports of the original withdrawing CP. This "rebalancing" feature of the agreement has been one of the more significant factors for maintaining the discipline of the tariff-schedule obligations.[20]

Negotiating Tariff Concessions: Item-by-Item Procedures

In the first five GATT tariff negotiating rounds—that is, before the Kennedy Round (1962–1967)—the procedure for negotiation was followed on an item-by-item basis.[21] Each country tabled, with each other country that had a potential to import from it, a "request list" of products and tariff concessions desired. Then each country prepared an "offer list" of concessions it was prepared to make in return. The national negotiators would then meet in two-country meetings to negotiate reciprocal concessions. The whole process was supervised by the GATT negotiating committee and the secretariat, with copies of all lists and notifications being kept by the secretariat and normally available for inspection by any negotiating party. Because each concession was applied on an MFN basis, a pair of nations that had arrived at preliminary agreement on their mutual concessions would then each try to obtain other concessions from other contracting parties that would benefit from the concessions.

For example: If country A agreed to limit its tariffs on bicycle imports to 8 percent, in exchange for B's agreement to limit its tariffs on cheese imports to 12 percent, and if country C also exported bicycles to A, then A would ask C for a concession on radio imports from A. If C refused, then A and B might have to rethink their tentative agreement. None of these preliminary agreements would be final until the end of the negotiation, when all parties were notified and all agreements were assembled into one treaty document by the GATT Secretariat. At that time each contracting party would have to decide whether on balance it was willing to sign the "tariff protocol." Its decision would be based partly on the total balance of what it would give up, compared to what it expected to receive.

Needless to say this process was very complex, and in later years it became increasingly cumbersome. When the EC was formed by the 1957 Treaty of Rome, it began negotiating as an entity for its six member states. But each bargaining position had to be internally worked out within the EC, and this contributed greatly to the difficulty of the GATT negotiating process. Consequently, a search for a different procedure was undertaken.

Negotiating Tariff Concessions: The Linear Procedure

During the sixth round, the Kennedy Round, (1962–67) the GATT CONTRACTING PARTIES decided to conduct the main portions of the tariff negotiations on a "linear" basis.[22] Under this procedure, most industrial countries (the developing countries and a few primary product nations were allowed to opt out of the linear offer) were required to make their initial "offer," an across-the-board cut in tariffs of 50 percent for nonprimary products (agriculture products were not included in this offer). The 1962 U.S. statute set a limit on the U.S. president's authority to agree to a tariff cut at 50 percent, and this figure strongly influenced the GATT decision on the linear-cut offer. Under such a maximum cut, a 14 percent ad valorem tariff would become 7 percent.

Each nation was then allowed to table "exceptions lists," which had to be defended in the negotiating committee, and thus became the focus of the negotiation. The advantage of this procedure was that the negotiations focused primarily on the "exceptions," and not on every item in the tariff schedule. Agricultural goods, however, and all goods for those countries that stayed out of the linear procedure, were negotiated on an item-by-item basis.

The result of this new procedure at the end of the Kennedy Round in 1967 was an average tariff reduction of about 35 percent—not as good as the original goal of 50 percent, but quite significant nevertheless.

Negotiating Tariff Concessions: The Tokyo Round and the Uruguay Round

When the Tokyo Round was launched in 1973, it was assumed that a linear-cut approach would be used again. The authorizing U.S. statute this time allowed the president to agree to up to a 60 percent cut, but the negotiations in Geneva took a somewhat different approach. It was argued by some countries, and especially the EC, that higher tariffs should be cut deeper than lower tariffs.[24]

The argument was made that tariffs that were fairly low already did not have the actual protectionist effect at the border that their levels might imply. On the other hand, a high tariff, say 20 percent, might have a very powerful effect in keeping out imports. At some point a tariff becomes virtually prohibitive and keeps out almost all imports. If that point were, for example, 30 percent, with a current tariff of 60 percent, a 50 percent reduction of that high tariff would result in almost no additional imports. The EC approach was influenced also by the fact that the EC Common External Tariff (CET) was a relatively level one, because it had been set primarily from averaging the various tariffs of the EC member states. On the other hand, the EC argued, the U.S. tariff had more "peaks and valleys," and therefore for proper reciprocity to occur in a tariff reduction negotiation, the peaks should be lowered further than the average or the valley tariffs.

Although the objective for the Tokyo Round negotiation was to place priority on nontariff measures, the search for an appropriate linear "tariff-cutting formula" was a protracted and extensive part of the negotiation. Whether it was worth it, in tariff-cutting terms, is uncertain.[25] But some observers noted that during many months and even years, when very little progress was made in the Tokyo Round negotiation, the tariff-cutting discussions were the only aspects of the effort that seemed to engage the participants' attention. For that reason, the tariff negotiations have sometimes been called the "glue" that held the negotiation together.

Much staff effort and many computer runs were regained by the process of evaluating a variety of proposals for tariff cuts. In the end, the negotiators agreed on an interesting formula for tariff cutting (subject to "exceptions list" item negotiations, like those in the Kennedy Round). This formula is expressed as follows:

$$Z = \frac{AX}{A + X},$$

where X was the starting tariff (before the Tokyo Round), Z was the resulting tariff, and A was some constant coefficient. This coefficient could differ for different contracting parties, and so some of the negotiation was about the level of this coefficient. For the United States it was set at 14; for the EC it was set at 16.[26]

Taking these two coefficients and the formula above, the following example enables us to see the effect of the agreement.

$A =$	Start tariff $X =$	End tariff $Z =$	Calculation
EC = 16	10%	6.15	$(16 \times 10)/(16 + 10) = 160/26$
	20%	8.89	$(16 \times 20)/(16 + 20) = 320/36$
United States = 14	10%	5.83	$(14 \times 10)/(14 + 10) = 140/24$
	20%	8.24	$(14 \times 20)/(14 + 20) = 280/34$

As noted, the tariff-cutting results of the Tokyo Round, for dutiable industrial products imported to industrial countries, has been estimated to be about 35 percent, reducing weighted average tariffs to about 6.3 percent.[27]

For a variety of policy reasons, some nations in the Uruguay Round, particularly the United States, did not accept the procedure of linear- or formula-tariff reductions, preferring instead an item-by-item or, in some cases, a sectorial approach. Nevertheless, the results of the Uruguay Round include some substantial tariff reductions, as well as a few "zero-for-zero" sectors, meaning that for subjects such as pharmaceuticals, electronics, medical equipment, and paper, steel, and oilseed products a substantial number of the countries agreed reciprocally to zero tariffs phased in over time, and applied to all other members of the WTO through MFN.[28]

The Question of Reciprocity

The GATT does not require reciprocity (and indeed by amendments made during the mid-1960s urges industrial countries to refrain from seeking it from developing countries).[29] Usually, U.S. statutes authorizing U.S. participation in GATT negotiations also did not explicitly require reciprocity. Nevertheless, the practice in GATT among the major negotiating parties was always to seek reciprocity—whatever that means. The 1934 U.S. statute, it will be recalled, was entitled the Reciprocal Trade Agreements Act;[30] and it was implied, and the Congress assumed, that tariff and other barrier reductions would be agreed on a mutual and equivalent basis.

In fact, it may be argued as a matter of economic policy that reciprocity does not make much sense. The theories of comparative advantage can demonstrate that a country can often gain a welfare advantage even by unilaterally reducing its tariffs.[31] Of course, if more than one nation reduces its tariffs, this creates even greater welfare. Thus there is some advantage in a country using various "bargaining chips," including reducing its own tariffs to persuade other countries to reduce theirs as well. Regardless of the economics of these moves, one thing is very clear: the principle of reciprocity has had a very powerful political effect. It has been a significant motivator of public and government opinion in favor of inducing tariff reductions, even if the principle is fallacious, or partly so.

Assuming a goal of reciprocity, however, the question is: How do nations measure it? One way, often used but rather simplistic, is to measure the value of a particular tariff concession by multiplying the total value of imports of the product, in the most recent year for which statistics are available, by the number of percentage points of the tariff reduction. Thus, if bicycle imports to country A totaled $100 million last year, and the tariff concession being considered would reduce the tariff from 14 percent to 7 percent, the value of the concession would be $.07 \times 100$ million, or 7 million dollars. If one-half of these imports came from country B, then the value of the concession to B is $3.5 million, and A would ask B to give A in return a concession worth that amount.

This "trade coverage" approach, however, does not get at what is really desired by reciprocity, which is to influence roughly the same amount of *future* trade. Under an approach to estimate the "future value" of trade, one would try to estimate the amount of additional trade that would occur if the tariff were lowered a certain amount. This would require using "price elasticities of demand," which are figures not always easy to obtain and are sometimes suspect. Nevertheless, using the hypothetical case in the previous paragraph, one would take such elasticity and compute how much additional bicycle imports would occur if the tariff were lowered from 14 percent to 7 percent. This should have an effect on the importing country price of imported bicycles of slightly less than 7 percent (even less of the retail price, given that imports are normally valued at wholesale). If one ascertained that the effect would be to sell 25 percent more imported bicycles, the value would arguably be 25 million dollars, and A would seek that amount of equivalent concessions from all the bicycle-exporting countries in the negotiation.

Although some countries in the negotiation tried to utilize these calculations in their appraisal of offers and reciprocal offers,[32] this process is obviously rather imprecise as well as difficult. In the end, the negotiators generally admit that reciprocity is mostly a political judgment. Thus, at the end of a negotiation, nations that had been negotiating with each other may both claim to have "won" the negotiation! Different techniques of calculating the reciprocity effects of the agreement could enable both of them to make such a claim. Furthermore, it has been suggested to me that at the end of the Kennedy Round, for example, when the political judgment "at the highest level" was made to approve the results for a major country, the political leader nevertheless required his officials to return to their offices and recalculate the "advantage" for his country, so that when made public the advantage would look more favorable!

Another problem of a tariff negotiation is the differences in classification and valuation techniques in various countries. For example, most GATT countries use a CIF (cost, insurance, freight) valuation for imported products, whereas the United States uses a free-on-board (FOB) valuation ("free on board", which is generally lower because it excludes insurance and freight costs). When calculating the reciprocity value of a tariff reduction, some allowance must be made for the different effects of a tariff resulting from the different techniques of valuing goods. A change from a 15 percent tariff to a 10 percent tariff for imports to the EC, which uses CIF valuation, might be worth somewhat less reciprocally speaking than a like change by the United States using an FOB method.[33]

Can other principles be politically useful to encourage trade liberalization? One idea that became reasonably prominent in the legislative consideration of the Trade Act of 1974 was "sector harmonization."[34] Under this principle, an attempt would be made to reach an international agreement among key nations to achieve in each of them, for a particular product sector (e.g., "aircraft" or "steel"), roughly the same level of import restraint. Whereas under traditional reciprocity concepts, concessions could be swapped across sectors (A reduces bicycle tariffs in exchange for B reducing radio tariffs), in a sector approach the goal would be to achieve, at the end of the negotiation, approximately the same level of restraint for a product sector in all agreeing nations. An important enhancement of this principle is to include nontariff measures also, and to add up the values of the effects of those measures, probably as some sort of "tariff equivalents."[35]

Economically this approach has much merit. It means that firms are competing on a level playing field against other firms in the same business, regardless of nationality. It is very difficult to negotiate under this approach, however. Indeed, although this approach was stated in U.S. legislation to be an important goal for the Tokyo Round, in the end only one trade-liberalizing sectorial agreement—that on aircraft—was completed in that round. The difficulty is clear when one considers that two nations might begin the negotiation with vastly different levels of protection in a particular sector. Suppose country A has a 15 percent tariff on imports of steel and various nontariff restraints on imports that are the equivalent of another 10 percent tariff. This total of 25 percent protection could be compared to that of B for steel, and if the latter totals only 5 percent, how can B induce A to reduce its protection to the 5 percent level? Maybe B can offer A some comparable inducement in another sector where the ratios are inverse, but often there is little incentive for the higher-restraint country to move its protection toward a harmonized level. During the Uruguay Round, more progress was made in the direction of sectorial tariff reductions, including goals of "zero tariff" sectors, as indicated above.

During the early 1980s the U.S. Congress began discussing yet another concept of reciprocity.[36] Legislation was proposed that would have the U.S. government impose new import restraints on products from foreign countries (often meaning Japan) that did not reciprocally allow imports of U.S. products.[37] This "negative reciprocity" approach had much political appeal, but obviously poses many questions. If used as a sector-by-sector approach, it defeats some of the results of traditional reciprocity whereby cross-sector swaps have induced reduction of tariffs and other restraints. It also is likely to cause violation of current GATT and other international obligations, not the least of which is MFN.[38] For some of these reasons, many nations oppose these negative-reciprocity proposals, although this approach seems to some particularly attractive for certain service trading sectors, such as banking, or brokerage.

An extremely difficult question is how to utilize reciprocity concepts in negotiating nontariff measures. Theoretically, one might try to compute tariff-equivalent values of various nontariff measures. Some scholars have tried this, but obviously it is difficult, and it does not address some important issues. For example, when nations draft and sign an agreement on the treatment of subsidies in international trade, how can "reciprocity" play a role? First, how can one calculate the trade effect of such an agreement (especially when certain ambiguities or imponderables exist about future implementation)? Second, all nations may receive a value from the establishment of certain common and predictable rules of behavior regarding international trade, even if the value each receives is not always equal.[39]

5.3 Classification for Tariff Purposes

Virtually every tariff system depends on descriptions of products contained in a classification system. If a tariff were the same on all imported goods (similar to many sales taxes), then presumably no such classification system would be needed (except for statistical and reporting purposes). Given that tariffs vary greatly, however—from zero to high levels such as 30 percent or 40 percent or more—it is necessary to classify imported products in order to ascertain what tariff level will apply. The difference between a "work of art" and a "toy" may not always be obvious to a customs official, but it may make the difference between tariff-free treatment and a 25 percent duty. Thus, officials at the border must constantly make classification judgments; and in most major trading countries, like the United States, a system is in place to appeal these judgments to the courts.[40] An elaborate jurisprudence with principles of classification, such as *ejusdem generis* and *noscitur a sociis*, has grown up to aid courts, administrators, and importers in predicting the classification of goods. The GATT obligates contracting parties to publish regulations and provide for fair and judicial-type procedures (Article X). It also contemplates the importance of classification rulings and the danger that these could undermine the value of a concession. In such a case it provides for negotiation and "compensatory adjustment" (Article II:5).[41]

Negotiating tariff reductions and evaluating reciprocity is further complicated by differences in nomenclature. Translation tables are needed. Because these problems occur even between negotiating rounds, for purposes of "compensatory concessions" in an escape clause or binding withdrawal case, the nomenclature problem is a constant one.

In the past, many countries, including the EC and Japan, have used the Brussels Tariff Nomenclature (BTN) of product classification for tariff purposes, which was developed by the Customs Cooperation Council in Brussels.[42] The United States, on the other hand, previously adhered rather resolutely to its own classification system, known as the Tariff Schedules of the United States (TSUS).[43]

For reasons noted above and from a desire to improve statistical reporting, in the 1980's a number of nations (including the BTN members and the United States) negotiated a unified and revised product classification system that they all could accept. This Harmonized Commodity Description and Coding System was opened for signature in 1984 and has been adopted by many nations.[44] The implementation of the Harmonized Code by the United States, however, was complicated by the political battles over the 1988 trade act[45] which delayed its enactment until the statute became law in September 1988.

The MFN obligation often has the effect of increasing the complexity of classifications. If nation A is willing to grant a concession to nation B, but discovers that if it does so in an MFN manner it will benefit C while C will not reciprocate, then A has an incentive to subdivide the classification of the product so that even on an MFN basis it will tend to allow B's goods into A, without extending such benefit to C. This will work if there are identifiable differences between B's exports and C's exports. The classic and well-known example of this occurred in the 1904 Swiss-German treaty reducing German tariffs on the imports of: "... large dapple mountain cattle or brown cattle reared at a spot at least 300 meters above sea level and having at least one month's grazing each year at a spot at least 800 meters above sea level....[46]

A 1982 GATT panel decision, however, upheld a Brazilian challenge to the subdivided classification of coffee imports by Spain, saying that the "tilt" against types of coffee produced in Brazil was inconsistent with the phrase "like product" in the GATT MFN obligation.[47] A later GATT panel decision in 1989 however upheld a tariff classification that was challenged as an MFN violation.[48]

5.4 Valuation for Customs Purposes

Classification and valuation comprise the two important "pillars" of administering a customs tariff. Of course a tariff may be "specific" (for example, $0.50 per pound) and not need valuation. But most tariffs are ad valorem (e.g., 12 percent). Gradually many nations have shifted specific tariffs to ad valorem, because the latter tend to keep pace with inflation.[49] After the customs official values and classifies the products, he can calculate the actual tariff amount that must be collected, that is, he "liquidates" the import entry.

As with classification, many problems are associated with valuation. It has already been noted that differences in valuation methods make tariff-reduction negotiations more complex. Whereas most countries use a CIF basis for customs valuation, the United States has always used an FOB method of valuation.[50] It has even been argued that the U.S. Constitution requires this.[51] Prior to the Tokyo Round, the U.S. law was particularly troublesome. For various historical reasons, this law contained nine different methods of valuing goods for customs purposes, depending sometimes on classification and other times on different facts.[52] One objective of many countries in the Tokyo Round was to reduce the costs and delays associated with troublesome valuation systems. The result was a code (side agreement) entitled, Agreement on Implementation of Article VII, or the "valuation code", GATT Article VII being the article that governs customs-valuation procedures.[53] This "Code" as revised became part of the single package mandatory text (WTO Annex 1A) in 1994 and thus is binding on all WTO members.

The Valuation text establishes a series of definitions of value for customs purposes, with a ranking of how they are to be used. First, a contracting party should use a "transaction value" (i.e., the value set by the price of the goods in the particular transaction leading to the importation, provided it is genuine). Second, if the first approach will not work for stated reasons, the contracting party should use the "transaction value" of identical goods exported at about the same time and place. Third, if the first two approaches for some reason do not work, the transaction value of similar goods shall be used. If these three approaches cannot be used, two more approaches are mentioned, along with some choice as to which to use. Fourth, the price at which similar or identical goods are sold, adjusted by subtracting commissions, transport, and insurance incurred within the country of import, should be used. Fifth, the contracting party shall use a "constructed" value method by adding to the original cost of materials and fabrication, to make this method comparable to the transaction costs of the first few methods.

This code was one of the more successful of the Tokyo Round results, with over 30 countries (including the EC as one "country") accepting the code. In the United States the rules of this code have replaced the prior archaic and complex valuation system, and the result has been a dramatic decrease in appeals to the courts from administrative determinations of valuation—another good sign of success for the code.[54] The modifications to this text resulting from the Uruguay Round were very minor.[55]

With the growth over several decades of various preferential agreements, free trade areas, customs unions, etc., the process of liquidation of a customs entry also must take into account the "origin of goods." This has added another dimension to the work of customs officials at the borders in establishing the appropriate tariff rate. This will be discussed in the next chapter, which is devoted to MFN, at Section 6.4.

5.5 Quantitative Restrictions and Other Nontariff Measures

GATT Article XI prohibits the use of quotas or measures other than duties to restrict either imports or exports. Other articles in GATT provide exceptions for balance-of-payments reasons[56] and for developing countries.[57] In section 5.1, I outlined the reasons why government officials and economists generally think that quotas are a less desirable import restraint than tariffs. The experience of widespread and escalating use of quotas during the 1930s also influenced the ITO-GATT drafters to try to abolish this technique of trade restraint.[58]

Despite this GATT obligation, the attempt to eliminate the use of quotas has not been nearly so successful as the tariff-reduction obligations of GATT. During the early years of GATT, many nations other than the United States could claim some legal cover for quotas under the balance-of-payments (BOP) exceptions of GATT. When in 1958 the major western European trading nations established external currency convertibility, the BOP excuse began to fade, and the GATT undertook a program to try to get quotas eliminated. This program had some success, but it was least successful with respect to agricultural products, partly because the United States was using quotas on such products under the 1951 statute for which it had obtained a waiver. Other countries in GATT argued that, waiver or no waiver, if the United States could use quotas, they would also. With respect to nonagricultural products, many countries continued to maintain at least some quotas. These quotas gradually came to be known as "residuals," and many of them still exist.[59]

The government procedures for administrating quotas can be abused, leading to corruption or to delay and expense from the procedures themselves. For these reasons, the Tokyo Round negotiations completed an Agreement on Import Licensing Procedures designed to impose fair and efficient procedures in cases where quotas are used.[60] The agreement, (now part of the Uruguay Round mandatory text) obligates nations to avoid using licensing procedures in a manner that would have trade-restricting effects, calling for published information about quotas, equality of opportunity to apply for quotas, reasonable duration of quota periods, and so on.[61]

Some indication has been given that the Tokyo Round Agreement on licensing was not very effective in achieving its objectives. During the Uruguay Round this text was strengthened somewhat, but not changed dramatically.[62]

NonTariff Measures

The ingenuity of man to devise various subtle as well as explicit ways to inhibit the importation of competing goods is so great that any inventory of such measures quickly becomes quite large. In addition, it is clear that this ingenuity will never cease: like ways to avoid income tax, human invention of nontariff barriers will undoubtedly go on forever. The international and national institutions designed to cope with this problem must recognize this as part of the circumstances that they must contend with.

In the 1960s the GATT undertook an exercise to catalog nontariff barriers of all participating countries. One purpose of such an inventory was to prepare factual background that could be used in the next trade-negotiating round. By 1973 the catalog contained well over eight hundred NTBs, listed by country.[63] The UNCTAD has also conducted a research project to inventory trade barriers, and by 1986 had many more items on its country-by-country lists.[64] Some restrictions are the results of valid domestic policies, such as those to do with product standards or pollution control. The key question, as I will explain in later chapters, is whether such valid domestic policies have been implemented in a way that unnecessarily or arbitrarily restrict international trade.

Scholars have tried to estimate the "tariff-equivalent" effect of the various nontariff measures but have found this to be no easy task. A monograph by Morici and Megna of the National Planning Association is an example of such an effort. It suggests that the aggregate tariff-equivalent value of most U.S. nontariff measures is approximately 9 percent.[65] Stern and Deardorff of the University of Michigan have written about the conceptual difficulties of such measurements, and have made tentative estimates of their own.[66]

Examples of measures that appear to be designed to restrict the amount of imports are sometimes amusing. For example, in one case a country required canned foods to have labels in the language of that country *and no other* (so that economies of scale are lost by the requirement of different labels for different markets). Another example: an importing nation requires VCRs to be imported only through one customs office, which is located in an interior city and has a limited amount of staff to process the goods. Sometimes inspection requirements handily exclude imports, such as the case of the importing nation that requires inspection of the production process itself, but will not send an inspector abroad![67]

In recent years, several major trading countries (including the United States, the European Community, Japan, and Canada) have begun publishing an annual report that proports to inventory trade barriers of other nations. Some of these reports are quite voluminous, and perusing them can illustrate the wide variety of governmental measures used to help insulate domestic producers from foreign competition.[68]

One particularly important measure has been the "variable levy" utilized by the EC for its Common Agriculture Policy. Under the various CAP systems of levy, a tariff is charged on imports, but the tariff varies frequently, even day to day. The tariff is usually set at a level to offset any price advantage that foreign agricultural goods might have over goods produced within the EC. Given that the levy is a tariff, and that the EC either does not have bindings on some of the imported products or withdrew bindings on other imported products (and paid the "renegotiation compensation"), the EC can argue that the variable levy is consistent with GATT, in that it functions as a tariff on unbound items. The variable aspect of the levy, however, certainly defeats one of the basic policies behind the GATT preference of tariffs as a trade restriction. If the tariff is fixed, then efficient foreign producers may be able to "hurdle" it by becoming more efficient and lowering their prices. A maximum amount of protection against foreign competition is set, and when domestic producers become unable to compete even with the advantage of such a tariff, pressure to become more efficient will be put on them by imports. When the tariff varies, however, in a manner explicitly designed to prevent foreign competition at virtually any price, then the "hurdle possibility" of other tariffs is defeated.[69]

6 The Most-Favored-Nation Policy

6.1 Most-Favored-Nation Obligation and Its Politics

MFN has been a central pillar of trade policy for centuries. Article I of GATT has established the benchmark of a very broadly worded unconditional MFN obligation with respect to trade in goods. With the results from the Uruguay Round, the number of challenging MFN issues is on the rise, particularly with reference to the application of the MFN concept to the new subjects of trade in services and trade-related intellectual property matters. It is not always entirely clear that the MFN concept as applied to goods will easily transfer to services or intellectual property. The language of MFN in the Uruguay Round treaty text for services and for intellectual property is not identical to the language found in GATT Article I, which raises the question of how this new language will be interpreted. How significant will the analogy from goods dispute-settlement cases, or other policy declarations and interpretations, be for application of MFN for services or intellectual property? In this chapter, I focus primarily on the MFN concept as it has been elaborated and applied to trade in goods.

Two important principles of "nondiscrimination" are included in GATT and most international trade policies. The first is that of the MFN principle, expressed in Article I of GATT and in a number of bilateral and other treaties. Despite some confusion over the phrase "most favored"—which seems to imply a specially favorable treatment—the concept is one of equal treatment, but to that other party which is most favored. In the GATT the MFN obligation calls for each contracting party to grant to every other contracting party the most favorable treatment that it grants to any country with respect to imports and exports of products.

The second obligation of nondiscrimination—that of "national treatment"—is to treat foreign goods equally to domestic goods, once the foreign goods have cleared customs and become part of the internal commerce. In this chapter I deal with MFN, deferring until a later chapter the issue of national treatment (GATT Article III).[1]

The MFN obligation has a long history that is easily traced back to the twelfth century,[2] although the phrase seems to have first appeared in the seventeenth century. Growth of commerce in the fifteenth and sixteenth centuries seemed to be a major cause of MFN-type treaty clauses, as European nations competed with one another to develop networks of trading relationships. The United States included an MFN clause (albeit "conditional") in its first treaty, a 1778 treaty with France.[3] It has been speculated that early MFN clauses were a "shorthand" means of including a series of trade obligations in new treaties, without laboriously writing out these obligations.[4] In the 1800s and 1900s, the MFN clause, either conditional or unconditional, was included frequently in a variety of treaties, particularly in the Friendship, Commerce, and Navigation treaties.[5]

One question that has been debated is whether any sort of MFN or economic nondiscrimination obligation independent of a treaty clause exists under customary international law. The prevailing view of scholars is that such an obligation exists only when a treaty clause creates it. Lacking a treaty, nations presumably have the sovereign right to discriminate against foreign nations in economic affairs as much as they wish. It may be that the national treatment obligation differs in this respect, however.[6]

What are the policy arguments that underpin the MFN principle? We now turn to an examination of some of these arguments, as well as to some arguments against the MFN idea.

Sometimes MFN is equated with the concept of "multilateralism," but it must be recognized that the two concepts can be distinguished. Multilateralism is an approach to international trade and other relations that recognizes and values the interaction of a number—often a large number—of nation-states. It recognizes the dangers of organizing relations with foreign nations on bilateral grounds, dealing with them one by one. On the other hand, MFN is a standard of equal treatment of foreign nations. Many policies that favor MFN also favor multilateralism. It is of course possible to have multilateral approaches that do not depend on MFN; but the reverse seems relatively unlikely, although not impossible (for example MFN clauses can be contained in bilateral agreements).

At least two groups of arguments buttress the policy of MFN: first are the arguments that may loosely be called "economic," and second are the arguments that are political or "not-so-economic." With respect to the first category, several economic policy arguments in favor of MFN can be stated. To begin with, nondiscrimination can have a salutary effect of minimizing distortions of the "market" principles that motivate many arguments in favor of liberal trade. When governments apply trade restrictions uniformly without regard for the origin of goods, the market system of goods allocation and production will have maximum effect. Lamb meat will not be shipped halfway around the world when nearby markets could just as easily absorb it. A second economic argument is that MFN often causes a generalization of liberalizing trade policies, so that overall more trade liberalization occurs (the multiplier effect of the MFN clause). Third, MFN concepts stress general rules applicable to all participating nations, which can minimize the costs of rule formation (such as the difficulty of negotiating a multitude of bilateral agreements). Some theoretical arguments incidental to the "prisoner's dilemma" suggest that an optimum approach to avoid mutually destructive actions is to enter into an agreement that effectively restrains attempts by any party to engage in "exploitative" behavior. When many parties are involved (such as 128 members of the WTO), a generalized rule seems the best approach. In addition, of course, attention must be given to making the rule effective. Finally, MFN helps minimize transaction costs, because customs officials at the border may not need to ascertain the "origin of goods" to carry out their tasks with respect to goods controlled by MFN.

Turning to the second group of arguments, that is, the "political" side of MFN policies, we first can note that without MFN, governments may be tempted to form particular discriminatory international groupings. These special groupings can cause rancor, misunderstanding, and disputes because the countries that are "left out" resent their exclusion. Thus MFN can both lessen tensions among nations and inhibit government temptation to rely on short-term ad hoc policies that could result in creating more tension in a world already too tense.

It must be recognized, however, that counterarguments do exist, and that certain categories of nations take positions on some MFN policies that run contrary to the full implementation of MFN obligations. During recent decades this has been particularly true of developing countries,[7] which have argued that the GATT world trade system operates in a manner that inhibits the economic development of societies with weaker international economic status. In the view of these countries, "preferences" should be arranged to compensate for the operation of this system, and generally for charitable reasons to assist the poorer nations to develop faster. Obviously, these arguments have merit. The risk, however, is always that these arguments will be used to rationalize preferential systems that do not have the intended function of promoting economic development, but rather are used to assist national governments in fulfilling certain short-term nationalistic political objectives that are not materially related to overall economic development. In addition, during the last twenty-five years or so, the experience of the Generalized System of Preferences in the GATT System has been that for a number of reasons the preference-granting national entities (i.e., the industrialized countries) often succumb to the temptation to use the preference systems as part of the "bargaining chips" of diplomacy.

A second set of counterarguments stresses the risks posed by a unilateral unconditional MFN approach. These are the "foot-dragger" and "free-rider" arguments. To negotiate a general rule applicable to all nations in a system that stresses unanimity and consensus often means that a holdout nation can prevent agreement or cause its provisions to be reduced to the least common denominator. This can greatly inhibit needed improvement in substantive or procedural rules.[8]

On the other hand, for like-minded nations to go ahead with reforms and agreements without the "foot dragger," but to grant (as unconditional MFN requires) all the benefits of the new approach to the non-agreeing parties, gives the foot dragger unreciprocated benefits without any of the obligations. This furnishes an incentive to nations to stay out of the agreement. This is what led the United States to require nations to accept the Subsidies Code obligations as a condition to receiving beneficial U.S. treatment in countervailing duty cases (as specified in the Tokyo Round code).[9]

The Uruguay Round, of course, changed some of these issues in important respects. With the single-package idea and the requirement that all countries must accept all parts of the Uruguay Round results (except the Annex 4 plurilateral agreements), the question of MFN with regard to subordinate portions of the agreement is mostly eliminated. Some issues remain because of the existence of special exceptions (such as how the services agreement relates to financial services). And of course there are a number of de facto possibilities for departure from MFN through the use of definition of goods, or of service sectors, or the way that specific obligations are placed in schedules by member governments.

6.2 The Meaning of MFN

Introduction

What does MFN treatment mean? Essentially it is an obligation to treat activities of a particular foreign country or its citizens at least as favorably as it treats the activities of any other country. For example, if nation A has granted MFN treatment to B, and then grants a low tariff to C on imports from C to A, nation A is obligated to accord the same low-tariff treatment also to B and its citizens. The result of a nation being a beneficiary of an MFN clause is that that nation can comb all of the treaties and all of the actual treatment of the granting nation, to see if some obligation or real treatment is more favorable than that granted to it—in which case, the beneficiary can argue that such better treatment is owed to it.[10]

The subject to which MFN applies depends on the treaty clause. The GATT clause (Article I), for example, applies to trade in goods—both imports and exports. It does not, however, apply to the "right of establishment" (often found in FCN treaties), nor to "services" trade (e.g., banking, insurance, etc.).[11] Nevertheless, the GATT language is quite broad and covers a lot of territory.

Most-favored-nation clauses can be "conditional" or "unconditional," and in recent decades yet another MFN concept has appeared, which I will call "code-conditional."

Conditional and Unconditional MFN: Code Conditionality

Under conditional MFN, when country A grants a privilege to country C while owing MFN to country B, then country A must grant the equivalent privilege to B—but only after B has given A some reciprocal privilege to "pay for it."

Under unconditional MFN, in the case above, A must grant the equivalent privilege to country B without receiving anything in return from B. The United States pursued a "conditional MFN" policy prior to World War I, although by that time many major nations had moved to an unconditional approach. The United States, for its part, changed to an unconditional policy in 1923.[12]

Several arguments are often given for the unconditional approach over the conditional. In the first place, it is very difficult to negotiate for reciprocal concessions from a third-party beneficiary of benefits. When A grants to C a privilege, and B knows that MFN obligations require that privilege to go to B also, albeit after "payment," the incentive is not very strong for B to be too forthcoming in a bargaining process with A. Such negotiations can generate more rancor and trouble than they are worth. Second, unconditional MFN can help spread trade liberalization faster, given that any concession by a particular country is generalized to apply very broadly.[13] The GATT MFN clause is clearly unconditional.

A different type of MFN concept has arisen in connection with various codes or side agreements on trade matters negotiated in the Tokyo Round. In some of these codes, certain code members took the position that the benefits of code treatment would only be granted to nations that became members of the code (or at least reciprocated with code treatment). Thus, if A, B, and C belonged to a code that called for an "injury" test requirement before countervailing duties can be applied to imports, A could argue that it need not give such "test" to the imports from X, which was not a code member.[14] Sometimes this has been called "conditional MFN," but in fact it is not the same as the traditional "conditional MFN" concept, given that it does not require a particular negotiation of reciprocal benefits. Instead, the code itself defines the nature of the reciprocity that is owed in order to receive the advantage of this type of MFN. The advantage of "code conditionality" is that it creates an incentive for other nations to join a code and submit to its discipline. If a general MFN obligation (e.g., in GATT) required all code nations to grant the favorable code treatment to nations that did not become code members, there would be substantially less incentive for such nations to join. They can take a "free-rider" approach and claim the benefits without having to incur the discipline of code membership.

Although the Uruguay Round greatly diminishes issues of this type, the possibility still exists of such issues arising under the optional or plurilateral agreements of Annex 4. Indeed, Annex 4 in some ways may be *the locus of the texts* for important innovative and potential evolutionary activities of the WTO, as it faces new issues such as environment, competition policy, and investment rules. Some of these could be designed with a code-conditional MFN as a way to make progress that might otherwise be stymied by problems discussed earlier in this chapter.

Applying the Clause

It is not always easy to determine the way the MFN obligation applies. First, in the GATT and many other agreements, the language of the obligation speaks of MFN treatment for "like products." So the question often arises as to what "like products" are.[15] This question relates frequently to the question of classifications for tariff purposes which I discussed in chapter 5. When country A wishes to differentiate its treatment of countries B and C, regarding tariffs on radios, for example, one way to do this is to analyze the imports from B and from C to discern any distinguishing characteristics. If it is discovered that B ships FM radios, while C ships

AM radios, then A will be tempted to charge a higher tariff on FM radios, if it intends to favor C or disfavor B. As I noted in section 5.3, this is one of the reasons for narrower classifications within tariff schedules.

A 1952 GATT dispute case reveals an important consideration in the process of applying MFN clauses.[16] Norway and Denmark complained that a Belgian law levying charges on imported goods differed according to the nature of family allowances in the exporting country. Although the language of the report in this case was not very clear, the report did conclude that Article I of GATT had not been fulfilled. The case can be interpreted to support the proposition that although treatment can differ if the characteristics of goods themselves are different, differences in treatment of imports cannot be based on differences in characteristics of the exporting country that do not result in differences in the goods themselves. On the other hand, as chapter 5 noted, a 1982 GATT panel found in favor of Brazil that Spain had not lived up to GATT MFN obligations when it subdivided its customs classification of coffee and applied a much higher duty on those types of coffee imported from Brazil. The panel stated that the coffees were so nearly the same that they were "like products," and that this must be treated nondiscriminatorily even though no tariffs were binding by Spain on the product.[17] (But contrast the Japan Dimension Lumber Case of 1989, noted in section 5.3.)

6.3 Exceptions to MFN and Potential for Bilateralism

The Variety of Exceptions

Despite the policies and legal obligations that support MFN, it is widely recognized that substantial departures from MFN in international trade practice are evident. Indeed, it has been estimated that 25 percent of all world trade moves under some form of discriminatory regime that is a departure from MFN principles.[18]

Some of these departures were anticipated by the original drafters of the MFN clauses, such as in GATT. For example, it has been recognized for centuries that although a tariff may be established on an MFN basis, classifications of tariff items can to some extent operate effectively to discriminate among the goods of various countries (as I noted in the previous section).[19]

In addition, when the GATT was drafted, a number of preferential systems were in existence, most prominently the Commonwealth Preference System. The final GATT text recognized that some of these preferential systems could continue as something like grandfather exceptions to the GATT, with the assumption that in due time the effect of those preferences would decline. Thus, annexes to GATT explicitly provide for such exceptional treatment from MFN.[20]

Other exceptions, such as the problem of Article XIX (escape clause),[21] questions that have arisen in the context of the Tokyo Round codes,[22] and the opportunity for nations to "opt out" of a GATT relationship pursuant to Article XXXV of GATT,[23] are discussed elsewhere in this book. It should be noted that if the WTO authorizes a responding action under the dispute settlement rules, such action need not be taken on an MFN basis.[24]

Furthermore, waivers can sometimes authorize departures from MFN. Two important examples of this are the United States-Canada Automotive Products Agreement (which allows a free trade area for automotive products),[25] and the United States preferences granted to the Caribbean basin.[26] The Generalized System of Preferences (GSP) program to favor trade of less developed countries operated under the benefit of a waiver from GATT MFN from 1971 to 1981.[27] Later it was presumed to be authorized by the Tokyo Round understanding, called the "enabling clause" but officially entitled the understanding on "Differential and More Favorable Treatment, Reciprocity, and Fuller Participation of Developing Countries."[28] The "enabling clause" is presumed to continue in the WTO, although its status may not be entirely clear.

GATT Article XX "general exceptions"[29] can allow departures from MFN, but there is in that article another "soft" MFN obligation.[30]

Quantitative restrictions often pose an important conceptual challenge to the MFN principle. If a licensing system is used that is based on a "global quota," open to all equally on a first-come, first-served basis, or on a system of auctioning licenses to the highest bidder, then MFN seems realized. But, as is often the case, when quotas or licenses are allocated on a geographical or enterprise basis—even if they are related to historical trading patterns—then to some extent MFN is not completely fulfilled, because different countries or enterprises will have different types of fixed rights. GATT Article XIII establishes a "quasi"—MFN principle for many such cases, which primarily relies on historical patterns of prior allocation of quotas.

In a similar context, the explosion of the use of export-restraint arrangements in world trade provided one of the most significant recent challenges to the MFN principle of GATT. In the widespread use of so-called voluntary restraint agreements, or orderly market arrangements, the typical application is on a bilateral basis and often provides de facto discrimination. Thus, countries that have proved most successful in rapidly expanding their exports of particular products become the targets of importing country governments' pressures to adopt export restraints of one form or another. In this context Japanese automobile restraints on the U.S. market immediately come to mind.[31] Whether or not the new Uruguay Round Agreement on Safeguards (see chapter 7) will succeed in prohibiting the use of voluntary restraint arrangements is unclear, although the text language purports to do so.

Finally, this brief inventory of some of the discriminatory or non-MFN activities within the current world trading system is not complete without noting the real difficulty of this problem for nonmarket economies. When the enterprises that do the trading—either imports or exports—are doing so not according to market principles but according to government commands, it is very hard to police any notion of MFN nondiscrimination. A government can always argue that it is not discriminating, and can often conceal the noneconomic motivations that have led to command differential orders for imports or treatment for exports. In this connection, the problem of reconciling the forms of economic organization of nonmarket economies with the particular obligations of GATT, which were designed for market economies, is not unique.[32] This problem comes up in a number of different types of obligations of GATT.[33] Similar problems arise in the context of so-called countertrade.

Customs Unions and Free Trade Areas

One of the most prominent and difficult problems engendering exceptions to MFN and GATT is found in GATT Article XXIV, which provides exceptions for customs unions (CUs), free trade areas (FTAs), and interim agreements leading to either. This article has furnished an extremely large loophole for a wide variety of preferential agreements.[34] An article in the Uruguay Round Services Agreement that has a similar thrust could also pose problems, although it is too soon to know.

GATT Article XXIV is based partly on the historical precedent of special regimes of frontier traffic between adjacent countries, and partly on the policy that total world welfare can be enhanced by regimes of trade that totally eliminate restrictions to trade among several countries. This is sort of an "all or nothing" idea, which tolerates some of the disadvantages of preferential treatment of trade in exchange for substantial liberalization of trade among several nations. It recognizes the "free-rider" or "foot-dragger" disadvantages of MFN, allowing particular departures from MFN to facilitate trade liberalization if such liberalization goes far enough to provide substantial global advantages. This article is also designed to allow such departures from the MFN principle for the purpose of trade creation, while discouraging regimes leading to trade diversion.

For these reasons, the GATT exceptions for customs unions and free trade areas provide several significant limitations.[35] First, the MFN departures are in theory allowed only for CUs or FTAs that are defined to require liberalization on "substantially all" the trade involved. Second, regarding the CU, the GATT article requires that the common tariff arrangements of the preferential group toward third-country "external" trade not be "on the whole" more restrictive than the "general incidence of" duties and regulations before the CU was formed. These are difficult legal concepts to apply, however, and they have caused much controversy in the GATT. In addition, the GATT exception allows an "interim agreement"—one that leads to a CU or FTA within a reasonable time—to depart from MFN. This has opened a loophole of considerable size, because almost any type of preferential agreement can be claimed to fall within the exception for interim agreement, and "reasonable time" is exceedingly imprecise.[36] Indeed, despite notification of over one hundred Article XXIV-type arrangements—some of which provide very loose preferences as interim agreements and no set date for completion of the FTA—no formal record of GATT "disapproval" of such arrangements exists.[37]

The Uruguay Round results include an "Understanding on the Interpretation of Article XXIV of the General Agreement on Tariffs and Trade 1994," which was designed by the negotiators to address some of these problems. Although not changing the actual language of Article XXIV of GATT 1994 (which of course is part of WTO Annex 1A), the understanding sets forth certain interpretations and guidelines for handling some of the ambiguities in Article XXIV. Significantly, the understanding also provides that the dispute-settlement provisions of GATT 1994 (which presumably now means the WTO dispute-settlement procedures) may be invoked with respect to any matter arising under Article XXIV relating to customs unions, free trade areas, or interim agreements. This was an issue that came up in cases brought against the European Community for its regulations on bananas. The negotiators resolved to reinforce the opinions in the two panel reports on bananas, which indicated that Article XXIV could be invoked, despite an argument that Article

XXIV has some separate procedures that could arguably be applied to some disputes.[38]

6.4 Rules of Product Origin

The customs laws of many nations require identification of the country of origin for imported goods. If true MFN were followed for all goods and all origins, then presumably no need would exist for such rules.[39] In fact, however, there is considerable differentiation of treatment of imports, depending on their origin. For example, if six GATT parties form a customs union so as to free all trade among them from tariffs, then at least three levels of tariffs may apply to goods imported into one of those six: the GATT bound-tariff level for GATT parties that are not in the customs union; tariff-free treatment for customs-union goods; and tariffs on goods from other countries that are not GATT parties. Thus, when widgets are imported, it may be necessary to determine from which of the three groups of countries the goods originated. In some cases there can be more than three categories, when other special preferential areas exist.[40]

In addition to the problem mentioned, there is also the "transshipment" question. Let us say that countries A, B, and C belong to GATT, but country X does not. Suppose X ships tires to B, which then ships them to C, where C plans to charge a tariff of 12 percent. If C's tariff binding on tires is 10 percent, and C actually charges 8 percent on tires from A, can B claim benefits from either the GATT binding (10 percent maximum) or GATT's MFN clause for its tire shipment to C? The answer is no, because the products are not products of B. They are products of X, and the GATT obligations apply only to the products of GATT members.

Now imagine that X produces plastic pellets, which are shipped to B. In B these are melted and extruded into combs. Can B ship the combs to C and claim GATT benefits? The key question is whether the products are those of B. Merely transshipping, or even merely repackaging X products, would probably not obtain for B the GATT treatment for the combs. But when substantial processing occurs, then B can claim the goods are now B's product. But how much processing is necessary?

GATT does not offer a single definitive answer to this question. Instead, each country, within the bounds of reasonableness, has a sovereign right to define the "rules of origin" that will govern the determinations of its customs officials about the origin of goods presented for import. Indeed, the same country may have several different "rules of origin," depending on the purpose of the regulation governing the particular imports. There is, however, a multilateral convention covering rules of origin. The Kyoto Convention (concluded under the auspices of the Customs Cooperation Council in 1974) contains, in Annex D:2, certain rules for the determination of origin.[41] The EC adopted this convention in 1977. The United States, however, only partially ratified the convention in 1983,[42] and did not accept the provisions on rules of origin.

The U.S.-Canadian FTA contains a measure regarding rules of origin that has already proven somewhat controversial.[43] Likewise, NAFTA contains a number of measures regarding rules of origin, some of which are extraordinarily complicated, and give rise to the suspicion that they are designed to inhibit nonpartner trade into the free trade area.[44] The Uruguay Round negotiators tried to address this lacuna in rule structure, but had only moderate success. The resulting text on rules of origin provide certain basic obligations regarding these rules, but mostly provide for a future study and negotiation with a view toward eventually harmonizing them.[45]

Two fundamental approaches to the rules of origin problem have been widely used. One approach is based on the "substantial transformation" principle, under which a product becomes attributed to the most recent exporting country only if within that country there has been a "substantial transformation" of the input goods obtained from another country. One test, sometimes mentioned, is whether the goods have been changed sufficiently to cause them to be listed under a different heading in the tariff classification. The problem with this approach is that different parts of the tariff classification have different levels of detail, and somewhat arbitrary results can occur.[46]

A second approach is a "value-added," or percentage-value, approach. Under this principle, goods are attributed to the last country of export if that country has added a certain percentage of value to those goods. For example, the U.S. rule-of-origin law governing goods imported to the United States under the GSP rules is that the goods must in general contain 35 percent of their value in materials or processes originating in beneficiary developing countries.[47]

Occasionally, rules of origin generate complaints from exporting countries when such rules are deemed to unfairly restrict imports from the complainant. For example, the United States became quite upset about standards for rules of origin in some free trade agreements between the EC and other European countries (former EFTA partners). Allegedly, the rule required 95 percent of the value of goods to be attributed to the free trade partner,[48] thus reducing the opportunity for the United States to sell parts or partially completed products to EC countries in competition with favored third-country goods.

The North American Free Trade Agreement (NAFTA) among the United States, Mexico, and Canada contains an entire chapter on rules of origin (chapter 4). One of the most complex and convoluted rules in that chapter is in Article 403 concerning automotive goods. It appears that this Article can only be read to have an intent to restrain import competition for automotive parts and automotive goods from third countries. The key question is whether this restraint would be seen as a fair restraint to limit the benefits of the NAFTA to the participating country producers, or whether there is an additional element of "trade distortion."[49]

6.5 MFN, Bilateralism, and Possible Trends: Some Conclusions

One of the earliest post-1945 departures from MFN by the United States was its exclusion of communist countries from such treatment in 1951.[50] During the 1960s, however, the United States began a series of moves that related to its more traditional trading partners, with the development and 1965 implementation of the United States-Canada Automotive Products Agreement.[51] The United States obtained a GATT waiver from its MFN obligations for this agreement, and at least some observers commented at the time that the agreement and waiver efforts helped undermine U.S. advocacy of MFN and multilateralism in connection with other GATT exercises such as GSP.[52]

Despite various U.S. reservations about GATT and some of its rules (chronicled in other chapters),[53] in general the United States has been a strong supporter of both the principles of multilateralism and non-discrimination as embodied in the unconditional MFN clause of GATT. These principles were pillars of United States policy during the drafting of GATT and its formative years. Through the 1960s, for example, the United States continued to express skepticism and hostility toward the proposal of developing countries to carve out an exception to MFN to allow a "generalized system of preferences" to provide particularly favorable conditions of trade for developing country exports. The United States was the last major industrialized country to implement the GSP policy, which had been called for by the international and multilateral institutions, including the GATT.[54]

Likewise, although the United States had tolerated and perhaps even favored the formation of the European Community, partly for broader strategic reasons, the United States found itself well into the 1970s increasingly skeptical about the benefits and directions of that and other regional trade groups in international trade. The United States particularly viewed a series of agreements between the European Community and four or five dozen developing countries—the so-called Lomé Convention and its predecessors—as detracting from MFN principles of GATT. These conventions provided preferential treatment between the EC and each other member of the convention. The Congress specified certain conditions regarding this convention in its 1974 legislation, refusing to extend GSP benefits to developing countries that afforded preferential treatment to developed countries (so-called reverse preferences).[55]

In the Tokyo Round (1973–1974), the United States also took steps that departed from unconditional MFN. In the 1974 trade act the Congress mandated that the United States try to offset the "free-rider" problem, at least of industrial countries, by withholding MFN treatment from certain countries if they did not provide reciprocal advantages in the results of a negotiation. In addition, the United States refused to give unconditional MFN status to all GATT members in connection with the obligations of three of the Tokyo Round Codes.[56] Clearly, however, the United States was again concerned about the "free-rider" problem, and the need to provide an incentive for countries to enter into the discipline of the codes.

More recently, one of the most visible and acrimonious trade relationships has been between the United States and Japan. The United States has essentially dealt with this on a bilateral level, rarely going to a multilateral forum, possibly in part because it distrusted the effectiveness of that forum. At the end of the Tokyo Round, the United States entered into bilateral negotiations with Japan for additional and special concessions under the Government Procurement Code, for purchases by the Japanese telephone company, Nippon Telegraph Telephone, (NTT).[57] Subsequently, they have engaged in frequent bilateral meetings, and institutional mechanisms have been set up to try to ameliorate their problems.[58] Europe also had similar difficulties with Japan. Yet neither the United States nor Europe—nor for that matter Japan—seemed inclined to focus these troubled bilateral relationships in the multilateral forum of GATT, although some specific cases and representations have been made in GATT about the "Japan problem."[59]

From the beginning of the Reagan administration in 1981, statements by the U.S. trade representative and his deputies hinted at a willingness of the administration to consider the potential of bilateral actions, at least where multilateral activities seemed ineffective. For example, in November 1985, Ambassador Yeutter said:

> We simply cannot afford to have a handful of nations with less than 5 percent of world trade dictating the international trading destiny of nations which conduct 95 percent or more of international commerce in this world....
>
> We would still like to go the GATT route with a new round.... That is the preferred course of action; but if those discussions bog down in Geneva 2 weeks from now to where it becomes evident that a new GATT round is not likely to occur, or simply could not occur with those issues included, then we would prefer to pass on a GATT round. In our judgement, this is not a negotiable issue. Services, in particular, must be in the round or we are just not going to have a new GATT round from the US standpoint; and we will have to confront those issues in a different way—plurilaterally or multilaterally.[60]

President Reagan reiterated this tough stance taken by his administration:

> To reduce the impediments to free markets, we will accelerate our efforts to launch a new GATT negotiating round with our trading partners, and we hope that the GATT members will see fit to reduce barriers for trade in agricultural products, services, technologies, investments and in mature industries. We will seek effective dispute-settlement techniques in these areas. But if these negotiations are not initiated or if insignificant progress is made, I am instructing our trade negotiators to explore regional and bilateral agreements with other nations.[61]

Later, additional statements by high administration officials hinted at a growing U.S. impatience with multilateral approaches.[62] Congressional efforts to promote reciprocity also seemed to tilt away from multilateralism toward bilateralism in many respects.[63]

Even when an MFN policy is ostensibly being carried out, an examination "beneath the surface can" sometimes detect a strong bilateral effect. For example, in the escape-clause case on motorcycles, the quotas that were actually implemented seem to affect Japan, but very few other countries.[64] Likewise, during the massive group of antidumping and countervailing duty cases on steel brought in 1982, the United States found it convenient to negotiate extensively with the EC. In many ways, the EC and the United States bypassed the GATT in working out their conflicts in the context of that series of cases.[65]

In 1983, the United States proposed and subsequently implemented a preference for Caribbean Basin nations.[66] Some suggested that this may have represented a major watershed in United States policy, although it was not particularly noticed to be such at the time. Later, a bilateral free trade area was negotiated and implemented with Israel.[67] Subsequently, a free trade agreement between the United States and Canada was completed.[68]

Later, NAFTA was negotiated; and the United States has begun to show interest in other regional possibilities, such as the Asian Pacific Economic Cooperation (APEC) group and even a trans-Atlantic "dialogue." In a broader context, an important question facing the new WTO is the relationship of regionalism to the multilateral trading system. In a 1993 article, I wrote that

> "All these factors make it reasonably clear that the GATT and its Article XXIV, as well as the more ambiguous legal framework of the 1979 Enabling Clause, are grossly inadequate for the tasks required of a multilateral system to provide some sort of adequate supervision and discipline on certain of the more dangerous tendencies of trading blocs. GATT Article XXIV is out of date, and some would say fatally flawed from the outset (given its inability to impose some GATT discipline.) This raises the question of what needs to be done in the future.
>
> Some subjects for consideration in this regard might include:
>
> 1. Strengthened GATT/MTO review of new agreements, with strong emphasis on transparency. In many ways, the preferential agreements are justified (even in some cases when they don't meet the Article XXIV criteria). They provide an outlet for smaller groups of countries to go well beyond what the GATT seems able to design in the way of rules and disciplines for international trade relations, and this is often commendable. Likewise, they provide an opportunity for experimentation with various rules which can then later be assimilated into the broader multilateral system. But it can be argued that a more detailed report should be presented to the GATT and available to all Contracting Parties, and opportunity to comment (and in some cases, depending on specific rules such as those in the Dunkel text, to impose a requirement of change) be made available.
> 2. Regular periodic reviews should be strengthened. Periodic reviews of preferential trade blocs could be developed along the lines of the new TPRM (Trade Policy Review Mechanism) of the GATT.
> 3. GATT dispute settlement provisions should be available, as suggested by the Dunkel Draft, to challenge "nullification or impairment" imposed on third parties by preference arrangements.
> 4. There should be an opportunity to develop some specific rules which would obligate the preference partners and the preference arrangement institutions, so as to provide the basis of a complaint under dispute settlement processes. These rules might require, for example, regulatory actions to be the "least trade restrictive" possible. The rules of origin provisions in the GATT Dunkel text are also highly relevant and could be extremely important.[69]

As this is written in 1997, the World Trade Organization has established a committee with jurisdiction over regional trade blocs, and the development of principles to review the operation and relationship of these blocs. But in the view of this author, it must be recognized that there are policy objectives one could call "noneconomic" in this context also.

Of course, there are links between the rules of trading blocs and a multilateral trading system, with such subjects as investment, monetary policy, environmental quality, etc. But there are also clearly links to subjects such as human rights, democratization, demilitarization, and other political relationships, such as arms control. These links cannot be totally ignored, and indeed it has sometimes been said that economic integration, such as that experienced in some of the trading blocs (especially Europe), simply would not work satisfactorily even to achieve economic goals, without the help of a strong political goal to motivate economic integration. In Europe this goal was seen from the inception of the European economic integration institutions (the Coal and Steel Community of 1952, and the Treaty of Rome of 1957) as relating to the overwhelming objective of preventing World War III, and particularly preventing conflict between France and Germany. In other regional blocs, political goals may not be so obvious, but they surely exist in the background. Thus, in considering the relationship of a multilateral trading system to trade blocs, we must be cognizant of noneconomic goals.

In sum, the inconsistent history of U.S. policy makes it difficult to forecast its future, but much has taken place, particularly during the last decade, to suggest the possibility that the United States has gradually moved away from its earlier adamant support for MFN and multilateralism toward a more "pragmatic"—some might say "ad hoc" approach—of dealing with trading partners on a bilateral basis and "rewarding friends." Whether the new WTO and its evolution will have influence on U.S. and other member thinking about multilateralism remains to be seen.

7 Safeguards and Adjustment Policies

7.1 The Policies and History of the Escape Clause and the International Structure for Safeguards

Introduction to the Policies of Safeguards

The term "safeguards" is generally used to denote government actions responding to imports that are deemed to "harm" the importing country's economy or domestic competing industries. These mechanisms often take an "import restraining" form, whether they be increased tariffs, quantitative restrictions, "voluntary" restraints by the exporting countries, or other measures. As such, the term "safeguards" embraces a number of legal and political concepts, including that of the escape clause, which for many decades has been built into national and international rules regarding international trade.[1] For the first time in the history of GATT, the Uruguay Round negotiators were finally able to come up with a new safeguards agreement, one that contains a number of interesting principles. It is too soon to evaluate how successful this code will be in bringing an additional measure of international trade-rule discipline to a variety of government restrictive activities, but the code text is very ambitious. Negotiators in the earlier Tokyo Round tried valiantly to develop a code on safeguards, but that effort totally failed. Thus special credit must be given to the Uruguay Round negotiators for their success (so far) with safeguards.

If "liberal trade" policies and practices did not exist, we would not need to consider safeguards as such. It is only because international economic policies have emphasized reduction of border barriers to trade that the subject of safeguards, as an exception to the general rule of liberal trade opportunities, comes into play. Thus, the question arises, why should there be this type of exception to normal liberal trade policies? In other words, what are the policies that justify the use of import restraints for escape-clause or safeguard reasons?

In general two arguments have been put forth for safeguard/escape clause actions. Other arguments for the use of import restraints, such as those related to national security needs.[2] Have been mentioned, but for safeguard actions—often described as actions of a temporary nature taken to impede imports that are causing "injury" to competing domestic industries—the policies seem to focus on an "economic-adjustment" goal, plus a more general "pragmatic" recognition of practical politics.[3]

The economic-adjustment argument for safeguards can be briefly stated as follows: Imports, particularly recently increasing imports, often cause harm to selected groups within an importing society, even though they may in the long term and in the broader aggregate increase the welfare of that society. Competing domestic firms will be forced to "adjust" to the imports, either by improving their competitiveness (productivity, price, quality, etc.), or by moving resources out of production of the competing products into production of other products. This adjustment process has often been viewed as "temporary," although it may be costly. Consequently, it is argued that a temporary period of time of some relief from imports will allow the domestic competing industry the opportunity to take the necessary adjustment measures.[4]

The problem, of course, is not this simple. Many other causes of adjusment exist in an economy: consumer tastes change; government programs (pollution controls, defense spending, fiscal and monetary measures, energy conservation) change; and these also can create great adjustment costs and pressures.[5] Why then should adjustment caused by imports be a justification for government intervention and aid, when adjustment caused by other forces is not? Answers vary. First, adjustments caused by forces other than imports do sometimes cause government responses to soften their impact; special additional unemployment compensation, investment aids, community actions, and so on, are all occasionally employed to assist those affected by onerous adjustments demands.[6]

Second, it is often observed that producers are better organized to bring pressure on government than are consumers.[7] In addition, if adjustment is analyzed as an action required by a relative few to bring about broadly spread benefits to a great many (like the government taking of property for public purposes such as a highway), an equity argument may be made for shifting the burdens of adjustment, from concentration on those few to the many who benefit, by distributing the burdens through taxes or higher prices.[8]

This leads easily into the second category of argument for safeguard policies, that is, the pragmatic or political argument. This argument also recognizes that producers often are better organized to influence governments. It also recognizes that with respect to imports, an important interested party is the foreign producer-seller. This party, however, does not vote in the importing country, so its influence in the decision-making process of that country is likely to be very small. In short, the political forces for border protection against imports are often formidable. Those who accept the policy arguments favoring liberal trade (i.e., disfavoring import barriers) feel that to insist too rigidly on the fullest application of their principles could lead to a general dismantling of the policies of the last several decades that have reduced import barriers. Consequently, they argue, it is better pragmatically to give in to the idea of temporary and limited import barriers for specific (and hopefully not too significant) cases as a way not only to alleviate some of the burdens of adjustment, but also to diminish the pressures for a more drastic departure from the general approach to imports. Some would describe this approach as "buying votes."

Of course, burdens of adjustment can be alleviated by means other than import barriers (and some would challenge whether border barriers really do alleviate adjustment burdens). Direct government assistance (or tax relief) is another way to provide relief. Programs of this type also have been utilized in varying degrees. In the United States, for example, since the 1962 Trade Expansion Act various programs of "trade-adjustment assistance" have been developed, as we will see later in this chapter.[9]

The concept of safeguards, when safeguards are justified on "adjustment" grounds, bears a strong relation to concepts of so-called industrial policy. If adjustment truly is the rationale for temporary safeguard actions to limit imports, then it follows that it might be appropriate for the government to demand an effective adjustment program from the industry concerned and/or to tailor government policies (including direct or tax aids) to encourage and assist such adjustment. It is commonly thought that the government of Japan does a fairly effective job in this regard (although some would challenge that proposition), and it is clear that Europe has tried this approach, albeit with varied success.[10]

What has been said in this section does not depend on the import trade being in any way "unfair." Traditionally, in trade policy circles "fair" trade has been sharply distinguished from "unfair" trade.[11] "Unfair" trade is normally deemed to include trade that has been influenced or promoted by activities such as "dumping," providing government subsidies, or foreign sellers attempting to evade legitimate regulations regarding the environment, fair competition, intellectual property protection, and so on. To counter these activities, it is often said that an importing nation is justified in taking import-restraining actions of various types. Safeguards policies, on the other hand, are justified for those imports that are perfectly "fair"—that is, untainted by any of the activities just described. Even if they are "fair," imports can cause burdens of adjustment for which an argument can be made to grant government relief.

It often becomes extremely difficult, however, to keep the concepts of fair trade separate from those of unfair trade. First, what is fair in an increasingly interdependent world with a variety of economic systems is very hard to define.[12] Second, unfair trade also causes burdens of adjustment, and so arguably qualifies for safeguards policies. The traditional GATT (and many national systems) often try to distinguish between unfair trade policies and safeguards polices by requiring a higher standard of harm to domestic competing industries, and a more stringent test of "cause by imports," for the safeguard policies to come into play. In practical institutional terms, as a result in part of the vagueness of the concepts involved (How does "serious injury" differ form "material injury"? How does "substantial cause" differ form "ordinary cause"?), nations have found it very difficult to keep these categories separate. Domestic complainants facing major burdens of adjustment comb the statutes and laws for ways to prevent imports, whether those laws be designed for unfair imports or based on safeguard policies. Escape-clause cases are sometimes brought when industries feel that imports are "unfair" but have difficulty in establishing the proof of unfairness required by the national administrative processes.[13]

In a world of increasing economic interdependence, additional arguments may exist to support safeguard programs. For example, let us suppose that two countries with different economic systems are engaged in trade. If one country is primarily "market-economy oriented" and the other is "nonmarket" oriented, entrepreneurs in one may feel that economic practices in the other pose an unfair competitive threat.[14] American firms sometimes argue that they can compete as long as they do not have to compete against the treasury of the foreign country.

This argument is somewhat valid. But to try to design national or international rules to respond to this type of situation is difficult. Many foreign practices are not unfair in the eyes of the foreign firms. The problem is rather that the differences between the two economies create stresses on one of the economies when the two trade extensively. Nothing may be unfair about the practices of either, but the differences cause perceptions of unfairness, and in fact these differences may create political and adjustment pressures in one of the societies to change its system. Foreign government subsidies of exports cause importing-country government officials and businessmen to consider offsetting subsidies or other practices to preserve the values of their own economic system. In preserving them, however, the system may in fact be altered. Arguably international trading rules should be designed to allow at least some measure of independent choice of economic systems for societies. (I will explore these issues further in later chapters.[15])

One possible solution could be included in a safeguards policy. In this sense, safeguards become a sort of "border buffer" to prevent too much pressure for change of the domestic economic structure resulting from increased international trade originating in economies that are structured differently. But this "solution," as is true of so much of safeguards policy, runs the considerable risk of eroding the basic principles of liberal trade.

History of Safeguards Measures

The modern era of safeguards measures stems from the beginning of the U.S. Reciprocal Trade Agreements program of its 1934 act. This statute launched the program of trade liberalization that is still a fundamental part of U.S. trade policy today. Even in that original program, however, the germ of a safeguards policy was evident.[16]

The "escape clause," as we currently think of it (a provision to allow temporary border barriers to imports when imports are increasing and can be shown to "injure" domestic competing industry), was first introduced into a U.S. reciprocal trade agreement in the U.S.-Mexico Agreement of 1943.[17] In 1947, as the United States and twenty-one other countries began negotiating the texts of GATT and an ITO,[18] President Truman issued an executive order requiring that an escape clause be included in every trade agreement entered into under the authority of the U.S. Reciprocal Trade Agreements program. This order was amended slightly by subsequent executive orders until 1951, when the escape clause was included by Congress in the Trade Agreements Extension Act.[19] It has remained a part of U.S. statutory law ever since, revised from time to time in the various extensions or amendments to the U.S. trade law.

The evolution of the language of the U.S. escape clause provides an interesting barometer of liberal or protectionist sentiment in Congress (but this is not a story for this book[20]). But it can be said that the GATT escape clause (Article XIX) was a direct descendant of the U.S.-Mexican Trade Agreement clause of the same nature.

Types of Safeguard Actions

Although Article XIX is the central and most prominent safeguards provision of GATT, a number of other measures are taken under GATT (or in evading GATT) that also can be termed "safeguards."[21] Various GATT clauses afford an opportunity to nations to impose border-import restraints, some of which may be "safeguards" in the sense discussed above. For example, Article XXVIII of GATT provides a means by which a contracting party can permanently withdraw a tariff "binding" (obligation as to a maximum tariff). In doing so, a country becomes obligated to negotiate with other GATT parties interested in exporting the product concerned, with a view to establish "compensation" by equivalent other concessions, or counterwithdrawals or concessions by the exporting countries.

Article XII of GATT provides some exceptions for balance-of-payments situations, while Article XVIII also provides some exceptions for BOP problems of developing countries. These measures, as well as other measures of Article XVIII designed for developing countries, can often provide GATT legal cover for various border-import restraints that are motivated by safeguards policies. Waivers can be voted under GATT Article XXV, and one could analyze other GATT explicit exceptions and see the possibility of using them for safeguards reasons. Finally, of course, there are a variety of techniques other than those permitted by GATT to effectively burden imports for safeguards reasons. The most prominent of these in recent years has been the "voluntary export restraint" (discussed later in this chapter).

During its history, the GATT has been more or less permanently concerned with the safeguards issue. From time to time, discussions have been held in GATT on various aspects of the problem. Some of the later discussions, those in the Tokyo Round and after, relating to a proposed safeguards code and concerning "adjustment," will be discussed in section 7.8. Other exercises on the subject in GATT include the elaborate textiles program (with a series of textile agreements or "arrangements" being negotiated, even though they probably violate GATT obligations). During the early 1960s, partly in connection with textiles problems, the GATT CONTRACTING PARTIES discussed generally the concept of "market disruption," and in November 1960 adopted a decision describing it and expressing the desirability of establishing consultative procedures for dealing with it.[22]

7.2 The Escape Clause in GATT/WTO and the United States

The most significant safeguard mechanism of the international trading system has been the escape clause. This mechanism exists in GATT as Article XIX. The escape clause also exists in the law of the United States and of other GATT contracting parties.[23] It will be recalled from section 7.1 that the GATT article was essentially drawn from earlier versions of U.S. law, but U.S. law has evolved through a number of texts over the more than thirty years of GATT history, whereas the GATT article has remained virtually the same as it was in the original GATT text.[24]

To grasp an overall picture of the mechanics of the escape clause, it is necessary to analyze it in five parts.

1. prerequisite of increasing imports
2. prerequisite of injury caused by increasing imports
3. permitted responses or remedies
4. responses of exporting countries or "compensation"
5. procedures

In this section I will introduce both the GATT and the U.S. escape clauses, make a few comments about the strengths or weaknesses of some of the details of these clauses, and try to compare them. In the next section I will deal with the two prerequisites for import-restraining action that would be permitted under Article XIX. And in the final section I will discuss what actions are permitted and the response to which other interested parties are entitled, and provide a brief note about procedures generally.

To further map the law of the GATT escape clause, the analysis proceeds as follows:[25]

1. It must be shown that imports of a product are increasing either absolutely or relatively, *and* such increase must be a *causal* result of (a)unforeseen developments, *and* (b) GATT obligations.

2. It must also be shown that domestic producers of competitive products are seriously injured *or* threatened with serious injury, *and* that this injury or threat is *caused* by the increased imports.

3. If one and two are shown, then an importing nation is entitled to suspend "such" GATT obligations in respect of such product for such time as necessary to prevent or remedy the injury.

4. The importing nation must consult with contracting parties having a substantial interest as exporters. If agreement is not reached, exporting CPs have the right to suspend "substantially equivalent concessions."

5. Various procedures are defined under GATT or national laws.

As we shall see in the next section, for each of the two prerequisites for action under Article XIX, namely, that (1) imports be increasing, and (2) that these increasing imports be causing injury to domestic industry (or a threat thereof), several variable concepts exist that can give considerable difficulty to persons attempting to interpret the language of Article XIX (or comparable escape clauses in domestic law such as that of the United States). These variable concepts include the concept of "like or competitive product" and the concept of "domestic producers of competitive products" (i.e., the "industry"). For many cases, these two concepts can become extremely significant. This is also true, incidentally, for injury tests applied under other trade policies, such as subsidy/countervailing duty policy and antidumping policy.[26]

In general, the GATT language of Article XIX as to these variable concepts, as well as to the various criteria, is quite ambiguous. This becomes particularly obvious when one compares this language to U.S. domestic law, which has evolved under the pressure of conflicting special and policy interests over thirty years of congressional activity. The language in the U.S. law has become increasingly detailed and elaborate, with particular definitions offered for much of it. The language of GATT is so general and ambiguous (and for the most part has not been articulated by interpretive decisions during its history) that nations can often claim to fulfill the GATT language prerequisites in many plausible but marginal circumstances.[27]

One interesting feature of the United States' relationship to GATT is that the increasingly detailed articulation of the U.S. escape-clause law has led to a situation in which some (but not all) respects the U.S. escape clause is a much more rigorous and disciplined body of law than the GATT. This means that industry groups within the United States who seek escape-clause relief find that in many circumstances they are not eligible under U.S. law for that relief, although they might well be eligible for such relief if the GATT language were the applicable legal standard.[28] This does not mean that the United States should abandon its own law and reembrace the ambiguous GATT standards. There may be sound policy reasons, and certainly the congressional drafters thought there were sound policy reasons, to define U.S. law as has been done. Even so defined, many observers believe that the U.S. International Trade Commission has been given extraordinarily broad discretion and leeway within the U.S. statute to act either affirmatively or negatively in response to a petition for import relief.[29] On the other hand, it is probably true that the United States' law and procedures have led the United States to not utilize the explicit measures of escape-clause relief in cases (such as the 1980 automobile case[30]) where clearly other governments would not be so inhibited. One question then is whether such a restraint leads to pressures on the U.S. government to evade its own law in applying safeguard measures that are not explicitly provided for in the statutes.

In summarizing some of these escape-clause requirements in the following sections, I will mention just a few of these troubles.

The United States has a specified procedure for escape-clause cases spelled out in its law. This procedure illustrates beautifully the uneasy tension among the branches of the United States government, particularly between the Congress and the president.[31] An escape-clause procedure is initiated by petition to the U.S. International Trade Commission where six commissioners, sitting as an impartial body, must make the various determinations I have listed. Only if this body rules affirmatively on the existence of the necessary prerequisites (by a majority or tie vote) can a case be eligible for the remedies specified in the statute. If the determination is negative, the president has no authority to invoke the escape-clause remedies. He may try invoking other measures, such as "voluntary restraints," but often constitutional or other constraints prevent him from doing so. If the ITC finds affirmatively, the case is forwarded to the president with a recommendation of remedial action. The president may, however, decide differently from the ITC whether any remedy is warranted, or what remedy to grant. Prior to the 1983 Supreme Court case that held legislative vetoes unconstitutional, the Congress was authorized in the statute to override a presidential determination that differed from that of the ITC.[32] Since then, however, although the Congress could enact a law changing a presidential escape clause determination, it would need a two-thirds vote of both Houses to override a president's veto of such a law.

Since 5 January 1975 through the end of August 1996, the U.S. ITC has received sixty-six petitions for the escape clause.[33] It has turned down thirty of these. Of the thirty-four cases sent to the president, the president imposed some sort of import restraining measure on at least eleven occasions. In some cases, however, although the president technically turned down the ITC case, he has with the help of other laws proceeded with action that has had an import-restraining effect. The most notable case of this type was that of steel in the early fall of 1984. A petition on carbon and certain alloy steel products[34] had been purposely timed so that the ITC ruling would land on the president's desk only several months prior to a presidential election—an obvious attempt to put the president under political pressure to give some relief. The ITC found that the domestic steel industry was injured with respect to some steel products, but not with respect to others. The ITC recommended to the president that quotas be imposed. Although technically rejecting the proposed form of relief, the president ordered his officials to embark on a worldwide extensive program of negotiating "voluntary restraint arrangements," to effectively lower the amount of steel being imported into the U.S. market.[35]

A GATT document lists 150 explicit invocations or notifications of the GATT escape clause through 1994, but also notes that the list is likely to be incomplete.[36] In many cases of explicit reliance on GATT Article XIX, no notification is sent to the GATT secretariat. Even more questionable, however, is the use of a large variety of import-restraining techniques, including voluntary restraints and "customs officials bottlenecks" (e.g., those operating in France on video cassette recorders[37]), essentially for safeguards reasons without any explicit reference to safeguards rules. In most of these "implicit safeguard" cases, some of which in recent years have been called "gray area measures,"[38] little or no GATT discipline has been effectively applied.

7.3 The Escape Clause: Legal Prerequisites and Practice

Introduction and the Problem of the "Variable" Legal Concepts

In the previous section I presented an overview analysis of escape-clause law, as we know it from both GATT and U.S. statutes. Of the five parts of that analysis, in this section we take up the two which concern the "legal prerequisites" of the privilege to utilize escape-clause remedies, namely:

1. It must be shown that imports of a product are increasing either absolutely or relatively, *and* such increase must be a *causal* result of (a) unforeseen developments, *and* (b) GATT obligations.

2. It must also be shown that domestic producers of competitive products are seriously injured, *or* threatened with serious injury, *and* this injury or threat is *caused* by the increased imports.

As I indicated, several problematic "variable" concepts cut across these prerequisites and thus merit some attention. First, regarding the "product" definition: is the product to be defined broadly, like "motor vehicles," or more narrowly, like "passenger vehicles with a value less than six thousand dollars"? The definition of the product can often be the determining factor of whether imports have increased, or whether these increases are causing injury to domestic producers of "like or directly competitive products."[39]

Second, the concept of "industry" is a variable one that causes great difficulty. In GATT the phrase is "domestic producers"; the phrase "domestic producers" is used in U.S. law, but more often the phrase "domestic industry" is determinative. Once again, whether this phrase is interpreted broadly or narrowly can be very significant. If the industry is deemed to consist of all "specialty steel" producers, a significant decline in employment and other harmful effects to only the producers of tools may not provide the basis for an affirmative determination for relief.

A third variable concept is implicit in GATT Article XIX and comparable domestic laws, but is not expressed precisely. This is the contemplated time frame, particularly in the cause test. When trying to ascertain whether imports have increased, should one use a one- or two-year period, or is it appropriate to use a much longer period? Obviously the longer the period, the more likely it is that one can find at least some increase in imports in a world where trade generally is increasing. Likewise, in considering a causal relationship, suppose that a GATT obligation was incurred in 1960, but that only in 1980 imports began to increase. Does the twenty-year gap insulate the relationship of the two events as being linked by cause?

Now I will turn to some of the specific legal elements of the escape-clause prerequisites, partly to illustrate some of the points we have made previously—namely, that the ambiguity of some of these elements reduces the effective discipline that the GATT escape clause was at least partly designed to impose on the use of "exceptional" import-restraining measures.

Increased Imports and Cause Thereof

What might seem to the layperson to be a simple concept on close examination turns out to be very complex. Under GATT Article XIX, several questions are involved in examining the first prerequisite of safeguard relief, that of "increased imports." The language of GATT Article

XIX states: "If, as a result of unforeseen developments and of the effect of the obligations incurred by a Contracting Party under this agreement, including tariff concessions, any product is being imported into the territory of that Contracting Party in such increased quantities ..."[40] Questions include:

1. What are "unforeseen developments"?
2. What are the obligations mentioned? Which type of obligations are meant?
3. What is the time frame for increased imports?
4. How is "product" to be defined—broadly or narrowly?
5. Must the increase be "absolute," or will a "relative" increase suffice?

I will examine questions, 1, 2, and 5 here. (Questions 3 and 4 involve the variable concepts already mentioned. Also, the jurisprudence of the USITC is quite extensive in its coverage of these concepts.)[41]

With respect to one of the tests for the "first cause requirement" (i.e., that the increased imports be a result of "unforeseen developments"), a major case was brought to the GATT early in its history concerning a U.S. escape-clause action regarding imports of hatters' fur. In October 1951 a GATT working party reported on this case, and a portion of that report focused on the question of whether "unforeseen developments" had existed. It appeared that the basic development that had occurred since the negotiation of the concession was a change in the style of women's hat bodies. The United States argued that this change was an unforeseen development, whereas the chief exporting country, Czechoslovakia, argued the contrary. The working party basically fudged the issue. It said that it was "satisfied that the United States authorities had investigated the matter thoroughly on the basis of the data available to them at the time of their inquiry and had reached in good faith the conclusion that the proposed action fell within the terms of Article XIX..."

Furthermore the working party noted that "any view on such matter must be to a certain extent a matter of economic judgment and that it is natural that government should on occasion be greatly influenced by social factors, such as local employment problems." Thus it concluded that there was "no conclusive evidence that the action taken by the United States under Article XIX constituted a breach of that government's obligations under the General Agreement."[42]

One is tempted to conclude that if change of style of women's hats is deemed to be an "unforeseen development," then anything could be an unforeseen development! (The same could be said for the width of men's neckties!) In short, it is argued that the prerequisite cause of "unforeseen developments" has been essentially "read out" of the GATT agreement. Almost any increase in imports could arguably be an "unforeseen circumstance" itself. The need for follow-up to review this language of GATT was noted in a 1963 GATT report, but follow-up has not occurred.[43]

The causal prerequisite that increased imports be a result of "obligations" on the part of GATT requires a more extensive examination. The language seems to clearly include GATT obligations other than tariff concessions. Given that certain parts of the GATT obligations (such as Article XI prohibiting the use of quantitative restrictions) apply to all goods, it can be concluded that an escape-clause case is possible for any imported good whatsoever, not just those that are listed on the schedule of concessions of a GATT member. Of course, if the schedule of concessions of a GATT member does not include the product concerned, then the country has the freedom under GATT to raise the tariff on the product at its own discretion. It is only bound to a maximum tariff on those items that it has agreed to place on its schedule.[44]

Until 1974 the U.S. law provided a causal-link requirement between GATT obligations and increased imports. The expression of this causal link differed in various statutes. For example, in the 1951 statute the language read "increased quantities ... as a result, in whole or in part, of the duty or other customs treatment reflecting such concession...." Thus, earlier U.S. law seemed to be focused on a tariff concession of a previous trade agreement. In reviewing U.S. trade policy in the early 1970s, the Williams Commission noted that this causal-link requirement of the U.S. law had been responsible in a large number of escape-clause cases for a negative determination. The Williams Commission concluded that the credibility of the U.S. escape-clause procedures was lessened by the rarity of affirmative determinations, which placed pressure on government alternative and on less explicit procedural devices. For these reasons the Williams Commission recommended that the United States change its law, and the Congress subsequently complied in the 1974 Trade Act. The causal-link requirement between obligations of GATT and the increased imports was deleted from United States law.[45]

It therefore can be argued that U.S. law, at least in this respect, no longer complies with its obligations under GATT. A counterargument, however, is that because in every escape clause case there is an applicable GATT obligation (such as Article XI), and because if there were no GATT obligation the United States would have the freedom to prevent such imports, any increased imports automatically have been at least partly caused by GATT obligations. Furthermore, the argument continues, the U.S. practice can in fact never be found to be a violation of a GATT obligation in this regard, even though the U.S. law makes no explicit mention of the particular GATT prerequisite.

Turning to a third issue—whether or not the increased imports can be relative, compared to "absolute"—the GATT has generally been interpreted to include the concept "relative increase." Thus, the absolute level of imports may remain constant or even decline, but if there is an increase relative to total domestic consumption in the percentage that these imports represent, there has been a "relative increase" of imports that satisfies the first prerequisite of GATT Article XIX. This interpretation stems from action in drafting the ITO charter at the 1948 Havana Conference, where the word "relatively" was inserted in the comparable text. Although this word was not added to the GATT text, a working party report adopted by the GATT CONTRACTING PARTIES in September 1948 stated that it was the understanding that the existing language of Article XIX was intended to cover such cases.[46]

It may be asked whether a "relative increase" should ever be the basis of a safeguards measure, given that it would be hard to argue that imports are a cause of injury in such circumstances. (The cause would, arguably, be found in the reasons for overall decline in consumption, such as change of taste, general economic decline, increase in consumer interest rates, or the like.) On the other hand, it might be argued that a "relative increase" concept addresses some of the "buffering" and "share the burden" policies necessary for an increasingly interdependent world.

The 1988 Trade Act retained the essential criteria for the U.S. escape clause, but the language of the new law places much more stress on the issue of "adjustment," giving both the ITC an opportunity to recommend actions to facilitate adjustment and the president more opportunity to use remedies toward that end. Whether the actual results of a case will differ from those under the prior law is hard to predict.[47]

The "Serious Injury" Test and Cause Thereof

The GATT language states that the increased imports must be such as "to cause or threaten serious injury to domestic producers in that territory of like or directly competitive products ..." This language also poses a series of interpretive problems, including: (1) the degree of causal link required between increased imports and the serious injury; (2) the definition of "threat" of injury; (3) the definition of "like or competitive product"; (4) the definition of "domestic producers," that is, the scope of the "industry"; and (5) how to define "serious injury."

The problem of defining "industry" or domestic producers" in this context is similar to the problem of identifying what are to be considered "like or directly competitive products." It should be noted that the word "competitive" is included—which is not the same as the phrase "like product," found in a number of other GATT clauses (such as Article I relating to Most-favored-nation status). This inclusion is clearly appropriate, because the objective in the escape clause is to ascertain when the imports are harming domestic industry, and obviously competitive products can so harm. The question remains, however, which products will be construed as being in a "competitive" relationship with others? Are apples competitive to oranges? Are black-and-white television sets competitive to color sets? Presumably, economists could develop a kind of "cross-elasticity" test, and thereby provide some interpretive assistance here. Nevertheless, GATT jurisprudence being so sparse, considerable leeway seems to exist for interpreting this phrase. The approach taken by a government on this issue can strongly influence the outcome of whether an industry or group of firms is eligible for escape-clause relief.

I will put aside the time-frame matter again (which lurks in a number of these issues), leaving three additional issues for discussion here: the cause, the "threat," and the question of how to define "serious injury."

With respect to cause, one should note how broad and simple the GATT language is. The question of cause in the U.S. law has been an extremely important one, being the determinative factor in the largest escape-clause case ever brought (the 1980 automobile case). Over the years contending factions in Congress have struggled with the definition of cause. The Williams Commission in 1972 recommended some relaxation of the causal test, suggesting the words "primary cause" in lieu of the statutory language that at the time required that imports be "the major factor in causing or threatening to cause, such injury."[48] This language had been interpreted to denote a cause that was more significant than all other causes put together. In the Trade Act of 1974, the Congress went even a little further than the Williams Commission recommendation, by lowering the cause requirement with the phrase "substantial cause." Standing alone, the phrase "substantial cause" could be very relaxed or ambiguous (implying anything that is not "insubstantial"?), but in close negotiations, the contending parties in Congress developed a definition that states "the term 'substantial cause' means a cause which is important and not less than any other cause."[49]

One critical question is how one disaggregates causes. If, for example, a general depression or general conditions of slack demand is considered one single cause, it would be very difficult for imports to override or equal that in importance. On the other hand, if one disaggregated the "depression" cause into components such as higher interest rates, increased oil prices, declining government programs, then it would be easier to find that imports were not only important, but also not less so than any other cause.[50]

The GATT has no jurisprudence to address this question. Thus, governments in GATT can often justify their safeguard actions under the loose language of Article XIX, although the United States would not be able to act under its own escape clause, which has a more rigorous standard. Again, this does not necessarily mean that the United States should change its law, given that important policy reasons were behind the careful formulations of that law. Nevertheless, it is clear that if the policy reasons were to change, the United States would have scope to relax the criteria of its escape clause while still complying with its GATT obligations.[51]

"Serious injury" is also a phrase that is considerably ambiguous. It should be noted that GATT clauses concerning antidumping and countervailing duty measures require "material injury," a concept that should be contrasted with the "serious injury" concept of Article XIX. United States law likewise tracks this difference (and also has several other degrees of injury).[52]

It is generally thought that the escape-clause standard for injury should be the highest or most difficult to establish, given that the escape clause is designed to respond to situations that do not necessarily involve any unfair action by foreign exporters. Antidumping and countervailing duty law, by contrast, are designed to respond to actions deemed improper, and therefore a less rigorous standard of injury is thought appropriate.

Nevertheless, it is often difficult to determine what precisely should be the criteria for determining serious injury. The United States statute has a detailed list of factors,[53] but the GATT jurisprudence is once again very sparse. The question of "threat of serious injury" is even more ambiguous. Because the concept of threat suggests trying to predict the future, even greater discretion is granted by this concept to national government authorities who desire to justify their safeguard actions under Article XIX of GATT.

It can be seen from the discussion in this section that the GATT escape clause can be quite easily abused or ignored. In any sort of strict jurisprudential sense, it is probably virtually impossible to determine with any degree of precision or clarity if a nation has not fulfilled its obligations under Article XIX. There will of course be cases in which reliance on Article XIX would clearly be considered subterfuge. Nevertheless, considerable room exists for clarification and negotiations leading to greater discipline in connection with safeguard measures as compared to Article XIX of GATT. The Uruguay round safeguards text, discussed in Section 7.8, could be a major step for greater discipline.

7.4 The Escape Clause: Remedies and Procedures

In this section, I turn from the prerequisites for invoking the escape clause to the nature of the remedies under that clause and the procedures involved in obtaining them.[54] I will describe these under three subtopics. First, I will look at the remedy afforded by Article XIX. Second, I will consider the "compensation" negotiations, which are the compliance or enforcement technique of GATT Article XIX and, more basically, of the bindings and concessions in the schedules. Third, I will turn briefly to a few other procedural questions.

The description in this section deals mostly with the language of the GATT agreement itself, now sometimes affected (and arguably superseded) by the safeguards agreement. In a later section I will take up the safeguards agreement directly.

Escape-Clause Remedies

The GATT language states that if the prerequisites of Article XIX are found, "the Contracting Party shall be free, in respect of such product, and to the extent and for such time as may be necessary to prevent or remedy such injury, to suspend the obligation in whole or in part or to withdraw or modify the concession."[55] Apparently what is contemplated is a temporary measure. This can be contrasted with Article XXVIII, where the privilege of a permanent withdrawal of a concession or tariff binding is given, subject to conditions and compensatory negotiations.[56]

Three questions come immediately to mind. First, what type of government action is contemplated by the remedies mentioned in Article XIX? Second how long may such remedies remain in force? And, third, what is the significance of MFN (discussed in section 7.5)?[57]

It will be noticed from GATT Article XIX that a contracting party is given the freedom to "suspend the obligation in whole or in part or to withdraw or modify the concession" of "such product." It seems clear that this concept embraces more than simply withdrawing or modifying the tariff concessions; it appears to apply to any of the GATT obligations, including the obligation of Article XI which prohibits the use of quantitative restrictions. Certainly the practice in GATT, and in U.S. law under GATT, has been to utilize nontariff barriers on a number of occasions.[58] United States law explicitly authorizes not only an increase in tariff, but the use of quantitative restrictions, tariff quotas, combinations of these, and orderly marketing agreements.[59] The 1988 Trade Act puts more stress than does previous law on the use of the measures "to facilitate adjustment"—which, however, include the above remedies as well as adjustment assistance.[60] Other countries have likewise used all these measures, but have not always notified GATT that they are acting under Article XIX. In any event, the practice seems well-enough established in GATT that almost any import barrier can find legal cover in the language of Article XIX when responding to the prerequisites of an escape-clause situation. In policy terms, of course, it can be forcefully argued that any import restraints should be "price" and not "quantity" oriented. Any use of quotas or restraints based on quantity will unfortunately reduce incentives of producers to be competitive in price or other product characteristics.[61] Yet it seems the GATT rules, at least in practice, do not reinforce these policy goals.

The time requirement is also ambiguous. The language says "for such time as may be necessary to prevent or remedy such injury," which seems to suggest a temporary measure, although the language at the end of the sentence, about "withdrawing or modifying" could imply a more permanent measure. In any event, a country has Article XXVIII if it wishes to do something permanent.[62] Article XIX seems designed for the application of temporary measures. The U.S. law, for example, has a five-year time limit for measures under its escape clause. This limit was extended to eight years under the 1988 Trade Act.[63] How long a measure may be invoked as "temporary," in the Article XIX sense, is again a subject that needs clarification. The UR safeguards text specifies a four year period, with extensions possible up to a total of eight years.

The remedy language of Article XIX also says "to the extent ... as may be necessary to prevent or remedy such injury...." How much in the way of import restraints is necessary to "remedy" the serious injury caused by imports is obviously a determination that is subject to great discretion of national governments.

Compensation and Compliance

In general, observers believe that the GATT tariff concessions and bindings, resulting from eight rounds of trade negotiations and embodied in many thousands of pages of country tariff concessions, have been among the most stable and most followed of the GATT obligations. For some reason, although the temptation to evade the GATT obligations has been very great over the years (and some would say has grown stronger), the tariff concessions, perhaps because of their attention to detail, have been widely complied with. One reason for this compliance may be the visibility or explicitness of a government's departure from a tariff binding. Some suggest that another reason for compliance is the effective "sanction" built into the GATT structure for departure from tariff obligations.

The GATT does not use the terms "sanction" or "retaliation," but it has a structure for requiring a "payment" from a country that departs from its schedule obligations in the context of the escape clause of Article XIX or elsewhere. This structure has been embellished by considerable practice over more than four decades of GATT history, and is not immediately apparent in the GATT language. Article XIX requires that a contracting party using the escape clause shall give notice to the GATT. Article XIX also gives to exporting countries having a substantial interest in the product concerned an opportunity to consult (unless the "critical circumstance" exception is invoked). If consultations do not result in any "agreement," the importing country can nevertheless act under Article XIX, but in that case "the effected Contracting Party shall be free ... to suspend ... such substantial equivalent concessions or other obligations under this Agreement ... which the CONTRACTING PARTIES do not disapprove." This is deemed to be the "compensation" requirement of Article XIX.

Because it is generally recognized that suspension of obligations has a negative impact on the general policies of liberalization under GATT, it has been the practice in GATT for negotiations to include the possibility that the importing country invoking the escape clause will grant to interested exporting countries alternative concessions on other products by way of compensation, so as to avoid the need of the exporting countries to counter the escape clause by suspending liberal trade concessions.[64]

In fact, in the political discourse of countries considering import barriers, one can note the importance of arguments that potential "retaliation" or "compensation" will be damaging and therefore provide reasons to avoid using import restraints. One of the problems in recent years, as the general average of tariffs has declined to a very low point, is that it has become increasingly harder for countries invoking safeguard measures to be able to effectively compensate affected countries by way of granting alternative concessions. Usually the "compensation bill" is sufficiently large that it becomes extremely difficult to find any products that have a tariff high enough to make an alternative concession meaningful, except for products that are already very sensitive and subject to the pressures of domestic interests who claim they are already harmed by imports. This "compensation bill" then adds pressure on governments to find an alternative or "non–escape clause" safeguarding technique, such as voluntary restraints. One option that contracting parties might consider in negotiating a more disciplined safeguard system would be to relax the compensation requirement in appropriate circumstances, such as in cases where higher degrees of the otherwise ambiguous criteria have been fulfilled.[65] The safeguards text of the Uruguay Round seems to have introduced this concept.

The risk of any such reform, however, might be to lessen the effective enforcement or compliance with the GATT schedule obligations. Indeed, when escape-clause measures are contemplated, it has sometimes been the case that the interested exporting nation has "leaked" lists of potential products that might be subject to "retaliation," as a way to focus the importing country's attention on the possible consequences of its action.[66]

Under U.S. law, the executive sometimes did not have authority to give "compensation" to foreign governments by lowering alternative U.S. tariff rates. When the so-called general negotiating authority[67] was in effect, the president could use that authority to enter a "trade agreement" that supplied the compensation; but in some periods (such as 1967 to 1975) this general authority had lapsed, leaving the president without the authority to offer compensation when the United States exercised escape-clause remedies. Section 123 of the Trade Act of 1974 remedied that lacuna, explicitly giving the president a certain amount of compensation authority.[68] This is an interesting example of the influence of GATT on U.S. law[69] and of a U.S. statutory provision that makes sense only in the context of U.S. participation in GATT.

Some Procedural Questions

GATT Article XIX requires notice, as I have mentioned, and also establishes time limits for the completion of compensation negotiations. Almost invariably these time limits are missed, and the GATT, by concerted action, or by agreement of the parties (including the negotiating parties), extends the time limits.[70]

The procedural requirements of Article XIX do not speak of the nature or process by which a nation shall determine its own escape-clause procedures. This raises the question whether a nation has complete freedom in this regard. For example, a nation that has a powerful executive endowed with the authority to limit imports whenever it desired might invoke Article XIX by a simple statement of the executive, arguing that the prerequisites of Article XIX have been fulfilled. Nothing in GATT explicitly prevents that possibility, although the Uruguay Round safeguards text now establishes some limitations on national government actions, requiring notification, consultation, and publicity. On the other hand, it is possible that a parliamentary body, such as the U.S. Congress, could make the necessary "findings" that the prerequisites of Article XIX have been fulfilled, and could take action that it could defend as permissible under Article XIX.[71] Of course, in all such cases, the "compensation" requirement could be an inhibitory factor.

7.5 The Escape Clause MFN Question

In the past decade, the most controversial issue of Article XIX of GATT has been the question of whether a remedy under it must be applied in a nondiscriminatory manner, that is, on an "MFN" basis. What does this mean?[72]

If a country becomes authorized to utilize Article XIX, because it has met the prerequisites, then when it applied the remedy (which would generally be import restraints of one type or another), it might do so in two ways. First, if it applied that remedy in an MFN manner, and if it were to utilize tariffs, there would be one tariff for the products of all MFN (GATT) nations. If it were to utilize quantitative restrictions, the concept of MFN would become considerably more difficult. Quotas are almost "inherently discriminatory," unless a country uses so-called global quotas, or auctions the quotas.[73] Generally speaking, however, given that global quotas can cause a rush by importers to fill them early in a prescribed time period (and thus result in no trade at the end of a time period), and that governments have not used an auction system very often, governments tend to prefer a more explicit allocative system of quotas. Usually quotas are granted on a country-by-country basis. In practice and under the language of GATT Article XIII that deals with quotas, as well as in the general practice under that article and in GATT history, it is considered that a nondiscriminatory quota system establishes the amount of quotas by referring to a recent historical period, "a previous representative period," and the amount or proportion of trade that each country had during that period. This of course often discriminates against any new entrants to the market.

This is a source of considerable bitterness for countries, such as developing countries, that are trying to develop new industries. It is probably not entirely a fair approach for that reason, and consequently countries may use some discretion to try to accommodate new market entrants. The result, of course, is that governments have considerable discretion in setting quotas, and thus, although they may claim to be applying import restraints on an MFN basis, on close examination impartial observers might determine that considerable discrimination has resulted from their actual application of quotas.[74]

Moreover, a government may expressly desire to depart from MFN application under Article XIX. Often the argument is made that it is wise to do so, as only a few countries can actually "cause" the increase of imports that has led to the invocation of Article XIX. These would be countries whose share of the importing country's market has grown fairly rapidly and recently. Obviously, these are likely to be the new market entrants. Some argue that in applying a safeguard measure, it is least disturbing to do so to only a few countries, rather than in a nondiscriminatory across-the-board manner. It is sometimes asked: Why should countries who are not responsible for the increase in imports have to bear the burden of anescape-clause action?

The counterpolicy argument is that the escape clause is designed to provide temporary relief from fair imports, not to respond to unfair imports.[75] Countries whose share of the importing country's market have been increasing most rapidly are doing exactly what they are supposed to do under world trade policies of the GATT. They have become more efficient, producing better and less expensive goods, and therefore the market is responding by favoring them. To penalize these economies is to target the very industries that have been achieving the results that international trade policy is designed to achieve. It is therefore argued that only MFN or nondiscriminatory application of the escape-clause import barriers will allow the more efficient industries to continue on their praiseworthy path of providing better goods for less cost.

These are the basic policy arguments. Now I will turn to the "legal" arguments.[76] The language of Article XIX states that the invoking contracting party shall be free "to suspend the obligation" of GATT that is deemed to be linked to the increased imports. It is not explicit as to which obligations are considered. It is therefore argued that the Article I MFN obligations of GATT are within the scope of those that can be "suspended" in Article XIX. For this reason, it is claimed that Article XIX legally and technically allows a discriminatory import-restraint remedy.

A counterargument focusing on the language of Article I is that it is unlikely that the MFN obligation is responsible for the increased imports. The increased imports are related causally to the domestic demand for imports of the goods generally, and the domestic consumer is usually indifferent to their origin.

An important interpretive practice in GATT is invoked by the latter argument. One result of the 1948 negotiations for an ITO charter held in Havana was an interpretive note inserted in the draft charter that stated: "It is understood that suspension, withdrawal or modification under ... [the escape clause provision] must not discriminate against imports from any Member country, and that such action should avoid to the fullest extent possible, injury to other supplying Member countries."[77]

A GATT working party in 1953 indicated that the same approach was taken for the GATT escape clause.[78] Despite its ambiguity this language has provided one basis of the legal argument that GATT Article XIX requires MFN application.

Starting in the Tokyo Round safeguards negotiations, the contrary position has been taken by the European Community. The EC, as well as some Scandinavian countries, have offered arguments mentioned previously that they are authorized to take discriminatory measures under Article XIX. This position has aroused intense opposition from many developing countries that see themselves as the potential targets (as "new entrants" to the market) of safeguards measures. It has also resulted in some debate on this subject among scholars.[79]

One of the arguments used in favor of a discrimination approach is that in fact the practice in GATT for several decades has shown a tolerance for the use of discriminatory safeguards measures. For example, it is noted that there are many voluntary-restraint agreements, and that these agreements are inherently discriminatory in their approach.[80] It has also been pointed out that on several occasions the United States and others have either used quotas in a de facto discriminatory manner or have negotiated orderly marketing agreements under U.S. domestic escape-clause law that were effectively discriminatory.[81] In addition, in at least one case there has been a fairly explicit application of a discriminatory safeguards measure by another country.[82]

In a 1981 GATT panel determination, however, the panel seemed explicitly to endorse an MFN obligation for Article XIX remedies, saying: "The Panel was of the view that the type of action chosen by Norway, i.e., the quantitative restriction limiting the importation of the nine textile categories in question, as the form of emergency action under Article XIX was subject to the provisions of Article XIII which provides for nondiscriminatory administration of quantitative restriction."[83]

The United States position in the GATT negotiations has varied a bit. In early phases of the Tokyo Round negotiations it began by strongly supporting the nondiscriminatory approach of Article XIX. At one point, however, it seemed to relax this stance. In later years, however, the United States took a very strong pro-MFN approach to Article XIX.[84]

Where does this all leave us? As is true of so many legal issues in the GATT (or other international obligations), it is hard to say with complete assurance and precision what the interpretation of an international obligation should be. Pragmatically, one would try to predict (as U.S. lawyers often do with respect to the U.S. Constitution and the Supreme Court) what would be the outcome of the controversy in the procedures of GATT, such as a panel determination if a dispute were taken under Article XXIII of GATT. More difficult, one would try to predict what practice would be considered and tolerated in GATT as consistent with the GATT obligations, over a longer period of time. It is very hard to make such predictions, given the fairly strong opposing stands of important trading partners. It does seem that if the MFN matter were to go to a panel in GATT, the panel would likely rule on the basis of the Havana Charter and the early GATT report that MFN is required by Article XIX remedies. The fact that we have witnessed departures from the rule over time, and that those departures have been "tolerated" (but not tolerated as fulfilling or changing the legal obligation) is not evidence of practice of an interpretation of an international agreement. Virtually all agreements are violated at some point or another, and some are violated more than others. A pattern of violations should never be the basis on which to argue that the underlying obligation itself has been changed. Something more would be needed, such as expressions consistent with the customary international law concepts of *opinio juris*.[85]

In addition, because of the existence of at least some ambiguity in the MFN question, it seems important to examine the underlying policies of the GATT agreement as a whole, and particularly of Article XIX in the context of the GATT agreement. These policies seem to reinforce the concept of MFN. As I have stated, it seems doubtful that one could argue that the MFN obligation is one that is "casually linked" to the increase of imports. In addition, the economic concepts of comparative advantage and the goal of liberal trade policies to allow more efficient producers to develop and enter the market reinforce an approach that would negate discriminatory application of Article XIX remedies.

It can be argued pragmatically, however, that given the existence of so many substantial deviations from the nondiscriminatory approach in safeguards, world welfare would be better served by some (even grudging) recognition of those deviations if they could then be channeled and disciplined so that the worst abuses would be inhibited. This is a "second-best" (or third-best) argument for the real world.[86] The dilemma is that to "recognize" the deviations might be to entrench or encourage more of them. One diplomat has therefore argued (somewhat cynically, perhaps) that the "law" should not be changed, even though "Professional trade policy administrators know that measures can usually be devised which deal with the category of imports which give rise to the perceived problem."[87] The Uruguay Round safeguards text seems to opt for the MFN interpretation of Article XIX, stating that "safeguard measures shall be applied to a product being imported irrespective of its source."[88] The U.S. Government's Statement of Administrative Action regarding the Uruguay Round texts notes that Article XIX actions "must be applied on a most-favored-nation (MFN) basis...." The safeguard code, however, does make some special provision for developing country members, prohibiting safeguard measures against a product from the developing country as long as its share of the imports concerned does not exceed 3 percent (with some other provisos.)

Article 5 of the UR Safeguards text also contains some measures that would apparently allow any member (industrial or otherwise) to depart from a strict MFN approach. Thus we see a certain tension concerning this question, even in the finished new text regarding safeguards.

7.6 Law and Practice Regarding Adjustment

Adjustment and Adjustment Assistance

Early in this chapter I noted a significant argument that supports government intervention in the market to ease the pain of the costs of adjustment that are caused by imports.[89] I suggested the eminent-domain analogy. Import restraints, of course, do some of this, but they may be not only costly but self-defeating in the long run, when uncompetitive industry sectors are induced to continue production by the subsidization that import restraints confer. Many economists would argue that it is preferable to grant government financial assistance to the adjusting producers, especially if this assistance is designed to "nudge" the recipients toward effective adjustment policies. These policies may involve moving completely out of production of particular uncompetitive products, or restructuring the producer plants and organization so that they can become competitive.[90] Given that the source of such aid is spread generally through the government fiscal policies, financial assistance is arguably fairer than import restraints, which impose costs only on certain segments of the population. For example, restraints on the imports of computer chips impose additional costs on domestic companies that use such chips in their products. Whether these costs can be passed on to another limited segment of the population—that is, those who buy computers—may depend in turn on whether restraints are imposed on the imports of computers.[91]

The problem is that many observers feel that the adjustment-assistance programs that have been tried in the United States and elsewhere have failed to accomplish their purpose and also have been very expensive. In times of budget constraints, as well as skepticism about government "welfare" subsidies, it has become increasingly difficult to persuade political leaders to fund adjustment assistance.

International Norms

Very little exists in the way of legal norms or explicit institutional obligations—in the sense of a positive obligation to promote or create advantageous conditions for adjustment in world trade. Most of the international legal and institutional activity concerning adjustment has been in the context of safeguards and escape-clause questions. From time to time, the issue has been raised as to whether an international obligation on nations could be designed to promote internal structural adjustment to facilitate the economic policies that lie behind the GATT/Bretton Woods System for international trade. It is possible that some sort of obligation could be implied from some of the looser or more general clauses of GATT. For example, Article XXXVI of GATT expresses a desire that developed countries provide favorable and acceptable conditions of access to world markets for products on which developing countries depend. Likewise, in Article XXXVII of GATT, developed contracting parties are called on to "give active consideration to the adoption of other measures designed to provide greater scope for the development of imports from less-developed contracting parties...." Article XXXVIII of GATT also reinforces this viewpoint, with general admonitions for contracting parties to collaborate "in seeking feasible methods to expand trade for the purpose of economic development."

In addition, from time to time committees and working parties in GATT have met to study the problem of structural adjustment. For example, in November 1980, the GATT Council established a working group on structural adjustment that examined several studies by the secretariat with respect to this problem.[92]

At the November 1982 ministerial meeting of the GATT contracting parties, the CONTRACTING PARTIES decided to continue the "work on structural adjustment and trade policy in order to focus on the interaction between structural adjustment and the fulfillment of the objectives of the General Agreement...."[93] Subsequent GATT activities have not changed this picture of little progress.[94]

By way of comparison, it is interesting to note the impact of International Monetary Fund actions, including the IMF standby agreements. With the pressure it can bring with the bait of financial resources and threat of withdrawal of those resources, it can be argued that the IMF has had a profound impact on economic policies of its members.[95] Whether it has been able to influence micropolicy to achieve "structural adjustment" would be a subject for another study.

Although it has occasionally been suggested that an international norm should be adopted that would obligate structural adjustment measures in the context of GATT and safeguard actions, so far such a norm seems to be only a question for future discussion.

United States and Adjustment Assistance

An innovation of the 1962 Trade Expansion Act in the United States was the introduction of the concept of "adjustment-assistance" payments to workers dislocated because of imports. The act provided for special unemployment compensation benefits for workers and certain tax benefits and other assistance to import-affected firms. These benefits, however, were tied to the escape-clause criteria as they existed at the time; and as noted in section 7.3, under those criteria few escape clause cases succeeded. Likewise, few petitions for adjustment assistance succeeded. (A similar but slightly relaxed provision put into the legislation implementing the U.S.-Canada Automotive Products Agreement also provided little actual relief.)

One of the 1971 Williams Commission recommendations was to make the adjustment-assistance prerequisites easier to fulfill than those for the escape clause, and thus to suggest a policy preference for such assistance. The 1974 Trade Act accomplished this, establishing easier criteria for units of workers to obtain "certification," so that workers could receive special benefits because of the imports. These criteria were that a "significant number or proportion" of workers in a unit be totally or partially separated from employment and that sales or production of the unit be declining, all because imports had "contributed importantly" to these conditions.

At the same time, the benefits for workers were considerably improved, including weekly unemployment compensation often much better than that provided by state unemployment benefit plans, plus special allowances for retraining, job search, and relocation. (In addition, although assistance to firms was cut back, some modest provision for assistance to "communities" affected by imports was provided.)

One result was a surge in cost of the program, which peaked in 1980 when five hundred thirty thousand workers received a total of $1.6 billion. At that point the "budgeteers" interceded, and in subsequent years the program was cut back by various administrative and legislative changes. In 1985 the Reagan administration urged repeal of the program, but in 1986 the Congress extended it for six years. The 1988 Trade Act added further refinements to the program, and in addition changed the language in the basic escape clause to stress the adjustment goal.[96]

Although seemingly based on sound economic principles, adjustment assistance has in the view of many failed to achieve its goals of either assisting adjustment or winning additional support for a liberal trade policy. Labor unions have called it "burial insurance" and have refused to be overly impressed by the program. Costs have been difficult to contain without imposing inequities on workers (why should *trade*-affected workers be treated more favorably than other unemployed workers?). Possibly part of the reason for this less-than-happy appraisal is that the program assumes workers are "mobile," when in many cases they are not. Workers have deep ties to their communities, own homes there, have spouses with jobs there, have children with school and activity ties there. May be they do not want to move. Why, then, should a government program be based on measures that seem to ignore such preferences? Alternatives to the program need study. Would it be better to use a "regional aides" approach (as in Europe) to assist communities to develop new businesses that would utilize the idled manpower resources already there? Or would this approach too closely resemble the notion of "industrial policy" despised by some?

7.7 Export Restraints, Agreements, and Arrangements

ERAs and Their Policies

One of the most troublesome and increasingly common types of safeguard action seen in recent decades has been the export restraint imposed by an exporting country on behalf of or at the request of an importing country.[97] A variety of terms have been used for these, including export restraint agreement (ERA), orderly marketing agreement (OMA), voluntary export restraint (VER), and voluntary restraint agreement (or arrangement)" (VRA). No one term is definite or preferred although a number of different types of arrangements exist, and some of the terms fit the different types better than others. For example, one can identify three particular categories of arrangements:

1. government-to-government arrangement
2. private exporting industry to private domestic competing industry
3. importing government contact with the private exporting industry

Other variations exist, of course, and another dimension is the degree of formality that is involved. The formality could be as high as an explicit international agreement between governments, or something considerably lower, such as merely "predictions" by an exportation industry association as to what would be their "likely" exports to a given country during the next brief time period. On many occasions, an exporting government will act "unilaterally," without any formal indication of international agreement or even any consensus arrangement, but of course it will have done so because it has received signals of one type or another from the importing government or competing industry that there are risks in continuing to export at the existing or potential level.[98]

These arrangements have been extremely troublesome and have been the subject of considerable criticism from GATT bodies as well as from economists and government officials. One of the problems is their "lack of transparency": many of the arrangements are secret, or at least attempts are made to keep them secret. Another problem is that almost invariably these arrangements have not been subjected to the scrutiny or checks of concrete domestic or international proceedings. Consequently, there is considerable lack of discipline over the issues that have been analyzed in previous sections of this book. One suspects that the arrangements can often result from particular political favors being rendered by governments to certain domestic constituent groups to enhance the possibility of reelection or other favors from the constituent groups. Finally, in most cases the arrangements have dubious legal status. Again, the safeguards text of the Uruguay Round has important provisions here, with an objective of prohibiting ERAs, with certain provisos and exceptions.

Legal questions involve both international obligations and national laws. In many countries, no essential inhibition exists on these types of arrangements in national law, with the possible exception of restriction of executive authority to enter into the arrangements without some parliamentary action. When legal obstacles appear to be present, often a very informal type of arrangement is utilized, so that no sustainable constitutional argument of *ultra vires* is possible. In the United States, the *ultra vires* argument has considerable importance, given the constant tensions between the executive and legislative branches and the limited nature of delegations of authority under the Constitution to either body.[99] But as to very informal arrangements, it is probably the case that the executive has very broad discretion to "encourage" or "inform" foreign governments that are inclined to impose some sort of export restraints on a product that has been causing "difficulties" for a competing domestic market in the United States. In addition, in the light of the Tariff and Trade Act of 1984, the U.S. government has somewhat stronger arguments that even explicit export-restraint agreements with foreign governments are authorized by Congress—at least for steel.[100]

U.S. Law

In the United States, an extremely important additional legal inhibition exists on certain types of arrangements for export restraints, namely the U.S. antitrust laws.[101] Under the "effects doctrine" of that law, private firms abroad who collude to limit exports to the U.S. market may find themselves liable to either criminal prosecution under U.S. law or to private civil treble damage actions by aggrieved plaintiffs in the United States. Given that the arrangements are often at least tacitly encouraged by the U.S. government, the risk of criminal or civil prosecution by bodies of the U.S. government is usually small. Under existing U.S. law, however, the government is not able to control the possibility of private treble damage actions, and it is the threat of the exposure to these actions that has been a major inhibiting factor for the United States to utilize voluntary or other kinds of export-control arrangements as a major part of its trade policy. Consequently, the United States generally wants the exporting country's restraints to be in the form of governmental measures that could sustain the "sovereign compulsion" defense in an antitrust lawsuit.[102]

Of course, under the U.S. law of its escape clause, the president has explicit authority (when there is an affirmative ITC ruling) to negotiate "orderly marketing agreements" on a government-to-government basis, and this authority has been used on a number of occasions.[103] In addition, the president has certain other explicit statutory authorities to enter into arrangements with foreign governments whereby these governments will limit exports of certain commodities to the United States.[104] This is true in categories of agricultural commodities and textiles. When the products do not fall within those categories, the legal situation becomes more complicated.

GATT and ERAs

Under the GATT obligations, many and probably most of the so-called export restraint arrangements are more than likely inconsistent with the obligations of GATT. The GATT does not apply to the actions of private companies, so this amounts to a major loophole that allows those governments not inhibited by antitrust or other laws from encouraging private-firm restraints on exports from doing so. But with respect to government actions that restrain exports, GATT Article XI is clearly attracted. This article states: "No prohibitions or restrictions other than duties, taxes or other charges, whether made effective through quotas, import or export licenses or other measures, shall be instituted or maintained by any Contracting Party on the ... exportation or sale for export of any product destined for the territory of any other Contracting Party." This sweeping language would seem to embrace virtually any export control maintained by governmental authority,[105] but not those caused by private-firm action.

The problem in GATT is a more pragmatic one: Who will make any sort of formal complaint? The country establishing the restraints is usually doing so at the behest or signal of an importing country. The country that establishes the export restraints would hardly complain against itself in

GATT. The country that is most affected, namely, the importing country that sent the signal, would hardly complain either, because the action is precisely what it had hoped for. Other countries in GATT would find it difficult or awkward to complain, because they normally would not be able to establish that they themselves have been harmed (under doctrines of nullification or impairment of Article XXIII, or other less-formal considerations). Thus, there have been a paucity of cases in GATT with respect to export restraints. One possible complainant country in the GATT context might be a country C, believing as a result of an export-restraint arrangement between A and B, exports of A were diverted from the B market, thus putting greater competitive pressure on the market in C. This was basically the U.S. steel industry's complaint in a domestic U.S. proceeding under the U.S. Section 301, in 1976.[106] In that proceeding, however, the United States government declined to take the case because no adequate evidence of actual diversion or harm had been established.[107]

More recently, in GATT the European Community has successfully challenged a U.S.-Japanese agreement concerning Japanese exports of computer chips. The panel found, inter alia, that Japanese monitoring (with "administrative guidance") of export prices was inconsistent with GATT Article XI commitments.

Economists generally view the export-restraint agreement as one of the more damaging devices affecting principles of trade policy of the GATT. In addition, from the point of view of the importing country, it is probably economically the most costly procedure that could be followed. Unlike a tariff, the export restraint does not give the government any revenue to offset some of the general welfare economic costs of the import restraints.[108] Indeed, it generally appears that the exporting country, or at least the exporting industry, can reap substantial "monopoly rents" through the process. This probably explains why some countries seem to be so willing to enter into such arrangements. Indeed, these rents have in some cases been viewed as a substitute for the GATT compensation requirement.

Textiles and the Multifiber Arrangement

One of the most pronounced anomalies of the GATT system and the liberal-trade policies of the post–World War II period is the elaborate system of "voluntary agreements," which perpetuates a quota system for international trade in textiles and clothing. Today this is called the Multifiber Arrangement (MFA).[109] An extensive study entitled "Textiles and

Clothing in the World Economy" was completed by the GATT Secretariat in 1984,[110] and this report (noting origins dating back to 1936) describes the thirty-year history of this arrangement—starting with a short-term arrangement (STA) on textiles in 1961 and 1962, followed by a succession of long-term agreements (LTAs) lasting from 1962 to 1973, when the LTA was replaced by the first MFA in 1974. Subsequently, MFA II entered into force in 1978, and MFA III in 1982 (extended in 1986 to last until 1991).[111] The MFA was further extended on 9 December 1993 until 31 December 1994. This extension was intended to bridge the time until the expected implementation of the results of the Uruguay Round. The Uruguay Round Agreement on Textiles and Clothing, which entered into force on 1 January 1995, as part of the WTO agreements, replaced the MFA and provides for the gradual and complete integration of textile products into the GATT/WTO regime over a ten-year transition period.

All of these arrangements involved a substantial departure from the policy and rules of GATT. It is noted in the GATT study that "the most common feature of trade policy in the textiles (and later clothing) area over the past century is the above-average level of government intervention." The study observes that most developed countries, especially in western Europe, began the postwar period with very restrictive trade regimes, and trade policies affecting textiles remained largely untouched by GATT trade liberalization. In some cases, countries invoked various GATT articles to justify their action. These GATT departures, however, were developed in the textile and multifiber arrangements into a regularized and constant form of government intervention for textile and clothing trade. It is recognized that this intervention is inconsistent with GATT, but the countries that have accepted the textile or multifiber arrangements have arguably partially "waived" their GATT rights. Of course, the pressure to enter into these agreements for the textile-exporting countries was very great, and the fear was that the importing countries would make matters worse without the arrangements. At least the arrangements were a result of the tugging and pulling of international negotiations, and the argument was that these arrangements would allow the progressive and predictable liberalization of trade for the products concerned.

The basic approach of these arrangements is to set up a framework by which the importing countries (the developed or industrial countries) negotiate bilaterally with the exporting countries for the establishment of a series of voluntary-restraint arrangements, subsidiary to the overall textile or multifiber arrangements. Certain rules in the overall agreements constrain the nature of the bilateral agreements. For example, a target was introduced in some of the agreements for annual expansion or gradual liberalization of the imports into the importing countries. This figure stood nominally at 6 percent since 1973, but it is clear that exceptions introduced in the agreement provide a number of circumstances in which nations may use a much lower rate of increase in imports. If agreement could not be reached on the level of imports to be accepted, the arrangement provided that a limit within certain boundaries be set by the importing country. Provision was also made for interim "emergency" restraining agreements on measures. In addition, a textiles surveillance body (TSB) was set up to provide a forum for disputes and generally to supervise the arrangement.

Some of the factors that seem to have influenced these special arrangements in the textile and clothing sectors are well known. In particular, clothing industries are often a very large sector of an economy, employing many people; and these are often distributed among a wide variety of locations, which adds to their political importance. The original short-term arrangement is traced by many persons to commitments made by John F. Kennedy during the 1960 presidential election campaign in the United States.[112] The GATT report notes the arguments that were used by proponents of these arrangements, including the concern that developing countries often find it most convenient to begin their industrialization in the textile sector, because the machinery to do so is not too complex, and because clothing for the domestic market is an important marketing consideration. Thus, low-wage textile employees in developing countries became a threat to textile workers in developed countries.[113]

Approximately forty countries were formal participants in the MFA, and of these about nine (including the EC as one) are developed importing countries.[114] The 1984 GATT report, as well as other studies, has pointed out the very high costs to consumers (worldwide) caused by textile trade restraints. Cline notes in his book:

> Yet the reality ... has been one of successive tightening of practices under the MFA and the creation of a protection regime of unrivaled longevity and scope ...
>
> In sum, quota protection for textiles and apparel appears to have been rising over time through the successive tightening of the MFA and its implementing mechanisms. By 1994 the tariff equivalent of apparel quotas was probably in the range of 25 percent (beyond the tariff), and that on textiles some 15 percent ...
>
> Total consumer costs of such protection amount to $17.6 billion annually in apparel and $2.8 billion in textiles .... The average American household thus pays $238 every year to retain some two hundred thirty-five thousand jobs in the tex-

tile and apparel sectors rather than elsewhere in the economy. The consumer cost per-job saved is approximately $82,000 in apparel and $135,000 in textiles.[115]

The Uruguay Round Agreement on Textiles and Clothing was a major initiative by the negotiators. The intention of this agreement is to phase out the quota system for textile protectionism over a period of ten years. The agreement sets a number of intermediate goals and requirements during this period, but generally it is thought that the most significant trade liberalization and phaseout of quotas will occur near the end of the period. In addition, the agreement provides a special safeguard measure during this transition period for textile goods. These textile transition safeguard measures need not necessarily comply with the rules under the general agreement on safeguards. In addition, the agreement provides for a separate dispute-settlement mechanism from that of the general procedures of the WTO, (with appeal to the normal dispute procedure). Although many compromises are manifest in the Textile Agreement, it does appear to be an important achievement of the Uruguay Round, and a good start in the direction of liberalization, provided that in the end it will be effectively implemented. Of course, governments can negotiate item by item on the tariffs that they may charge for textile product imports. With the statement of policy inherent in this Textile Agreement, it does appear that the risk of the textile quota approach of the past being considered as a model for other sectors—such as steel—has decreased.

7.8 Reforms and the Uruguay Round Safeguards Text

The Attempts to Negotiate an International Safeguards Code: The Tokyo Round and After

One of the major objectives of the Tokyo Round negotiation, reflected in the September 1973 Tokyo ministerial declaration, was to develop a new "safeguards code" that would enhance the international discipline of safeguards.[116]

It is well known that this objective of the Tokyo Round negotiation ended largely in failure. The contracting parties could not come to a mutual agreement on the subject of safeguards during that negotiation, despite extensive sessions and hard work. The director-general's report, at the end of the Tokyo Round in 1979, acknowledged the difficulties of this negotiation, mentioning the controversy about discriminatory application of safeguards measures, as well as difficulties having to do with surveillance and dispute settlement, the definition of "serious injury," and the broader issues of "structural adjustment."[117] In addition, the question of how to bring some discipline to the burgeoning and chaotic use of export restraints was addressed, again, with little agreement.

At the conclusion of the Tokyo Round, the negotiating parties did agree that a committee of the GATT contracting parties continue negotiations. At the November 1982 ministerial meeting, the ministerial declaration noted the need for a comprehensive understanding, to include inter alia the following elements:

1. transparency
2. coverage
3. objective criteria for action including the concept of serious injury or threat thereof
4. temporary nature, degressivity, and structural adjustment
5. compensation and retaliation
6. notification, consultation, multilateral surveillance, and dispute settlement with particular reference to the role and functions of the safeguards committee."[118]

The Uruguay Round Agreement on Safeguards

With this history in mind, it seems eminently fair that, despite various reservations about how well it will be implemented, the Uruguay Round Agreement on Safeguards is a substantial achievement, and indeed a heroic statement of principle. In many ways the safeguards agreement brings into international law obligation many of the checks and safeguards that exist in the U.S. escape-clause legislation. Indeed, the U.S. Government Statement of Administrative Action explicitly comments on this, noting that the agreement "incorporates many concepts taken directly from Section 201 [of the U.S. law]." To briefly summarize the provisions of the agreement, it sets forth reasonably specific and explicit rules on the following aspects of safeguards.

1. Very important, it establishes a series of procedural rules standards of transparency, procedural fairness, public notice to interested parties, etc.
2. The agreement remedies some of the broader ambiguities of GATT Article XIX, with more explicit language and definitions of some of the concepts such as "serious injury," "threat of serious injury," "domestic industry," etc. It also interprets the nature of the causal link between increased imports and the serious injury, albeit not too precisely.

3. The agreement provides additional language and explanation of the nature of safeguard measures (basically tariffs or quotas) and defines some limits about how quotas shall be administered so as to respect a fair allocation of shares in the quota with all other members. It also establishes a limit on their duration (basically eight years.)

4. One of the more interesting provisions relaxes somewhat the compensation requirements under the prior GATT rules, provided that the safeguard measure has been taken as a result of an "absolute increase in imports and that such a measure conforms to the provisions of this agreement." If these conditions are fulfilled, there shall be no "right of suspension" (retaliatory or compensatory measure) for exporting countries affected during the first three years of the safeguard measure. This appears to introduce something of a "two-tier" approach to safeguards, whereby a quid pro quo for adhering to more precise and higher standards and criteria will be an escape from retaliatory type measures for this limited period of three years.

5. The agreement appears to impose severe prohibitions on the use of any safeguard measures, or the use of voluntary export restraints, other than that permitted under the agreement. There is a period during which existing measures shall be phased out (four years after the date of entry into force of the WTO), although provision is made for one exception per importing member to maintain a restriction until the end of 1999. (Under this provision the European Community is explicitly given only one exception, namely, to its provisions with Japan regarding passenger-car imports into the EC.)

There does not, however, appear to be any provision in the safeguard agreement for adjustment assistance or structural adjustment promotion. Probably such a provision would be very hard to implement and enforce anyway. In short, the safeguards text is an ambitious and admirable agreement, although the key to appraising it will be some years hence after observing the effectiveness of its implementation. Nevertheless, even if it is half implemented, it would appear that it will be a substantial improvement in the policy framework for safeguards in the world trading system.

8 National Treatment Obligations and Nontariff Barriers

8.1 The Policies and History of the National Treatment Obligation

The second major obligation of nondiscriminatory treatment, after MFN, is the national treatment obligation (expressed primarily in Article III of GATT).[1] Whereas MFN requires equal treatment among different nations, the national treatment obligation requires the treatment of imported goods, once they have cleared customs and border procedures, to be no worse than that of domestically produced goods. Obviously, an important policy behind this rule is to prevent domestic tax and regulatory policies from being used as protectionist measures that would defeat the purpose of tariff bindings. It should be noted, however, that this obligation applies to all products, not just to bound products. Thus, this rule assists the general goal of reducing restraints to imports.

A national treatment obligation can be found in many treaties, some dating back to earlier centuries.[2] The scope of the obligation may vary from treaty to treaty, however, and may apply to various activities, not only to products. For example, a common application of national treatment obligations is to criminal procedures when used for foreign citizens. Another example is national treatment obligations for the "right of establishment," so that a foreign business can set up branches and offices in another country.[3]

The national treatment obligation is often a source of complaint or dispute among nations.[4] Because it refers to domestic regulatory and tax measures, it is intimately related to various governmental measures that are based on legitimate policy reasons not necessarily designed for purposes of restraining imports. In some cases the domestic measures will overreach or be shaped to significantly and unnecessarily restrain imports. In other cases legitimate policy goals, including those mentioned in the article on general exceptions to GATT (Article XX), will prevent a measure from being inconsistent with GATT obligations.[5] The temptation of legislators and other government officials to shape regulatory or tax measures to favor domestic products seems to be very great, and proposals to do this are constantly suggested. This clash of policies raises some of the broader issues described in chapters 10 and 14, about whether a "harmonization" or "interface" approach is preferable.[6]

The national treatment clause is quite central to the new subjects negotiated in the Uruguay Round (services and intellectual property). Indeed, a difficult question is the degree to which the national treatment obligation as found in GATT (for goods) can be appropriately applied in the context of services (or intellectual property). A quick inspection of the services text illustrates the complexity of developing a meaningful national treatment obligation in the context of services.

8.2 The Contours and Application of the GATT Obligation

Article III of GATT sets out the national treatment obligation pertaining to treatment of imported products. The first paragraph is a general statement of policy, but includes an important phrase obligating contracting parties to avoid using taxes or regulations "so as to afford protection to domestic production."[7]

The second paragraph of Article III requires that internal taxes on imported products shall not be in excess of those applied to domestic goods, and expressly refers to the general goal of paragraph 1. The fourth paragraph of this article imposes essentially the same obligation (although without reference to paragraph 1) with respect to regulations and other "requirements affecting ... [the] internal sale ..." of imported products. Paragraphs 5 and 7 prohibit the use of mixing requirements to favor domestic products. Other paragraphs, however, provide some exceptions to the general national treatment rule, the most notable of which is the exception for government purchases (to which we return in section 8.6.)

A 1958 dispute-panel report, concerning Italian government measures relating to the sale of tractors, provides a fundamental interpretation for the national treatment clause. In this case the United Kingdom complained about an Italian banking measure that provided more favorable loans to farmers buying domestically made tractors than for buying imported tractors. The panel report, accepted by the CONTRACTING PARTIES,[8] stated that "... the intent of the drafters was to provide equal conditions of competition once goods had been cleared through customs..." and particularly stressed the fact that "... the assistance by the State was not given to producers but to the purchasers of agricultural machinery ..."[9]

Thus, once the imported goods have entered the internal stream of commerce, no government regulatory measure should assist the purchase of the domestic goods without likewise doing the same for imported goods. Even though the domestic *producer* may be subsidized under the GATT rules (an explicit exception for such subsidy appears in paragraph 8(b) of Article III of GATT), when the subsidy has the effect of directly influencing the purchaser's choice, it is inconsistent with the GATT.

The problem of "domestic-content" rules has been troublesome. As a condition of certain regulatory or license permissions such as might be required to build a new factory or to invest in a country, some nations have required formal or informal commitments that products produced in the new plant or assembled from imported parts be comprised of a certain minimum percent of domestic "value added." The United States brought a complaint against the Canadian government Foreign Investment Review Act (FIRA) partly on these grounds, arguing a violation of GATT Article III:4 and 5. The United States argued that the necessity of a commitment to the purchase of Canadian goods, when "competitively" or otherwise available from Canadian suppliers, as a requirement for investing in Canada violated GATT Article III:4. The panel report in 1984 supported this view even when the requirement was "informal."[10] The brief four-page text of the Uruguay Round "TRIMs" (trade-related investment measures) agreement addresses domestic content issues, and states that a requirement to use or purchase products from a domestic source as a condition for privilege or required by rule is inconsistent with paragraph 4 of Article III.[11]

A separate complaint was made by the Canadians against a U.S. law and practice under it, known as "Section 337."[12] This law provides a procedure whereby an American industry can complain about "unfair trade practices" of foreign parties shipping goods to the U.S. market. These practices might be infringement of copyright or patents, or attempts to monopolize, and so on. Canada alleged that the Section 337 procedure, when compared to similar U.S. domestic procedures for attacking unfair trade practices (through the Federal Trade Commission [FTC] or through patent or copyright domestic procedures) in effect discriminated against imports. A 1983 GATT panel report concluded that GATT Article XX general exceptions, which allowed "necessary" differences in treatment of imports in order to secure compliance with patent, copyright, and certain other laws, were applicable.[13] The report then went on to determine whether the Section 337 measures were either a "disguised restriction on international trade" or an "arbitrary or unjustifiable discrimination," and concluded again in the negative. The report, however, did not give Section 337 an entirely clean bill of health, noting that in cases with different facts, it could not exclude the possibility that "there might be cases ... where a procedure before a United States court might provide ... an equally satisfactory and effective remedy."[14]

In an action brought under the so-called New Commercial Policy Instrument of the EC, Akzo, a Dutch supplier of high-technology fibers, complained to the European Commission concerning a Section 337 ban requested by the U.S. company DuPont.[15] The Section 337 action alleged infringement by Akzo of patents held in the United States by DuPont. The commission brought a GATT panel proceeding arguing that Section 337 subjected imported goods to a separate and distinct procedure by virtue of their non-U.S. origin, and that such discrimination could not be justified as "necessary" under Article XX(d) of the GATT. The panel reported in January 1988, agreeing with a number of the EC's arguments.

8.3 De Facto or Implicit Discrimination

One of the more difficult conceptual problems of GATT rules has to do with the application of the national treatment obligation in the context of a national regulation or tax that *on its face* appears to be nondiscriminatory, but that, because of various circumstances in the marketplace or elsewhere, has the effect of tilting the scales against the imported products. As sophistication about GATT rules has increased among various national officials, the number of these "implicit discrimination" cases has seemed also to increase.

A classic example of this situation occurred in U.S. taxation of alcoholic beverages. A U.S. law (predating GATT and therefore benefiting from grandfather rights) provided for a tax of $10.50 on "each proof gallon or wine gallon when below proof." This taxing phrase applied to domestically produced as well as imported alcoholic beverages. A wine gallon is simply a gallon of the beverage, no matter how diluted the alcohol. A "proof gallon," however, is a gallon of liquid that is 100 proof, or 50 percent alcohol, by volume. If a producer can have his liquid taxed while at full proof, then later when the liquid is diluted to the percentage of alcohol used in the beverage sold at retail, (e.g., 86 proof or 43 percent for certain whiskeys), the effective tax per gallon of liquid sold at retail is $9.03, rather than $10.50. Domestic producers were able to achieve this.

Their concentrated whiskey was kept in cask under bond, and tax was paid on that basis. Only after the tax was assessed was the liquid diluted and bottled for retail sale. Importers, however, preferred to import the whiskey bottled at their home place of production, and the tax was assessed at the time of importation at the wine gallon rate, thus, effectively taxing the imported whiskey more per retail bottle. The importer *could* import the concentrated beverage, but then could not advertise it as "bottled in Scotland." Also, the bottling process might be more expensive in the United States.

In several interesting cases, foreign producers challenged this U.S. tax law as a violation of certain bilateral treaties.[16] Because the U.S. law was grandfathered under GATT, the GATT language was not directly involved.[17] A U.S. court held that because the tax law applied equally to domestic and imported products, the national treatment clauses of the treaties were not violated. However, these clauses did not have the language found in GATT Article III paragraph 1, prohibiting taxes arranged "so as to afford protection." Partly because of this language, under the GATT it can be strongly argued that even though a tax (or regulation) appears on its face to be nondiscriminatory, if it has an *effect* of affording protection, and if this effect is not essential to the valid regulatory purpose (as suggested in Article XX), then such tax or regulation is inconsistent with GATT obligations.

This brings to mind a number of hypothetical or not-so-hypothetical measures. One type of taxing proposal that has been considered is structured as follows. A uniform "excise" or sales tax (or value-added tax) is imposed on the sale of a product, for example automobiles (whether domestic or imported). Then the company paying this tax is allowed to credit the amount paid against U.S. employment taxes it would otherwise pay on behalf of its employees (such as social security taxes). Again, on its face, the provision appears neutral. Only when we learn that importers have very little liability for U.S. employment taxes, and thus have little opportunity to use these "credits," do we see that the effect can be essentially discriminatory.[18]

As another example, suppose a nation's tax laws provide for accelerated depreciation deduction allowances for capital purchases when the materials or machinery purchased are produced domestically, but not when they are imported. It appears clear that this is even *explicit* discrimination. But suppose the law instead provides that the deduction is allowed only when the goods are made by persons who are paid more than an average of $25,000 per year. Again, it is clear that this is not a very well disguised discrimination. The GATT obligation does not allow for differential treatment based on characteristics of the production process rather than the product itself.[19]

In 1994 a GATT panel report concluded that a U.S. luxury tax on autos priced over $30,000 (later adjusted to $32,000) was not inconsistent with Article III national treatment obligations. It was argued that although the tax nominally applied to both domestic and imported autos, it had a heavier effect on imports. Panel reasoning that has been quite controversial struggled with the question whether autos over and under the price threshold were "like products," and "recognized ... that two individual products could never be exactly the same in all aspects ... differences between products formed the basis of regulatory distinctions by governments ... Thus the practical interpretive issue under paragraphs 2 and 4 of Article III was: which differences between products may form the basis of regulatory distinctions by governments that accord less favorable treatment to imported products?" The panel then reasoned "that Article III serves only to prohibit regulatory distinctions between products applied so as to afford protection to domestic production. Its purpose is not to prohibit fiscal and regulatory distinctions applied so as to achieve other policy goals." It continued to suggest that examination of "so as to afford," suggested both "aim and effect," and concluded the tax did not have the aim of targeting imported autos. Some argue that in the light of the later WTO Appellate Body report (October 1996) on Japanese taxation of alcoholic beverages, the "aim and effect" test is not likely to be used again.[20]

A more subtle case is that in which a regulation for standardization or safety is used to effectively discriminate against imports. I take up this question in section 8.5.

8.4 Border Tax Adjustments

One of the more perplexing trade-policy problems, related to the national treatment obligation but also to several other GATT obligations, is the subject of border tax adjustments (BTAs). Under GATT, upon importation a nation may charge a tax (in addition to other tariffs) equivalent to a like internal tax imposed on domestic products of the same type. With respect to trade in the opposite direction (i.e., exports), a nation is allowed to *rebate* the amount of any internal tax imposed on the exported goods. Thus, in theory, the goods travel in international trade "untaxed," and are taxed at their destination under whatever rules apply there to domestic goods as well as imported goods. It sounds equitable and reasonable, but these measures have been the source of considerable acrimony in international trade relations, and were considered by the Supreme Court of the United States in one of the few international trade cases it has ever considered. [21].

First, it is useful to examine the legal structure of GATT that provides for the measures described in the preceding paragraph. The language calling for this treatment is sprinkled through a number of GATT clauses. On the import side, Article II, paragraph 2(a) grants an exception from the rule limiting border charges to the amount of the scheduled tariff binding, for "a charge equivalent to an internal tax imposed consistently with the provisions of paragraph 2 of Article III ..." It is important to note that both Article III and the remainder of the language of Article II refers to taxes on *products*.

As to the export side, matters are a bit more complex. An interpretative note to Article XVI, paragraph 4 states that a rebate of internal taxes on products shall not be considered a "subsidy" for purposes of the obligation against export subsidies.[22] In addition, a clause in Article VI likewise states that such a product tax rebate shall not be the basis of either an antidumping duty or a countervailing duty in the country of import. Again one can note that the taxes involved are those on *products*.

These product taxes (such as a sales tax, excise tax, or tax on a product at each stage of production), are often called "indirect taxes," to distinguish them from income or corporate taxes or other taxes imposed on a firm (not a product). Thus, the latter are often termed "direct taxes." Although an argument might possibly be made to the contrary, the value-added taxes, such as those in the European Community, have for a long time been considered in GATT to be "indirect," that is, taxes on products, and thus eligible for border tax-adjustment treatment. Given that these taxes are often as much as 20 percent or more, this obviously has considerable potential effect on imports and exports when border adjustments are applied.

In countries (like the United States) that do not generally have significant "product taxes," but instead rely heavily on income taxes for their revenue, border tax adjustments are either not used or are relatively insignificant. Income or "direct" taxes are *not* eligible for border tax adjustment, and this has been the source of considerable criticism among political and business leaders in the United States who see this disparity of treatment as unfair to the United States.[23] What is (or was) the rationale for this special approach of GATT toward border tax adjustments?

Probably when these rules were drafted not too much thought was given to their potential impact in the future, because at that time tariffs themselves were relatively much more important. The BTA question, like so many others involving nontariff measures, was in early GATT years not the focus of much attention. As tariffs declined, however, these alternative methods of affecting trade flows became much more significant.

One theory supporting the BTA system is that taxes on products (indirect taxes) tend to be effectively borne by the purchaser or consumer of these products. It is thus said that such a tax burden is "shifted forward" to the purchaser, or is a "destination" approach. In contrast, it was thought that income or "direct" taxes were borne primarily by the suppliers of capital investment (i.e., were shifted "backward," or were "origin" based). Thus it seemed fair to impose the product taxes at the destination on a basis equal to that imposed there on like domestic products. Certainly domestic producers in the importing country would perceive unfairness if the imported products were not taxed equally to their products.

To leave the products subject to the product taxes of the exporting country, however, would mean that products moving in international trade would be double-taxed: at the place of production, and again at the place of purchase or consumption. Therefore it was thought necessary to exclude the products from the product taxes of the exporting countries, by allowing a rebate of those taxes if necessary.

The problem, as any economist can demonstrate, is that both types of taxes have some burden on both the purchaser and the provider of capital, depending often on particular characteristics of the market structure. For example, if competition is keen, a product tax may mean that a producer will find it necessary to charge less than otherwise (to partly offset the tax effect on purchasing demand). In such a case, profitability will be lowered, and thus the return to capital is less (i.e., investors bear part of the burden of the tax). Likewise, an income tax affects the net after-tax return to capital and (if the market permits) induces the producer to charge a higher price to purchasers so as to offset the income-tax effect on net profit. Thus the purchaser bears part of the burden of the income tax. No simple way exists to find the dividing line or to know the percentage of each type of tax borne by the various participants for any particular product. The division probably differs from product to product.[24] Some economic comment suggests that even for a corporate tax, up to 20 percent of the burden is shifted forward to the consumer in the short run, and as much as 60 percent to 75 percent of the burden is shifted forward eventually. Evidence of this (if it exists) would provide substantial arguments that income taxes should receive some border tax-adjustment treatment also. Without such treatment for income taxes, countries that depend much more on such taxes argue that goods from countries with substantial border tax rebates have not shouldered their share of the costs of government, and therefore are in essence subsidized.

How to resolve this problem? There seems to be no good way. First of all, it is very unlikely that the GATT will be changed on this point. Even if it could be changed, it is hard to state a rule that would be more accurate. Perhaps the present rule is as good a rough approximation of equity as can be found, and it is at least administrable. In a floating exchange-rate world, at least where the product taxes are generally uniformly applied to all products, it can be argued that the exchange rate adjusts to any border tax adjustment, so that over a few years (at least) most distortion effects of the BTA are neutralized. Another approach for the "income tax" nations, is to shift to a value-added or product tax for a much larger portion of revenue, and then to apply a border tax adjustment. It seems much like the "tail wagging the dog" to change an otherwise desirable tax system to try to achieve some uncertain and perhaps dubious advantage for the international trade, but if such a product tax system has other merit to commend it, it does not hurt that a by-product might be less concerned about perceptions of unfairness of the international trade rules.[25]

The issue of "pass-through" of indirect taxes was raised in a case before the United States Court of International Trade in which a U.S. producer challenged, inter alia, the assumption of the Commerce Department that an indirect tax would be completely passed through to the eventual purchaser.[26] Commerce argued that it knew of "no reasonable method" for accurately measuring the incidence of a tax. The CIT rejected this approach, stating that "a conclusion that full pass-through occurred in all cases is not supported by substantial evidence," and remanded the issue back to Commerce. In a later administrative review, Commerce continued to work on the assumption that full pass-through occurred, and stated that the government was considering an appeal against the decision of the CIT.[27]

8.5 Technical Standards

Implicit discrimination against imports is often found in the context of so-called product standards. Examples are numerous. A nation that uses metric measures for tools and small fasteners might require all such products to be marked in metric measures. A valid domestic consumer protection policy might support such requirement, but it might also be introduced because troublesome import competition stems from products that are measured in other units, such as inches or feet.[28] Likewise, in chapter 5 I mentioned one nation's requirement that packages of food products be in its own language *and no other*. Although ample policy grounds appear to exist to require the labels to have the language of the country of import, to require that no other language appear on the label is to prevent the use of a cost-saving multilingual label.

Sometimes it is alleged that agencies or industry groups that set standards consciously try to "gerrymander" those standards to make it comparatively more difficult for foreign producers to comply. In this way a market for electronic components might be protected for domestic producers by certain quality or standards specifications. Likewise drug or cosmetic standards might be "shaped" to allow domestic manufacturers to accommodate them easily.

The process of obtaining clearance of a product subject to inspection, for health or safety reasons, may also add enough of a burden to the importation of goods as to "afford protection" to domestic manufacturers. Even though the country of export may test and examine goods that are exported, the importing country might require this to be done again. In some cases it may have good reason to do this. The exporting nation's tests may be unreliable or may not require as high a standard as that of the importing nation. If the exporting nation's tests are specifically for exports (and not domestically consumed products also), that nation may not have a strong incentive to provide stringent testing, in contrast to the nation whose consumers will purchase the good. On the other hand, delay and costs of processing tests in the importing nation, whether because of understaffing of the testing agency or a tacit understanding by that agency that "slowness helps the balance of trade," clearly are contrary to the liberal trading policies of the international system.

Much of the controversy and, indeed, anger over Japan's apparent unwillingness to import is centered on practices such as those just mentioned. The Japanese government has responded with various programs designed to prevent such measures from inhibiting imports and to mute the criticism leveled at Japan for taking these measures.[29]

Because of the risk that these various problems can become increasing sources of protectionism and conflict among nations, the GATT contracting parties negotiated a new code in the Tokyo Round designed to address these questions. This Agreement on Technical Barriers to Trade (TBT) expanded the GATT Article III obligations slightly, stating:

Parties shall ensure that technical regulations and standards are not prepared, adopted or applied with a view to creating obstacles to international trade. Furthermore, products imported from the territory of any Party shall be accorded treatment no less favorable than that accorded to like products of national origin and to like products originating in any other country in relation to such technical regulations or standards. They shall likewise ensure that neither technical regulations nor standards themselves nor their application have the effect of creating unnecessary obstacles to international trade.[30]

The Uruguay Round negotiators built on the experience of the Tokyo Round code, and it appears that they substantially enhanced the obligations. Even though once again, the major thrust of the Agreement on Technical Barriers to Trade (TBT) of the Uruguay Round is aimed at the procedures of standard making, the paragraph that seems to most nearly parallel the text quoted above from the predecessor agreement (article 2.2) reads as follows:

Members shall ensure that technical regulations are not prepared, adopted or applied with a view to or with the effect of creating unnecessary obstacles to international trade. For this purpose, technical regulations shall not be more trade-restrictive than necessary to fulfil a legitimate objective, taking account of the risks non-fulfillment would create. Such legitimate objectives are, inter alia: national security requirements; the prevention of deceptive practices; protection of human health or safety, animal or plant life or health, or the environment. In assessing such risks, relevant elements of consideration are, inter alia: available scientific and technical information, related processing technology or intended end-uses of products.

It will be noted that the new obligation goes substantially beyond the mere requirement of nondiscrimination, and addresses more fully than language of the predecessor agreement the question of the scientific justification necessary for standards that might inhibit imports. A provision was also included for reference to international standards when they exist. It is still not very clear what the burdens of a regulating government are to establish the legitimacy of its regulation in the light of scientific evidence. But nevertheless, the Uruguay Round text obviously goes another step further in this direction. Another Uruguay Round agreement, namely, the Agreement on the Application of Sanitary and Phytosanitary Measures, or SPS agreement, contains obligations concerning technical standards type barriers in the area of agriculture and food products.[31] The U.S. Statement of Administrative Action in regard to this notes that, although similar, the two texts "differ fundamentally in the means used to determine whether a measure is protectionist in nature. The TBT agreement relies primarily on a test of whether a measure discriminates against imported products (including against imports from one WTO member compared to imports from another member or a nonmember). By contrast the SPS agreement focuses on whether a measure is based on scientific principles and on a risk assessment."[32]

The UR TBT text specifies a number of obligations regarding the *procedure* by which product standards are developed in each of the signatory nations. Under this text, governments must, to the extent possible (recognizing that many product standards are developed by nongovernment groups), ensure that foreign nations and their producers with an interest in exporting shall have the opportunity to be heard and to present facts and arguments to standards-making bodies during the formulation of standards. In addition the text calls for "transparency" of standards, which is adequate notice and opportunity to comply. It urges the development of international standards, and encourages parties to recognize testing that has been appropriately done in the country exporting products. It also contains a preference for performance rather than design specifications.

Some consider the Tokyo Round TBT Code to be one of the more successful results of the Tokyo Round, because it had the largest number of acceptances of any of the codes (forty-two, including both developing and nonmarket economies).[33] (The United States implemented the code in Title IV of the 1979 Trade Agreements Act.)[34] Its operation in practice, and the activity of its committee of signatories, seem to have engendered satisfaction among governments and businesses. Some disputes brought under this code's dispute-settlement mechanism were satisfactorily resolved.[35] Of course, the TBT text of the Uruguay Round is part of the mandatory portion of the WTO Agreement, so all members are now bound by it, and disputes will proceed under the unified dispute settlement procedures.

My discussion here has focused on the standards for products themselves. Another important problem is that of standards relating not to the product itself but to the manufacture or processing of the products, and its impact on the environment, and on the safety of workers. I take this up in chapter 9.[36]

8.6 Government Procurement

The most important exception to the national treatment obligation in GATT Article III is found in paragraph 8, relating to government procurement. The language provides some interpretative difficulties but generally exempts, from Article III national treatment obligations, purchases by "governmental agencies of products purchased for governmental purposes ..."[37] Because the Article I MFN obligation of GATT makes reference to the obligations of Article III, paragraphs 2 and 4, it is argued that government procurement is also an exception to MFN rules.[38] Practice Under GATT confirmed this argument.

Early preparatory drafts of the ITO charter and GATT would have included government procurement in the discipline of these instruments, but government negotiators objected, so the final drafts included explicit exclusions.[39] Apparently government procurement was too close to sovereignty to permit regulation at that time. Given, for example, that military procurement would have been exempted in any event, the drafters worried that any attempt to draw lines between exempt and included government procurement would be too difficult.

Several important reasons can be given for why this exception had become very troublesome by the 1970s. First, a trend of increasing the government sector of a number of economies had become evident, so that in some nations over 40 percent of gross national product would pass through government budgets.[40] Where major industry sectors, such as steel or utilities were nationalized, an increasing amount of economic activity was beyond the reach of the GATT rules. Manufacturers of heavy electrical equipment (such as turbines) in the United States saw great exporting potential if foreign restrictions on government purchases of imports could be softened.

A second important (and related) reason for concern was the difficulty of finding an agreed definition of either "government agency" or "governmental purposes." Nations have a wide variety of ideas as to what is the appropriate sphere of government activity. In some countries it is automatically assumed that the government should own and run railroads, telephone systems, all electricity generation, travel bureaus, airlines, and many other activities that private enterprise conducts elsewhere. Some countries have added to the list basic "smokestack" industries, including steel and coal, as well as major related service sectors, such as banking. Such an important exception from the GATT trading rules would clearly diminish the liberalizing effects of these rules.

Nonmarket economies of course posed even greater problems in this regard. With the general world developments of a shift from government-owned or operated economic activities to "privatization," some of these problems may be ameliorated.

Nevertheless at the time of the Tokyo Round, and indeed even in the Uruguay Round, the negotiators felt that it was important to have an agreement on government procurement. The Tokyo Round government procurement agreement was accepted by only thirteen nations, basically the industrialized economies. The Uruguay Round text is also optional. It is described as a "substantial improvement over the Tokyo Round code"[41]. The obligations are quite far reaching. The starting point is the following text in Article III, paragraph 1 (which closely parallels the Tokyo Round code, with, however, the addition of services):

1. With respect to all laws, regulations, procedures and practices regarding government procurement covered by this Agreement, each Party shall provide immediately and unconditionally to the products, services and suppliers of other Parties offering products or services of the Parties, treatment no less favorable than:
a) that accorded to domestic products, services and suppliers; and
b) that accorded to products, services and suppliers of any other Party.

The code outlines detailed rules to implement this general principle, including rules governing the bidding procedures. These regulate the type of technical specifications that can be required in bids: the tendering procedures, including public announcement, qualification of bidders, time limits, tender documents, and so on. Foreign bidders are entitled to obtain a statement of reasons why their bids were rejected, and a dispute-settlement mechanism is established to follow through on complaints. Several complaints were processed through this procedure of the Tokyo Round Code.[42]

Although the requirements may seem far reaching, the important limitation of the code is that it only applies to the governmental "entities" on a list appended to the agreement for each signatory. The scheme has characteristics very similar to those of tariff bindings in GATT. Each country specifies by name to which entities the code applies, as part of a process of reciprocal negotiation among the code signers. The basic goal of the drafters was to have the code establish a framework for truly effective discipline against governmental discriminatory purchasing, recognizing that such stringent requirements would make governments somewhat hesitant to include entities on their list. Once the code came into existence, with reciprocal negotiated lists of entities, later negotiations were contemplated for adding more entities to the list. Some negotiations have been held,[43] and more are contemplated.

The scope and coverage of the Government Procurement Agreement additionally depends on certain other clauses in it. A minimum threshold for covered contracts is set in various parts of each party's annexed schedule. The annexes containing each party's schedule are divided into five parts:

Annex 1 contains the central government entities.

Annex 2 contains subcentral government entities.

Annex 3 contains all other entities that procure in accordance with the provisions of this agreement.

Annex 4 specifies services covered by this agreement.

Annex 5 specifies covered construction services. Exception is provided for national security, and in a qualified way, for national measures to protect public morals, order, safety, health, and similar goals.[44]

Telecommunications has been a large issue in connection with the agreement, and this issue has figured prominently between the United States and Japan. In the United States, telecommunications has not been government owned, and even its monopoly power has been diluted by the trend to "deregulation." Thus, the United States argues that foreign suppliers have the opportunity to sell telecommunication equipment in the U.S. market. On the other hand, most other nations have a government-owned telecommunications monopoly, although several have recently decided to "privatize" or deregulate also. From the end of the Tokyo Round onward, the United States and Japan have negotiated strenuously over U.S. demands that U.S. companies have better opportunity to sell products to the Japanese telephone monopoly. From the U.S. perspective, these negotiations have had only moderate success. On the other hand, in at least one case, the Japanese demonstrated that a U.S. telephone company, AT&T, refused a purchase of Japanese fiberoptics equipment (which was the low bid in a competition), for "Buy American" reasons.[45] What effect the Japanese "privatization" of NTT will have is not yet clear.

In the United States, many "Buy American" regulations are on the books, both at the federal and state levels.[46] A 1979 International Trade Commission study found some twenty-five instances of regulatory preferences for U.S. goods at the federal level alone.[47] The United States is not unique in requiring preferences for domestically produced goods.[48]

The best example of U.S. law is the Buy American Act, which essentially requires acquisition of domestically produced articles for "public use."[49] In an important exception, the law authorizes the federal authorities to deviate from this rule if the cost of foreign-produced articles is lower by specified amounts.[50]

Although federal procurement policies now limit "Buy American" provisions in order to open government markets in accordance with the MTN agreement, state "Buy American" statutes have proliferated in recent years. The Tokyo Round Code did not apply to subfederal units, but an important achievement for the Uruguay Round text is to extend its application to subfederal units, as they are scheduled in the annexes.

9 Competing Policies and Ingenious Devices

9.1 Protecting the Value of Tariff Concessions and Competing Policies

In chapters 5 through 8 I examined some of the most important regulatory principles affecting contemporary international trade. In chapters 10 and 11 I will explore more such principles, but mostly in the context of permitted national government unilateral responses to certain so-called unfair practices in exporting nations. In this chapter I take up several regulatory principles that can be quite important, but that for one reason or another can be treated more briefly. Two basic common threads run through most of the sections in this chapter: the existence of important policies competing with those of comparative advantage and liberal trade, and the desirability of protecting the value of tariff and other trade rules by plugging "loopholes" and preventing the protectionist use of a variety of ingenious import restraints.

As already noted, the ingenuity of man in devising import restraints that skirt the formal rules of international trade seems boundless.[1] Nevertheless, there are a number of situations where import-restraining activity is required by legitimate government goals.

9.2 National Security

One exception to liberal trade policies that has always been recognized by economic theorists and statesmen is that of national security. Here the competing policy of protecting a nation's continued existence is obviously more important than economic welfare or other potential benefits of comparative advantage. On the other hand, it is not always clear that the best way to protect a nation's national security is by using import restraints or other trade-distorting measures. In a world where some wars could be over in minutes, traditional notions of the need for production facilities are not always applicable. In another context, the overall economic well-being of a nation, and such subtle attributes as the scientific advancement of its research and the technical proficiency of its workforce, are to some observers more important as longer-term protections of national security than traditional shorter-term goals of stockpiled war material or factories.[2]

Even if one acknowledges the importance of having viable and working production facilities in some sectors of the economy, some economists suggest that import restraints to protect such facilities from decline as a result of import competition may be the wrong approach. Such a policy can let the domestic sector slide into noncompetitiveness and lack of productivity, which can worsen its position and even render it unfit in an emergency. On the other hand, alternative measures, if some protection from competition is deemed necessary, may work better in the economy. One such alternative to applying import restraints is to subsidize the sector or some of its facilities, as a way to keep it viable. "Moth-balling" may be one type of subsidy, but another might stem from government purchases, and yet another technique would be direct payments possibly tied to particular activities needed for national security which might not otherwise be compensated in the marketplace. For example, certain equipment might need to be much more reliable if used for military rather than for civilian purposes.

Despite these various considerations, nations still occasionally feel the national security need to use border restraints or other measures not consistent with international trade rules. The GATT (now GATT 1994) recognizes this in Article XXI, which provides for a general exception to all GATT obligations with respect to disclosure of national security information, regulation of fissionable materials, regulation of traffic in arms, and action in pursuance of UN Charter obligations relating to maintenance of international peace and security. Article XXI has a catch-all clause that allows action that a contracting party "considers necessary for the protection of its essential security interests ... taken in time of war or other emergency in international relations."[3]

This language is so broad, self-judging, and ambiguous that it obviously can be abused. It has even been claimed that maintenance of shoe production facilities qualifies for the exception because an army must have shoes![4] Because of this danger of abuse, contracting parties were extremely reluctant to formally invoke Article XXI, even in circumstances when it seemed applicable. Thus only a few cases have been reported regarding Article XXI in GATT's history.[5] In general, the GATT approach to Article XXI was to defer almost completely to the judgment of an invoking contracting party.

The United States has severed trading relations (and therefore GATT relations) with certain contracting parties in GATT on a number of occasions. In 1951 the U.S. Congress required the nonapplication or withdrawal of application of MFN treatment for communist countries; and at that time one communist country—Czechoslovakia—was a GATT contracting party, so the United States had to terminate the application of the GATT between it and that country. There was no explicit authority in GATT for doing this,[6] but the CONTRACTING PARTIES adopted a "declaration" authorizing the two countries to suspend GATT obligations toward each other, and this action could be interpreted as a "waiver."[7] Several other comparable situations are recorded in GATT.[8] In 1985 the U.S. president decreed an embargo on trade between the United States and Nicaragua, and Nicaragua challenged the U.S. action in GATT.[9] The U.S. position in the GATT process was that because the U.S. was invoking Article XXI and because that article deferred to national judgments about national security, GATT had no business discussing this matter further.[10]

The United States has a number of domestic trade law measures based on "national security" considerations. The most often used of these are the export control laws, under the Export Administration Act.[11] The United States tries to prevent shipments to certain countries of products that it has included on a list of products having some strategic importance. These include advance computers, various electronic devices, certain weapons and their technology, and similar items. In addition this act gives certain powers to the president to limit exports for reasons of foreign policy or short supplies.[12] In the post–Cold War world, these regulations have been quite controversial in the United States, and have been undergoing agonizing scrutiny.

On the import side, the United States has a law on its books—Section 232 of the 1962 Trade Expansion Act—that permits the executive to limit imports of products when necessary for national security purposes.[13] As of mid-1996, over twenty petitions to use this statute had been received. In only three cases—all involving petroleum products—was the authority actually used, although a 232 petition led to "voluntary" export restraints on machine tools from 1986 until 1993. Under this statute, citizens can petition their government to apply import restraints, and the government must respond within one year (with a few exceptions), with action restricting imports, or the reasons for not doing so must be published. In practice, the U.S. government looks at a wide variety of factors to determine whether or not import restrictions, for national defense reasons, are justified.[14]

One of the most interesting cases concerning the Article XXI exception of GATT was a complaint by Nicaragua against the United States in relation to the U.S. embargo against Nicaragua during the problems of the civil war in Nicaragua in the 1980s. A 1986 panel report, which has not been adopted, included the following paragraph.

> The panel did not consider the question of whether the terms of Article XXI precluded it from examining the validity of the United States' invocation of that Article as this examination was precluded by its mandate. It recalled that its terms of reference put strict limits on its activities because they stipulated that the Panel could not examine or judge the validity of or the motivation for the invocation of Article XXI:(b)(iii) by the United States ... The Panel concluded that, as it was not authorized to examine the justification for the United States' invocation of a general exception to the obligations under the General Agreement, it could find the United States neither to be complying with its obligations under the General Agreement nor to be failing to carry out its obligations under that Agreement.[15]

Language similar to the GATT Article XXI is contained in both the Services and the Intellectual Property Agreements of the Uruguay Round.[16]

9.3 The General Exceptions and Legislation for Health and Welfare

A very broad list of exceptions to GATT obligations is found in Article XX, and is entitled "General Exceptions." It includes governmental measures undertaken in order to effectively implement policies such as those to protect or promote:[17]

- public morals
- protection of human, animal, or plant life or health
- gold or silver trade
- customs enforcement
- monopoly laws (antitrust)
- patents, trademarks, and copyrights
- preventing deceptive practices
- banning products of prison labor
- protecting national treasures

- conserving natural resources
- carrying out an approved commodity agreement
- export restrictions because of short supply
- export restrictions to implement a price stabilization program

Most of these measures might be thought of as falling within the general "police powers" or "health and welfare powers" of a government. Article XX thus recognizes the importance of a sovereign nation being able to act to promote the purposes on this list, even when such action otherwise conflicts with various obligations relating to international trade.

A difficult interpretive question is raised by the relationship of this article of GATT to some of the other texts in Annex 1A of the WTO Agreement (such as the Technical Standards Agreement, or the Agreement on Agriculture or the Agreement on Textiles and Clothing.) In addition the texts regarding new subjects, such as services, contain reference to exceptions like those of GATT article XX, not always worded identically to the GATT language.[18]

Many of the article XX exceptions can relate to the national treatment obligations of Article III. Take, for example, a government regulation imposing a minimum standard of purity for certain drugs. If this regulation applies not less favorably to imported goods than to domestic goods, then no need exists to invoke Article XX: the national treatment standard is fulfilled (unless there is implicit or de facto discrimination as described in section 8.3). On the other hand, it may be the case that, in order to achieve its objective of protecting consumers against impure drugs, a nation would find it necessary to impose some special regulations to take care of imports. Perhaps the manufacture of imported goods cannot be readily inspected because of the cost of sending inspectors to a foreign country. In such case it might be reasonable for the importing country to require that the drug imports be subjected to testing at or after importation. Article XX contemplates this possibility and allows it to occur without breaching GATT.

Many of these exceptions are quite general, for example, "public morals" or "human health." Obviously, clever argumentation could be used to justify practices that have as their secret goal preventing import competition. This article therefore includes clauses designed to protect against such abuse. Its opening paragraph, called the "chapeau", allows an exception to all GATT obligations for items on the list, provided that "measures are not applied in a manner which would constitute a means of arbitrary or unjustifiable discrimination between countries where the same conditions prevail, or a disguised restriction on international trade ..."[19]

These phrases can be characterized as "softer" obligations of MFN and national treatment. They allow departure from the strict language of Article I (MFN) and Article III (national treatment), to the extent necessary to pursue the goals listed in Article XX, but not to the extent of non-MFN discrimination or protection of domestic production, if either is not unnecessary to pursue those listed goals.

Various disputes have been brought to GATT concerning this language. For example, a 1982 GATT panel ruled that a U.S. embargo on imports of tuna and tuna products from Canada was inconsistent with GATT Article XI obligations and not justified by Article XX.[20] The United States had argued that its action was taken as an enforcement measure to ensure proper conservation and management of certain fish stocks. The panel noted, however, that Article XX(g) required complementary domestic conservation measures that appeared to be missing in this case. The history of the case suggested that the United States was using trade measures to enforce its view of a disputed sea boundary.

In the first case under the WTO to go all the way through the appellate procedure, the Appellate Body Panel held that the U.S. government environmental regulations on gasoline were not consistent with U.S. obligations under GATT. This case also turned on an examination of the exception in Article XX(g). However, the WTO Appellate panel held that Article XX(g) had been fulfilled by an objective to protect "clean air." Nevertheless, the panel then carefully looked at the chapeau of Article XX, and concluded that the U.S. regulations did not escape the disciplines required by the chapeau language. As the first WTO appellate body report, this report has considerable importance. In its approach to Article XX(g), the Appellate panel seems to be enlarging the potential choices of a nation regarding the methods it wishes to pursue for environmental protection reasons. (See discussion in section 4.4.)[21]

As discussed elsewhere,[22] Section 337 of U.S. law, a measure most often applied to imports that offend patent rights, has several times been challenged, raising the question under GATT Article XX(d) of whether Section 337 is "necessary to secure compliance" with patent protection.

In general, the question of the protection of intellectual property rights has become prominent in trade policy discussions. The United States in particular has passed many motions to control counterfeiting and violation of patents and copyrights by firms within its borders. The United States has used Section 337 (described in section 10.7 below) and Section

301 (described in chapter 4) to apply pressure to these issues. The 1988 Trade Act has a number of measures relating to this concern. Most prominently, the act (1) specifically mentions lack of protection of intellectual property rights as "unreasonable" in its definitions under the Section 301 amendments,[23] and (2) changes U.S. Section 337 law so that an "injury test" is no longer a necessary prerequisite for an order excluding imports that abuse intellectual property rights.[24] The Uruguay Round texts now include new rules regarding intellectual property, and presumably these rules will affect some of the U.S. actions, such as its "special 301" cases.

Several legitimate domestic policies pose particularly difficult conceptual problems for trade policies. I take up two of these in the next two sections, namely, the problem of pollution from the manufacturing process and the problem of restrictive business practices and monopolies policies.

9.4 Pollution and Regulation of the Manufacturing Process

If an imported product has the effect when used of creating a health or pollution hazard, the Article III and XX rules make it relatively easy for a nation to take measures to deal effectively with this problem. A nondiscriminatory regulation can be adopted, applying to domestic and imported products alike and requiring certain standards. For example, a law could prohibit automobiles from issuing more than a certain amount of pollutants, or it could prohibit the use of materials in residential buildings that are flammable or tend to issue noxious gas when burning.

The more difficult conceptual problem comes from the impact on competitiveness of industry when a government imposes a requirement of pollution prevention, safety, or health protection on the manufacturing process. Take, as an example, the production of a certain type of plastic toy. The toy itself, let us suppose, is perfectly safe, poses no health hazard, and cannot burn or emit gases. Thus, neither the domestic nor the imported models of this toy will constitute a hazard to be guarded against. Assume, however, that the manufacture of these toys can be quite hazardous, perhaps because the processing of chemicals to make and mold the plastic involves noxious fumes, danger of explosion, or inhalation of carcinogenic gases.

Likewise assume that the factory producing this toy emits noxious smoke, affecting the environment. In such a case governments will impose requirements to protect health and safety of the workers and the environs on the manufacturing company, and these will have costs that must be included in the price of the product. Now suppose that imports of identical toys come from a country that is not so careful about the health of its employees or environs and imposes no such regulation. All other things being equal, the imports, can be priced cheaper and could cause competitive distress to the domestic producers. Is this fair? What can be done about it? Could the importing nation take a countermeasure such as (1) impose a ban (or limitation) on imports of goods that are manufactured by processes that cause health, safety, or environmental problems; or (2) impose an additional charge at the border on the imported goods, to equal the amount of the cost that domestic producers incur through compliance with health, safety, or environmental standards; or (3) impose a tax on all goods, domestic and foreign, related to the cost of the regulation, then rebate that tax to domestic manufacturers or subsidize them so as to offset their costs of compliance?

Arguably the importing nation may not do any of these, given that the national treatment requirement of Article III of the GATT imposes the obligation to treat the "like products" equally, and the products may be considered as "like." The article does not allow discrimination on the basis of differences in the country of export or its manufacturing environment.[25] Indeed, to a certain extent, this is what comparative advantage is all about: differences in environments of production, including the environment of government regulation.[26]

Article XX does not seem to help here either. The language prohibits actions that are a "disguised restriction on international trade," and allows exceptions for human health, safety, and so on. Although not explicitly restricted to the health and safety of the *importing* country, it can be argued that this is what Article XX means. It allows exceptions from GATT obligations, which in general apply to "like products," implying a focus on the product itself, and not on the production process (unless that process affects the *product*).[27]

In addition, some possible measures could also be inconsistent with MFN requirements of Article I of GATT. For example, suppose country A imports the toys from countries B and C. Country B regulates the same way that A does, but C does not; and goods from C are therefore cheaper. If A imposed a "regulatory equalization tax" on goods from C and not from B, then an MFN objection could be raised. Country C would argue that the products are "like products," that Article I requires equal treatment of like products, and that it makes no allowance for unlike production processes.[28] One approach might be to apply a uniform border tax on all imported products, to provide *on the average* for imports to carry the same regulatory cost burden as domestic products, but this, of course, would effectively penalize countries that do apply such regulatory costs. The products from these countries would be doubly burdened, and this measure would have the perverse effect of providing an incentive to avoid such regulation.

Of course, if the manufacturing process in the exporting country itself causes hazards or pollution in the importing country, such as from smoke or gases that drift across the border, other ways may be found to approach the problem. This is a problem similar to one faced by the United States and Canada in connection with acid rain. One solution is a bilateral or multilateral treaty dealing with the problem. Another, but less likely to be successful, is a direct international law proceeding arguing wrongdoing in the nature of an "international tort."[29] In some cases (such as Rhine water pollution), regional treaties may already exist that can be relied on to help.[30]

Whether an importing nation could use border restrictions or taxes to equalize the price of imported goods with domestic costs of health and safety regulation is as yet an unresolved issue for the world trading system. It is an issue fraught with dangerous potential. If this principle were extended to many types of government regulation—for example, minimum wage or other labor regulations—it could be the basis of a rash of import restrictions, often defeating the basic goals of comparative advantage. Government regulations vary so greatly that the already difficult conceptual questions of the world's rules on subsidies[31] would pale in significance beside the problems that the costs of regulation equalization would create.

Alternatively, to never allow such equalization measures might appear somewhat callous. At one time, Brazil allegedly argued that its capacity to absorb pollution was a feature of its comparative advantage in the production of paper and pulp products. Yet, more recently, Brazilians have realized that even they cannot ignore the environmental effects of some of their factories. The tourism industry is often an important counterlobby against the manufacturers on this point. Some suggest that the best approach is at least temporary "benign neglect," with the possibility that over time many of these problems will sort themselves out as the necessity of health and safety regulation becomes more apparent to more nations.[32]

Perhaps the best-known GATT case concerning some of these matters was the tuna-dolphin case, brought against a U.S. restriction on imports of tuna from Mexico. The 1993 report of the panel (which was not adopted by the GATT contracting parties) struggled with the concepts outlined above. The United States restricted the imports of tuna that came from countries that did not protect against the killing of dolphins in the process of netting the tuna. The U.S. standard on this was a unilateral one, imposed by statute passed by Congress reflecting various pressures from environmental interest groups in the United States. The argument of Mexico, accepted by the panel, was that the tuna was a like-product to U.S. domestically produced tuna, and tuna imported from other countries. The U.S. regulation was trying to reach a *process* of harvesting the tuna, not affecting the characteristics of the *product*. Near the end of its report, the panel said as follows:

> It seemed evident to the panel, that, if the CONTRACTING PARTIES were to permit import restrictions in response to differences in environmental polices under the General Agreement, they would need to impose limits on the range of policy differences justifying such responses and to develop criteria so as to prevent abuse. If the CONTRACTING PARTIES were to decide to permit trade measures of this type in particular circumstances it would therefore be preferable for them to do so not by interpreting Article XX, but by amending or supplementing the provisions of the General Agreement or waiving obligations thereunder. Such an approach would enable the CONTRACTING PARTIES to impose such limits and develop such criteria.

This language seems to imply a attitude of "judicial restraint," with deference to the negotiating and other rule-making processes under the GATT. However, this case received an enormous amount of criticism from environmental groups. A subsequent case, sometimes called "Tuna II," also rules against similar U.S. measures applied to prevent transhipment through third countries. It appears very likely that environmental cases will be quite important, as the first completed WTO case suggests.[33]

9.5 Restrictive Business Practices

The international law rules generally apply only to nations, not to individual citizens or business firms. The number of exceptions to this principle is growing, particularly in the areas of responsibility for war and treatment of prisoners, and of human rights.[34] Nevertheless, most economic international rules, certainly including those of GATT, apply almost exclusively to nations. The wording of GATT, or the IMF charter, and of most FCN treaties[35] reinforces this approach. Article XVII of GATT, applying to state trading enterprises, could be a modest exception, but even here the language requires that "each contracting party undertakes that if it establishes or maintains a State enterprise, ..." that contracting party will do certain things. In some clauses the contracting party is obligated to require or ensure that the trading enterprise follow certain rules, but the obligation itself does not appear to fall on the enterprise. In any case most enterprises contemplated by Article XVII would be subject to the control of the national government.

In chapter 13 I will address the difficulty that GATT principles pose for economic systems that rely extensively on state trading agencies or monopolies. The language of most GATT obligations does not easily stretch to such nonmarket economies and their practices which affect trade. In market economies, however, an important group of practices exists that can defeat the underlying purposes of the world trading rules and that are not reached by the GATT language. These are various restrictive business practices.

For example, several nations may assiduously apply all GATT rules, allowing trade to flow freely among them. But a large corporation in one nation, for purposes of its own, may decide that it will buy only domestically produced parts for its products. If these purposes are not based on efficient economic principles, their effect is to undo the governmental liberal trade policies. Perhaps the corporation is owned by a parent that also owns parts producers and mandates (or "encourages") purchases from the sister company. Perhaps the domestic product preference is the result of informal pressure of the employees, or a mutual back-scratching pact among various domestic industries. Perhaps the domestic buyers rely on domestic producers for a majority of their parts inputs, and these domestic producers have conspired to prohibit sales of their parts to any domestic buyer that also buys imported goods (a "loyalty rule," sometimes encouraged by a "loyalty rebate," might have this effect).[36]

Many of these practices raise questions of government antitrust or restrictive business practice policies. There is a very large range in the degree to which governments regulate to minimize such practices. The United States, for example, is often thought to have one of the most stringent antitrust laws in the world, strongly reinforced by treble damage awards to diligent complainants (sometimes called "private attorneys general"). Yet even in the United States there have been well-publicized instances of private "buy domestic" attitudes.[37]

The draft Havana Charter for an ITO contained an entire chapter devoted to the problem of restrictive business practices (RPBs), recognizing the important link between these practices and liberal trade policies generally.[38] When the ITO failed, the GATT had to step into the trade-regulation role. The GATT, however, contains nothing addressed to the RBP problem, and when a suggestion was made in 1954 to bring this subject under the GATT, the GATT CONTRACTING PARTIES decided only to provide for consultations on the subject and not bring it within the procedures of GATT Article XXIII (on disputes).[39]

Thus, to a certain extent a gap exists in the world trade-regulation system. Perhaps part of this gap was filled by several voluntary codes that have been developed to address the problem, including the 1976 OECD *Guidelines for Multinational Enterprises*[40] and the 1980 UNCTAD *Set of Multilaterally Agreed Equitable Principles and Rules for the Control of Restrictive Business Practices.*[41]

The problem of restrictive business practices has been raised in recent years in another GATT context. It has been argued (usually in the United States where strong RBP laws exist) that toleration by a foreign government of RBPs that tend to exclude imported goods amount to unfair trade practice or a "subsidy" to the local business. In the 1988 Trade Act, for example, Section 1301, which amended Section 301, includes in the definition of "unreasonable" acts to which Section 301 refers the "toleration by a foreign government of systematic anticompetitive activities by private firms or among private firms in the foreign country that have the effect of restricting ... access of United States goods to purchasing by such firms."[42]

The measure once again points out the gaps in the international trade rules because of the absence of rules on RBP such as those in the ITO charter. The problem with the U.S. approach, of course, is that it is not tied to an internationally agreed standard for RBP rules. Governments and societies differ greatly in their notion of the appropriate level of RBP rules, and few governments view the rules in the United States as the best approach. Yet U.S. law now seems to imply that the United States could take unilateral action to "retaliate" against countries that do not measure up to the U.S. view of appropriate RBP rules. Considerable scholarly and professional attention has been paid to the problem of this regulatory gap, but a great deal of controversy continues about what to do about it. There are discussions in the context of OECD, and the WTO, and various proposals to develop some kind of international agreement. It remains to be seen what will happen. Some of the Uruguay Round texts, such as those on services and intellectual property, include provisions relating to this subject.

9.6 Balance-of-Payments Exceptions and Currency Obligations

When GATT was drafted, balance-of-payments problems were severe both for developing countries and for countries faced with postwar reconstruction. For many years, economists spoke of the "dollar shortage," which reflected the relative strength of the U.S. economy and the need of many nations to buy capital goods from the United States. One of the purposes of the International Bank for Reconstruction and Development (the World Bank), which was created at the Bretton Woods Conference along with the International Monetary Fund, was to assist in the postwar reconstruction of devastated countries. The IMF provided a series of obligations to prevent currency restrictions and manipulations from becoming important barriers to trade, while recognizing that BOP considerations would necessitate short-term exceptional governmental interference with currency transactions.[43] The original IMF charter obligated its member nations to pursue policies to support fixed par values for their currencies.

In light of these conditions, the GATT drafters recognized the necessity for exceptions from the other GATT obligations in the face of a severe balance-of-payments crisis. In GATT Articles XII, XIII and XIV, they authorized certain trade restrictions when a need related to BOP conditions could be demonstrated. The restrictions they authorized were quotas, not tariffs. It is interesting to speculate why, in the face of a general policy preference for the "price mechanism" approach of tariffs, the GATT drafters opted instead to allow quantitative restrictions. One possibility was that, in many nations, quotas (at least temporary ones) were under the control of executive portions of the government which could act without parliamentary approval. The contrary was normally true for tariffs, which legislatures preserved as their prerogative. Thus, the drafters (representatives of executives) may have seen the practical advantage of quotas, particularly given that a BOP crisis often requires swift action and confidentiality before such action is taken.

History has dealt with this subject differently, however, and has posed one of the persistently most difficult jurisprudential questions for GATT. In fact, many contracting parties in the face of BOP difficulties have resorted to tariff "surcharges." (A tariff surcharge is an across-the-board ad valorem tariff on all imports, added to the tariff otherwise charged on imports.) In general, a surcharge is supposed to be applied uniformly to all goods, and to apply to otherwise nondutiable goods as well as those that otherwise are subject to duties. A 10 percent surcharge, for instance, would apply this additional amount of tariff for all goods. Those already subject to a 5 percent tariff would now be subject to 15 percent. Those otherwise duty-free goods would now be subject to the 10 percent surcharge.[44]

In some cases waivers have been given for the application of such a surcharge, but in other cases the surcharge has been used without any GATT legal cover.[45] Given that a surcharge inevitably results in a tariff charged on most goods that exceeds the tariff binding of that country's GATT schedule, it is in these cases that it is quite clearly inconsistent with GATT obligations. On the other hand, the economic policies would support the tariff surcharge as preferable to the use of quotas.[46] Thus, the GATT BOP rules are anomalous. It has been argued that the GATT rules should be changed. On the other hand, an argument against changing the rule has been made that by keeping the GATT rule as it is, the CONTRACTING PARTIES, although (to a certain extent) tolerating the use of surcharges, have more "leverage" to urge the withdrawal of the surcharge than they would have if it were technically legal. This is an interesting but troublesome argument, and it usually overlooks the subtle longer-term damage done to the fabric of the legal structure involved.

A major BOP tariff surcharge was imposed by the president of the United States in August 1971. The level was set at 10 percent, although some exceptions were made, particularly because the basic tariff statute had lower tariffs, and under the U.S. Constitution the president did not have authority to go above these statutory limits. The surcharge was part of a broader program designed to correct a serious currency crisis for the United States. Other parts included the closing of the "gold window": that is, ceasing to buy dollars with gold at a set price; introducing the Domestic International Sales Corporation (DISC) legislation;[47] and imposing internal price controls on certain products.[48] All of these measures had serious domestic and international legal problems. Closing the "gold window" essentially left the dollar to float in world markets, and was a violation of U.S. government obligations under the IMF. Subsequently, the IMF charter was amended to accommodate floating, which had been strongly recommended by many economists for more than a decade. The DISC was challenged in GATT.[49] Domestic price controls were authorized by very broad ambiguous language in a statute that the president had not sought and had earlier intimated he would never use.[50] All parts of this program except the DISC were challenged in court litigation in the United States, but ultimately all were upheld.[51]

In a world with floating exchange rates, it has been suggested that the use of trade restrictions for balance-of-payments reasons is no longer justified.[52] In theory, the exchange rate is supposed to shift and cause automatic adjustment in the balance-of-trade and payments. The GATT BOP language, which allows use of the quota exception, tends to condition the exception in monetary reserves. With floating exchange rates, however, on the decline or need for increase reserves are no longer such a central feature of the world economic system, and it can be argued that the GATT criteria will almost never be met. On the other hand, the experience of more than two decades of floating exchange rates leaves many questions unanswered, and the voices articulating the need for trade measures because of the misfunctioning of the exchange-rate system are growing in number.[53]

As a result of the Tokyo Round, the CONTRACTING PARTIES adopted a Declaration on Trade Measures Taken for Balance-of-Payments Purposes.[54] The first article of this declaration states that "The procedures for examination stipulated in Articles XII and XVIII shall apply to all restrictive import measures taken for balance-of-payments purposes. The application of restrictive import measures taken for balance-of-payments purposes shall be subject to the following conditions in addition to those provided for in Articles XII, XIII, XV and XVIII without prejudice to other provisions of the General Agreement."[55]

Although this language in its own terms does not modify the GATT, it nevertheless seems to contemplate measures other than quotas, so arguably gives some "legal comfort" for the use of surcharges. As is the case with many GATT rules, the ambiguity appears studied and intentional!

United States law regarding the use of a tariff surcharge is also interesting. The president was challenged in court for imposing the 1971 surcharge, but ultimately the courts upheld him under the emergency powers of the U.S. Trading with the Enemy Act.[56] The Congress was sufficiently disturbed, however, about presidential encroachment on its tariff domain that it included in the 1974 Trade Act a section designed to clarify the president's authority in this regard.[57] This section gives explicit authority to impose a surcharge, but limits it in amount and duration unless Congress approves differently. The section also calls on the president to "seek modifications in international agreements aimed at allowing the use of surcharges in place of quantitative restrictions ..." in BOP cases, and some authorities of this enactment are tied to international obligations.[58]

Developing countries can often argue that the BOP exceptions of GATT (Article XVIII contains some that are targeted to such countries) permit them to use quotas, given that many of these countries are perennially in BOP difficulties. This exception to GATT therefore has been a major "legal cover" for many developing countries acting without the normal disciplines of international trade rules,[59] and was a source of scrutiny and negotiation in the Uruguay Round of trade negotiations.[60]

The Uruguay Round negotiators struggled with this history and the conflicting policies embedded in it. The result in the Uruguay Round text is an Understanding on the Balance-of-Payments Provisions of the General Agreement on Tariffs and Trade 1994. This text includes the 1979 Tokyo Round declaration mentioned above, and it establishes additional procedures for balance-of-payment consultations, and norms about the application of such measures, with citations to Articles XII and XVIII. The most concrete aspects of this text are that members utilizing balance-of-payment measures must notify the WTO of their use, and must submit to consultation procedures with the Committee on Balance-of-Payments Restrictions, which will report to the General Council. Then the text reads "whenever the general council has made specific recommendations, the rights and obligations of members shall be assessed in the light of such recommendations." Thus the text is studiously ambiguous, although it appears to imply that if a general council recommendation is not complied with, other members complaining against a balance-of-payments measure would have a better chance of arguing a breach that entitles them to take compensatory measures. But as of 1996, these issues are very fluid and not well defined.

9.7 Other Policies for Future Consideration: Investment and Labor Standards

The GATT, as such, has been considered not to apply to investment measures. Indeed, in the complaint by the United States against Canada on the Canadian FIRA—Foreign Investment Review Act,"[61] the terms of reference to the panel were worded so as to avoid taking up purely "investment issues." Nevertheless, one of the agenda items for the Uruguay Round was the TRIMS (trade-related investment measures, and one of the results of the Uruguay Round is a brief agreement on TRIMS, which has very little rule content and mostly relates to interpreting the national treatment measures of Article III). When one examines some of the other texts of the Uruguay Round, however, particularly the Services Agreement, it can be readily seen that these new obligations have considerable impact on investment and potential capital flows. For example, an effective investment often involves "establishment" of branches or offices in a particular country, and this gives rise to the general question of the right of establishment. The NAFTA agreement (U.S., Canada, and Mexico) went considerably further than the Uruguay Round agreements, and included a chapter on investment measures that covers much of the ground of bilateral investment treaties, including investor-state arbitration and measures constraining expropriation.[62] In many ways, the link between trade and investment is so intimate that it would be difficult to see how the investment subjects can be kept out of the WTO.

Thus it is not entirely surprising that a strong push has been made to develop new international cooperative legal norms relating to investment and capital flows. Some of this has been developed in the context of the OECD; others propose, however, that the matter be taken up directly in the WTO.[63]

Labor standards as a subject for the WTO, or other international treaty cooperation, have been extremely controversial. Labor standards were an issue in the negotiation of NAFTA, ending in a rather ambiguous and contorted side agreement among the NAFTA participants.[64] Some countries have been proposing that some type of attention in the WTO be given to labor standards; however, almost all of the world's developing countries are adamantly opposed because they fear the use of international explicit legal exceptions for labor standards questions will result effectively in trade restrictive measures based on cultural and political considerations within the large industrial countries—to the detriment of developing low-wage countries. The issue is very complicated, and it relates also to the International Labor Organization and its one hundred seventy or so labor standards conventions. It is still too soon to predict how some of these issues will develop in the WTO context.[65]

10 Unfair Trade and the Rules of Dumping

10.1 The Level Playing Field and the Policies of Managing Interdependence

Unfair Trade Rules and the Policies of International Trade

Other than import restraints, a number of policies of firms or governments are designed to influence international trade flows. In particular, both governments and enterprises may wish to promote exports through the use of discriminatory pricing or subsidies. For decades, many versions of these practices have been considered by the international system and many national systems to be "unfair." To such practices the international rules have permitted certain responses from the importing nations, such as antidumping duties or countervailing duties.[1]

In this context the distinction between responses to "fair trade," and those to "unfair trade" has long been understood. The escape clause, for example, allows import-restraining responses regardless of whether imports have benefited from "unfair practices." Responses to dumping or subsidies, however, are based on a totally different theory. In these and other cases, the basic idea is that the response of importing nations is designed partly to offset the effects of the "unfair" actions, and perhaps to go further and have a sort of "punitive" effect, to inhibit such actions in the future.[2] The distinction between fair and unfair trade has become increasingly blurred, however, in recent years, partly because of some fundamental disagreement about what should be called "unfair." Arguments in "fair" cases, such as escape-clause proceedings often include reference to "unfairness," while invocation of some of the "unfair trade" proceedings sometimes occurs in circumstances in which it is reasonably clear that the petitioners seek a sort of safeguard relief, even though no clear agreement among nations exists that the practices they complain about are "unfair."[3]

A commonly expressed goal of trade policy in connection with "unfair" practices is that of the "level playing field."[4] This evokes the notion of economic activity as a game, and the idea that competition in this game should be defined according to a set of rules that all participants share. Unfortunately, it is often very difficult to carry this analogy too far. Societies and their economic systems differ so dramatically that what seems "unfair" to members of one society may seem perfectly fair to those of another society.

The Interface Question

Many of the "unfair" trading practices that we will examine have been considered unfair because they interfere with or distort free market economic principles. GATT, of course, was largely based on such principles. It is not surprising, therefore, that it is often difficult to apply GATT's trading rules to nonmarket economies. In addition, even among the relatively similar western industrial market economies, wide differences exist with regard to the degree of government involvement in the forms of regulation or ownership of various industrial or other segments of the economy. As world economic interdependence has increased, it has become more difficult to manage relationships among various economies. This problem is analogous to the difficulties involved in trying to get two computers of different designs to work together. To do so, one needs an "interface" mechanism to mediate between the two computers.[5] Likewise in international economic relations, particularly in trade, some "interface mechanism" may be necessary to allow different economic systems to trade together harmoniously.

These problems will become clear in this and the next chapter, where it will be shown that part of the definition of dumping is selling for export at below-cost prices. But do meaningful costs and prices exist in nonmarket economies? In the case of subsidies, it may be easy to identify cash payments to an exporter, but myriad government policies affect the competitiveness of a business. If the goal is really to achieve a level playing field, does that imply that all governments must adopt uniform policies? If not, how will it be possible to analyze the effect of different policies? Besides, isn't trade to some degree based on differences between countries (as discussed in chapter 1)?

In some cases, the problem involves questions of preventing or inhibiting what are deemed unfair practices, such as dumping or export subsidies. As the subject of unfair practices develops, however, it becomes clear that it reaches deeply into matters of domestic concern to governments, and the questions of unfairness become more controversial. In many cases of subsidies, for example, the government providing such subsidies considers them to be an essential and praiseworthy tool of government, sometimes useful to correct disparities of income or to help disadvantaged groups or regions. With respect to dumping, it is argued that such a practice, a form of "price discrimination," actually has beneficial effects on world and national prosperity, encouraging competition. The rules for responding to some unfair trade practices allow use of import restrictions, such as added duties, (and also quantitative measures applied pursuant to settlements of dumping or countervailing cases), which can be anticompetitive and can be detrimental to world welfare. In some cases, exporting nations feel bitterness toward these import restrictions on their trade, and argue that the rules on unfair trade are being manipulated by special interests for effectively protectionist reasons.

An example of the interface problem and the difficulty of defining unfairness can be seen in the following problem, which focuses on so-called variable cost analysis. It may arise in the context of two economies that differ only slightly in their acceptance of basic free-market economic principles. As the problem demonstrates, given such similarities, differences may exist between the ways the respective economies operate over the course of the business cycle that could create situations that are considered unfair, even though these differences may not have resulted from any consciously unfair policies or practices.

Take an industrial sector (such as steel) in two economies (such as the United States and Japan) with the following characteristics:

Society A is characterized by:
Worker tenure (no layoffs of workers)
Capitalization with a high debt-equity ratio (e.g., 90 percent debt)

Society B is characterized by:
No worker tenure (wages for workers are therefore variable costs)
Capitalization with low debt-equity ratio (e.g., less than 50 percent; dividends can be skipped)

In times of slack demand, economists note that it is rational for a firm to continue to produce as long as it can sell its product at or above its short-term variable costs. This is true because it must in any event pay its fixed costs. Of course, this is true only for limited periods; presumably over the regular course of the business cycle, the firm must not incur losses in the long term.

An analysis of the short-term variable cost of firms in Societies A and B can be detailed as follows:

Costs of a firm (per unit of production)	Society A	Society B
Plant unkeep	20 fixed	20 fixed
Debt service	90 fixed	50 fixed
Dividends (cost of capital)	10 variable	50 variable
Worker costs	240 fixed	240 variable
Cost of materials	240 variable	240 variable
Total "costs"	600	600
(per unit of production)		
Fixed	350	70
Variable	250	530

I use the word "cost" to include use of capital—which some may dislike—but it makes the point.

Thus, total average "costs" in both societies are the same, but as noted here, it will be rational for producers in Society A to continue production as long as they can obtain a price of 250, whereas producers in Society B need to receive a price of 530. Thus, in a period of falling prices and demand, the producers in Society A can be expected to garner, through exports to Society B, an increasing share of Society B's market. Suppose this happens and the firms in Society B go out of business. Are Society A's exports to Society B unfair?

No easy answers exist to such questions. Indeed, they are much more complicated than the foregoing case indicates. For example, whatever general rules exist, it is argued that special considerations should apply to developing countries.[6] In addition, it must be recognized that economic structural characteristics vary from sector to sector within a country, and that advantages that tilt one way for one sector might tilt in the opposite direction for another sector. Furthermore, these differences may alter across time, and the direction of the tilt might reverse. One of the questions I pose in section 10.6 is whether the antidumping rules of trade policy are actually performing an "interface" or buffering role, rather than a role of response to "unfairness."

10.2 The Policies of Antidumping Rules

What Is Dumping?[7]

For almost one hundred years international trade policy rules have recognized that "dumping" is a practice that "is to be condemned," and have allowed an importing country to take certain countermeasures, at least when the dumped goods cause "material injury" to competing industries in the importing country.[8]

The definition of dumping as described in GATT and elsewhere, is often expressed as the sale of products for export at a price less than "normal value," where normal value means roughly the price for which those same products are sold on the "home" or exporting market.[9] In other words:

home-market sales price − export sales price = margin of dumping

When that margin is greater than zero, there is "dumping" in the sense used in international trade policy.

So defined, the concept of dumping is relatively simple. As applied, however, it is anything but simple. Each term of the equation involves complex calculations. A threshold question is what level of trade should be used to judge price, that is, wholesale or retail? Presumably whatever is used should be the same for both home market and export sales.[10] Then with respect to the home-market sales price, how is it to be calculated? Often an "average" of prices at which the product is offered in the home market is used, but a complex series of adjustments may be necessary to align that price with comparable prices for exports. Suppose, however, the goods are not sold in the home market, or too few are sold to use as the basis of a valid home-market average price. Then laws may call for comparison to one of several other measures of "normal value," such as comparison to prices for sale to other countries (third markets) or to a "constructed price" composed of an evaluation of cost plus reasonable profit.

Whenever a "constructed cost" calculation is required, matters can beome extremely complex. A foreign country may have different accounting systems, the firm involved may produce many products with costs that will have to be allocated, a foreign language is often involved, and methods of doing business vary greatly. Under some national laws, home-market prices that do not represent full recovery of cost plus a reasonable profit must be excluded from the home-price average. In such cases a "constructed cost" methodology must be followed to determine which home-market sales to exclude from the average, and this methodology introduces virtually all the same complexities of constructed cost computations in the absence of home market sales.

Likewise, finding the "export price" can become very complex. Often a number of adjustments to the transaction price actually used in an export sale will be necessary to try to keep comparisons with home prices fair. Adjustments might include packaging, advertising costs, warranty services, and so on.

Under most national systems of dumping law, after (or while) a finding of "dumping" (or in U.S. law, "less-than-fair-value" [LTFV] sales) has been made, a separate determination is made regarding whether the requisite "injury" has been caused by the dumping. If both dumping and injury findings are affirmative, then duties will be applied at the border up to the amount of the margin of dumping.

Why Do Enterprises Dump? Profit Maximizing and Marginal Costs

Why would enterprises dump? In fact there are understandable profit-maximizing reasons that a firm might want to engage in such discriminatory pricing. Suppose, for example, a firm produces one million radios per year from a single plant that operates only a day shift. Suppose that it prices these radios on its home market at the equivalent of $20 each, and makes about $4 profit each. Suppose further that the variable or "avoidable" costs of these radios (workers wages, cost of materials, etc.) are about $10 each, thus suggesting that the fixed or unavoidable costs (capital equipment, the plant, etc.) are about $6 each. Given that the firm is making a $4 profit per unit with its one million sales per year, it has apparently covered all of its fixed costs with these sales. It could now sell more radios at anything above its variable costs of $10 and make an additional profit.[11]

For example, suppose the plant could add a night shift and produce another million radios per year. The plant and equipment costs are presumably already covered by the first million radios produced. If it could somehow sell another million without affecting the price it is receiving for its first million, then any price above the $10 variable costs will add to the firm's total profit. If it sold the night production at $14, for example, it would add $4 million to its previous profit of $4 million per year, that is, doubling its profits. The catch, of course, is not to affect the price received for the first million produced. This implies somehow segmenting the available market, or in other words, seeking a totally different market for the firm's night production. But, in addition, the new market must be such that buyers there cannot easily ship back to the home or first market; otherwise the price of the day production will be undercut.

How can this segmenting be done? One way is to charge different prices in different geographical areas, in circumstances such that the return shipment costs will inhibit buyers in the lower-price region from reselling into the higher-price region. In some respects this evokes normal "discriminatory pricing" questions discussed within national boundaries, such as those connected with the U.S. law known as the Robinson-Patman Act, which may prohibit such dual-pricing behavior. In fact, at present, the U.S. government apparently does not enforce the Robinson-Patman Act,[12] and the economic policy literature urging the repeal of this act is considerable. Furthermore, many respected economists do not see anything wrong with discriminatory pricing as such.[13]

The Policies of International Antidumping Rules

With respect to the core idea (export sales at prices lower than home-market sales), what is the underlying policy that has led the international trading community for more than a century to consider "dumping" to be an action that is somehow "unfair"? This is a question that is not easy to answer. The original focus on the "price difference" can be described as a focus on "price discrimination." There seems to be a notion that sales at different prices to different persons is somehow unfair. Perhaps some of this is a leftover from medieval notions of "fair price."[14]

The differences can go either way, however. The person charged more can be just as "aggrieved" as those (usually the competing sellers) who complain that some persons have been charged less. Clearly part of the worry has to do with monopoly or competition policy. This is true not only for international but also for domestic transactions, as the U.S. Robinson-Patman Act bears out. Discussions about the formulation of laws relating to price discrimination often include concerns about large and economically powerful firms using market leverage to drive small concerns out of business, thus reducing competition so the predatory larger firms can then raise prices and reap monopoly profits.[15] This is often called "predatory behavior" or "predation." If the seller prices his goods in a particular market so as to drive out the competition, with a view to later raising his prices (which he can do when the competition has exited), this may be "monopolistic" behavior of a type that is condemned by other laws.[16] Economists, including Jacob Viner in his classic 1923 work, tend to be skeptical of the predation argument, however, because they doubt that the chances for success of the predation are very good.[17] If a number of firms are producing for a market, they would need to collude to raise prices later. They would also need to keep out potential new producers, and if prices go up this can be very difficult to do.

One complaint about dumping is that government-imposed barriers may exist at the border to prevent reshipment of the goods into the home market. Thus, if there is a 40 percent tariff on imported radios, the night production can be shipped abroad at a price as low as $12 without much fear that foreign buyers would try to reintroduce these radios into the home market to undercut the home-market price. Therefore it has been argued that international trade dumping depends heavily on import barriers of the exporting country, and that this is unfair.[18] A counter-argument is that the problem in such a case is the import barriers, *not* the dumping as such, and that the sanctions against dumping are an inefficient way to get at the real problem.[19]

In section 10.4, I consider certain questions about sales below costs. Apart from predation, economists note that firms have several incentives to sell at a price that may be below costs.[20] One incentive arises when production has had to be scheduled before prices are known, and when prices become known, production costs are already "sunk" (e.g., the crop is planted). A second incentive arises when costs fall as production experience accumulates (the learn-by-doing argument), so that the benefit from current production exceeds the price for which the output is sold. A third incentive is when a firm finds it advantageous to build market share so as to make consumers more familiar with its product and ultimately expand their demand for it. In all these cases, economic policy suggests that overall welfare is improved by the below-cost sales and so these practices should not be punished, whether in domestic or export trade. Total consumer welfare is greater than the loss to producers caused by the new competition. Thus, such policies would counsel against the use of anti-dumping duties.

(There may also be some distorted firm internal incentives for increasing market share for certain products, perhaps because of internal power struggles or historical trends within a firm. These may not be welfare enhancing, but it can be argued that the market will punish a firm that indulges itself in these practices.)

Of course, if government decision makers are more responsive to producers than to consumers (as is often the case), the loss to competing *producers* may be given more weight in government policy. In this connection a meaningful safeguards policy to limit imports can be justified.[21] For "safeguards," however, the fact that imports are or are not "dumped" is mostly irrelevant. If antidumping duties are used, it is for "safeguard" reasons, and not because these practices are "unfair" or damaging to economic welfare of the importing nation.

In light of these various considerations, it is interesting that when the negotiators added the extensive new Uruguay Round text for trade in *services*, they did not include provisions relating to dumping or antidumping duties. Indeed, it would be conceptually difficult to see how the antidumping principles could be applied in many areas of services trade.

10.3 The Antidumping Rules and Their Sources

History and Origins

The concept of "dumping" in international trade has a long history. Jacob Viner reports mention of "bounty" practices by Adam Smith. Likewise, Viner notes statements by Alexander Hamilton in debates in the United States in 1791, warning about foreign country practices of underselling competitors in other countries, thus to "frustrate the first efforts to introduce [a business] ... into another by temporary sacrifices, recompensed, perhaps by extraordinary indemnifications of the government of such country ..."[22] Other instances of allegations of dumping by British manufacturers into the new American market were reported, and public discussion of this problem as well as various legislative attempts to deal with it were reported during most of the nineteenth century.[23] Indeed, one of the first U.S. laws relating to international trade was concerned with practices we might identify as dumping.[24]

Viner reports that during the early twentieth century dumping was most widespread by firms in Germany.[25] During and after World War I, the U.S. Congress enacted several antidumping statutes.[26] During the 1930s the United States embarked on its reciprocal trade agreements program, negotiating about thirty bilateral treaties for the mutual reduction of tariff barriers. Many of these agreements recognized the "problem" of dumping and allowed national government treaty partners to use antidumping duties to offset dumping.[27]

The International Rules: GATT and the Codes

Given the long history of national and international concern with dumping, it is not surprising that when the GATT was negotiated in 1947 special provision was made for cases of dumping. Article VI of GATT allows GATT contracting parties to utilize antidumping duties to offset the margin of dumping of dumped goods, provided that it can be shown that such dumping is causing or threatens to cause, "material injury" to competing domestic industries.[28] Today this is still the core international rule regarding dumping.

As time passed, however, some countries in GATT began to feel that other countries, in applying their antidumping laws, were doing it in such a way as to raise a new barrier to trade. Some believed that antidumping procedures—such as delay, or certain calculations of dumping margins, or certain applications of the injury test—were causing restrictions and distortions on international trade flows, sometimes by creating a period of risk and uncertainty to traders in a particular product. Thus, during the Kennedy Round of GATT trade negotiations (1962–1967), the GATT CONTRACTING PARTIES negotiated an Antidumping (AD) Code, which set forth a series of procedural and substantive rules regarding the application of antidumping duties, partly as a result of the desire to limit antidumping duty practices and procedures of governments that were damaging international trade.[29]

This code caused a major constitutional problem in the United States, which was ironic given that it was a major proponent of the AD code. As an international agreement the Code had been signed by authority of the president, but without any participation of the U.S. Congress, either through the constitutional Senate advice-and-consent procedure or by statute adopted by the Congress as a whole. The president's officials argued that the code could be implemented within the existing constitutional and statutory powers of the president, but the Congress disagreed with him. The Congress enacted legislation that prohibited the executive and the Tariff Commission (later the International Trade Commission) from following the rules of the GATT AD code in certain circumstances.[30] Although the United States argued consistently that the internal measures it took complied adequately with the code, many other nations did not agree.[31]

Although at the outset of the Tokyo Round negotiation in 1973 the subject of dumping was not on the agenda, a rather sudden turn of events late in that negotiation[32] caused the negotiators to take it up; and, partly to provide symmetry with the drafting that was occurring in the negotiations for the Subsidies Code, the GATT parties developed a new Antidumping Code, which came into effect in 1979 replacing the 1967 AD Code.[33] This code had twenty-six signatories, and among them, it prevailed over any prior agreements on dumping, including the 1967 code.[34] The Uruguay Round text on dumping, building on the prior AD Codes, further modifies the AD rules, and of course prevails over them for all WTO members, given that it is now a mandatory agreement.[35]

Thus the international commitments concerning dumping are now set forth in the GATT, particularly Article VI, and in the 1994 Uruguay Round antidumping text, officially titled, "Agreement on Implementation of Article VI of the General Agreement on Tariffs and Trade 1994."[36] These commitments are briefly summarized below.

To begin, nothing in these agreements obligates nations or firms to refrain from practices that are construed as dumping. The GATT Article VI language does say that dumping "... is to be condemned if it causes or threatens material injury to an established industry," but the wording is far short of a binding obligation to prevent dumping.[37] Of course, these international treaties do not apply to private persons or firms; rather, they apply to nations that accept the treaties. But the wording of obligations does not require nations themselves to refrain from dumping, nor does it require nations to see to it that firms refrain from dumping. This contrasts with the international obligations concerning subsidies and countervailing duties, which include commitments against certain types of subsidies. This difference has sometimes been overlooked or misrepresented by political leaders or diplomats.[38]

On the other hand, the GATT and code language do provide for a permitted response to dumping in certain circumstances. This permitted response is the "antidumping" duty (which otherwise might be prohibited by GATT commitments on tariff maximums and MFN treatment). The treaty obligations specify three types of obligations constraining the use of such duties: (1) detailed rules about what facts constitute "dumping," (2) detailed rules about the "injury requirement," and (3) detailed rules about the procedures under which governments determine and apply these antidumping duties.

The basic overall pattern of antidumping law, derived from these rules and the national implementations of them, is that dumping requires a certain comparison of export price with "normal" price (usually home-market price). For responding duties to be permitted, "material injury" or threat occurring to the competing domestic industry in the importing country (or retarding the establishment of such an industry) must also be found. If, and only if, these two conditions are found to exist (dumping plus injury), then the importing country may apply antidumping duties. That country, however, is obligated to see to it that its procedures and provisional remedies for dumping are kept consistent with a number of international rules in the GATT and the code.

The National Rules: The United States and Its Procedures

Although various GATT reports indicate that more than twenty countries used antidumping laws from time to time before 1990,[39] it is commonly understood that three nations—the United States, Canada, and Australia—and the EC were the principal users of antidumping laws. Until recently, these four have accounted for the vast majority of antidumping cases brought in the world, although other countries are "learning this game," and may increasingly use antidumping laws as a means of inhibiting imports.[40]

In the United States, antidumping laws were enacted in 1916 and 1921.[41] The 1916 act, however, was primarily patterned after U.S. antitrust acts, and provides a private right of action by domestic producers who feel they are harmed by dumped imports, provided that a certain predatory intent can be proven. There has never been a case in the United States which has been successful under this statute. In 1970 a landmark case was brought under the 1916 act, but in the end after much litigation (some of it mingled with antitrust litigation), the U.S. courts determined that the case had not been made for recovery under the 1916 act.[42] Although proposals to enhance the possibility of 1916 act litigation have been circulated,[43] none have become law.

The principal U.S. law regarding antidumping, which has in fact been applied, is the 1921 antidumping act as often amended.[44] It is this law that provides for application of antidumping duties by federal government authorities, when it is ascertained that imported goods have been dumped and are causing injury in the United States. It will be noted that there is a two-part test (as required under international law), namely, the determination of "dumping," and then the determination of "injury". The injury test is the same as that for subsidy cases, and I will describe that in section 10.5.[45]

Since the introduction of the new antidumping regime in 1979, and through 1995, nearly seven hundred fifty petitions have been filed for antidumping cases. A small number of these in turn resulted in suspension agreements, but material injury was finally determined to exist in about two hundred eighty cases. Thus, approximately 35 percent of the petitions filed have resulted in actual antidumping duty orders.

Prior to 1974, the laws of dumping in the United States were sufficiently vague to allow the administrating authorities considerable discretion. In addition, it was not clear that any opportunity would be given to appeal to the courts to overturn administrative determinations. In the 1974 Trade Act, the Congress took its first steps to remedy what it perceived to be an improper mode of implementation of antidumping laws. Thus, in this statute, the Congress provided time limits and judicial review.[46]

By the mid-1970s the pressure of domestic interests for a more diligent application of antidumping duties had become very strong, partly because other major trade barriers, particularly the tariff, had been substantially dismantled since 1948 under the GATT rules. Thus considerably more attention was focused on the antidumping rules; and, as we shall see in the next chapter (on the subsidy and countervailing duty rules), some of these pressures had been building for years and were responsible for the congressional antagonism to the U.S. participation in the 1967 AD Code.

In 1979, as a result of the Tokyo Round negotiations which led to a new international antidumping code, the Congress embodied in the Trade Agreements Act of 1979 (implementing the Tokyo Round results) a new statutory framework for U.S. antidumping law. This new statute, in the context of implementing the new international code, substantially overhauled the U.S. rules for antidumping duties.[47] Again, in the 1994 Uruguay Round Implementing Act, the Congress revised U.S. antidumping rules in order to achieve what in the U.S. view was consistency with the Uruguay Round antidumping text. Whether true consistency was achieved is somewhat controversial and beyond the scope of this work.[48] These various rules will be addressed in later sections, but a brief overview of the procedural steps of an antidumping case may be useful here.

Under the current U.S. law, antidumping cases (as well as subsidy/countervailing duty cases) are handled by at least two U.S. administrative agencies.[49] A complaint must be filed simultaneously with the Commerce Department and with the International Trade Commission (ITC). The Commerce Department is responsible for examining whether dumping exists, that is, whether there is a margin of dumping. The ITC is responsible for examining whether the dumping or dumped goods are causing "material injury" (or threat) of the competing industry within the United States. A fairly elaborate series of procedural steps is mandated by the statute, roughly outlined as follows:

1. Filing of the complaint with both Commerce and the ITC.
2. Within forty-five days, an ITC preliminary determination of whether any reasonable chance exists of finding injury (a negative finding would halt the procedure).

3. A preliminary determination by the Commerce Department of whether dumping margins exist. If this determination is affirmative, customs-entry "liquidations" are suspended on the goods, and all imports of these goods thereafter are subject to the ultimate antidumping duties which are applied. There are also provisions for retrospective application to earlier imports. The preliminary determination is followed by a fairly elaborate additional "verification," undertaken by Commerce Department investigators who travel abroad to ascertain various facts, such as the foreign-market price.

4. A final determination by the Commerce Department of whether a margin of dumping exists. If this is negative, the case ceases. If it is affirmative, the case then proceeds to the ITC.

5. Final determination by the ITC of the existence of "material injury" (or threat) caused by the dumped imports.

6. If both the Commerce Department and ITC final determinations are affirmative, then the Commerce Department will issue an antidumping order that must be implemented by the Customs officials at all the ports of entry into the United States with respect to the goods from the sources stipulated in the antidumping order.

The original complaint procedures, undertaken by administrative agencies, and the antidumping order, can apply either to specific producers abroad or to all producers in a particular country.[50] To ascertain the necessary facts, it is useful to have the cooperation of foreign producers. Needless to say, such producers do not have an overwhelming incentive to cooperate, except for the fact that U.S. law allows the administrators, in the absence of cooperation, to use "best information available," or "BIA." The United States has sometimes been criticized for the way it uses "BIA." It has been argued that sometimes the BIA is little more than the allegations of the complaint brought by the competing domestic U.S. interest, and thus can operate to the substantial detriment of the foreign producers. All this induces considerable cooperation from foreign producers.[51]

Once the antidumping order has been issued, an extremely intricate set of procedures is put in place, which can only be briefly outlined here. Essentially, each customs entry of goods from the producer sources or producer country identified in the antidumping order must be compared to see whether the price of the goods in that transaction is less than some benchmark price determined to be the "normal" price (e.g., the home-market price in the foreign-producing market). In some countries, by way of contrast, a flat ad valorum or specific antidumping duty amount is assessed on all goods from the identified sources. In the United States, however, an attempt is made to match each entry retrospectively with the fair market price that has been ascertained as part of the procedure, although for administrative reasons, certain annual determinations are made and certain estimates are utilized in the process. These calculations are used to set new duty deposit levels and, on rare occasions, to revoke the antidumping order. In addition, there is a retrospective review in the light of actual trading patterns, from which a revised antidumping order can result with adjustment of duties. This system offers the possibility of precise duty assessment, but at the cost of an elaborate and costly procedure, and a delay in calculating the duties actually owed.[52]

In earlier years, even though a fair number of countries signed both the 1967 and 1979 Antidumping Codes, relatively few regularly used their antidumping legislation. This, however, seems to be changing. A recent report from the new WTO shows that for approximately a one-year period in (1994–1995), nineteen countries initiated one hundred sixty antidumping actions and had in force a cumulated number of eight hundred and five antidumping measures. The largest number of initiations (thirty-seven) was in the EC (treated as one country) and the second largest (thirty) in the United States. Other relatively high numbers are shown for Brazil and Mexico.[53]

10.4 Dumping Margins and Less Than Fair Value

Introduction

To determine if dumping has taken place, we have noted that the rules compare the price for export with some fairness benchmark. At one time this was essentially a price-discrimination test—a comparison of the price for export with the price on the home (exporting) market. Allowance was always made, however, for the case where the home price was not comparable, either because there were no home market or third country sales or for other reasons. The traditional approach for such cases has been to turn to comparisons with sales to third markets, or to a "constructed-cost" method of arriving at a "fair" home price. During recent decades, however, more attention has been focused on the "cost" of the goods produced abroad, for reasons I will explore. Thus there has been a shift from exploring potential "price discrimination" to a determination of whether the exported goods have been sold at a price that is "below cost."

In this section I will briefly examine some of these concepts, looking first at the determination of "export price," and then to the prices used for comparison. In U.S. law this is called the less-than-fair-value (LTFV) or "less than normal value" determination, which is carried out by the Commerce Department. As previously noted, this determination process can be extremely complex, partly because of the large number of potential "adjustments" that can be made either to the export price figures or to the comparable "normal" or home-market price in order to arrive at what is deemed a fair comparison. In this chapter I can only scratch the surface and suggest general approaches, leaving to specialized treatises the lawyers' details of how these computations and comparisons are made.[54]

Under the U.S. law, if it is determined that LTFV sales exist, then the authorities determine a "margin of dumping" by making the comparison discussed later in this chapter. This margin can, if injury is found, determine the amount of the antidumping duty to be applied at the border. For this reason it is often assumed that the LTFV determination is essentially the task of determining the margin of dumping.

In the past the U.S. authorities have generally refused to proceed with cases when the dumping margin is less than a de minimis, defined as 0.5 percent or less. During the Uruguay Round, the negotiators felt that this de minimis should be higher, so they set the level of de minimis at 2 percent.[55] The negotiators also established a minimum percentage of imports of the like product, as a threshold for successful petitions, with some exceptions. This is stated to be 3 percent of imports of the like product in the importing member. The U.S. law was changed in the Uruguay Round Implementing Act to reflect these new rules for investigations but not for reviews.[56]

The Price Comparison: Export Sales Price ("United States Price") and the Normal Value

The price of goods exported is the starting point of the analysis. The U.S. law specifies that this shall be the "export price" or the "purchase price," whichever is appropriate. Other adjustments are necessary also. Essentially the rules aim at an FOB or ex factory price, at the wholesale level, in the country of export.[57] Under U.S. law this price must exclude the freight. Supposedly, shipping costs are responsible for part of the natural comparative lack of advantage of imported goods, so it is considered unfair to allow these to be considered part of the price for comparison purposes. Likewise the price must not include duties paid in the United States.

The figure to compare is the home-market price, or as U.S. law specifies, the "normal value." This is the price normally offered for sale in the usual wholesale quantities. Prior to the Uruguay Round, the U.S. approach to the comparison was arguably quite tilted. For the export sales price, a single price could be matched to determine if dumping or LTFV exists, while the foreign market value or normal price would be an average. In many cases this almost assured the finding of a dumping margin. If prices on the home market vary over some time span—for example, if ten sales are at an average price of $95 but range from $90 to $100—then the foreign market value is this average of $95. Yet ten *export sales* may be at exactly the same distribution of prices, averaging $95 but ranging from $90 to $100, and in this case about half of the export sales will be at a price below the foreign market value; and thus dumping or LTFV has been established.[58] This disparity of treatment in U.S. law was criticized, and the Uruguay Round text provides that the comparison should "normally" be established "on the basis of a comparison of a weighted average normal value with a weighted average of prices of all comparable export transactions, or by a comparison of normal value and export prices on a transaction-to transaction basis." The U.S. law was changed to make this average-to-average approach possible, but it opens up a bit of a crack for alternative methods of comparison.

Many attorney hours are spent on numerous potential adjustments to each of the prices to be compared.[59] For example, if the exported goods benefit from a superior warranty, or from better after-sale service than the home market goods receive, adjustments will be made to try to make the prices comparable. Differences in quality or financing assistance must be taken into account. A troublesome and perplexing issue during many years has been the difference of treatment of sales expenses and commissions for goods sold by the exporter to an independent importer compared to those sold by that exporter to a subsidiary.[60]

If no comparable home market prices exist, for example, on a product sold only for export (the classic case of golf carts from Poland), then the rules provide alternative benchmarks. One benchmark is to look to comparable sales in third markets as an indication of the home-market price.[61] Again, care must be taken to establish comparability. The goods may differ in quality, or type, or other characteristics, thus making them hard to compare.

If third-market sales are not to be used to determine the dumping comparison, then the traditional rules allow a "constructed cost" approach. In this situation the export sales price will be compared to a price that is "constructed" as the "normal" or "home-market" price. This constructed price is developed by examining the costs of the product and then adding to it a profit amount to establish what shall be deemed the normal price.[62] It is easy to see how difficult this can sometimes be.

In addition, U.S. law since the 1974 Trade Act has added another wrinkle. This act now requires that even if home-market sales are found, in establishing the average home-market price that will be the benchmark for comparison, all sales that are at a price below cost plus profit must be excluded from the average.[63] This will tend to raise that average and thus make it more likely that a dumping margin will be found. For example, if, in our specific case above with an average price of $95, the costs plus profits of the product are deemed to be, say $92, then the home-market "average" price will be the average of sales excluding those below $92. Thus the average is likely to move up to $96, and more export sales will be found to be under that level—ergo, dumped.

Logic certainly supports this shift in average, if there is reason to think that below-cost sales are somehow unfair also, and if (a big "if") the methods of computing the constructed costs are "fair." I will now address this issue.

Constructed Cost and Its Conceptual and Practical Difficulties

Many difficulties are associated with computing the constructed cost of a product, and some of these difficulties raise questions about the administration of antidumping laws of various countries. To begin with, investigators of the importing country must explore in considerable depth the accounting procedures and data of foreign firms to establish benchmark figures. This means a considerable intrusion into a foreign society and into foreign firms. Reluctant cooperation is obtained by rules of the importing country such as the "best evidence available." In addition, we have noted that differences in language and accounting methods make the investigators' tasks formidable and cast some doubts on the validity of the process. But besides these practical administrative problems, there are also some very worrisome conceptual problems.

If a firm produces multiple products, it may be quite difficult to allocate costs among products. This difficulty may be compounded if the product for the export market differs slightly (for marketing and customer acceptance reasons) from the products sold at home. More significant, however, is the extremely difficult problem of selecting which longer-term costs to include in a "constructed cost."

As I noted at the beginning of this chapter, firms can rationally sell products at a price that is only slightly larger than so-called short-term variable cost. This is because the firm must pay the longer-term fixed "costs" (debt service, etc.) regardless of whether it produces goods. Thus, if it is able to produce at slightly more than a short-term variable cost, it has incentive to do so. Unfortunately, however, the U.S. law regarding the calculation of the foreign-market price does not always seem to recognize this. Thus, in times of slack demand, if the foreign enterprise must price for export at a level that includes all of these long-term costs, even when it would be rational for the enterprise to price at a much lower level both at home and abroad, it is placed at a disadvantage in world markets.

The 1974 Trade Act, which introduced the requirement that below-cost sales be discarded from the information on which the average home-market price is based, speaks of prices being based on figures that "permit recovery of all cost within a reasonable period of time in the normal course of trade ...." One could expect that "reasonable period of time" should be interpreted in a manner consistent with normal business practice. Thus recovery of costs should here mean shorter-term variable costs, with an understanding that over a business cycle or product life cycle the firm should demonstrate that it can recoup all costs, including fixed ones. During a period of slack demand this would mean that prices for export need not be based on full average-cost recovery. Nevertheless, the U.S. administration of its antidumping laws seems to ignore these economic realities, by imposing on foreign producers an obligation to price at a higher level than, for example, competing domestic producers within the United States would find necessary in the same circumstances.

Needless to say, these and other peculiarities of the antidumping law render it suspect in many ways. When politicians rail against "dumping prices," one has to be wary of what they are talking about, because prices that are deemed "dumping" under U.S. law may really be based on artificial and arbitrary calculations. It is not coincidental that such arbitrary calculations tend to restrict imports more than would be the case if the concepts were more genuinely attuned to economic and accounting practices.

Finally, we need only mention how difficult these concepts are in relation to nonmarket economies. This is a subject to which I will return in chapter 13.

10.5 The Material Injury Test

Under international rules, both antidumping duties and countervailing duties require fulfillment of the "material injury test."[64] The basic idea is that in the case of imported dumped or subsidized goods, the importing country is not authorized to respond with the antidumping or countervailing duties (as an exception to other obligations in GATT), unless it can be established that the imported goods have caused "material injury" to the competing industry of the like product in the importing country. The rules concerning this injury test are fundamentally the same both for dumping and for subsidies. There is no particular inherent reason, however, why they need to be. The policies concerning a permitted response to dumped goods are substantially different from those concerning subsidized goods. One might easily think of a separate set of material-injury rules for each of these subjects, so that the rules would be more carefully tuned to the policies of each subject.

The basic overall approach is that in order to respond when goods that are dumped or subsidized are imported, the importing country must show a harmful impact on the total industry producing the like product in the importing country. This is not just a matter of harm to a particular firm, rather it must be "material injury" to the industry as a whole. If the industry is generally thriving, even though several firms are going out of business, arguably there is not material injury.

Trade law and policy are full of different kinds of injury tests, and in previous chapters I have mentioned a few.[65] Although the phraseology of the tests differ (e.g., for the escape clause it is "serious injury"), the definitions of the various injury tests are not very precise. Thus it is difficult in an abstract way to compare the tests. It is generally thought, however, that the "serious injury" test of the escape clause and safeguards is the most stringent, in the sense of being the hardest to show that it is fulfilled. This approach accords with the general policies that the safeguards questions are addressed to fair trade. On the other hand, the material injury test of dumping and subsidies is thought to be somewhat easier to fulfill than the serious injury test, and one rationale offered is that in the case of "unfair trade practices," the competing domestic industries ought to find it easier to obtain a response (antidumping duties or countervailing duties).[66]

United States law concerning the material injury test for both the antidumping and the countervailing duty cases has not always been completely consistent with the GATT rules. The original GATT (Article VI) called for the material injury test in antidumping and subsidy cases, and the language of this test has been carried over in the three codes concerning antidumping and countervailing, namely, the two Antidumping Codes of 1967 and 1979 and the Subsidies Countervailing Duty Code of 1979. Likewise, this phrase is included in the Uruguay Round texts for both dumping and countervailing duty. Prior to 1979, the U.S. law of dumping merely specified an "injury" test, without the additional word "material."[67] United States law concerning countervailing duties had no injury test prior to the 1974 Trade Act.[68] Because these U.S. laws preceded the GATT, the United States benefited from grandfather rights established in the Protocol of Provisional Application under GATT 1947, with respect to injury test matters. The side codes of the Tokyo Round, however, were not subject to provisional application and did not include an exception for existing legislation; thus grandfather rights did not apply. Likewise, under the Uruguay Round, there are no grandfather rights. In fact, at the end of the Tokyo Round in the 1979 Act, the United States added the word "material" to the material injury test, as we see below.

The development (some would say "tortured development") of the international rules concerning antidumping duties presents a rather interesting history both with regard to international negotiations and in connection with United States domestic constitutional procedures. Because the United States accepted the 1967 AD Code, which reiterated the material injury test, it could claim no grandfather rights to avoid its international obligations under that code. Thus, from 1967 until 1979, the U.S. statute was phrased in a manner different from its material injury obligations under the international code. As I related in a previous section, the 1967 AD Code was accepted with presidential authority only and was not referred to Congress—which clearly angered the Congress. One of the reasons for its anger was its belief that the president did not have authority to accept the material injury test, thereby relinquishing the grandfather rights (which allowed a softer test). After 1967 the United States was annually pilloried in the GATT Antidumping Code Committee because its statute did not live up to the material injury wording of the code. The response of the United States was to claim that even though the statute did not include the word "material," in fact when it applied the statue, the U.S. government was fulfilling the requirements of material injury.[69] This was an interesting argument, because it is very difficult for a foreign nation to refute. A refutation would require not only an examination of what in fact was obligated by the phrase "material injury," but also a difficult factual inquiry into each of the specific cases brought in the United States, to determine whether the facts of these cases lived up to the code's material injury standard. At one point in the United States administration of its dumping law, the then Tariff Commission (now the ITC) was apparently applying a fairly soft definition of injury, sometimes termed de minimis. The theory of this, propounded by the ITC commissioners,[70] was that any injury more than de minimis fulfilled the U.S. statutory injury requirement. It seems to me likely that such a de minimis test did not fulfill the material injury test of U.S. international obligations.

When the 1967 Antidumping Code was revised in the Tokyo round, and a new code put forth for signature and implementation, the matter was revisited before Congress in connection with the adoption of the 1979 Trade Agreements Act. During the preliminary deliberations held by the appropriate congressional committees, committee members seemed inclined to retain the older U.S. statutory language, which omitted the word "material." An interesting facet of the diplomacy that occurred on trade laws at this time was a protest that was registered by the European Community and transmitted to the congressional committees. The EC argued that the failure to include the word "material" in the U.S. implementing statute for the Tokyo Round results would be considered by the EC to be inconsistent with U.S. obligations under the Tokyo Round agreements. The congressional committees acquiesced in this viewpoint and reluctantly added the word "material" to the U.S. statute, so that the current version of the statute on the injury test (for both antidumping and countervailing) reads "material injury." Nevertheless, the Congress then preceded to define "material injury" as "harm which is not inconsequential, immaterial, or unimportant." The committee reports on this matter went further, stating that it was the understanding of the committees that the phrase "material injury" meant the same level of injury standard as that which had been applied during the preceding five years in the Tariff Commission. The committee reports, however, did explicitly reject the de minimis test of an earlier period.[71] Thus, the view of the U.S. Congress was that material injury should be understood to be a level of injury that can be inferred from the injury cases that actually occurred before the Tariff Commission during the period from 1974 to 1979.[72]

In discussing the matter with practitioners who must speak on these issues before the ITC, it is very difficult to try to generalize as to the meaning of the material injury test. Indeed, some practitioners seem to think that it depends more on who the particular ITC commissioners are, at any given time, than on any statutory formula or committee attempt to define that formula.[73]

The current state of international obligations regarding the material injury test (for antidumping and countervailing) is not very satisfactory. Prior to the Tokyo Round, the GATT Article VI definition of material injury was embellished by the 1967 AD Code. In the context of the Tokyo Round negotiations for a subsidy code, the injury test was considerably changed. The treaty language defining material injury was extended, and it can be argued that it was made much "looser" with excessive verbiage. Although this treaty language was worked out in the context of the negotiations on rules of subsidies (as I have previously indicated), late in the Tokyo Round negotiation it was decided to redraft the antidumping code, and this subsidies injury test language was also included in the new code.[74] In the Uruguay Round, the negotiators kept much of the language that defined injury, including some of the language described below.

This language is very broad indeed. For example, it calls for an examination of both "the volume of the subsidized imports and the effect of the subsidized imports on prices in the domestic market for like-products and ... the consequent impact of these imports on the domestic producers of such products."[75] The language then goes on to add considerable explanation for "volume" of subsidized imports, "either in absolute terms or relative to production or consumption in the importing member." A long list of factors is suggested, including potential decline in output, sales, market share, profits, productivity, return on investments, and utilization of capacity. Included in the language is the explanation of effect on prices, which directs the investigating authorities to "consider whether there has been a significant price undercutting by the subsidized imports ... or whether the effect of such imports is otherwise to depress prices to a significant degree or to prevent price increases, which otherwise would have occurred, to a significant degree." Arguably, any competition, including import competition, should have some of these effects. Consequently, if a nation wished to push to the outer limits of the permissible range of definition for "material injury," such national authorities would find comfort in this extremely broad and permissive language of the new GATT and Uruguay Round text.

In the United States, of course, the matter is constrained by the U.S. statutory test,[76] which is more precise and controlled than that of the international treaty obligation. Fortunately, at present there is little evidence of any important trend on the part of national authorities to move to the outer limits of this permissive international language regarding the material injury tests, but some potential for this exists and presumably should be guarded against, possibly by paying attention to it in new rounds of negotiation.

Several other important issues have arisen in connection with the injury test. To begin, it must be recognized that this test also includes the concept of "threat of material injury." In evaluating whether or not "threat" exists, the national authorities have more leeway than in the case of existing injury, because they are expected to evaluate trends for the future, which in many cases are not clear.

In addition, two other issues have been particularly troublesome in connection with the way the United States applies its material injury tests in these types of cases. These are the issues of cumulation and "margins analysis."

Cumulation is the proposition that when dumping and/or subsidization has occurred in several different countries that export to the United States, then these various cases can be lumped together for purposes of evaluating the presence of material injury. Thus, suppose countries A, B, C, and D each import into the United States a fairly small quantity of goods, let us say 5 percent of the U.S. market for each. If each of these four countries is determined to be dumping, then the cases go to the ITC for determination of injury. It might well be that the ITC would decide that no single country's dumping could be the cause of material injury to the competing U.S. industry. However, when dumping of all four countries is combined, the dumped products now take 20 percent of the U.S. market, and it would be much easier for the ITC to make an affirmative injury determination. Prior to 1984, the ITC cumulated in some cases but had the discretion to refrain from doing so. It had developed some general guidelines of when to cumulate.[77] The Congress, with the 1984 Tariff and Trade Act, imposed a requirement on the ITC to use cumulation in almost all cases.[78] The result of this has in some ways been insidious.

Let us take, for example, a situation in which two or three larger exporting countries ship significant quantities to the United States and are found to be dumping. In addition, assume that two other countries ship very small quantities to the United States, but are also found to be dumping. These latter two countries will be lumped together with the larger countries to determine material injury, thus exposing the very small traders in the latter countries to the vicissitudes of a dumping finding. This means a much greater exposure to the costs and burdens of a U.S. unfair trade practice case for start-up entrepreneurs who desire to enter the U.S. market. Obviously this dumping rule can have a considerable restraining effect, apart from the underlying policies of the AD or CV rules, on world trade. One solution is to have a de minimis cutoff to eliminate from such exposure the truly small cases.[79] This is the approach that was adopted by the Uruguay Round negotiators, so that the Uruguay Round text allows accumulation of a particular country only if all exporters of such country itself has more than a nonnegligible volume of imports.[80] One troublesome aspect about the small cases is that in some situations the amount of trade does not warrant paying for the attorney and other costs that would be required to defend against an antidumping or countervailing duty case, even when a defense would almost certainly prevail. The question has also been raised of whether the imports that are dumped should be cumulated with imports that are subsidized for an even greater cumulation effect in determining material injury.[81]

A second troublesome direction in the U.S. application of its unfair trade laws in connection with the injury test is usually discussed under the rubric "margins analysis" or "imports analysis." Prior to 1982 the ITC tried to show the causal connection between the extent of dumping or the extent of subsidization (the so-called margins), on the one hand, and the material injury, on the other hand. It was not enough merely to show that there was material injury in the United States: it had to be shown that this injury was caused not only by the imported goods that had been dumped or subsidized, but by the amount of the dumping or the subsidization. Thus, if the dumping margin were determined to be 5 percent, whereas the price undercutting caused by the imports were 15 percent, it could be argued that the dumping was not the cause of the material injury, because the imports would easily undersell domestic producers in the U.S. market anyway. If the purpose of unfair trade law is to eliminate the effect of the unfair action, policy would seem to support a margins analysis.

During 1981–1982, pursuant to memoranda coming from the ITC General Counsel's Office,[82] the ITC began to consider a different approach. The commissioners were urged not try to show a causal relationship between the margin of dumping or margin of subsidy, on the one hand, and material injury, on the other hand. Rather, the only causal relationship that need be shown was that between the dumped or subsidized *imports* as a whole. Thus the ITC could enjoy the luxury of ignoring the extent of the margin of dumping or subsidization, and could look merely at the amount of imports that were tainted by the dumping or subsidization and connect these to the injury.[83]

The argument in favor of this approach seems to hinge primarily on the language of the 1979 act defining material injury, which speaks of "imports of the merchandise" rather than more specifically about a margin. The counterargument, however, is the long-established practice following a margins approach (some have challenged whether this was a consistent practice).[84] In the absence of any expression of congressional intent to change this practice, it is argued no change was intended. In addition, the GATT Subsidies Code explicitly states: "It must be demonstrated that the subsidized imports are through the effects of the subsidy, causing injury within the meaning of this Agreement."[85] This would seem to establish an international obligation to pursue a causal connection that would relate to the actual subsidization—that is, the margin. A similar clause existed in the 1979 Antidumping Code and now is in the Uruguay Round text.[86] A counterargument has been raised in connection with footnotes to these clauses. These footnotes refer to paragraphs 2 and 3 in a way that have led some to argue that the notion of an obligation to use margin analysis has softened. Such a conclusion, however, appears to me somewhat improbable.

Thus, it can be argued that the U.S. government is obligated to use a margins analysis in evaluating the material injury resulting from dumping or subsidization, and that at the very best the U.S. statute is ambiguous enough that the general principle in U.S. jurisprudence that calls upon the statutory interpretation to be consistent with international obligations when it is possible to do so comes into play.[87]

10.6 Remedy and Reflection on Dumping Rules and Policies

The discussion in the preceding section should amply demonstrate that even if there is some underlying validity to the notion of the international and national antidumping rules when properly managed, in reality it is fair to express considerable doubt about the policy soundness of the implementation of some of these rules. There seems to be a considerable "tilt" against imports, and any close observer of the processes of governments—whether of the United States, the European Community, Canada, or Australia (i.e., the four principal historical users of the antidumping law)—can discern the considerable pressures brought by competing domestic producer groups to influence the governmental implementation of the antidumping laws in order to limit import competition.[88]

United States law, in particular, is especially vulnerable to this type of criticism, partly because the Congress has made that law so mandatory, limiting the discretion involved in government implementation. In the European Community, the antidumping rules grant to the Community officials a discretion "in the interests of the Community" to refrain from applying antidumping duties; and they also give the Community officials discretion to apply an antidumping duty that is lower than that of the margin of dumping, if such lower duty will "remove the injury."[89] Indeed, this concept has been written into the Antidumping text, which states that such lower duties are "desirable."[90] The U.S. law does not permit this amount of discretion, a fact that reflects congressional suspicion of executive-branch implementation of these laws, as well as the pressures of domestic producers who are seeking to use the antidumping laws as a way to limit the importation of competing goods.[91]

Another aspect of the unfair trade laws (both dumping and subsidies) is the advantage they tend to give to the larger economic entities in the world. By allowing a unilateral national response (antidumping duties or countervailing duties), the more economically powerful nations can have a considerable impact on smaller trading nations, whereas the reverse may not be true. For example, for Canada, exports to the United States are an extremely significant portion of the Canadian economy, whereas exports from the United States to Canada are only a small part of the U.S. economy.[92] Thus, the United States finds that it can more easily apply antidumping duties to Canadian products without a worry of retaliation or symmetrical application by the Canadians of such duties on U.S. products. This is because when the Canadians apply the duties, they have only a very small effect on the U.S. economy or U.S. producers. Thus, part of the frustration of other countries, particularly those smaller than the big three (the United States, Japan, and the EC), is the feeling that there is a lack of symmetry regarding the application of unfair trade laws. When this lack of symmetry is combined with relative freedom for unilateral sovereign definitions and determinations, it effectively grants considerable trade-policy power to the larger trading entities.

Finally, an additional aspect might be mentioned. Some political leaders liken antidumping laws to criminal or tort statutes, and argue that the statutes should provide a penalty for dumping.[93] This obviously misconceives the very nature of the antidumping rules under international and even national laws. From an examination of the policies of dumping and antidumping duties, we have seen that these policies reflect a certain tentativeness about the "wrongfulness" of dumping. Thus, it is not merely dumping, but rather dumping that causes injury, for which the international system allows the permitted response of antidumping duties.

Nevertheless, in pursuing these concepts of wrongfulness, some parties advocate that domestic-competing producers in the importing country should be given a "private right of action" under which they could sue the foreign exporting producers who are dumping and recover damages that would go directly to the "harmed" interests in the importing country.[94] Indeed, sometimes it is argued, by way of analogy to the terms of the U.S. antitrust statutes, that the recoverable damages should be treble those of the actual harm. Clearly such proposals would dramatically change the trade-policy impact of the antidumping (and subsidy) rules, and would substantially increase the risk of exporting to markets that introduce such "private-rights" laws. Indeed, unless there were a comparable domestic statute allowing domestic producers to seek similar recoveries from domestic producers who engaged in the pricing activities comparable to dumping, these private right-of-action proposals would most surely be a violation of GATT.[95]

Despite all the policy hesitations that can be expressed about antidumping laws, it is unlikely that these laws will either be abolished, or substantially overhauled in the near future. Consequently, it seems advisable that additional attention be given to the shape and implementation of the world's antidumping rules in the context of a multilateral trade institution such as the WTO.[96]

Finally, it is both interesting and potentially provocative to suggest the possibility that, for all its faults, the system of antidumping rules may be performing a useful function in world trade, *not* as a response to so-called unfairness, but rather as an "interface" or buffer mechanism to ameliorate difficulties such as those discussed in section 10.1, which are caused by interdependence among different economic systems. Could it be that the antidumping rules are acting as a crude or blunt instrument to cause different economic systems to share more equitably the burdens of adjusting to shifts of world trade flows? If so, perhaps we should view antidumping rules as part of the subject of "safeguards" (described in chapter 7) rather than as part of a subject of "unfair trade."

10.7 Beyond Dumping and Subsidies

What Is Unfair?

For almost a century, dumping and certain types of subsidies have been deemed by international trading governments to be "unfair" exporting measures, and thus vulnerable to permitted responses from importing countries and subject to certain types of international rule constraints. But in addition to these activities a number of other actions have also been challenged—if not by the international rules, then at least by one or more importing nations—as "unfair" when affecting international trade.

The most prominent category of other practices are those related to "restrictive business practices" described in section 9.5. Closely related to these is a group of practices deemed "unfair" by domestic law when they are undertaken with respect to domestic trade. Activities such as patent, copyright, or trademark infringement, deceptive business practices, or other monopolistic actions can be challenged in some countries on the basis of common-law rules or statutory provisions designed to reinforce "fairness" in trade. It would therefore seem natural to apply such concepts to imported goods although this practice poses some difficult procedural problems. The United States has probably been the most aggressive in developing a procedure (its Section 337) to handle these situations, so consequently I will explore this further, below.

Apart from the Section 337 responses to "unfair" trade, there are a number of other possible importing-nation counterattacks on certain types of trade practices. Focusing just on the United States, for example, we find a variety of relatively unknown laws that are designed for this purpose.[97] One dramatic example is a provision of U.S. law potentially connecting certain unfavorable income-tax treatment of a company to foreign nation practices affecting exports. As I noted in section 4.5, the U.S. law of Section 301 has language allowing the potential of unilateral U.S. definition of what is "unfair" as a trigger for possible retaliatory actions.

In the current rapidly changing world, with the problems that economic interdependence has created, it is not surprising that many political leaders have a number of candidates to bring within national and international disciplines on "unfair actions" in international trade. One general category of potential new rules, suggested for trade negotiations, is that of international trade in services, already addressed in the Uruguay Round but clearly requiring further ongoing negotiations. Another subject that has been much discussed is that of "targeting."[98] By this I mean the practice of some countries of using various government favors and "guidance" to encourage some industry sectors, and discourage others. This is closely related to "industrial policy" ideas.[99] Somehow the possibility of this type of government "interference" with market processes seems to have struck a chord of fear in the hearts and minds of some political leaders. In turn, these leaders suggest that certain aspects of these practices should be deemed "unfair" under trade rules, and should trigger certain import-restraint responses. The issues raised are extraordinarily complex, and they go to the heart of some of the trade-policy dilemmas of today. They also raise questions about the validity of the traditional comparative advantage theories, suggesting the idea of "dynamic comparative advantage."[100]

It should be recognized that not all possible international trade policies, rules, responses, and restraint techniques can be covered in this book. There is almost an infinite variety of subjects that relate to the flow of trade across borders. I have selected for inclusion here issues that normally are considered to be a part of "international trade policy," but the reader should not overlook other issues that can also have a large influence on international trade. Product liability issues, for example, pose considerable difficulties for the interdependent world.[101]

U.S. Law Section 337 Actions

A 1922 statute, modified and reenacted as Section 337 of the Tariff Act of 1930, and amended in the Trade Act of 1974 and the Omnibus Trade Act and Competitiveness Act of 1988, provides an important remedy for certain types of "unfair trade practices" involved with imports into the United States. Since the 1974 amendments, this remedy has become increasingly invoked and its importance has been growing. Over three hundred ninety cases have been brought between 1974 and 1995, and remedies have been directed against imports in approximately one hundred of these cases.

The statute provides a remedy against "unfair methods of competition and unfair acts in the importation of articles into the United States, or in their sale ... the effect or tendency of which is to destroy or substantially injure industry; efficiently and economically operated, in the United States, or to prevent the establishment of such an industry, or to restrain or monopolize ... "[102] The 1988 act added a provision so that an "injury" test is no longer required when the unfair practices involve intellectual property rights such as patents, trademarks, and copyrights.[103] The ITC carries out the procedure, with appeal being directly to the Court of Appeals for the Federal Circuit.

Unfair acts within this statute are most often deemed to be violations of intellectual property rights, such as patent, copyright, or trademark infringements. In addition, however, monopoly or other actions against competition can be the basis of remedy under this statute. All of these unfair actions have counterpart remedies in the courts of the United States, and in some instances are also the subject of regulatory actions by the Federal Trade Commission. Thus, it can be argued that, given the 337 remedy, discrimination does not exist regarding imports because counterpart remedies exist in domestic U.S. law when domestic goods are involved. A big difference, however, is in the procedure. The 337 remedy is *in rem*—a lawyer's term that means that the procedure is against the goods (imports) themselves, rather than against firms or individuals for actions relating to the goods. The advantage of this is that difficult procedural problems of service or process, or carrying out a court's judgment, are avoided. The 337 remedy can be an "exclusion order," preventing further importation of the goods.

Complaints to initiate this procedure are directed to the ITC, which then has a strictly limited time (twelve to eighteen months) within which to complete its process. Normally an administrative law judge (ALJ) will "try" the case and report to the commission, which must then make the final determination. An interesting facet is that after the commission's ruling, the law provides an opportunity for the president of the United States to "veto" or overrule the commission (and he has done so in approximately five cases) for reasons he deems sufficient.

The essential elements of a complaint (other than in intellectual property cases) include: (1) unfair acts or methods of competition, (2) the importation of goods, (3) effect to destroy or injure, (4) a U.S. industry, which (5) is efficiently and economically operated. The ITC cases provide a certain amount of interpretative exegesis for each of these elements. The "injury test" when applicable, for example, is clearly not as stringent as tests in the escape clause or in AD or CV cases.[104] On the other hand, the requirement that the industry be "efficiently and economically operated" imposes a burden on the domestic industry. The ITC must also consider whether an exclusion order would have an effect on the "public health, welfare or competitive conditions" of the U.S. economy.[105]

This U.S. law has been challenged several times in GATT, as I described in chapter 8, because it is argued that Section 337 effectively discriminates against imports compared to domestic goods, and therefore, concerning national treatment, is inconsistent (at least) with GATT Article III.[106] A GATT panel report that was adopted in November 1989 accepted this argument and held the U.S. Section 337 inconsistent with GATT. This report, however, did leave open the possibility of some procedural differences, such as an "in rem" approach, being justified under Article XX of the GATT.[107]

11 The Perplexities of Subsidies in International Trade

11.1 Introduction: The Policies

In chapter 10 I discussed some of the general policies regarding so-called unfair trade practices in international trade,[1] as well as the problem of dumping and antidumping duties. In chapter 11 I now turn to the partner of dumping: namely, the problem of subsidies and the response of countervailing duties.[2]

Both of these unfair trade practices depend (under international rules) on an injury test. Thus, in order for a nation to be permitted under GATT rules to respond to subsidized imports by imposing a countervailing duty, that nation must show that the subsidized imports are causing "material injury" to the domestic industry of the like product. As I noted in section 10.5,[3] the rules regarding the injury test are virtually the same for dumping as for subsidies, although there is no inherent policy reason why this should be so. Perhaps this is partly for purposes of symmetry and simplicity. Indeed, during the Tokyo Round, when a number of new provisions and criteria were worked out for injury in the context of subsidies and countervailing duties, the negotiators decided late in that negotiation to bring the antidumping injury rules into basic conformity with those of the subsidy rules.[4] For these reasons, I will not repeat the description of injury in this chapter, but instead will concentrate here on the substantive issues of subsidies: how they are identified, and what are the policies regarding them with respect to international trade.

Discussions of subsidies in international trade begin by drawing the distinction between "export subsidies," on the one hand, and "domestic," "production" or "general" subsidies, on the other hand. Export subsidies are granted only to products when they are exported. Some people view export subsidies as particularly pernicious,[5] and indeed it has been argued that because export subsidies are such an obvious attempt to impose burdens on other countries (burdens that are more political or producer oriented than they are economic in a broader sense), perhaps an injury test should not even be a criterion for responding with countervailing duties in such cases. Indeed, if this logic is followed, it might even be argued that an importing country should have the obligation to counter export subsidies by imposing countervailing duties on the products concerned.

Domestic or production subsidies, on the other hand, are subsidies that are granted for the benefit of products regardless of whether those products are exported or not. These are clearly the most perplexing, because they involve a vast range and number of government policies, many of which are perfectly justifiable as exercises of sovereign activity within a country.

It should be noted that by way of contrast with dumping matters, in the case of subsidies, we are almost always talking about government action, rather than individual enterprise action. Thus, issues of subsidies and countervailing duties are often significantly more visible and involve a higher level of government-to-government diplomacy than do many other trade policy matters. If an importing nation decides to counter a foreign subsidy, it is acting rather confrontationally toward a foreign sovereign's act. It can certainly be expected that the foreign sovereign will not be pleased to have this reaction from another nation.

Apart from the different types of subsidies mentioned above, it should be noted that there are at least three effects of subsidies. For example, subsidies of country A can enhance the exportability of products into an importing nation, country B. In such a case, nation B may wish to respond with countervailing duties. Second, subsidies from country A can enhance the exportation of its products to a third country, C, where they compete with similar products that are exported from country B. In such a case, country B does not have easy recourse to a response. Its own countervailing duties are not effective. It may not wish to competitively subsidize its exports. Thus it must somehow induce the importing country, country C in this case, to respond to the subsidized imports. Country C, however, may be quite happy to receive such subsidized goods. Consequently, country B's grievance against country A may have to be aided by some other technique, such as recourse to an international forum like the GATT.

A third effect of subsidies can be to restrain imports into the subsidizing country. Thus, if country A subsidizes its bicycles even when all of those bicycles are sold in its home market, one effect is to make it harder for other countries such as B or C to export bicycles to country A. The subsidy in this situation has become an import barrier, and economists can demonstrate that the effect is in some ways similar to a tariff.[6] Once again, countervailing duties will not provide a remedy, because the country that is "harmed" is not receiving subsidized imports.

In the next section, I will look at the overall landscape of national and international rules that affect subsidization in international trade. Basically, there are two sets of such rules: those regarding the use of countervailing duties and those providing certain substantive international obligations against the use of subsidies that may affect international trade. With respect to the use of countervailing duties, it should be noted that at the present time the United States is the principal user of this response to subsidized goods. Although several other countries have had a few countervailing duty cases, and more have a law on their books that permit them,[7] the United States is the only country in the world that has extensively used countervailing duties. The number of countervailing duty cases in the United States since 1979 and through 1995 is more than 440.[8]

As is the case with dumping and antidumping duties, the economic and other policies concerning the use of subsidies in international trade, and the permitted responses to those subsidies, are perplexing and controversial.[9] Particularly regarding whether an importing nation should use countervailing duties to respond to imports that are subsidized, there is a considerable amount of economic literature that would suggest that such response is unwise. The basis for this view is that if a foreign government wishes to subsidize the exports to an importing country, the importing country—or at least its consumers—should be grateful for the gift that has been sent to it. The appropriate response in such a case, so it is said (tongue-in-cheek), is to send a "thank-you note" to the subsidizing nation. Although certain subsidies may correct rather than distort the most efficient allocation of resources, a reasonably careful economic analysis[10] suggests that in the case of a subsidy—whether export subsidy or domestic subsidy (with products exported)—the country that does the subsidizing loses in net national economic welfare, while the rest of the world gains. The particular distribution of the gains within the rest of the world may not always be predictable, although certainly the consumers in the importing countries would usually benefit sufficiently to offset the harm to producers in the same countries. And in net exporting countries and elsewhere in the world where that is not the case, consumers gain sufficiently to offset the harm to their own producers. This has been the rationale of many economists who have urged that all countervailing duty laws should be abolished.

Economists recognize, however, that there are certain types of situations, sometimes called "strategic," for which an import restraint such as a countervailing duty might have a welfare-enhancing effect for the importing country. However, they also believe that this effect is unrelated to whether the goods are subsidized or not. The effect usually arises because of the market power of the importing country. If this country is large enough that by restraining imports it causes a reduction in the world price of the commodity (an "optimum tariff" concept[11]), then certain situations exist in which the tariff (including the countervailing duty) can enhance the overall welfare of the importing country.

The basic problem with all of these views, however, is that they focus on too narrow a perspective—that of the importing country. When one moves to a worldwide perspective—that is, in order to explore which actions will enhance or decrease worldwide net welfare—then a stronger case can be made for providing some kind of international or national disciplines on the use of subsidies of internationally traded goods. The economists would apparently admit that in such circumstances some subsidies tend to distort international production and trading patterns, and reduce efficiency and thus reduce world welfare.[12] This is, however, a rather peculiar argument to use within an importing nation for the application of countervailing duties. It is certainly not the basis of most of the arguments heard. Most of the arguments originate from competing producer groups, and they are most interested in their own welfare, and not that of the world in general. On the other hand, it can be argued that if such relatively parochial or selfish motivations result in the use of measures, such as countervailing duties, that coincidentally in the long run tend to inhibit a practice (subsidization) that reduces world welfare, then why not take advantage of such parochial/selfish motivations? This argument would support the use of countervailing duties.

Other arguments have been used concerning the traditional international trade policies of countervailing duties. One of these arguments notes the adjustment costs when new subsidies are put in place. For an importing nation, the subsidies may dramatically shift the competitive relationship between its domestic products and the imports, and cause domestic industry to go out of business or "adjust outward." If subsidies are short-lived, there may soon come a time when the reverse adjustment will occur. Adding up the two adjustment costs (in and out) may establish that the adjustment costs are greater than the net welfare addition to the importing country. Thus, in the case of short-lived subsidies, special argument could be made for using countervailing duties at the very beginning.

If one believes that subsidies are inherently unstable, because they involve favoritism by the public fisc of the subsidizing country (which will stimulate opposing political forces to get rid of them), one might think that this argument has some weight. Observers note, however, that subsidies are often very long term and very stable. Thus, this argument of "in and out adjustment costs" is relatively weak.

Another possible argument is very similar to that made in the case of dumping. It can be argued that subsidies can be used for "predatory purposes," to enable a subsidizing nation's industry to obtain market share abroad to the point where it has sufficient monopoly power that it can then raise prices, reduce the subsidy, and extract "monopoly rents."[13] There are some curious dimensions to this argument. For one, it will be noted that subsidization is primarily a government activity, so this argument is essentially accusing a foreign government of predatory intent. That accusation seems not too polite from a sovereign's viewpoint, but of course it may nevertheless be deserved. On the other hand, given that a government is more likely to have a broader impact on its own firms and to be a single decision-making entity, it may have greater opportunity to actually effectuate a predatory intent than would a sector of economic activity in which a number of firms existed—each suspicious of the other. I discussed these problems in the context of dumping, and it will be recalled that many economists are skeptical of predatory intent because of the difficulty of "succeeding."[14] In the case of subsidies, a single relatively powerful economic national government can more easily "succeed." Thus, if predation can in fact be proven, this fact may also be an argument against subsidies, and in favor of such policies that would tend to prevent the effectiveness of subsidies (including countervailing duties). Some of these arguments may relate to the notion of "targeting," which has been discussed during recent years.

Of course, there may be some policies relating to subsidies that are relatively unrelated to the question of total economic net welfare. For example, national defense policies may suggest that an importing nation must defend itself against the competition of subsidized imports in certain sectors.[15] Likewise, income-distribution arguments can be made, as can short-term arguments with respect to various governmental fiscal and budgetary considerations, or political considerations (e.g., maintaining a majority in the parliament by avoiding unemployment in certain districts).

Finally, there may be some policies relating to subsidization that are connected to national government's general approach to its economic system. Entrepreneurs in a market economy, such as that of the United

States, often say that they can compete against "fair imports," but they cannot compete against a foreign government's treasury. What they mean, partly, is that an additional layer of risk is involved in competing in a world trade environment when other than market and profit-maximizing considerations of foreign firms are motivating those firms' exports. If the motivation is some set of policies carried out by the foreign government, the importing country's entrepreneurs say that this is unfair and tends to reduce the efficacy of the importing country's economic system when that system is geared toward a free-market orientation. In short, it is fair to worry about escalating competitive subsidization that would be occasioned by strong political pressures within an importing country when its entrepreneurs feel aggrieved by foreign government subsidies. Such competitive subsidization would tend to change the economic system within the importing country, and arguably the importing country ought not be put to that choice. Thus, a "buffering response," such as countervailing duties on the imports that are subsidized, might be appropriate as a way to assist the importing nation to maintain the relative purity of its free-market economic system. This argument is so vague, it is even hard to articulate, much less prove. Nevertheless, it certainly appeals in a visceral way to entrepreneurs who would argue that the entrepreneurial spirit is important to the free-market economy.

The reader may now detect that there is great controversy about the economic policies with respect to subsidies in international trade. It is not possible at this point in time to resolve these issues. One thing is clear: for more than a century, the international trade rules and some national systems have been established on the basis of the proposition that imports that are subsidized by foreign governments are somehow "unfair." The politicians, perhaps because they respond more to the arguments and pressures of producer groups than to those of consumer groups, constantly repeat these notions. Thus it is all too likely that whatever the underlying economic merits of these cases, these are not clear enough to establish movement toward radical change, and that the countervailing duty regimes of the world (currently mostly in the United States, but probably to be emulated by other countries soon) will continue.

In arguing against the use of countervailing duties in the United States, persons have sometimes noted that the world perspective, that might justify unilateral national government actions that generally could help to inhibit the use of subsidies worldwide, is not persuasive because the United States does not have that much impact on the world. Discussions and experience with specific cases, and with specific individuals and foreign governments, however, suggest that through its trade policies the United States does indeed have a very great impact on the world. In the 1970s and 1980s Canada, for example, was shocked by its own vulnerability to what Canadians often call "contingent protectionism" of the United States, which means the application of U.S. antidumping and countervailing duty laws. Some would say that the very large and important U.S. countervailing duty cases against lumber from Canada were a major motivation leading the Canadians to seek a bilateral free-trade agreement with the United States.[16] Comparable instances of U.S. countervailing duty law impact on other government policies can be noticed.[17] Thus, if one believes that the world would be better off if there were a general reduction of the use by governments of subsidies relating to products which flow in international trade, one could argue that the U.S. policies, motivated for entirely different reasons, may be fortuitously or coincidentally having a salutary effect on the world economy.

11.2 Evolution of the Rules on Subsidies and Countervailing Duties in National and International Law

National rules that provide a response from the importing country to imports that have been subsidized by foreign governments can be traced back to the nineteenth century.[18] Indeed, certain generalized statements about unfair trade seem to fuse together the concepts that we now separate into "dumping" and "subsidization," and some of these concepts can be traced back much further than the nineteenth century.[19] In the United States, the original countervailing duty statute is taken to be that of 1897.[20] A number of treaties, particularly bilateral treaties, touched on this subject,[21] including general wording in some of the U.S. bilateral reciprocal trade agreement treaties of the 1930s and 1940s.[22]

But the elaborate development of multilateral international rules concerning subsidized trade began primarily with the GATT. In the original GATT agreement of 1947 there was very little discipline on the question of subsidizing, except for the permitted response of countervailing duties. There was a fairly general reporting requirement in Article XVI of the original GATT, plus a general obligation in Article II, paragraph 4 against the use of new subsidies to inhibit imports into the subsidizing country when that country had "bound" its tariff on the product concerned.[23] But no other substantive international rules existed on subsidy practices.

The 1955 review session amendments to the GATT introduced the first substantive obligations regarding subsidies into the GATT (paragraphs 2 through 5 of Article XVI).[24] However, this portion of GATT related only to export subsidies and did not apply to general, production, or domestic subsidies. Even then, the discipline of GATT was attenuated. In addition, the GATT rules were divided between applications to "primary" and "nonprimary" products. With respect to primary products, GATT Article XVI, paragraph 3 admonished countries to "seek to avoid" their use for exports and stated that they should not be applied "in a manner which results in that contracting party having more than an equitable share of world export trade in that product ..." This "equitable share" language was very troublesome for its ambiguity, and thus it is not surprising that it has been changed in the Uruguay Round text.

In addition, paragraph 4 of Article XVI of GATT provided that "from 1 January 1958 or the earliest practicable date thereafter," contracting parties should cease to grant subsidies on exports of nonprimary goods, when the subsidy resulted in a sale at a price for export lower than that for the domestic market. This obligation thus had two significant conditions: a date before which it would not apply, and the "bilevel pricing" test, which has also proved troublesome in subsequent developments.[25] Because of the structure of this amendment to GATT, the paragraph 4 obligation for nonprimary goods would not come into effect until additional action was taken by countries concerned. For some years, the GATT CONTRACTING PARTIES adopted an annual standstill declaration, but finally, in 1962, a declaration applying the paragraph 4 obligations was opened for signature.[26] However, partly because of the differentiation of treatment between primary and nonprimary goods, many developing and primary goods countries believed that the GATT was discriminating against their trade. Consequently, not all countries were prepared to adopt the declaration implementing paragraph 4 of Article XVI. Until the Uruguay Round, therefore, the GATT Article XVI paragraph 4 commitments regarding subsidies were only binding on a small portion of the contracting parties of GATT. Of course, the Tokyo Round Subsidies Code bound the signatories to that code in ways that superseded GATT Article XVI, as I discuss below.

GATT Article VI allows governments to impose duties on imported products otherwise subject to GATT obligations in cases of dumping and subsidization. This "exception" to GATT obligations, however, only operates when imports cause material injury to the competing domestic industries of the importing country.

The U.S. countervailing duty law anteceded the GATT, and thus according to the Protocol of Provisional Application, which applied grandfather rights to Article VI of GATT, the U.S. 1897 statute[27] that provided for countervailing duties against subsidized goods without the necessity of showing "material injury" did not technically violate the U.S. obligations under GATT.

As tariffs declined under GATT, domestic-producing interests in a number of GATT countries began to search for other ways to inhibit import competition, and more attention was devoted in the United States to the U.S. antidumping and countervailing duty laws. Thus, during the 1960s and early 1970s new attention was given to countervailing duties and a higher risk that such duty cases in the United States would succeed. Because the U.S. law was relatively short and sketchy, considerable discretion was exercised by the U.S. administrative agency that applied it (then the Department of Treasury), and the application of U.S. countervailing duty laws was relatively hesitant.[28] This hesitancy, however, angered the domestic interests and the Congress. Partly because of this anger, Congress in 1980 succeeded in obtaining the transfer of jurisdiction of countervailing and antidumping duties from the Department of Treasury to the Department of Commerce.[29]

At the beginning of the Tokyo Round of GATT negotiations in 1973 and 1974, the U.S. government developed a statutory framework for the U.S. negotiating position, and in that statute the Congress demanded a tightening of the countervailing duty laws.[30] This resulted in specific time limits being applied to the administrating agency's consideration of complaints, the opportunity for judicial review of those decisions, and a tightening of the criteria for the mandatory application of countervailing duties to subsidized goods. In addition, in this statute, the executive branch and the Congress agreed to extend the application of countervailing duties to nondutiable goods. Prior to this statute, countervailing duties in the United States only applied to dutiable goods. This change reflected the fact that an increasing amount of trade was entering the United States duty free, and that a new generalized system of preferences for developing country trade would extend duty-free treatment to much more trade in the future.

The reader will note, however, that U.S. grandfather rights (allowing it to avoid applying a material injury test) only applied to the pre-GATT existing statute that covered dutiable goods. Therefore, in a careful exercise of obedience to international obligation, the Congress enacted the 1974 statute with an injury test imposed for those subsidy cases where the goods could be entered duty free.[31] Thus, for the first time the United States established an injury test in connection with countervailing duties on subsidized goods. The history of the U.S. congressional action on this point is a salutary example of the Congress studiously confining its action to those that are consistent with U.S. international obligations.

The United States was much criticized at this time for its lack of a general injury test in its countervailing duty statute, and so the United States indicated to its trade-negotiating partners in the Tokyo Round that it was prepared to put this issue on the table, provided that other nations would join with it in establishing a new international discipline on the use of subsidies in international trade. Negotiations leading to a code concerning subsidies and countervailing duties were begun in the Tokyo Round, resulting in 1979 in an agreement on that subject. This agreement, the Subsidies Code,[32] was the first general comprehensive multilateral discipline of the use of subsidies in international trade and the first elaboration of the subsidy rules since the 1955 GATT amendments. In addition, the 1979 code contained the first international obligations of a multilateral character that explicitly concerned so-called domestic subsidies, and not just export subsidies.[33]

The 1979 GATT Subsidies Code covered substantive obligations essentially in two parts, sometimes called "Track I" and "Track II." Track I dealt entirely with countervailing duties, establishing international rules on what national governments could do in implementing their countervailing duty rules (including constraints on the procedures for those cases) and rather elaborate definitions of material injury. The one thing that was lacking, however, was any definition of "subsidy" in the context of national countervailing duty rules. This meant that national governments enjoyed a considerable amount of latitude in defining "subsidy" for countervailing duty purposes, a latitude that the United States—as principal user—found significant. Indeed, the U.S. administration of the subsidies/countervailing duty issues has been very significant in the development of the conceptual thinking at a broader multilateral level.

Track II of the 1979 code was devoted to the substantive obligations under international law regarding how governments should refrain from granting subsidies that affect goods in international trade. Some of these rules were further elaborations of Article XVI of GATT, and applied only to export subsidies. The code's Track II reiterates the obligation to avoid the use of export subsidies on primary products (defined slightly differently) when the result would be "larger than an equitable share" of the world market. Regarding nonprimary goods, the code was more stringent than the GATT, although it purported merely to be interpreting the GATT. For this category of goods, the code flatly prohibited the use of export subsidies, and did not repeat the bilevel pricing test found in Article XVI of GATT.

An important additional feature of Track II of the Subsidies Code, however, was found in Article 11, entitled "Subsidies Other Than Export Subsidies." It was this article that contained the first general multilateral treaty discipline on government use of domestic subsidies which have an impact on international trade. The language of the article was relatively tortured and ambiguous, clearly because there was not much agreement among the negotiating countries regarding this subject. The language noted that domestic subsidies "are widely used for the promotion of social and economic policy objectives," and that the code did not "intend to restrict the right of signatories to use such subsidies to achieve these and other important policy objectives which they consider desirable." On the other hand, the language of the article recognized that the use of subsidies "may cause or threaten to cause injury" to the domestic industry of other signatories, or "serious prejudice to the interests," or "may nullify or impair benefits" to the other signatories. Then the language imposed the obligation on signatories to "seek to avoid such effects through the use of subsidies." Needless to say, it is not surprising that the Subsidies Code had a difficult history subsequent to the completion of the Tokyo Round, given its very language reflects considerable ambivalence about its obligations.

An interesting feature of the 1979 code is an annex that listed a series of practices entitled "Illustrative List of Export Subsidies." This annex was a revision of a 1960 GATT document resulting from a working-party study that also listed practices that would be deemed to be export subsidies.[34] Thus, for purposes of Track II of the code, language that applied to export subsidies, the Illustrative List was an important source of interpretive material for defining "export subsidies."

The United States implemented the 1979 code through its 1979 Trade Agreements Act (which generally implemented the results of the Tokyo Round[35]). In that statute, the Congress wrote the specific rules of U.S. law regarding subsidies and countervailing duties, doing so in a way that the Congress felt fully implemented U.S. obligations under the new Subsidies Code of the Tokyo Round. As I have noted elsewhere, the Congress explicitly indicated that the code would not be "self-executing," and that therefore it would not be part of domestic U.S. law.[36]

The U.S. Congress limited the full benefits of the code obligations (and its application of the injury test) to products of nations that became "a country under the agreement." Generally this meant a country that accepted the Tokyo Round's Subsidies Code and its obligations, or a country that accepted the obligations, even though it did not sign the code. For developing countries that benefited from an extraordinarily broad exception in article 14 of the Tokyo Round Subsidies Code, the United States was not prepared to grant its domestic law provisions implementing the code unless certain special commitments were entered into to follow some of the broader obligations of the code. This U.S. position was questionable under the MFN clause of GATT and was challenged, but no definitive ruling on this occurred under GATT. At the end of the Uruguay Round and of GATT's existence, twenty-four countries had ratified the Subsidies Code, some with exceptions or reservations. The Uruguay Round now changes all of this.

The Uruguay Round text on subsidies, mandatory for all members, is a substantial change from the Tokyo Round Subsidies Code, and in my view, a substantial improvement, although it is still subject to some criticism and the obvious need for further negotiating changes in the future. Indeed, the Uruguay Round Subsidies Code follows an overall conceptual outline that was proposed during the Tokyo Round negotiation, but which negotiators were not able to achieve. This is sometimes called the "red, green, yellow light approach." The basic concept is that subsidies can be put into various "baskets" that include "prohibited (red)," "actionable (yellow)," and "nonactionable (green)" categories.

The Uruguay Round subsidies text, officially entitled "Agreement on Subsidies and Countervailing Measures" is sufficiently extensive and detailed that for most purposes it seems to supersede the text of GATT Articles VI and XVI, although there may still be a few concepts that would remain embedded in those articles of GATT 1994. As mentioned in an early chapter, the relationship of some of these "agreements" or "texts" in the Uruguay Round to the GATT itself, is not entirely clear, but given that the UR subsidies text provides a rather complete and overall framework, it seems quite clear that on subsidies matters the starting point will be the new Uruguay Round text. What are the outlines of that text?

Similar to the 1979 code, the new subsidies text addresses both the issue of international obligations (1979 Track I) and the issues of application of countervailing duties (1979 Track II). The basic parts of the new code provide a somewhat broader landscape, however. They are as follows:

Part I. General provisions (definition and specificity)

Part II. Prohibited subsidies (red light?)

Part III. Actionable subsidies (yellow or amber?)

Part IV. Nonactionable subsidies (green light?)

Part V. Countervailing duty measures

The subsequent parts then deal with institutions, surveillance, developing-country questions, transitional arrangements, and dispute-settlement and final provisions, followed by a series of annexes. The first annex to the subsidies text, Annex 1, is again (similar to prior versions) an "Illustrative List of Export Subsidies" that largely follows the language of the 1979 code illustrative list, with some important differences.

A few words about each of these five substantive parts should help the reader grasp the overall "landscape" provided by this text. For example, in Part I the text provides a "definition of a subsidy" in Article 1 which has some intriguing elements. Unlike the 1979 code, the Uruguay Round's text basic definition of subsidy appears to apply to all parts of the agreement, including that of countervailing duties. The definition requires a "financial contribution by a government or any public body," which can occur by several different devices such as foregone revenue, or provision of goods or services, or a direct transfer. In the alternative, a form of income or price support "in the sense of Article XVI of GATT 1994" can be part of this definition. In addition, there is the requirement that "a benefit is thereby conferred."

One of the key concepts that developed in the U.S. statute, and the jurisprudence implementing it, is the concept of "specificity" as a prerequisite of certain kinds of responses to the subsidies, such as countervailing duties, or an international procedure. The definition of specificity is fairly complex, but it basically strives to provide a focus on subsidies that assist particular enterprises, industries, or group of enterprises, and are thus not "generally available."

Parts II, III, and IV then take up the international obligations regarding subsidies, dealing with the three "baskets." However, there are certain "sub-baskets" or particular exceptions to some of the rules. Thus, one cannot assume that all subsidies fall neatly into one of three categories. For example, under the yellow light category of "actionable subsidies," there are some types of subsidies that have been colloquially characterized as "dark amber" where a "serious prejudice" type injury test is "presumed."

Part II regarding prohibited subsidies (red light) focuses primarily on export subsidies, and refers to the Annex I list. Also included in that prohibited category are subsidies that are contingent upon the required use of domestic over imported goods. There are certain exceptions in the agreement, including those for developing countries. The basic thrust, however, provides that in the case of prohibited subsidies, a member can complain without the need to show any sort of injury or prejudice.

Part III actionable subsidies (the yellow light) is in some sense a residual category for subsidies that are not explicitly included under "prohibited" in Part I, or "nonactionable—green" in Part IV. It should not be surprising that most subsidies will fall under this yellow or amber category. In this case, "no Member should cause, through the use of any subsidy ... adverse effects to the interests of other Members, i.e.: a) injury to the domestic industry of another Member, b) nullification or impairment of benefits directly or indirectly to other Members under GATT 1994 ... c) serious prejudice to the interests of another Member." (Agricultural subsidies are handled in a different agreement.)

Thus there are basically three different kinds of injury tests embraced in this category, and each of these have certain definitions and exceptions.

Part IV covers "nonactionable subsidies," the so-called green category. These are sometimes referred to as the "green box" or "green basket" subsidy. The basic idea is that subsidies that fall within this category shall not be subject to either an international complaint procedure or to countervailing duties.[37]

Finally, Part V covers countervailing measures, which are fairly similar to the previous 1979 code and to the practice under GATT Article VI. One notable difference is the explicit provision of a de minimis threshold of 1 percent.[38] The rules for determining injury are very close to those provided for antidumping (see the previous chapter), and the other rules now set forth in the new subsidies text add details to the international obligations concerning the determination of subsidies, the procedures of an investigation, the methods of calculating the amount of a subsidy (which can be quite complex), and so on.

Unlike the subject of dumping, subsidies is a topic that is explicitly recognized in the Uruguay Round Agreement on Trade in Services. Even here, however, the relevant Article (Article XV) merely calls upon members to enter into negotiations "with a view to developing the necessary multilateral disciplines to avoid such trade-distortive effects." It also exhorts the negotiators to address the "appropriateness of countervailing procedures" and to "recognize the role of subsidies in relation to the development programs of developing countries ..." The article also provides any member "which considers that it is adversely affected by a subsidy of another member" the opportunity to request consultations. There is no mention in the intellectual property Uruguay Round text of the problem of subsidies.

11.3 Defining Subsidies and "Actionable Subsidies"

The definition of "subsidy" has always perplexed policymakers, partly because the word "subsidy" can mean so many different things. If the term "subsidy" is defined in a rather broad way, as is sometimes the case, it can include an enormous range of government activities. For example, if an economic definition of subsidy contends that it is deemed to mean a "benefit conferred on a firm or product by action of a government,"[39] then the concept of subsidy could include such typical and universal governmental activities as providing fire and police protection, roads, and even schools or education. Highly effective fire and police protection would obviously reduce the insurance costs of producing firms, and thus reduce part of their costs of production. Likewise, other types of societal infrastructure can reduce the costs that are "internalized" in the accounting of a firm that is evaluating the price of its goods.[40] The problem is that if such a broad definition were used, and international rules permitted governments to respond with countervailing duties against such subsidies, the whole system of post–World War II GATT liberal trade (including the reduction in tariffs) would be undermined: governments would be able to impose many countervailing duties, because virtually every product would benefit from these kinds of governmental assistance.

Therefore, the problem becomes one of defining "subsidy" in such a way as to avoid these broad, damaging effects on international trade. This problem has been primarily connected to the use of countervailing duties by unilateral national government actions. Of course, these definitional problems occur with respect to the substantive international obligations against the use of subsidies; but in that context generally there is an international procedure, and governments do not have as much unilateral scope or freedom to define subsidy.

A basic approach is to recognize that there is a vast universe of governmental activity that can be called "subsidy" under broad definitions, but to recognize that the international system should not be concerned about all of the contents of this vast universe. Rather, the international system should be trying to define a subset of a certain type of "subsidy" with which it will be concerned.

Behind all this it must be recognized that subsidies are an exceedingly important, even crucial tool of national governments in facilitating their sovereign capacity to promote legitimate governmental policies to serve their constituents. There is no way that a government can "give up subsidies" under any broad definition of the term "subsidies." One needs only to recall a variety of different kinds of subsidies to realize this, including: aid to the poor, aid for technological development, special aids for education, aid to handicapped persons, aid to disadvantaged groups and regions, aid to offset certain disadvantages that have been created by other government policies, national security policies, and so on.[41]

Although many subsidies, particularly the so-called production or general subsidies, have legitimate government policies behind them, as implemented these subsidies may transgress on foreign governments' legitimate aspirations on behalf of their own producing interests. Thus we may have a clash of competing policy goals: on the one hand, governments have legitimate reasons for implementing subsidies, but on the other hand, importing nations have legitimate reasons for being concerned about the importation of subsidized goods when those goods cause distress to their own industries. The basic problem is how to balance these competing interests. It is in this connection that the injury test is crucial: it acts as a sort of "mediating principle" to help governments accommodate these diametrically opposed competing interests. If the subsidized goods are not harming or causing injury in the importing country, then why bother about any response? On the other hand, if the subsidized imports create sufficient distress in the importing country to rise to some threshold level of "material injury," or "serious prejudice", perhaps at that point a response such as a countervailing duty is justified (although at this point the economic policies outlined in section 1 of this chapter may introduce reasons why, even with material injury, countervailing duties may be inappropriate).

With these caveats in mind, we can turn to some of the concepts that are currently being used to constrain the breadth of a definition of "subsidy," and also think a bit about other concepts that could be likewise used. The Uruguay Round text on subsidies provides two important such concepts. First, in Article 1 it provides a definition of subsidy that applies to the entire agreement, and that limits somewhat the type of subsidy that will be considered in the agreement. The second concept is the important constraint of "specificity."

Concerning the first concept and its definition, an initial question is sometimes asked by policymakers, namely: does the subsidy impose a cost on the granting government and/or a benefit on the production of a particular product that moves in international trade? According to one approach, in order for a subsidy to be brought under the GATT rules, it must be established that the government has incurred a cost. According to a different viewpoint (that prevailing in the U.S. administration), "cost" is not the relevant consideration. Instead, the key question is whether the subsidy activity has conferred a benefit on a firm, compared to what that firm would receive under normal market conditions without the government intervention.

An example is useful to illustrate this difference in approach. Suppose that the government is prepared to make special loans to a particular industry sector at a cost of 8 percent interest. Suppose, at the same time, the government can borrow its own funds at a cost of about 6 percent. On the other hand, suppose that the normal private-market lending would require an interest rate of 10 percent. In this situation, it might be argued that there has been no cost to the government for its 8 percent loans, given that the government receives its funds for 6 percent. It will be further noted that the recipient firm is receiving a benefit because it obtains the loan at 8 percent, instead of the market rate of 10 percent. Under U.S. administration of its countervailing duty law, it is very clear that the benefit approach is being used and that the loan would be considered a "subsidy."[42] Arguably the U.S. approach is the correct one, if one of the basic policies of the international discipline on subsidies is to prevent "distortions." The benefit conferred on the firm by an interest rate lower than the market's interest rate induces that firm to produce goods that it might not otherwise produce, and induces a certain allocation of resources that is not "fine tuned" to economic principles and to the needs of society or the world.[43]

Of course, if one wanted to push the frontiers of this concept, it would be possible to note that when the government lends at 8 percent (even though it borrows at 6 percent), it has incurred an "opportunity cost" by giving up a portion of the interest it *could* obtain. If the "cost approach" includes this opportunity cost, then we see the opposing approaches converge. Perhaps this is another reason why the benefit approach seems to be preferable.

Article 1 of the Uruguay Round text provides a definition of subsidy that combines elements of the cost as well as the benefit approach. That text requires a "financial contribution by a government or any public body" that can be a direct transfer of funds, foregone revenue, providing goods and services, or government payments to particular funding mechanisms, or forms of income or price supports. But then it also requires that "a benefit is thereby conferred." An important implication of this definition may be to prevent the use of the Urugury Round subsidies obligations to attack what is sometimes called "regulatory subsidy," namely, to attack as a subsidy the failure of a foreign government to provide certain levels of regulation (such as environmental protection, or labor standards), and to argue that these are a subsidy within the obligations of the WTO.

A second very important concept, which basically was developed in the U.S. administrative and statutory implementation of countervailing duty law, is the concept of "specificity." This was introduced explicitly in the U.S. Countervailing Duty Statute of 1979 (implementing the Tokyo Round Code), but was not necessarily required by the 1979 code and is probably not found in the laws of other nations.

To some degree, the specificity concept is the reverse side of the coin of what has in the recent past been called "general availability."[44] The basic idea is that when there is a foreign government subsidy that affects exports, in order for an importing country to respond with countervailing duties it must be established that the subsidy is "specific" and not one that is so "generally available" that everyone in the exporting society can use it.

The U.S. 1979 law defines subsidy this way: "The following domestic subsidies, if provided or required by government action to a specific enterprise or industry, or group of enterprises or industries, whether publicly or privately owned, ..."[45] This is the source of the "specificity test," which has been an important and pivotal concept in the U.S. administration's application of countervailing duties, and on which there is considerable jurisprudence both at the administrative level and in court appeals from administrative determinations.[46] There was doubt, however, whether the international rules then required the same approach. There is nothing in GATT or in the 1979 Subsidies Code that so explicitly focuses on a "specificity test," although in the 1979 code at Article 11, paragraph 3, there is reference to "the aim of giving an advantage to certain enterprises." The UR text clearly embraces specificity.

What are the policy arguments supporting a "specificity test"?[47] It seems that there are at least two. First, there is some economic argument that could be made that if a subsidy is generally provided across the board to all of society and all of the producing sectors of society, it does not "distort." This argument has to be made with some caution, of course, although it might be modified simply to say that the distortions are quite minimal in such cases. Furthermore, in the context of a floating exchange-rate world, given a moderate time for adjustment of exchange rates, the *international* distorting effects of a generally available subsidy may normally be quite minimal. Thus some economic argument can be used to buttress the notion that generally available subsidies—that is, nonspecific subsidies—should not be "actionable."

But these economic arguments can only go part of the way toward explaining a rationale for the specificity test. If we recognize the need to eliminate from the subset of subsidies called "actionable" the general activities that all governments undertake (such as societal infrastructure like police, fire protection, roads, schools, etc.), the specificity test can offer a very useful method for doing so. Thus, it can be argued that part of the rationale for the specificity test is that it is useful as a tool of administration (albeit sometimes blunt) to get rid of a number of cases which really ought not to be brought into a countervailing duty or other international rule process.

A specificity test, however, is not itself free of problems. An immediate question that arises is the difference between de jure and de facto specificity. A government subsidy may be worded so that it appears to offer a benefit to everyone in society, or at least to offer benefits broadly to many sectors of the producing part of society. Yet, the underlying reality may be such that only a few producers or sectors can really take advantage of it. For example, Canadian provinces offer "stumpage," which gives to firms the right to remove trees from government property, to use as a material input in production of a variety of goods. In theory, this offer is open to all comers. In practice, obviously there may be only a more limited set of industries that can profitably utilize the privilege.[48] Likewise, the Mexican government may ostensibly offer to all comers the opportunity to have ammonia at a very favorable price compared to the world market price, but it may be that only fertilizer makers are really interested in taking up such an offer.[49] Thus United States jurisprudence, at both the administrative and the court levels, has pushed the concept of specificity to a de facto test,[50] such that in order for the specificity test to be fulfilled, it must be demonstrated that not only as a legal matter are the benefits available, but also that in fact a broad segment of the economy is able to take advantage of the benefits.

Problems still remain, of course. Probably no "nonspecific subsidy" is uniformly applied across all of society. For example, in the income tax law an accelerated depreciation privilege could be offered to all who can take advantage of it, but in fact it will likely benefit those firms that use more capital goods than other firms (such as service firms) that do not. Yet, it seems generally understood that such a tax measure would be "non-specific," and therefore not "actionable."[51] Likewise, is something which is available to the entire agricultural sector nonspecific because there are a number of subsectors of agriculture (grains, beef, etc.), and thus agriculture is broad enough to be considered "nonspecific"?[52] What other perimeters can be placed around the concept?

In approaching these questions, it seems that the issue is not so much an abstract one of what is or is not "specific," but is one that must be understood as an administrative tool that can assist even low-level officials to determine "actionability," in the light of some of the economic and "administratability" principles that have been outlined above. National government administrators need some leeway in making these determinations, which will allow them to provide some guideposts for lower-level officials. Otherwise, the processes become so expensive that they themselves are a "nontariff barrier" to liberal world trade. The Uruguay Round subsidies text at Article 2 incorporates the specificity idea into the international treaty obligations of the WTO, and provides some additional definitions of "specificity". It also embraces the "de facto" test, so that specificity may have to be measured by what in fact occurs in the market place.

Another possible approach to these problems of constraining the breadth of a subsidy definition (which, however, is not explicitly embraced in the Uruguay Round subsidy text language) is to look at whether the subsidy "distorts" economic activity by comparison with some notion of "normal free-market" conditions. This comparison is obviously very tricky and indeed some writers would suggest that there is no such thing as "normal market activity."[53]

It does seem possible, however, to use a "distortion test," at least to some extent, for ascertaining some guideposts for our problem of defining "subsidy." It seems, however, that not just any "distortion" should suffice for the international system to take action. In some sense, every governmental action that impinges on the economy creates a "distortion." With their graphs and deadweight triangles, the economists will show, that many of these subsidy activities will reduce overall national welfare.[54] However, it is a legitimate choice for a national sovereign to accept lower economic welfare in order to promote certain societal and governmental objectives (such as redistribution of income, or support for the handicapped). As long as the government's actions are taken in such a way that the costs are borne only by that society, it seems inappropriate for other nations in the world to complain.[55] It is when the government's subsidy activity not only creates distortions within its own economy, but also significantly distorts the economies of other societies, that the international system has a legitimate concern.

A hypothetical example will partly illustrate this point. Suppose in a country, say Italy, private entrepreneurs would gladly invest in the production of a glass factory in a port city. The object would be to produce both for the home and the export market. Suppose, in addition, the government of Italy prefers that the factory be located in a depressed area in the mountains, so as to uplift that area economically. Suppose, further, that the government is prepared to pay a subsidy to the firm just equal to the additional costs of locating in the mountain region rather than in the port. In such a case, presumably the government's subsidy will distort economic activity within its national boundaries, and will somewhat lower its overall national economic welfare. However, it has a legitimate reason for wanting to do this and for bearing the costs of doing it. If the subsidy, however, is no more than enough to offset the additional costs of the factory's more remote location, it can be argued that there will be no change in the amount of glass exported and thus no distortion outside the borders of the country. In such a case, it can be further argued that the international system should not be concerned about this "regional aid" subsidy.

Although the current international and national rules do not approach the "subsidy" issue this way, it would seem that it would be wise to develop the notion that there should be a prerequisite to bring actions within the concept of "actionable subsidy," namely, that there be "distortion across the border." Of course, administering this concept may not be easy. That process could require a fairly detailed and sophisticated economic analysis of each case. In addition, it would have to be recognized that in the interdependent world of today, there is no clean case in which there is zero distortion across the border; instead, some sort of concept of a minimal threshold of distortion across the border would have to be developed, as an outer limit for the definition of "actionable subsidy." With respect to countervailing duties, at least, to some extent the application of the material injury test could measure this "distortion across the border." It must be recognized, however, that this "distortion" prerequisite would not necessarily be a sufficient criterion for the test.

The problem with relying on the injury test is two-fold. First, as I noted in chapter 10, certain methods of employing the injury test venture considerably beyond the distortion caused by the foreign subsidy. Second, the injury test tends to be applied in a later stage of a CVD investigation, thus requiring the foreign exporter to undergo considerable procedural costs. If a "distortion across the border" test could be applied as part of the process of defining an "actionable subsidy" (or at least a "preliminary injury" determination that recognized the need to show a casual relation between the injury and the subsidy), then a certain number of cases could be easily disposed of.

11.4 Perspectives and Reflections on the Subsidies Subject

From the previous sections, it may be seen that the whole area of subsidies activity in international law, including the rules designed to constrain the use of subsidies and the other rules designed to allow national governments the unilateral privilege of responding to subsidies with countervailing duties, is not only extremely complex but holds the potential, if misapplied, of undermining the basic policy goals of the post–World War II liberal trade system. On the one hand, governments can use subsidies to evade a liberal trade system, by subsidizing so as to inhibit imports, or subsidizing so as to enhance exports. On the other hand, responses to subsidies, particularly the unilateral national government response of countervailing duties, can be implemented in such a way as to undermine liberal trade policies. The countervailing duty becomes, in a sense, a substitute for the older normal tariff. Indeed, the processes of determining the appropriate application of countervailing duties can become so convoluted and expensive themselves that they play into the hands of domestic producing interests in an importing country.[56]

Many of these troublesome aspects are being worked out in a series of specific issue contexts that have become incorporated into U.S. statutory law, and, to some extent, into the Uruguay Round text. These include attention to some of the specific characteristics of "natural resource subsidy," or "upstream subsidies," and so on. The lack of consensus that still remains concerning the appropriate definition of subsidy for both countervailing duty purposes and for substantive international obligations on subsidization is still a potentially troublesome feature of international trade policy. The Uruguay Round negotiators were appropriately motivated to include subsidies as a major item on their agenda, and have achieved considerable success in ameliorating some of the problems. Many problems remain, however. Perhaps a brief inventory of some of these problems or potential improvements would be useful. They include:

1. National governments should recognize the principle of "generalizability" of what they do in the context of their countervailing duty laws. When a government, such as the United States, begins to apply countervailing duties to a particular subsidy practice, it must recognize that this will aid and comfort other governments who wish to emulate that approach. But in addition, countries which have substantially greater economic power in the world should recognize that they owe the world trading system an additional obligation of responsibility not to use that power merely because they can get away with it.

2. A prerequisite needs to be developed for an international response to a subsidy, that such subsidy have some kind of "cross-border effect" that is not merely insubstantial.

3. Further elaboration and definition of the two categories of "prohibited (red)" subsidies, and "nonactionable (green)" subsidies, need to be achieved. These categories are relatively more precise for guidance to business enterprises and entrepreneurs in the world than the "actionable" category.

4. Like various parts of the subsidies agreement, however, the specific exceptions mentioned for inclusion in the "green box," namely, nonactionable treatment for certain assistance for research activities, for certain assistance to disadvantaged regions, and for assistance to promote adaptation of existing facilities to new environmental requirements with certain restraints, need to be better defined. There has been considerable attention given to the ambiguity of these clauses and the danger that that poses for abuse in the future.

5. The injury test, and particularly the "material injury" test for countervailing duties, is an important mediating principle to help balance the clash of policy goals, especially those in the context of so-called domestic subsidies. This test must be preserved and its implementation probably needs more attention, given that some of its defining clauses are extraordinarily broad. The "cumulation test" and the possible decline of "margins analysis" described toward the end of chapter 10 could give cause for concern in the future of unduly weakening the discipline provided by the injury test.

6. The provision of a more explicit and slightly higher de minimis cutoff for the percentage of subsidization required for countervailing duties, is

welcome. Further study, however, might reveal that this de minimis should be even higher than that set in the agreement.

7. Constant efforts must be made to reduce the procedural costs of applying a countervailing duty system. There is already much commentary on the fact that these costs are too high, and the threat of countervailing duty procedures therefore can unnecessarily inhibit trade. To some extent these costs are necessary in order to provide a more liberal trading system than that which would otherwise be available. However, when the costs become very high compared to the value of imports of certain commodities, then domestic competing interests are tempted to bring processes simply to impose those costs on foreign imports, and to inhibit such imports. In addition there is an effect on foreign exporters that will lead them to hesitate in attempting to penetrate a market when they feel there is great vulnerability to process costs.

8. In general, countervailing duty procedures ought not to be based on practices that have occurred far in the past (as has been sometimes suggested). To open up the possibility of countervailing duty suits against subsidies that have ceased ten or fifteen or more years ago, simply because there is a "continuing effect," is very dangerous indeed, because it would expose a great deal of international trade to the costs of such processes. A corollary to this, however, would seem to be that the rules ought to be able to look better into the future. Thus, the "threat of material injury" may become more significant. In addition it may be that certain kinds of countervailing duty-type procedures should be allowed even before imports actually occur.

By way of conclusion, it can of course be asked again whether there is any rational justification for the countervailing duty rules of the GATT system, or even of the substantive obligations regarding subsidies in the GATT system. I asked those questions at the beginning of this chapter, and I noted that we would not be able to resolve those issues or answer those questions in any satisfactory way. I think the reader can now readily see why that is so. Consequently, a reasonable prediction based on empirical observation of the world and the many conflicting interested parties in it suggests that both the international subsidy system and the national government countervailing duty systems will continue for many years, and probably will see a greater number of national governments using countervailing duty actions. Thus, even though it may not be the optimal approach for an international system regarding subsidies, it seems wise to continue the process of elaborating the rules of this system, particularly in the context of international agreements developed either in WTO negotiations. Thus at least two provisions of the subsidies agreement seem particularly appropriate in this context. Article 31 provides for a review of certain core provisions (Article 6, paragraph 1 and Articles 8 and 9) at the end of five years, and Article 24 not only provides for the usual "Committee on Subsidies and Countervailing Measures" composed of member representatives, but also establishes a five-person "Permanent Group of Experts" that may be consulted by any member on the nature of any proposed subsidy, and may even render a confidential "advisory opinion" about such proposals. The subject probably merits other efforts of elaboration and definition also.

12 The Uruguay Round "New Subjects": Extending the Scope and Competence of the World Trading System

12.1 Introduction

One of the major goals and subsequent achievements of the Uruguay Round was to embrace within the GATT rule system a series of new (or almost new) subjects. Four subjects in particular were high priority, three of which could be termed "new," while the fourth had been relatively intractable for the GATT system although it technically was subject to the GATT rules. These four subjects are trade in services, trade-related intellectual property measures (TRIPS), trade-related investment meaures (TRIMS), and trade in agricultural goods. There were many other objectives of the Uruguay Round relating to trade rules of the GATT and subject to major negotiation in the previous Rounds. These included such subjects as textiles, antidumping and dispute settlement, etc. But the four subjects of this chapter were particularly designed to bring the trade rule system to bear on subjects that heretofore had largely escaped those rules.

As might be expected, there was a great deal of opposition in the early 1980s from many countries of the world to the idea of incorporating at least some of these subjects into the GATT. At the September 1986 launching of the ministerial meeting at Punta del Este, Uruguay, there was heavy negotiating attention and controversy, particularly about the incorporation of services and intellectual property into the GATT system. By 1986, however, several years of intricate diplomacy had resulted in persuading most of the countries of the world, including some of the staunch opponents in the developing world, to accept the proposition that the Uruguay Round negotiation would include attention to these subjects. The question of whether the result of such negotiations would be embraced in a GATT-type structure, or in some other fora or institutions, was left open at that time.[1]

In this chapter I take up each of these four subjects, although not in great detail. The objective here will be to present the overall outline of the agreements which resulted. In many cases, further negotiations will be required to flesh out some of the detail of these negotiation results. In some other cases, the detail is extraordinarily intricate and complex, and beyond the scope and context of this book.

At the end of the negotiation, it was partly the fact that considerable success had been achieved in developing treaty text agreements on these new subjects that led the negotiators to realize that some new institutional structure would be needed. It was not very feasible to simply extend the uneasy GATT institutions (the "nonorganization") to services, or intellectual property, for example. Thus, the development of a WTO charter as an umbrella for all of the texts of the Uruguay Round was, in some views, virtually inevitable.

12.2 Trade in Services in the Uruguay Round

Although the Uruguay Round text concerning trade in services did not entirely live up to some of the aspirations expressed at the outset of the negotiation, nevertheless the text is a considerable positive achievement for the negotiators. For more than a decade, various policy groups and interested enterprises had foreseen the need for some kind of international rule discipline for trade in services. The service "sector" is extraordinarily complex, consisting of perhaps one hundred fifty specific service sectors,[2] but in the aggregate, services were beginning to represent a larger portion of gross domestic product of many of the western industrialized countries, than was the production of goods.[3] Some service providers were exploring the possibility of exporting their activity, and they had begun to encounter foreign government actions designed to restrict their activity and to preserve businesses for domestic service providers in those importing countries. Thus, various groups began to urge an international cooperative mechanism that would develop rules against such protectionist activity before those activities became entrenched and multiplied.

However, there were a number of conceptual difficulties for a negotiation on the trade in services. First and perhaps most fundamental, was the question whether the normal economic principles of "comparative advantage" would apply to services trade, as well as to trade in goods. Some economists and other writers argued that it would,[4] and although the evidence does not seem to this writer overwhelmingly clear, a judgment to go ahead with international rules seemed appropriate. In addition, apart from the more intricate economic arguments of comparative advantage, there was the observable phenomena that increasing competition among service providers tended to increase the efficiency and lower the cost of the services provided, just as could be observed for trade in goods.

Another difficult conceptual question about the negotiation on services is whether the well-established and well-known principles regarding trade in goods, could be applied by analogy to trade and services. These principles included the most-favored-nation principle, the national treatment principle, and concepts of market access such as "scheduled concessions" reciprocally negotiated. National treatment in particular was problematical because certain kinds of services seemed to call for special principles to handle some particular policy risks that are posed by imports, compared to domestic service providers. This was the case for financial services and the need to protect consumers with various prudential governmental regulations. Thus, it was argued, that to apply a national treatment concept to services required considerable expertise about particular service sectors, and this could result in changes needed to the basic concepts of national treatment so as to effectively balance the need for trade liberalization against appropriate national government regulatory and prudential policies related to the particular service sectors—banking, insurance, brokerage, and so on.[5]

In addition, there was a question whether services as a whole, or only specific subparts of that total landscape, should be addressed in the Uruguay Round. And there were questions about how to structure the negotiation so as to maximize the opportunity for trade liberalization rules on services.

The Uruguay Round succeeded in developing the General Agreement on Trade in Services—GATS as a sort of a framework agreement for the entire landscape of services trade. The Agreement went relatively far in embracing the traditional GATT concepts (MFN, national treatment, schedules of concessions), but clearly had to adapt those concepts for the new terrain encountered. Furthermore, this services agreement leaves a great deal open, in some cases calling for specific ongoing negotiations, in other cases simply leaving it to the future to see what negotiators will be able to do. Again, by an analogy to goods, one can argue that there should be at least fifty years of ongoing negotiations about service concessions, and some of these negotiations will probably never end. After all, in the goods area the GATT existed almost fifty years with eight major rounds of negotiations, with later rounds pushing the frontiers of the GATT regulatory concepts beyond what was probably understood at the time in 1947 when the GATT was originally negotiated.

The major substantive part of the GATS is divided into three parts. The first of these lists a series of fifteen "general obligations and disciplines," including MFN, the requirement of transparency and publication of regulations, and a number of traditional GATT-type exceptions such as safeguards, unfair trade (namely, subsidies), general exceptions (health, etc.), and national security. In addition, these clauses go a bit beyond the original GATT, and briefly address the problem of competition and business restrictions, and government procurement. The MFN clause is worded differently from that of GATT (and the full implications of that are not yet known). In addition, there is provision for members to table certain exceptions or exemptions to MFN but only at the time when the agreement enters into force for a member.

The second portion of the substantive obligations is entitled "specific commitments" and establishes the framework for a schedule of commitments from each member. The obligations require each member to accord to services and service suppliers of any other members treatment "no less favorable than that provided for under the terms, limitations and conditions agreed and specified in its schedule." This is a bottom-up approach, so that the GATS applies only to the tabled or bound sectors established in the schedules. (This can be contrasted to the NAFTA, which has a top-down approach whereby all service sectors are covered unless an exception is tabled.)[6]

The specific commitments in the schedules are listed by modes of supply outlined in Article I of GATS and summarized by one author[7] as:

- cross border
- commercial presence
- movement of consumer
- movement of personnel

The treatment for scheduled service concessions is also covered by text that limits six "prohibited" actions (unless exceptions are listed in a Schedule), defined as:

- limits on the number of service providers
- limits on the total value of service transactions or assets imported
- limits on the number of service operations or quantity of service imports

• limits on the number of natural persons that may be employed in a particular service sector

• measures that restrict or require specific types of legal entity or joint venture for supplying the service

• limits on the participation of foreign capital in shareholding or investment.

In addition, a more general national treatment clause is included, requiring members to give treatment to service imports from other members "no less favorable than that it accords to its own like services and service suppliers."

Third, there are several articles on "progressive liberalization," dealing with approaches to negotiating the various specific commitments to be included in schedules. Again, the commitments are considerably more complex than the analogous tariff commitments under GATT. Article XX of the GATS requires that

> with respect to sectors where such commitments are undertaken, each schedule shall specify:
>
> (a) terms, limitations and conditions on market access;
>
> (b) conditions and qualifications on national treatment;
>
> (c) undertakings relating to additional commitments;
>
> (d) where appropriate the time-frame for implementation of such commitments; and
>
> (e) the date of entry into force of such commitments.

Thus, obviously the important effects of the GATS Agreement are contained in the scheduled concessions, and there are several thousand pages of those concessions as part of the overall Uruguay Round Agreement. To really ascertain what the GATS Agreement means for a particular business, it is necessary to examine with some care these commitment schedules. As this is written (mid-1997) the availability of the information about these schedules is not always optimal, thus posing some problems to entrepreneurs and enterprises who would like to take advantage of the services commitments of foreign countries.

Several further remarks can be made about the GATS Agreement. For one thing, to some extent this agreement is also an agreement on "investment." The subject of "investment" is not technically within the current WTO, although there are proposals to bring that subject to the WTO.[8] However, when one examines the actual text of the GATS, it is easy to see a number of clauses which in fact relate to investment, to the extent that sometimes persons have suggested that the agreement is actually an "investors' agreement." This is particularly true for investment which is related to service providers, such as investment to establish branches, offices, or personnel, in the country of delivery.

It has already been remarked that there are provisions in this agreement concerning competition policy, which make it somewhat different from the traditional GATT rules which (after the failure of the ITO Charter) do not apply competition policy rules.

Finally, there is the question of how future negotiations on services will move forward. In the Uruguay Round, there were a few service sectors that gained considerable attention, including financial services, basic telecommunications, maritime transport, and audiovisual services. Various tough negotiations occurred, and in some cases resulted in uneasy compromise, or even impasse (such as in financial services). How the WTO members will proceed in the future to develop additional agreements in additional service sectors is not yet clear. How they will be able to incorporate the results of such future negotiations into the WTO treaty text is also unclear.

12.3 Intellectual Property Rights

One of the surprisingly strong achievements of the Uruguay Round was the development of a very important and impressive agreement on intellectual property rights (IPR). Technically the agreement is entitled "Agreement on Trade-Related Aspects of Intellectual Property Rights," sometimes called "TRIPS." The reason for relating it particularly to trade was to make it more plausible that the agreement be negotiated and placed in the context of the GATT trading system (and now the WTO).

When ideas for developing an important and quite broad scope treaty on intellectual property were first suggested in the late 1970s and early 1980s, there was a great deal of opposition. In particular, developing countries felt that they had a lot to lose and very little to gain from such an endeavor, because to extend intellectual property rights as obligations upon developing countries, would, presumably, mean that developing countries would be paying for many of the technological advancements that they then had been receiving without payment, with very little in return, because they did not feel they had the capacity to develop new intellectual property.[9]

The proponents of intellectual property obligations were primarily from the industrialized countries, and they formed a very strong and sophisticated coalition that developed policy advocacy, both at the national government levels (sometimes coordinated by groups from different nations meeting together), and at the international level (namely, the Uruguay Round). Various IP groups argued that their societies were losing billions of dollars through the "stealing" of intellectual property in many countries, including activities of counterfeiting,[10] and reproduction of works such as music recordings, as well as software for computers. These attitudes played an important role in the early years of the Uruguay Round, and were part of the overall negotiating strategy of countries such as the United States, which felt that it was important to develop certain quid pro quo agreements that would meaningfully give some advantages to developing countries (such as revising the textile agreement, providing more assurances and discipline for safeguards, developing restraints on agriculture subsidies, etc.). While some of these latter measures developed in an arguably somewhat meager way, nevertheless, by the time of the Dunkel text in December 1991, there seemed to be an enormous change in attitudes, including attitudes of developing countries, which led many such countries to be willing ultimately to accept the IP Agreement as part of the very broad package of the Uruguay Round.

Intellectual property embraces a number of subjects, including copyright, patents, special extensions of those two property concepts to living organisms, software, and additional subjects such as trademarks and industrial designs. The proponents of IPR in the Uruguay Round were quite eager to have the GATT system embrace IPR in competition with, or to some extent, in preference to, the WIPO—World Intellectual Property Organization. There were a number of reasons for this, partly because the WIPO did not have a good record of assuring effective implementation of treaty obligations (it supervises dozens of intellectual property treaties, including the very important Paris Convention for the Protection of Industrial Property, and the Berne Convention for the Protection of Literary and Artistic Works (focused on copyright)). Perhaps one of the most significant reasons why the IPR interests wished to move their subject into the GATT context, was the admiration of the GATT dispute settlement mechanism which had been evolving to a point where it appeared to be a reasonably effective procedural mechanism for establishing relative enforceability of international treaty norms.

The agreement that resulted in the Uruguay Round is reputed to have exceeded the aspirations of many of the intellectual property rights groups, although certain portions of the agreement, particularly the long transitional and phase-in clauses, were rather strongly criticized toward the end. One of the developments that was perhaps not entirely foreseen at the outset of the UR negotiation, was that as time went on, the controversy was less and less between developing countries and industrial countries, and more and more between the industrial societies, such as the tensions between the United States and Europe and other industrial countries, concerning some particulars of patent or copyright protection. This was an interesting example of some of the broader problems of international regulatory cooperation in economic matters. "Harmonization," or promoting congruence between regulatory systems and laws that diverge, poses significant problems with respect to certain habits, cultural and vested interests in various societies, and those came into play rather strongly towards the end of the IPR negotiation.

The resulting agreement in the Uruguay Round, is however, strong and perhaps the one that most nearly represents fulfillment of the original agenda aspirations of Punta del Este of September 1986. The agreement builds upon the important existing intellectual property treaties, including the Paris and Berne Conventions (with some adaptation),[11] and overall provides a series of minimum standards of intellectual property protection which all members of the WTO must conform.

The TRIPS agreement opens with a series of general obligations, including reference to the Paris and Berne Conventions and an indication that members must meet the obligations of those conventions, or at least portions of those conventions. In addition, there are the ubiquitous clauses of national treatment and MFN. These clauses are adapted, partly to make them consistent with similar obligations in previous IP treaties. Then the Uruguay Round agreement proceeds with a series of specific intellectual property subjects, with basic minimum standard requirements for each of those subjects. Thus, there are a series of articles on copyright, another group on trademarks, some clauses on geographical indications (e.g., wines and spirits), industrial designs, patents, layout designs, integrated circuits, other types of undisclosed information, particularly with respect to governmental regulatory processes that require and use secret business information, and some attention to anticompetitive practices in licensing.

The IPR text then provides a series of obligations relating to "enforcement of intellectual property rights." These require governments to "ensure that enforcement procedures as specified in this part are available under their law, so as to permit effective action against any active infringement...." There are even some clauses that mandate certain elements of civil judicial procedures (written notice, representation by counsel, procedures that are not overly burdensome, etc.) And if these types of obligations are not fulfilled, then there is recourse by nations or members of the WTO against other members for enforcement procedures under the normal WTO dispute settlement processes.

One example of the "harmonization" effect of the agreement is the development of a minimum patent protection period of twenty years (somewhat longer than the United States previously had), although the measurement of that period extends from the filing of an application, rather than the granting of the patent period. In the copyright area, considerable controversy was manifested among the negotiators about such things as "moral rights," or "neighboring rights," and in the end members were largely left alone to choose their approach.[12]

12.4 Agriculture

Commentators and observers about the GATT system have sometimes stated that agriculture was exempt from GATT. This statement is not correct, but it reflects the unfortunate reality that agriculture has been the most difficult part of international trade to bring under international treaty rule discipline of the GATT. For a variety of domestic, political, and international market circumstances, many nations in the world, particularly the industrialized countries, have been largely unwilling to allow the GATT rules to constrain their policies designed to assist and protect their agriculture population. Quite often this is related to the political makeup of the society concerned, where agriculture had, in some circumstances, an undue weighted influence on the electoral system. It is also partly because of the extraordinary adjustment that has occurred during the twentieth century with increased efficiencies of agricultural production so that the number of persons needed in agriculture work dropped dramatically.

For the United States this has been particularly worrisome, because it believes that it has a strong comparative advantage in the production of many agricultural goods, and that its agriculture producers were thwarted by other country limitations on imports of agricultural goods, often in direct defiance of GATT rules. Thus, in the Kennedy Round in the 1960s, the United States and other countries such as Canada and Australia made an effort to bring agriculture "into the GATT." That largely failed, and once again in the Tokyo Round (1970s) agriculture was made a high priority issue by the United States and other countries, particularly with an attempt to restrain a number of practices of the European Community that were having considerable damage to world agricultural trade. This too failed. Thus, when it came to the Uruguay Round, U.S. officials were joined by a number of other agricultural producing countries of the world (many of them combined in the so-called Cairns group, which included countries such as Canada, Australia, New Zealand, Brazil, Argentina, etc.). These mounted an almost do or die effort to make sure that the Uruguay Round would finally succeed in bringing agriculture under the trading rule system. In fact, it did succeed in making an important beginning in this respect. Some of the initial objectives of negotiating partners, such as to completely phase out export subsidies and other subsidies on agricultural goods within a decade, largely failed, even though such objectives had been the cause of several negotiating impasses and stalemates. Indeed, agriculture was the central negotiating issue for the Uruguay Round, and to a large extent, the Uruguay Round proceeded at a pace only to the extent it was permitted by the U.S. and the EC negotiators who were locked in a very intense political struggle over the issues of agriculture.

Thus it is not surprising that the results of the agriculture negotiation of the Uruguay Round are not one of the more solid "achievements" of the Round, at least when measured by the initial aspirations. Nevertheless, the Agreement on Agriculture does have considerable promise for the future. At this point, it seems that this agreement will in fact be a beginning of rule application and liberal trade principles pursuant to GATT policies, even for the agricultural sector.

The U.S. relationship to all this has some ambivalent and troubling aspects. Early in the history of GATT, in the early 1950s, the U.S. Congress mandated a series of measures restricting imports of certain types of agricultural goods, although it was quite clear that the U.S. statutory provisions were inconsistent with U.S. GATT obligations. In the 1955 session of the GATT Contracting Parties, the United States obtained a "waiver" for these agricultural measures, arguing that the failure to provide a waiver would lead the U.S. Congress to be even more hostile to the GATT. The contracting parties were confronted with a de facto situation that led them to feel it was necessary to give the United States what it desired. The waiver had no time limit, and broadly gave the United States a legal cover for the statutory measures on agricultural imports. Some people have argued that this was a major event or circumstance that led other governments to refuse to comply with their GATT obligations regarding agriculture, possibly under the notion that if the United States would not do so, even though it had legal cover, reciprocally other nations should not be required to comply. For several decades thereafter, the waiver was one of the problems in achieving a better integration of agricultural trade discipline into the GATT. Clearly in the Uruguay Round, the waiver was "on the table," and the U.S. was prepared to negotiate its relinquishment. The legal situation at the end of the Uruguay Round appears to confirm that the U.S. waiver is no longer retained, although the new agricultural agreement[13] may in some cases permit "special safeguard" measures that would allow measures previously covered by the waiver (or similarly by other provisions for other countries), but essentially the perception seems to be that the U.S. agricultural waiver is "no more." Under the WTO Charter provisions concerning waivers, it appears that waivers can no longer be perpetual.[14]

The agreement is very complex and does many things. The following are considered its major characteristics. The agreement addresses the agricultural problem in basically four subject categories. The first of these is the obligation in the agreement to phaseout nontariff barriers (including quotas, many of which violated Article II of GATT), and "convert" the effect of such measures to tariffs. This is called "tariffication," and is a central feature of the agreement. In addition to tariffication, countries negotiated to place concessions in their schedules providing minimum access for certain products, tariff reductions for certain products, and tariff bindings for all agricultural goods. Some have argued that the results of tariffication and the other commitments will result in rather a meager increase in agricultural trade. For example, some nontariff barriers for certain products were "tarrified" to yield a tariff of 800 or even 1,000 percent! It is not likely that much trade will flow with those kinds of border protections. Nevertheless, a scheme is now embedded in the agreements that permits policy focus on the world welfare costs of agricultural barriers, and hopefully an opportunity for negotiations to result in further reduction of those barriers. A slight back-step or political "insurance" is contained in a "special agricultural safeguard" clause that allows certain temporary restraints on imports particular difficulties due to agricultural imports occur.

The second major subject area of the agreement is a series of commitments on domestic supports (particularly domestic subsidies). There is a "green box" list of measures that are exempt from these commitments, including domestic food aid, decoupled income support, social safety net programs and income insurance, and so on. The general commitment for measures not included in the green box, however, is the reduction over time of the domestic subsidies under scheduled commitments, taking into account all trade distorting support programs. The basic concept for measuring these support problems is the "aggregate measurement of support" (AMS). This is a very intricate process of calculating a number which should more or less represent the total amounts of domestic support, and then providing some requirements for lowering the amount of the AMS over time.

The third general category of attention by the agricultural agreement is a focus on export subsidies. Although some negotiators wanted to see a scheduled and phased elimination of all export subsidies, that did not prove possible. Nevertheless, there are a series of basic obligations that should result in lowering the amount of export subsidies over a period of time.

Fourth, the agreement includes a so-called peace clause, which establishes an obligation for governments to refrain for the first nine years of the agreement from taking domestic countervailing duty proceedings, or initiating WTO dispute-settlement proceedings, in connection with certain types of practices and products.

Finally, the agricultural agreement is coupled with a second agreement called "Agreement on the Application of Sanitary and Phytosanitary Measures," which addresses the various product standards and other health or safety limitations with respect to health risks from plant or animal-born pests or diseases, or additives, toxins or disease-causing organisms in foods, beverages, or feed stuff. This agreement is parallel to the basic standards agreement or Technical Barriers to Trade Agreement (TBT), but it takes precedence over TBT for the products covered by the phytosanitary agreement.

It should also be noted that the general subsidies agreement also must defer to the agriculture agreement with respect to handling of subsidies on agricultural products.

12.5 Agreement on Trade-Related Investment Measures

Finally, in this chapter, we deal with another relatively short agreement, which has been conceptually included among the "new issues" for the Uruguay Round. This addresses the subject of investment measures that relate to trade.[15] Although it could be a very broad subject, and indeed there are more recent proposals and discussions about developing much broader reaching treaty obligations for investments (perhaps analogous to the clauses contained in the NAFTA, or in many bilateral investment treaties), the Uruguay Round did not attempt this broader agenda. Instead, it confined its attention to just a few specific measures that had proven somewhat troublesome in past trade policy disputes and discourse. Basically, the agreement reaffirms the national treatment obligation, and the prohibition on quantitative restrictions, as related to particular types of investment measures. For example, the agreement includes an Annex with an "illustrative list" of "TRIMS that are inconsistent with the obligation of national treatment," and included on that list are clauses prohibiting:

- a requirement of purchase of domestic goods as a prerequisite to obtain an advantage under administrative rulings
- limitations on purchases or use of imported products for use in producing goods under an investment
- certain restrictions on access to foreign exchange
- requirements about exportation or sale for export by an enterprise of its products.

The four-page agreement includes obligations on "transparency," and several other practices such as notification.

13 Economies with Special Circumstances

13.1 Economies That Do Not Well Fit the Rules of the World Trading System

In this chapter, I take up several types of national economies that for one reason or another do not well fit the post-World War II Bretton Woods world trading system and the market-oriented rules of GATT. First, we will focus on the problems of developing countries, that is, countries that have low living standards and usually low wages. This subject has been extensively treated elsewhere, however, and generally involves the expertise of economists rather than lawyers, so here I will be relatively brief. The GATT system "legal rules" concerning developing countries are remarkably vague and "aspirational" in approach, although under the Uruguay Round texts, at least the more advanced developing countries will be increasingly subject to the general discipline of the trade rules. Later in this chapter we will also deal with the perplexing problems of state trading and nonmarket economies (and those now called "economies in transition").

Throughout the forty years of GATT history, there has been much discussion and considerable perplexity about the position of developing countries in world trade. The economics literature is extensive[1] and a number of different problems can be posed or debated. Here I will address a few of those problems.

The first is the question whether the world trading rules are fair to developing countries. At various times it has been alleged that these rules operate in such a way as to disadvantage the nonindustrial countries. Indeed, some of the controversy during the GATT drafting process and at the Havana Conference in 1948 turned on this question. After the Havana Conference, a number of developing countries, particularly Latin American countries, were sufficiently dismayed by the rules that had evolved that they opted to stay out of the GATT system for years and even decades. (Mexico, for example, only recently joined the GATT.)[2] In 1958 the GATT commissioned a special study by a group of eminent experts, headed by Gotfried Haberler, to comment on the application of the world trading rules regarding trade of developing countries.[3] The GATT itself had only two provisions that explicitly allowed differential treatment for developing countries—namely, Article XVIII, and the Articles in part IV of GATT. For the most part, the GATT rules do not otherwise distinguish between trade of developing and developed countries.

A number of the 1979 Tokyo Round Codes had special provisions for developing countries, some of which have provoked troublesome policy responses.[4] In addition, one "Understanding" resulting from the Tokyo Round explicitly contemplated industrial-country actions favoring developing countries, while noting the possibility of improving the capacity of those countries to "participate more fully in the framework of rights and obligations under the General Agreement."[5] In addition, there were some special arrangements between certain groups of countries (sometimes permitted by a GATT waiver or justified as a free trade area under GATT Article XXIV), which were designed to benefit developing countries. The most prominent of these were the EC's Lomé agreements with over sixty African, Caribbean, and Pacific (ACP) nations.[6] The U.S. "Caribbean Basin Initiative" can also be mentioned as an example.[7]

The question of whether the rules operate fairly for developing countries, however, is a complex one involving several layers of analysis.[8] The first level of analysis asks which rules of GATT explicitly discriminate against the trade of developing countries. The answer to this question is generally none. The GATT rules tend not to explicitly distinguish between trade of developing and developed countries, except to give benefits to developing countries.

A slightly deeper layer of analysis would look at whether the nominally nondiscriminatory rules of GATT and the trading system in fact have a discriminatory effect, given the facts and circumstances of the real world. Attention could be given to the way the rules apply to different kinds of trade; as I have noted, some of the GATT rules distinguish between primary and nonprimary goods,[9] and insofar as this distinction might adversely affect developing countries, some case could be made that a problem exists.

An even deeper analysis might look at the institutional structure of the trade-rule system, to ascertain if some countries are put at a disadvantage in that system. Here it could be argued that because the GATT did not have a very effective enforcement mechanism,[10] large and powerful economic countries could "get away with more" than could the weaker countries. Given that the developing countries tend to be the weakest economically, they might argue that they are at some disadvantage in this process.

Against all this, however, would have to be balanced the observation that many developing countries were able to take advantage of either explicit or implicit exceptions in GATT so as to be able to pursue almost at will any form of trade policy they wish. For example, the balance-of-payments rules of Article XII and XVIII of GATT gave a claim to legitimacy for many measures implemented by developing countries, including quantitative restrictions, despite the nominal prohibitions in GATT against such measures,[11] (and these texts continue to have some role, as we discussed in chapter 9).

Another approach would be to analyze certain patterns that lead to what is called the "effective tariff rate" problem, whereby developing countries can sometimes demonstrate that industrial importing countries' tariff structures impose little tariff on raw materials, but increasingly higher tariffs as one goes up the scale of processing. One result of this, it has been alleged, is to discourage developing countries from developing downstream value added industries, and therefore to inhibit their economic development.[12]

Of course, any appraisal of the effects of the world trading rules on developing countries must also recognize certain advantages of these rules. For example, flawed as the rules are, the MFN clause does extend many privileges to developing countries (without reciprocal obligations) which might not be available otherwise.[13] A trade "deal" between two large economic entities will often, through MFN, give benefits to economically smaller entities. In addition, the dispute settlement procedures, although also flawed, occasionally gave some added leverage to the trade diplomacy of weaker nations[14] compared to what they would have when acting unilaterally or bilaterally. This was one of the motivations for them to enter the GATT or participate in specific Tokyo Round Codes.[15]

The Uruguay Round strengthened dispute settlement procedures should be even more interesting for the diplomacy of developing countries, as the early cases suggest. (More than a third of the complaints have been brought by developing countries or jointly with developing countries.)[16]

A second issue of considerable importance in the GATT-Bretton Woods world trading system is whether there are valid reasons to give special privileges to developing countries. There are two different questions raised by this broad general one, namely: what is the moral basis for favorable discrimination toward developing countries? Is favorable discrimination actually helpful, or does it merely perpetuate undesirable policies in the developing countries?[17]

These questions lead to a third general policy issue, which has been highly debated in recent years, namely, whether the more advanced developing countries should now be required to accept more fully the general nondiscriminatory discipline of the GATT and trade rules. This is the so-called graduation issue.[18] Recently, for example, the United States has been vigorous in pushing the idea of graduation, partly at the behest of Congress. One manifestation of this has been a U.S. disposition to revoke the benefits of its GSP (Generalized System of Preferences) program for certain key developing countries.[19] The Uruguay Round, with its single package idea, amounts to an important thrust in this direction of graduation, since governments will no longer be able to pick and choose among a series of codes, but must all adhere to more than 95 percent of the obligations. Developing countries will generally have longer phase-in periods, however.

Finally, the whole question of debt must be noticed. Developing-country debt is an obvious and extraordinarily difficult problem, and of course it relates to trade and the trade rules. Insofar as the rules tend to inhibit the ability of developing countries to export in such a way as to obtain the necessary foreign exchange to service their debt, those rules can be deemed faulty.[20]

To works that are more focused on the economic considerations of world trade, I will leave the task of sorting out these and many other questions. The legal structure of the generalized system of preferences, however, merits a bit more exploration here.

13.2 The Generalized System of Preferences

International Law

At the first United Nations Conference on Trade and Development (UNCTAD I) in 1964, the secretary general of that United Nations organization shepherded through the adoption of a report designed to focus international attention on the need for special rules for the trade of developing countries. In particular, the report promoted the idea of lower tariff rates for imports into industrial countries from developing countries. This idea of preferences clearly was inconsistent with the GATT MFN principle.[21] Thus it was necessary to develop a new legal exception to MFN for the benefit of developing countries.

This exception was developed in a variety of international institutions.[22] It was recognized, however, that the final legal authority for a GSP program would have to be taken in GATT, in the form of a GATT waiver to the MFN clause. This waiver was granted in 1971 for a ten-year period.[23] The waiver authorized each industrial country to establish its own GSP program, providing that each of those programs benefited all "developing countries." However, it was left to each industrial country to define what was a "developing country" for purposes of benefiting from the GSP program. Thus, although the GATT waiver established the GSP framework, a great deal of individual discretion was left to each of the sovereign industrial nations implementing it. There was no international law requirement to grant GSP, and no particularly detailed requirements as to what should be the shape and framework of GSP. As actually put into effect, each country's GSP program has its own features. Furthermore, different countries implemented their programs at different times, the United States being the last major nation to implement GSP.[24] (The U.S. program is described below.) Some countries granted lower tariffs or zero tariffs, but hedged them with quota limits.

The degree to which these programs provided actual benefits to developing countries is somewhat controversial. Various estimates come up with various results.[25] Nevertheless, the programs have been highly popular among developing countries, which view them as an important part of the evolving world trading system.

Given that the GATT waiver was limited to a ten-year period, it technically expired in 1981. As part of Tokyo Round negotiations, however, the CONTRACTING PARTIES developed and adopted a declaration entitled "Differential and More Favorable Treatment, Reciprocity and Fuller Participation of Developing Countries."[26] In this declaration, adopted as a "decision" of the CONTRACTING PARTIES but not explicitly labeled a "waiver", it was stated that "CONTRACTING PARTIES may accord differential and more favorable treatment to developing countries, without according such treatment to other Contracting Parties ...," notwithstanding the provisions of the GATT MFN clause. This declaration or decision has been called the "enabling clause" and is seen by some essentially to perpetuate the authority for GSP. This decision, however, does speak of the possible improvement of the ability of developing countries to make "contributions or negotiated concessions" under the provisions of GATT.

This oblique language, in the minds of some, constitutes a potential "graduation requirement."[27]

The situation in the WTO after the Uruguay Round continues with even more ambiguity. The Uruguay Round text provides that most of the legal instruments under GATT 1947 still in force when the WTO came into existence would be carried over as part of GATT 1994. Thus it appears that these measures continue to apply, although the special provisions for developing countries distributed in many Uruguay Round texts may largely supersede the 1979 Tokyo Round Declaration.

GSP and U.S. Law

Originally, the United States was generally opposed to any concept of special or general preferences of developing countries, and it was not until 1967 that the president announced a shift in U.S. policy toward being more favorably inclined to a GSP program.[28] Although the GATT waiver of 1971 authorized GSP programs, the United States was the last to implement it, and it did so in Title V of the 1974 Trade Act.

Under the 1974 act, the Congress provided authority to the President that was very broad and gave him much discretion, both to determine the countries which would benefit from the program and in many cases to determine when the benefits could be withdrawn. The Congress also had a number of ideas for attaching strings to these benefits, including, for example, prohibiting GSP benefits to countries who expropriated property without compensation or nullified existing contracts with U.S. citizens, or to communist countries unless they received MFN treatment from the United States and were members of GATT and the IMF.[29]

Countries who are members of OPEC or are engaged in activities to "withhold supplies of vital commodity resources" so as to increase prices are also excluded from the U.S. GSP program.[30] The Congress also exempted certain "import sensitive articles" from the application of its GSP program.[31]

Essentially the U.S. GSP provided a zero tariff on all articles except those excepted, for the countries who were designated as beneficiary countries. The U.S. law had something called a "competitive need formula," however.[32] Under this provision, when a particular GSP beneficiary country was shipping a quantity of an eligible article to the U.S. market in an amount that exceeded a certain threshold either in dollars ($25 million, adjusted for inflation) or in a percentage of total imports of such article (e.g., 50 percent), then GSP treatment for that product would be withdrawn for that country. The basic idea was that when such a threshold was reached, the GSP beneficiary country no longer could claim that its industry was "infant" and needed such special privileges. Another idea was that by removing the GSP privileges from the more advanced industries of the third world, the lesser-developing countries would be able to better take advantage of the program.[33]

Overall, under the U.S. program one hundred forty countries have at one time or another been eligible under the GSP program, and at its peak the system covered upwards of $19 billion worth of imports.[34] This figure, however, only represented around 3 percent to 4 percent of imports.[35]

The U.S. statute was limited to ten years and so needed renewing in 1984.[36] The Congress enacted the renewal in the 1984 Tariff and Trade Act, but a number of modifications were made: in particular, a policy of graduation was specified. Under these provisions and subsequent evolution of the system, the United States has taken significant steps to graduate both countries and products from its GSP program.[37]

The graduation policy and annual reviews provide domestic producers and other lobbies opportunity to petition for the withdrawal of GSP status. For example, in December 1987, the president withdrew the GSP status from Chile because Chile had not taken steps to afford workers internationally accepted rights.[38]

In August 1996 the U.S. GSP legislation was renewed through May 1997.[39]

13.3 State Trading and the GATT System

The post–World War II international trading system is obviously based on rules and principles that more or less assume free market-oriented economies. The rules of GATT certainly were constructed with that in mind.[40] Yet important parts of the world do not have economies based on these principles, and even in market economies there are many institutions that do not operate under free-market principles, such as state trading agencies or monopolies, government-owned industries, and the like. These circumstances pose some difficult conceptual problems for the GATT trading system. Can that system continue to exist and improve if it embraces economies and institutions that do not follow the assumed economic structure of free markets? Should that system remain primarily one that consists of economies which are relatively "market oriented?" Should major nonmarket or transition economies, such as China or Russia, be incorporated into this system? If so, on what terms? Likewise, can this system accommodate, without increasing tension and rancor, a situation in which current participants have major portions of their economies essentially outside the normal GATT rule discipline because these portions are government owned or operated? I will explore these questions below.[41]

First, I will examine how the GATT rules fail to accommodate the state trading or nonmarket situation. A hypothetical case will illustrate the problem. Suppose that the government of Xonia maintains a state trading monopoly for the importation of bicycles. No bicycles can be imported except through this state trading enterprise. Suppose further that this government has accepted a binding in GATT for tariffs of 5 percent on bicycles. In addition, it will be remembered that GATT prohibits the use of quantitative limitations on the importation of bicycles (or any other goods). Thus, exporting nations might think they have an opportunity to sell bicycles to Xonia.

Instead, however, as a matter of proprietary direction, Xonia may inform the bicycle trading enterprise that during the next year, it shall purchase for import no more than one million bicycles. With such an order, Xonia evades the impact of Article XI of GATT, prohibiting the use of quantitative restrictions. In addition, suppose that Xonia directs the state trading enterprise that, when they are resold on the domestic market the markup on all imported bicycles must be larger than a normal market markup. Likewise, part of the effect of this order is to evade the tariff binding, given that the markup can partly operate like a tariff. Article II, paragraph 4 of GATT, does provide that when a government maintains a monopoly on importation of a product which has been bound, the operation of this monopoly should not "afford protection on the average in excess of the amount of protection provided for . . ." under the binding. Nevertheless, this has been a difficult measure to police.[42] In addition, many products may be unbound.

GATT Article XVII addresses the problem of state trading enterprises, but its provisions are not very rigorous. Arguably, the activity mentioned in the hypothetical case above is completely consistent with GATT, even though it undermines two of the fundamental obligations of GATT: the tariff binding and the rule against quantitative restrictions. Article XVII requires state trading enterprises to "act in a manner consistent with general principles of non-discriminatory treatment prescribed in this Agreement . . ." This obligation has been deemed by some interpretations of GATT to apply only as a sort of MFN measure. Such an approach argues that no "national treatment" Article III-type obligation exists with respect to how state trading enterprises operate. There is an alternative view, which was mentioned in a GATT panel report.[43] Nevertheless, the general thrust of Article XVII of GATT is weak as it relates to the possibility of governments using state trading measures to evade the other obligations of GATT. Needless to say, if an entire economy is based primarily on state trading principles such that we would call it a "nonmarket economy," then most of the economic activity of this economy evades the effective responsibilities and policies of GATT, even though this economy can be in complete conformity with the technical rules of GATT.

Thus, there are several important problems facing GATT. Perhaps the most serious problem is how to manage the acceptance into the GATT system of economies with major nonmarket sectors. I will take that up in the next section. In addition, however, there has been considerable criticism of the GATT as it applies to current WTO members, because it allows many members to evade the GATT discipline through the use of government-owned industries and state trading monopolies. Some proposals for legislative revision of United States law would attempt to impose greater disciplines on state trading of other countries in connection with the GATT obligations, and the whole state trading question is one of those which was addressed during the Uruguay Round of GATT trade negotiations.[44] However, the Uruguay Round "Understanding on the Interpretation of Article XVII of GATT 1994" basically only provides for notification, review of policies, and the opportunity of other members to raise questions and disputes. Whether it will be possible politically to tighten the discipline of GATT concerning state trading is questionable. It is very difficult to amend the text of GATT,[45] and how one would design a separate code on state trading and induce countries to accept this such discipline (without any apparent advantage or quid pro quo) is not clear.

In recent years there has been a fair amount of comment about the problem of countertrade.[46] Countertrade describes a situation in which governments or enterprises barter and exchange products rather than simply pay a price for goods. Some forms of countertrade can be accomplished through state trading enterprises or other government monopolies or regulations. In some cases these are set up under bilateral treaty frameworks. Of course, countertrade can also be carried on purely by private enterprises in a free-market context, in which case the GATT may not have rules that apply. Countertrade mandated by governments, however, may be inconsistent with certain GATT obligations,[47] such as MFN, or obligations prohibiting the use of quotas, or with national treatment.

13.4 Nonmarket Economies and Economies in Transition in China and Russia

For various historical and other reasons, the GATT has always had a few nonmarket economies as contracting parties. These are now WTO members. In some cases, these were nations that were contracting parties to GATT before they shifted to a nonmarket economy structure (such as Czechoslovakia or Cuba). In other cases, the GATT explicitly accepted into membership certain nonmarket economies under special provisions or protocols (such as Poland, Hungary, Romania, and Yugoslavia).[48] Sometimes it is said that because of these precedents, GATT and WTO should have no problem accepting new nonmarket economies. Commentators are quick to note, however, that the contracting parties who were nonmarket economies in GATT were relatively small in terms of their impact on trade. Furthermore, relations between the GATT and its nonmarket contracting parties were always troublesome.[49] Arguably, the trading relationship does not work well, but the other members of GATT were willing to tolerate the situation because they either had special arrangements of their own with the countries concerned, or the amounts of trade are small. Neither of these circumstances would apply in the case of a country like China or Russia, both of which are very large and therefore very significant in terms of potential trade impacts in the GATT/WTO context.[50]

Some countries mentioned argue that they have a substantial portion of their economies which operate under market- and price-oriented systems, and some argue that the trend is more in that direction, so that they should not be branded with the label "nonmarket." Commentators point out, furthermore, that even in so-called market-oriented economies, such as those in Europe or in certain developing countries (e.g., India and Brazil), a very large proportion of the economic resources of such nations may be owned and controlled by government operation, either through state trading enterprises or directly through government-owned industrial complexes.[51] Nevertheless, some of the countries mentioned are those which are deemed to be "more nonmarket" than the other members of GATT. In some cases trade relations between these countries, and between certain contracting parties of GATT, are handled under bilateral regimes—some of which include quota measures (which may not be technically consistent with GATT obligations). This seems to be the case for the European Community, for example.[52]

In some cases, special "safeguard measures" have been designed to try to address the conceptual difficulties of a GATT relationship with nonmarket economies. In the United States, for example (as I will show in the next section), this approach has been taken. In particular, such special safeguard measures tend to be "selective," that is, targeted just at the particular nonmarket economy and thus not consistent with the general notions of Article XIX of GATT and its MFN requirement.[53]

China poses some particularly interesting questions, both legal and economic, for the GATT. China was one of the original twenty-three contracting parties of the GATT when it came into force under the Protocol of Provisional Application at the beginning of 1948, and so the current government in Beijing argues that China continues to be a contracting party and merely needs to resume its position. The legal situation, however, was somewhat more cloudy.[54] During the early years of GATT, China was in the midst of a civil war. In 1950 the GATT headquarters received a cable from a Chinese government then located on the island of Taiwan, which purported to withdraw China from GATT membership. Since that time, there was no China that acted as a Contracting Party in GATT, although a government located on Taiwan took an observer position in GATT from 1965 to 1971. The current government of Beijing argued, however, that the 1950 cable to GATT was null and void, because it did not originate from the government which was then in control of "China." It also argued, by analogy with credentials actions taken in other international organizations such as the United Nations and the International Monetary Fund, that the mainland Chinese government of today should be the beneficiary of the various memberships of China in international organizations.[55]

The form of Chinese accession or renewal to GATT was not resolved, but the GATT contracting parties agreed that the mainland Chinese government would negotiate for membership in GATT as if the new accession procedures of Article XXXIII of GATT would apply. In fact, a pure "resumption approach" would probably not have been satisfactory to either the GATT contracting parties or the Chinese government, since a 1948 tariff schedule is totally out of date, grandfather rights would have been handled differently and less favorably, and there was a question of the Article XXXV opt out provision and whether China could exercise some opt out rights. The Chinese were quite interested in obtaining GATT membership before the WTO came into effect, so they would be an "original member" of the WTO, but that did not occur. As of mid-1997, negotiations continue for Chinese accession as a new member under

Article XII WTO. Some of these prior issues are no longer significant or even relevant (for example, there are no longer grandfather rights).

The assimilation of China into the WTO and GATT is a formidable task. Not only has China been a nonmarket-oriented economy (although it has argued that it is now evolving more toward price and market orientation), but China claims the status of a developing country with its special privileges in WTO and GATT. Many producers, both in the industrialized western countries and in other major developing countries, are eyeing potential Chinese competition with considerable apprehension. The method by which China could be drawn into a satisfactory WTO and GATT relationship is not easy to foresee. In all probability, it will involve a number of different measures embodied in a protocol of WTO accession. Many of these measures may not be entirely consistent with the traditional habits of GATT policymakers, and may involve departures from some of the generally accepted norms of GATT which apply primarily to market- and price-oriented economies. For example, some western WTO members argue there should be special safeguard rules for Chinese products. In addition, certain special rules regarding the so-called unfair trade practices may be necessary. With respect to China's importing regime, other GATT members will undoubtedly want some assurances from China beyond its mere acceptance of GATT and of a tariff schedule. Already suggested have been such measures as requiring China to: accept an obligation to unify its national customs rules and institutions; accept some of the pluralateral Annex 4 agreements such as the Government Procurement Agreement; publish its import regulations and take other "transparency measures." Because the accession is now to a WTO that includes agreements on services and intellectual property (as mandatory agreements), obviously the Chinese will be required to accept those obligations. Intellectual property has been a particular troublesome subject between some western industrial countries and the Chinese.

The China negotiation for WTO membership is of course important not only because China is important, but also because the rules for accommodation that are worked out in the China context will set an important precedent for future similar activities of the GATT, including the possible accession of Russia and other former Soviet Union states, and revisions of Article XVII relating to state trading.

Before its breakup, the Soviet Union manifested considerable interest in membership in the GATT. The contracting parties of GATT, however, seemed quite cool to the idea. After the events of 1989 and the so-called end of the Cold War, as well as the breaking apart of the Soviet Union into its constituent nations, attitudes and circumstances changed. Russia began to pursue more actively its interest in membership in the GATT and now the WTO. Likewise a number of the other former Soviet states are pursuing similar objectives. Many of these countries are now "observers" to GATT, which is often the first step toward membership.

It seems quite clear that neither China nor Russia should be kept out of the WTO for very long. This would not be in the interest of world economic relations, because both nations are having an increasingly profound effect on world trade. Similar attitudes would apply towards the other former Soviet Union countries. However, some of the considerations described earlier in this chapter pose important difficulties for membership of Russia and its former Soviet partners. Even though they may claim to be market economies, or at least nearly market economies, a great deal of skepticism about this remains.

This raises some other important policy considerations for the new WTO, namely, should it be preserved as a more purely "market-oriented" institution or, given the lack of alternative universal trade institutions, should the WTO reach out to embrace economic systems that are not particularly market oriented? If the latter course is chosen, the question then becomes how to create an appropriate "interface" for the different economic systems of the world to belong to the general organizational structure of the WTO.

Although some are tempted to use WTO membership as a bait to try to force different national economic systems to change, it can be argued that the WTO also has a responsibility to change and to figure out an appropriate way to accommodate the different economic systems. This might involve buffering mechanisms, such as some of those just suggested in the case of China. Once again, buffering mechanisms might involve a number of measures which are not very "pure" in the eyes of market-oriented economic policies. It is also important that these mechanisms adequately protect the market-oriented economies from abuse by the fact that nonmarket economies and state trading agencies can too easily evade the disciplines of the GATT rules and policies. All of this is a tall order, but certainly not an impossible one to fill.

One possible way to develop an "interface mechanism" for nonmarket economies in WTO, while at the same time accommodating the possibility that portions of such economies might move toward a market orientation, would be to establish a "two-track" safeguard system. A protocol of accession/resumption could first provide for transparency (publication of regulations and administration of customs), procedural fairness, and a working party or other committee established under the protocol to meet annually to review problems of the relationship (with the review clearly able to look in both directions—that is, not only to compliance with obligations by the nonmarket economy, but also to compliance of other WTO members in their trade relations with the nonmarket economy). All of the other obligations of WTO would be assumed.

A second track could then be designed for certain exceptional cases involving the difficult interface between nonmarket economies or state trading institutions and the WTO/GATT. This might include certain special safeguards measures, certain particular consultation and negotiating requirements to alleviate injury caused by the differences, and so forth.

Clearly, such measures may not be entirely consistent with liberal trade economic arguments. But they might furnish a fairly pragmatic way for the WTO and GATT to accommodate the state trading countries in a manner that would minimize the suspicions and tensions that could otherwise occur. Furthermore, the two-track system has the advantage of accommodating evolution in the economic system of the state trading country. At that point in time when such a country becomes truly a "market system," obviously the second track will not be invocable. In between, if certain sectors of the state trading country achieve sufficient "market orientation," they could be eligible for the full regular GATT treatment instead of the second track.

13.5 The United States and Nonmarket/Transition Economies

The United States has a special and sometimes unfortunate legal regime for its trading relationship with communist countries. This legal regime poses certain problems in connection with the accommodation of nonmarket economies into the WTO system. It stems principally from a congressional impetus in the early 1950s, as a reaction to the Cold War. In 1951 the U.S. Congress enacted a law which prohibited the United States from granting MFN status to countries controlled or dominated by world communism.[56] With respect to the contracting parties then part of GATT, only Czechoslovakia was really affected, but the result of the U.S. enactment was to require the U.S. government to cease to apply the GATT, at least as a de facto matter, to Czechoslovakia. When Czechoslovakia complained to the GATT about this, the GATT approach was to adopt a resolution that merely recognized this state of affairs between the United States and Czechoslovakia.[57] By 1960 political relations between the

United States and some Eastern bloc nations were such that the United States was willing to allow Poland entry into the GATT, and willing to establish trading relationships with Yugoslavia.[58]

In 1972 the United States negotiated a bilateral trade agreement with the Soviet Union, with the understanding that the Congress would have to approve key actions to be taken under that agreement. When the executive branch began to draft a potential trade bill during the early 1970s,[59] part of the bill authorized the president to enter into bilateral trade agreements, including the extension of MFN treatment, with communist countries under certain conditions. At this point, however, an important movement in the Congress, generated by U.S. citizens interested in promoting the opportunity for emigration (particularly of Jewish persons) from the Soviet Union led to the Jackson-Vanik amendment. Under these statutory proposals, which were included in the trade bill versions voted on by the House and later the Senate, a communist country would be entitled to receive MFN treatment from the United States only if it permitted free emigration, with the possibility of being granted a waiver if the president determined that certain progress toward the goal of free emigration was being achieved. This waiver was subject to various checks and actions by the Congress.[60] After prolonged negotiations between the executive and legislative branches of the U.S. government, measures to this effect were finally included in Title IV of the Trade Act of 1974.[61] One result of this series of events was the rejection by the Soviet Union of the trade agreement because it was not prepared to conform to the U.S. Congress measures included in the act.[62]

Thus, the United States is constrained in terms of how it can enter into trade relations with communist countries. This constraint prevents the United States from fully accepting new members of WTO when such members are communist countries. Indeed, because of the legislation, the United States is required to exercise its opt-out of a WTO relationship with a member which is communist. The United States may then enter into a bilateral trade agreement with such a country—which trade agreement will incorporate WTO treatment but also the essential clauses mandated by U.S. legislation, including the review of the trade relationship which must occur annually before the Congress. Needless to say, this is not an entirely satisfactory state of affairs for the countries concerned.[63]

Another feature of Title IV of the Trade Act of 1974 is Section 406, regarding "market disruption," which is a special escape-clause channel that applies only to communist countries. To a certain extent, Section 406 is partly based on a recognition of the difficulty of applying normal unfair trade laws, such as antidumping and countervailing duties, to the case of nonmarket economies.[64]

The potential membership of China in WTO raises some of these same issues for the U.S. administration, which would like to support such a role. In all likelihood the United States is required under current U.S. statutes to opt out of a WTO relationship between it and China and establish such a relationship by means of a bilateral agreement subject to the provisions of the statute. Perhaps, however, when the negotiations have proceeded further, it may be possible for the U.S. executive branch to obtain some sort of explicit change in the statute from Congress that would permit a more regular GATT relationship with China.

The Omnibus Trade and Competitiveness Act of 1988 contains a rather intriguing provision relating to this subject.[65] Section 1106 of that act, entitled "Accession of State Trading Regimes to the General Agreement of Tariffs and Trade," provides that before any major country with significant state trading enterprises can enter the GATT, the U.S. president must determine whether trade between the United States and that country is significant and unduly burdens the United States. If so, the act provides that the GATT rules will apply between the United States and that country only if the state trading enterprises are conducted on a commercial basis, or (and this is perhaps the most interesting feature) if the extension of GATT rules is approved by Congress under "fast-track" procedures. This implies the possibility that, in a relatively comprehensive settlement agreement between a potential nonmarket entrant into the WTO and U.S. interests, the Congress might be willing to alter or soften some of the existing measures of United States law that make it difficult for the United States to enter into a full relationship with nonmarket economies. Clearly, a potential Russian membership in the WTO raises these issues also.

13.6 Unfair Trade Practice Laws and Nonmarket/Transition Economies: Antidumping and Countervailing Duties

The rules regarding antidumping duties and those regarding countervailing duties are difficult (some say impossible) to apply in the case of nonmarket economies. With respect to responses to subsidized goods and the determination of subsidies in nonmarket economies, the matter is so difficult that the U.S. administrating authority, ultimately backed by the Court of Appeals, finally determined that the U.S. countervailing duty law did not apply to products from nonmarket economies. This was based partly on the failure of the U.S. countervailing duty statute to mention any special regime for applying countervailing duties to nonmarket economies (in contrast to the antidumping laws, which did so mention).[66]

Take first the problem of dumping. Dumping requires a comparison of the price for export with the home-market price to see if the former is lower than the later so that there is a "margin of dumping."[67] However, what is the "price" in the home market of a nonmarket economy? Almost by definition, given that such an economy is not based on pricing principles, the nominal price of goods may bear little relation to prices that would be set by enterprises in a market/price-oriented economy. The prices may be set by a state planning commission, and may vary according to end user. Furthermore, the prices may bear little relation to the costs of an enterprise, or "profitability."

Thus in U.S. application of its antidumping law, the practice has developed of seeking to compile a "constructed cost" method of establishing the home-market price, while using information from market economies. In particular, as established in the landmark Polish golf-cart case,[68] and embellished by later cases,[69] the U.S. procedure can be explained like this. In a case involving alleged dumping from a nonmarket economy, the U.S. authorities would examine the product in the nonmarket economy, and determine all the various input components (parts, labor, overheads, etc.). Then the U.S. authorities would seek a "surrogate country," which would be a market-oriented country at approximately the same level of economic development as the allegedly dumping nonmarket economy. The U.S. authorities would take the list of inputs, a sort of "shopping list," to the surrogate country, and price each of those inputs on the market of the surrogate country. With this information it would then compile an overall constructed cost, and by adding the (later abandoned) statutorily mandated amounts for administration and profit (the latter being 8 percent), the U.S. authorities would find the home-market price, which would be compared to the export price, to establish whether dumping had occurred.

Needless to say, this process is very cumbersome. First, a great deal can depend on which country is chosen as a surrogate. Second, any country selected to be a surrogate has very little incentive to cooperate or to allow U.S. investigators to enter its territory and investigate prices there. Neither the surrogate country nor any of its enterprises are, after all, parties to the procedure. (It is even alleged that in one case a surrogate country later found it was the object of a dumping investigation in the United States, which investigation may partly have relied on the information ascertained during the surrogate procedure!)[70] Also, it is argued that a fair amount of manipulation of the data can occur, giving a wide latitude to administrative discretion so that its decisions can become biased, depending on the antidumping procedure. In any event, many feel that the process is not satisfactory.

With respect to countervailing duties and responses to subsidized goods, the matter has been somewhat different. There has never been (so it is claimed) an application of countervailing duties in U.S. law to products imported from a nonmarket economy. Until the fall of 1983, no such case had been brought.[71] Then, the U.S. textile industry brought a case alleging that textile imports from China were subsidized and therefore should be subject to countervailing duties. Partly for reasons relating to the general evolving political relationship of the United States and China, the U.S. administration was very concerned about this case. Furthermore, the Chinese had formally intimated their distaste for the process and indicated the possibility of counter responses of China (such as a reduction in the purchase of grains from U.S. farmers) if the United States actually applied countervailing duties. The matter was further complicated because of the U.S. law that requires insulation of the administrators of antidumping and countervailing duty laws from the diplomatic and other political arms of U.S. government. In the end, a settlement was obtained and the case was withdrawn, but not before considerable comment and concern.[72] In a sequence of later cases, the U.S. administration[73] took the position that U.S. countervailing duty laws do not apply to nonmarket economies, and the U.S. courts upheld[74] the administration on this position. Attempts by some in the Congress to legislate on this subject failed.[75]

The rational for nonapplication of countervailing duty law to nonmarket economies bears some similarity to arguments in dumping cases. It was argued by the Commerce Department that the concept of subsidization has no real meaning in an economy that is not market- or price-oriented in the first place. In some sense, one could argue that everything is subsidized in such an economy. In any event, there was no benchmark against which to compare the activities of economic entities, government or otherwise, in order to ascertain what was the level of subsidization.[76] Because the U.S. statute and legislative history was silent on the question of whether it applied to nonmarket economies,[77] the administrators found it possible simply to rule that the law did not apply.

The U.S. Uruguay Round Implementing Act of 1994 did not explicitly change the U.S. jurisprudence described above, but Article 29 of the Subsidies Agreement concerns "Transformation into a Market Economy," and provides for a grace period of nonapplication for some subsidy rules, after which it seems the normal subsidy rules will apply.[78] Since the grace period does not apply to countervailing duties, and since the U.S. Uruguay Round Implementing Act of 1994 is silent on the question of CV and nonmarket or transition economies, it is not now clear how the United States will administer its CV law in relation to "transforming economies." Thus it appears the U.S. courts will determine this issue for U.S. law sometime in the future.

The conceptual problems of these and similar international trade policies as they relate to nonmarket economies are clearly not resolved. Various proposals have been made as to how to handle these questions. Many of these proposals can be lumped under the rubric "benchmark approaches."[79] The basic concept of the benchmark proposals is that the imports from a nonmarket economy will be compared to some sort of benchmark price, and whenever the imports are priced below the benchmark, they will be presumed to have been dumped or subsidized and a duty equal to the difference between the price and the benchmark will be applied. In some proposals the presumption is conclusive; in others it can be rebutted. In any event, the critical question is how to set the benchmark. It was on this question that the House Ways and Means Committee of the U.S. Congress floundered in trying to make a concrete legislative proposal in 1984.[80]

One proposed benchmark is simply the average price in the U.S. market of U.S.-produced goods. Obviously this tends to be more restrictive of imports. Another benchmark proposal is to look towards the price of imports from market economies. Still another is to look at the home-market prices of like products in market economies. An approach that seeks some intermediate level of restrictiveness for trade is to set the benchmark equal to the lowest average price of a substantial quantity of imports of like products from a market economy. All of these approaches, of course, to a certain extent undermine the concepts of comparative advantage, and make it harder for a nonmarket economy to compete on the world market, at least in price. On the other hand, the purpose of these approaches is to assure competing producers in importing market economies that they do not have to face competition which is deemed "unfair" under long-established traditional international trade policies. There is no easy solution, and some sort of benchmark approach may be the "least worst" solution to the problem, if the benchmark is chosen with great care.

14 Conclusions and Perspectives

14.1 The "Trade Constitution"

What we have explored in the preceding chapters can be characterized overall as the "constitution" for international trade relations in the world today. It is a very complex mix of economic and governmental policies, political constraints, and above all an intricate set of constraints imposed by a variety of "rules" or legal norms in a particular institutional setting.

This constitution imposes different levels of constraint on the policy options available to public or private leaders. Some of its rules are virtually immutable. Others can be changed more easily. Part of the complexity of the whole system is this variety of constraints, which limit the realistically available options for solving problems. In addition, there are different contexts or levels for these constraining rules. Some of these constraints come from national or sovereign state governmental systems (e.g., the Constitution of the United States, or statutes of a WTO member country). Other rules come from the international system and its treaty mosaic, centering for our purposes on the WTO System, but also influenced by other elements of the Bretton Woods System and indeed the entire structure of international law (weak as it may be).

Some of these "constitutional" constraints are sources of great annoyance to both decision makers and economists. The rules, they say, too often "get in the way." Indeed, with respect to the "trade constitution," they are probably right. As I will explain, there is considerable reason to be discontented with that constitution as it exists today, and to worry about its weaknesses and defects in the context of the type of interdependent world with which we are faced.

Some of the constraints, however, are the result of important and necessary principles, resulting from competing policy goals of the total system (not just that for international trade). For example, there is no doubt that the U.S. constitutional separation-of-powers principles are the source of great annoyance for decision makers, who must cope with the constant tensions of the executive-Congress power struggles. Yet the great genius of the draftsmen of this Constitution was their understanding of the need to disperse power so as to avoid its abuse. Thus, in a broader context, the separation-of-powers principle can be seen to have greater importance than the needs for short-term solutions to disagreeable international economic and trade problems.

Likewise, a rule-oriented structure of the portion of the skeleton devoted to international treaties for trade is often a source of annoyance and aggravation. Yet that rule structure itself, as outlined in chapter 4, has potential value for creating greater predictability, redressing unfair power imbalances, and preventing escalating international tensions. In some instances it is more important that international disputes be settled quietly and peacefully than that they conform to all correct economic policy goals, although the long-term impact of a "settlement" on the rule structure must also be considered.

Like almost all government activity, the international trading system and its constitution contain conflicting and competing policy goals. Thus, like most government institutions, methods for resolving or "compromising" these competing goals are crucial to the potential long-range success of the system. For example, the worthy objectives of liberal trade (based on economic principles such as comparative advantage) will often conflict (at least in the short run) with goals of protecting poorer or weaker parts of a society's citizenry. Thus, as we saw in the chapter on safeguards, the "pureness" of liberal trade policies is relaxed somewhat to accommodate some competing goals of helping the poorer to adjust. (Of course, the constitutional structure of the system sometimes perversely also assists the more privileged of the world's producers to perpetrate that privilege at the expense of others—merely illustrating one of the many imperfections in the system.) The "conservative social welfare function" so ably described by Max Corden[1] realistically explains the approach of many national governments in today's world. Even if Corden and his admirers (including me) do not always feel that this function is wisely administered, it can be defended in some circumstances as an appropriate governmental goal that also competes with purer versions of liberal trade policy.

With these observations we can now see some approaches to solutions for the puzzles posed in chapter 1. How vulnerable is a small country to blocking by other nations of the small country's exports? As we have seen, at the moment nearly the only recourse or inhibition on such action by importing nations is the WTO system. Defective as it is, it nevertheless plays a crucial role in constraining some of the more rampant national governmental actions that would otherwise restrict trade and defeat important expectations of small (and large) exporting countries.

Likewise, one puzzle was that faced by the investor who needed some long-term dependability of export markets for his new plant to be a viable investment. Again, in such cases the WTO system is crucial (albeit not necessarily too comforting). Without this system, the degree of predictability would be even considerably less.

Why do governments choose fourth-best economic policy options? It should now be clearer. The intricate interplay of the international rules and the national constitutions and norms gives us the necessary clues. National executives prefer to avoid going to Congress or parliaments to obtain the necessary authority for certain approaches, and this may rule out some options. The international rules provide in some circumstances the onus of "compensation" or rebalancing of negotiated benefits, which impose constraints. Thus governments may pursue informal measures or other approaches that are less advantageous in economic terms to avoid some of the national or international rule-imposed costs of particular actions. The use of export-restraint arrangements particularly comes to mind.

14.2 How the System Works

We can now summarize, or at least characterize, how the world's "trade constitution" works, such as it is. As the previous section noted, this system is a complex interplay of both national and international norms, institutions, and policies. It cannot be understood if only the international part is studied, nor can it be understood if only the sovereign national states are studied. The linkages are extremely significant: the GATT is what it is at least partly because of the U.S. constitutional structure, and more recently, the structure of the European Community. U.S. law is what it is at least partly because of the GATT. To explore how to achieve certain policy options, one must know not only the WTO procedures for rule formulation or treaty change, but also the similar procedures in at least some of the key EC/nation-state WTO members.

Within major WTO trading nations, a cardinal principle of the administrating (executive) authorities is often to avoid seeking legislation from the legislature. Thus the constitutional allocation of powers, embellished by existing legislation, often produces significant constraints on policy selection.

A core part of the system is the vast body of GATT tariff bindings, made significant and relatively enforceable because of the GATT, and now the WTO institutional makeup. An additional part of the system (perhaps less effective) is the codes of conduct established by the many other WTO texts.

Important additions to the system come from national government laws and institutions, most particularly those relating to unfair trade practices. In many cases national procedures provide for initiation of complaints by private entrepreneurs, and various nations have rules that differ in the extent to which government officials are mandated to carry out certain actions, or have discretion to choose among various possibilities. We have seen that, at least for dumping and subsidy countermeasures, the U.S. Congress has strongly pushed U.S. law in the direction of mandatory import restraints, and this is posing certain threats to the liberal trade policies of the system. Part of the congressional impetus for this approach is the distrust by the Congress of executive-branch handling of trade policy in the past, but some of the impetus stems from the natural proclivity of members of Congress to please particular constituents.

All in all, however, the system does work; or perhaps it would be better to say that the GATT system operated better than anyone had a reason to expect, given the uncertain beginnings and the various gaps in this trade constitution, which all hope have now been corrected with the WTO, so that the WTO system should work even better.

14.3 Weaknesses of the Trade Constitution: Are They Now Corrected?

The first edition of this book, and other writings by this author, have flagged a number of institutional and legal problems of the GATT, with its various "birth defects." With the Uruguay Round Agreement establishing a new institution—the World Trade Organization—one can happily report that most of the institutional and legal problems of the GATT have indeed been corrected or at least improved. Yet no institution is perfect, nor for that matter complete and final. The WTO has a number of institutional problems. It will have to adapt and evolve to meet the rapidly changing circumstances of international economic relations. A key question in that context is whether the new charter for the WTO will allow the organization to efficiently adapt.

Every treaty (like every statute and constitution) will require attention to various interpretive difficulties, due to unforeseen ambiguities or compromises in the drafting process. In previous chapters, a number of these difficulties have been noted. This is not really a criticism of the institution; the more important question is whether the institution has the capability of resolving these interpretive difficulties, and the new dispute settlement procedures of the WTO, as well as its institutional measures, provide considerable promise that it can meet this challenge.

Rather than focus on problems that would face virtually any human institution, I think it more useful to outline a few particular characteristics of the new organization that may pose important problems.

- Amending the GATT was almost impossible, and so trading nations turned to other measures such as "side-codes" (1979). Indeed, in order to bring the results of the Uruguay Round efficiently into effect, the GATT was essentially abandoned and terminated, and a whole new institutional and treaty structure created. The new treaty structure and the WTO Charter rules also are designed to make amending very difficult. This could prove to be a problem almost as serious as it was in the GATT, and could lead to a number of ad hoc or other "end-run" type measures. Of course, the difficulty of amending is designed to protect national sovereigns in an imperfect voting structure, which the WTO shares with many international organizations.
- One of the particular problems that resulted from the long and somewhat agonizing period of negotiation for the Uruguay Round, is that the relationship of the various parts of the overall Uruguay Round Agreement to each other are often not clear. This is particularly acute with respect to a number of the texts in Annex 1A. Their relationship to GATT 1994 is sometimes quite ambiguous, as has been pointed out. Whether, for example, some of the GATT standard exceptions (general exceptions of Article XX, or national security exception of Article XXI) apply to some of these other texts, is not clear.
- In order for the WTO to evolve, it may be necessary to develop texts for new subjects (such as environmental protection, competition policy, investment, etc.), which would not necessarily be acceptable to all of the members of the very large membership of the WTO. Thus an approach now embraced in Annex 4 with the "plurilateral" optional agreements, may be an important institutional focus for change and adaptation (sometimes experimental). Yet, unfortunately, additions to Annex 4 under the WTO Charter language must be by full consensus, which could result

in stale-mate. There may indeed be ways around this, such as the development of a "practice" by which new proposed agreements for Annex 4 which fulfill certain characteristics (MFN, open to all WTO members, etc.), would be "normally" accepted and to which governments would refrain from objecting. It is too soon to tell whether such an approach will be necessary or feasible.

• With a membership of 129 at the end of 1996, and still growing, it is very hard to manage the WTO, and this raises the question of whether some small steering group of countries could be designed to provide a more centralized management which would still be responsible to the total membership. This has proven impossible to institute in the past, and there are still no indications that it will be easier now with the WTO. But certainly something will have to be developed, or the likelihood will be increased of small ad hoc groups of very powerful members, settling a number of issues affecting the WTO between them without as broad a representation as a more formal steering group could provide.

• The GATT did not have the ability to house amicably under its single roof vastly different economic systems, including those called "non-market," or "economies in transition." The WTO and the Uruguay Round results do not really change this. How this new institution can respond to the challenges of nations like China or Russia is yet to be seen. Clearly more thought is needed.

• There has been a strong "regionalist" movement in the last decade, and to some extent these regional economic organizations challenge the multilateral WTO. How regional organizations will relate to the WTO, and hopefully be in a symbiotic relationship that compliments each other, is also as yet unknown.

However, it is not only the international institutions that can be criticized. The laws and procedures of national governments leave much to be desired. For example, in the United States there is much ambiguity and potential for troublesome delay in situations when a WTO dispute-settlement panel and procedure rules that the U.S. is obligated to change its law because of WTO treaty obligations. The Congress or the administration does not always efficiently implement such international rulings, a fact which tends to induce other countries also to resist such rulings and to generally reduce the respect for and predictability of the rules of the trading system.

In the United States there is some concern about the inefficiency of the U.S. national laws and procedures relating to "unfair trade practices," particularly those involving dumping or subsidies. This concern includes worry that the procedures are cumbersome, slow, and very costly, in some cases becoming themselves barriers to liberal trade among nations.

In addition, there is general concern about the functioning of the U.S. Congress. Its vulnerability to narrow local constituency interests and to certain powerful lobbies, especially in the absence of strong presidential leadership, is a worry expressed by many about the U.S. Constitution. The performance of the Congress in trying to shape a trade bill during 1985, 1986, 1987, 1988 and 1994 must be seen as evidence of the weakness of some of the congressional processes, confirming those worries.

Concerns may also be expressed about the trade laws of other governments. The European Community is in the process of an agonizing constitutional evolution which sometimes renders its relations to the WTO system less than satisfactory from the point of view of other nations.

Likewise, the influence of approaching national elections (and when is there none?) on international trade policy and negotiations often raises worries.

More could obviously be said, but we need to turn to some key policy questions.

14.4 Some Fundamental Policy Questions

Clearly the implications of the preceding section are that considerable attention to the basic constitutional structure of the GATT/WTO system is warranted. Another particularly fundamental question, not often discussed, is the issue of what techniques are appropriate to "manage interdependence." Several alternative approaches can be suggested:[2]

- Harmonization, a system which gradually induces nations toward uniform approaches to a variety of economic regulations and structures. An example would be standardization of certain product specifications. Another example would be uniformity of procedures for applying countervailing duties or escape clause measures.

- Reciprocity, a system of continuous "trades" or "swaps" of measures to liberalize (or restrict) trade. GATT tariff negotiations follow this approach.

- Interface, which recognizes that different economic systems will always exist in the world and tries to create the institutional means to ameliorate international tensions caused by those differences, perhaps through buffering or escape-clause mechanisms.

Obviously a mixture of all these techniques is most likely to be acceptable, but that still leaves open the question of what is the appropriate mixture. For example, how much should the "trade constitution" pressure nations to conform to some uniform "harmonized" approaches, or is it better to simply establish buffering mechanisms that allow nations to preserve diversity but try to avoid situations in which one nation imposes burdens (economic or political) on other nations?

Closely connected to this previous point is an issue which may be loosely characterized as that similar to federalism. This is the issue about the appropriate allocation of decision-making authority at different levels of government. Each federal nation faces this issue—that is, what is the appropriate allocation of power between the national government and subordinate state or municipal governments? The international system broadly and the international trade system particularly, also face this question. As interdependence drives nations to more concerted action, there also arises the question of whether a gradual drift of decision-making authority upward to international institutions is always best for the world. How much power do we want to delegate to such international institutions? In what instances do we wish to preserve local or subordinate government control on the ground that such government is closer to the affected constituents? To what degree does a "harmonization" approach to managing interdependence unduly interfere with these federalist principles of maintaining decision making closer to affected individuals and firms?

One very perplexing issue is that of the appropriate linkage of international economic policies and measures to "noneconomic" policies such as human rights, or to geopolitical considerations. Many enterprises and their leaders (at least in the United States) have been arguing against any such linkage. They argue that measures such as trade boycotts, or removing MFN privileges, often tend to be self-defeating and only allow competing nations and firms to move in with trade to fill the gap. Yet national leaders of powerful states cannot easily eschew the use of economic measures, particularly since the use of more "active" or military approaches have become less and less feasible. Economic measures are often the sole usable instruments of diplomacy. No one denies that if a nuclear war can be avoided by the use of an economic trade measure, such is appropriate. However that type of causal connection is never presented. But if the "trade constitution" were to provide for a more effective channel of concerted economic actions to encourage better human rights treatments in some states, or to discourage risky national military moves or terrorism, to what degree should such economic actions be allowed or encouraged?

Clearly there are some causal connections between economic measures and other policy goals, even though in many instances it appears that the economic measures do not work very well.[3] Enlarging the EC to include Greece, Spain, and Portugal had a large component of noneconomic policy in it. Other examples can be readily cited. It has been argued that economic interchange and discourse can play an important role in promoting understanding among nations and their citizens, and that it can also build constituencies for identity of interests which cross national boundaries and thus discourage resorts to force.

There is an important policy issue in connection with the "trade constitution's" principles of nondiscrimination, particularly the MFN principle discussed in chapter 6. It must be recognized that MFN policies have some costs as well as benefits. Thus the question arises, in connection with many trade measures, whether MFN principles should be observed or not. Closely related but not identical is the question of multilateralism versus bilateralism. Which of these approaches best promotes the long-term interests of the system?

Within national governments there are also a number of fundamental policy issues closely linked to the international "trade constitution." One of these is the degree to which a legalistic and adversarial system (such as the U.S. antidumping and countervailing duty systems) of administrating trade laws is best. A more legalistic or litigious approach has its costs, including attorney and consultant fees, time delay, and government costs. On the other hand, it may in some situations provide better information to decision makers, allow interested parties to make their cases and give them the feeling that they have had their "day in court," and use transparency to avoid corruption.[4]

Also pertaining to national governments is the question of the appropriate distribution of power to courts and administrative officials. What is the appropriate role of courts in reviewing trade measures undertaken by administration officials? Should the courts exercise great deference toward the administrators on the grounds of the courts relative lack of expertise and information-gathering techniques? Or will such deference result in increasing abdication of judicial responsibilities to maintain fairness and completeness of decisions, as interdependence extends to more human endeavors?

14.5 Regulating International Economic Behavior: The Broader Framework for Policy Analysis

This book has focused on trade, including the broader trade subjects now embraced in the Uruguay Round texts. However, a broader problem lurks behind the issues in this book and relates to a number of other questions of international economic relations in the world's interdependent economy. A long list of subjects can also be explored, some but not all of them appropriately allocated to the WTO. For example, an inventory of relevant subjects could include labor standards, product standards, insurance, banking and fiduciary institutions, securities regulation, shipping and transport, intellectual property, taxation, investment, competition policy, environmental regulations, monetary policy, etc. This raises the question of whether we can develop some sort of more general framework for policy analysis on such a broad landscape.

Look first at typical economic analysis of regulation.[5] Generally speaking, market-oriented economists talk about avoiding governmental interference, except when there is something called "market failure." Market failure can be caused by externalities, information asymmetries, monopolization, or public goods problems such as national defense. Economists note that often one can find in these situations of market failure that social costs differ from the market costs. In such cases it is suggested that governments can respond in a variety of ways. Governments can provide goods (highways, education, services). Governments can tax, they can regulate, or they can restructure incentives. And in any event, the governments have to struggle with competing goals in those cases.

What happens, then, when the economy becomes globalized? I would suggest that these concepts of market failure and ideas of government responses can shift quite dramatically. For example, when you are trying to detect whether there is a market failure, globalization can affect that judgment. A local monopoly may not be so damaging if a nation's borders are open to trade and you are really in a global market for a product. There are many other comparable examples.

Likewise the government *responses* may have to be different. Some of the governmental responses suggested in the event of market failure cannot easily be used in a globalized situation. How is a government going to tax foreign people? Suppose a government tries to regulate but a foreign government sees an opportunity to assist its own business participants by lax regulations, a so-called race to the bottom idea or regulatory competition. Thus many of the tools for government responses will not work the same way in a globalized situation. And that forces us to consider the problems of regulatory competition, race to the bottom and downward harmonization, something that the environmentalists have warned us about during the last few years. When one begins to analyze these situations, sometimes with the aid of game theory (particularly the so-called prisoner's dilemma),[6] one is pushed towards international cooperation as a necessary ingredient for handling these issues.

There are arguments for and against such internationalization. Governments may or may not be acting in the best interests of their society because of the distortions on governmental policy that are sometimes described by public choice theories. For example, a government leader wants to get reelected this fall and therefore won't vote for a trade treaty. There are all sorts of examples of that type. There is also a reverse side. An international institution can provide an additional buffer for national policy officials to make arguments in favor of the goals of an international institution. They can say that their nation is constrained by the international law and must obey these obligations.

However, there are risks in international cooperative activity or international governance. Some of those risks are in the institutional details, such as the danger of decision rules like "consensus" that lead to the lowest common denominator approach that inhibit some countries from embracing higher standards concerning product safety or environmental considerations. There are situations where it is going to be very hard or impossible to get agreement because of the cultural differences and the economic diversities in the world. And we have to worry that some institutions can be abused, that when we yield sovereignty to some institutions, we could find down the road (as has been alleged in some of the existing international organizations) corruption or misallocation of resources, or a distortion of the voting patterns.

Trade liberalization, the economists teach us, creates more goods or more welfare for everyone overall, but you can't say that every particular person will be better off. There will be some winners and some losers, and that is the problem. What do you do about the losers, particularly if they are the disadvantaged of some sort? This raises the question of adjustment costs. As noted in chapter 1, the economist Max Cordon's explains some of these problems in the terms of the "conservative social welfare function."[7] Basically he says, whether you like it or not, governments pay more attention to avoiding the reduction in welfare of any class of its citizenry than they do in maximizing the total welfare.

Beyond that there clearly are goals that are not so economic oriented. And one of them I mentioned at the outset: keeping the peace. That is an important element of international relations theory and international economic theory also. But it is often not considered. So we have to construct the institutions that will follow or mediate among these various goals, which will include human rights, crime abatement, drug traffic reduction, etc.

Furthermore, even though globalization may affect a nation's decision as to market failure and the need for government intervention, that does not necessarily lead to the desirability of international intervention. It could be that the market failure consequences are confined to the domestic economy, even though they have been partly caused or influenced by globalization effects. Or, it could be that national government action could effectively correct the problem with international action.

There are at least two kinds of effects across the border that have to be analyzed. First, the activity generated by the market may have a direct effect across the border, such as the flow of polluted water or atmosphere, or export of defective or dangerous goods. Second, there may be a world market effect from activities of market failure activities. For example, a domestic subsidy may lower the price of some goods shipped across the border, which will then affect the world market price in a variety of ways, sometimes depending on whether the exporting country is large enough to affect world market prices. Economists (including Alan Deardorff)[8] can then analyze what some of these market effects might be to try to ascertain if they really create conditions that call for some kind of international regulation.

After working through the various policy questions explored above, it may be concluded that an international cooperative mechanism, or institution of some kind is necessary to achieve the optimal governmental response.

These considerations lead essentially to the broader subject of constitution making, and relate both to world trade institutions such as the WTO and to national government constitutional and legal processes. It is with some satisfaction that we can note that the WTO is in place and operating, and is already achieving some success. But we also have noted that there are additional problems facing it that will need to be addressed in the not too distant future.

14.6 Some Conclusions

The WTO and the Uruguay Round results are clearly an important and indeed splendid achievement, warranting the extraordinary number of years and resources devoted to this negotiation. Whether this approach can be repeated with a new Round, or we will now need to rethink the fundamental procedures for ongoing institutional and rule evolution, is still open. The WTO would appear to have sufficient institutional flexibility to address a number of the questions and concerns that I raised in the preceding chapters. But it still remains to be seen whether the WTO can mediate on such a wide landscape of policy goals as we have outlined in the previous section, or will the WTO be essentially a somewhat more narrow trade organization. Can it successfully accommodate many diverse policy approaches in areas such as environment, competition policy, labor standards, economies in transition, developing country particular needs, and so on? And do we want an organization to have much control or a relative monopoly of the international regulatory activity concerning economics in the world? Rather, do nations prefer to have a number of organizations so they can each be kept relatively weaker?

Finally, we can observe that national governments often have tensions between executive institutions and legislative institutions. These tensions are part of a process of checks and balances. This process is often very messy, but arguably it leads to a more satisfactory governing structure, meeting some of the problems that have been noted above. Legislatures tend to look after specific constituents. Executive bodies tend to look at matters more nationally oriented, but sometimes have their own particular "public choice" goals, and sometimes become more remote from constituents while developing affinity to certain elites. These tensions are a real dilemma for constitution making. We see them in the United States, and we see them in the process of the gradually federalizing European Community development. Thus we can ask the question whether there will inevitably be some parallels necessarily develop at the international multilateral level. This brings me to two final quotations which I will close with: One is Tip O'Neill's statement that "all politics is local."[9] The other is by Drucker in a recent *Foreign Affairs* article, which states "All Economics is International."[10] This is a tension that we face in the new World Trading System, as well as in national governments.

Notes

Chapter 1

1. WTO Document WT/L/113/Rev. 6, 5 Dec. 1996, and WTO pages on the World Wide Web.

2. See Thomas L. Friedman, "U.S. is to Maintain Trade Privileges for China's Goods," *New York Times,* 26 May 1994, A1; John H. Jackson, Hyman Soloway Lecture: "The Uruguay Round, World Trade Organization, and the Problem of Regulating International Economic Behavior," in *Policy Debates/Debats Politiques* (Ottawa: Centre for Trade Policy and Law, 1995).

3. Nobel Prize winners Douglas C. North and Robert Fogel for 1993, Economics. See, e.g., Douglas C. North, *Institutions, Institutional Change, and Economic Performance* (New York: Cambridge University Press, 1990).

4. "The OECD Member Countries" *OECD Observer* 145 (1987), 22–23.

5. Lester C. Thurow, "America, Europe, and Japan: A Time to Dismantle the World Economy," *Economist* 297 (1985), 21. See also statement of Canadian ambassador Gotlieb, *International Trade Reporter* 4 (1987), 655: "The diplomacy of interdependence, characterized by compromise and mutual concessions, is profoundly unsatisfying to national feeling. It is unable to strengthen governments against their political opponents or attract popular support. In an international negotiation, a concession will always attract more attention than an advantage it is designed to deliver. It will be perceived by the media and electorate as a sign of weakness and betrayal of the national interest."

6. See Richard N. Cooper, "U.S. Position on International Economic Relations," *Department of State Bulletin* 77 (1977), 696, 698; Paul W. McCracken, "Economic Policy in the U.S.," *Wall Street Journal* 27 August 1981, 18.

7. See generally Jackson, supra note 2.

8. C. Fred Bergsten, *Managing International Economic Interdependence: Selected Papers of C. Fred Bergsten, 1975–1976* (Lexington, MA: D.C. Heath, 1977).

9. See generally John H. Jackson, *World Trade and the Law of GATT* (Indianapolis: Bobbs-Merrill, 1969); John H. Jackson, William Davey, and Alan Sykes, *Legal Problems of International Economic Relations* (St. Paul: West, 3d ed., 1995); and John H. Jackson, Jean-Victor Louis, and Mitsuo Matsushita, *Implementing the Tokyo Round* (Ann Arbor: University of Michigan Press, 1984).

10. Paul Samuelson, *Economics* (New York: McGraw Hill, 11th ed., 1980), 651. See also Peter Kenen, *The International Economy* (Englewood Cliffs, NJ: Prentice Hall, 1985), and Jagdish Bhagwati, *Protectionism* (Cambridge, MA: MIT Press, 1988).

11. *Trade Policies for a Better Future: Proposals For Action*, (Geneva: GATT, 1985), 23 (also called the Leutwiler Report).

12. History of the Committee on Finance, Sen. Doc. 91-57, 91st Cong., 2d sess., 1970.

13. *United States International Economic Policy in an Interdependent World, Report to the President Submitted by the Commission on International Trade and Investment Policy* (Washington, DC: U.S. Government Printing Office, 1971).

14. Richard N. Cooper, "Trade Policy as Foreign Policy," in *U.S. Trade Policies in a Changing World Economy*, Robert M. Stern, ed. (Cambridge, MA: MIT Press, 1987), 291–336.

15. Harry Hawkins, *U.S. Department of State Commercial Policy Series* 74 (Pub. no. 2104, 1944), 3. See also Jackson, supra note 9, 38.

16. United States Proposals, *U.S. Department of State, Commercial Policy Series* (Pub. no. 2411, 1946), 1–2.

17. For example, *Trends in International Trade* (Geneva: GATT, 1958) (also called the Haberler Report). See also Jackson, supra note 9, section 25.4.

18. See Kenen, supra note 10, 1.

19. Adam Smith, *An Inquiry into the Nature and Causes of Wealth*, Edwin Canaan, ed. (New York: Random House, 1937) (1789), 424.

20. Paul A. Samuelson, 1949. "Gains from International Trade Once Again," reprinted in *International Trade: Selected Reading*, Jagdish N. Bhagwati, ed. (Cambridge, MA: MIT Press, 1981), 1–161. See also Kenen, supra note 10, chapters 2, 3, and 4.

21. See Alan V. Deardorff, "Testing Trade Theories and Predicting Trade Flows," in *Handbook of International Economics*, Ronald Jones and Peter Kenen, eds. (Amsterdam: North-Holland, 1984), 487–517. See also infra note 29.

22. See, for example, *International Trade 1983/84*, 2 (table 1). See also Kenen, supra note 10, chapter 6.

23. See Economic Effects of Export Restraints (332-TA-117), U.S. International Trade Commission Pub. 1256 (1982).

24. Joseph Norton, "Industrial Policy and American Renewal," *Journal Economic Literature* 24 (1986), 1, 3, 27.

25. Robert M. Stern, "Tariffs and Other Measures of Trade Control: A Survey of Recent Developments," *Journal of Economic Literature* 11 (1973), 857.

26. See, for example, Paul Krugman, "Strategic Sectors and International Competition," and Avinash Dixit, "How Should the U.S. Respond to Other Countries' Trade Policies?" in *U.S. Trade Policies in a Changing World Economy*, supra note 14, 207–243; 245–282.

27. See Alan V. Deardorff, "Gains from Trade in and out of Steady Stage Growth," *Oxford Economic Papers* 25 July (1973), 173.

28. See Kenen, supra note 10, 526–527. See also Zysman and Cohen, "Double or Nothing: Open Trade and Competitive Industry," *Foreign Affairs* 61 (1983), 1113.

29. Alan V. Deardorff, "Major Recent Developments in International Trade Theory," in *International Trade and Exchange Rates in the Late 1980's*, Theo Peeters, Peter Praet, and Paul Reding, eds. (New York: Elsevier Science Pub. Co., 1985).

30. See, in general, the so-called Stolper-Samuelson model. For more recent analyses of the problems, see *Handbook of International Economics*, supra note 21.

31. W. Max Corden, *Trade Policy and Economic Welfare* (Oxford: Clarendon Press, 1974), 107. See also W. Max Corden, *The Theory of Protection* (Oxford: Clarendon Press, 1971).

32. See, for example, Ambassador Yeutter speaking after his nomination as U.S. trade representative, where he declared that he supports "free and open, but fair trade, on a level playing field" (*International Trade Reporter* 2 [1985], 510). The concept has also appeared in certain presidential statements; see *Federal Register* 49 (1984), 36813.

33. See infra chapters 10 and 11.

34. See Kenen, supra note 10, 169–172; Charles P. Kindleberger, *International Economics* (Homewood, Ill.: Irwin, 5th ed., 1973), 126.

35. Adam Smith, *The Wealth Of Nations* (1776), book 4, chapter 2. See also Kenen, supra note 10, 169–172.

36. See Kenen, supra note 10, 171; Kindleberger supra note 34, 126–127.

37. See Robert Reich, *The Next American Frontier* (New York: Times Books, 1983), 235.

38. Of course, such choices can be rationalized as reflecting merely one aspect of the preferences of consumers and laborers, but the question remains: Does the market create efficiently the environment most of its citizens would choose to live and work in?

39. See Kenen, supra note 10, 213; Kindleberger, supra note 34, 113.

40. See infra chapter 13.

41. See Kindleberger, supra note 34, 113.

42. See, for example, Gerard Curzon, *Multilateral Commercial Diplomacy* (London: Michael Joseph, 1965), 187–191, 206 for a discussion of the role of the farmers' union in the Swiss decision to retain agricultural protectionism.

43. See Pieter VerLoren van Themaat, *The Changing Structure of International Economic Law* (The Hague: Martinus Nijhoff, 1981). See also John H. Jackson, "Economic Law, International" in *Encyclopedia of Public International Law* (Amsterdam: North-Holland, 1985); Dominique Carreau, Patrick Juillard, and Thiebaud Flory, *Droit International Economique* (Paris: Pichon et Durand-Anzias 3d ed., 1990); Paolo Picone and Giorgio Sacerdoti, *Diritto Internazionale Della Economia* (Milan: Franco Angeli, 1982); John H. Jackson, *International Economic Law: Reflections on the "Boilerroom" of International Relations* 10 *American University Journal of International Law and Policy*, no. 2 (winter 1995), 595.

44. Concerning a "GATT for investment," see Charles P. Kindleberger and Paul M. Goldberg, "Toward a GATT for Investment: A Proposal for Supervision of the International Corporation," and Charles P. Kindleberger, "A GATT for International Direct Investment: Further Reflections," in *Multinational Excursions* (Cambridge, MA: MIT Press, 1984), 202–231; 247–265.

45. Louis Henkin et al., *International Law* (St. Paul: West, 3d ed., 1993), 54–94; Ian Brownlie, *Principles of Public International Law* (Oxford: Clarendon Press, 4th ed., 1990), 4–11.

46. See American Law Institute, *Restatement of the Law (Third): Foreign Relations Law of the United States,* 1987, §712. §511c. Brownlie, supra note 45, 180–183; Henkin, supra note 45, 1244.

47. See Georg Schwarzenberger, "The Principles and Standards of International Economic Law," *Receuil des Cours* 117 (1966), 14; Jackson, Davey, and Sykes, supra note 9, 269.

48. See infra chapter 6.

49. For example, Georg Schwarzenberger, "Equality and Discrimination in International Economic Law," *Yearbook of World Affairs* 25 (1971), 163. See infra section 6.1.

50. For example, the abduction of Adolf Eichmann in 1960, described in detail in Louis Henkin, *How Nations Behave: Law and Foreign Policy* (New York: Council On Foreign Relations/ Columbia University Press, 2d ed., 1979), 269–278. See also Harold G. Maier et al., "Appraisals of the ICJ's Decision: *Nicaragua v. United States* (Merits)," *American Journal of International Law* 81 (1987), 77.

51. See Henkin, supra note 50, 26–42; Roger Fisher, *Improving Compliance with International Law* (Charlottesville: University Press of Virginia, 1981), 12–16.

52. See infra chapters 4 and 14.

53. Frederick W. Maitland, "Prologue to a History of English Law," *Law Quarterly Review* 14 (1898), 13.

54. For example, see the Trade Act of 1974, Pub. L. 93-618, 121, 123, and 126, 88 Stat. 1986 et seq. Section 121(b) (19 USC §2131 [1980 and Supp. 1988]) directs the president inter alia to make trade agreements conform with GATT principles; section 123 (19 USC §2133 [1980 and Supp. 1988]) permits the president to grant new concessions or to modify existing agreements in order to compensate for any trade restrictions increased by the United States.

Chapter 2

1. See chapter 1.

2. See Article 31 of the *Vienna Convention on the Law of Treaties,* done at Vienna, 23 May 1969.

3. See generally John H. Jackson, *World Trade and the Law of GATT* (Indianapolis: Bobbs-Merrill, 1969); John H. Jackson, William Davey, and Alan Sykes, *Legal Problems of International Economic Relations* (St. Paul: West, 3d ed., 1995); and John H. Jackson, Jean-Victor Louis, and Mitsuo Matsushita, *Implementing the Tokyo Round* (Ann Arbor: University of Michigan Press, 1984). See also Robert Hudec, *The GATT Legal System and World Trade Diplomacy* (New York: Praeger, 1975).

For an overview of GATT's troubled history, see William Diebold, *The End of the ITO* (Princeton, NJ: Princeton University Press, 1952); Richard N. Gardner, *Sterling-Dollar Diplomacy* (Oxford: Clarendon Press, 1969); William A. Brown, *The United States and the Restoration of World Trade* (Washington, DC: Brookings Institution, 1950); Clair Wilcox, *A Charter for World Trade* (New York: Macmillan, 1949).

4. Charles H. Alexandrowicz, *The Law-Making Function of the Specialized Agencies of the United Nations* (Sydney: Angus and Robertson, 1973); Henry Schermers and Niels Blokker,

International Institutional Law (Rockville, MD: Sijthoff and Noordhoff, 3d ed., 1995); Marcel A. G. Van Meerhaeghe, *International Economic Institutions* (Boston: Martinus Nijhoff, 4th ed., 1985).

5. Margaret Garritsen de Vries, *The International Monetary Fund, 1966–1971: The System Under Stress* (Washington DC: IMF, 1976).

6. See Edward Mason and Robert Asher, *The World Bank Since Bretton Woods* (Washington DC: Brookings Institution, 1973); Roberto Lavalle, *La Banque Mondiale et Ses Filiales* (Paris: Librarie Générale de Droit et de Jurisprudence, 1972); Aart van de Laar, *The World Bank and the Poor* (The Hague: Martinus Nijhoff, 1980).

7. Union of International Associations, *Yearbook of International Organizations* (Munich: K. G. Saur, 32nd ed., 1995/96).

8. The International Bank for Reconstruction and Development (the World Bank) is a sister organization to the IMF, all members of the bank being obliged to be members of the IMF. The Articles of Agreement of the IBRD as amended in 1965 are found in 16 UST 1942, TIAS 5929, 606 UNTS 294. The IBRD has two affiliates, the International Development Association (IDA) (11 UST 2284; TIAS 4607; 439 UNTS 249) and the International Finance Corporation (IFC) (as amended 24 UTS 1760; TIAS 7683; 563 UNTS 362).

9. See OECD, Annual Reports; Goran Ohlin, "The Organization of Economic Cooperation and Development," *International Organization* 22 (1968), 231; Van Meerhaeghe, supra note 4, chapter 8; Miriam Camps, *"First World" Relationships: The Role of the OECD* (New York: Council on Foreign Relations, 1975).

10. Robeat S. Walters, "UNCTAD: Intervenor Between Poor and Rich States," *Journal of World Trade Law* 7 (1973), 527.

11. See generally Walter Sharp, *The United Nations Economic and Social Council* (New York: Columbia University Press, 1969); Ali Syed Amjad, *The Record and Responsibilities of the Economic and Social Council* (New York: United Nations, 1952).

12. On the FAO, see documents relating to the Food and Agriculture Organization of the United Nations, 1 August–14 December, 1944 (1945); Gove Hambidge, *FAO, Food and Agriculture Organization of the United Nations, Cornerstone for a House of Life* (Washington DC: FAO, 1946).

On the ICAO, see Thomas Buergenthal, *Law-Making in the International Civil Aviation Organization* (Syracuse, NY: Syracuse University Press, 1969).

On the ILO, see Anthony Alcock, History of the International Labor Organization (New York: Macmillan, 1971); David Morse, *The Origin and Evolution of the ILO and Its Role in the World Community* (Ithaca, NY: Cornell University Press, 1969).

On the International Maritime Organization, see Samir Mankabady, ed., *The International Maritime Organization* (London, NH: Croom Helm, 1984).

13. By the Treaty on the European Union, a European Union was created, consisting of three "pillars": the first pillar is made up of the three communities, the European Economic Community (now called "European Community"), the European Coal & Steel Community (ECSC) and the European Atomic Energy Community (EURATOM); the second pillar relates to cooperation in the field of common foreign policy and security; and the third pillar relates to cooperation in the field of justice. The distinction is important; for example, the Court of Justice is only competent for the first pillar. Given that commercial policy falls within the first

pillar, under the European Community treaty, I will consistently use the term "European Community" or "EC"; see also "Names After Maastricht," *Common Market Law Review* 1 (1994), 4–7.

14. See Robert Stern, Philip Trezise, and John Whalley, eds., *Perspectives on a U.S.-Canadian Free Trade Agreement* (Washington, DC: Brookings Institution, 1987); William Diebold, ed., *Bilateralism, Multilateralism, and Canada in U.S. Trade Policy* (Cambridge, MA: Ballinger, 1988); George A. Bermann, Roger J. Goebel, William J. Davey, and Eleanor M. Fox, *Cases and Materials on European Community Law* (St. Paul: West, ed., 1993).

15. Frederick Meyer, *The European Free Trade Association: An Analysis of "The Outer Seven"* (New York: Praeger, 1960); Robert Middleton, *Negotiating on Non-Tariff Distortions of Trade: The EFTA Precedents* (London: Macmillan/TPRC, 1975).

16. See Van Meerhaeghe, supra note 4, 350.

17. See *North American Free Trade Agreement Implementation Act,* Section 107, Pub. L. 103-182, 107 Stat. 2057 (1993).

18. On commodity agreements, see Fiona Garden-Ashworth, *International Commodity Control: A Contemporary History and Appraisal* (London: Croom-Helm, 1984); Ervin Ernst, *International Commodity Agreements: The System of Controlling the International Commodity Market* (Boston: Martinus Nijhoff, 1982); Kabir-ur-Rahman Kahn, *The Law and Organization of International Commodity Agreements* (Boston: Martinus Nijhoff, 1982).

19. For example, the International Tin Council ceased trading in 1985, and the resulting upheaval brought about a number of interesting cases in the U.K. courts. See Ilona Cheyne, "The International Tin Council" *International and Comparative Law Quarterly* 36 (1987), 931–935.

20. 22 UST 320, TIAS No. 7063, 157 UNTS 129. See also the "International Convention on the Simplification and Harmonization of Customs Procedures (Kyoto Convention)." Done at Kyoto, 18 May 1973. Entered into force in the United States, 28 January 1984. The convention is under the auspices of the CCC, and attempts to harmonize customs procedures.

21. See infra section 5.3.

22. 21 UST 1749, TIAS No. 9964, 828 UNTS 3. See United International Bureau for the Protection of Intellectual Property, *Intellectual Property Conference of Stockholm, Documents* (1967).

23. TS 548. See Charles Bevans, *Treaties and Other Agreements Of The United States Of America 1776–1949* (Washington, DC: U.S. Department of State, 1974). See generally Louis Bloomfield and Gerald Fitzgerald, *Boundary Waters Problems of Canada and the United States* (Toronto: Carswell, 1958).

24. See Ernst Fraenkel, *Military Occupation and the Rule of Law; Occupation Government in the Rhineland, 1918–1923* (London: Oxford University Press, 1944).

25. Eric V. Youngquist, "United States Commercial Treaties: Their Role in Foreign Economic Policy, Studies in Law and Economic Development," *George Washington University International Law Society,* vol. 2, study no. 1 (1967).

26. See, for example, investment treaties with Latvia, Albania, Mongolia, Trinidad and Tobago, Estonia, Georgia, Ukraine, Jamaica, Belarus, Ecuador, Moldova, Kazakhstan, Kyrgyzstan, Argentina, and Bulgaria.

27. See Youngquist, supra note 25.

28. See Schermers and Blokker, supra note 4, 681–683.

29. For example, GATT and many UN bodies. See Van Meerhaeghe, supra note 4.

30. See Pieter VerLoren van Themaat, *The Changing Structure of International Economic Law* (Boston: Martinus Nijhoff, 1981); Pieter Van Dijk, ed., *Supervisory Mechanisms in International Economic Organizations* (Deventer: Kluwer/TMC Asser Institute, 1984); Stephen M. Schwebel, ed., "The Effectiveness Of International Decisions" (Papers and Proceedings of a Conference of the American Society of International Law [1971]).

31. See generally Jackson, supra note 3.

32. VerLoren van Themaat (infra note 34, at p. 1) makes the history begin in the Middle Ages, in the Hansa context.

33. Edmund Heward, *Lord Mansfield* (Chichester: Barry Rose, 1979), 99–105.

34. See Pieter VerLoren van Themaat, "Restructuring the International Economic Order; Some Keynotes," in *Restructuring the International Economic Order: The Role of Law and Lawyers*, Peter van Dijk, Fried van Hoof, Alfred Koers, and Kamiel Mortelmans, eds. (Deventer: Kluwer, 1987), 1. See also Sir Charles Petrie, *Earlier Diplomatic History 1492–1713* (London: Hollis and Carter, 1949), chapter 23.

35. See Georg Schwarzenberger, "The Principles and Standards of International Economic Law," *Recueil des Cours—Academie de Droit International* (1965/1), 1.

36. See infra chapters 6 and 8.

37. See Amos Peaslee and Dorothy Xydis, *International Governmental Organizations—Constitutional Documents* (The Hague: Martinus Nijhoff, 2d ed., 1961), 1506.

38. See Hans Aufricht, *Guide to League of Nations Publications* (New York: Columbia University Press, 1951), 217–230.

39. See Jackson, supra note 3, 37.

40. See, for example, Richard N. Cooper, "Trade Policy as Foreign Policy." in *U.S. Trade Policies in a Changing World Economy*, Robert M. Stern, ed. (Cambridge, MA: MIT Press, 1987), 291–336.

41. The conference was held from 1–22 July 1944, at Bretton Woods, NH. See Jackson, supra note 3, 40.

42. See United Nations Monetary and Financial conference (Bretton Woods, NH, 1–22 July 1944), Proceedings and Documents 941 (U.S. Department of State Pub. No. 2866, 1948).

43. See Act to Extend the Authority of the President under section 350 of the 1930 U.S. Tariff Act as amended, and for other purposes, 5 July 1945, Pub. L. 79-130., 59 Stat. 410.

44. 1 UN ECOSOC Res. 13, UN Doc. E/22 (1946).

45. Estimate based on examination of the documents. GATT headquarters in Geneva, of course, has a practically complete collection. In the United States, the UN library in New York and the U.S. Department of State in Washington, DC, also have fairly complete collections. Most of the records are also available on microfiche.

46. For example, if a tariff commitment for a maximum 10 percent tariff charge were made, a country might nevertheless decide to use a quantitative restriction to prevent imports and thus would evade the trade-liberalizing effect of the tariff commitment.

47. See GATT, Article XXV, and Jackson, supra note 3, 126.

48. See infra chapter 5.

49. See GATT, Article XXIX. Cf. Jackson, supra note 3, chapter 2.4.

50. See infra chapter 7. See also Jackson, supra note 3, 20 et seq., 48–49.

51. See the works of Diebold, Gardner, and Wilcox, supra note 3.

52. Susan A. Aaronson, *Trade and the American Dream: A Social History of Postwar Trade Policy* (Lexington, KY: University Press of Kentucky, 1996).

53. U.S. Department of State, *Analysis of General Agreement on Tariffs and Trade* (Washington, DC: U.S. Department of State, 1947), 112–125, 147–171.

54. See Jackson, supra note 3, 62; UN Doc. EPCT/TAC/7, 3 (1947).

55. See supra note 43. The act expired on June 12, 1948. See Jackson, supra note 3, 37.

56. See UN Doc. EPCT/TAC/4, 8 (1947).

57. 55 UNTS 308 (1947).

58. See Jackson, supra note 3, section 3.3.

59. See Edwin Vermulst and Marc Hansen "The GATT Protocol of Provisional Application: A Dying Grandfather?" 27 *Columbia Journal of Transnational Law* (1987).

60. See infra chapter 11.

61. GATT, BISD 31 Supp. 74-94 (1985).

62. See Jackson, supra note 3, 92, and Appendix D. Under the Annecy Protocol, Denmark, the Dominican Republic, Finland, Greece, Haiti, Italy, Nicaragua, Sweden, and Uruguay acceded; and under the Torquay Protocol, Austria, the Federal Republic of Germany, Peru, and Turkey did so.

63. See Jackson, supra note 3, 154.

64. Ibid., chapter 6.

65. GATT, BISD 14 Supp. 17 (1966).

66. See Jackson, supra note 3, 51.

67. See Jackson, supra note 3, section 6.3.

68. See "Securing the Foothold," *Time* 91 (17 May 1968), 92; "The Kennedy Round: Sick, Sick, Six," *The Economist* 223 (1967); "The Politics of the Success," *The Economist* 223 (1967), 814. See also John W. Evans, *The Kennedy Round in American Trade Policy: The Twilight of GATT* (Cambridge, MA: Harvard University Press, 1971), 235, 272.

69. Protocol Amending the GATT to Introduce a Part IV on Trade and Development, GATT, BISD 13 Supp. 2 (1965).

70. See infra sections 5.4, 8.5, and 8.6, and chapters 10 and 11.

71. See generally Ernest Preeg, *Traders in a Brave New World: The Uruguay Round and the Future of the International Trading System* (Chicago: University of Chicago Press, 1995); Hugo Paemen and Alexandra Bensch, *From the GATT to the WTO: The European Community in the Uruguay Round* (Leuven: Leuven University Press, 1995); Jackson, Davey, and Sykes, supra note 3.

72. John H. Jackson, *Restructuring the GATT System* (London: Royal Institute of International Affairs, 1990).

73. OECD, *The New World Trading System*, table 1, 47.

74. *United States International Economic Policy in an Interdependent World, Report to the President Submitted by the Commission on International Trade and Investment Policy* (Washington DC: U.S. Government Printing Office, 1971), vol. 1, 627.

75. GATT Article XXX.

76. On the basis of the Protocol of Provisional Application to the General Agreement on Tariffs and Trade, 30 October 1947, 61 Stat. pts. 5, 6, TIAS No. 1700, 55 UNTS 308. See generally Jackson, supra note 3, section 2.1.

77. Cf. Jackson, supra note 3 at section 9.2.

78. GATT Article XXX. Cf. Jackson, supra note 3, chapter 3.6.

79. See Jackson, supra note 3, chapter 26.

80. Jackson, Davey, and Sykes, supra note 3, section 13.3. See also Ernst-Ulrich Petersmann, "Grey Area Measures and the Rule of Law," *Journal of World Trade Law* 22/2 (1988), 23.

81. Gary Sampson and Richard H. Snape, "Identifying the Issues in Trade in Services," *World Economy* 8 (1985), 171; Robert Stern and Bernard Hoekman, "Issues and Data Needs for GATT Negotiations on Services," *World Economy* 10 (1987), 39; William Diebold and Helena Stalson, "Negotiating Issues in International Services Transactions," in *Trade Policy in the 1980s*, William Cline, ed. (Washington DC: Institute of International Economics, 1983), 582.

82. See Wolfgang Friedmann, *The Changing Structure of International Law* (New York: Columbia University Press, 1964), chapter 4; Ian Brownlie, *Principles of Public International Law* (Oxford: Clarendon Press, 4th ed., 1990), section 2.4 and chapter 24; Louis Henkin et al., *International Law* (St. Paul: West, 3d ed., 1993), section 5.6.

83. Cf. Jackson, supra note 3, chapters 14 and 1. See infra section 4.6 and section 13.2.

84. See infra section 9.5.

85. Francis G. Jacobs (ed.), *The Effect Of Treaties On National Legislation* (London: Sweet and Maxwell/KCCCL, 1987); John H. Jackson, "Status of Treaties in Domestic Legal Systems: A Policy Analysis," *The American Journal of International Law 86* No. 2 (1992), 310–340; John H. Jackson, "The European Communities and World Trade: The Commercial Policy Dimension," in William James Adams, ed., *Singular Europe: Economy and Polity of the European Community After 1992* (Ann Arbor: University of Michigan Press, 1992).

86. See generally John H. Jackson, "The General Agreement on Tariffs and Trade in United States Domestic Law," *Michigan Law Review* 66 (1967), 249; Robert E. Hudec, "The Legal Status of GATT in the Domestic Law of the United States," in *The European Community And GATT*, Meinhard Hilf, Francis Jacobs, and Ernst-Ulrich Petersmann, eds. (Deventer: Kluwer, 1986), 187–249.

87. Jackson, supra note 86, 297-311. See also Jackson, Louis, and Matsushita, supra note 3, 142 et seq. See also Jackson, Davey, and Sykes, supra note 3, section 3.6 and Hudec, supra note 86.

88. "Understanding on the Interpretation of Article XXIV of the General Agreement on Tariffs and Trade 1994," *1995 Documents Supplement to Legal Problems of International Economic Relations*, 3d ed., John H. Jackson, William Davey, and Alan Sykes.

89. GATT Doc. SR.7117 (1952); GATT, BISD 1st Supp. 86 (1953). Cf. Jackson, supra note 3, chapter 22, especially section 22.3, and chapter 5, especially section 5.6.

90. See, for example, the 1955 U.S. agriculture waiver, Waiver to the United States Regarding the Restrictions under the Agricultural Adjustment Act, GATT, BISD 3 Supp. BISD 32 (1955); and the 1971 waiver allowing developed countries to depart from MFN to the extent necessary to grant tariff preferences to developing countries, Generalized System of Preferences Waiver, Decision of 25 June 1971, GATT, BISD 18 Supp. 24 (1972).

91. At their thirty-eighth session, the contracting parties agreed to examine the issue of services (GATT, BISD 29 Supp. 21 [1983]) and set up a procedure to examine the issue. A report on the matter was presented in 1985 (GATT, BISD 32 Supp. 70 [1986]). The matter was formally adopted by the contracting parties at Punta del Este. See GATT ministerial declaration, BISD 33 Supp. 19 (1987); GATT/1396, 25 September 1986, part 2, 11. See also John H. Jackson, *The Constitutional Structure for International Cooperation in Trade in Services and the Uruguay Round of GATT* (Washington, DC: Institute for International Economics, 1988), and bibliography contained therein.

92. Jackson, supra note 3, section 20.3.

93. Section 8 of the Agreement on Trade-Related Aspects of Intellectual Property Rights.

94. See Jackson, supra note 3, section 20.2, 520, 521.

95. See, for example, GATT Article XVI.3 and Article 10 of the 1979 Subsidies Code (GATT, BISD 26 Supp. 56 [1980]).

96. Jackson, supra note 3, section 27.6.

97. See U.S. waiver request regarding the restrictions under the Agricultural Adjustment Act, supra note 90.

98. The multifiber arrangement (MFA), signed originally in 1973 (25 UST 1001, TIAS 7840), was extended on 31 July 1986, for five more years. See Henry Zheng, *Legal Structure of International Textile Trade* (New York: Quorum Books, 1988). See also symposium "Perspectives on Textiles," *Law and Policy in International Business* 19 (1987), 1–271.

99. 1994 Agreement on Textiles and Clothing.

100. Douglas C. North, *Institutions, Institutional Change and Economic Performance* (New York: Cambridge University Press, 1990).

101. See generally Jackson, supra note 3, section 4.6. It was felt that it would be unreasonable to force a nation to accept an agreement with another nation when it might have compelling political reasons not to enter into such a relationship with another country. As of 6 June 1988 thirteen contracting parties were exercising such an option (see GATT L/6361 [1988]).

102. See Jackson, supra note 3, 98–102.

103. All but three of the 1979 MTN arrangements had measures permitting nonapplication of the rights and obligations between signatories. The three that contained no such waiver provision were the Arrangement Regarding Bovine Meat (GATT, BISD 26 Supp. 84 [1980]), the International Dairy Arrangement (GATT, BISD 26 Supp. 91 [1980]), and the Agreement on the Implementation of Article VII (GATT, BISD 26. Supp. 116 [1980]).

104. See Jean Groux and Phillipe Manin, *The European Communities in the International Order* (Brussels: European Commission, 1985), part 2, chapter 1; see also Ernst-Ulrich Petersmann, "Participation of the European Communities in GATT: International Law and Community Law Aspects," in *Mixed Agreements*, David O'Keeffe and Henry Schermers, eds. (Boston: Kluwer, 1983), 167–198; Ernst-Ulrich Petersmann, "The EEC as a GATT Member: Legal Conflicts between GATT Law and European Community Law," in *The European Community and GATT*, Meinhard Hilf, Francis Jacobs, and Ernst-Ulrich Petersmann, eds. (Deventer: Kluwer, 1986), 23–71.

105. See Chung-chou Li, "Resumption of China's GATT Membership," *Journal of World Trade Law* 21 (1987), 25; Robert Herzstein, "China and GATT: Legal and Policy Issues raised by China's Participation in the General Agreement on Tariffs and Trade," *Law and Policy In International Business* 18 (1986), 371. See infra section 13.2.

106. China became a signatory to the GATT MFA on December 15, 1983, the agreement having effect on 18 January 1984 (*Status of Legal Instruments*).

107. For example, Hong Kong has brought an action before a GATT panel, although the request for the establishment of the panel was placed by the United Kingdom (see GATT, BISD 30 Supp. 129 [1984]).

108. See GATT/1384, 24 April 1986.

109. See supra section 2.2.

110. See GATT Article XXV.1.

111. See Jackson, supra note 3, sections 4.6, 5.6, and 22; see also Jackson, Davey, and Sykes, supra note 3, section 6.4(B).

112. See Jackson, supra note 3, chapters 6 and 7, Edmond McGovern, *International Trade Regulation* (Exeter: Globefield Press, 2d ed., 1986), chapter 1.14. See also GATT, INF/236 (1987), "List and Index of Documents Issued by Bodies," which lists the committees of GATT).

113. See, for example, GATT, BISD 32 Supp. 44 (1986).

114. See Jackson, Louis, and Matsushita, supra note 3. See Gilbert R. Winham, *International Trade and the Tokyo Round Negotiations* (Princeton, NJ: Princeton University Press, 1986), chapters 6 and 9. See also "Symposium on the Multilateral Trade Agreements II," *Law and Policy In International Business* 12 (1980), 1–334, in particular, John H. Jackson, "The Birth of the GATT-MTN System: A Constitutional Appraisal," 21. See also Donald McRae and C. Thames, "The GATT and Multilateral Treaty Making: The Tokyo Round," *American Journal of International Law* 77 (1983), 51; the contributions in *Cornell International Law Journal* 13 (1980), 145–290; and the MTN studies commissioned by the Senate Finance Committee, 96th Cong., 1st sess., 1979, Comm. Prints 96-11 to 96-15.

115. See infra sections 4.3 and 4.6.

116. A listing of LLDC countries is provided in the Statistical Yearbook (United Nations). U.N. Doc ST/ESA/STAT/SER. 5/16, at 823, 824. Other indicators are, in some case, approximate and can differ with different definitions. U.N. Doc E/1996/76 of May 1996 contains the list also.

117. See Jackson, supra note 114, 40.

118. See Jackson, supra note 3, chapter 4.

119. See supra note 91. See also Results of the GATT Ministerial Meeting Held in Punta del Este, Uruguay: Hearings before the Subcommittee on Trade of the Committee on Ways and Means, 99th Cong., 2d. Sess., 17-23 (1986). See also the comments of U.S. Trade Representative Yeutter to the U.S. Congress, 3-11; and *International Trade Reporter* 3 (1986) 1151 and *International Trade Reporter* 3 (1986), 1182.

120. See Alan Deardorff and Robert M. Stern, *An Economic Analysis of the Effects of the Tokyo Round on the United States and Other Industrialized Countries, Subcommittee on International Trade, Senate Finance Committee*, 96th. Cong., 1st. Sess. III–IV, 1979, Comm. Print 96-15. See also Robert E. Baldwin, Robert M. Stern, and Henryk Kierzkowski, *Evaluating The Effects Of Trade Liberalization* (Leiden: Sijthoff, 1979).

121. See Jackson, supra note 3, chapter 10.

122. See Jackson, Davey, and Sykes, supra note 3. Cf. Peter Kenen, *The International Economy* (Englewood Cliffs, NJ: Prentice-Hall, 1994) 229–250. See also Michael Daly and Hiroaki Kuwahara, *Examining Restraints on Trade,* The OECD Observer, No. 203, December 1996–January 1997, p. 27.

123. Agreement on the Implementation of Article VI of the General Agreement on Tariffs and Trade (GATT, 15th. Supp. BISD 74 (1968). See infra chapter 10.

124. See infra chapter 10.

125. *Agreement on the Interpretation of Article VI of the General Agreement on Tariffs and Trade* (GATT, BISD 26 Supp. 171 (1980).

126. See Thomas Curtis and John Vastine, *The Kennedy Round and the Future of American Trade* (New York: Praeger, 1971), chapters 9 and 10; Evans, supra note 68, 90–2, 227–9, 285–6. See also Jackson, Davey, and Sykes, supra note 3, 411.

127. See supra chapter 2.2

128. The texts of the agreements and understanding can be found in GATT, BISD 26 Supp. (1980). See also Jackson, Louis, and Matsushita, supra note 3.

129. See Robert Stern, John H. Jackson, and Bernard Hoekman, *An Assessment of the GATT Codes on Non-Tariff Measures* (Brookfield, VT: Gower, 1988). See also Jackson, supra note 114.

130. The United States left the International Dairy Agreement at the end of 1984 after the EC had made sales of subsidized butter to the Soviet Union (see *International Trade Reporter* 2 [1985], 12. Austria followed suit in March 1985 (*International Trade Reporter*, 2 [1985], 429).

131. GATT, BISD 26 Supp. 201 (1980).

132. See especially *Declaration on Trade Measures Taken for Balance-of-Payments Purposes* (GATT, BISD 26 Supp. 205 [1980]) and *Decision on Differential and More Favorable Treatment Reciprocity and Fuller Participation of Developing Countries* (GATT, BISD 26 Supp. 203 [1980]).

133. See *Action by the Contracting Parties on the Multilateral Trade Negotiations* (GATT, BISD 26 Supp. 201 [1980]).

134. See infra section 6.5.

Chapter 3

1. Wolfgang Friedmann, *The Changing Structure of International Law* (New York: Columbia University Press, 1964), chapter 3; Wolfgang Friedmann, "National Sovereignty, International Co-Operation and the Reality of International Law," *U.C.L.A. Law Review* 10 (1963), 739.

2. See supra section 2.2

3. See John H. Jackson, William Davey, and Alan Sykes, *Legal Problems of International Economic Relations* (St. Paul: West, 3rd ed., 1995), section 14.3(a). See also infra chapter 10.

4. See infra section 3.4.

5. Opinion 1/94 of 15 November 1994, [1994] ECR 5267; see also Jacques Bourgeois, "The EC in the WTO and Advisory Opinion 1/94: An Echtermach Procession," *Common Market Law Review* 1995, 763–787.

6. See John H. Jackson, Jean-Victor Louis, and Mitsuo Matsushita, *Implementing the Tokyo Round* (Ann Arbor: University of Michigan Press, 1984), 164.

7. 299 US 304, 57 S.Ct. 216, 81 L.Ed. 255 (1936).

8. Raoul Berger, "The Presidential Monopoly of Foreign Relations," *Michigan Law Review* 71 (1972), 1; Louis Henkin, "Foreign Affairs and the Constitution," *Foreign Affairs* 66 (1988), 284.

9. U.S. Constitution, Art. I, sec. 8, cl. 3.

10. See, for example, Trade Reform Act of 1974, S. Rep. No. 1298, *Senate Finance Committee*, 93rd Cong., 2d Sess., 1974, 14.

11. 343 U.S. 579, 72 S.Ct. 863, 96 L.Ed. 1153 (1952).

12. *United States v. Guy W. Capps, Inc.*, 204 F.2d 655, (4th Cir. 1953). See also Jackson, Davey, and Sykes, supra note 3, 104–106.

13. However, see Harold Hongju Koh, "Congressional Control on Presidential Trade Policy-Making after *INS v. Chadha*," *New York University Journal of International Law and Politics* 18 (1986), 1191; Thomas M. Franck and Clifford A. Bob, "The Return of Humpty-Dumpty: Foreign Relations Law after the Chadha Case," *American Journal of International Law* 79 (1985), 912. See also infra note 69.

14. See supra section 2.1(b).

15. The American Law Institute, *Restatement of the Law, Foreign Relations Law of the U.S.*, 1987 §§301–308; John H. Jackson, "The Application of International Conventions in Domestic Law of the United States," in *The Effect of Treaties in Domestic Law*, Francis G. Jacobs, ed. (London: Sweet and Maxwell, 1987); Myres S. McDougal and Asher Lans, "Treaties and Congressional-Executive or Presidential Agreements: Interchangeable Instruments of National Policy," *Yale Law Journal* 181 (1945), 181; Berger, supra note 8.

16. See *Restatement*, supra note 15, §308.

17. Bruce Ackerman and David Golove, "Is NAFTA Constitutional?" *Harvard Law Review* 18, no. 4 (February 1995); Laurence Tribe, "Taking Text and Structure Seriously: Reflections on Free-Form Method in Constitutional Interpretation" *Harvard Law Review* 108, no. 6 (April

1995); Memorandum of Law, Re: Statutory Procedure for Approval of the Uruguay Round Negotiations and the WTO.

18. See, supra note 15.

19. See Jackson supra note 15; Yuji Iwasawa, "The Doctrine of Self-Executing Treaties in the United States: A Critical Analysis," *Virginia Journal of International Law* 26 (1986), 627.

20. Jackson, Louis, and Matsushita, supra note 6, at 198–210.

21. Jackson, supra note 15.

22. The use of the term "presidential" is intended to extend to all acts of the executive branch.

23. Supra note 12. See also Jackson, Davey, and Sykes, supra note 3.

24. Bernard Schwartz, *Super Chief: Earl Warren and His Supreme Court—Judicial Biography* (New York: New York University Press, 1983), 165–66.

25. 506 F.2d 136 (1974), cert. denied, 421 U.S. 1004, 95 S.Ct. 2406, 44 L.Ed. 2d 673 (1975). See also Jackson, Davey, and Sykes, supra note 3, 106–112.

26. Section 607 of the Trade Act of 1974. See Jackson, Davey, and Sykes, supra note 3, at 112.

27. See Stanley D. Metzger, "The Mills' Bill—Domestic Implication and Foreign Repercussions," *Journal of World Trade Law* 5 (1971), 235.

28. See Richard N. Cooper, "Trade Policy as Foreign Policy," in *US Trade Policies in a Changing World Economy*, Robert M. Stern ed. (Cambridge, MA: MIT Press, 1987), 291–336. See also I. Mac. Destler, *American Trade Politics: System Under Stress* (Washington DC: Institute for International Economics, 1986), 9–10. Cf. Barry Eichengreen, *The Political Economy of Smoot Hawley* (Washington, DC: National Bureau of Economic Research Working Paper No. 2001, 1986).

29. Omnibus Trade and Competitiveness Act of 1988, Pub. L. 100-418, 102 Stat. 1107 et seq.

30. As to the effects of such programs in general, see David Tarr and Morris Morkre, *Aggregate Costs to the United States of Tariffs and Quotas on Imports: General Tariff Cuts and the Removal of Quotas on Automobiles, Steel, Sugar and Textiles* (Washington, DC: Federal Trade Commission, 1984).

31. See Morkre and Tarr supra note 30. See also Michael Levine, *Inside International Trade Policy Formulation: A History of the 1982 US-EC Steel Arrangements* (New York: Praeger, 1985).

32. See Morkre and Tarr supra note 30; Jackson, Davey, and Sykes, supra note 3, chapter 13.3(E). See also Crandall, "The Effects of US Trade Protection for Autos and Steel," *Brookings Papers on Economic Activity* (1987), 271–298.

33. *Schechter v. United States*, 295 U.S. 495, 79 L.Ed. 1570, 55 S.Ct. 837 (1934).

34. *J. W. Hampton and Co. v. United States*, 276 US 394, 409; 72 L.Ed 624; 48 S. Ct. 348 (1928). See generally Laurence H. Tribe, *American Constitutional Law* (Mineola, New York: Foundation Press, 1978) at §5-17, p. 284 ff. (2d ed. 1988 at p.362)

35. Amalgamated Meat Cutters and Butcher Workmen of North America, *AFL-CIO v. Connally*, 337 F. Supp. 737 (D.D.C. 1971).

36. Trade Act of 1974, Pub. L. 93–618, § 101a, 88 Stat. 1983, 19 USC § 2111, (1980 and Supp. 1988). Note the breadth of the authority contained therein. See also Jackson, Davey, and Sykes, supra note 3, Sections 3.2(C), 3.4, 3.5.

37. See infra Section 3.2(e) and (f)

38. See, for example, the Curtiss-Wright case, supra note 7. See also Jackson, Davey, and Sykes, supra note 3, 98–102.

39. *Chicago v. Southern Air Lines, Inc. v. Waterman S.S. Corp.*, 333 U.S. 103, 68 S.Ct. 431, 92 L.Ed. 568 (1948).

40. Ibid., 111.

41. *Haig v. Agee*, 453 U.S. 280, 101 S.Ct. 2766, 69 L.Ed. 2d 640 (1981) at 291, citing *Zemel v. Rusk*, 281 U.S. 1, 17 (1965).

42. See infra chapter 14.

43. See infra chapter 10.

44. See infra chapter 11.

45. *Missouri v. Holland*, 252 U.S. 416, 40 S.Ct. 382, 64 L.Ed. 641 (1920). See also Jackson, Louis, and Matsushita, supra note 6 at 142–145.

46. See Jackson, Davey, and Sykes, supra note 3, section 3.6.

47. See Matthew Schaefer, Note on State Involvement in Trade Negotiations, at p. 180 of Jackson, et al., note 3 supra. Schaefer outlines approaches taken in the Uruguay Round and its U.S. Implementing Legislation.

48. Agreement on Government Procurement, GATT BISD 26 Supp. 33-55 (1980).

49. See Lesly Alan Glick, *Multilateral Trade Negotiations: World Trade After the Tokyo Round* (Totowa, N.J.: Rowman and Allenheld, 1984), 31.

50. See, International Trade Reporter 4 [1987], 1503, 1505, and International Trade Reporter 5 [1988], 296.

51. See Jackson, Louis, and Matsushita, supra note 6, at 21–23; Joseph H. H. Weiler, The European Parliament and Foreign Affairs: External Relations of the European Economic Community, in *Parliamentary Control Over Foreign Policy*, Antonio Cassese, ed. (Germantown, Md.: Sijthoff and Nordhoff, 1980), 151, 156. See also infra section 3.4.

52. See supra section 3.2.

53. Jackson, Davey, and Sykes, supra note 3, quoting from remarks before 18 July 1985 conference on the Export Administration Amendments Act of 1985, reported in *International Business Review* 4 (1985), 3.

54. See Jackson, Davey, and Sykes, supra note 3.

55. Jackson, Davey, and Sykes, supra note 3 at 139. See generally John H. Jackson, *World Trade and the Law of GATT* (Indianapolis: Bobbs-Merrill, 1969).

56. Jackson, Davey, and Sykes, supra note 3 at 140, fn. 18.

57. See supra note 29.

58. Senate Rep. No. 258, 78th. Cong., 1st. Sess. 47, 48 (1943). See Jackson, Davey, and Sykes, supra note 3 at 140.

59. Trade Act of 1974, Pub. L. No. 93-618, 88 Stat. 1978.

60. Trade and Tariff Act of 1984, Pub. L. 98-618, 88 Stat. 1978.

61. See supra note 29.

62 See Uruguay Round Agreements Act, Pub. L. 103-465, 8 December 1994.

63. See supra sections 2.1 and 2.2(b), (c) and (d).

64. On the Trade Act, see Jackson, Davey, and Sykes, supra note 3, Section 3.4(d). See also Jackson, Louis, and Matsushita, supra note 6, 146–149.

65. See supra note 59. See also Senate Report No. 93-1298, 93d Cong., 2nd. Sess. 1974. Reprinted in *U.S Code Congressional and Administrative News*, 4 [1974] 7186, 7253. See also Jackson, Louis, and Matsushita, supra note 6, 146–149.

66. See Jackson, Louis, and Matsushita supra note 6, 162–168.

67. Ibid., 163.

68. See Barbara Hinkson Craig, *Chadha* (New York: Oxford University Press, 1988).

69. Immigration and Naturalization Service v. Chadha, 462 US 919, 103 S. Ct. 2764. 77 L. Ed. 2d 317 (1983). See Jackson, Louis, and Matsushita, supra note 6, 162–168. See also supra note 13.

70. See, for example, section 203 of the Trade Act 1974 as amended by the Tariff and Trade Act of 1984, Pub.L 98-573, Title II, §248(a), 98 Stat. 2998, codified at 19 USC §2253(c)(1) and (2) (1980 and Supp. 1988).

71. After the Senate Finance Committee proved hostile to the use of "fast-track" (see below), Canadian Finance Minister Michael Wilson said, "At this point in time we are not withdrawing our proposal" (International Trade Reporter 3 [1986], 497). The next week, in the Senate Finance Committee, George Mitchell (D-Maine) said that Canada had too much to lose if it were to pull out of the FTA simply because of lack of "fast-track." John Chaffee (R-RI) disagreed, stating that Canadian Premier Mulroney had put himself on a limb over the proposal and was unlikely to renew the FTA talks if the Senate disapproved "fast-track" (International Trade Reporter 3 [1986], 530 and 721).

Cf. Negotiation of United States-Canada Free Trade Agreement, S. Hrg. 99-743, Senate Committee on Finance, 99th Cong., 22d sess., 1986. Eventually the Senate Finance Committee approved the use of the "fast track" procedure (International Trade Reporter 3 [1986], 565).

72. See Jackson, Louis, and Matsushita, supra note 6, 55–56.

73. Jackson, Davey, and Sykes, supra note 3, section 6.2. See also John H. Jackson, "The General Agreement on Tariffs and Trade in U.S. Domestic Law," *Michigan Law Review* 66 (1967), 285–286.

74. Proclamation 2761A, Federal Register 12 (1947), 8863. See Jackson supra note 73, 293–294 and Robert E. Hudec, "The Legal Status of GATT in the Domestic Law of the United States," in *The European Community and GATT*, Meinhard Hilf, Francis Jacobs, and Ernst-Ulrich Petersmann (eds.) (Deventer: Kluwer, 1986), 187–249.

75. Jackson, Louis, and Matsushita, supra note 6, 169–172.

76. Ibid. See The American Law Institute, *Restatement of the Law, Foreign Relations Law of the U.S.*, supra note 15, §135; Jackson, supra note 15.

77. See Senate Report No. 249, 96th Cong., 1st Sess. 4, 36 (1979); House Report No. 317, 96th Cong., 1st Sess. 26, 41 (1979). See also Jackson, Louis and Matsushita, supra note 6, 167, text and accompanying note 153; Jackson, Davey, and Sykes supra note 3, 143–147.

78. See Restatement of the Law, Foreign Relations Law of the U.S., supra note 15, §134.

79. Trade Agreements Act of 1979: Statements of Administrative Action, H.R. Doc. No. 153, 96th Cong., 1st Sess. Pt 2, 1979. Reprinted in *U.S Code Congressional and Administrative News* (1979) 665.

80. Senate Report No. 249, supra note 77, 6.

81. Section 101: Approval and Entry into Force of the Uruguay Round Agreements [Title I-Approval of, and General Provisions Relating to, the Uruguay Round Agreement, Item 47 (1994) 1167].

82. "But these roles have been cut back somewhat compared to former times." See the annual *United States Government Annual* (Washington D.C.: USGPO). See also Jackson, Louis, and Matsushita, supra note 6, 172–173.

83. For the statutory basis of the Office of the USTR, see section 141 of the Trade Act of 1974 (19 USCA §2171[c] 1980 and Supp. 1988]) as amended by section 1601 of the Omnibus Trade and Competitiveness Act of 1988 (supra note 28). See also Jackson, Davey, and Sykes, supra note 3, 149–151.

84. For a general discussion of the ITC, see Robert Baldwin, "The Political Economy of U.S. Import Policy" (Cambridge, MA: MIT Press, 1985), chapter 3.

85. See Jackson, Louis, and Matsushita, supra note 6, 203 et seq.

86. For example, in the United States, section 301 of the Trade Act of 1974 (19 USC §2411 (1980 and Supp. 1988) and in the EC, the so-called "New Commercial Policy Instrument," Council Regulation (EEC) 2641/84 on the strengthening of the common commercial policy with regard in particular to protection against illicit commercial practices, OJ [1984] L.252/1. See infra section 4.5.

87. See infra section 10.1 and chapter 14.

88. See Jackson, Louis, and Matsushita supra note 6; Hans Smit and Peter Herzog, *The Law of the European Economic Community* (New York: Matthew Bender, 1976, looseleaf); Eric Stein, Peter Hay and Michel Waelbroeck, *European Community Law And Institutions In Perspective: Text, Cases And Readings* (Indianapolis: Bobbs Merrill, 1976) (with Supplement) (1985); Jacques Megret, Michel Waelbroeck et al, *Le Droit de la Communaute Economique Europeenne* (Brussels: Presses Universitaires de Bruxelles, 1970).

89. Jackson, Louis, and Matsushita, supra note 6; John H. Jackson and Alan Sykes, *Implementing the Uruguay Round.* Volume of works by thirteen authors including analysis of eleven different countries' implementation processes. Forthcoming in 1997 (Oxford Press).

90. GATT, The Tokyo Round of Multilateral Trade Negotiations, Volume II, Supplementary Report of the Director-General, chapter IV. See also John W. Evans, *The Kennedy Round in American Trade Policy: The Twilight of the GATT?* (Cambridge, MA: Harvard University Press, 1971), sections 4 and 12; Gilbert Winham, *International Trade and the Tokyo Round Negotiation* (Princeton, NJ: Princeton University Press, 1986), 146–155, 156–158, 247–255.

91. The three basic treaties that establish the European Communities are the Treaty establishing the European Coal and Steel Community (ECSC) (Treaty of Paris 1951); the Treaty establishing the European Economic Community (EEC), (Treaty of Rome 1957); and the Treaty establishing the European Atomic Energy Community (Euratom) (1957). The 1965 "Merger Treaty" established a single council and commission for the European Communities. Treaties of Accession were signed in 1972 with Denmark, Eire, and the United Kingdom, in 1980 with Greece, and in 1985 with Spain and Portugal. See Jackson "United States-EEC Trade Relations: Constitutional Problems of Economic Interdependence," *Common Market Law Review* 16 (1979) 453. Later treaties include the Single European Act which came into effect in 1987, the Treaty on the European Union (TEU) which came into effect in 1993 (also called the Maastricht Treaty), and the Treaties of Accession with Austria, Sweden, and Finland.

92. For the text of the act, see Bulletin of the European Communities, Supp 2/86. See also the articles found in *Common Market Law Review* 24 (1987), 9–64, and Ehlermann, "The Internal Market following the Single European Act," *Common Market Law Review*, 24 (1987) 361.

93. Under Article 189(b) and (c) of the Treaty of Rome, as amended, the European Parliament is now able to amend and in some circumstances reject legislation.

94. See Title III of the Single European Act, repealed by Article P(2) TEU.

95. See 31 International Legal Materials (A.S.I.L.), p. 237 (1992), for texts.

96. The Maastricht Agreement created a new entity, the European Union. This is "founded on the European Communities, supplemented by the policies and forms of co-operation" (Article A of TEU). These policies and forms of cooperation are the common foreign and security policy, and the cooperation in the field of justice. The European Union thus comprises the EC, the ECSC and Euratom together with two "policies and forms of co-operation."

97. See Part Five, Title I, Chapter I, Section 3 of the European Community (EC) Treaty as amended.

98. Article 189 of the European Community (EC) Treaty.

99. See Part Five, Title I, Chapter I, Section 4 of the European Community (EC) Treaty.

100. Article 113 of the European Community (EC) Treaty, as amended by Article G(28) TEU.

101. See Eric Stein, with Louis Henkin, "Towards a European Foreign Policy? The European Foreign Affairs System from the Perspective of the United States Constitution," in *Integration Through Law*, Mauro Cappeletti, Monica Seccombe, and Joseph Weiler, eds. (New York: Walter de Gruyter, 1985) vol. 1, book 3.

102. Article 229 of the EC Treaty of Rome states that it shall be for the Commission to ensure the maintenance of appropriate relations with GATT. Because of the exclusive competence of the Community in commercial relations, the Community tends to represent the interests of the Member States in the GATT. However some debate exists as to the exclusive power of the Community to sign agreements under the auspices of the GATT. In the Tokyo Round, the Community felt it had exclusive competence to sign all the multilateral and bilateral agreements. Some debate arose as to the extension of Community competence to standards and trade in aircraft and so largely as a political gesture, the Member States were allowed to sign the Civil Aircraft Agreement and the Standards Code. The Member States also signed the Tariff Protocols with respect to products covered by the ECSC. For an excellent discussion of this process, see Jackson, Louis, and Matsushita, supra note 6, chapter 2.

103. See Jackson, Louis, and Matsushita, supra note 6, 47–61; Clans Dieter Ehlermann, "Application of GATT Rules in the European Community," in Hilf, Jacobs, and Petersmann, supra note 74, 187–249, at 201; Ernst-Ulrich Petersmann, "Application of GATT by the Court of Justice of the European Communities," *Common Market Law Review* 20 (1983), 397–437.

104. See Chalmers Johnson, *MITI and the Japanese Miracle* (Stanford, CA: Stanford University Press, 1982), 47–49.

105. See Jackson, Louis, and Matsushita, supra note 6, chapter 3.

Chapter 4

1. See supra Section 1.4.

2. See, for example, William B. Lockhart et al., *Constitutional Rights and Liberties* (St. Paul: West, 7th ed., 1991), 815–921, 1138–1186 and Gerald Gunther, *Constitutional Law* (Mineola, NY: Foundation Press, 12th ed., 1991, supplement 1995), 586–642, 855–968. For a historical look at the problem, see Richard Kluger, *Simple Justice* (New York: Knopf, 1976).

3. See Louis Henkin, *How Nations Behave* (New York: Council on Foreign Relations, 2d. ed., 1979), 38–88.

4. Examples include the change of U.S. law on DISC (Domestic International Sales Corporation). In reference to GATT, a compromise was reached between the parties leading to a rather vague and contradictory council statement (GATT, BISD 28 Supp. 114 [1982]). In 1984 the United Stated replaced the DISC system by the FSC (Foreign Sales Corporations) system (26 USC §§ 921-7). See also the 1986 customs users' fee case: During congressional consideration of the 1986 Tax Reform Act, certain committees decided to impose a customs users' fee to add to tariffs at the border in order to partially fund the U.S. Customs Service. The initial proposals were clearly contrary to GATT bindings and obligations. As a result of committee staff members' criticisms, the proposals were redrafted so as to tie the amount of revenue raised to the total expenditure of the Customs Service. This would have allowed the United Stated to claim that the measure was consistent with Article VIII of the GATT. The provisions were challenged, however, and a GATT panel held that the provisions were incompatible with GATT obligations (see *International Trade Reporter* 4 [1987], 1450). Also, in 1982, at the request of the European Community, a GATT panel was established to consider the compatibility with the agreement of the U.S. "manufacturing clause" (17 USC § 601). The panel reported in May 1984 (GATT, BISD 31 Supp. 74 [1984]) that the clause was inconsistent with Article XI and that its extension beyond 1 July 1982 was not excused by U.S. grandfather rights. In 1986 a bill (S 1822 - HR 4696) was introduced that attempted to make the clause a permanent feature of U.S. copyright law. In the hearings in the House, Ambassador Yeutter said that:

We have to be concerned about the fact that the manufacturing clause has been declared GATT illegal. Here we are attempting to strengthen the GATT, respond to the criticisms of the GATT that exist throughout the world, including in this subcommittee, appropriate criticisms in my judgment, but how do we go about reaching that objective, which all of us share, if we patently violate GATT ourselves. We have a definitive GATT decision against the United States on this clause. We have no defense whatsoever for the continuation of the manufacturing clause. How can we possibly go to other countries and say don't violate the GATT, if we cavalierly and flagrantly violate it ourselves.

(Hearing on HR 4696, Ways and Means Committee, 99th. Cong., 2nd Sess. [1986] 2). However, the bill did not pass, and the legislation lapsed.

5. See infra chapters 10 and 11.

6. See Philip R. Trimble, "International Trade and the 'Rule of Law,'" *Michigan Law Review* 83 (1985): 1016.

7. See supra chapter 2.2 and infra section 9.6.

8. Unlike the one-nation-one-vote system in the GATT, the IMF and the World Bank both have voting weighted on the basis of total contribution to the fund, with a minimum number of votes per nation to ensure representation of developing and poorer nations. See Richard W. Edwards, *International Monetary Collaboration* (Dobbs Ferry, NY: Transnational Publishers, 1985), 32–35. See also John H. Jackson, William Davey, and Alan Sykes, *Legal Problems of International Economic Relations* (St. Paul: West, 3rd ed., 1995), 259–263, 284–288; Henry Schermers, *International Institutional Law* (Rockville, MD: Sijthoff and Noordhoff, 2d ed., 1980), 681–683.

9. See, for example, Robert Triffin, *The World Money Maze: National Currencies in International Payments* (New Haven, CT: Yale University Press, 1966); Robert V. Roosa, *Monetary Reform for a World Economy* (New York: Council on Foreign Relations, 1965); Joseph Gold, "Unauthorized Changes of Par Value and Fluctuating Exchange Rates in the Bretton Woods System," *American Journal of International Law*, 65 (1971), 113.

10. Adapted from John H. Jackson, "Governmental Disputes in International Trade Relations: A Proposal in the Context of GATT," *Journal of World Trade Law* 13 (1979), 3–4, and John H. Jackson, "The Crumbling Institutions of the Liberal Trade System," *Journal of World Trade Law* 12 (1978), 98–101.

11. See supra section 2.2.

12. See generally Leo Gross, ed., *The Future of the International Court of Justice* (Dobbs Ferry, NY: Oceana 1976); Partan, "Increasing the Effectiveness of the International Court," *Harvard International Law Journal* 18 (1977), 559.

13. Olivier Long, *Law and its Limitations in the GATT Multilateral Trade System* (Boston: Kluwer, 1985) at 73 citing Kenneth Dam, *The GATT: Law And International Economic Organization* (Chicago: University of Chicago Press, 1970), 356.

14. Arthur Dunkel, GATT/1312 (1982).

15. See Long, supra note 13, 21: "GATT is at the same time a legal framework and a forum for negotiation." See also Robert E. Hudec, "GATT or GABB?", *Yale Law Journal* 80 (1971), 1299.

16. See Long, supra note 13, 71, citing Dam, supra note 13, 335–336.

17. Statement of Harry Hawkins, representing the United Stated, speaking about the proposed ITO charter at the London meeting of the Preparatory Committee of the United Nations Conference on Trade and Employment, UN Doc. EPCT/C.II/PV.2,9 (1946).

18. See charter of the ITO, Chapt. VIII, Articles 92–97, UN, Final Act and Related Documents, UN Conference on Trade and Employment, held at Havana, Cuba, from 21 November 1947 to 24 March 1948, Interim Commission for the International Trade Organization, Lake Success, New York, April 1948. UN Doc. E/Conf. 2/78. See also Clair Wilcox, *A Charter for World Trade* (New York: Macmillan, 1949), 159, 305–308.

19. See Wilcox, supra note 18, 159.

20. Ibid., 160

21. See supra section 4.1(b).

22. GATT, BISD 14 Supp. 18 (1967).

23. GATT, BISD 11 Supp. 95 (1963).

24. John H. Jackson, *World Trade and the Law of GATT* (Indianapolis: Bobbs-Merrill, 1969), 167–171.

25. Ibid. Generally on the GATT dispute-settlement procedure, see William Davey, "Dispute-Settlement in GATT" *Fordham International Law Journal*, 11 (1987), 51; Rosaline Plank, "An Unofficial Description of How a GATT Panel Works and Does Not" *Swiss Review of International Competition Law*, 29 (1987), 81.

26. Jackson, supra note 24, 164–166.

27. Ibid., 175.

28. An action may also be brought under Article XXIII when the attainment of any objective of the agreement is being impeded.

29. *Australian Ammonium Sulphate*, GATT, BISD Vol. II, 188 (1952). This case is sometimes called the "Marbury v. Madison" of GATT. See Robert E. Hudec, "Retaliation Against Unreasonable Foreign Trade Practices," *Minnesota Law Review* 59 (1975), 461; Robert Hudec, *The GATT Legal System and World Trade Diplomacy* (New York: Praeger, 1975), 144–153; Hudec, supra note 15, 1341.

30. *The Australian Subsidy on Ammonium Sulphate* case and the *German Duty on Sardines* case (GATT, BISD 1 Supp. 53 [1953]) both endorsed the view that the GATT should be construed to protect "reasonable expectations" of the contracting parties. See Hudec, *The GATT Legal System*, supra note 29, 144–153, and Hudec, supra note 15 at 1341. On the notion of protecting reasonable expectations generally, see Edward Allen Farnsworth, *Contracts* (Boston: Little Brown, 1982), 19.

31. GATT, BISD 3 Supp. 224 (1955). See infra chapter 11.

32. GATT Doc. L/1222/Add. 1 (1960). See also Jackson, supra note 15, 182.

33. See Hudec, *GATT Legal System* supra note 29, 66–96.

34. Some of this information is developed from private conversations with senior GATT officials closely associated with the early development of GATT.

35. *Understanding Regarding Notification, Consultation, Dispute Settlement and Surveillance*, GATT, BISD 26 Supp. 210 (1980), especially paragraphs 10–21.

36. *Netherlands Measures of Suspension of Obligations to the United states*, GATT, BISD 1 Supp. 32 (1953). This was one fallout result of the U.S. Congress's enactment of Section 22 of the Agriculture Act in 1951. See Jackson, Davey, and Sykes, supra note 8, 956.

37. The Netherlands never enforced the quota, arguably because of its ineffectiveness in removing the U.S. quota on dairy products. See Hudec, "Retaliation Against Unreasonable Foreign Trade Practices," supra note 29, 57.

38. As a result of the panel decision in the so-called Superfund case (GATT, BISD 34 Supp. 136 [1988]), the EC requested that the CONTRACTING PARTIES authorize retailiation (*International Trade Reporter*, 5 [1988], 681 and 1303–1304.

39. For example, in the Citrus case, as a result of the failure of the EC to accept the findings of a 1985 GATT panel (*International Trade Reporter* 50 [1985], 261430. In the light of continuing discussion between the EC and the United Stated, however, the president issued Proclamation 5363 of 15 August 1985 (*Federal Register* 50 [1985] 337110, suspending the application of the duty until 1 November 1985. The duties became effective until 21 August 1986, when the president revoked the increased rates of duty as a result of a settlement of the Citrus case (*Federal Register*, 51 [1986], 30146). It must be noted, however, that trade in pasta between the United Stated and the EC was itself a problem, and so retaliation against a problematic product may have had a certain added attraction.

40. See supra note 35.

41. Ibid.

42. GATT, BISD 29 Supp. 13 (1983).

43. See GATT ministerial declaration, BISD 33 Supp. 19, 25 (1987) and decision of 28 January 1987 GATT, BISD 33 Supp. 31, 44-45(1987). See also, for example, Clayton Yeutter, "The GATT Must Be Repaired—and Fast!", *The International Economy* (March/April 1988), 44-47-48; Address by Lamb (U.S. Department of State, *Current Policy*, No. 585 [1984]). Improvement of the dispute-settlement procedures of GATT is also listed in the 1988 Trade Act (Omnibus Trade and Competitiveness Act of 1988, Pub. L. 100-418, Section 1101(b)(1), 102 Stat. 1121) as a U.S. objective under the Uruguay Round.

44. Agreement on Technical Barriers to Trade, GATT, BISD 26 Supp. 8 (1980).

45. On compliance with ICJ rulings, see Guenter Weissberg, "Role of the International Court of Justice in the UN System: The First Quarter-Century," in *The Future of the International Court of Justice*, Leo Gross ed. (Dobbs Ferry, NY: Oceana, 1976), 137–150, 170–174.

46. Based on an inventory of GATT disputes developed over a number of years by the author, one article that describes some of this work is John H. Jackson, "Dispute-Settlement Techniques Between Nations Concerning Economic Relations—With Special Emphasis on GATT," in *Resolving Transnational Disputes Through International Arbitration*, Thomas Carbonneau, ed., (Charlottesville: University Press of Virginia, 1984), 39–72. See also Robert E. Hudec, "Reforming GATT Adjudication Procedures: The Lessons of the DISC Case," *Minnesota Law Review* 72 (1988), 1443; Robert E. Hudec, "Legal Issues in U.S.-EC Trade Policy: GATT Litigation 1960–1985," in *Issues in U.S.-EC Trade Relations*, Robert Baldwin, Carl Hamilton, and Andre Sapir, eds. (Chicago: National Bureau of Economic Research, 1988), 17–58; see also, Robert E. Hudec, *Enforcing International Trade Law: The Evolution of the Modern GATT Legal System* (Salem, NH: Butterworth Legal Publishers, 1993); Robert E. Hudec, *The GATT Legal System and World Trade Diplomacy* (Salem, NH: Butterworth Legal Publishers, 1990); Robert E. Hudec and Jagdish Bhagwati, *Fair Trade and Harmonization: Prerequisites for Free Trade?* (Cambridge, MA: MIT Press, 1996).

47. Hudec, *Enforcing International Trade Law*, supra note 46, 353.

48 *Agreement on Interpretation and Application of Articles VI, XVI and XXIII of the General Agreement on Tariffs and Trade*, 12 April 1979, GATT, BISD 26 Supp. 56 1980).

49. Agreement was reached on 5 August 1987 (*International Trade Reporter*, 4 (1987) 1004), and was implemented on the U.S. side by Proclamation 5712 of 30 September 1987 (*Federal Register* 52 [1987] 36895) and on the EC side by Council Decision 87/482/EEC of 7 August 1987 (OJ [1987] L.275/36). Paragraph 10 of the settlement states that agreement is without prejudice to the position of the parties on the GATT consistency of the original EC mea-

sures. The implementation of the settlement of the dispute was also enacted by section 1122 of the Omnibus Trade and Competitiveness Act of 1988, Pub. L.100-418; 102 Stat. 1143.22.

50. *U.S. Export Weekly*, 18 (1983) 899 (1983). See Massimo Coccia, "Settlement of Disputes in GATT Under the Subsidies Code: Two Panel Reports on EEC Export Subsidies," *Georgia Journal of International and Comparative Law* 16 (1986), 1.

51. See *U.S. Export Weekly*, 19 (1983) 371; *U.S. Import Weekly*, 8 (1983) 468. See Coccia supra note 11, and Garcia Barcero "Trade Laws, GATT and the Management of Trade Disputes between the U.S. and EEC" *Yearbook of European Law* 5 (1985), 149.

52. See Hudec, *Enforcing International Trade Law*, supra note 46, 287.

53. The Vienna Convention on the Law of Treaties, with annex, done at Vienna, 23 May 1969. (Text: UNGA UN Doc. A/Conf. 39-27, 23 May 1969). The revised restatement closely follows the Vienna Convention. See American Law Institute, *Restatement of the Law (Third), Foreign Relations Law of the United States*, part 3.

54. Vienna convention, supra note 11, Article XXXII. "Further reference may be made to supplementary means of interpretation, including the preparatory work of the treaty and the circumstances of its conclusion, in order to confirm the meaning resulting from the application of Article XXXI, or to determine the meaning when the interpretation according to Article XXXI: (a) leaves the meaning ambiguous or obscure; or (b) leads to a result which is manifestly absurd or unreasonable."

55. Annex I, Notes and Supplementary Provisions. Volume IV of the *Basic Instruments* (Geneva: GATT/1969-7) contains the text of the general agreement (of which the Annex I is an integral part) which entered into force 27 June 1966.

56. See supra section 2.5.

57. GATT, *Analytical Index*, Guide to GATT Law and Practice, The *Analytical Index* currently in use is the 1995 edition (2 volumes).

58. This is a critical question for Article XIX concerning safeguards; see infra section 7.5.

59. John H. Jackson, supra note 24, chapter 3.

60. See Ian Brownlie, *Principles of Public International Law* (Oxford: Clarendon Press, 4th ed., 1990), 21–23. Cf. Edmond McGovern, Dispute Settlement in the GATT—Adjudication or Negotiation? In *The European Community and the GATT*, Meinhard Hilf, Francis Jacobs, and Ernst-Ulrich Petersmann, eds. (Deventer: Kluwer, 1986), 73–84, 78–79.

61. Statute of the International Court of Justice, 59 Stat. 1055, T.S. 993. Article 59 reads: "The decision of the Court has no binding force except between the parties and in respect of that particular case."

62. See GATT *Analytical Index*, supra note 56, Article I:12. See also Article I:15 (chairman); Article I-16 (chairman); Article II:20 (secretariat).

63. Some have even cast doubt on about this. See supra section 4.2.

64. Vienna Convention on the Law of Treaties, supra note 53, Article XXXI:3: "There shall be taken into account, together with the context ... (b) any subsequent practice in the application of the treaty which establishes the agreement of the parties regarding its interpretation...."

65. See, for example, *Articles of Agreement of the International Monetary Fund* (60 Stat. 1401; TIAS 1501), Article XXIX, and *Articles of Agreement of the International Bank for Reconstruction and Development* (60 Stat. 1440; TIAS 1502), Article VIII.

66. See supra section 2.2.

67. International Court of Justice, *Reports of Judgments, Advisory Opinions, and Orders.*

68. Havana (ITO) Charter articles 92–97. See Jackson, supra note 24, section 5.5, 135.

69. See Richard Sutherland Whitt, "The Politics of a Procedure: An Examination of the GATT Dispute Settlement Panel and the Article XXI Defense in the Context of the US Embargo of Nicaragua," *Law and Policy in International Business* 19 (1987), 603, 611–615. For the details of the dispute(s), see Report of the Panel, GATT, BISD 31 Supp. 67 (1984). See also *Case Concerning Military and Paramilitary Activities in and Against Nicaragua (Nicaragua v. United States)*, Merits, Judgment of 27 June 1986. ICJ Reports 1986.

70. See Articles 3:1, 3:2, 3:5, 3:7, 19, 21:1; 21:5, 6, 22:1, 22:8, 23:2(b), 26:1(b) of the Understanding on Rules and Procedures Governing the Settlement of Disputes.

71. See, For example, Ruggiero, Director General of the WTO, Special Report for the Ministerial Conference in Singapore on 9 December 1996, including an annual review. In Part III, WTO Activities in 1996, the report says "... the WTO's reinforced dispute settlement system continues to prove its effectiveness ..." *WTO Focus*, December 1996, No. 14 at page 7. In another speech by the Director General on 18 September 1996, the DG also commented about the importance of the dispute settlement system, describing it as "the major success story ..." *WTO Press*/56, 18 September 1996, page 4. The United States Office of the U.S. Trade Representative has also commented on U.S. satisfaction with the new WTO procedures. An October 1, 1996, document readable on the USTR Web page, entitled "Identification of Trade Expansion Priorities" (Super 301) Pursuant to Executive Order 12901, states: "The WTO dispute settlement procedures have already yielded positive results: ..."

72. WTO Document "Overview of the State-of-Play of WTO Disputes" dated January 7, 1997, downloaded from the WTO Web page.

73. WTO Case: United States—Standards for Reformulated and Conventional Gasoline, Appellate Body Report and Panel Report, WTO Document WTO/DS2/9 of 20 May 1996.

WTO Case: Japan—Taxes on Alcoholic Beverages, Report of the Appellate Body, WTO Document WT/DS8/AB/R of 4 October 1996.

74. WTO Case: United States—Standards for Reformulated and Conventional Gasoline, Appellate Body Report and Panel Report, WTO Document WT/DS2/9 of 20 May 1996, p. 30.

75. See Brownlie, supra note 60, 495–505.

76. Governments do not have a duty to exercise diplomatic protection. Charles E. Rousseau, *Droit International Public* (Paris: Dalloz, 10d. 1984), 116. Cfr. Barcelona Traction, Light, and Power Co., Ltd. (*Belgium v. Spain*), 1970 L.C.J.

77. Trade Expansion Act of 1962, §252, Pub. L. 87-794, 75 Stat. 879.

78. Bart S. Fisher and Ralph G. Steinhardt III, "Section 301 of the Trade Act of 1974: Protection for U.S. Exporters of Goods, Services, and Capital," *Law and Policy in International Business* 14 (1982), 569; see also Hudec, "Retaliation Against 'Unreasonable' Foreign Trade Practices," supra note 29.

79. The enactment of the 1988 Omnibus Act met with a great deal of criticism from foreign nations, particularly the EC and Japan. The EC protested the passing of the act at the September GATT council meeting (*International Trade Reporter* 5 [1988], 1302) and on 26 September 1988, the EC council of ministers released a statement expressing "serious concern" over the act (*European Community News*, No. 24/88). Japanese officials also expressed concern over the act: see "New U.S. Trade Bill Raises Fears in Asia and Europe," *Financial Times*, 5 August 1988, 1 and "Japan Fumes at U.S. Steps in Trade Bill," *Wall Street Journal*, 9 August 1988, 26.

80. 1974 trade act (as amended through 1988), Sections 301-306, 19 USC §§2411–2416 (1980 and Supp 1988). As to application to services, see 19 USC §2411(e)(1)(A) (1980 and Supp 1988); as to scope of retaliation, §2411(a)(2)(A) (1980 and Supp 1988). See also *United States v. Star Industries* 462 F.2d 557, cert. denied 409 US 1076, 93 S. Ct. 678, 34 L.Ed. 663 (CCPA, 1972).

81. The legislative history of the 1974 trade act made it clear that the president was not obliged to refer a Section 301 action to the GATT, see Senate Finance Committee, 93rd Cong. 2nd Sess. (1974) (Comm. Rpt. No. 93-1298), reprinted in *US Code Congressional and Administrative News*. 4 (1974) 7186, 7304. The Trade Agreements Act of 1979 (§901, 93 Stat. 295, 19 USC §§2413-2414 [1980 and Supp. 1988]), however, introduced a new section, Section 303, that requires the USTR to refer the matter to international dispute-settlements procedures where applicable. It is clear that the dispute-settlement procedure need not be fully completed (in the GATT case the adoption on the panel report by the council) before the USTR can recommend action.

82. 19 USC §2411(e)(3) (1980 and Supp. 1988). See Hansen "Defining Unreasonableness in International Trade: Section 301 of the Trade Act of 1974," *Yale Law Journal* 96 (1987), 1122.

83. 19 USC §2411(a)(1)(B)(ii) (1980 and Supp. 1988).

84. Action 301-58. On 30 December 1986, the United Stated and Canada concluded an agreement under which the Department of Commerce terminated a countervailing duty case after Canada agreed to levy a 15 percent *ad valorem* duty on certain softwood exports to the United Stated (*Federal Register* 52 (1987), 229, 231, and 232). See also Alan F. Holmer and Judith H. Bello, "The U.S.-Canada Lumber Agreement: Past as Prologue" *International Lawyer* 21 (1987), 1185; Charles Doran and Timothy Naftali, *U.S.-Canadian Softwood Lumber: Trade Disputes Negotiations* (Washington DC: Foreign Policy Institute, Johns Hopkins University, FPI Case Study No. 8, 1987).

85. Action 301-48. Petition was filed in 1985 (*Federal Register* 50 [1985], 28866). The action resulted in the Arrangement Between the Government of Japan and the United States of America Concerning Trade in Semiconductor Products, 2 September 1986, (reprinted in *International Legal Materials*, 25 [1986], 1409). The Section 301 action was suspended as a result in 1986 (*Federal Register* 51 [1986], 27811) but certain sanctions for breach of the agreement were imposed in 1987 (*Federal Register* 52 [1987], 13412). These were later partially withdrawn (*Federal Register* 52 [1987], 22693 and 43146).

86. For legislative history of original 1974 trade act, see *US Code Congressional and Administrative News* 4 (1974) 7186.

87. See Fisher and Steinhardt, supra note 78, 577 et seq.

88. See supra note 83. In a Section 301 steel complaint filed by the American Iron and Steel Institute, for example, the USTR decided not to initiate an investigation (*Federal Register*

[1983], 8878), inter alia, because "the petition fails to present evidence to demonstrate that U.S. benefits under the GATT have been nullified or impaired by reason of the GATT-inconsistent measure." The petition does not include specific information relating to the impact on petitioners and on U.S. commerce arising from the alleged foreign practices.

89. In 1981 the U.S. specialty steel industry filed a Section 301 complaint, alleging that Austria, Belgium, Brazil, France, Italy, Sweden, and the United Kingdom had subsidized their specialty steel industries. The complaint placed the executive branch in a difficult position because it was not limited to GATT-countervailable subsidies. Therefore an affirmative determination would likely have created an uproar among U.S. trading partners. Following a USTR recommendation to that effect, the president in 1982 suspended the Section 301 proceeding, while requesting the ITC to conduct an expedited Section 201 (safeguards) proceeding (*Federal Register* 47 [1982], 51717). The ITC issued an affirmative finding and in 1983 the president decided to grant relief in the form of tariff increases and quotas (*Federal Register* 48 [1983], 31177).

90. Council Regulation (EC) No. 3286/94 of 22 December 1994 laying down Community procedures in the field of the common commercial policy in order to ensure the exercise of the Community's rights under international trade rules, in particular those established under the auspices of the World Trade Organization (OJ No L 349, 31.12.1994, p. 71).

91. Council Regulation (EEC) No 2641/84 of 17 September 1984 on the strengthening of the common policy with regard in particular to protection against illicit commercial practices (OJ No L 252, 20.09.1984, p.1) as last amended by Regulation (EC) No 522/94 (OJ No L66, 10.03.1994, p.10).

92. Articles 3, 4, and 6 respectively of Regulation 3286/94.

93. Article 12(2), Article 13(2), Article 14 Regulation 3286/94.

94. Article 12(2) and (3), Article 13(3) Regulation 3286/94.

95. Article 12(2) and (3), Regulation 3286/94.

96. Article 15 Regulation 3286/94.

97. Kapteyn, VerLoren van Themaat, Inleiding tot het recht van de Europese Gemeeschappen, Na Maastricht, Vijfde geheel herziene druk, Kluwer, Deventer, 1995, p. 798.

98. See John H. Jackson, "Governmental Disputes in International Trade Relations," supra note 10, 15–16; Jackson, "MTN and the Legal Institutions of International Trade, MTN Studies" Comm. Print 96-14, 96th Cong., 1st Sess., 1979, 17.

99. See, for example, the U.S.-Canada Free Trade Agreement, *International Legal Materials* XXVII (1988), 281; On the U.S. side implementation of this provision was carried out by section 401(c)(g)(7) of the United States-Canada Free Trade Implementation Act of 1988, Pub. L. 100-449; 102 Stat.

100. John H. Jackson, Jean-Victor Louis, and Mitsuo Matsushita, *Implementing the Tokyo Round* (Ann Arbor: University of Michigan Press, 1984), 208–209.

101. Giorgio Malinverni, *Le Reglement des Differends dans les Organizations Intérnationales Economiques* (Leiden: Sijthoff, 1974), 106 quoted in Olivier Long, supra note 13, 7.

102. See supra notes 13 and 14. See also Edmond McGovern, *International Trade Regulation* (Exeter: Globefield Press, 2d ed., 1986), 32.

103. GATT, BISD 18 Supp. 149, 158, 166 (1970–1971); 19 Supp. 97 (1972); 20 Supp. 145-209 (1973).

104. See ministerial declaration (GATT, BISD 33 Supp. 19; GATT/1396, 25 September 1986), part 1 (e) (i), which states that the negotiations aim to develop understandings and arrangements: to enhance the surveillance in the GATT to enable regular monitoring of trade policies and practices of contracting parties and their impact on the functioning of the multilateral trading system. See also Olivier Long et al., *Public Scrutiny of Protection: a Report on Policy Transparency and Trade Liberalization* (New York: Trade Policy Research Centre, 1987).

105. See GATT, *Review of Developments in the Trading System*, a biannual survey of developments affecting international trade, issued by the GATT secretariat.

Chapter 5

1. John H. Jackson, *World Trade and the Law of GATT* (Indianapolis: Bobbs-Merrill, 1969), chapter 10.

2. See Jackson supra note 1, 305–308, 625–638; John H. Jackson, William Davey, and Alan Sykes, *Legal Problems of International Economic Relations* (St. Paul: West, 3rd ed., 1995), 373 et seq.

3. See Jackson, supra note 1, at chapter 14.

4. Ibid., chapters 15 and 16.

5. Ibid., chapter 25. See also infra chapter 12.

6 Peter Kenen, *The International Economy* (Englewood Cliffs, NJ: Prentice-Hall, 1985), 175–177; Charles Kindleberger, *The International Economy* (Homewood, IL: Richard D. Irwin, 5th ed., 1973). See also Alan V. Deardorff, "Safeguards and the Conservative Social Welfare Function," in *Protection and Competition in International Trade*, Henryk Kierzkowski, ed. (Oxford: Basil Blackwell, 1987), 22–40.

7. Frank W. Taussig, *The Tariff History of the United States* (New York: G.P. Putnam's, 8th ed., 1931).

8. See Kenen, supra note 6, 224–232.

9. Supra chapter 2.5. See also Jackson, Davey, and Sykes, supra note 2, section 8.2; and Michael Daly and Hiroaki Kuwahara, "Examining Restraints on Trade," *The OECD Observer*, No. 203, December 1996–January 1997, p. 27.

10. See supra section 2.5.

11. This concern was crucial among Canada's reasons for negotiating the U.S.-Canada Free Trade Agreement (International Legal Materials XXVII [1988], 181).

12. Alan V. Deardorff and Robert. M. Stern, "An Economic Analysis of the Effects of the Tokyo Round of Multilateral Trade Negotiations on the United States and the Other Major Industrialized Countries," Subcomm. on International Trade, Senate Finance Comm., 96th Cong., 1st Sess., 1979 III–IV (Comm. Print 96-15). See also Alan V. Deardorff and Robert M. Stern, *The Michigan Model of World Production and Trade: Theory and Application* (Cambridge, MA: MIT Press, 1985), 54–55.

13. Articles VII–X, GATT, BISD, Vol. IV (1969):

Article VII. Valuation for customs purposes

Article VII. Fees and formalities connected with importation and exportation

Article IX. Marks of origin

Article X. Publication and administration of trade regulations

14. See generally Jackson, supra note 1, chapter 10; Kenneth Dam, *The GATT: Law and International Economic Organization* (Chicago: University of Chicago Press, 1970), 17; Gerard Curzon, *Multilateral Commercial Diplomacy* (London: Michael Joseph, 1965), 70–123.

15. Reciprocal Trade Agreements Act of 1934, Act of 12 June, 1934, 48 Stat. 943, 19 USC §1351. See Jackson, Davey, and Sykes, supra note 2, 13, 140.

16. An ad valorem duty is a duty expressed as a percentage of the import price—for example, 34 percent. A specific duty is a duty expressed as a fixed amount per unit, weight or measure; for example, the duty is $0.10 per pound of fish.

17. See Jackson, supra note 1, 203 et seq.

18. This has occurred, for example, in Canada and Japan.

19. See Jackson, Davey, and Sykes, supra note 2, 384.

20. GATT, Article XXVIII details some of the procedures by which these renegotiations occur. See Jackson, supra note 1, 229 et seq.

21. See Jackson, supra note 1, 219 et seq.; John W. Evans, *The Kennedy Round in American Trade Policy: The Twilight of the GATT?* (Cambridge, MA: Harvard University Press, 1970), 221 et seq.

22. See Jackson, supra note 1, at 223 et seq.; Evans, supra note 21, 140 et seq.; John Rehm, "The Kennedy Round of Trade Negotiations," *American Journal of International Law*, 62 (1968), 403. See also *Operation of the Trade Agreements Program, 19th Report*, United States International Trade Commission Publication 287 (1967), 167–170.

23. See *Operation of the Trade Agreements Program*, supra note 22, 236 et seq.

24. See Jackson, Davey, and Sykes supra note 2, 381; A.H.M. Albregts and A. van de Gevel, "Negotiating Techniques and Issues in the Kennedy Round," in *Economic Relations after the Kennedy Round*, Frans A. M., Alting von Geusau, ed. (Leiden: Sijthoff, 1969), 20–47; Thomas B. Curtis and John R. Vastine, *The Kennedy Round and the Future of American Trade* (New York: Praeger, 1971), 82–91.

25. See Deardorff and Stern, supra note 12. See also Alan V. Deardorff and Robert Stern, "Economic Effects of the Tokyo Round," *Southern Economic Journal* 49 (1983), 605.

26. The Tokyo Round of Multilateral Trade Negotiations, Volume I, Report of the Director-General of GATT (Geneva: GATT, [1979]), 46–48.

27. The Tokyo Round of Multilateral Trade Negotiations, Volume II, Supplementary Report of the Director-General (Geneva: GATT, 1980), 3–7. See also note 9 supra.

28. Uruguay Round Agreements Act, presidential statement, p. 701.

29. See, for example, Article XXXVI:8 of GATT: "The developed contracting parties do not expect reciprocity for commitments made by them in trade negotiations to reduce or remove tariffs and other barriers to the trade of less-developed contracting parties."

30. See supra note 15.

31. Kenen, supra note 6, section 2.2.

32. Ibid.

33. See, for example, U.S. Tariff Commission Customs violation, report to Senate Comm. on Finance, 93d Cong., 1st Sess. (1973). Reprinted in Jackson, Davey, and Sykes, supra note 2, 409–410.

34. See Trade Act of 1974, Title I, §104, 88 Stat. 1985, 19 USC §2114 (1980 and Supp. 1988).

35. See Peter Morici and Laura Megna, *U.S. Economic Policies affecting Industrial Trade: A Quantitative Assessment of Non Tariff Barriers* (Washington, DC: National Planning Association, 1983).

36. The so-called Danforth Bill, S. 2094, 97th Cong. 2nd. Sess., *Congressional Record* 128 (1982) S678. There were, however, numerous other proposals, see Michael Gadbaw, "Reciprocity and Its Implications for US Trade Policy," *Law and Policy in International Business,* 14 (1982), 691, 692 n.4.; see also William Cline, "Reciprocity: A New Approach to World Trade Policy?" *Policy Analyses in International Economics,* no. 2 (1982) Jagdish Bhagwati and Douglas Irwin, "The Return of the Reciprocitarians: U.S. Trade Policy Today," *World Economy* 10 (1987), 109.

37. See Trade and Tariff Act of 1984, Title III, Barriers to Market Access, 98 Stat. 3000 et seq., 19 USC §2111 et seq (1980 and Supp. 1988).

38. See infra chapter 6.

39. See supra note 35.

40. For useful secondary books on customs law, including classification, see Ruth Sturm, *Customs Law and Administration* (New York: American Importers Association, 3d ed., looseleaf 1985); David Serko, *Import Practice: Customs Law and International Trade* (New York: Practicing Law Institute, 2d ed., 1991). The court with exclusive primary jurisdiction over customs matters is the Court of International Trade, whose decisions are published in the Federal Supplement. Appeals are to the Court of Appeals for the Federal Circuit, whose decisions are published in *Federal Reporter,* 2d ed.

41. See Jackson, supra note 1, section 10.3.

42. The Brussels Tariff Nomenclature is also known as the Nomenclature for the Classification of Goods in Customs Tariffs and the Customs Cooperation Council Nomenclature. The text is reproduced in Customs Cooperation Council, *Nomenclature For The Classification Of Goods In Customs Tariffs* (5th ed. 1976) (supplemented from time to time).

43. The first United States tariff schedule came into being only four months after the Constitution of the United States became effective. The current tariff schedules of the United States became effective on 31 August 1963. See, in general, Jackson, Davey, and Sykes, supra note 2, 373 et seq.

44. The Convention on the Harmonized Commodity and Coding System was approved by the CCC on 14 June 1983, and was to enter into force on acceptance by no less than 17 states or customs or economic unions, but in no case no *earlier* than 1 January 1987. It was submitted to Congress on 15 June 1987. See also the Geneva (1987) Protocols to the Introduction of the Harmonized Commodity Description and Coding System, GATT, BISD 34 Supp. 5 (1988).

45. The implementation of the code was carried out by sections 1201–1217 of the Omnibus Trade and Competitiveness Act of 1988, Pub.L. 100-418; 102 Stat. 1147–1163.

46. See Curzon, supra note 14, 60, note 7.

47. GATT, BISD 28 Supp. 102 (1982). See also Jackson, Davey, and Sykes, supra note 2, 378.

48. GATT panel report adopted July 1989, 36th Supp. BISD 167 1990, Japan-Tariff on Import of Spruce Pine-Fir (SPF) dimension lumber (complaint brought by Canada). See Jackson, Davey, and Sykes, supra note 2, p. 445.

49. A number of GATT waivers have been granted to various countries over the years to facilitate their shift from specific to ad valorem tariffs. See Jackson, supra note 1, sections 22.3 and 23.4.

50. An FOB price is the price of the point of shipment for the goods only, while a CIF price is the price for the goods plus an amount covering transportation and insurance to buyer's port. The statutory basis for the United States use of the FOB valuation method is 19 USC 1401a(b)(4)(A), providing that dutiable value excludes any costs, charges, or expenses, or expenses incurred for transportation, insurance, and related services incident to the international shipment of the merchandise to the United States.

51. See supra note 33.

52. See Jackson, Davey, and Sykes, supra note 2, 403 et seq.

53. Agreement on Implementation of Article VII of the General Agreement on Tariffs and Trade, GATT BISD, 26 Supp. 116 (1980). See also Protocol to the Agreement on Implementation of Article VII of the General Agreement on Tariffs and Trade, GATT BISD, 26 Supp. 151 (1980).

54. Twenty-seven countries (including the European Community as one signatory) have accepted the code. Spain withdrew in November 1987 as a result of its accession to the EC (GATT L/6212/Add.3). Turkey has signed the code but has not accepted the code as of the time of this writing. For detailed information on the signatories, see GATT Doc. L/6453 (1989), and Analytical Index, 6th ed., 1995, 1167.

55. Note presidential statement on Uruguay Round at p. 897, which is the statement of administrative action on the customs valuation code.

56. See GATT Articles XII, XIII, XIV, and XV.

57. See GATT Article XVIII, and Part IV, Articles XXXVI, XXXVII, and XXXVIII. Compare the discussion of the safeguards system in chapter 7.

58. See Jackson, supra note 1, 309 et seq.

59. See Jackson, supra note 1 at chapter 26.8. See also for example, Senate Finance Committee, The Quantitative Restrictions in the Major Trading Countries, Executive Branch Study No. 6, 93d. Cong., 2nd. Sess., 1974.

60. Agreement on Import Licensing Procedures, GATT BISD 26 Supp. 154 (1980).

61. Ibid., Articles 2 and 3.

62. Statement of Administrative Action at President's statement, p. 907.

63. GATT Doc. NTM/W/6/Rev.2 and Addenda. The information therein is summarized in "Quantitative Restrictions and Other Non-Tariff Measures," Report (1984) of the Group on Quantitative Restrictions and Other Non-Tariff Barriers, GATT BISD 31 Supp. 211 (1985). See also Jackson, Davey, and Sykes, supra note 2, section 8.1(B).

64. UNCTAD, *Non-Tariff Barriers Affecting the Trade of Developing Countries and Transparency in World Trading Conditions: The Inventory of Non-Tariff Barriers* (Geneva: UNCTAD, 1983).

65. Morici and Megna, supra note 35.

66. Alan V. Deardorff and Robert M. Stern, *Methods of Measurement of Non-Tariff Barriers*, UNCTAD/ST/MD/28 (New York: United Nations, 1985).

67. For example, French regulations stipulated that French inspectors must inspect the factory of any pharmaceutical sold in France, but "French inspectors do not travel." See *U.S. Export Weekly* 20 (1984), 953. See also infra section 8.5.

68. Examples of such reports include: United States Trade Representative, 1996 National Trade Estimate Report on Foreign Trade Barriers, U.S. Government Printing Office, 1996 Services of the European Commission, 1996 Report on U.S. Barriers to Trade and Investment, Brussels, May 1996. Services of the European Commission, Summary of Market Access Problems in Japan, Brussels, June 28, 1996; Industrial Structure Council of Japan, 1996 Report on the WTO Consistency of Trade Policies by Major Trading Partners. Department of Foreign Affairs and International Trade, Canada, Register of U.S. Barriers to Trade, 1994. Recently, Web or Internaet cites were opened with information on foreign trade barriers: by the European Commission (http://makaccdb.eu.int) and the United States Trade Representative (http://www.ustr.gov/reports/nte/1996/contents.html).

69. For a general overview of the EC's common agricultural policy, see Hudson, The European Community's Common Agricultural Policy in Trade Policy Perspectives: Setting the State for 1985 Agricultural Legislation, Senate Fin. Comm. on Agricultural, Nutrition and Forestry, 98th Cong. 2d Sess. 323, 1984, 323. On the variable levy, see Edmond McGovern, *International Trade Regulation* (Exeter: Globefield Press, 2d ed., 1986), 456–458.

Chapter 6

1. See generally John H. Jackson, *World Trade and the Law of GATT* (Indianapolis: Bobbs-Merrill, 1969), chapter 11; John H. Jackson, William Davey, and Alan Sykes, *Legal Problems of International Economic Relations* (St. Paul: West, 3d ed., 1995), chapter 9; John H. Jackson, "Equality and Discrimination in International Economic Law (XI): The General Agreement on Tariffs and Trade," *Yearbook of World Affairs* 37 (1983), 224; Report of the International Law Commission, "Draft Articles on Most-Favored-Nation clauses and commentary," *Yearbook of the International Law Commission* [1978], 8-73 (Vol. II, Pt 2. 1979) Gardner Patterson, *Discrimination in International Trade: The Policy Issues 1945–1965* (Princeton, NJ: Princeton University Press, 1966), Gros Espiell, "The Most-Favored-Nation Clause," *Journal of World Trade Law* 5 (1971), 29; Theodore C. Sorensen, "Most Favored and Less Favorite Nations," *Foreign Affairs*, 52 (1974), 273; Gary C. Hufbauer, J. Shelton Erb, and H. P. Starr, "The GATT Codes and the Unconditional Most-Favored-Nation Principle," *Law and Policy in International Business*, 12 (1980), 59.

2. See *The Most-Favored-Nation Provision*, Executive Branch GATT study, No. 9, 93d Cong., 2d Sess. 1974, 1.

3. Ibid. Also, Jackson, *World Trade*, supra note 1, section 11.1.

4. Ibid.

5. See, for example, "A Convention to Regulate the Commerce Between the Territories of the United States and of His Britannick Majesty," 3 July 1815, Article the Second 8, Stat. 228, Treaty Series 110 (reprinted in Charles Bevans, *Treaties and Other International Agreements of the United States of America 1776–1949* (Washington, DC: Department of State, 1974), 49.

6. See, for example, Georg Schwarzenberger, "Equality and Discrimination in International Economic Law (I)," *Yearbook of World Affairs* 25 (1971), 163; Pieter VerLoren van Themaat, *The Changing Structure of International Economic Law* (The Hague: Martinus Nijhoff, 1981), Chapter 1. See also Ian Brownlie, *Principles of Public International Law* (Oxford: Clarendon Press, 4th ed., 1990), chapter 23, especially section 4.

7. See infra chapter 13.

8. Cf. Section 126 of the Trade Act of 1974, Pub. L. 93-618; 88 Stat. 1978; 19 USCA §2136 (1980 and Supp. 1988), providing for "reciprocal non-discriminatory treatment." Senate Report no. 93-1298, 93d Cong., 2d Sess., 1974, 94-495, explains the national behind these sections. See also Hufbauer, Erb, and Starr, supra note 1.

9. Trade Agreements Act of 1979, Pub. L. 96-39; Title I, section 101, 93 Stat. 151, 19 USCA §1671(b) (1980 and Supp. 1988). See S. Rep. 96-249, Senate Finance Committee, 96th Cong., 1st Sess., 1979, 45. See also infra section 11.2.

10. See John H. Jackson, "Equality and Discrimination in International Economic Law (XI): The General Agreement on Tariffs and Trade," supra note 1, 225. See also *Schieffelin v. United States*, 424 F. 2d 1396 (U.S. CCPA, 1970).

11. See cases cited in Jackson, Davey, and Sykes, supra note 1, 456–458.

12. See supra note 2, 2. Cf. *John T. Bill Co. v. United States*, Court of Customs and Patent Appeals, 104 F. 2d 67, 26 CCPA (Customs) 67 (1939).

13. See Gerard Curzon, *Multilateral Commercial Diplomacy* (London: Michael Joseph, 1965), 67–68, quoting John Evans, director of Commercial Policy of GATT in 1956, from a speech given at the Bologna Center of the School of Advanced International Studies of Johns Hopkins University, 20 February 1956; see also Jackson, "Equality and Discrimination in International Economic Law (xi): The General Agreement on Tariffs and Trade," supra note 1 at 231 et seq. See also supra note 2.

14. If, however, both A and X are GATT members, or for other reasons have granted each other MFN treatment, a legal issue arises, which I discuss in section 6.5.

15. This was an important issue in one of the earliest GATT cases: German Sardines, GATT, BISD, 1 Supp. 53-59 (1953). See also GATT Analytical Index, (Geneva: GATT, 1995).

16. Belgian Family Allowances, GATT, BISD, 1 Supp. 59 (1953).

17. See Jackson, Davey, and Sykes supra note 1, 467, and Spanish Coffee, GATT, BISD 28 Supp. 103 (1982).

18. Michel M. Kostecki, "Export-restraint Arrangements and Trade Liberalization," *World Economy* 10 (1987), 425, 429.

19. See supra sections 5.3 and 6.2.

20. See Jackson, *World Trade* supra note 1, section 11.5; Article I:2 and 3 and Annex A–F to the agreement.

21. See infra chapter 7.

22. See infra section 6.5.

23. See supra section 2.4.

24. See supra section 2.4.

25. 1965 United States-Canadian Automotive Products Agreement, 17 UST 1372, TIAS No. 6093; see also Stanley D. Metzger, "The United States-Canadian Automotive Products Agreement of 1965," *Journal of World Trade Law* 1 (1967), 103.

26. The Caribbean Basin Initiative was established under the Caribbean Basin Economic Recovery Act, 19 USC §§2701–2706; 19 CFR §§10.191–10.198 (1985). Cf. GATT, BISD, 31 Supp. 20 (1985) where GATT CONTRACTING PARTIES granted the United States a waiver for the program. See W. Charles Sawyer and Richard L. Sprinkle, "Caribbean Basin Economic Recovery Act," *Journal of World Trade Law* 18 (1984), 429; Bruce Zagaris, "A Caribbean Perspective of the Caribbean Basin Initiative," *International Law* 18 (1984), 563. See also infra Section 12.1.

27. *Differential and More Favorable Treatment, Reciprocity and Fuller Participation of Developing Countries*, GATT, BISD, 26 Supp. 203 (1980). See generally Abdulgawi A. Yusuf, "Differential and More Favorable Treatment: The GATT Enabling Clause," *Journal of World Trade Law* 14 (1980), 488; Bela Balassa, "The Tokyo Round and the Developing Countries," *Journal of World Trade Law* 14 (1980), 93. See also chapter 13.

28. See infra chapter 9.

29. See infra section 9.3.

30. See infra section 7.7.

31. See infra section 10.1.

32. See infra chapter 13.

33. See infra chapter 13.

34. In a customs union, customs duties between the parties are eliminated and a common tariff with regard to third countries is adopted by all parties to the union. In a free trade area, the parties eliminate tariffs as between themselves but not adopt a common external tariff. Free trade areas are therefore prone to a type of trade diversion where goods from third countries enter the free trade area at the point of the lowest external tariff and then move to their ultimate destination within the free trade area duty free. This can be dealt with by differential and more strict rules of origin.

35. Kenneth W. Dam, "Regional Economic Arrangements and the GATT: The Legacy of a Misconception," *University of Chicago Law Review* 30 (1963), 615; Jackson, *World Trade*, supra note 1, chapter 9.4.

36. Article XXIV of GATT, particularly XXIV, paragraph 8, which provides that a "customs union" is understood to mean the "substitution of a single customs territory for two or more customs territories, so that ... duties and other restrictive regulations ... are eliminated with respect to substantially all the trade between the constituent territories, ... and, substantially the same duties and other regulations of commerce are applied by each of the members of the union to the trade of territories not included in the union."

With respect to the "free trade area," the definition in paragraph 8 of Article XXIV reads that it shall be understood to mean "a group of two or more customs territories in which the duties and other restrictive regulations of commerce ... are eliminated on substantially all the trade between the constituent territories in products originating in such territories."

37. See GATT *Analytical Index*, supra note 15, Article XXIV, 818. See also supra note 35; Edmond McGovern, *International Trade Regulation* (Exeter: Globefield Press, 2d ed., 1986), 262.

38. "Findings and Conclusions of GATT Panel on EC Bananas Imports," Special Report Inside U.S. Trade, 4 June 1993; and EEC-Import Regime for Bananas, GATT Panel Report, 18 January 1994, ILM No.1, Vol. 34, January 1995, 180.

39. See supra section 6.1.

40. The preference-giving developed countries also will have special (law) tariff rates for certain products from developing countries. In addition, special rules of origin may apply to certain *products*—for example, textiles (see 19 CFR §§12.130–.131 [1985]). See also note, "The 1984 'Country of Origin' Regulations for Textile Imports: Illegal Administrative Action Under Domestic and International Law," *Georgia Journal of International and Comparative Law* 14 (1984), 573.

41. The International Convention on the simplification and harmonization of Customs procedures (signed at Kyoto, 18 May 1973, entered into force 25 September 1974).

42. The Senate gave its advice and consent to the convention on 21 June 1983 (see *Congressional Record* 129 [1983] S8803 and 8814; *U.S. Import Weekly* 8 [1983]), 535). The U.S. instrument of accession was deposited with the Customs Cooperation Council on 8 October 1983, and entered into force for the United States on 28 January 1984.

43. See chapter 3 of the U.S.-Canada Free Trade Agreement, *International Legal Materials* 27 (1988), 281. The rules were implemented in the United States by Section 202 of the U.S.-Canada Free Trade Agreement Implementation Act of 1988, Pub. L. 100-449; 102 Stat. 1856. For some statements critical of the rules of origin, see *International Trade Reporter* 4 (1987), 1579 and 5 (1988), 576 and 953.

44. See part 2, chapter 4, Articles 401–415 of the North American Free Trade Agreement.

45. Agreement on Rules of Origin in John H. Jackson, William J. Davey, and Alan O. Sykes *1995 Documents Supplement to Legal Problems of International Economic Relations* 3d ed. (St. Paul: West, 1995), 235.

46. Thus, the EC preferential rules generally focus on whether the four-digit tariff classification number of the product changes, although there are many special exceptions. On EC rules of origin, see Jan S. Forrester, "EEC Customs Law: Rules of Origin and Preferential Duty Treatment," *European Law Review* 5 (1980), 167, 257.

47. See Trade Act of 1974, supra note 8, section 503; 19 USC §2463 (1980 and Supp. 1988); 19 CFR §§10.171–178 (1985).

48. U.S. Department of Commerce, *EEC and EFTA Rules of Origin Governing Preferential Trade* (Overseas Business Reports, OBR 74-04 (April 1974).

49. Article 403 on Automotive Goods, North American Free Trade Agreement (NAFTA), entered into force January 1, 1994. See also: Sabrena A. Silver, *"NAFTA's Rules of Origin for Automobiles: A Need for Reform," Fordham Law Review*, May 1994, Vol. 62, No. 7, p. 2245. See also Jonathan Cooper, *"NAFTA's Rules of Origin and Its Effect on the North American Automotive Industry," North Western Journal of Int'l Law and Business*, Winter 1994, Vol. 14, No. 2, 442.

50. Briefing Materials Prepared for Use of the Committee. On the Subject of Foreign Trade and Tariffs, House Ways and Means Committee, 93d Cong., 1st Sess., 1973, 189–190.

51. See supra section 6.3.

52. *Canada/United States Agreement on Automotive Products*, GATT, BISD 13 Supp., 112, 119 (1965); *United States—Imports of Automotive Products*, GATT, BISD 14 Supp., 181, 185 (1965). See also Jackson, Davey, and Sykes, supra note 1, section 7.4(B).

53. See supra chapter 3.

54. See supra section 6.3 and infra chapter 13. See Rachel McCulloch, "United States Preferences: The Proposed System," *Journal of World Trade Law* 8 (1974), 216, at para. 217. The original U.S. GSP scheme was authorized by Title V of the 1974 trade act and most recently renewed in the Trade and Tariff Act of 1984, Pub. L. 98-573; 98 Stat. 3109; 19 USCA §2462 et seq. (1980 and Supp. 1988).

55. See infra chapter 13.

56. See supra section 6.5 and infra section 11.2; see also John H. Jackson, Jean-Victor Louis, and Mitsuo Matsushita, *Implementing the Tokyo Round* (Ann Arbor: University of Michigan Press, 1984), 171–172.

57. See, for example, *International Trade Reporter* 2 (1985), 474. NTT purchases equipment from U.S. suppliers (see *International Trade Reporter* 3 [1986], 710). This purchase, however, was not then repeated and there was some indication that NTT resumed its "buy Japanese" policy (see *Business Week*, 13 June 1988, 46). See also Timothy J. Curran, "Politics and High Technology: The NTT Case," in *Coping with U.S.-Japanese Economic Conflicts*, Mac Destler and Hideo Sato, eds. (Lexington, MA: Lexington Books, 1982), 185–241.

58. In 1977 the Trade Facilitation Committee was established with the aim of assisting U.S. firms to gain access to Japanese Markets. The bilateral committee was staffed by members of the U.S. Department of Commerce and the Japanese Ministry of International Trade and Industry. In September 1981, a bilateral subcabinet body called the U.S.-Japan Trade Subcommittee was established to monitor and review broad-ranging trade policy issues. There are also numerous other sector-specific groups operating under the general rubric of Market-Oriented Sector Selective (MOSS). These aim to deal with specific industry issues. See also General Accounting Office *U.S.-Japan Trade/Interim Report on Sector Selective Agreements* (Washington, DC: U.S. Government Printing Office, 1987).

59. Japanese Measures on Leather, GATT, BISD 26 Supp. 320 (1979); see also *U.S Export Weekly* 401 (1982) 768; *U.S. Import Weekly* 8 (1983), 136.

60. S. Hrg. 99-624, Senate Finance Committee, 99th Cong. 1st. Sess., 1985, 11 and 41–42.

61. Remarks by the President to Business Leaders and Members of the President's Export Council and Advisory Committee for Trade Negotiations (ibid., 18, 20).

62. See *International Trade Reporter* 1 (1984), 625. See also the statements of Treasury Secretary James A. Baker, Department of the Treasury, *Treasury News*, B-1277, 5. See also *International Trade Reporter* 5 (1988), 620.

63. Reciprocal Trade and Investment Act of 1982, amendment to the Trade Act of 1974, S.2094, 97th Cong., 2d Sess. (1982); Reciprocal Trade and Investment Act of 1982, Committee on Finance, U.S. Senate, S. Rep. No. 97-483, 97th Cong., 2d Sess., 1982.

64. *Heavyweight Motorcycles and Engines and Power Train Subassemblies Therefore*, 201-TA-47, USITC Pub. 1342 (1983). The president granted temporary import relief (Proclamation 5050,

15 April 1983, *Federal Register* 48 [1983], 16639), but this was terminated in 1987 (Proclamation 5727, 14 October 1987, *Federal Register* 52 [1987], 38075).

65. "Tentative Steel Agreement Reached by U.S. Commerce Department and European Community Negotiators," *U.S. Import Weekly* 141 (1982), 620.

66. Caribbean Basin Economic Recovery Act of 1983, Pub. L. No. 98-67, 97 Stat. 384 (1983); "Democracy and the Path to Economic Growth, Address by Secretary George Schultz," *Department of State Bulletin* 85 (January 1985), 1; Bruce Stokes, "Reagan's Caribbean Basin Initiative on Track But Success Still in Doubt," *National Journal* 17 (1985), 206.

67. *International Trade Reporter* 1 (1984), 540 and 624. See also the U.S.-Israel Free Trade Agreement, signed on 22 April 1985 and entered into force on 19 August 1985 (*International Legal Materials* 24 [1985] 653), implemented in the United States by the United States-Israel Free Trade Area Implementation Act of 1985, Pub. L. 99-47, 99 Stat. 82; 19 USC §2112b.

68. See William Diebold, *Bilateralism, Multilateralism, and Canada in US Trade Policy* (Cambridge, MA: Ballinger, 1988). Cf. *Canada not for Sale: The Case Against Free Trade* (Toronto: General Paperbacks, 1987).

69. John H. Jackson, "Regional Trade Blocs and GATT" 16 *The World Economy*, No. 2 (March 1993), 121–131.

Chapter 7

1. See generally John H. Jackson, *World Trade and the Law of GATT* (Indianapolis: Bobbs-Merrill, 1969), 553; Alan Wolff, "The Need for New GATT Rules to Govern Safeguard Action," in *Trade Policy in the 1980s*, William Cline, ed. (Washington, DC: Institute for International Economics, 1983), 363.

2. See generally John H. Jackson, William Davey, and Alan Sykes *Legal Problems of International Economic Relations* (St. Paul: West, 3d. ed., 1995), chapter 13. See also infra section 9.2.

3. See Jackson, Davey, and Sykes, supra note 2, chapter 13.

4. See Senate Rep. No. 93-1298, infra note 14.

5. See Robert Lawrence and Robert Litan, *Saving Free Trade: A Pragmatic Approach* (Washington, DC: Brookings Institution, 1986), chapter 2.

6. Ibid. See also the 1982 Job Training Partnership Act, intended in part for dislocated workers, Pub. L. 97-300 Stat. 1322.

7. See, for example, Mancur Olsen, *The Rise and Decline of Nations* (New Haven, CT: Yale University Press, 1982). See also Ingo Walter, "Structural Adjustment Trade Policy in the International Steel Industry," in *Trade Policy for the 1980s*, supra note 1, 483.

8. This argument is invoked by union representatives, such as those for the United Auto Workers (UAW). See statement of Douglas A. Fraser, UAW vice president, Trade Adjustment Assistance the House Committee on Foreign Affairs, 92d Cong., 2d sess. (1972).

9. See infra section 7.6.

10. See Alexis Jacquemin, ed., *European Industry: Public Policy and Corporate Strategy* (Oxford: Clarendon Press, 1984).

11. Note the structure of the 1974 trade act, infra note 14, where Title II deals with "fair trade" and Title III deal with "unfair trade." See Sections 201, 301, 341 (88 Stat. 2011, 2041, 2053). See also infra chapter 10.1.

12. See Jackson, Davey, and Sykes, supra note 2, 666–668. See also infra section 10.1.

13. It is possible that the steel Section 301 petition in 1983 may have been brought partly for this reason, although in the end the executive branch referred the case to the International Trade Commission under the escape clause provisions (see infra Section 10.1, fn. 3.). See *Twenty-Sixth Annual Report of the President of the United States on the Trade Agreements Program*, 11981-82, 196.

14. Trade Act of 1974, Title IV, Section 406, Pub. L. No. 93-618, 88 Stat. 2062 (1975); Trade Reform Act of 1973, S. Rep. 93-1298, Senate Finance Committee, 93d Cong., 2d Sess., 1974, 210–213, reprinted in *U.S. Code Congressional and Administrative News* 4 (1974), 7186.

15. See infra chapters 10 and 11.

16. Amended Tariff Act of 1930: Reciprocal Trade Agreements, H. Rep. No. 73-1000, House Ways and Means Committee, 13–14 (1934).

17. Reciprocal Trade Agreement with Mexico, 23 December 1942, Art. XI, 57 Stat. 833 (1943); E.A.S. No. 311 (effective Jan. 30, 1943); Hearings on the Extension of the Reciprocal Trade Act House Ways and Means Committee, 79th Cong., 1st Sess., 1945, 277, 280. See Jackson, supra note 1, 663 et seq.

18. See Jackson, supra note 1, *World Trade*, chapters 2 and 23; William Diebold, *The End of the ITO* (Princeton, NJ: Princeton University, 1952).

19. See Executive Order 9832 of 25 February 1947, §3 CFR §634 (1947). See also Trade Agreements Extension Act of 1951, ch. 141; 65 Stat. 74. For a general history of the U.S. escape clause, see Jackson, supra note 1, 553–555, and Jackson, Davey, and Sykes, supra note 2, 541 et seq.

20. Ibid., 541.

21. See Jackson, supra note 1, chapter 23. See also Jackson, Davey, and Sykes, supra note 2, 27.2.

22. *Avoidance of Market Disruption*, GATT, BISD, 9 Supp. 26-28 (1961).

23. The United States escape clause is contained in Section 201 of the Trade Act of 1974, supra note 14, as amended by the Trade Agreements of 1979, Pub. L. No. 96-39, §§106(b)(3), 1106(a)(1)–(7), 93 Stat. 193, 312; and the Trade and Tariff Act of 1984, Pub. L. No. 98-573, §§248(a), 249, 98 Stat. 2998 codified in 19 USC § 2251 (1980 and Supp. 1988). The main EC escape clause is Council Regulation (EC) 288/82, OJ (1982) L.35/1.

24. The only change in the language of the escape clause in GATT, Article XIX, was as follows: (1) In paragraph 1(a), "relatively" had been inserted between "such" and "increased" in the Havana Charter, but it was not included in GATT Article XIX; and (2) In the ninth session, "obligations or concessions" was substituted for "concessions or other obligations" in paragraph 3. GATT *Analytical Index*, Guide to GATT Law and Practice (Geneva: WTO, 6th ed., 1995), 516.

25. The text of Article XIX, 1(a) reads: "If, as a result of unforeseen developments and of the obligations incurred by a contracting party under this agreement, including tariff concessions, any product is being imported into the territory of that contracting party in such

increased quantities and under such conditions as to cause or threaten serious injury to domestic producers in that territory of like or directly competitive products, the contracting party shall be free, in respect of such product, and to the extent and for such time as may be necessary to prevent or remedy such injury, to suspend the obligation in whole or in part or to withdraw or modify the concession." GATT, BISD, Vol. IV, Article XIX, 1(a) (1969).

26. See infra chapters 10 and 11.

27. In contrast to United States administrative and judicial practice, there are very few interpretations of Article XIX in the GATT documentation. *See* GATT, *Analytical Index*, supra note 24.

28. This is especially true of the 1980 U.S. escape clause in the concerning automobiles. *See Certain Motor Vehicles and Certain Chassis and Bodies Thereof*, Inv. (TA-201-44), USITC Pub. No. 1110 (1980).

29. The 1974 Trade Act speaks of factors which must be considered, but is worded so as not to confine the ITC attention to the factors listed. The legislative history notes that "it is not intended that a mathematical test be applied by the Commission." S. Rep. No. 93-1298, supra note 14, 120. See also Walter Adams and Joel B. Dirlam, "Import Competition and the Trade Act of 1974: A Case Study of Section 201 and Its Interpretation by the International Trade Commission," *Indiana Law Journal*, 52 (1977), 535, 539–540.

30. See supra note 28. However, the attempt by the American automobile industry to obtain protection from import competition did not end with the negative ITC determination. Legislation introduced in the U.S Congress to authorize a VRA in the automobile sector and to impose quotas or automobile imports from Japan was not pushed after an exchange of letters between U.S. Attorney General Smith and Japanese Ambassador Okawara, whereby the Japanese government agreed to unilaterally restrain the export of cars to the United States. See Jackson, Davey, and Sykes, supra note 2, 630–635. See also David Tarr and Morris Morkre, *Aggregate Costs to the United States of Tariff Cuts and Removal of Quotas on Imports: General Tariff Cuts and Removal of Quotas on Automobiles, Steel, Sugar and Textiles* (Washington, DC: Federal Trade Commission, 1984).

31. See supra chapter 3.

32. One of the significant issues in the drafting of the Trade Act of 1974 was how much discretion to give the president to depart from the findings or recommendations of the ITC. The 1974 Act tried to achieve a balance between those who wanted more and those who wanted no presidential discretion. Thus, the president was given the right to decline to order relief "in the national economic interest." Section 203, however, established a legislative veto in order to check (override) the presidential decision. After the Chadha case, Congress replaced the veto with a provision that enables Congress to override the president (two-thirds of the votes of each House required) and cause the recommendation of the ITC to come into effect by adapting a joint resolution to that effect. See Jackson, Davey, and Sykes, supra note 2, section 13.3.

33. Information concerning such actions can be obtained from the ITC *Annual Report* and from the annual report, *Operation of the Trade Agreements Program*, also issued by the ITC.

34. *Carbon and Certain Steel Alloy Products* (TA-201-51), USITC Pub. No. 1533 (1984). The petition was brought by the United Steelworkers of America, AFL-CIO and Bethlehem Steel Corporation on 24 January 1984. On June 12, 1984, the ITC (by a 3 to 2 decision) voted that the domestic steel industry was injured with respect to plates, sheets and strip, wire and wire products, structural shapes and units, ingots, blooms, billets, slabs, sheet, and sheet bars.

They also found that the domestic industry was *not* injured with respect to wire-rods, railway-type products, bars, pipes and tubes and blanks thereof. On 11 July 1984, the ITC recommended to the president that quotas be imposed for over a five-year period. The president rejected the proposed form of relief, and instead directed USTR Brock to negotiate VRAs with foreign governments.

35. "Steel Import Relief: Memorandum from the President, September 18, 1984," *Weekly Compilation of Presidential Documents* 20 (1984), 1307. See Jackson, Davey, and Sykes, Op. cit. supra note 2, at p. 1195, section 26.5.

36. GATT, *Analytical Index*, supra note 24, XIX-27.

37. See infra section 5.5.

38. See infra section 7.7. See also the articles by Jackson, Kostecki, and Petersmann, infra note 97.

39. For details of the U.S. law resulting from administrative and court opinions on these subjects, see in particular *International Trade Reporter Decisions* (BNA, biweekly), which contains both the ITC and CIT administrative decisions. With respect to Section 201, see Section 58 in the Classification Guide.

40. See supra note 25 for the text of Article XIX: 1(a).

41. See supra note 39. Regarding product definition, see 58.07. Regarding limitations on relief, see 58.121.

42. See *Report on the Withdrawal by the United States of a Tariff Concession Under Article XIX of the GATT (the Hatter's Fur Case)* (Geneva, GATT/151-3, 1951); Jackson, supra note 1, 560; Jackson, Davey, and Sykes, supra note 2.

43. Jackson, supra note 1, 563.

44. Ibid., 201–211.

45. See supra note 14. See also Jackson, Davey, and Sykes, supra note 2, 604–610, 641–642.

46. *Modifications to the General Agreement*, Working Party Report, GATT BISD, Vol. II, 39, 44–45 (1952); Jackson, supra note 1, 557–559; Jackson, Davey, and Sykes, supra note 2; GATT, *Analytical Index*, supra note 24, 6th revision, 1995, 515.

47. The Omnibus Trade and Competitiveness Act of 1988, Pub. L. 100-418, Title I, Subtitle D, Part 1, 102 Stat. 1225-1241; H. Rpt. 100-40, Pt. 1, House Ways and Means Committee, 100th Cong., 1st Sess., 1987; S. Hrg. 100-419, Pt. 1, Senate Finance Committee, 100th Cong., 1st Sess., 1987. See also *Proposals to Reform the Escape Clause*, S. Hrg. 99-898, Senate Finance Committee, 99th Cong., 2d Sess., 1986. For a brief commentary, see Alan Holmer and Judith H. Bello, "The 1988 Trade Bill: Is it Protectionist?" *International Trade Reporter* 5 (1988), 1347, 1350–1351.

48. See *United States International Economic Policy in an Interdependent World*, supra note 3, volume 1, 49. See also *Administration Analysis of the Proposed Trade Reform Act of 1973*, House Ways and Means Committee, 93d Cong., 1st Sess., *1973; Press Release and Other Materials Relating to the Administration Proposal Entitled the "Trade Reform Act of 1973," including the Message of the President, Text, Summary, and Section-by-Section Analysis of the Proposed Bill*, HR 6767, 70-72 (1973); Jackson, Davey, and Sykes, supra note 2, 604–610.

49. See supra note 14, Section 201(b)(1), (4), 19 USC §2551(b)(1), (4). See, for example, *Certain Motor Vehicles* (TA-201-44), USITC Pub. No. 1110 (1980); *Heavyweight Motorcycles*

(TA-201-47), USITC Pub. No. 1342 (1983); *Non-Rubber Footwear* (TA-201-50), USITC Pub. No. 1545 (1984); *Non-Rubber Footwear* (TA-201-55), USITC Pub. No. 1717 (1985).

50. See *Certain Motor Vehicles* and *Heavyweight Motorcycles*, supra note 49.

51. Jackson, supra note 1, 566–567; Jackson, Davey, and Sykes, supra note 2, 604–610.

52. Other injury tests in United States law include: the "market disruption" phase in the Trade Act of 1974, supra note 14, Title IV, Sec. 406(e)(2); the original provision for trade adjustment assistance, "contributed importantly," in the Trade Act of 1974, supra note 14, Title II, Sec. 222; and the provisions of Section 337 which use, "to destroy or substantially injure an industry," supra note 14, Title III, Section 341(a). See also the "material injury" standard in antidumping and countervailing duty proceedings, infra chapters 10 and 11.

53. See supra note 14, Title II, Section 201(a)(2)(A), which mentions the significant idling of productive facilities in the industry, the inability of a significant number of firms to operate at a reasonable level of profit, and significant unemployment or underemployment within the industry. This list is not exhaustive.

54. See generally Jackson, supra note 1, chapter 23; Jackson, Davey, and Sykes, supra note 2, 13.3.

55. See supra note 25 for the full text of GATT Article XIX, 1(a).

56. See Jackson, supra note 1, Section 10.6; Jackson, Davey, and Sykes, supra note 2, 387 et seq.

57. See infra chapter 7.5.

58. See *Norwegian Restrictions on Hong Kong Textile Imports*, GATT, BISD, 27 Supp., 119, at 125 (1981). For United States escape-clause cases where quotas were imposed, see *Clothespins*, (TA-201-36), USITC Pub. No. 933 (1978); "Clothespins Imports," Proclamation 4640, *Weekly Compilation of Presidential Documents* 15 (1979) 325; *Heavyweight Motorcycles*, supra note 49; "Imports of Heavyweight Motorcycles," Proclamation 5050, *Weekly Compilation of Presidential Documents*, 19 (1983) 550; *Stainless Steel and Alloy Tool Steel*, (TA-201-48), USITC Pub. No. 1377 (1983); "Imports of Specialty Steel," Proclamation 5074, *Weekly Compilation of Presidential Documents* 19 (1983), 1023.

59. See supra note 14, section 203.

60. See supra note 47, Title I, Subtitle D, Part 3.

61. Charles P. Kindleberger, *International Economics* (Homewood, IL: Irwin, 5th ed., 1973), 107–110, 122–123; Marco C. E. J. Bronckers, "The Non-Discriminatory Application of Article XIX GATT: Fact or Fiction," *Legal Issues of European Integration* (1981/2), 39; Marco C. E. J. Bronckers, "Reconsidering the Non-Discrimination Principle As Applied to GATT Safeguard Measures: A Rejoinder," *Legal Issues of European Integration*, (1982/3), 114. See generally Bo Sodersten, *International Economics* (New York: St. Martin's Press, 2d. ed., 1980).

62. GATT, *Analytical Index*, supra note 24, 6th revision, 1995, 933. In 1983, Brian Hindley ("Voluntary Export Restraints and the GATT's Main Escape Clause," *World Economy* 3 [1980], 313, n.25) pointed out that a West German restriction under Article XIX was still in force even though it was begun in 1958.

63. See supra note 14, section 203(h)(1).

64. See Jackson, supra note 1, 565–566; Jackson, Davey, and Sykes, supra note 2, 652–654.

65. See infra section 7.8 and OECD, *Policy Perspective for International Trade and Economic Relations* (Paris: OECD, 1972), 81–84 (the "Rey" Report).

66. Supra note 23, section 123. See also Marco C. E. J. Bronckers, *Selective Safeguard Measures in Multilateral Trade Relations* (Boston: Kluwer, 1985), chapter 3. See also *U.S. Import Weekly* 9 (1983), 305.

67. See Trade Expansion Act of 1962, and other negotiating authorities. See supra section 5.2.

68. See supra note 14. See also Jackson, Davey, and Sykes, supra note 2, 652–654.

69. See supra chapters 1 and 3.

70. See *Article XIX—Action by the United States—Specialty Steel—Extension of Time-Limit* (as to Austria, Korea, Brazil, Sweden, and Japan), GATT Doc. L/5524/Adds. 44–49 (1985); *Article XIX—Action by Canada—Footwear, other than Footwear of Rubber or Canvas,* GATT L/4611/Add.50 (1985). See also GATT *Analytical Index,* supra note 24.

71. *Fair Practices in Automotive Products Act of 1982,* H.R. 5133, 97th Cong., 2d Sess., 1982; *Fair Practices in Automotive Products Act,* H.R. Rep. 97-842 Committee on Energy and Commerce, House of Representatives, 97th Cong., 2d Sess., 1982.

72. See Bronckers, supra note 66; Marco Bronckers, "The Non-Discriminatory Application of Article XIX GATT: Tradition or Fiction?", supra note 61; Mark Koulen, "The Non-Discriminatory Application of GATT Article XIX(1): A Reply," *Legal Issues of European Integration* (1983/2), 89; Marco Bronckers, "Reconsidering the Non-Discrimination Principle As Applied to GATT Safeguard Measures: A Rejoinder," *Legal Issues of European Integration,* supra note 61; Cf. Ernst-Ulrich Petersmann, "Economic, Legal and Political Functions of the Principle of Non-Discrimination," *World Economy* 9 (1986), 113. See also Hugh Corbet, "Reform of the GATT Provision for Emergency Protection" *EFTA Bulletin* 27 (1986), 1; Alan Wolff, supra note 1; Prem Kumar, "Critical Issues in the Talks on Emergency Protection," *World Economy* 5 (1982), 241; Patrizio Merciai, "Safeguard Measures in GATT," *Journal of World Trade Law* 15 (1981), 41; Jan Tumlir, A Revised Safeguard Clause for GATT, *Journal of World Trade Law* 7 (1973), 404.

73. Section 1102 of the Trade Act of 1974, supra note 14 authorized the President to sell import licenses at public auction. This applied inter alia to the Section 201 procedures. Section 1401 of the Omnibus Trade and Competitiveness Act of 1988, supra note 47 amends Section 203 to include at Section 203(a)(3)(F) the optional auction of quotas as an explicit presidential remedy. For the arguments for the use of such auctions, see C. Fred Bergsten, Kimberly Ann Elliott, Jeffrey J. Schott, and Wendy E. Takacs, *Auction Quotas and U.S. Trade Policy,* Policy Analyses in International Economics No. 19 (Washington, DC: Institute for International Economics, 1987). Cf. N. David Palmeter "Turkeys Masquerade as Peacocks," *Journal of Commerce* (10 June 1988). See also Alan V. Deardoff, "Safeguards Policy and Conservative Social Welfare Function," in *Protection and Competition in International Trade,* Henryk Kierzkowski, ed. (Oxford: Basil Blackwell, 1987), 22–40.

74. See *Heavyweight Motorcycles,* supra note 49; Bronckers, "Reconsidering the Non-Discrimination Principle As Applied to GATT Safeguard Measures: A Rejoinder," supra note 61, 117–120; Bronckers, supra note 66. 75. Of course, the problem of distinguishing "fair" and "unfair" trade, discussed supra chapter 7.1, is part of this question. See also infra section 10.1.

76. See articles, supra note 72, in particular the debate between Marco Bronckers and Mark Koulen, published in *Legal Issues of European Integration* [1983/2].

77. Havana (ITO) Charter, Interpretative Note, ad art. 40, at 65. See Jackson, supra note 1, 564, fn. 6.

78. GATT L/76 (1953); Marco Bronckers, "Reconsidering the Non-Discrimination Principle As Applied to GATT Safeguard Measures," supra note 61, 114–117.

79. Supra note 72. Regarding the concerns of the developing countries, see *The Tokyo Round of Multilateral Trade Negotiations: Report of the Director-General of GATT* (Geneva: GATT, 1980), 14–15. See also Gilbert Winham, *International Trade and the Tokyo Round Negotiation* (Princeton, NJ: Princeton University Press, 1985), 243–247.

80. Marco Bronckers, "Reconsidering the Non-Discrimination Principle As Applied to GATT Safeguard Measures," supra note 61, 130.

81. See supra note 74; *Artificial Fibers from the United States,* Commission Regulation (EEC) 388/80, OJ [1980] L45/5; Commission Regulation (EEC) 388/80, OJ [1980] L45/7; *Norwegian Restrictions on Hong Kong Textiles Imports,* GATT, BISD, 27 Supp. 119 (1981). See also Commission Regulation (EEC) 539/83, OJ [1983] L63/15 (EC restricted imports of certain textile products from Turkey, based on bilateral preferential agreement).

82. For example, in 1977, the United Kingdom introduced an annual quota on the import of portable television sets from South Korea (see GATT L/4613 [1977]). According to the GATT Secretariat at the time, "this case is the only one in the history of the GATT in which Article XIX action has unilaterally been taken on a discriminatory basis with regard to a simple source of supply in a fully transparent manner" (GATT L/4679, 10 et seq [1978]).

83. See *Norwegian Restrictions on Hong Kong Textile Imports,* GATT, BISD, 27 Supp. 119, 125 (1981). Note that the panel report was adopted by the contracting parties "in principle." See GATT, C/M/141, 11 (1980). This could cast some moderate doubt on the binding character of the panel report. See also Bronckers, supra note 66.

84. See *Twenty-Eighth Annual Report of the President of the United States on the Trade Agreements Program, 1984–5* (Washington, DC: Office of the USTR, 1986), 50–51.

85. Louis Henkin et al., *International Law* (St. Paul: West 3d ed., 1993), 78–82; Ian Brownlie, *Principles of Public International Law* (Oxford: Clarendon Press, 4th ed., 1990), 7–11.

86. See Bronckers, supra note 66, chapter 3. Cf. Petersmann, supra note 72.

87. Rodney R. Grey, A Canadian Comment on the Tokyo Round, in *Aides et Mesures de Sauveguarde En Droit International Economique* Seminaire de la Commission Droit et Vie des Affaires de l'Université de Liege (Paris: Feduci, Editions du Moniteur, 1979), 286–287.

88. Article 2 of Item 15 "Agreement on Safeguards" p. 295 of John H. Jackson, William J. Davey, and Alan O. Sykes, *1995 Documents Supplement to Legal Problems of International Economic Relations,* 3d ed. (St. Paul: West, 1995).

89. See supra section 7.1.

90. See generally Gary C. Hufbauer and Howard F. Rosen, *Trade Policies for Troubled Industries* (Washington, DC: Institute for International Economics, Policy Studies in International Economics No. 15, 1986); David Richardson, Worker Adjustment to U.S. International Trade, in *Trade Policy in the 1980s,* William Cline, ed. (Washington DC: Institute for International Economics, 1983), 393–424; Jackson, Davey, and Sykes, supra note 2, 660–665.

91. See David Richardson, "Worker Adjustment" supra note 90.

92. The working party was set up by the GATT council (GATT, C/M/144, 21 [1980]) as a result of the Report of the Consultative Group of Eighteen. The Working Party Report (L/5120 [1981]) was presented in 1981.

93. *Ministerial Declaration of 29 November 1982*, GATT, BISD 29 Supp. 9, 41 (1983).

94. Working Party on Structural Adjustment and Trade Policy, *Report to the Council*, GATT L/5568 (1983); Council of Representatives, *Report on Work Since the Thirty-ninth Session—Addendum*, GATT L/5734/Add. 1, 21-24 (1984).

95. See John Williamson, ed., *IMF Conditionality* (Washington, DC: Institute for International Economics, 1983).

96. See supra note 47.

97. See Ernst-Ulrich Petersmann, "Gray Area Measures and the Rule of Law," *Journal of World Trade* 22/2 (1988), 23; Michel Kostecki, "Export Restraint Arrangements and Trade Liberalization," *World Economy* 10 (1987), 425; John H. Jackson, "The GATT Consistency of Export Restraint Arrangements," *World Economy* 11 (1988), 485.

98. See Jan Tumlir, *Protectionism: Trade Policies in Democratic Societies* (Washington, DC: American Enterprise Institute, 1985), chapter 3, esp. 39–55; *Consumers Union v. Kissinger*, 506 F. 2d 136, 146–152 (1974), cert. denied, 421 U.S. 1004 (1975); *Safeguards*, chairman's report, GATT, BISD, 30 Supp. 216, 217-218 (1983); *Committee on Safeguards—Minutes of Meeting of 2 April 1982*, GATT Doc. L/5310 (1982).

99. See Jackson, Davey, and Sykes, supra note 2, 699–700, 1062–1107. See also Joel Davidow, "Cartels, Competition Laws and the Regulation of International Trade," *New York University Journal of International Law and Politics* 15 (1983) 351, 366–375.

100. Trade and Tariff Act of 1984, Title VII, Section 805, Pub. L. No. 98-573, 98 Stat. 2948, 3045 (1984); Steel Import Stabilization Act, H.R. Rep. No. 98-1089, House Ways and Means Committee, 98th Cong., 2d Sess., 1984; Trade Act of 1974, supra note 14, Title II, Section 201. See also Section 607 of the Trade Act of 1974, supra note 14, which contains a congressional grant of immunity from antitrust laws with respect to voluntary arrangements of steel.

101. See the exchange of letters, supra note 99. See also Harvey Applebaum, "The Antitrust Implications of Trade Law Proceedings," in *The Trade Agreements Act of 1979: Four Years Later* (New York: Practicing Law Institute, 1983), 33; OECD, *Competition and Trade Policies: Their Interaction* (Paris: OECD, 1984).

102. See exchange of letters, supra note 99; *Consumers Union v. Kissinger*, 506 F. 2d 136, 146–152 (1974), cert. denied, 421 U.S. 1004 (1975). See also Spencer Weber Waller "Redefin ing the Foreign Compulsion Defense in US Antitrust Law: The Japanese Auto Restraints and Beyond," *Law and Policy in International Business* 14 (1982), 747; Mitsuo Matsushita and Lawrence Repeta, "Restricting the Supply of Japanese Automobiles: Sovereign Compulsion or Sovereign Collusion?" *Case Western Reserve Journal of International Law* 14 (1982), 47.

103. See supra note 14, Title II, Section 203. This authority was used in "Specialty Steel," Presidential Proclamation No. 4445, *Federal Register* 41 (1976), 24101; "Nonrubber Footwear," Presidential Proclamation No. 4510, Federal Register 42 (1979), 32430; and "Color Television Receivers and Assemblies," Presidential Proclamation No. 4511, *Federal Register* 42 (1977), 32747.

104. Agricultural Act of 1956, Pub. L. No. 540, 70 Stat. 188 (1956).

105. GATT Article XI, BISD, Vol. IV (1969). For a discussion of Article XI, see Jackson, supra note 1, chapter 13; Jackson, Davey, and Sykes, supra note 2, section 8.4.

106. American Iron and Steel Section 301 complaint, *Federal Register* 41 (1976), 45628; Discontinuance of Investigation, *Federal Register* 43 (1978), 3962.

107. See also the 1982 American Iron and Steel Institute's Section 301 complaint. In that case, the USTR decided not to initiate an investigation. See *Federal Register* 48 (1093), 8878. The 1982 case is discussed in Bronckers, supra note 66, 195 et seq.

108. Concerning the economics of voluntary restraint agreements, see "Economic Effects of Export Restraints" USITC Pub. No 1256 (1982); Colleen Hamilton, Economic Aspects of Voluntary Export Restraints, in *Current Issues in International Trade*, Brian Greenaway, ed. (London: St. Martin's Press, 1985), 99–117; Tarr and Morkre, supra note 30.

109. The Short-Term Arrangement (1961–1962) and the Long-Term Arrangement (1962–1973) were the first attempts to deal with textiles. For an overview of the problem, see Henry R. Zheng, *Legal Structure of International Textile Trade* (Westport, CT: Quorum Books, 1988), chapter 1; William R. Cline, *The Future of World Trade in Textiles and Apparel* (Washington, DC: Institute for International Economics, 1987; Rev. ed. 1990).

110. *GATT Textiles and Clothing in the World Economy* (Geneva: GATT, 1984). See also *GATT A study on Cotton Textiles* (Geneva: GATT, 1966).

111. *Arrangement Regarding International Trade in Textiles* (MFA), GATT, BISD, 21 Supp. 3 (1975); 25 UST 1001; TIAS 7840. Regarding the protocols extending the MFA, see *MFA II*, GATT, BISD, 24 Supp. 5 (1978); *MFA III*, GATT, BISD 28 Supp. 3 (1982); and *MFA IV*, GATT, BISD 33 Supp. 7 (1987). See also Zheng, supra note 109, 8.

112. The speech was reported in the *New York Times*, 3 September 1960, 1 and 38. After his election, President Kennedy then issued a formal plan for textiles: see *New York Times*, 3 May 1961, 1.

113. However, the GATT report, supra note 110, paragraphs 1.6 to 1.8, notes that this argument only holds good as long as the production of textiles is dependent upon abundant low-skilled labor. The increased levels of automation in the textile industry have possibly moved the comparative advantage back to industrialized, developed countries. This conclusion seems to be partially supported by Ambassador Clayton Yeutter in an article in the *Washington Post*, 5 August 1987, reprinted in *Congressional Record* 134 (1988), S11134.

114. See GATT, *Analytical Index* (Geneva: GATT, 1995).

115. Cline, supra note 109, 158, 167, and 15.

116. *Declaration of Ministers*, GATT, BISD 20 Supp. 19, 21 (1973).

117. See *Report by the Director-General of GATT*, supra note 79, 14–17 and Annex C. See also Lesly Alan Glick, *Multilateral Trade Negotiations: World Trade After the Tokyo Round* (Totowa, NJ: Rowman and Allenheld, 1984), 112–126, 152, 157 and Appendix III; Winham, supra note 79, 123–125, 197–200, 240–247, 278–279.

118. *GATT Ministerial Declaration of 29 November 1982*, GATT, BISD 29 Supp. 12-13 (1982).

Chapter 8

1. Article III GATT, BISD, Vol. IV (1969). See, for example, John H. Jackson, *World Trade And The Law Of GATT* (Indianapolis Bobbs-Merrill, 1969), chapter 12; John H. Jackson,

William Davey, and Alan Sykes, *Legal Problems Of International Economic Relations* (St. Paul: West, 3rd ed., 1995), chapter 11.

2. See Pieter VerLoren van Themaat, *The Changing Structure of International Economic Law* (Boston: Nijhoff, 1981), 16 et seq., who notes that nondiscrimination clauses (in the sense of national treatment) were developed as early as the twelfth and thirteenth centuries, especially in the Hansa context. United States FCN treaties with a national treatment clause included Reciprocal Trade Agreement with Iceland, 27 August 1943, Art. II, 57 Stat. 1075, E.A.S. No. 342; Treaty of Friendship, Commerce, and Consular Rights with Finland, 13 February 1934, Art. VII, 49 Stat. 2659, T.S. No. 868; Treaty of Friendship, Commerce, and Consular Rights with Germany, 8 December 1923, Art. VIII, 44 Stat. 2132, T.S. 725.

3. The right of establishment is a critical concern with respect to the provision of services (although it may be important with respect to trade in goods). As such, right of establishment was an important issue in the service negotiations in the Uruguay Round. See Jonathan Aronson and Peter Cowhey, *Trade in Services: A Case for Open Markets* (Washington, DC: American Enterprise Institute, 1984), 25–26.

4. Our rough calculations indicate that of the 6123 disputes formally brought to GATT, 51 concern Article III. See list of some of these disputes in Robert Hudec, *The GATT Legal System And World Trade Diplomacy* (New York: Praeger, 1975); Jackson, supra note 1, chapter 12.3–12.4; and Jackson, Davey, and Sykes, supra note 1, 504–541.

5. See section 9.3.

6. See infra chapters 10 and 14.

7. See, in general, Jackson, supra note 1, section 12.3; Jackson, Davey, and Sykes, supra note 1, chapter 11.

8. *Italian Discrimination Against Imported Agricultural Machinery*, Report by the Panel, GATT, BISD 7 Supp. 60 (1959).

9. Ibid., paragraph 5.

10. *Canada: Administration of the Foreign Investment Review Act*, Report of the Panel, GATT, BISD 30 Supp. 140 (1984).

11. The following extract is from John H. Jackson, William J. Davey, and Alan O. Sykes, 1995 *Documents Supplement to Legal Problems of International Economic Relations*, 3d ed. (St. Paul: West, 1995), 173:

1. TRIMs that are inconsistent with the obligation of national treatment provided for in paragraph 4 of Article III of GATT 1994 include those which are mandatory or enforceable under domestic law or under administrative rulings, or compliance with which is necessary to obtain an advantage, and which require:
a) the purchase or use by an enterprise of products of domestic origin or from any domestic source, whether specified in terms of particular products, in terms of volume or value of products, or in terms of a proportion of volume or value of its local production; or
b) that an enterprise's purchases or use of imported products be limited to an amount related to the volume or value of local products that it exports.

12. See infra section 10.7.

13. *United States: Imports of Certain Automotive Spring Assemblies*, Report of the Panel, GATT, BISD 30th Supp. 107 (1984).

14. Panel Report, supra note 13, paragraph 66.

15. See Ross Denton, "The New Commercial Policy Instrument and *Akzo v. DuPont*" *European Law Review* 13 (1988), 3; Litowitz, "European Community Regulation No. 2641/84: A New Challenge to U.S. International Trade Commission's Section 337," *International Business and Trade Law Reporter* (1986), 3.

16. See *Schieffelin & Co. v. United States*, 424 F. 2d 1396 (CCPA, 1970); *Bercut-Vandervoort & Co. v. United States*, 46th Court of Customs and Patent Appeals, C.A.D. 691 (1958), cert. den., 359 U.S. 953, 79 S. Ct. 739, 3 L. Ed. 2d 760 (1959). See also Jackson, Davey, and Sykes, supra note 1, chapter 11.

17. In Schieffelin, the treaties involved were the Ireland-U.S. Treaty of Friendship, Commerce and Navigation of 1950, and the British-U.S. Treaty of Friendship, Commerce and Navigation of 1815. The Customs Court had accepted that the British imports were entitled under the MFN clause in the British treaty to whatever tax treatment was required with respect to imports of Irish origin.

18. See generally Jackson, Davey, and Sykes, supra note 1, section 11.2, 504.

19. See *Belgian Family Allowances (Allocations Familiales)*, GATT, BISD, 1 Supp. 59 (1953). Belgian law imposed a charge on foreign goods purchased by public bodies when these goods originated in a country whose system of family allowances did not meet certain requirements. The panel noted that this discrimination was inconsistent with the provisions of Article I "and possibly with those of Article III, paragraph 2." See Hudec, supra note 4, chapter 13.

20. United States—Taxes on Automobiles, Report of the Panel, GATT Document DS31/R, 29 September 1994; WTO Case: Japan—Taxes on Alcoholic Beverages, Report of the Appellate Body, WTO Document WT/DS8/AB/R of 4 October 1996.

21. See *Zenith Radio Corp. v. United States*, 437 U.S. 443, 98 S. Ct. 2441, 57 L. Ed. 2d 337 (1978). See also Jackson, Davey, and Sykes, supra note 1, 136.

22. See Annex I, Ad Article XVI, *General Agreement on Tariffs and Trade*, GATT, BISD, Vol. IV (1969): "The exemption of an exported product from duties or taxes borne by the like product when destined for domestic consumption, or the remission of such duties or taxes in amounts not in excess of those which have accrued, shall not be deemed to be a subsidy."

23. For example, Section 1101(b)(16) of the 1988 Trade Act (Omnibus Trade and Competitiveness Act of 1988, Pub. L. 100-418, 102 Stat. 1125.) states that a principal negotiating objective of the United States in the Uruguay Round regarding border taxes is "to obtain a revision of the GATT with respect to the treatment of border adjustments for internal taxes to redress the disadvantages of countries relying primarily for revenue on direct taxes rather than indirect taxes."

See also *Tax Adjustments in International Trade: GATT Provisions and EEC Practice*, Executive Branch GATT Study No. 1, 93d Cong., 1st Sess. 1973.

24. See, in general, Ballentine, "Uncertainty and the Short-Run Shifting of the Corporate Tax," *Oxford Economic Papers* 19 (1967), 95–110; J. Gregory Ballentine, *Equity, Efficiency and the U.S. Corporation Income Tax* (Washington, DC: American Enterprise Institute, 1980); Lawrence H. Goulder, John B. Shoven, and John Whalley, "Domestic Tax Policy and the Foreign Sector Formulations to Result from a General Equilibrium Tax Analysis Model," in *Behavioral Simulation Methods in Tax Policy Analysis*, Martin Feldstein, ed. (Chicago: University of Chicago Press, 1983), 333–364; Oswald Brownlee, *Taxing the Income form U.S. Corporation Investments Abroad* (Washington DC: American Enterprise Institute, 1980); Douglas Kahn and Pamela Gann, *Corporate Taxation and Taxation of Partnerships and Partners* (St. Paul: West, 3d ed., 1989).

25. See John Whalley, *Trade Liberalization among Major World Trading Partners* (Cambridge, MA: MIT, 1985).

26. *Zenith Electronics Corporation v. United States*, 633 F. Supp. 1385 (CIT 1986).

27. "Television Receivers from Japan; Final Results of an Antidumping Duty Administrative Review," *Federal Register* 53 (1988), 4050.

28. The following are some examples:

1. The French requirement that French inspectors inspect the source factory of any pharmaceutical sold in France, combined with the fact that French inspectors do not travel abroad (see *United States Export Weekly* 20 [1984], 953)

2. Belgian rules that margarine in Belgium must be sold in cubes, and not in oblong sticks, as in the rest of the Common Market (see, for example, Case 261/81, *Walter Rau Lebensmittelwerke v. De Smedt* PVBA [1982] ECR 3961, [1983] 2 CMLR 496)

3. German requirements that prevent importation of non-fizzy mineral water on the basis that such mineral water, as opposed to fizzy mineral water, does not help kill bacteria (see *The Economist* [23 June 1984], 29)

4. Pre-1983 Japanese practice of requiring "lot" or "unit" approval for imported products, while allowing "type" approval for Japanese-produced products.

(See John H. Jackson, Jean-Victor Louis, and Mitsuo Matsushita, *Implementing the Tokyo Round* [Ann Arbor: University of Michigan Press, 1984], 110.)

29. See Peter B. Edelman, "Japanese Product Standards as Non-Tariff Barriers: When Regulatory Policy Becomes a Trade Issue," *Stanford Journal of International Law* 24 (1988), 289; Jackson, Louis, and Matsushita supra note 28, 107–115.

30. *Agreement on Technical Barriers to Trade*, GATT, BISD, 26 Supp. 8 (1980), T.I.A.S. 9616, 31 U.S.T. 405. See R. W. Middleton "The GATT Standards Code," *Journal of World Trade Law* 14 (1980), 201; Robert E. Sweeney "Technical Analysis of the Technical Barriers to Trade Agreement," *Law and Policy in International Business* 12 (1980), 179; Jacques Nusbaumer "The GATT Standards Code in Operation" *Journal of World Trade Law* 18 (1984), 542.

31. Jackson, Davey, and Sykes, Item 5: Agreement on the Application of Sanitary and Phytosanitary Measures, p. 121 of 1995 Documents Supplement to *Legal Problems of International Economic Relations*, 3d ed. (St. Paul: West, 1995).

32. U.S. Statement of Administrative Action, Uruguay Round Agreements Act, p. 742–786.

33. *Analytical Index*, guide to GATT Law and Practice (1995), 1147.

34. Trade Agreements Act of 1979, Pub. L. 96-39, Title IV, 93 Stat. 242 et seq., 19 USC §2531 et seq. (1980 and Supp. 1988).

35. See Robert Stern, John H. Jackson, and Bernard Hoekman, *An Assessment of the Implementation and Operation of the Tokyo Round Codes*, 66–68 (Brookfield, VT: Gower, 1988). In the case involving metal bats from the United States, the United States claimed that Japanese "lot" inspection (see supra note 1) of American imports was discriminatory. A formal bilateral complaint was lodged in August 1982. In March 1983 the Japanese changed the law and permitted U.S. producers to obtain "type" approval. See Edelman, supra note 29, 406–410.

36. See particularly infra section 9.4.

37. Article III, par. 8 GATT, BISD, Vol. IV (1969). For example, paragraph 8(a) used the phrase "products purchased for governmental purposes." The question of what is a

"governmental purpose" can be very troublesome indeed. See, for a U.S. example, *Bethlehem Steel Corp. v. Board of Commissioners*, 276 Cal. App. 2d 221, 80 Cal. Rptr. 800 (1969).

38. See also supra chapter 6. Cf. Edmond McGovern, *International Trade Regulation* (Exeter: Globefield Press, 2d ed., 1986), 213.

39. Kenneth Dam, *The GATT: Law And International Economic Organization* (Chicago: University of Chicago Press, 1970), 199–200.

40. Ibid., 199. See Jackson, Davey, and Sykes supra note 1, 550–558; for a European view, Jacques Bourgeois, "Tokyo Round Agreements on Technical Barriers and on Government Procurement in International and EEC Perspective," *Common Market Law Review* 19 (1982), 5.

41. See Statement of Administrative Action in the U.S. President's submittal to Congress of the Uruguay Round Agreements, for approval (103rd Congress 2nd Session House Document 103-316, Vol. 1) at page 368 (of the SAA, which is page 1037 of the document), 1994. This SAA text lists those countries which had signed the 1996 Government Procurement Code, numbering ten plus the European Union and its member states.

42. For example, the complaint of the United States against EC deductions of value-added tax in calculating whether the contract value exceeds the threshold figure. See *Report of the Panel on Value-Added Tax and Threshold*, GATT, BISD, 31st Supp. 247 (1985). A second dispute concerned a French code-covered entity's procurement of a substantial number of microcomputers with allegedly Code-inconsistent procedures. The United States has proposed establishment of a working party to study the problem.

43. See, for example, *International Trade Reporter* 3 (1986), 1427.

44. Agreement on Government Procurement, Article II, paragraph 1, GATT BISD, 26th Supp. 33, 35 (1980).

45. In 1981 Fujitsu submitted a bid to supply fiberoptic cable to AT&T. When AT&T considered accepting the bid, which AT&T freely admitted was the lowest, Congressman Timothy Wirth wrote to the FCC pointing out the national security implications of such a purchase (*Wall Street Journal*, 19 October 1981, 26; *New York Times*, 12 December 1981, 33 and 34). AT&T later rejected Fujitsu's bid, and decided in favor of Western Electric, the manufacturing arm of AT&T (*New York Times*, 18 January 1983, D4). In 1982, however, MCI awarded a similar contract to Fujitsu (*Wall Street Journal*, 18 June 1982, 12).

46. On state "Buy American" acts, see Leslie Alan Glick, *Multilateral Trade Negotiations: World Trade After the Tokyo Round* (Totowa, NJ: Rowman and Allenheld, 1984), 138.

47. MTN Studies No. 6, Pt. 3, 96th Cong., 1st Sess. 233, 265 (1979).

48. McGovern, supra note 38, 213–219.

49. Sections 1 to 3 of Act of 3 March 1933, c.212 Title III, 47 Stat. 1520, are commonly known as the "Buy American" Act. See 41 USCA §102, (1980 and Supp. 1988); 41 CFR §1-61, 48 Federal Register 14899 (1983).

50. The president has set this cost difference at 6 percent, 48 C.F.R. §25.105.

Chapter 9

1. For example, the variable levy of the EC Common Agricultural Policy has been criticized as skirting the former rules of GATT. See John H. Jackson, William Davey, and Alan Sykes,

Legal Problems of International Economic Relations (St. Paul: West, 3d. ed., 1995), 1161–1173. An "import deposit" is another device. In addition, the extensive use of so-called "voluntary restraint arrangements" also skirts the formal rules of GATT. However, cf., John H. Jackson, "Export Restraints and the Law of GATT," *World Economy* 11 (1988), 485. For a general discussion of NTBs, see supra chapters 5 and 8.

2. See Peter Kenen, *The International Economy* (Englewood Cliffs, NJ: Prentice Hall, 1st ed., 1985), 167 et seq.

3. Article XXI(b), especially iii, GATT, BISD, Vol. IV (1969). See also John H. Jackson, *World Trade and the Law of GATT* (Indianapolis: Bobbs-Merrill, 1969), 748–752; Jackson, Davey, and Sykes, supra note 1, 983–990; Barry Carter, *International Economic Sanctions* (New York: Cambridge University Press, 1988); David D. Knoll, "The Impact of Security Concerns Upon International Economic Law," *Syracuse Journal of International Law and Commerce* 11 (1984), 567.

4. See, for example, Santon, "The National Security Exception to Free Trade," *Federal Business News and Journal* 30 (1983), 293, and Robert Reich, "Beyond Free Trade," *Foreign Affairs* 61 (1983), 773, 787.

5. In 1949, Czechoslovakia brought a complaint against the United States practices of export control licenses, see GATT CP.3/33 (1949); CP.3/38; CP.3/SR.22 (1949); CP.3/20 (1949). In 1961, Ghana imposed a ban on all imports from Portugal, invoking Article XXI, see GATT Doc. SR.19/12, at 196 (1961). The 1951 dispute between the United States and Czechoslovakia and the 1955 conflict between Peru and Czechoslovakia may also have involved Article XXI, see Jackson, supra note 3, 749–750. The 1985 dispute between the United States and Nicaragua is discussed infra notes 9 and 10.

6. This contrasts with the provisions of Article XXXV of GATT, which authorized any GATT contracting party to "opt out" of its relationship with any other GATT contracting party or prospective party, at one time only: the time at which one of the two parties enters GATT. There was no provision for such an "opt-out" at some subsequent point in time during GATT Membership.

7. GATT, BISD, Vol. II, 36 (1952). See Jackson, supra note 3, 749–750.

8. See cases cited supra note 5.

9. The embargo was imposed by Presidential Executive Order No. 12,513 of 1 May 1985 (*Federal Register* 50 [1985], 18629). See Richard S. Whitt, "The Politics of Procedure: An Examination of the GATT Dispute Settlement Panel and the Article XXI Defense in the Context of the US Embargo of Nicaragua," *Law and Policy in International Business* 19 (1987), 603.

10. A GATT panel report, presented to the Council on 6 November 1986, ruled that the U.S. embargo did not constitute a violation of GATT. The panel, however, noted that its mandate did not allow it to rule on whether the embargo was consistent with GATT law. The panel also noted that irrespective of Article XXI, the embargo was contrary to the basic objectives of GATT. See *International Trade Reporter* 3 (1986), 1368.

11. Export Administration Act of 1979, Pub. L. 96-72, 93 Stat. 503, as amended, Pub. L. 97-145, 95 Stat. 1727, and Pub. L. 99-64, 99 Stat. 120 (1985), 50 U.S.C. §2402.

12. See 50 U.S.C. §§2404(a), 2405(a); Jackson, Davey, and Sykes supra note 1, 941–972, 983–990.

13. Section 232 of the Trade Expansion Act of 1962, Pub. L. No. 87-794, 76 Stat. 872 et seq., 19 U.S.C. §1862 (1980 and Supp. 1988). See *Threat of Certain Imports to National Security,*

S. Hrg. 99-1041, Senate Finance Committee, 99th Cong., 2d sess., 1986. Section 1501 of the Omnibus Trade and Competitiveness Act of 1988 (Pub. L. 100-418, 102 Stat. 1257) amended 232 to shorten the period in which the president may respond to a petition. The secretary of commerce is also to notify and consult with the secretary of defense concerning any petition. See also Jackson, Davey, and Sykes, supra note 1, 983–990. Note also the case of machine tools. Following an investigation which concluded that imports of machine tools could affect U.S. national security, the president sought voluntary export restraints with the countries in question (statement by the president, 20 May 1986, Public Papers [1986], 661). The export-restraint agreements were announced in December 1986 (*Weekly Compilation of Presidential Documents* 22 [1986], 1654). See also *Operation of the Trade Agreements Program*, 38th Report, USITC Pub No. 1995 (1987), section 5-20.

14. See Section 232, op. cit. supra note 13 as amended in 1988.

15. L/6053, dated 13 October 1986 (unadopted), paras. 5.1–5.3.

16. John H. Jackson, William Davey, and Alan Sykes, *Documents Supplement to Legal Problems of International Economic Relations*, 3d ed. (St. Paul: West, 1995), 365, Item 17, Annex 1C, Agreement on Trade-Related Aspects of Intellectual Property Rights, Art. 73, and p. 316, Item 16, Annex 1B, General Agreement on Trade in Services, Article XIVbis.

17. Article XX GATT, BISD, Vol. IV (1969). See supra note 3, 741–747; Jackson, Davey, and Sykes, supra note 1, 519–520.

18. Article XIV of the General Agreement on Trade in Services, see supra note 16.

19. Article XX, GATT, BISD, Vol. IV (1969). See Jackson, supra note 3, 741–747.

20. Prohibition of Imports of Tuna Fish and Tuna Products from Canada, GATT, BISD 29 Supp. 91 (1983).

21. WTO Report of the Appellate Body, United States—Standards for Reformulated and Conventional Gasoline, AB-1996-1, WTO Document WT/DS2/AB/R of 29 April 1996, at page 25.

22. See infra section 10.7.

23. See supra note 13, Omnibus Trade and Competitiveness Act of 1988, Section 1301(a), amending section 301(d)(3)(B)(II). the pre-1988 version of section 301 has, however, been used to challenge the intellectual property policies (or lack thereof) of foreign governments. The most notable examples are Docket 301-49, "Brazilian Informatics Policy" (Federal Register, 51 [1986] 35993, 52 [1987] 1619, 4207 and 24971), Docket 301–61, "Brazilian Patent Protection of Pharmaceuticals" (*Federal Register* 52 [1987], 28223 and 53 [1988], 28100 and 30894), Docket 301-68, "Argentinean Intellectual Property Protection of Pharmaceuticals" (*Federal Register* 53 [1988], 37668), and Docket 305-32, "South Korean Patent Protection" (*Federal Register* 53 [1988], 22758).

24. See supra note 13, section 1342(a)(1).

25. See supra section 8.3.

26. See Charles Kindleberger, *International Economics* (Homewood, IL: Irwin, 5th ed., 1973), 53–69.

27. See, for example, Frederick L. Kirgis, "Effective Pollution Control in Industrialized Countries: International Economic Disincentives, Policy Responses, and the GATT," *Michigan Law Review* 70 (1972), 859, 889–895; Seymour Rubin and Thomas Graham, eds., *Environment and*

Trade: The Relation of International Trade and Environmental Policy (Totowa, NJ: Allanheld, Osmun, 1980).

28. Kirgis, supra note 27.

29. See, for example, *United States v. Canada* (Trail Smelter case), *United Nations Reports of International Arbitration Awards,* Vol. III, 1907 et seq. See also Emmanuel du Pontavice, "Compensation for Transfrontier Pollution Damage," in *Legal Aspects of Transfrontier Pollution Damage* (Paris: OECD, 1977), 409.

30. For example, the 1977 Berne Convention on the Protection of the Rhine Against Chemical Pollution; the 1975 Paris Convention for the Prevention of Marine Pollution from Land-Based Sources; the 1976 Barcelona Convention on the Protection of the Mediterranean Sea Against Pollution.

31. See infra chapter 11.

32. The United Nations Environment Program, established in 1972 as a coordinating agency, might play a role in international regulation or harmonization of pollution controls. Cf. Pieter VerLoren van Themaat, *The Changing Structure of International Economic Law* (The Hague: Martinus Nijhoff, 1981), 101–102.

33. United States—Restrictions on Imports of Tuna, Report of the Panel, GATT Doc. DS29/R, 16 June 1994, at par. 6.3. Also International Legal Materials, v.33, p. 839 (1994).

34. See, for example, Wolfgang Friedmann, *The Changing Structure of International Law* (New York: Columbia University Press, 1964), 40–45, 232–253.

35. See Jackson, supra note 1, at 8, 187, 402. See, on FCN Treaties, Eric V. Youngquist, "United States Commercial Treaties: Their Role in Foreign Economic Policy," *Studies in Law and Economic Development,* Vol. 2, Study No. 1, Washington, DC: George Washington University International Law Society, 1967.

36. During the 1960s, the British Steel Corporation offered a rebate to its customers if they certified that they had not used imported steel in their products. This was challenged by the US in the GATT and eventually the measure was withdrawn. More generally, see Kozo Yamamura, "Caveat Emptor: The Industrial Policy of Japan," in *Strategic Trade Policy and the New International Economics,* Paul Krugman, ed. (Cambridge, MA: MIT Press, 1986), 167–210, 180–181. The issue of loyalty rebates in order to prevent import penetration was raised in the massive *Zenith v. Matsushita* litigation. Such rebates, however, were also arguably assisted in the alleged predation of the U.S. market, secret rebates being a way of circumventing U.S. antidumping regulation. A criminal case was brought against Sears Roebuck for false declaration on customs documents since the price declared was overstated to the extent of the secret rebate received. See also *Dealers Wholesale Supply Inc. v. Pacific Steel and Supply Co., and Mitsui & Co. (USA), Inc.,* 1984-2 Trade Cas. P66, 109.

37. See "GM Switch: Will Now Buy Foreign Steel," *Dunn's Business Month* 125 (1985), 30.

38. *Final Act and Related Documents,* UN Conference on Trade and Employment, held at Havana, Cuba, from 21 November 1947 to 24 March 1948; Interim Commission for the International Trade Organization, Lake Success, New York, April 1948; UN Doc. E/Conf.2/78, (Chapter V of this charter, E/Conf.2/C.4/1-25, dealt with restrictive business practices); Havana Charter for an International Trade Organization, U.S. Dept. of State Commercial Policy Series 114 Pub. No. 3117, 1948.

39. *Proposal of Denmark, Norway, Sweden,* GATT L/283 (1954). Proposal of West Germany, GATT L/261/Add.1, 41 (1954). See also *Restrictive Business Practices* (Geneva: GATT, 1959). See also Jackson, supra note 3, 522–527.

40. *OECD Guidelines for Multinational Enterprises* (OECD: International Investment and Multilateral Enterprises, rev. ed., 1979) as amended. Robert Grosse, "Codes of Conduct for Multinational Enterprises," *Journal of World Trade Law* 16 (1982), 414. See also the UN Draft Code of Conduct for Transnational Corporations, *International Legal Materials* 24 (1984), 624.

41. The Set of Multilaterally Agreed Equitable Principles and Rules for the Control of Restrictive Business Practices, U.N. Doc. TD/RBP/10 (1980). See Philippe Brusick, "UN Control of Restrictive Business Practices," *Journal of World Trade Law* 17 (1983) 337; Debra Miller and Joel Davidow, "Antitrust at the U.N.: A Tale of Two Codes," *Stanford Journal of International Law* 18 (1982), 347.

42. See supra note 22, Section 1301(a), amending Section 301(d)(3)(B)(III).

43. On the IMF, see, in general, Jackson, Davey, and Sykes, supra note 1, 282–288; Kenneth Dam, *The Rules of the Game: Reform and Revolution in the International Monetary System* (Chicago: University of Chicago Press, 1982); Joseph Gold, *Legal and Institutional Aspects of the International Monetary System: Selected Essays* (Washington, DC: IMF, 1984); Gold, "Developments in the International Monetary Fund, and International Monetary Law Since 1971," *Receuil des Cours* 174 (1982), 107. See also John K. Horsefield, ed., *The International Monetary Fund,* 1945–1965, 3 vols. (Washington, DC: IMF 1969); Margaret Garritsen de Vries, *The International Monetary Fund, 1966–1971: The System Under Stress* (Washington, DC: IMF 1976); Richard W. Edwards, *International Monetary Collaboration* (Dobbs Ferry, NY: Transnational Publishers, 1985).

44. See Jackson, supra note 3, 711–716; Jackson, Davey, and Sykes, supra note 1, 1051–1059. A list of tariff surcharges coming within the cognizance of GATT can be found in GATT COM.TD/F/W.3 (1965). Of course, a number of subsequent tariff surcharges have not been included.

45. See Jackson, supra note 3, 711–716. A list of documents for each surcharge case can be found in GATT COM.TD/F/W.3, at 4-3 (1965). The following is a list of the action taken in each case: GATT, BISD, 3 Supp. 26 (1955) (France); GATT, BISD, 7 Supp. 37 (1959), (Peru); GATT, BISD, 8 Supp. 29 (1960), (Chile); GATT, BISD, 8 Supp. 52 (1960), (Nicaragua); GATT, BISD, 10 Supp. 35 (1962), (Ceylon); GATT, BISD, 10 Supp. 51 (1962), Uruguay; GATT, BISD, 11 Supp. 57 (1963), (Canada); GATT Doc. L/2477 (1965), (India), (Statement of removal without action taken); GATT Doc. C/50 (1964), and L.2651 (1965), United Kingdom; GATT L/3573 and L. 3647 (1971) United States.

46. See Kindleberger, supra note 26, chapter 7, Kenen, supra note 2, 172–177; Jackson, Davey & Sykes, supra note 1, 16–17. See also GATT COM.TD/F/W.3 (1965) (policy reasons).

47. See "Address to the Nation Outlining a New Economic Policy: 'The Challenge of Peace,'" *Public Papers of the President, Richard Nixon* (1971) 886–890.

48. Ibid. The decision was implemented by Executive Order No. 11615, *Federal Register* 36 (1971), 15727. See also infra note 51.

49. See, GATT, BISD 23 Supp. 98 (1977). See John H. Jackson, "The Jurisprudence of International Trade: The DISC Case in GATT," *American Journal of International Law* 72 (1978), 747. See also Robert Hudec, "Reforming GATT Adjudication Procedures," *Minnesota Law Review* 72 (1988), 1443. See Jackson, Davey, and Sykes, supra note 1, 774–776.

50. See Jackson, Davey, and Sykes, supra note 1, 113–115. Nevertheless, the Congressional delegation was upheld by the Court in *Amalgamated Meat Cutters & Butcher Workmen of North America, AFL-CIO v. Connally*, 337 F.Supp. 737 (D.D.C. 1971).

51. The tariff surcharge was upheld in *United States v. Yoshida International Inc.*, 526 F.2d 560 (C.C.P.A. 1975), reversing, 378 F.Supp. 1155); and in Alcan Sales, *Division of Alcan Aluminum Corp. v. United States*, 534 F.2d 920 (C.C.P.A.), cert. denied, 429 U.S. 986, 97 S.Ct. 506, 50 L. Ed. 598 (1976).

52. See, in general, Frieder Roessler, "Selective Balance-of-Payment Adjustment Measures Affecting Trade: The Roles of the GATT and the IMF," *Journal of World Trade Law* 9 (1975), 622.

53. Cf. C. Fred Bergsten and William Cline, *Trade Policy in the 1980s* (Washington, DC: Institute for International Economics, Policy Analyses in International Economics No. 3, 1982), 54–55, who recognize the link but recommend "a much greater degree of equilibrium among the major currencies . . . ."

54. *Declaration on Trade Measures Taken for Balance-of-Payment Purposes*, GATT, BISD, 26th Supp. 205 (1980).

55. Ibid.

56. See cases cited supra note 5.

57. Section 122 of the Trade Act of 1974, Pub. L. 93-618, 88 Stat. 1978, 19 U.S.C. §2132. See also Senate Report No. 93-1298, Senate Finance Committee, 93d Cong., 2d Sess., 1974, 87–89.

58. Ibid., Section 122(d)(4).

59. Cf. Bergsten and Cline, supra note 53, at 78.

60. Private discussions with government officials: see *GATT Focus* 52 (1988), 3, where it is stated that a number of views had been expressed supporting the continued existence of Article XVIII:B.

61. Jackson, Davey, and Sykes, supra note 1.

62. NAFTA, chapter 11.

63. See, for example, Thomas L. Brewer, "International Investment Dispute Settlement Procedures: The Evolving Regime for Foreign Direct Investment," Vol. 26, no. 3 (1995), 633; Michael A. Geist, "Toward A General Agreement on the Regulation of Foreign Direct Investment," *Law and Policy in International Business* Vol. 26, no. 3 (1995), 673.

64. North American Agreement on Labor Cooperation, Jackson, Davey, and Sykes, supra note 16, Item 38, p. 734 et seq.

65. David Greenaway and Chris Milner, "The World Trade System and the Uruguay Round: Global Employment Implications," *International Labor Review* 134, nos. 4–5 (1995), 497.

Chapter 10

1. See Jacob Viner, *Dumping: A Problem in International Trade* (New York: Kelley, 1966); Edwin A. Vermulst, *Antidumping Law and Practice in the United States and European Communities* (New York: North-Holland, 1987); Richard Dale, *Anti-Dumping Law In a Liberal Trade*

Order (New York: St Martin's Press, 1980); John H. Jackson, William Davey, and Alan Sykes, *Legal Problems of International Economic Relations* (St Paul: West, 3rd ed., 1995), chapter 14. See also John J. Barcelo, "The Antidumping Law: Revise It or Repeal It," *Michigan Yearbook of International Legal Studies* 1 (1979), 53; Peter D. Ehrenhaft, "What the Antidumping and Countervailing Duty Provisions (Can) (Will) (Should) Mean for US Trade Policy," *Law and Policy in International Business* 11 (1979), 1361.

2. See, for example, *The Unfair Foreign Competition Act 1985: Hearings on S. 1655*, S. Hrg. 99-643, Senate Judiciary Committee, 99th., 1st Sess., 1985 and *Remedies Against Dumping of Imports: Hearings on S. 1655*, S. Hrg. 99-897, Senate Finance Committee, 99th Cong., 2d Sess., 1986.

3. See, for example, a Section 301 action brought by the specialty steel industry resulted in a request from the President that the ITC opens a Section 201 action (*Federal Register* 47 [1982], 51717). A Section 201 action was initiated (*Federal Register* 47 [1982], 56218) and the positive determination of injury by the ITC (*Federal Register* 48 [1983], 22373) led to a presidential proclamation placing quantitative restrictions on some kinds of steel (*Federal Register* 48 [1983], 33233). See also Andreas F. Lowenfeld, "Fair or Unfair Trade: Does It Matter?", *Cornell International Law Journal* 13 (1987), 205; Phedon Nicolaides, "How Fair is Fair Trade?", *Journal of World Trade Law* 21 (1987), 147.

4. See Ambassador Clayton Yeutter's comments on the conclusion of the Punta del Este declaration (*International Trade Reporter* 3 [1986], 1150) where he stated that: "The Punta del Este meeting means that GATT can remain relevant to the needs of our economy. We have a chance to eliminate the unfair foreign trade practices that are hurting American farmers and establish new rules to expand trade in services, America's fastest-growing sector, and provide new protection for US intellectual property, including patents, copyrights and trademarks, establish international rules on foreign investment and improve out ability to settle disputes arising over interpretations of international trading rules. All these actions would help to level the playing field for American exporters." See also Senator John Dingell (*International Trade Reporter* 3 [1986], 1198): "all the companies and workers of this country ask is a level playing field. Yet with few exceptions, this Administration continues to turn the other cheek when country after country targets industry after industry.... First the intellectual property of our industry is stolen, then our foreign markets are flooded with counterfeit, profits are used to dump in the US market. Finally our firms are driven out of business, or close to it—and all the while, their markets are insulated from meaningful competition."

5. The infra text is adapted from Jackson, Davey, and Sykes, supra note 1, 668–671, and appears by permission of the authors. The concept first appeared in John H. Jackson, United States Policy Regarding Disruptive Imports from State Trading Countries or Government Owned Enterprises. In *Interface One: Conference Proceedings on the Application of US Antidumping and Countervailing Duty law to Imports from State-Controlled Economies or State-Owned Enterprises*, Don Wallace, George Spina, Richard Rawson, and Brian McGill, eds. (Washington, DC: Institute for International and Foreign Trade Law, Georgetown University Law Center, 1978), 1–20.

6. See infra chapter 13.

7. See supra note 1. The author also acknowledges the special assistance of Professor Alan Deardorff of the Department of Economics, University of Michigan, in the preparation of this section.

8. One should note, however, that certain economists believe that dumping *may* have beneficial effects in certain circumstances—for example, where the ability to dump allows a certain scale of production and consequent cost reduction which, without the ability to dump,

could not have been achieved. See, for example, Joan Robinson, *Economics of Imperfect Competition* (London: Macmillan, 2d ed,. 1969), chapter 16, 204–205. See also the speech of Milton Friedman, "In Defense of Dumping," reported in *International Trade Reporter* 4 (1987), 935.

9. See *General Agreement of Tariffs and Trade,* Article VI. See also *Agreement on the Implementation of Article VI of the General Agreement on Tariffs and Trade* (the "1979 Code"), GATT, BISD 26 Supp. 171 (1980); 31 UST 4919; TIAS No. 9650.

10. 19 USC §1677b (1980 and Supp. 1987). See also 19 CFR §353.19 (1987).

11. See William Wares, *The Theory of Dumping and American Commercial Policy* (Lexington, MA: Lexington Books, 1977), 68; Bart S. Fisher, "The Anti-Dumping Law of the United States: A Legal and Economic Analysis," *Law and Policy in International Business* 5 (1973), 85.

12. "An Act to amend Section 2 of the act entitled 'An Act to supplement existing law against unlawful restraints and monopolies, and for other purposes' approved October 1914 as amended" (the Robinson Patman Act), ch. 592, 49 Stat. 1526 (1936) amending §2 of the Clayton Act (current version at 15 USC §13[a] [1976 and Supp. 1982]). See U.S. Department of Justice, *Report on the Robinson-Patman Act* (Washington, DC: U.S. Government Printing Office, 1977); Philip Areeda and Louis Kaplow, *Antitrust Analysis: Problems Texts, Cases* (Boston: Little, Brown, 4th ed., 1988, supp. 1994), chapter 6. See also "The Robinson-Patman Act: A Symposium on Its Fiftieth Anniversary," *Antitrust Bulletin* XXXI (1986), 571; "The Robinson Patman Act Revisited in its 50th Year," *Antitrust Law Journal* 55 (1986), 133; "Living with the Robinson-Patman Act," *Antitrust Law Journal*, 53 (1985), 845, in particular Terry Calvani, "Government Enforcement of the Robinson-Patman Act," 921.

13. See Richard Posner, *The Robinson-Patman Act: Federal Regulation of Price Differences* (Washington, DC: American Enterprise Institute, 1976); Edward H. Levi, "The Robinson-Patman Act—Is it in the Public Interest?", *ABA Antitrust Section* 1 (1952); Thomas W. Ross, "Winners and Losers under the Robinson-Patman Act," *Journal of Law and Economics* 27 (1984), 243.

14. See Frank W. Taussig, *Principles of Economics* (New York: Macmillan, 3d ed., 1928, revised 1935), volume 1, 153.

15. See, for example, *Matsushita Electric Industrial Co. v. Zenith Radio Corp.*, 475 U.S. 574. In the domestic context, see, for example, *Cargill v. Monfort of Colorado*, 479 U.S. 104 (1986).

16. Sherman Act, ch. 647 §2, 26 Stat. 209 (1890) (current version at 15 USC §2 [1973]). See Areeda & Kaplow, supra note 12, 541–549.

17. See Viner, supra note 1, 120: "In the absence of world-wide monopoly, the dumping concern will have to share with rival concerns in its own country or in other foreign countries the benefit accruing from the destruction of the native industry in the country dumped on." However, he continues: "There are, however, sufficient instances of trusts and combinations, many of them international in their membership or affiliations, that are within reach of a world-wide quasi-monopolistic control of their industry, to make the danger of predatory competition a real one even if this reasoning is unqualifiedly accepted."

In *Matsushita v. Zenith* (supra note 15, 588–593), the Supreme Court noted that *conspiracies* to predate were even more unlikely than single predatory actions. However, a growing body of literature, while accepting that price predation is unlikely, emphasizes *nonprice* predation. For a summary of these ideas, see Ordover and Wall, "Proving Predation After Monfort and Matsushita: What the 'New Learning' Has to Offer," *Antitrust* 1 (1987), 5.

18. See Fisher, supra note 11 and the comments of Senator Dingell, supra note 4.

19. See Barcelo, supra note 1.

20. See supra note 7.

21. See supra chapter 7.

22. Alexander Hamilton, *Report on Manufactures* (1791), quoted in Viner, supra note 1, 37.

23. See Viner supra note 1, 38–39.

24. Viner states that the Tariff Act of 1816 was "the first distinctly protectionist tariff of the United States, and it has been claimed that the threat to American industries from English dumping, and especially Brougham's frank utterances with respect thereto, was an important influence contributing to this, as well as to subsequent, protectionist legislation." (See Viner, supra note 1, 40–44.) However, cf. Frank W. Taussig, *The Tariff History of the United States* (New York: G.P. Putnam's, 8th ed., 1931, Johnson Reprint, 1966), 68.

25. See Viner, supra note 1, 51.

26. The Revenue Act of 1916, ch. 463, Sections 800-801, 39 Stat. 798 (commonly referred to as the "Antidumping Act of 1916," 15 USC §72 [1976]); "An Act Imposing temporary duties upon certain agricultural products to meet certain emergencies, and to provide revenue; to regulate commerce with foreign countries; to prevent dumping of foreign merchandise on the markets of the United States; to regulate the value of foreign money, and for other purposes ..." (The Emergency Tariff Act of 1921, ch. 14, Title II, 42 Stat. 9 [current version, Tariff Act of 1930, Title VII §731, as added July 26, 1979, Pub. L. 96-39, Title I, §101, 93 Stat. 162, 19 USC §1673 (1980 and Supp. 1988)]).

27. See, for example, Article IX:2 of the 1938 *Reciprocal Trade Agreement between the United States and United Kingdom* (54 Stat. 1897), where a provision allowed the United Kingdom to take measures that it deemed necessary to act as an effective deterrent to the practice. No mention was made of an equivalent U.S. right. Cf. the 1938 Reciprocal Trade Agreement between the United States and Canada (54 Stat. 2348), where no such antidumping provision is to be found.

28. *General Agreement of Tariffs and Trade,* Article VI. 30 October 1947, 61 Stat. (5), (6), TIAS No. 1700, 55 UNTS 194 (1948) as amended and Vol. IV BISD. However, NB *Protocol of Provisional Application to the GATT,* 30 October 1947, 61 Stat. (5), (6), TIAS No. 1700, 55 UNTS 308.

Article VI, entitled "Antidumping and Countervailing Duties," at paragraph 1 reads as follows:

1. The Contracting Parties recognize that dumping, by which the products of one country are introduced into the commerce of another country at less than the normal value of the products, is to be condemned if it causes or threatens material injury to an established industry in the territory of a Contracting Party or materially retards the establishment of a domestic industry. For the purposes of this Article, a product is to be considered as being introduced into the commerce of an exporting country at less than its normal value, if the price of the product exported from one country to another
a. is less than the comparable price, in the ordinary course of trade, for the like product when destined for consumption in the exporting country, or,
b. in the absence of such a domestic price, is less than either
   i. the highest comparable price for the like product for export to any third country in the ordinary course of trade, or

ii. the cost of production of the product in the country of origin plus a reasonable addition for selling cost and profit

Due allowance shall be made in each case for differences in conditions and terms of sale, for differences in taxation, and for other differences affecting price comparability.

29. *Agreement on the Implementation of Article VI* (the "1967 Code") 651 UNTS 320, GATT, BISD 15 Supp. 24 (1968). See Jackson, Davey, and Sykes, supra note 1, 691–716. See also John W. Evans, *The Kennedy Round in American Trade Policy: The Twilight of the GATT?* (Cambridge, MA: Harvard University Press, 1971), 106–110.

30. Section 201 of the 1968 Renegotiations Amendment Act, Pub. L. No. 90-634, 82 Stat. 1345. See Jackson, Davey, and Sykes, supra note 1; John H. Jackson, Jean-Victor Louis, and Mitsuo Matsushita, *Implementing the Tokyo Round* (Ann Arbor: University of Michigan Press, 1984), 146; Thomas Curtis and John Vastine, *The Kennedy Round and the Future of American Trade* (New York: Praeger, 1971), chapter 14; See also Eugenia S. Pintos and Patricia J. Murphy, "Congress Dumps the International Code," *Catholic University Law Review* 18 (1968), 180.

31. See Jackson, Louis, and Matsushita, supra note 30, 164–165; Vermulst, supra note 1, 544–545; J. F. Beseler and A. N. Williams, *Anti-Dumping and Anti-Subsidy Law: The European Communities* (London: ICC/Sweet and Maxwell, 1986), 11–13.

32. *The Tokyo Round of Multilateral Trade Negotiations: Report by the Director-General of GATT* (Geneva: GATT, 1979), 181, and *The Tokyo Round of Multilateral Trade Negotiations: Supplementary Report by the Director-General of GATT* (Geneva: GATT, 1980), chapter 3(b).

33. The 1979 Code, had a number of significant alterations. First, the injury test was arguably weakened since the causation standard was reduced. Article 3 of the 1967 code talked of the dumped imports being "demonstrably the principal cause of material injury," whereas the 1979 Code did not have such a provision, merely stating in Article 3(4) that the dumped imports through the effects of dumping are causing the injury. Second, the criteria for assessing what amounted to injurious effects on a domestic industry were made more explicit. Third, the rules on price undertakings were expanded. Fourth, a provision on dispute settlement was added (Article 15). Fifth, signatories were obligated under Article 16(6)(b) to notify any changes in its laws or regulation to the Committee on Antidumping Practices of any changes in its laws or regulation. Finally, there was a new article (Article 13) inserted, concerning developing countries.

34. In general, see Article 59 of *Vienna Convention on the Law of Treaties* (UN Doc. A/CONF.39/27, [1969]). In addition, see Article 16(5) supra note 9 of the 1979 Anti-Dumping Code: "Acceptance of this Agreement shall carry denunciation of the Agreement on the Implementation of Article VI of the General Agreement on Tariffs and Trade, done at Geneva on 30 June 1967, which entered into force on 1 July 1968, for Parties to the 1967 Agreement. Such denunciation shall take effect for each Party to this Agreement on the date of entry into force of this Agreement for each such Party."

35. Jackson, Davey, and Sykes, *Documents Supplement to Legal Problems of International Economic Relations*, 3d ed. (St. Paul: West, 1995), 174, Item 9, Agreement on Implementation of Article VI of the General Agreement on Tariffs and Trade 1994.

36. See the 1979 code, supra note 9, Article 2. See Ehrenhaft, supra note 1; Shelley A. Lorenzen, "Technical Analysis of the Antidumping Agreement and Trade Agreements Act," *Law and Policy In International Business* 11 (1979), 1405.

37. Indeed, a GATT panel (GATT, BISD 30 Supp. 140, 164 [1984] has stated: "in particular, the General Agreement does not impose on contracting parties the obligation to prevent enterprises from dumping."

38. Malcolm Baldridge, "There Won't Be a Trade War," *Washington Post*, 10 April 1987, A27: "Dumping is ... anti-free trade and is illegal under US laws as well as under the General Agreement on Tariffs and Trade. In short, sanctions against illegal dumping and for opening markets are pro-, not anti-free trade." See also Clyde Prestowitz, Jr., in his book *Trading Places* (New York: Basic Books, 1988), where at page 38 he states: "The only problem was that dumping is illegal under both U.S. trade law and under the international rules of GATT." See statement of Senator Heflin, in *The Unfair Foreign Competition Act of 1985: Hearings on S.1655 Senate Judiciary Committee*, supra note 2, 72 where he says, "Dumping is clearly unlawful." Cf. John H. Jackson, *World Trade and the Law of GATT* (Indianapolis: Bobbs Merrill, 1969), 412, nn.9, 10, and accompanying text.

39. The Committee on Antidumping Practices publishes the relevant figures as an appendix to its report, which can be found in the BISD volume for that year. Its first report can be found in GATT, BISD 16 Supp. 43 (1970). This committee produced eleven reports before being reconstituted following the signing of the 1979 Code. The first report of the "new" Committee on Antidumping Practices can be found in GATT, BISD 27 Supp. 44 (1981).

40. On 24 December 1986, the Japanese government issued new guidelines to strengthen the implementation of the 1979 Antidumping Code. See Shintaro Hagiwara, Yasuhiko Noguchi, and Kazohito Masui, "Antidumping Laws in Japan," *Journal of World Trade* 22/4 (1988), 35. See also Jackson, Louis, and Matsushita, supra note 30, 102–107; Matsushita, comment in Jackson and Vermulst, supra note 7.

41. See supra note 26.

42. In re *Japanese Electronic Products Antitrust Litigation*, 723 F. 2d 238 (CA3 1983); 513 F. Supp. 1100 (ED Pa. 1981). See also *Zenith Radio Corp. v. Matsushita Electric Industrial Co.*, 494 F. Supp. 1190 (ED Pa. 1980); In re *Japanese Electronics Products Antitrust Litigation*, 723 F. 2d 319 (CA3 1983); *Matsushita Electric Industrial Co. v. Zenith Radio Corp.*, 475 U.S. 574.

43. See, for example, S. 1655, 99th Cong., 1st Sess. (1985), and hearings, supra note 2. The House version of the 1987 trade bill (HR 3, 100th Cong., 1st Sess., 1987 §166) provided for a repeal of the criminal sanction in the 1916 Antidumping Act, and the introduction of a private right to obtain single damages. Another provision would have allowed domestic industries injured by dumped imports to apply to have some or all of the antidumping duties paid to them as some form of compensation (see HR 3, 100th Cong., 1st Sess., 1987 §167. Neither provision made it into the bill which eventually formed part of the Omnibus Trade and Competitiveness Act of 1988 (Pub. L. 100-418, 102 Stat. 1107 et seq.).

44. "An Act Imposing temporary duties upon certain agricultural products to meet certain emergencies, and to provide revenue; to regulate commerce with foreign countries; to prevent dumping of foreign merchandise on the markets of the United States; to regulate the value of foreign money, and for other purposes ..." (The Emergency Tariff Act of 1921), ch. 14, Title II, 42 Stat. 9 [current version, Tariff Act of 1930, Title VII §731, as added 26 July 1979, Pub. L. 96-39, Title I, §101, 93 Stat. 162, (19 USC §1673 [1980 and Supp. 1987])]).

45. See infra section 10.5

46. Trade Act of 1974, Pub. L. 93-618, §321(f)(3), 88 Stat. 1978 amending 28 USC §§2632.

47. Trade Agreements Act of 1979, Pub L. 96-39, Title I, section 101, 93 Stat. 144, amending the Tariff Act of 1930, 19 USCA 1671 et seq. (1980 and Supp. 1988).

48. Alan F. Holmer, Gary N. Horlick, and Terence P. Stewart, "Enacted and Rejected Amendments to the Antidumping Law: In Implementation or Contravention of the Antidumping Agreement," *The International Lawyer* 29 (no. 2), 483 et seq.

49. See 19 USC §§1330-1338 (International Trade Commission). See also Vermulst, supra note 1, 37–40; Jackson, Davey, and Sykes, supra note 1, 611–612. However, one should note that in the case of third-country dumping, under Section 1317 of the 1988 Trade Act (supra note 43) the USTR is required, upon determination that products are being dumped and that injury results to a U.S. industry, to request that the third nation undertake an investigation.

50. A single- or multiple-firm action is in theory possible under the 1979 Code, but most jurisdictions do not use them either for fear of the action being manipulated to suit the domestic industry—for example, when a U.S. firm imports Korean cars and then brings a single-firm action against a Korean producer (while excluding its own imports from the scope of the investigation). The U.S. Department of Commerce discourages petitioners from attempting such a case. The EC has, however, opened a single-firm action against two named Japanese firms (OJ[1987]C.256/16). However, cf. Beseler and Williams, supra note 31, 186. EC antidumping law is governed by Council Regulation [EC] 3283/94, OJ [1994] L/349/1 as amended by Council Regulation 355/95, OJ [1995] L/41/95, which raises issues similar to single-firm actions. In theory, an EC petitioner may request that the commission impose duties upon a foreign firm, already found to be dumping, who assembles in the EC, and not have similar duties imposed on itself, even though it uses exactly the same parts in the same amounts as the foreign assembler.

51. See the 1979 Antidumping Code, supra note 9, Article 6, paragraph 8, and *Recommendations Concerning Best Information Available in Terms of Article 6:8*, GATT BISD 31st. Supp 283 (1985). In the U.S., see 19 CFR §207.8 (1988); 19 CFR §353.51 (1988). See also Vermulst, supra note 1, 61–64, 207–208.

52. See generally Vermulst, supra note 1; Peter Feller, *US Customs and International Trade Guide* (New York: Matthew Bender, 1979), chapter 18.

53. WTO Focus Newsletter, No. 7, December 1995, p. 10.

54. See *The Commerce Department Speaks on Import and Export Administration 1984* (New York: Practicing Law Institute, 1984), vols. 1 and 2; Vermulst, supra note 1; Feller, supra note 52, chapter 18.

55. Article 5.8 of the Agreement on Implementation of Article VI of the General Agreement on Tariffs and Trade 1994.

56. Title VII of the 1930 Tariff Act as amended by the 1979 Trade Act, the 1984 Trade Act, the 1988 Trade Act and the 1994 Uruguay Round Agreements Act.

57. See Vermulst supra note 1, 495. See also Feller, supra note 52, §18.02[1]. Cf. *Report of Group of Experts on Anti-Dumping and Countervailing Duties* (Geneva: GATT, 1961), 7.

58. See Vermulst, supra note 1, 384–386; Thomas Schoenbaum, *Antidumping and Countervailing Duties and the GATT: An Evaluation and a Proposal for a Unified Remedy for Unfair International Trade* (Athens, GA: Dean Rusk Center for International and Comparative Law, University of Georgia Law School, 1987), 10–15.

59. See Peter D. Ehrenhaft and Charlotte G. Meriwether, "The Trade Agreements Act of 1979: Small Aid for Trade," *Tulane Law Review* 58 (1984), 1107, 1131. Cf. Statement of Gary Horlick, *Options to Improve the Trade Remedy Laws: Comm. Ser. 98-15*, House Ways and

Means Committee, 98th Cong., 1st Sess., 1983, 565. Horlick points out that, at least as far as the complainant is concerned, a dumping action need cost them no money or effort because the actual investigation is carried out by the Department of Commerce and International Trade Commission. Most of the time and money expended by the complainants is used to check on the governmental agencies' results.

60. The so-called ESP offset (19 CFR §353.15c) problem has become one of the most notorious elements of antidumping law in the United States. See *SCM Group v. United States,* 713 F. 2d 1568 (Fed. Cir. 1983) cert. den., 104 S. Ct 1274. Senator Hollings proposed an amendment to the 1987 Trade Bill bringing the ESP offset into line with the more rigorous version used in the EC. This was adopted by voice vote on 30 June 1987 (*International Trade Report* 4 [1987], 864) and became §339 of HR3 as passed by the Senate. The amendment was seen as very significant (see statement of Senator Bentsen, *International Trade Reporter,* 4 [1987], 810). In October 1987, a report was released quantifying the effects of the Hollings amendment on imports to the United States. The report was very critical of the amendment, saying that up to 800,000 US jobs could disappear and that a decline in living standards of close to $39 billion may occur (*International Trade Reporter,* 4 [1987], 1290). The Hollings amendment was not included in the 1988 Omnibus Trade and Competitiveness Act (supra note 43).

61. 19 USC §1677b (1980 and Supp. 1987), 19 CFR §353.5 (1987).

62. 19 USC §1677b(e) (1980 and Supp. 1987), 19 CFR §353.6 (1987).

63. See supra note 46, Title III, chapter 2, §321(d), amending 28 USC §164 (current version 19 USCA §1677b[b] [1980 and Supp. 1987], 19 CFR §353.7 [1988]).

64. See GATT, Article VI, see also the code, supra note 9.

65. See supra chapter 7.

66. See S. Rep. No. 1298, Senate Finance Committee, 93d Cong., 2nd Sess., 1974, reprinted in *U.S Code Congressional and Administrative News,* 7187, 7317: "In short the Committee does not view injury caused by unfair competition, such as dumping, to require as strong a causation link to imports, as would be required for determining the existence of injury under fair trade conditions."

67. See Jackson, Louis, and Matsushita, supra note 30, 154-55; Vermulst, supra note 1, 544–545; Beseler and Williams, supra note 31, 11–13.

68. See supra note 46, Title III, chapter 3, §331, amending 28 USC §1303 (current version 19 USCA §1303 and §1671b and d [1980 and Supp. 1988].

69. See statement of Richard O. Cunningham, *Comparison of Recommendations Received from Public Witnesses on Multilateral Trade Negotiations Implementing Legislation,* WMCP 96-20, Subcommittee on Trade, House Ways and Means Committee, 99th Cong. 1st Sess., 1979 46,50. See also Jackson, Davey, and Sykes, supra note 1, 622-629; Jackson, Louis, and Matsushita, supra note 30, 164.

70. See, for example, *Cast Iron Soil Pipe, Poland,* USTC Pub. 214 (1967), 6. This interpretation of the commission lasted until 1975. See Vermulst, supra note 1, 546–547.

71. HR Rep. 96-317, House Ways and Means Committee, 96th Cong., 1st Sess., 1979, 46.

72. S. Rep. 96-249, Senate Finance Committee, 96th Cong., 1st sess., 1979, 87. See also supra note 71.

73. Private discussions with the author.

74. The injury test found in Article 6 of the Subsidies Code (*Agreement on the Interpretation and Application of Articles VI, XVI and XXIII of the General Agreement on Tariffs and Trade,* 31 UST 513, TIAS No. 9619, 26 BISD 56 [1980]) differs in some respects from the test found the Antidumping Code (Article 3). It includes most of the definition of industry found in a separate article (Article 4) in the Antidumping Code. Also, the Subsidies Code does not have the explicit reference to threat of material injury or material retardation found in footnote 3 of the Antidumping Code. It is unclear whether this is significant, given that Article VI:6(a) of the GATT seems to extend the application of countervailing duties to these other situations.

75. Article 15.1 of the Agreement on Subsidies and Countervailing Measures.

76. 19 USC §1677(7) (1980 and Supp. 1987). See supra notes 71 and 72. See also section 1329(b) of the *1988 Trade Act,* supra note 43.

77. See, for example, *Certain Carbon Steel Products, Certain European Countries,* USITC Pub. No. 1064, 14-15 (views of Vice Chairman Alberger) and 64-67 (views of Commissioner Stern); *Certain Carbon Steel Products, Certain European Countries,* USITC Pub. No. 1221, 16-17 (views of Commissioners Alberger, Stern, and Eckes). See also Vermulst, supra note 1, 575–583; William B. T. Mock, "Cumulation of Import Statistics in Injury Investigations before the International Trade Commission," *Northwestern Journal of International Law and Business* 7 (1986), 433.

78. Trade and Tariff Act of 1984, Pub. L. 98-573, §612, 98 Stat. 2948 amending 19 USC §1677 (current version 19 USCA §167[(7)][C][iv)][1980 and Supp. 1988]).

79. The 1988 Trade Act, supra note 43, contains a provision (section 1330[b]) on negligible imports. Under it the ITC is not required to cumulate imports as required under Section 1330(a) if they have "no discernable impact on the domestic industry."

80. Article 3.3 of the Agreement on Implementation of Article VI of the General Agreement on Tariffs and Trade 1994; Article 15.3 of the Agreement on Subsidies and Countervailing Measures.

81. See also Section 1330(a) of the 1988 Trade Act, supra note 43. Under this provision the ITC *may* cross-cumulate among various actions in the assessment of *threat* of material injury.

82. See *ITC General Counsel Memoranda,* GC-E-065 (17 March 1981), Memo from General Counsel to Commissioner Stern, and GC-F-345 (8 October 1982) Memo from General Counsel to the Commission. See also Vermulst, supra note 1, 563-575; Edward R. Easton, "Administration of the Import Trade Statutes: Possibilities for Harmonizing the Investigative Techniques and Standards of the ITC," *Georgia Journal of International and Comparative Law* 10 (1980), 78; Elward R. Easton and Willam E. Perry, "The Causation of Material Injury: Changes in the Antidumping and Countervailing Duty Investigations of the International Trade Commission," *UCLA Pacific Basin Law Journal* 2 (1983), 43.

83. In *Hyundai Pipe Co. v. U.S. International Trade Commission* 670 F. Supp. 357 (1987), the CIT held that the Commission is not required to examine margins, but that it is not barred from examining them if it so wishes. See also Easton, and Easton and Perry, supra note 82.

84. See Vermulst, supra note 1, 570–571. Cf. Easton, supra note 82.

85. The 1979 Subsidies Code, supra note 74, Article 6, paragraph 4.

86. The 1979 Antidumping Code, supra note 9, Article 3, paragraph 6.

87. The American Law Institute, *Restatement of the Law, Foreign Relations Law of the U.S.,* 1987, 329–330.

88. See in general Alan Rugman and Andrew Anderson, *Administered Protection in America* (London: Croom-Helm, 1987) in particular 6–8. See also Vermulst, supra note 1, 703.

89. See Article 9(4) of Council Regulation (EC) 3286/94 on *Protection against Dumped or Subsidized Imports from Countries not Members of the European Economic Community* (OJ [1994] L.369); Article 13(3) Commission Decision 2424/88/ECSC, *Protection against Dumped or Subsidized Imports from Countries not Members of the European Coal and Steel Community* (OJ [1988] L.209). See also the decision of the European Court of Justice in case 53/83, *Allied Corporation v. Council of the European Communities* ("Allied II") (1985) ECR 1621, (1986) 3 CMLR 605, where the court held that the council must ascertain whether the amount of duty imposed "is necessary in order to remove the injury."

90. See the 1979 code, supra note 9, Article 8, paragraph 1.

91. 19 USC §1673 (1980 and Supp. 1988).

92. The United States share of Canadian merchandise exports was 70.2 percent in 1983, 75.6 percent in 1984 and 78 percent in 1985 was 78 percent (compared with 65 percent in 1975). By way of contrast, U.S. merchandise exports destined for Canada in 1984 were 21.4 percent of the total; in 1985, 22.2 percent; and they fell to 20.9 percent in 1986. In the United States in 1986, exports of goods and services accounted for 8.8 percent of GNP; in Canada in 1986, exports of goods and services accounted for 27.3 percent of GDP. In 1986, Canadian exports were worth $110.4 billion; U.S. exports were worth $373 billion. Imports into Canada in 1986 were $104 billion; and imports into the United States were $477.3 billion (figures complied from the Economic Intelligence Unit, *Economic Indicators* [London: Economic Intelligence Unit]).

93. A number of attempts have been made to introduce an effective private right of action for dumping in the United States. Concern has been expressed as to whether *any* remedy other than duties would be compatible with GATT. There is also a question of to what extent the United States can alter the 1916 act without losing the grandfather rights. At the moment, Section 801 of Revenue Act 1916 (ch. 463, 39 Stat. 798, current version 15 USC §72 [1976]), contains a criminal prohibition on predatory dumping. The requirement of intent has never been legally satisfied.

94. See HR3, 100th Cong., 1st Sess., 1987, §167. This provision was not accepted into the trade bill which eventually became the Trade Act of 1988 (see supra note 43).

95. Article III of GATT provides for national treatment, under which imported goods should be treated no worse than the domestic equivalent. It has been suggested that since the United States does not enforce a prohibition on price discrimination within the United States, it may not treat imports any more stringently [see letter from John H. Jackson to the Honorable Dan Rostenkowski, 13 March 1987 [unpublished]; see also *Hearings on S.1655,* supra note 2 (statements of Alan Holmer, 28, and Gary Horlick, 132)]. It has also been suggested that the clear implication of Article VI:2 of GATT is that the only legitimate response to dumping is the imposition of duties, this narrow remedy being an exception to Article III: see *Hearings on S.1655,* supra note 2 (statements of Alan Holmer, 28, Gilbert Kaplan, 37, and Gary Horlick, 130). Cf. *The Unfair Foreign Competition Act of 1985: Hearings on S.1655,* Senate Judiciary Committee, supra note 2 (statements of Peter Ehrenhaft, 55 and Richard O. Cunningham, 43), 1985.

96. See *Decision of 28 January 1987,* GATT, BISD 33 Supp. 28, 43 (1987).

97. See Jackson, Davey, and Sykes, supra note 1, 508–517; 874–884.

98. The unfair trade practice of export targeting is included in the 1987 Trade Bill, (supra note 43, Section 1301). For an analysis of targeting practices, see *Foreign Industrial Targeting*

and Its Effects on US Industries, Phase I: Japan, USITC Pub. No. 1437 (1983); *Foreign Industrial Targeting and Its Effects on US Industries, Phase II: The European Community and Member States,* USITC Pub. No. 1517 (1984); *Foreign Industrial Targeting Practices,* S. Hrg. 98-522, Joint Economic Committee, 98th Cong., 1st Sess., 1983. There is also great debate as to the effectiveness of targeting from an economic standpoint: see Paul R. Krugman, "The U.S. Response to Foreign Industrial Targeting," *Brooking Papers on Economic Activity* (1984/1), 77. Cf. *The Effect of Government Targeting on World Semiconductor Competition* (Cupertino, CA: Semiconductor Industry Association, 1983). See also Jackson, Davey, and Sykes, supra note 1, section 22.2.

99. Industrial policy is extremely difficult to define. See, for example, William Diebold, *Industrial Policy as an International Issue* (Washington DC: Council on Foreign Relations, 1980); John Pinder, ed., *National Industrial Strategies and the World Economy* (London: Croom Helm, 1982); Brian Hindley "Empty Economics in the Case for Industrial Policy," *World Economy* 7 (1984), 277; "Industrial Policy: An Unfair Trade Practice?", *Congressional Quarterly Weekly Reports* 41 (1983), 211.

100. See supra sections 1.2 and 1.3.

101. See, for example, *Product Liability Reform Proposals,* S. Hrg. 99-1004, Senate Commerce, Science and Transportation Committee, 99th Cong., 2d Sess., 1986 (testimony of Secretary Baldridge); *Problems Confronting Small Manufacturers in Automating Their Plants,* S. Hrg. 100-455, Senate Committee on Small Business, 100th Cong., 1st Sess., 1987. See also Sara F. Liebman, "The European Community's Products Liability Directive: Is the U. S. Experience Applicable?", *Law and Policy in International Business* 18 (1986), 795; Jon R. Maddox, "Products Liability in Europe," *Journal of World Trade Law* 19 (1985), 508; *U.S. Export Weekly* 18 (1983), 684, 686.

102. 19 USC §1337(a) (1980 and Supp. 1988).

103. See the 1988 Trade Act, supra note 43, section 1342. See also *Congressional Record* 134 (1988), H2043.

104. See Jackson, Davey, and Sykes, supra note 1, 717-756; 622–629.

105. 9 USC §1337(e) (1980 and Supp. 1988). The ITC has refused to provide relief on these grounds in at least two cases: *Automatic Crankpin Grinders,* USITC Pub No. 1022 (1979), and *Inclined Field Acceleration Tubes,* USITC Pub. No. 1119 (1980).

106. See supra Chapter 8.2. See also GATT, BISD 30 Supp. 107 (1984).

107. United States - Section 337 of the Tariff Act of 1930, GATT Panel Report adopted 7 November 1989, 36 Supp. BISD 345 (1990) at page 508 of Jackson, Davey, and Sykes, see supra note 1.

Chapter 11

1. See supra section 10.1.

2. See generally Gary C. Hufbauer and J. Shelton Erb, *Subsidies in International Trade* (Washington, DC: Institute for International Economics, 1984); John Barcelo, "Subsidies and Countervailing Duties—Analysis and a Proposal," *Law and Policy in International Business* 9 (1977), 779; *The Commerce Department Speaks on Import and Export Administration 1984* (New York: Practicing Law Institute, 1984), volume I; Don Wallace, Frank Loftus, and Van Krikorian, eds., *Interface III, Legal Treatment of Domestic Subsidies* (Washington, DC: International Law Institute, 1984); John H. Jackson, *World Trade and the Law of GATT* (Indianapolis: Bobbs-Merrill Co., 1969), 365–438; Harald B. Malmgren, *International Order for Public Subsidies*

(London: Trade Policy Research Centre, 1977); Richard Rivers and John Greenwald, "The Negotiation of a Code on Subsidies and Countervailing Measures: Bridging Fundamental Policy Differences," *Law and Policy in International Business* 11 (1979), 1477.

3. See supra section 10.5.

4. See *The Tokyo Round of Multilateral Trade Negotiations, Report by the Director-General* (Geneva: GATT, 1979), 181; *The Tokyo Round of Multilateral Trade Negotiations: Supplementary Report by the Director-General* (Geneva: GATT, 1980), 10. See also Daniel Tarullo, "The MTN Subsidies Code: Agreement Without Consensus," in *Emerging Standards of International Trade and Investment*, Seymour Rubin and Gary Hufbauer, eds. (Totowa, NJ: Rowman and Allenheld, 1984), 63–99.

5. See, for example, John Barcelo, "Subsidies, Countervailing Duties, and Antidumping after the Tokyo Round," *Cornell International Law Journal* 13 (1980), 257, 282–285; Barcelo, supra note 2, 794–835.

6. See, for example, Geoffrey Denton and Seamus O'Cleirearain, *Subsidy Issues in International Commerce* (London: Trade Policy Research Centre, 1972), 33–45, 52–59. If the government of an importing country has accepted a tariff binding and the government of the exporting country could, at the time of the negotiation of the tariff binding, not reasonably have expected the subsequent introduction of a subsidy, then it is possible that such a subsidy constitutes a prima facie case of nullification or impairment in the sense of GATT Article XXIII.

7. See, for example, for the EC: Council Regulation 3284/94 on protection against subsidized imports from countries not members of the European Community, OJ (1994) L/369; and Decision 2424/88/ECSC, OJ (1988) L.209; for Canada: Special Import Measures Act 1984, 32-33 Eliz. II, c. 25.

8. Based on the Annual Reports from the United States Trade Representative (1980–1996).

9. See, for example, Alan Deardorff and Robert M. Stern, "Current Issues in Trade Policy: An Overview," and Avinash Dixit, "How Should the United States Respond to Other Countries' Trade Policies?", in *U.S. Trade Policies in a Changing World Economy*, Robert M. Stern, ed. (Cambridge, MA: MIT Press, 1987), 15–68 and 245–282, respectively; Alan Sykes, "Countervailing Duty Law: An Economic Perspective," *Columbia Law Review* 89 (1989), 199. James A. Brander, "Rationales for Strategic Trade and Industrial Policy," in *Strategic Trade Policy and the New International Economics*, Paul R. Krugman, ed. (Cambridge, MA: MIT Press, 1986), 23–46; W. Max Corden, *Trade Policy and Economic Welfare* (Oxford: Clarendon Press, 1974), chapter 2; Steven J. Warnecke, ed., *International Trade and Industrial Policies* (New York: Holmes and Meier, 1978).

10. See Dixit, supra note 9.

11. Ibid. 252; see also Deardorff and Stern, supra note 9.

12. Deardorff and Stern, supra note 9, 55.

13. On subsidies and predation, see, for example, Januse Ordover, Allan Sykes, and Robert Willig, "Unfair International Trade Policies," *New York University Journal of International Law and Politics* 15 (1983), 323, 332; Barbara Epstein, Foreign Predation against U.S. Firms: Reconciling International and Domestic Policies, in *1984 Fordham Corporate Law Institute*, Barry Hawk, ed. (New York: Matthew Bender, 1985), 41–61.

14. See supra section 10.2.

15. Arguably, the subsidy on the imports is irrelevant in this context. This may, again, show that the difference between measures against fair and unfair trade is often very vague. See supra section 10.1. On trade actions and national security, see generally Jackson, supra note 2, 748–752.

16. See, for example, Paul Wonnacott, *The United States and Canada: The Quest for Free Trade: An Examination of Selected Issues* (Washington, DC: Institute for International Economics, Policy Analyses in International Economics No. 16, 1987), 7.

17. A clear, but controversial, example of this is the U.S. "commitments" policy. See, for example, "Brass Sheet and Strip from Brazil," *Federal Register* 51 (1986), 40837, 40840. On the "commitments" policy, see infra section 11.2, text accompanying notes 40–42.

18. See generally William N. Walker, *International Limits to Government Intervention in the Marketplace, Focus on Subsidies to the Private Sector* (London: Trade Policy Research Centre, Lectures in Commercial Diplomacy No.1, 1976), 2–3.

19. Alexander Hamilton, for example, stated in his 1791 Report on Manufacturers:

[T]he greatest obstacle of all to the successful prosecution of a new branch of industry in a country, in which it was before unknown, consists, as far as the instances apply, in the bounties premiums and other aids which are granted, in a variety of cases, by the nations, in which the establishments to be imitated, are previously introduced. It is well known ... that certain nations grant bounties on the exportation of particular commodities, to enable their own workmen to under sell and supplant all competitors, in the country to which the commodities are sent. Hence the undertakers of a new manufacture have to contend not only with the natural disadvantages of a new undertaking, but with the gratuities and enumerations which other government bestow. To be enabled to contend with success, it is evident, that interference and aid of their own governments are indispensable.

See also Alexander Hamilton's famous *Report on Manufactures* (Washington, DC: U.S. Department of Treasury, 1892), and Adam Smith, *Wealth of Nations* (1776), book IV, chapter 5.

20. Tariff Act of 1897, ch. 11; 30 Stat. 151, 205.

21. In 1923 Viner found twenty-nine treaties containing a pledge against subsidies, of which seven were signed after 1900: see Jacob Viner, *Dumping: A Problem in International Trade* (New York: Kelley, 1966), 166–168. Countervailing duties were also discussed in the framework of the League of Nations. For a discussion on countervailing duties and the most-favored-nation principle, see League of Nations, Committee of Experts for the Progressive Codification of International law, *Report of the Subcommittee* (V. Legal, 1927, V.10), reprinted in *American Journal of International Law* 22 (Supp., special no., 1928), 134.

22. A majority of the bilateral treaties concluded by the United States had only implicit references to the use of countervailing duties as a way of offsetting subsidies. See, for example, Article VI:2 of the 1942 Reciprocal Trade Agreement between the United States and Mexico (57 Stat. 833, 839). However, at least one (*1938 Reciprocal Trade Agreement between the United States and United Kingdom,* Article XI:2 [54 Stat. 1897]) had explicit provisions dealing with the use of countervailing duties. But this provision related to U.K. action against U.S. subsidies.

23. See Jackson, supra note 2, chapters 15 and 16.

24. Ibid., section 15.3.

25. See, for example, the DISC case, GATT BISD 23 Supp. 98 (1977), partially reprinted in Jackson, Davey, and Sykes, *Legal Problems of International Economic Relations* (St. Paul: West, 3d ed., 1995), 775.

26. GATT L/1864 (1962); 445 U.N.T.S. 294 (1962); See Jackson, supra note 2, 373.

27. See Tariff Act of 1897, supra note 20, 30 Stat. 151, 205; The language of this act evolved out of two earlier countervailing duty provisions that had been applicable only to sugar exports. These first U.S. countervailing duty provisions were Section 237 of the Tariff Act of 1890 (26 Stat. 567, 584) and Par. $182\frac{1}{2}$ of the Tariff Act of 1894 (28 Stat. 521). See also supra sections 2.2 and 2.3.

28. See, for trade reform, Hearings before the House Committee on Ways and Means, 99th Cong., 1st Sess. 4088-4097 part 12 (Testimony of Dan Gerhardstein, Director, American Institute for Imported Steel); see also John H. Jackson, Jean-Victor Louis, and Mitsuo Matsushita, *Implementing the Tokyo Round: National Constitutions and International Economic Rules* (Ann Arbor: University of Michigan Press, 1984), 156.

29. Reorganization Plan No. 3 of 1979, §2(a); Executive Order No. 12188, 3 CFR §131, (1981), *Federal Register* 44 (1979), 69273, 69274; 19 U.S.C.A. §2171 (1980 and Supp. 1988).

30. The Trade Act of 1974, Pub. L. No. 93-618, Title I, chapters 1 and 2, 88 Stat. 1978.

31. Section 331 of the Trade Act of 1974, supra note 32 amending Section 303 of the *Tariff Act of 1930*, 19 USCA §1303 (1980 and Supp. 1988). See also H. Rep. 93-571, House Ways and Means Committee, 93d Cong., 1st Sess., 1973, 185.

32. *Agreement on Interpretation and Application of Articles VI, XVI and XXIII of the General Agreement on Tariffs and Trade*, GATT, BISD 26 Supp. 56 (1980); 31 UST 513; T.I.A.S. No. 9619 (hereinafter cited as Subsidies Code). See *The Tokyo Round of Multilateral Trade Negotiations, Report by the Director-General*, supra note 4, 53–61; Rivers and Greenwald, supra note 2; Tarullo, supra note 4.

33. Subsidies Code, supra note 34, Article XI.

34. *Report adopted on November 19, 1960*, reprinted in GATT, BISD 9 Supp. 185, 186 (1961).

35. Trade Agreements Act of 1979, Pub. L. No. 96-39, 93 Stat. 144 (1979).

36. See supra section 3.3.

37. Article 8 of the Agreement on Subsidies and Countervailing Measures.

38. Article 11.9 of the Agreement on Subsidies and Countervailing Measures.

39. For example, the U.S. Economic Joint Committee in 1965 offered the following definition: "An act by a governmental unit involving either (1) a payment, (2) a remission of charges, or (3) supplying commodities or services at less than cost or market price, with an intent of achieving a particular economic objective, most usually the supplying to a general market a product or service which would be supplied in as great a quantity only at higher prices in absence of the payment or remission of charges." (*Subsidies and Subsidy-Effect Programs of the U.S. Government*, Joint Economic Committee Print, 89th Con., 1st Sess., 1965).

40. See generally William D. Hunter, and Susan A. Kuhbach, "Subsidies and Countervailing Duties: Highlights Since 1984," in *The Commerce Department Speaks, 1987* (New York: Practicing Law Institute, 1987), 491–625, 543–550.

41. Other examples are environmental and employment aid and aid for industrial restructuring. See Subsidies Code, supra note 32, Article 11(1).

42. For a detailed overview of the methodologies used by the U.S. Commerce Department for the calculation of a subsidy, see the Subsidies Appendix, "Cold-Rolled Carbon Steel Prod-

ucts from Argentina," *Federal Register* 49 (1984), 18006, 18018; See also, Alan Holmer, Sosau Haggerty, and William D. Hunter, "Identifying and Measuring Subsidies under the Countervailing Duty Law: An Attempt at Synthesis," in *The Commerce Department Speaks on Import and Export Administration 1984* (New York: Practicing Law Institute, 1984), vol. I, 301–562.

43. See, for example, Paul Samuelson, *Economics* (New York: McGraw-Hill, 10th ed., 1976), 470–462; Warren F. Schwartz and Eugene W. Harper, "The Regulation of Subsidies Affecting Trade," *Michigan Law Review* 70 (1973), 831, 843.

44. The specificity test in U.S. law was first applied in "Certain Steel Products from Belgium," *Federal Register* 47 (1982), appendix 4, 39304, based on explicit statutory language. The European Commission also later accepted the principle of specificity: see Decision 85/223/EEC, OJ (1985) L. 106/19, Recital 7.3.

45. Tariff Act of 1930 as amended, Section 771(5), 19 USCA §1677(5) (1980 and Supp. 1988).

46. See especially supra note 2 and infra note 50.

47. See Judith H. Bello and Alan F. Holmer, "Subsidies and Natural Resources: Congress Rejects a Lateral Attack on the Specificity Test," *George Washington Journal of International Law and Economics* 18 (1984), 297.

48. "Certain Softwood Lumber Products from Canada," *Federal Register* 48 (1983), 24159; "Certain Softwood Lumber Products from Canada," *Federal Register* 51 (1986), 37453, see supra note 60; Alan F. Holmer and Judith H. Bello, "The U.S.-Canada Lumber Agreement: Past as Prologue," *International Lawyer* 21 (1987), 1185.

49. "Anhydrous and Aqua Ammonia from Mexico," *Federal Register* 48 (1983), 28522; "Carbon Black from Mexico," *Federal Register* 48 (1983), 28564; "Lime from Mexico," *Federal Register* 48 (1983), 35672; "Portland Hydraulic Cement and Cement Clinker from Mexico," *Federal Register* 48 (1983), 43063.

50. U.S. Department of Commerce practice, several court cases, and Section 1312 of the 1988 Omnibus Trade and Competitiveness Act all stress the need for "de facto" or actual nonspecificity rather than mere "nominal" availability of benefits programs. See Gary N. Horlick, Judith H. Bello, and Michael K. Levine, "The Countervailability of Subsidies: Specificity," in *United States Import Relief Laws: Current Developments in Law and Policy* (New York: Practicing Law Institute, 1985), 47; *Cabot Corp v. United States*, 620 F. Supp. (CIT, 1985), appeal dismissed, 788 F. 2d 1539 (Fed. Cir., 1986); *PPG v. United States*, 661 F. Supp. 285 (CIT, 1987); *Al Tech v. United States*, 661 F. Supp. 1206 (CIT, 1987); *Can-Am v. United States*, 8ITRD 2510 (CIT, 1987). The legislative history of the 1988 Act states: "The amendment codifies the holding by the U.S. Court of International Trade in *Cabot Corporation v. United States*, 620 F. Supp. 722 (CIT, 1985) that, in the order to determine whether a domestic subsidy is countervailable, the Commerce Department must examine on a case-by-case basis whether the benefits provided by a program are bestowed upon a specific enterprise or industry, or group of enterprises or industries." (Omnibus Trade Act of 1987, S. Hrg. 100-71, Senate Finance Committee, 100th Cong., 1st Sess., 1987, 122.)

51. *Carlisle Tire and Rubber Co. v. United States*, 5 C.I.T. 229, 564 F. Supp. 834 (1983).

52. "Fresh Asparagus from Mexico," *Federal Register* 48 (1983), 21618. For a list of cases reflecting the Commerce Department's approach, see Holmer, Haggerty, and Hunter, supra note 42, 301–562.

53. See Tarullo, supra note 4. Also Horlick, "Current Issues in Countervailing Duty Law," in *The Trade Agreements Act of 1979—Four Years Later* (New York: Practicing Law Institute,

1983), 11, 35. See also Daniel Tarullo, "Logic, Myth and the International Order," *Harvard International Law Journal* 26 (1985), 533; Daniel Tarullo, "Beyond Normalcy in the Regulation of International Trade," *Harvard Law Review* 100 (1987), 546.

54. See, for example, Peter Kenen, *The International Economy* (Englewood Cliffs, NJ: Prentice-Hall, 1985), 203–205; Denton and O'Cleirearain, supra note 6, 52–59.

55. An exception to this should be made with regard to the responsibility of the industrialized countries for the development of the less developed countries.

56. See generally John H. Jackson, "Perspectives on the Jurisprudence of International Trade: Costs and Benefits of Legal Procedures in the United States," *Michigan Law Review* 82 (1984), 1570.

Chapter 12

1. Ministerial declaration of 20 September 1986 at Punta del Este, reprinted in *GATT Activities* 1986, 15.

2. See, for example, GATT Uruguay Round Document MTN.GNS/W/120, of 10 July 1991, including a Services Sectoral Classification list of approximately 122 or more sectors. See also document of the U.S. Department of Commerce, October 1994, Benefits to Service Industries of the General Agreement on Trade in Services, introduced by Jude Kearney, Deputy Assistant Secretary for Service Industries and Finance. At page 2, it reports there are about 150 service sectors and subsectors.

3. In 1994, approximately 70 percent of American jobs were tied to the service sector and total U.S. exports of services reached $200 billion, see 1994 Annual Report U.S. Trade Representative, 29; a 1991 report to the U.S. Congress estimated that the trade in services accounted for 25 percent of all world trade, see Report to the Congress of Fast-Track Procedures, 1 March 1991, at 51.

4. Geza Feketakuty, "Trade in Professional Services: An Overview," *University of Chicago Legal Forum* 1, 3–4 (1986).

5. See generally Claude E. Barfield, ed. *International Financial Markets: Harmonization v. Competition* (Washington, DC: American Enterprise Institute Press, 1996). See also Joel P. Trachtman, "The Applicability of Law and Economics to Law and Development: The Case of Financial Law," chapter 3 in Joseph J. Norton and Mads Andenas, eds., *Emerging Financial Markets and Role of International Financial Organizations* (London: Kluwer Law International, 1996).

6. Chapter 12, Articles 1201 and 1206 NAFTA; Article XX GATS.

7. Bernard Hoekman, *The General Agreement on Trade in Services*, in *OECD Documents, The New World Trading System: Readings* (Paris: OECD, 1995), 177.

8. Michael Geist, "Toward a General Agreement on the Regulation of Foreign Direct Investment," *Law and Policy in International Business* (1995), vol. 26 no. 3 673.

9. Alan Deardorff, "Welfare Effects of Global Patent Protection," *Economica*, February 1992 at 35; Jerome Reichman, "The TRIPS Component of the GATT Uruguay Round: Competitive Prospects for Intellectual Property Owners in an Integrated World Market," *Fordham Intellectual Property, Media & Entertainment Law Journal* 4 (1993), 171.

10. U.S. International Trade Commission, Foreign Protection of Intellectual Property Rights and the Effect on U.S. Industry and Trade, USITC Pub. No. 2065 (1988), at 4–2.

11. A compendium of the more important agreements, including the Paris and the Berne Convention, in M. Laeffer, ed., *International Treaties on Intellectual Property* (Washington, DC: Bureau of National Affairs, 1990).

12. J. H. Reichman, "Universal Minimum Standards of Intellectual Property Protection under the TRIPS Component of the WTO Agreement," *International Lawyer* 29, no. 2, page 345; U.S. Statement of Administrative Action; John H. Jackson, William Davey, and Alan Sykes, *International Economic Relations* (St. Paul: West, 3d ed., 1995).

13. See particularly Articles 4 and 5, and footnote 1 to Article 4.

14. See Article IX, paragraphs 3 and 4.

15. See *International Lawyer* 29, no. 2 (1995); see Hoekman, supra note 7; see the U.S. Statement of Administrative Action by the U.S. President in his message to Congress on the Uruguay Round Trade Agreements, U.S. Congress 103rd, 2nd Sess. House Document 103-316, Vol. 1, at page 656, 804, Agreement on Trade—Related Investment Measures; see also Jackson, Davey, and Sykes, supra note 12.

Chapter 13

1. See generally John H. Jackson, *World Trade and the Law of GATT* (Indianapolis: Bobbs-Merrill, 1969), chapter 25; John H. Jackson, William Davey, and Alan Sykes, *Legal Problems of International Economic Relations* (St. Paul: West, 3d ed., 1995), chapter 24. For more specific works, see Robert E. Hudec, *GATT and the Developing Countries* (Brookfield, VT: Gower/Trade Policy Research Centre, 1988); Jagdish Bhagwati, *The Economics of Underdeveloped Countries* (New York: McGraw-Hill, 1966); Jagdish Bhagwati, *The International Crisis and the Developing Countries* (Bombay: Economic Research and Training Foundation, 1975); Anne O. Krueger et al., eds., *Trade and Employment in Developing Countries*, 3 vols. (Chicago: University of Chicago Press, 1981); Richard Pomfret, "The Effects of Trade Preferences for Developing Countries," *Southern Economic Journal* 53 (1986), 18; Somitro Djojohadikusumo, "Common Interests of Industrial and Developing Countries," *World Economy* 8 (1985), 325; Tamotsu Takase, "The Role of Concessions in the GATT Trading System and Their Implications for Developing Countries," *Journal of World Trade Law* 21 (1987), 67.

2. T.N. Srinivasan, "Why Developing Countries Should Participate in the GATT," *World Economy* 5 (1982), 85; See also Jackson, Davey, and Sykes, supra note 1, 1109 et seq.

3. GATT, *Trends in International Trade* (Sales No. GATT/1958-3) (also known as the Haberler Report). See Jackson, supra note 1, section 25.4.

4. See supra chapter 2 and section 11.2 (the U.S. "commitments" policy). The four Tokyo Round codes having special provisions are the Agreement on Technical Barriers to Trade (Article XII), the Agreement on Government Procurement (Article III), the Subsidies Code (part III, Article 14) and the Antidumping Code (Article 14). The text of all the MTN codes can be found in GATT, BISD, 26 Supp. (1980).

5. *Differential and More Favorable Treatment Reciprocity and Fuller Participation of Developing Countries*, GATT, BISD 26 Supp. 203 (1980). See also infra section 12.2.

6. See supra section 6.3. The Fourth Lomé Convention was signed in Lomé on 15 December 1989, entered into force on 1 September 1991, and was implemented on the EC side by the

Decision of the Council and Commission, 91/400, OJ (1991), L229. Currently, sixty-eight African, Caribbean, and Pacific (ACP) states have signed the convention.

7. See supra chapter 6, notes 26 and 64.

8. See Jackson, supra note 1, section 25.7.

9. See, for example GATT Article XVI:3. See Jackson, supra note 1, sections 15.7 and 15.8.

10. See supra sections 4.3 and 4.4.

11. See *Declaration on Trade Measures Taken for Balance Purposes*, GATT, BISD 26 Supp. 205 (1980), and *Statement of the Chairman of the Committee on Balance of Payments Restrictions*, GATT, BISD, 31 Supp. 56 (1985).

12. Such tariff escalation was a major concern of developing countries during the Tokyo Round, because the linear-tariff method used in the Kennedy Round tended not to address this question, see GATT, *The Tokyo Round of Multilateral Trade Negotiations, Report by Director-General* (Geneva: GATT, 1979), 164–165. It should be noted, however, that the developing countries wanted the reduction in tariff levels on industrial goods to be on a preferential basis so as to preserve an advantage over developed exporters: see W. Cline, T. Kawanabe, T. Williams, and T. Kronsjo, eds., *Trade Negotiations in the Tokyo Round* (Washington, DC: Brookings Institution, 1978), 220–224.

13. See supra section 6.3.

14. See supra sections 4.3 and 4.4.

15. Mexico and the People's Republic of China have expressed such concerns. The accession of India to the Subsidies Code was also based upon such considerations. See supra section 6.5 and chapter 11.

16. WTO document "Overview of the State-of-Play of WTO Disputes," dated May 23, 1997, downloaded from the WTO Web page.

17. See Robert Hudec, *Developing Countries in the GATT Legal System*, supra note 1, 210 et seq.; Jagdish Bhagwati, *Anatomy and Consequences of Exchange Control Regimes* (New York: National Bureau of Economic Research, 1978); A. F. Ewing, "The Assault of Development Economics," *Journal of World Trade Law* 18 (1984), 189. See also W. R. Cline, Introduction and Summary, in *Trade Policy in the 1980s* (Washington, DC: Institute of International Economics, 1983), 1–54, 23–26. Cf. Abdulqawi Yusuf, "Differential and More Favorable Treatment: The GATT Enabling Clause," *Journal of World Trade Law* 14 (1980), 488.

18. Graduation refers inter alia to the removal of a country from GSP eligibility in general with respect to specific individual products based on the degree of competitiveness the developing country has achieved with the products. The policy is partly a result of the fact that certain countries, like Brazil and Mexico, have become major exporters of certain industrial products. The developing nations reject graduation as arbitrary and damaging. See Yusuf, supra note 17, 504, and "Address of Alister McIntyre, Acting Head of UNCTAD," reported in *International Trade Reporter* 2 (1985), 932. The U.S. Congress has been instrumental in encouraging the U.S. administration to undertake a graduation program: see Trade Agreements Act of 1979, Senate Report 96-249, 96th Cong., 1st Sess., 1979, 273.

19. The graduation rules are found at 19 USC §2464(a) (1980 and Supp. 1988). As noted in note 18, a country can be completely graduated or graduated with respect to particular articles. For a recent example of the operation of the rules with respect to individual products, see *Federal Register* 53 (1988), 1302, list 1. From this list it appears that the following coun-

tries have been partially "graduated": Argentina, Bahamas, Brazil, Chile, Colombia, Hong Kong, Israel, Mexico, Peru, Singapore, South Korea, Taiwan, Turkey, Yugoslavia, Zambia. See also Jackson, Davey, and Sykes, supra note 1, chapter 20.3(c).

20. See the "Address of Acting Head of UNCTAD," supra note 18; John A Bohn, "Governmental Response to Third World Debt: The Role of the Export-Import Bank," *Stanford Journal of International Law* 21 (1985), 461. See also Jackson, Davey, and Sykes, supra note 1, section 20.5.

21. See supra chapter 6.

22. See Jackson, Davey, and Sykes, supra note 1, section 24.3.

23. GATT, BISD 18 Supp. 24 (1972). See Hector G. Espiell, "GATT: Accommodating Generalized Preferences," *Journal of World Trade Law* 8 (1974), 341.

24. The U.S. GSP system was authorized by Title V of the 1974 Trade Act, Pub. L. 93-618, 88 Stat. 2067; 19 USCA §2461 et seq. (1980 and Supp. 1988): see Senate Rep. No. 93-1298 (1973), reprinted in *U.S. Code Congressional and Administrative News* 4 (1974), 7186. However, the system did not come into effect until January 1976. See infra section 12.3.

25. See, for example, supra note 1 and the annual *General Report on the Implementation of the Generalized System of Preferences,* prepared by the UNCTAD Secretariat. Cf. "Study of the Effects of the Generalized System of Preferences on U.S. Trade in the Program's First Year of Operation," *ITC Staff Research Study No. 12* (Washington, DC: International Trade Commission, 1978); "An Evaluation of U.S. Imports Under the Generalized System of Preferences," USITC Pub. No. 1379 (1983). See also Drusilla Brown, "General Equilibrium Effects of the U.S. Generalized System of Preferences," *Institute of Public Policy Studies Discussion Paper No. 237* (1985).

26. GATT, BISD 26 Supp. 203 (1980). See also Jackson, Davey, and Sykes supra note 1, 1126.

27. Cf. Yusuf, supra note 17, 504–505.

28. See R. Krishnamurti, "Tariff Preferences in Favour of the Developing Countries," *Journal of World Trade Law* 1 (1967), 643, 656–657. See also Jackson, Davey, and Sykes, supra note 1, 1160 et seq.

29. See supra note 24, Section 502(b), 88 Stat. 2067; 19 USCA §2462(b) (1980 and Supp. 1988). See also Senate Rep. No. 93-1298 (1973), reprinted in *U.S. Code Congressional and Administrative News* 4 (1974), 7186, 7351–7352. The system, however, did not come into effect until January 1976.

30. See supra note 24, Section 502(b)(2); 19 USCA §2462(b)(2) (1980 and Supp. 1988).

31. See supra note 24, Section 503(c); 19 USCA §2463(c)(1) (1980 and Supp. 1988). The articles are textiles under trade agreements, watches, certain electronic articles, certain steel articles, certain footwear, certain semimanufactured and manufactured glass products, and other items designated by the president as import-sensitive.

32. See supra note 24, Section 504; 19 USCA §2464 (1980 and Supp. 1988). See also Senate Rep. No. 93-1298 (1973), reprinted in *U.S. Code Congressional and Administrative News* 4 (1974), 7186, 7355–7357.

33. Ibid. See also S. Rep. 96-249, supra note 18.

34. The value of GSP duty-free imports in 1994 was about $19 billion, *1994 Annual Report of the United States Trade Representative.*

35. In 1982 the GSP coverage as a percentage of total U.S. imports was 3 percent, in 1983, 4.2 percent, in 1985, 3.9 percent, and in 1986, 3.8 percent.

36. Trade and Tariff Act of 1984, Pub. L. 98-573, Title V, 98 Stat. 3018, 19 USCA §2461 et seq. (1988 and Supp. 1988). For an overview of the GSP renewal program, see *Operation of the Trade Agreements Program,* 35th Report, USITC Publication No. 1535 (1984), chapter 1.

37. The amount of "graduation" with respect to products has been gradually increasing. In 1982 the president removed $651 million from the list of eligible items.

38. See Proclamation 5758 of 24 December 1987, *Federal Register* 52 (1987); 49129.

39. Public Law 104-188, August 20, 1996, 19 USC 2465.

40. See generally Jackson, supra note 1, chapter 2; Jackson, Davey, and Sykes, supra note 1, 293–298.

41. See generally Thomas Hoya, *East West Trade: COMECON Law: American/Soviet Trade,* (New York: Oceana, 1984); M. M. Kostecki, *East West Trade and the GATT System,* (New York: St. Martin's Press, 1979); Donald Wallace et al., eds, *Interface Two: Conference Proceedings on the Legal Framework of East-West Trade* (Washington, DC: International Law Institute, Georgetown University Law Center, 1982); Jozsef Nyilas, ed., *Integration in the World Economy: East-West and Inter-State Relations* (Leyden: Sijthoff, 1978). See also Jackson, Davey, and Sykes supra note 1, chapter 21.

42. See Jackson, supra note 40, chapter 14, section 7.

43. Panel report, GATT, BISD 30 Supp. 140, on the Canadian FIRA legislation where the panel said: "The Panel saw great force in Canada's argument that only the most favored nation and not the national treatment obligations fall within the scope of the general principles of nondiscriminatory treatment referred to in Article XVII:1(a). However, the Panel did not consider it necessary to decide in this particular case whether the general reference to the principles of non-discriminatory treatment referred to in Article XVII:1 also comprises the national treatment obligation since it had already found the purchase undertakings to be inconsistent with Article III:4 which implements the national treatment principle specifically in respect of purchase requirements."

44. See the report of a 1988 U.S. position paper on state trading under the GATT system: *International Trade Reporter* 5 (1988), 795.

45. See supra chapter 2.4(e).

46. Donald Zarin, "Countertrade and the Law," *George Washington Journal of International Law and Economics* 18 (1984), 235; Walsh, "The Effects on Third Countries of Mandated Countertrade" *Journal of World Trade Law* 19 (1985), 592; M. M. Kostecki, "Should One Countertrade?" *Journal of World Trade Law* 21 (1987), 7. See also Interface IV, East-West Countertrade, *Journal of Comparative Business and Capital Markets* 5 (1983), 327 et seq., S. Douglas Nugent, "US Countertrade Policy: Is it Economically Sound?" *George Washington Journal of International Law and Economics* 19 (1985), 829.

47. See Frieder Roessler, "Countertrade and the GATT Legal System," *Journal of World Trade Law* 19 (1985), 604; Michael Gadbaw, "The Implications of Countertrade under the General Agreement on Tariffs and Trade," *Journal of Comparative Business and Capital Markets* 5 (1983), 355; Vincene Verdun, "Are Governmentally Imposed Countertrade Require-

ments Violations of the GATT?" *Yale Journal of International Law* 11 (1985), 191; Howard M. Liebman, "GATT and Countertrade Requirements," *Journal of World Trade Law* 18 (1984), 252.

48. With respect to the NMEs that have joined GATT since its inception, see *Yugoslavia* Report of the Working Party on the Accession of Yugoslavia, GATT, BISD 14 Supp. 49 (1967) and Protocol for the Accession of Yugoslavia, GATT, BISD 15 Supp. 53 (1968). *Poland* Protocol for the Accession of Poland, GATT, BISD 15 Supp. 46 (1968). See also Report of the Working Party on the Accession of Poland, ibid., p. 109. *Romania* Protocol for the Accession of Romania, GATT, BISD 18 Supp. 5 (1972). See also Report of the Working Party on the Accession of Romania, ibid., p. 94. *Hungary* Protocol for the Accession of Hungary, GATT, BISD 20 Supp. (1974) 3. See also Report of the Working Party on the Accession of Hungary, ibid., p. 34.

49. See Eliza R. Patterson, "Improving GATT Rules for Non-Market Economies," *Journal of World Trade Law* 20 (1986), 185. See also Edmond M. Ianni, "The International Treatment of State Trading," *Journal of World Trade Law* 16 (1982), 480; K. Grzybowski, "Socialist Countries in GATT," *American Journal of Comparative Law* 28 (1980), 539.

50. Kevin C. Kennedy, "The Accession of the Soviet Union to the GATT," *Journal of World Trade Law* 21 (1987), 23; Erik Dirksen "What if the Soviet Union Applies to Join the GATT?" *World Economy* 10 (1987), 228.

51. See for example M. M. Kostecki, *East West Trade and the GATT System* (New York: St. Martin's Press, 1979), 43–52.

52. See, for example, *Agreement of July 28 Between the European Economic Community and the Socialist Republic of Romania on Trade in Industrial Products* (OJ [1980] L. 352/5) and *Trade and Economic Co-Operation Agreement Between the European Economic Community and the People's Republic of China* (OJ [1986] L.257/54).

53. See supra chapter 7. See also Trade Act of 1974, Pub. L. 93-618, §406, 88 Stat. 2062., 19 USC §2436 (1980 and Supp. 1988).

54. See Chong-Chou Li, "Resumption of China's GATT Membership," *Journal of World Trade Law* 21 (1987), 25; Robert E. Herzstein, "China and the GATT: Legal and Policy Issues raised by China's Participation in GATT," *Law and Policy in International Business* 18 (1986), 371; and Peter C. Sheridan, "The Accession to GATT of the People's Republic of China: New Challenges for the World Trade Regime," *Willamette Law Review* 23 (1987), 737.

55. The People's Republic of China was recognized as the representative of China in the IMF on 17 April 1980. See IMF *Summary Proceedings* 35 (1980), 99–103. See also documents regarding the recognition of the People's Republic of China as the representative of China in the World Bank in *International Legal Materials* 20 (1980), 777–781.

56. An act to extend the authority of the president to enter into trade agreements under section 350 of the Tariff Act of 1930, as amended, and for other purposes, Pub. L. No. 49, ch. 139, §5, 65 Stat. 73 (1951).

57. GATT, 2 BISD 36 (1952).

58. See Jackson, Davey, and Sykes, supra note 1, 997.

59. Ibid.

60. Trade Act of 1974, Title IV §409, 88 Stat. 2064, 19 USC §2439(b).

61. Ibid. See also Paula Stern, *The Water's Edge: Domestic Politics and the Making of American Foreign Policy* (Westport, CT: Greenwood Press, 1979); Paul Lansing and Eric Rose, "The Granting and Suspension of Most-Favored-Nation Status for Non-Market Economy States: Policy and Consequences," *Harvard International Law Journal* 25 (1984), 329.

62. See *Department of State Bulletin* 72 (1975), 139–140.

63. The risk of annual review in the U.S. Congress is not particularly desirable!

64. Trade Act of 1974, §406, 88 Stat. 2062, 19 USC §2436. See Vakerics, Wilson and Weigel *Antidumping, Countervailing Duty, and Other Trade Actions*, (New York: Practicing Law Institute, 1987), chapter 5. See also John P. Erlick "Relief from Imports from Communist Countries: The Trials and Tribulations of Section 406," *Law and Policy in International Business* 13 (1981), 617. See also Jackson, Davey, and Sykes, supra note 1, 586–589.

65. Section 1106 of the Omnibus Trade and Competitiveness Act of 1988 (Pub. L. 100-418, 102 Stat. 1133); 19 USC 2905.

66. The nonmarket economy rules with respect to antidumping actions are found in Trade Agreements Act 1979 Pub. L. 96-39, Title I §101, 93 Stat. 182, amending Tariff Act of 1930, currently at 19 USC §1677b(c) (1980 and Supp. 1988). See also 19 CFR 353.8 (1987). See Gary N. Horlick and Shauuon S. Shuman, "Non-Market Economy Trade and US Antidumping/Countervailing Duty Laws," *International Lawyer* 18 (1984), 807; Stanislaus Soltysinski, "US Antidumping Laws and State-Controlled Economies," *Journal of World Trade Law* 15 (1981), 251. See also Jackson, Davey, and Sykes, supra note 1, 711–729.

67. See supra chapter 10.

68. See Horlick and Shuman supra note 66. Robert L. Meuser "Dumping from 'Controlled Economy' Countries: The Polish Golf Car Case" *Law and Policy In International Business* 11 (1979), 777.

69. See, for example, William P. Alford, "When is China Paraguay? An Examination of the Application of Antidumping and Countervailing Duty Laws of the US to China and Other 'Nonmarket Economy Nations,'" *Southern California Law Review* 61 (1987), 79.

70. In an investigation concerning Finnish carbon steel plate (*Federal Register* 49 [1984], 8973), the Commerce Department stated: "The allegation of sales at less than fair value of this merchandise from Finland is supported by comparisons of the estimated Finnish home market prices (derived from data used by the Department of Commerce in its section 751 review of the suspension agreement in the antidumping proceeding on carbon steel plate from Romania) with the weighted average f.a.s. Finnish port value of the product imported into the U.S. ... In the Romanian case the value of the Finnish carbon steel plate was used as a surrogate for the foreign market value of Romanian carbon steel plate." For example, Cotton Shop Towels from the People's Republic of China, *Federal Register* 48 (1983), 37055.

71. See "Initiation of Countervailing Duty Investigations; Textiles, Apparel and Related Products from the People's Republic of China," *Federal Register* 48 (1983) 46600. The Commerce Department stated that the action contained "novel issues," including whether a bounty or grant may be found in a nonmarket economy.

72. "Textiles, Apparel and Related Products From the People's Republic of China; Termination of Countervailing Duty Investigations," *Federal Register* 48 (1983), 55492. The termination was without prejudice to the issues involved, see for example Carbon Steel Wire Rod From Poland: Initiation of Countervailing Duty Investigation, *Federal Register* 48 (1983), 56419.

73. "Carbon Steel Wire from Czechoslovakia, Final Negative Countervailing Duty Determination," *Federal Register* 49 (1984), 19370. During the course of the examination of the steel wire case, two new cases were brought and all three were decided in a similar manner and proceeded through the appeals together, see "Potassium Chloride from the Soviet Union, Recision of Initiation of Countervailing Duty Investigation and Dismissal of Petition," *Federal Register* 49 (1984), 23428. "Potassium Chloride from the German Democratic Republic, Recision of Initiation of Countervailing Duty Investigation and Dismissal of Petition," *Federal Register* 49 (1984), 23428.

74. *Continental Steel Corp. v. United States,* 614 F. Supp 548 (1985, CIT) *Georgetown Steel Corp. v. United States,* 801 F.2d 1308 (CAFC, 1986).

75. Section 325 of the Senate version of HR3, 100th Cong., 1st Sess. 1987 would have used a trade-weighted average price of comparable merchandise, as sold at arms-length in the United States, to determine the foreign market value of the non-market economy products. The provision was not included in the 1988 Trade Act (the Omnibus Trade and Competitiveness Act of 1988 [Pub. L. 100-418, 102 Stat. 1107 et seq.]).

76. For the reasoning of the Department of Commerce, see the decisions supra note 73.

77. See supra note 66.

78. Jackson, Davey, and Sykes, 3rd ed., 1995, Decument Supplement to International Economic Relations (St. Paul: West) p. 284, Article 29 of Agreement on Subsidies and Countervailing Measures.

79. This approach is typified by the so-called Heinz Bill. It was first proposed as S. 1966 in 1979 (96th Cong., 1st Sess.) and has been resubmitted subsequently under other numbers. However, see also, for example, the "Hecht" proposal, *International Trade Reporter* 4 (1987), 1064.

80. The Heinz Bill in its 1983 form (S.1531, 98th. Cong., 1st. Sess.) was adopted by the Senate but later dropped in conference at the end of the 1984 congressional session.

Chapter 14

1. See W. Max Corden, *Trade Policy and Economic Welfare* (Oxford: Clarendon Press, 1974). See also W. Max Corden, *The Theory of Protection* (Oxford: Clarendon Press, 1971).

2. See John H. Jackson, William Davey, and Alan Sykes, *Legal Problems of International Economic Relations* (St. Paul: West, 3d ed., 1995), section 27.4.

3. See Gary Hufbauer, Jeffrey Schott, and Kimberley Elliott, *Economic Sanctions Reconsidered* (Washington, DC: Institute for International Economics, 1985), and Barry E. Carter "Improving International Economic Sanctions: Improving the Haphzard US Legal Regime," *California Law Review* 75 (1987), 1159.

4. See, for example, John H. Jackson, "Perspectives on the Jurisprudence of International Trade: Costs and Benefits of Legal Procedures in the United States," *Michigan Law Review* 82 (1984), 1570.

5. See Richard Lipsey, Paul Courant, Douglas Purvis, and Peter Steiner, *Microeconomics* (New York: HarperCollins College Publishers, 10th ed., 1993), especially part 4.

6. Avinash K. Dixit and Barry J. Nalebuff, *Thinking Strategically* (New York: Norton, 1991.)

7. Max Corden, *Trade Policy and Economic Welfare* (Oxford: Clarendon Press, 1974.)

8. Alan V. Deardorff, "International Conflict and Coordination in Environmental Policies," prepared for the conference, "Economic Analysis of International Law," conducted by the George Mason University Law School, 5–6 May 1995, forthcoming in a volume of the conference proceedings. Economic Law Project, sponsored by *the Law and Economics Program*, Duquesne University (August 1994.)

9. See Thomas P. O'Neill and Gary Hymel, *All Politics is Local* (New York Times Books, 1994). "Tip" O'Neill was the Speaker of the U.S. House of Representatives.

10. Peter F. Drucker, "Trade Lessons from the World Economy," *Foreign Affairs*, Vol. 73, No. 1 (January/February 1994), 99.

Index

Absolute advantage. *See* Comparative advantage
Adjustment assistance. *See* Economic policy, structural adjustment; United States, Section 201
African, Caribbean and Pacific (ACP) Nations. *See* European Community, Lomé Convention
Agriculture, 2, 24, 48, 57–58, 305, 313–316. *See also* European Communities, common agricultural policy; GATT; United States
compliance problem, 313, 314–315
domestic supports, 315
export subsidies, 316
1994 Agreement on Agriculture, 2, 48, 233, 313–316
1994 Agreement on Sanitary and Phytosanitary Measures, 223, 224, 316
phaseout of non-tariff barriers, 315
Antidumping law, 2, 41, 168, 247–277. *See also* Dumping; United States, antidumping law, antidumping codes, 256, 267
antitrust and, 238–240, 249, 253, 258
Article VI and, 51, 256, 266
community interest and, 273
comparison of normal value with export price, 257, 262–264
constructed value, 251–252, 263
export price, 251
history of, 255–258
injury, 182, 155, 226, 227, 236–237, 239
causation, 256, 272
cumulation, 270
de minimis test, 262, 268, 271
margin of dumping, 261–262, 335
nonmarket economy rules, 334–338 (*see also* Nonmarket economies; United States)
NAFTA and, 135
1967 Antidumping Code, 80, 256, 267
1979 Antidumping Code, 256–257, 259
1994 Agreement on Antidumping, 262, 271–272
normal value, 251
predation, 253–254
sales, below cost, 254–264
services, 255
use of antidumping legislation, 261
Argentina, 314
Australia, 231, 242, 272, 313, 314

Balance of payments, 241–244. *See also* Quantitative restrictions
Committee on BOP Restrictions, 244
declaration on trade measures taken for balance of payments purposes, 243 (*see also* Multilateral trade negotiations, Tokyo Round, understandings)
import duty surcharge, 53, 241
Barter. *See* Countertrade
Berne Convention for the Protection of Literary and Artistic Works, 311, 312
Bretton Woods Conference, 7, 32
WTO as "missing leg" of Bretton Woods System, 4
Brazil, 163, 237, 314, 328
Brussels tariff nomenclature. *See* Tariffs, classification

Cairns Group, 314
Canada, 50, 89, 155, 231, 237, 242, 272, 273, 313, 314

Canada (cont.)
Canada-U.S. Free Trade Agreement (*see* United States)
FIRA legislation (*see* Panel reports)
initiative in promoting WTO, 45
North American Free Trade Agreement (*see* NAFTA)
Caribbean Basin Initiative. *See* United States, free trade agreements
Causation. *See* Antidumping, injury; Escape Clause, injury; United States, Section 201
Chile, 325
China. *See* People's Republic of China
CIT. *See* United States Court of International Trade
Cline, William, 208
Codes. *See* Multilateral trade negotiations
Commitments policy. *See* Subsidies; United States, subsidy and countervailing duty laws
Commodity agreements, 33
Comparative advantages, 8, 14–19, 22, 147, 237. *See also* Economic policy
absolute advantage, 16
factor endowments, 16
problems with, 276
proof of, 18–19
Conciliation. *See* Dispute settlement
Content, local or domestic. *See* Non-tariff barriers, content rules
Corden, W. Max, 20, 21, 340. *See also* Economic policy
Countertrade, 165, 327
Countervailing duties, 41, 279–303
1979 Agreement on Subsidies and Countervailing Duties, 41, 51, 256–257, 267, 279, 288–290, 296–299
1994 Agreement on Countervailing Measures, 41, 51, 256–257, 267, 288–290, 296–299, 300
Cuba, 328. *See also* Nonmarket economies
Customs Cooperation Council (CCC). *See* Tariff, classification
Customs union, 61, 153, 165. *See also* Most Favored Nation Clause
Customs. *See* Non-tariff barriers
Czechoslovakia, 231, 328, 332. *See also* Nonmarket economies

Deardorff, Alan V., 141, 154
Department of Commerce. *See* United States Department of Commerce
Developing countries, 2, 43, 60, 143, 319–325, 330
Article XVIII, 243, 320–321
balance of payments problems, 243–244, 321 (*see also* Balance of payments; Quantitative restrictions; United States, president, foreign affairs)
Caribbean Basin Initiative, 164, 171, 320
"Differential and More Favourable Treatment, Reciprocity and Fuller Participation of Developing Countries," 164, 323
debt, 322
dispute settlement, 321
effective tariff rate, 321
Enabling clause, 164, 320, 323
fairness of trading rules for, 319, 320–321
greater integration in world trading system under WTO, 2, 319, 322
Generalized System of Preferences, 160, 164, 168, 169, 322–325 (*see also* Most Favored Nation Clause; United States)
graduation, 322, 325
Haberler report, 320
intellectual property, attitude to protection of, 310–311
Lomé Convention, 71, 170, 320
position following Uruguay Round, 3, 60, 324
preferentiality, reason for, 321–322
tariff escalation, 322
Tokyo Round and, 320, 322
Discrimination. *See* Most Favored Nation Clause; National treatment
Dispute-settlement procedures, 3, 111, 112–127, 133–137, 206. *See also* Panel reports
adoption of reports, 125
appeal mechanism, 125
compensation, 125, 135
conciliation, 112, 134
disputes, information on, 118
effectiveness, 113–137
exclusive recourse, 124
focus of Uruguay Round negotiations, 45
future of, 133–137
GATT working party, 114, 115–116
invocation re customs unions and free trade areas, 166
1979 Understanding on Dispute Settlement, 116–117
1994 Understanding on Dispute Settlement, 47, 77, 96–98, 124–127

non-violation nullification and impairment, 115
nullification and impairment, 115
precedent, 126
prima facie nullification and impairment, 115
purpose of GATT dispute settlement procedure, 113, 116
retaliation, 116
statistical review of cases, 120, 127
unified system under WTO, 3, 125
United States' Section 301 (*see* United States)
Drucker, Peter, 351
Dumping, 21, 247–277. *See also* Anti-dumping law
economic analysis, 251–253
Viner, Jacob, 253, 255

Economic policy, 5–14, 140, 199, 206. *See also* National security
"Beggar-thy-neighbor," 8
Conservation Social Welfare Function (CSWF), 20, 21, 340 (*see also* Corden, W. Max)
liberal trade, 24, 28, 175
market economy basis, 13, 325
noneconomic aspects, 4, 13, 19, 23, 24, 346
structural adjustment, 18, 20, 199–263 (*see also* Escape clause; United States)
Environment control. *See* Non-tariff barriers
Environment & Trade, 235–238, 348
Escape clause, 3, 175–199. *See also* Multilateral trade negotiations; United States; Voluntary export restraints
adjustment, 199–203, 208–209 (*see also* Economic policy; United States, Section 201)
Article XIX, 180–182, 185–188, 190–192, 193, 195–199, 329
compensation, 143, 191–195
economic rationale for, 176–179
history of safeguards, 179–180
injury, 178, 181, 184, 185–191
1979 Agreement on Safeguards, 2, 165, 192, 199, 209–210
1994 Agreements on Safeguards, 2, 165, 192, 199, 210–211
procedures, 185–191
reform of safeguards policy, 165, 172, 175, 192, 194, 195, 199, 204, 209–211
safeguards and, 175–211
safeguards negotiations, 198, 175, 209
selectivity, 195–199 (*see also* Most Favored Nation Clause)
state trading nations, 325–327, 330
unforeseen developments, 181, 184, 185–187
usage of, 184
European Communities, 7, 33, 61, 70, 80, 89, 100–104, 110, 142, 144, 151, 155, 258, 272, 273, 328. *See also* Antidumping law
Commission of the European Communities, 61, 100, 101
common agricultural policy, 57, 118–119, 155
Common External Tariff (CET), 145
Council of Ministers of the European Communities, 100, 102
Court of Justice of the European Communities, 100, 103
decision-making process, 79–80
enlargement, 347
European Council, 100
European Parliament, 100, 101
foreign affairs system, 61, 80, 101
Lomé Convention, 170, 320
membership in GATT/WTO, 61–62
New Commercial Policy Instrument, 132, 216
negotiating authority for Uruguay Round, 164
selectivity (*see* Escape clause; Most Favored Nation Clause)
Single European Act, 101, 102
trade barrier legislation, 132–133
European Free Trade Area (EFTA). *See* Free trade agreements
Export restraint agreement or arrangement. *See* Voluntary export restraint
Expropriation, 26, 324

Feldstein, Martin, 3
Financial Services, 10, 307, 310
Floating exchange rates, 109, 153, 242. *See also* Balance of payments
Food and Agriculture Organization (FAO). *See* United Nations
France, 173. *See also* Non-tariff barriers, customs
Free Trade Agreements. *See also* Customs union; GATT, exceptions to; Most Favored Nation Clause; United States
Article XXIV, 165

Free Trade Agreements (cont.)
Asian Pacific Economic Cooperation (APEC) Group, 172
European Free Trade Area (EFTA), 33
North American Free Trade Agreement (NAFTA), 33, 95, 97, 135, 168–169, 172, 245, 295, 308, 316
Trans-Atlantic "dialogue," 172
Friedman, Thomas, 4

General Agreement on Tariffs and Trade. *See* GATT
GATT, 7, 8, 12, 25, 29, 31–78, 80, 95–96, 100, 107–137, 139–155, 163, 180, 186–189, 193, 196–199, 205–209, 221, 225, 230–232, 241–245, 248, 255–258, 266, 277, 280, 285–293, 296, 305, 310–313, 323, 328, 332, 343–345. *See also* Multilateral trade negotiations; Non-tariff barriers; United States
accession to, 59, 60, 61, 329–331
agriculture, coverage in GATT, 2, 24, 57–58, 153, 305, 313–316
analytical index, 121, 184
articles of
Article I (*see* Most Favored Nation Clause)
Article II, 150 (*see* Tariffs)
Article III, 214, 218, 219, 235, 277, 326 (*see* National treatment)
Article VI (*see* Antidumping law)
Article VII, 152
Article X, 150
Article XI, 153 (*see* Quantitative restrictions)
Article XII, 321
Article XIII, 164
Article XVI, 219, 285–286, 288, 291 (*see* Subsidies)
Article XVII, 140, 238–239
Article XVIII, 320, 321
Article XIX, 180–182, 185–188, 190–192, 193, 195–199, 329
Article XX, 164, 214, 215, 217, 233, 234, 236, 277, 309
Article XXI, 55, 230, 232 (*see also* National security)
Article XXIII, 114 (*see* Dispute settlement)
Article XXIV, 165–166, 326 (*see* Free Trade agreements, Customs union)
Article XXV, 55–57, 63, 123 (*see also* Waivers)
Article XXVI, 40, 60, 62
Article XXVIII, 180, 191–193
Article XXX, 69
Article XXXV, 60–62
Article XXXVI, 200
Article XXXVII, 201
Article XXXVIII, 201
Part IV, 43, 200–201, 320
application to subordinate government units, 54
"Balkanization" of, 76
Bretton Woods System and, 7, 8, 35–36, 200–319
"code of conduct," 50, 51–52, 342
compliance with, 117
consultative group of, 65
CONTRACTING PARTIES, 38, 59, 63, 123, 116, 144, 188, 201, 240
coverage of, 42, 53
decision making, 51, 53, 55, 56, 57, 58–62, 124–127
direct effect of, 54
dispute settlement within (*see* Dispute settlement procedures)
exceptions to, 54–62 (*see also* Most Favored Nation Clause; National treatment)
balance of payments problems, 242
customs union, 55, 67, 165–167
developing countries (*see also* Developing countries)
Escape clause, 55, 175–183
general exceptions and Article XX, 54–55, 164, 214, 232–235, 236
national security, 55, 229
"opt out" and Article XXV, 55, 58, 60–62, 164, 329, 330
renegotiations of tariff schedule (Article XXVIII), 55
state trading monopolies, 52, 139, 140, 239, 325–327
waivers, 52, 54, 55, 63, 77, 116, 153, 169, 320, 323
GATT Council, 63, 244
Grandfather rights under, 41, 48
history of, 35–49 (*see also* United States)
extension of influence post-Uruguay Round, 48
Havana Charter, 7, 38, 121–122, 239, 319
Havana Conference, 37, 39
ICITO, 42
intercessional committee of, 42, 115
International Trade Organization (ITO), 7,

32, 37, 38–39, 40, 41, 42, 43, 53, 57, 75, 93, 113, 114, 121, 123, 124, 139, 188, 197, 239
Organization for Trade Cooperation (OTC), 42, 75, 93
interpretation of, 120–124
negotiations, 73–78 (*see also* Multilateral trade negotiations)
rounds, 62, 74, 75, 91, 117, 209–211 (*see* also Multilateral trade negotiations)
tariffs, 37, 38, 51
nonmarket economies (*see* Nonmarket economies, GATT and)
observer status, 62
opt-out clause, 60–62
protocol of provisional application, 39–41, 50, 51, 286
reform of GATT system, 339–351
retaliation (*see* Dispute settlement)
review session, 42, 286
secretariat, 42
textiles, 58, 62, 206–209 (*see also* Multifiber arrangement)
termination of, 45, 47, 48, 50, 64
"trade constitution," 339–340, 341
waivers, 52, 54, 55, 63, 77, 116, 153, 169, 320, 323
withdrawal from, 40
Generalized System of Preference (GSP). *See* Developing countries; Most Favored Nation Clause; United States
Germany, 13, 173
Government procurement. See Non-tariff barriers
"Grandfather" rights. *See* GATT, protocol of provision application
"Gray area" measures. *See* Voluntary export restraints

Haberler report. *See* Developing countries
Hamilton, Alexander, 255
Harmonization, 214, 345
Hawkins, Harry, 13
Havana Conference. *See* GATT, history of
Hong Kong, 62
Hudec, Robert, 118, 120
Hull, Cordell, 90. *See also* United States, Reciprocal Trade Agreements Act of 1934
Human rights and trade, 325, 346
Hungary, 328. *See also* Nonmarket economies

IMF. *See* International Monetary Fund
Import licensing. *See* Non-tariff barriers
India, 61, 328
Individuals, as subjects of international law. *See* International law
Industrial policy, 8, 17–18, 22, 177, 275. *See also* Targeting
Infant industries, 24
Injury test, 9, 181–182. *See also* Antidumping law; Escape clause
Intellectual property, 2, 44, 234–235. *See also* Multilateral trade negotiations; United States, protection of intellectual property
1994 Agreement on Trade-Related Aspects of Intellectual Property Rights (TRIPS), 2, 60, 232, 244, 293, 305, 310–313
dispute settlement under, 311, 312
harmonization, 312, 313
history, 310–311
Interdependence, 22–23, 205
"Interface" concept, 178–179, 214, 248–250, 275–276, 284, 294, 331, 345
International Civil Aviation Organization (ICAO). *See* United Nations
International economic law, 25–28, 31–35. *See also* International law
International Labor Organization (ILO). *See* United Nations
International law. *See also* Treaties
customary law, 26, 27
effectiveness of, 27, 107
functional approach to, 27–28
individuals, recourse to, 83–84, 128–129
power-oriented diplomacy vs. rule-oriented diplomacy, 109–111, 340
sovereignty and, 79
treaties and conventions, 26
interpretation of, 112, 113, 114, 115, 129
International Maritime Organization (IMO). *See* United Nations
International Monetary Fund (IMF), 7, 32, 36, 48, 109, 111, 201, 242, 329
International Bank of Reconstruction and Development. *See* World Bank
International Court of Justice (ICJ). *See* International law, treaties, and conventions, interpretation of
International Trade Commission. *See* United States Trade Commission
International Trade Organization (ITO). *See* GATT

Interpretation, 35, 50, 56, 121–124, 238
analogizing goods' rules to services, 10, 25, 50, 157, 214, 307
direct effect, 54
interpretive notes as aid to GATT interpretation, 53
ITO preparatory history as interpretive aid, 38
standard of review, 127
Investment, 10, 25, 244–245, 305
Agreement on Trade-Related Investment Measures (TRIMS), 215, 244, 305, 316–317
Bilateral Investment Treaties (BIT), 34
Israel, 91, 171
Italy, 299
ITO. *See* GATT

Jackson-Vanik Amendment. *See* United States, nonmarket economies
Japan, 60, 70, 80, 142, 149, 151, 155, 170, 222, 273. *See also* Antidumping law
formulation of trade policy, 104–105

Kenen, Peter, 14. *See also* Comparative advantage
Kennedy Round. *See* Multilateral trade negotiations

Labor, 245
League of Nations, 35
Leutwiler report, 12
"Level playing field." *See* "Unfair" trade, concept of

Manufacturing clause, 41
Market disruption. *See* United States, Nonmarket economies
Megna, Laura, 154
Mercantilism. *See* Comparative advantage
Mexico, 238, 261, 320
MFN. *See* Most Favored Nation Clause
Morici, Peter, 154
Most Favored Nation Clause (MFN), 27, 35, 38, 41, 51, 144, 151, 157–173, 234, 236, 346. *See also* Customs union
Article XX, 164
"code conditionality," 77, 161–162
Conditional Most Favored Nation Clause, 161–162
"customary" basis, 158
customs unions, 165–167
exceptions to, 163–167
"free ride" problem, 160, 161, 165–166, 170
free trade agreements, 165–167
Generalized System of Preferences (GSP), 164, 169, 322–325
history of, 156
"like products," 162
multilateralism and, 158
preferentiality (*see also* Developing countries)
political basis, 160, 322–323
reciprocity, 27, 52, 59, 84
selectivity, 195–199
tariff reciprocity, 147–150
Multifiber Arrangement, 58, 62, 206–209
Long Term Agreements (LTA), 207
1994 Agreement on Textiles and Clothing, 207, 209, 233
origins, 58, 208
Short Term Agreements (STA), 207
Textiles, 2, 58, 180, 206–209
Textiles Surveillance Body, 208
Multilateral trade negotiations. *See also* Non-tariff barriers, 55, 121
Kennedy Round, 43, 73, 75, 148
American Selling Price (ASP), 75
Antidumping Code (AD), 75, 256, 259, 261
ongoing nature of future negotiations, 2, 307, 310, 343, 345
Tokyo Round, 43, 47, 70, 71, 74, 75–78, 84, 116–117, 118, 145–146, 170, 176 (*see also* non-tariff barriers)
1979 Agreement on Government Procurement, 76, 224–228
1979 Agreement on Safeguards, 2, 165, 192, 199, 210–214
1979 Agreement on Subsidies and Countervailing Measures, 41, 52–53, 76, 256–257, 267, 279, 288–290, 296
1979 Agreement on Technical Barriers, 76, 223,
1979 Antidumping Code, 76, 256–257, 259 (*see also* Antidumping law)
1979 Bovine Meat Code, 76
1979 Civil Aircraft Code, 76
1979 Dairy Code, 76
1979 Import Licensing Code, 76, 153–154
1979 Understanding on Dispute Settlement, 116–117
1979 Valuation Code, 76, 152

non-tariff barriers codes, 76–77
safeguards negotiations, 197, 209–210
understandings, 75–78, 164, 242, 320, 323
Uruguay Round, 1, 2, 12, 44, 62, 70, 80, 92, 117, 160, 209, 235, 295, 305–317 (*see also* Services; Intellectual property; Investment)
application to subordinate governmental units, 53–54
conclusion of, 1
"fast track," 95, 334
Future of GATT System (FOGS), 308
grandfather rights, elimination of, 41, 49
history, 1, 44–46
implementation by,
European Community, 80, 104
United States, 92, 95
material injury test, 269
1994 Agreement on Agriculture, 2, 48, 233, 313–316
1994 Agreement on Antidumping, 257, 262, 271–272
1994 Agreement on Government Procurement, 226–227, 228, 330
1994 Agreement on Import Licensing Procedures, 153–154
1994 Agreement on Sanitary and Phytosanitary Measures, 223, 224, 316
1994 Agreement on Safeguards, 2, 165, 192, 199, 210–211
1994 Agreement on Countervailing Measures, 41, 51, 256–257, 267, 288–290, 296–299, 300
1994 Agreement on Technical Barriers (TBT), 223, 290–293, 294, 300, 316, 336
1994 Agreement on Textiles and Clothing, 207, 209, 233
1994 Agreement on Trade-Related Aspects of Intellectual Property Rights (TRIPS), 2, 60, 232, 244, 293, 305, 310–313
1994 Agreement on Trade-Related Investment Measures (TRIMS), 215, 244, 305, 316–317
1994 Understanding on Dispute Settlement, 47, 77, 96–98, 124–127
1994 General Agreement on Trade in Services (GATS), 2, 60, 72, 232, 244–245, 292, 305, 307–310
problems with, 342
tariff reduction negotiation, 146
single package idea, 45, 160, 162
subsidies, 300
rules of origin, 168
overview, 2–4
Multilateral Trade Organization (MTO), 45

National security, 22, 24, 229–232, 283
Article XXI, 230–231
United States and Nicaragua, 231
United States and nonmarket economies, 231
National treatment, 35, 41, 51, 157, 213–228, 223
Article III and, 214, 236
history of, 213
implicit discrimination, 216–218
state trading and, 326
subsidies and, 214–219
taxation, 213, 218 (*see also* Non-tariff barriers, taxes as)
border tax adjustments, 218–221
Netherlands, 116
New Zealand, 314
Nicaragua, 231. *See also* National security, Article XXI
Nonmarket economies (NME). *See also* under individual country names; Antidumping law; United States
antidumping law, 334–337
Cuba, 328
Czechoslovakia, 328, 332
GATT and, 328–332
Hungary, 328
interface with market-based WTO system, 331, 344, 345
People's Republic of China, 325, 328, 329–330, 331, 336, 344
accession to WTO, 329–330, 334
Poland, 328, 333, 335
Romania, 328
Russia (ex-Soviet Union), 310–311, 325, 331, 332, 334
accession to WTO, 330–331, 334, 344
safeguard measures, 329
state trading, 326–327
Yugoslavia, 328, 333
Non-tariff barriers, 7, 154–155. *See also* Antidumping law; Subsidies
content rules, local or domestic, 215
customs, 51, 138
French VCR imports, 155, 184
valuation, 76, 151–153
environmental regulation, 235–238
government procurement, 170, 224–228

Non-tariff barriers (cont.)
1979 Agreement on Government Procurement, 76, 224–228
1994 Agreement on Government Procurement, 226–227, 228, 330
import licensing
marks of origin, 51
1979 Agreement on Import Licensing, 76, 153–154
origin rules, 167–169
restrictive business practices, 57, 238–240, 275
OECD guidelines for multinational enterprises (1976), 240
UNCTAD set of multilaterally agreed equitable principles and rules for the control of restrictive business practices (1980), 240
sectoral issues
1979 Bovine Meat Code, 76
1979 Civil Aircraft Code, 76
1979 Dairy Code, 76
tariff equivalent, 150, 154
taxes. *See also* National treatment
border tax adjustment (BTA), 218–221
destination principle, 218–220
double taxation, 220
origin principle, 220
personal vs. product, 219–221
Value Added Taxes (VAT), 219
technical standards, 221–224
1979 Agreement on Technical Barriers, 76, 222–223
North American Free Trade Agreement (NAFTA), 33, 95, 97, 135, 168–169, 172, 245, 295, 308, 316
"fast track" and, 95
investment rules, 245
rules of origin, 168, 169
North, Douglas, 58
Norton, Joseph, 18
Norway, 198

OECD. *See* Organization for Economic Cooperation and Development
O'Neill, Tip, 351
Opportunity costs. *See* Subsidies, cost versus benefit
Origin rules. *See* Non-tariff barriers, origin rules
Organization for Economic Cooperation and Development (OECD), 7, 32–33
OECD guidelines for multinational enterprises (1976), 246 (*see also* Non-tariff barriers, restrictive business practices)
Organization for Trade Cooperation (OTC). *See* GATT, history of

Panel reports, 117–120
automobiles, 218
Belgian family allowances, 163
Canadian FIRA legislation, 215
Czechoslovakian hatters fur, 186
EC pasta subsidies, 119–120
EC wheat flour subsidies, 118–119
implementation of, 134,
Italian agricultural machinery, 214–215
Japanese dimension lumber, 163
Japanese semiconductor measures, 206
Norwegian textile quotas, 198
Nicaraguan trade, 232
Spanish coffee restrictions, 151
Uruguay and foreign access complaint, 114
U.S. embargo on Canadian tuna, 234
U.S. embargo on Mexican tuna, 237–238
U.S. manufacturing clause, 41
U.S. restrictions on imports of tuna ("Tuna II"), 238, 1979
U.S. Section 337, 215–216, 234, 277
Paris Convention for the Protection of Industrial Property, 34, 311, 312
People's Republic of China, 62, 329–330, 331, 334, 336, 344. *See also* Nonmarket economies
accession to WTO, 329–330, 334
Poland, 328, 335. *See also* Nonmarket economies
Pollution. *See* Non-tariff barriers, national standards
Precedent. *See* Dispute settlement
Prima facie nullification and impairment. *See* Dispute settlement, nullification and impairment
Product Standards, 3, 221–224, 276

Quad Group, 64, 70
Quantitative restrictions, 5, 40, 139, 140, 153, 186, 196, 205–206. *See also* Voluntary export restraints
Article XI, 52, 205, 326
Article XI and balance of payments problems, 153,
Article XII, 180, 241, 321
Article XIII, 241

Article XIV, 241
"monopoly rents," 140, 206

Reagan, President, 170. *See also* United States, president
Reciprocal trade agreements system. *See* United States
Reciprocity. *See* Most Favored Nation Clause
Requests lists. *See* Tariffs, negotiating process
Restrictive business practices. *See* Non-tariff barriers
Ricardo, David, 14, 15. *See also* Comparative advantage
Romania, 328. *See also* Nonmarket economies
Rules of origin, 167–168
Russia (ex-Soviet Union), 310–311, 325, 331, 332, 334
accession to WTO, 330–331, 334, 344

Safeguards. *See* Escape clause
Samuelson, Paul, 12. *See also* Comparative advantage
Services, trade in, 2, 7, 19, 21, 47, 48, 72, 214, 232, 292–293, 305–306
anti-dumping law and, 255
comparative advantage, 306
1994 General Agreement on Trade in Services (GATS), 2, 44, 60, 72, 232, 244–245, 292, 305, 307–310
commitments, 308
history, 44
investment, 309–310
progressive liberalization, 309
prohibitions, 308
MFN, as applied to, 154, 214
Smith, Adam, 14, 17, 21, 255. *See also* Comparative advantage
Smoot-Hawley Act. *See* United States, Congress
South Africa, 61
Sovereignty, and international law. *See* International law
Soviet Union. *See* Nonmarket economies; Russia
Standards. *See* Non-tariff barriers
State trading monopolies. *See* Nonmarket economies
Stern, Robert M., 141, 154
Subsidies, 2, 21, 22, 24, 68, 139, 140, 279–303. *See also* Agriculture, Panel reports; Targeting; United States
"actionability," 293–300
Article VI, 286, 287
Article XVI, 52, 286, 288, 289, 290, 291
Article XIX, 180–182, 185–188, 190–191
bi-level pricing, 286
code conditionality, 293 (*see also* United States, subsidy and countervailing duty law)
cost v. benefit, 294
opportunity costs, 295 (*see also* United States, subsidy and countervailing duty law)
distortion across the border, 299
domestic subsidies, 279
effects of subsidies, 280–284
equitable share, 286, 288
export subsidies, 279
history of CVD law, 285–293
injury, 181, 279, 287, 296
causation, 272
commitments policy (*see* United States)
cumulation, 270
de minimis test, 262, 268, 271 (*see also* Antidumping, injury; United States, subsidy and countervailing duty law)
1979 Agreement on Subsidies and Countervailing Duties, 41, 51, 256–257, 267, 279, 288–290, 296–299
1994 Agreement on Countervailing Measures, 41, 51, 256–257, 267, 288–290, 296–299, 300
non-primary products, 119, 286
Permanent Group of Experts, 303
potential improvements, 301–303
predation, 283
reform of subsidy law, 300–303
regional subsidies, 298–300
"specificity," 294 (*see also* Multilateral trade negotiations; Non-tariff barriers)
"subsidy" definition, 288, 291, 293
track I, 288, 289, 290
track II, 288, 289, 290
"traffic light approach," 290–293, 301

Taiwan, 329
Targeting, 275, 283. *See also* Industrial policy
Tariff commission. *See* United States Tariff Commission
Tariff equivalent. *See* Non-tariff barriers

Tariffs, 5, 7, 41, 51, 139, 193, 229
Article II, 77, 142, 326
exception to obligation to bind, 119
classification, 150
Brussels tariff nomenclature, 151
Customs Cooperation Council (CCC), 151, 168
harmonized commodity description and coding system, 151
graduation, 322 (*see* Developing countries)
history of, 140–141
negotiating process, 143
item-by-item, 143–144
linear cut, 144–145
requests and offers lists, 144
reductions in, 74, 141, 145–146
renegotiation of tariff schedule (Article XXVIII), 55
schedule of tariff concessions valuation, 51 (*see also* Multilateral trade negotiations; Non-tariff barriers)
ad valorem, 151
cif, 148, 152
Customs Valuation Code, 152
FOB, 148, 152
Taxes. *See* National treatment; Non-tariff barriers
Textiles, trade in. *See* Multifiber arrangement
Telecommunications, 227–228
Tokyo Round. *See* Multilateral trade negotiation
Treaties, 26. *See also* International law, treaties, and conventions
friendship, commerce, navigation (FCN), 34, 35, 157, 238
International Union for the Publication of Customs Tariffs of 1890, 35
multilateral (*see* Multilateral trade negotiations)
Treaty of Utrecht of 1713, 35
United States-Canada Boundary Waters Agreement of 1907, 34

UNCTAD, 7, 33, 154
UNCTAD set of Multilaterally Agreed Equitable Principles and Rules for the Control of Restrictive Business Practices (1980), 240 (*see also* Non-tariff barriers, restrictive business practices)
"Unfair" trade, concept of, 21, 30, 149, 177–178, 247–248, 252, 274–276, 284
United Kingdom, 62
United Nations, 32, 36–38, 329. *See also* UNCTAD
ECOSOC, 33, 36
Food and Agriculture Organization (FAO), 33
International Civil Aviation Organization (ICAO), 33
International Labor Organization (ILO), 33
International Maritime Organization (IMO), 33
World Customs Organization, 33
World Intellectual Property Organization (WIPO), 34, 311
United States
agriculture, 58
antidumping law, 258–272 (*see also* Antidumping law)
Antidumping Act of 1916, 258
Antidumping Act of 1921, 258
comparison of normal value with export price, 262–264
constructed value, 264–265, 335–336
cumulation, 270
Department of Commerce, 260
Export Selling Price (ESP) offset, 252
Foreign Market Value (FMV), 263
grandfather rights, 49, 267
implementation of antidumping codes, 75, 80, 256, 259, 267–268
International Trade Commission (ITC), 259, 268
judicial review, 259
Less Than Fair Value (LTFV), 252, 262
margins analysis, 271
material injury, 267–272
nonmarket economy rules, 334–337 (*see also* Nonmarket economies)
normal value, 264
private right of action, 274–275
procedure, 259–261
ratification of Uruguay Round results, 83
bilateralism, 169–173
cases
Guy Capps, 85
Consumer Union v. Kissinger, 85
Curtiss-Wright, 81
INS v. Chadha, 95, 183
Schliefflin, 217
Youngstown Sheet and Tube, 82
Zenith v. U.S., 219

code conditionality, 176
Congress
foreign affairs powers, 84, 86–89, 140
Smoot-Hawley, 36, 86, 90, 140
Constitution, the, and foreign affairs, 29, 81–89
executive agreements, 82, 83
judicial interpretation of foreign affairs powers, 87
treaties, 82
direct applicability of international law, 82–84, 95–96
federal law, 88
state law, 88
DISC corporations, 242
free trade agreements, 172–173
Canada, 95, 164, 168, 169, 172
Caribbean Basin Initiative, 164, 171, 320
Israel, 91, 171
GATT and, 39, 40, 41, 43, 58, 69, 80, 92 (*see also* GATT, history)
International Trade Organization (ITO), 32, 37–39, 80
Organization for Trade Cooperation (OTC), 42, 75
Generalized System of Preferences (GSP), 322–325
coverage, 324–325
graduation, 322, 325
implementation of international economic obligations, 40, 81, 92–95, 224, 256, 287, 289
Agreement on Government Procurement, 88, 224–228
"fast track," 94–95
manufacturing clause, 41 (*see also* Panel reports)
nonmarket economies, 332–337 (*see also* Nonmarket economies)
Jackson-Vanik Amendment, 333
market disruption, 333–334
Omnibus Trade and Competitiveness Act of 1988, 86, 90, 92, 95, 129, 132, 188, 192, 235, 240, 334
president
foreign affairs power, 84–85, 86, 88
protection of intellectual property
Section 337, 215
Reciprocal Trade Agreements Act of 1934, 12, 35, 36, 142, 147, 179, 285
U.S.-Mexican Agreement of 1943, 179
Section 201, 182–184 (*see also* Escape clause)
adjustment assistance, 177, 201–203
causation, 186–187, 190
practice under, 183–184
presidential action, 183, 192, 194, 203–206
Section 232, 231 (*see also* National security)
Section 301, 127–132, 206, 235, 240, 275
discretion and, 131
"injury" requirements, 131
practice, 131–132
procedure, 129–130
Section 337, 275, 276–277 (*see also* Panel reports)
Statement of Administrative Action (SAA), 97–98
subsidy and countervailing duty law, 131, 279–303
cost versus benefit (*see* Subsidies)
"country under the agreement," 290
injury test, 287–288
nonmarket economies, 325–327
specificity test, 296, 298
Tariff Act of 1930 (Smoot Hawley), 36, 86, 90, 140
Tariff Schedule of the United States (TSUS), 151
Trade Agreements Act of 1979, 81, 91, 96, 97, 129
Trade Expansion Act of 1962, 128, 177
trade policy reform
trade policy structure, 98–99
Williams Commission, 12, 187, 189, 202
Trade and Tariff Act of 1974, 91, 129, 148, 184, 264, 265, 333
Trade and Tariff Act of 1984, 91, 204, 325
Uruguay Round Agreements Act, 13, 92, 259
Uruguay Round Implementing Act, 129, 259, 262, 336, 337
United States Department of Commerce, 88, 259. *See also* United States, antidumping law
United States International Trade Commission, 88, 98, 183, 259. *See also* United States, antidumping law
United States Trade Representative (USTR)
organization, 98
Yeutter, Clayton, 171

Uruguay, 114
Uruguay Round. *See* Multilateral trade negotiations; Intellectual property; Services
USSR. *See* Nonmarket economies; Russia
USTR. *See* United States Trade Representative

Vienna Convention on the Law of Treaties. *See* International law
Viner, Jacob, 253, 255. *See also* Dumping
Voluntary Export Restraint, 5, 53, 164, 183, 197–198. *See also* Multifiber arrangement; United States
 semiconductors, 206
 steel, 204, 206

Wilcox, Clair, 113
Williams Commission report. *See* United States, trade
 policy reform
World Bank, 7, 32, 33, 36, 65, 241
World Court. *See* International Court of Justice (ICJ)
World Intellectual Property Organization (WIPO). *See* United Nations
World Trade Organization (WTO), 1, 25, 31, 33, 41, 48, 49, 53, 64–65, 72–73, 77, 79, 111, 121, 128, 132, 133, 142, 143, 152, 159, 164, 172, 209, 224, 234, 245, 274, 296, 310, 312, 313, 324, 328–332, 339, 342–344, 350–351
 accession to, 59
 creation, 4, 12–13
 de facto application of GATT by, 50, 121
 dispute settlement, 70, 124–127
 future work, 274, 345–347
 General Council, 63, 64
 grandfather rights, 41, 49, 267
 history, 42, 44–46
 as international organization, 48, 58–59
 labor, 245
 membership, 1, 59–60, 64, 70–71, 159, 328–332
 "missing leg" of Bretton Woods "stool," 4, 32
 problems, 64, 343–347, 350
 review of regional trading blocs, 172–173
World Trade Organization Appellate Body, reports of,
 standard of review, 127
 Standards for Reformulated Gasoline, 127, 234
 Taxes on Alcoholic Beverages, 127, 218
World Trade Organization Charter, 4, 12, 46–47, 54, 55, 57, 123
 agreements
  1994 Agreement on Agriculture, 2, 48, 233, 313–316
  1994 Agreement on Antidumping, 257, 262, 271–272
  1994 Agreement on Countervailing Measures, 41, 51, 256–257, 267, 288–290, 296–299, 300
  1994 Agreement on Government Procurement, 226–227, 228, 330
  1994 Agreement on Import Licensing Procedures, 153–154
  1994 Agreement on Safeguards, 2, 165, 192, 199, 210–211
  1994 Agreement on Sanitary and Phytosanitary Measures, 223, 224, 316
  1994 Agreement on Technical Barriers (TBT), 223, 290–293, 294, 300, 316, 336
  1994 Agreement on Textiles and Clothing, 207, 209, 233
  1994 Agreement on Trade-Related Aspects of Intellectual Property Rights (TRIPS), 2, 60, 232, 244, 293, 305, 310–313
  1994 Agreement on Trade-Related Investment Measures (TRIMS), 215, 244, 305, 316–317
  1994 Understanding on Dispute Settlement, 47, 77, 96–98, 124–127
  1994 General Agreement on Trade in Services (GATS), 2, 60, 72, 232, 244–245, 292, 305, 307–310
  Plurilateral Trade Agreements, 43, 46, 48, 77–78
 ambiguity, 55, 57
 amending procedure, 52, 69, 71–73, 343
 annexation of 1979 Valuation Code, 152
 articles of
  Article IX, 56, 65, 123
  Article X, 68, 72
  Article XII, 59–60
  Article XIII, 61 (*see also* "opt-out")
  Article XVI, 31, 56–57, 58, 78, 112
 consensus, operation of, 65, 69, 124, 133
 customs unions/free trade areas, 166
 Dunkel Draft, 46, 311

decision-making under, 63, 65, 68, 71
interpretation, 124
legal framework, 46
MFN and, 214
restrictive trade practices and, 240
safeguards and, 165, 172, 175, 192, 194, 195, 199, 204, 210–211
Trade Policy Review Mechanism (TPRM), 47, 172
waivers under, 52, 55–57, 69, 71
voting, 65–68, 70
Wyndham-White, Sir Eric, 43, 115

Yeutter, Clayton. *See* United States Trade Representative
Yugoslavia, 328, 333